Information Management: Principles, Techniques and Technologies

Information Management:
Principles, Techniques
and Technologies

Edited by
Reuben Hammond

WILLFORD **P**RESS

www.willfordpress.com

Published by Willford Press,
118-35 Queens Blvd., Suite 400,
Forest Hills, NY 11375, USA

ISBN: 978-1-68285-410-5

Cataloging-in-Publication Data

Information management : principles, techniques and technologies / edited by Reuben Hammond.
p. cm.
Includes bibliographical references and index.
ISBN 978-1-68285-410-5
1. Information resources management. 2. Information technology. I. Hammond, Reuben.
T58.64 .I54 2018
658.403 8--dc23

For information on all Willford Press publications
visit our website at www.willfordpress.com

Contents

Permissions

List of Contributors

Index

Preface

Information management is concerned with the acquisition, archiving and distribution of information. As a field of study, information management includes topics such as planning, organizing, controlling and reporting. It plays a significant role in business strategy and processes. This book contains some path-breaking studies in the field of information management. The readers would gain knowledge that would broaden their perspective about this field. It strives to provide a fair idea about information management and to help develop a better understanding of the latest advances within this field.

Various studies have approached the subject by analyzing it with a single perspective, but the present book provides diverse methodologies and techniques to address this field. This book contains theories and applications needed for understanding the subject from different perspectives. The aim is to keep the readers informed about the progresses in the field; therefore, the contributions were carefully examined to compile novel researches by specialists from across the globe.

Indeed, the job of the editor is the most crucial and challenging in compiling all chapters into a single book. In the end, I would extend my sincere thanks to the chapter authors for their profound work. I am also thankful for the support provided by my family and colleagues during the compilation of this book.

Editor

Knowledge sharing behaviour and demographic variables amongst secondary school teachers in and around Gaborone, Botswana

Authors:
Isaac C. Mogotsi[1,2]
J.A. (Hans) Boon[1]
Lizelle Fletcher[3]

Affiliations:
[1]Department of Information Science, University of Pretoria, South Africa

[2]Department of Accounting and Finance, University of Botswana, Botswana

[3]Department of Statistics, University of Pretoria, South Africa

Correspondence to:
Isaac Mogotsi

Email:
Isaac.Mogotsi@mopipi.ub.bw

Postal address:
Business Information Systems Group, Department of Accounting & Finance, University of Botswana, Private Bag UB00701, Gaborone, Republic of Botswana

The purpose of this study was to investigate the relationships between knowledge sharing behaviour and the demographic variables gender, age, organisational tenure and professional tenure. Following a correlational survey approach, the study sourced its data from senior secondary school teachers in and around Gaborone, Botswana. Knowledge sharing behaviour was measured using an instrument sourced from the extant literature. No statistically significant relationship was detected between knowledge sharing behaviour and gender, age, or professional tenure. Only organisational tenure weakly negatively correlated with knowledge sharing behaviour. Thus, according to these findings, demographic variables do not appear to be important determinants of knowledge sharing behaviour.

Introduction

Contemporary economies place a high premium on knowledge. According to the now widely established knowledge-based theories of the firm (Grant 1996; Kogut & Zander 1992; Nonaka, Toyama & Nagata 2000; Prahalad & Hamel 1990; Spender 1996) organisations exist primarily to integrate knowledge. The essence of these theories is that in as much as production involves the transformation of inputs into outputs, the critical input in production, which is also the primary source of value, is knowledge (Grant 1996). By implication, organisations that effectively manage and leverage knowledge are more likely to prosper than those that do not. Indeed, empirical research (Bontis 1999; McKeen, Zack & Singh 2006) consistently links effective knowledge management to superior organisational performance.

As Botha and Fouché (2002:282) correctly argue, knowledge per se cannot be managed: as such, the focus of knowledge management is to positively influence the context in which people create, share, and generally exploit knowledge. Stimulating knowledge sharing, in particular, remains an important thrust of the knowledge management movement. Bouthillier and Shearer (2002) posit that the focus of knowledge management is knowledge sharing. It is when individuals share knowledge that organisational knowledge stocks grow and organisational learning occurs. Knowledge sharing helps organisations avoid reinventing the wheel and thus be better prepared to seize new opportunities as they arise, whilst avoiding past mistakes. Knowledge sharing also enables knowledge transfer, which is concerned with the flow of knowledge between larger organisational entities such as departments and organisations themselves (see Ipe 2003). That famous lament by a former executive of the Hewlert-Packard Company – 'if only HP knew what HP knows' (see Sieloff 1999) – was an endorsement of the importance of knowledge sharing to organisational effectiveness. As it has already been noted, effective knowledge sharing has a positive impact on organisational performance (Chen 2006; Du, Ai & Ren 2007; Jacobs & Roodt 2007; Lin 2007; Pai 2006; Yang 2007).

Knowledge sharing defined

Hansen and Avital (2005:6) defined knowledge sharing behaviour as '... behaviour by which an individual voluntarily provides other social actors (both within and outside an organization) with access to his or her unique knowledge and experiences'. An important aspect of this definition is the idea that knowledge sharing is voluntary. In this regard, Hansen and Avital's definition of knowledge sharing bears more than a passing resemblance to Jarvenpaa and Staples 2000's view of information sharing. According to Jarvenpaa and Staples (cited in Hansen & Avital 2005:6), it is the willingness to share that distinguishes 'information sharing' from 'involuntary information reporting'. Knowledge sharing similarly 'represents a volitional act of providing others with (…) access to one's own knowledge and expertise' (Hansen & Avital 2005:6).

It is also helpful to distinguish between knowledge donating and knowledge collecting. According to Van den Hooff and De Ridder (2004:118) knowledge donating refers to 'communicating to others what one's personal intellectual capital is' whilst knowledge collecting is 'consulting colleagues in order to get them to share their intellectual capital'. As Van den Hooff and De Ridder further note, both processes are active, in other words, in donating, the individual who plays the role of knowledge source actively communicates his or her knowledge to others, whilst in the role of knowledge receiver the individual actively seeks out knowledge from others. Van den Hooff and De Ridder's distinction between 'knowledge collecting' and 'knowledge donating' is similar to, though perhaps more general than, the distinction between 'knowledge seeking' and 'knowledge contribution' made by He and Wei (2009). The latter distinction appears to be limited to knowledge sharing through computer-mediated knowledge management systems. Nevertheless, He and Wei's approach supports Van den Hoof and De Ridder's conceptualisation of knowledge sharing as a two-dimensional construct.

Correlates of knowledge sharing behaviour

Researchers have identified a number of variables that are related to knowledge sharing behaviour. Ipe (2003) conveniently placed them into four main groups, namely, (1) the nature of knowledge, (2) motivation to share, (3) opportunity to share and (4) the culture of the work environment. It is perhaps trivially obvious that the nature of the knowledge being shared will influence knowledge sharing behaviour. For instance, explicit knowledge, being easily modifiable, would be easier to share than tacit knowledge. With respect to the motivation to share knowledge, empirical studies have shown that factors such as enjoyment in helping others and self-efficacy can be strong motivators of knowledge sharing behaviour (Lin 2007). However, even when individuals feel motivated to share knowledge, such sharing will be subject to the availability of the opportunity to do so, with information and communications technology – frequently in the form of electronic knowledge repositories – routinely used to facilitate knowledge sharing (Cabrera, Collins & Salgado 2006). The culture of the work environment also plays an important role, with researchers reporting that dimensions such as communication climate and organisational justice do in fact influence knowledge sharing behaviour (Kim & Lee 2006). For a more comprehensive review of the literature on the correlates of knowledge sharing behaviour, see Mogotsi (2009).

Problem statement

Whilst the body of empirical literature on the correlates of knowledge sharing behaviour is growing, literature that focuses on the role of demographic variables remains scarce. Furthermore, as Gaffoor and Cloete (2010) note, knowledge management studies tend to focus on the private sector, with scant attention paid to the public service sector. Moreover, in the few studies that do consider the public service sector, the focus tends to be on Western contexts with little focus on

developing countries. This study investigates the relationship between demographic variables (gender, age, organisational tenure and professional tenure) and knowledge sharing behaviour in the context of the public service sector in a developing country in Africa. Specifically, the study seeks to answer the following research questions:

- Are gender and knowledge sharing behaviour related?
- Does knowledge sharing behaviour vary with age?
- Is knowledge sharing behaviour related to organisational tenure?
- Is knowledge sharing behaviour related to professional tenure?

In the following section, we draw from the extant literature to derive the hypothesis tested in the present study.

Literature reviewed to formulate research hypotheses
Gender

Gender appears to influence knowledge sharing behaviour. Drawing from social exchange theory, Boardia, Irmer and Abusah (2006) investigated the influence of evaluation apprehension and perceived benefits of knowledge sharing on the intention to share knowledge. In their study, these researchers considered two contexts, namely, when sharing occurs directly between individuals and when sharing occurs through contributions to an electronic knowledge management system. Women exhibited higher perceptions of the benefits of knowledge sharing than men in both contexts, such as whether knowledge sharing occurred interpersonally or via a knowledge management system. Given these findings, one would expect women to be more likely to engage in knowledge sharing than men.

Findings from other studies, too, suggest that gender may influence knowledge sharing behaviour. Taylor (2004) found that the use of knowledge management systems was significantly influenced by gender, with men consistently reporting higher levels of usage of the email, data mining, knowledge repository and yellow page components of the knowledge management system investigated than women. Lin's 2006 study investigated the effect of instrumental and expressive ties on knowledge sharing behaviour. Instrumental ties are transactional in nature; they involve a person gathering information, advice and resources necessary to accomplish a task, whilst expressive ties involve expressions of interpersonal affect, which may be positive (e.g. friendships) or negative (e.g. enmities) (Umphress *et al.* 2003:742). Lin's study indicated that gender moderated the effect of instrumental and expressive ties on knowledge sharing; specifically, the relationship between instrumental ties and knowledge sharing was stronger for women, whilst that between expressive ties and knowledge sharing was stronger for men.

All these studies would seem to suggest that gender influences knowledge sharing behaviour even if only indirectly, in other words, by influencing other variables that are themselves directly related to knowledge sharing behaviour. In the present study, therefore, it is hypothesised that:

- **Hypothesis 1**: Women are more likely to engage in knowledge sharing behaviour than men.

Age

Riege (2005) includes differences in age amongst the 'three-dozen knowledge-sharing barriers managers must consider' that he lists in his paper, although he does not provide details of how age might act as a barrier to knowledge sharing. Presumably, though, individuals might be more willing to share with members of their age group than with significantly younger or older colleagues, a sentiment supported by Ojha's 2005 study involving members of software project teams. These arguments, however, do not consider how knowledge sharing behaviour would act as a function of age. For that, it would be instructive to cast the net wider and consider the broader organisational behaviour literature in order to draw parallels that might help predict the nature of the relationship between these two variables.

Knowledge sharing behaviour as defined in the present study bears a strong resemblance to organisational citizenship behaviour as defined by Organ, Podsakoff and MacKenzie (2006:3) as 'individual behaviour that is discretionary, not directly or explicitly recognized by the formal reward system, and in aggregate promotes the efficient and effective functioning of the organization'. Thus, one might expect the relationship between knowledge sharing behaviour and age to be akin to that between organisational citizenship behaviour and age. Here, the study by Garg and Rastogi (2006) is of particular interest because it considered the relationship between age and organisational citizenship behaviour amongst schoolteachers. In this study, older teachers exhibited more pro-social behaviour than their younger colleagues. In the present study, therefore, we hypothesise as follows:

- **Hypothesis 2**: Compared to younger teachers, older teachers are more likely to engage in knowledge sharing behaviour.

Organisational and professional tenure

Tenure appears to have some effect on knowledge sharing. Boardia, Irmer and Abusah (2006) found organisational tenure to be a good predictor of knowledge sharing when knowledge is shared interpersonally, although not so when sharing occurs through databases. Additionally, they reported negative correlations between tenure and evaluation apprehension whether knowledge was shared interpersonally or through databases, which would seem to suggest an indirect link between organisational tenure and knowledge sharing behaviour. Watson and Hewett (2006) argued that organisational tenure would be positively related to knowledge sharing behaviour because as tenure increases so do trust and commitment to the organisation and its process. Watson and Hewett's argument is reasonable

because both trust (Chowdhury 2005; Wang *et al.* 2007) and commitment (Van den Hooff & De Ridder 2004) have been found to be positively related to knowledge sharing behaviour. In fact, Watson and Hewett's findings supported their hypothesis.

Boardia, Irmer and Abusah (2006), and Watson and Hewett (2006) focused specifically on organisational tenure. However, it seems plausible that tenure in general will be related to knowledge sharing behaviour; tenure, generally, should also be positively correlated with trust and commitment, which in turn ought to be positively correlated with knowledge sharing behaviour. For instance, Bakker *et al.* (2006) reported a positive correlation (0.19; $p < 0.05$) between team tenure and knowledge sharing, indicating that the longer team members have been together, the more likely they are to engage in knowledge sharing behaviour. Intuitively, one would expect affective commitment to the profession to grow with tenure in the profession; consequently, knowledge sharing behaviour, driven by a desire to contribute to the growth of the profession, should grow with professional tenure. With regard to organisational and professional tenure, therefore, we hypothesise as follows:

- **Hypothesis 3**: Knowledge sharing behaviour will be positively correlated to organisational tenure.
- **Hypothesis 4**: Knowledge sharing behaviour will be positively correlated to professional tenure.

Methodology
Study context

The present study was designed as an analytical survey, with data collected from a sample of teachers selected from a six public senior secondary schools in and around Gaborone, Botswana. In Botswana, senior secondary schools refer to schools that prepare students for the Botswana General Certificate of Secondary Education (BGSE) examinations, deemed equivalent to Cambridge University's International General Certificate of Secondary Educations (IGSE). Students enter senior secondary schools after undertaking seven years of primary and three years of junior secondary schooling. Teachers in these schools generally have Bachelor's degrees or higher.

In order to undertake the study, permission had to be sought from a number of authorities. Firstly, it was necessary to get Botswana government approval and because schools fall under the Ministry of Education, permission was sought from the Permanent Secretary in the said ministry. Schools in Botswana are divided into a number of regions. Thus, having obtained the overall research permit from the ministry, it was then necessary to seek permission from the appropriate regional chief education officer. With this permit duly obtained, individual school heads could then be approached to seek their permission to approach teachers in their schools to participate in the study. Finally, each questionnaire had a covering letter requesting individual teachers to participate in the study. Teachers were informed that their participation was voluntary and that they could pull out of the study any time they wished.

Measuring instruments

Amongst the self–report knowledge sharing scales, the one developed by Van den Hooff and colleagues (De Vries, Van den Hooff & De Ridder 2006; Van den Hooff & De Leeuw van Weenen 2004; Van den Hooff & De Ridder 2004) is particularly attractive because of its ability to measure two dimensions of knowledge sharing, namely, knowledge donating, and knowledge collecting. Lin (2007) modified Van den Hooff & De Leeuw van Weenen (2004)'s knowledge sharing scale to produce one in which no reference is made to departments within the company. This is particularly useful in school contexts where teachers are assigned to departments on the basis of the subjects they teach, raising the possibility of a teacher belonging to more than one department. In any case, there is no intention in the current study to investigate the influence of the department (to which a teacher belongs) on knowledge sharing behaviour, and no suggestion from the reviewed literature that this might be a worthwhile endeavour to pursue. Lin's knowledge sharing instrument was adopted for the current study. For the purposes of this study, the scale was modified, replacing 'company' with 'school' to make the instrument directly relevant to the study participants. The final knowledge sharing behaviour used in the study is shown as Table 1.

Results

Sample description

Out of the 283 returned questionnaires, 147 (52%) were from female teachers, whilst 133 (47%) were from male teachers; 3 (1%) did not mention their gender, presumably because they were uncomfortable to do so, or did not see what its bearing would be on the study. Nevertheless, looking at these figures, it can be seen that the sample was fairly well balanced in terms of gender. Teacher age ranged from a minimum of 21 years to a maximum of 63 years (a range of 42 years), with a mean of 37.3 years and a standard deviation of 7.3. Most teachers were quite young, with approximately half under 36 years old. Professional tenure ranged from one month to 42 years, with a mean of 12.0 years and a standard deviation of 7.5. Half of the teachers had been teaching for no more than 10

TABLE 1: Knowledge sharing behaviour scale.

Item number	Description
1	When I've learned something new, I tell my colleagues about it (KD).
2	When they have learnt something new, my colleagues tell me something about it (KD).
3	Knowledge sharing among colleagues is considered normal in my school (KD).
4	I share information with my colleagues when they ask for it (KC).
5	I share my skills with colleagues when they ask for it (KC).
6	Colleagues in my school share knowledge with me when I ask them to (KC).
7	Colleagues in my school share their skills with me when I ask them to (KC).

Note: This table was modified from Lin, H.F., 2007, 'Knowledge sharing and firm innovation capability: An empirical study', *International Journal of Manpower* 28(3/4), 315–332, viewed 20 May 2010, from http://dx.doi.org/10.1108/01437720710755272.
KC, knowledge collecting; KD, knowledge donating.

years. With respect to organisational tenure, approximately 50% of the teachers had only been at their schools for no more than three years; the mean organisational tenure, though, was 3.9 years, with a standard deviation of 3.7.

Reliability of the knowledge sharing behaviour scale

Item analysis of the knowledge sharing behaviour scale (see Table 1) yielded a Cronbach's coefficient α of 0.82, with all the items strongly positively correlated with the scale total. The first three items were intended to measure knowledge donating, whilst the last four were intended to measure knowledge collecting. The knowledge donating items on their own yielded a Cronbach's coefficient α of 0.70, whilst the knowledge collecting items on their own yield a Cronbach's coefficient α of 0.87. However, principal axis factoring with both the Eigenvalue > 1 rule and inspection of the scree plot revealed that the seven-item scale was, for the sample under consideration, unidimensional, explaining 76% of the variance in the data. The reason for the unidimensionality of the scale might be that the differences in the items were too subtle for the respondents to notice. In particular, the use of the word share might have been construed as suggesting a bidirectional, rather than unidirectional, flow of knowledge and information, thus nullifying the distinction between knowledge donating and knowledge collecting. Further statistical analysis was thus based on the seven-item unidimensional knowledge sharing scale with a coefficient α of 0.82.

Hypothesis testing

The Pearson correlation coefficient was used to quantify the relationships between demographic variables (age, organisational tenure and professional tenure) and knowledge sharing behaviour. Age and professional tenure were not statistically significantly related to knowledge sharing behaviour, so hypotheses two and four were not supported. Organisational tenure and knowledge sharing behaviour were negatively correlated ($r = -0.14$, $p < 0.05$), providing some support for hypothesis three. The Levene test for variability ($F = 0.59$, $p = 0.44$) suggested that the difference in the variance of the knowledge sharing behaviour scores for men and women was not statistically significant. Furthermore, with $t (277) = -1.01$, $p = 0.31$, the difference in the mean knowledge sharing behaviour scores for men and women was not statistically significant. Thus, hypothesis one was also not supported.

Discussion

This study examined the relationships between gender, age, professional tenure and organisational tenure on one hand, and knowledge sharing behaviour on the other. The literature on the relationship between gender and knowledge sharing, whilst limited, would seem to suggest that women should be more inclined to both donate and collect knowledge than men. In this study, however, no statistically significant relationship was identified between gender and knowledge sharing behaviour. This may very well be due to our failure to distinguish between (biological) sex and (psychological) gender. Indeed, in this study, we used gender to refer to biological sex. As noted earlier in this paper, biological sex appears to influence knowledge sharing behaviour indirectly by influencing other variables that themselves influence knowledge sharing behaviour directly.

Bem (1974) devised an instrument for measuring psychological gender. Using this often cited instrument, it is possible to classify individuals as sex-typed (i.e. men exhibiting 'male' values and women exhibiting 'female' values), cross sex-typed (men exhibiting 'female' values or women exhibiting 'male' values), or androgenous (i.e. individuals showing little difference in their masculinity and feminity scores). Using this instrument, researchers (e.g. Todman and Day, 2006) have shown that in situations where biological sex does not matter, psychological gender does sometimes matter. Conceivably, therefore, psychological gender may be related to knowledge sharing behaviour even if the latter remains unrelated to biological sex.

Our findings regarding age and professional tenure, both of which turned out not to be related to knowledge sharing behaviour, are counter intuitive: one would have expected older and more experienced individuals to be eager to donate knowledge to younger and less experienced colleagues; conversely, younger and less experienced teachers were expected to eagerly engage in knowledge collecting. The results obtained in this study may be due to the fact that regardless of their age and professional tenure, teachers tend to have similar educational levels. For that reason, they may all feel that they possess the same level of expertise, and thus have little motivation for knowledge sharing, be it donating or collecting. Furthermore, a lot of the expertise they might require access to is likely to relate to subject content (e.g. Newton's Third Law of Motion for Physics teachers) that can be obtained from books and other information sources without the knowledge seeking individual necessarily having to consult other colleagues.

Knowledge sharing was negatively – albeit weakly related to organisational tenure. This is rather worrying because it suggests that the longer teachers stay at a particular school, the more unwilling they become to share knowledge. A possible explanation for this might be that when teachers initially arrive at a new school, either as new recruits or on transfer, they eagerly share knowledge with their colleagues as they try to find their way around the new environment. In time, however, the enthusiasm for knowledge sharing dies down because of a lack of reprocity on the part of other colleagues, or because of the feeling that knowledge sharing in general is not valued.

Conclusions & recommendations

This study investigated the relationship between knowledge sharing behaviour and four demographic variables, namely, gender (biological sex), age, organisational tenure and professional tenure. Contrary to the postulated hypotheses, gender, age, and professional tenure were not related to knowledge sharing behaviour, whilst organisational tenure only weakly negatively correlated with knowledge sharing behaviour. Thus, demographic variables do not appear to play any significant role in relation to knowledge sharing behaviour. Nevertheless, given suggestions from the literature that demographic variables do influence knowledge sharing behaviour, it is recommended that further research into the relationship between knowledge sharing behaviour and demographic variables amongst schoolteachers be prosecuted. Future studies should be more comprehensive in terms of the schools and teachers targeted, and also consider the role of other variables, such as a conducive working environment, that might influence how demographic variables interact with knowledge sharing behaviour.

Author acknowledgements

The work reported in this paper formed part of a doctoral research project undertaken by the first author at the University of Pretoria. The first author wishes to express his gratitude to the University of Botswana which financed the said doctoral study. All the authors would like to express their gratitude to the various officers in the Botswana Ministry of Edcuation for granting the requisite permits that allowed the authors to conduct this study. We would also like to sincerely express our gratitude to the teachers without whose input this study would never have seen the light of day. Finally, we wish to acknowledge the input of the reviewers who significantly improved the quality of this paper.

Authors' competing interests

The authors declare that they have no financial or personal relationship(s) which may have inappropriately influenced them in writing this paper.

Author contributions

This study was part of a doctoral study undertaken by Isaac Mogotsi (first author) under the supervision of Prof. Boon (second author) at the University of Pretoria. Dr Fletcher (third author) provided invaluable statistical input to the study.

References

Bakker, M., Leenders, Th. A.J., Gabbay, S., Kratzer, J. & Van Engelen, J.M.L., 2006, 'Is trust really social capital? Knowledge sharing in product development projects', *The Learning Organization* 13(6), 594–605, viewed 20 May 2010, from http://dx.doi.org/10.1108/09696470610705479

Bem, S.L., 1974, 'The measurement of psychological androgyny', *Journal of Consulting and Clinical Psychology* 42(2), 155–62, viewed 20 May 2010, from http://dx.doi.org/10.1037/h0036215, PMid:4823550

Boardia, P., Irmer, B.E. & Abusah, D., 2006, 'Differences in sharing knowledge interpersonally and via databases: The role of evaluation apprehension and perceived benefits', *European Journal of Work and Organizational Psychology* 15(3), 262–280, viewed 20 May 2010, from http://dx.doi.org/10.1080/13594320500417784

Bontis, N., 1999, 'Managing an organizational learning system by aligning stocks and flows of knowledge: An empirical examination of intellectual capital, knowledge management, and business performance', PhD thesis, Richard Ivey School of Business, University of Western-Ontario.

Botha D.F. & Fouché B., 2002, 'The assessment of corporate knowledge management parctices: The role of a reference model', in T. Bothma & A. Kaniki (eds.), *Progress in Library and Information Science in Southern Africa: Proceedings of the second biennial DISSAnet Conference*, Infuse Publishers, Pretoria, South Africa, October 24–25, 2002, pp. 279–293.

Bouthillier, F. & Shearer, K., 2002, 'Understanding knowledge management and information management: The need for an empirical perspective', *Information Research* 8(1), viewed 09 December 2009, from http://InformationR.net/ir/8-1/paper141.html

Cabrera, A., Collins, W. & Salgado, J.F., 2006, 'Determinants of individual engagement in knowledge sharing', *The International Journal of Human Resource Management* 17(2), 245–264, viewed 20 May 2010, from http://dx.doi.org/10.1080/09585190500404614

Chen, L.Y., 2006, 'Effect of knowledge sharing to organizational marketing effectiveness in large accounting firms that are strategically aligned', *Journal of the American Academy of Business* 9(1), 176–182.

Chowdhury, S., 2005, 'The role of affect- and cognition-based trust in complex knowledge sharing', *Journal of Managerial Issues* 17(3), 310–326.

De Vries, R.E., Van den Hooff, B.B. & De Ridder, J., 2006, 'Explaining knowledge sharing: The role of team communication styles, job satisfaction, and performance beliefs', *Communication Research* 33(2), 115–135, viewed 20 May 2010, from http://dx.doi.org/10.1177/0093650205285366

Du, R., Ai, S. & Ren, Y., 2007, 'Relationship between knowledge sharing and performance: A survey in Xi'an, China', *Expert Systems with Applications* 32(1), 38–46, viewed 20 May 2010, from http://dx.doi.org/10.1016/j.eswa.2005.11.001

Gaffoor, S. & Cloete, F., 2010, 'Knowledge management in local government: The case of Stellenbosch Municipality', *South African Journal of Information Management* 12(1), Art. #422, 7 pages. http://dx.doi.org/10.4102/sajim.v12i1.422

Garg, P. & Rastogi, R., 2006, 'Climate profile and OCBs of teachers in public and private schools of India', *International Journal of Educational Management* 20(7), 529–541, viewed 20 May 2010, from http://dx.doi.org/10.1108/09513540610704636

Grant, R.M., 1996, 'Toward a knowledge-based theory of the firm', *Strategic Management Journal* 17, Winter Special Issue, 109–122.

Hansen, S. & Avital, M., 2005, 'Share and share alike: The social and technological influences on knowledge sharing behavior', *Sprouts: Working papers on Information Systems* 5(13), 1–19.

He, W. & Wei, K.-K., 2009, 'What drives continued knowledge sharing? An investigation of knowledge-contribution and -seeking beliefs', *Decision Support Systems* 46(4), 826–838, viewed 20 May 2010, from http://dx.doi.org/10.1016/j.dss.2008.11.007

Ipe, M., 2003, 'Knowledge sharing in organizations: A conceptual framework' *Human Resource Development Review* 2(4), 337–359, viewed 20 May 2010, from http://dx.doi.org/10.1177/1534484303257985

Jacobs, E. & Roodt, G., 2007, 'The development of a knowledge sharing construct to predict turnover intentions', *Aslib Proceedings: New Information* 59(3), 229–248, viewed 20 May 2010, from http://dx.doi.org/10.1108/00012530710752034

Jarvenpaa, S. & Staples, D., 2000, 'The use of collaborative electronic media for information sharing: An exploratory study of determinants', *Journal of Strategic Information Systems* 9(2–3), 129–134, viewed 20 May 2010, from http://dx.doi.org/10.1016/S0963-8687(00)00042-1

Kim, S. & Lee, H., 2006, 'The impact of organizational context and information technology on employee knowledge-sharing capabilities', *Public Administration Review* 66, 370–385, viewed 20 May 2010, from http://dx.doi.org/10.1111/j.1540-6210.2006.00595.x

Kogut, B. & Zander, U., 1992, 'Knowledge of the firm, combinative capabilities, and the replication of technology', *Organization Science* 3(3), 383–397, viewed 20 May 2010, from http://dx.doi.org/10.1287/orsc.3.3.383

Lin C.-P., 2006, 'Gender differs: Modeling knowledge sharing from a perspective of social network ties', *Asian Journal of Social Psychology* 9(3), 236–241, viewed 20 May 2010, from http://dx.doi.org/10.1111/j.1467-839X.2006.00202.x

Lin, H.F., 2007, 'Knowledge sharing and firm innovation capability: An empirical study', *International Journal of Manpower* 28(3/4), 315–332, viewed 20 May 2010, from http://dx.doi.org/10.1108/01437720710755272

McKeen, J.D., Zack M.H. & Singh S., 2006, 'Knowledge Management and Organizational Performance: An Exploratory Survey', *Proceedings of the 39th Annual Hawaii International Conference on System Sciences (HICSS'06) Track 7*, 2006.

Mogotsi, I.C., 2009, 'An empirical investigation into the relationships among knowledge sharing behaviour, organizational citizenship behaviour, job satisfaction and organizational commitment', DPhil thesis, Dept. of Information Science, University of Pretoria.

Nonaka, I., Toyama, R. & Nagata, A., 2000, A firm as a knowledge creating entity: A new perspective on the theory of the firm, *Industrial and Corporate Change* 9(1), 1–20, viewed 20 May 2010, from http://dx.doi.org/10.1093/icc/9.1.1

Ojha, A.L., 2005, 'Impact of team demography on knowledge sharing in software project teams', *South Asian Journal of Management* 12(3), 67–78.

Organ, D.W., Podsakoff, P.M. & MacKenzie., S.B., 2006, *Organizational citizenship behavior: Its nature, antecedents, and consequences*, SAGE, Thousand Oaks, CA.

Pai, J.C., 2006, 'An empirical study of the relationship between knowledge sharing and IS/IT strategic planning (ISSP)', *Management Decision* 44(1), 105–122, viewed 20 May 2010, from http://dx.doi.org/10.1108/00251740610641490

Prahalad, C.K. & Hamel, G., 1990, 'The core competence of the corporation', *Harvard Business Review*, May – June, 79–91.

Riege, A., 2005, 'Three-dozen knowledge-sharing barriers managers must consider', *Journal of Knowledge Management* 9(3), 18–35, viewed 20 May 2010, from http://dx.doi.org/10.1108/13673270510602746

Sieloff, C., 1999, '"If only HP knew what HP knows": The roots of knowledge management at Hwelett-Packard', *Journal of Knowledge Management* 3(1), 47–53.

Spender, J.-C., 1996, 'Making knowledge the basis of a dynamic theory of the firm', *Strategic Management Journal* 17, Special Issue: Knowledge and the Firm (Winter), 45–62.

Taylor, W.A., 2004, 'Computer-mediated knowledge sharing and individual user differences: An exploratory study', *European Journal of Information Systems* 13(1), 52–64, viewed 20 May 2010, from http://dx.doi.org/10.1057/palgrave.ejis.3000484

Todman, J. & Day, K., 2006, 'Computer anxiety: the role of psychological gender', *Computers in Human Behaviour* 22(5), 856–869, viewed 20 May 2010, from http://dx.doi.org/10.1016/j.chb.2004.03.009

Umphress, E.E., Labianca, G., Brass, D.J., Kass E. & Scholten, L., 2003, 'The role of instrumental and expressive social ties in employees' perceptions of organizational justice', *Organization Science* 14(6), 738–753, viewed 20 May 2010, from http://dx.doi.org/10.1287/orsc.14.6.738.24865

Van den Hooff, B. & De Leeuw van Weenen, F., 2004, 'Committed to share: Commitment and CMC use as antecedents of knowledge sharing', *Knowledge and Process Management* 11(1), 13–24, viewed 20 May 2010, from http://dx.doi.org/10.1002/kpm.187

Van den Hooff, B. & De Ridder, J.A., 2004, 'Knowledge sharing in context: The influence of organizational commitment, communication climate and CMC use on knowledge sharing', *Journal of Knowledge Management* 8(6), 117–130, viewed 20 May 2010, from http://dx.doi.org/10.1108/13673270410567675

Wang, C.-H., Lee, Y.-D., Lin, W.-I. & Zhuo, L.-T., 2007, 'Effects of personal qualities and team processes on willingness to share knowledge: An empirical study', *International Journal of Management*, 24(2), 250–256.

Watson, S. & Hewett, K., 2006, 'A multi-theoretical model of knowledge transfer in organizations: Determinants of knowledge contribution and reuse', *Journal of Management Studies* 43(2), 141–173, viewed 20 May 2010, from http://dx.doi.org/10.1111/j.1467-6486.2006.00586.x

Yang, J., 2007, 'The impact of knowledge sharing on organizational learning and effectiveness', *Journal of Knowledge Management* 11(2), 83–90, viewed 20 May 2010, http://dx.doi.org/10.1108/13673270710738933

Information and knowledge sharing trends of small and medium-sized enterprises in the Western Cape, South Africa

Authors:
Faeda Mohsam[1]
Pieter A. van Brakel[2]

Affiliations:
[1]Faculty of Business, Cape Peninsula University of Technology, South Africa

[2]Faculty of Informatics and Design, Cape Peninsula University of Technology, South Africa

Correspondence to:
Pieter van Brakel

Email:
vanbrakelp@gmail.com

Postal address:
PO Box 652, Cape Town 8000, South Africa

Background: Small and medium-sized enterprises (SMEs), especially in the Western Cape Province of South Africa, are currently facing various financial and other obstacles, which may threaten their survival. Globalisation, the lowering of trade barriers and the reduction of import tariffs have resulted in increased international competition. Businesses are thus forced to undertake continuous improvements and innovation in order to survive, to keep abreast of change and to excel.

Objectives: Effective knowledge sharing and consequent knowledge management (KM) have been identified as definite approaches to enhancing competitive advantage. The research therefore aimed to establish to what extent small enterprises embrace their knowledge sharing activities and whether their knowledge sharing activities are managed at all. Furthermore, it examined how their knowledge sharing can contribute to their competitive advantage.

Method: A case study approach was followed for this research. Selected SMEs from the engineering sector were the subject of the case study and SME owners, directors and managers of consulting civil engineering firms were interviewed to determine whether there are mechanisms in place to ensure better knowledge sharing within SMEs.

Results: In general, respondents had stated that they possessed special factors that set them above their competitors:

- The company strategy and good reputation of completing projects within the required timeframe. In other words, they were well known for their track record in terms of service delivery.
- Their specialty in terms of different focus areas, namely structural and civil engineering, water supply and storm water design, transportation, sewer design and storm water traffic.
- The fact that they operated in silos. This means that the specialists in their specific fields operated independently in groups, separately from everyone else in the company.
- Their good relationship with local authorities and other companies in the field.
- Their multidisciplinary approach in incorporating all spheres of civil engineering, which gave them a niche in the market.
- The vast knowledge and experience of the owners and directors.

Conclusion: Each of the companies interviewed had unique skills that they can apply to their advantage. They were also found to be implementing KM processes such as sharing, creating and leveraging of information and knowledge, albeit in the absence of formal policies. It was therefore deduced that SME successes depend on how well they share their tacit and explicit knowledge; this will determine whether they would excel above their competitors.

Introduction

Small businesses form an integral part of the South African economy. The importance of the small business sector is widely recognised and it is therefore essential that small businesses survive and prosper. According to the South African Department of Trade and Industry, by 2004 approximately 45% of employed people in South Africa worked in the small business sector and it is predicted that this sector could contribute up to 60% – 80% of the gross domestic product over the next 5–10 years (*South Africa business guidebook* 2006:241). The importance of small business is stressed repeatedly in the important policy publication of the South African Government, namely *A framework to guide Government's programme in the electoral mandate period 2009–2014* (South African Government 2009).

In South Africa, the *National Small Business Act* (Act No. 102 of 1996) defines micro, small and medium businesses (SMMEs) as:

… a separate and distinct business entity, including co-operative enterprises and non-governmental organizations, managed by one owner or more which, including its branches or subsidiaries, if any, is predominantly carried on in any sector or sub-sector of the economy … and which can be classified as a micro-, a very small, a small or medium enterprise by satisfying the criteria … opposite the smallest relevant size or class …

(South African Government 1996)

The Act further defines a small business organisation as:

… any entity, whether or not incorporated or registered under any law, which consists mainly of persons carrying on small business concerns in any economic sector, or which has been established for the purpose of promoting the interest of or representing small business concerns, and includes any federation consisting wholly or partly of such association, and also any branch of such organization.

(South African Government 1996)

For the purpose of clarification, the term 'SMME' is one that is used only in the South African context, whereas 'SME' is mostly an international term that encompasses our SMME concept. In this article 'SME' is therefore preferred and will be used throughout.

In South Africa, there are presently approximately two million small, medium and micro enterprises (SMEs) registered to create long-term employment (South African Government 2009). Nearly a decade ago, Berry *et al.* (2002:4) already positively indicated the major economic roles SMEs fulfil in South Africa, for example, by manufacturing goods of value or by providing services to both consumers and or enterprises. SMEs also contribute to export performance by offering services and products to foreign clients. Akinwumi and Olawale (2010:2763) assert that, as a result of South Africa's current high unemployment rate, SMEs are expected to be an important mechanism to address the challenges of job creation, economic growth and development. They further state that SMEs are an important source of innovation when it comes to new products, services and technology. It is therefore clear that both small and medium enterprises play a significant role in the South African economy.

Research problem

From the above it is clear that SMEs can play a pivotal role in any national economy. Furthermore, for the purpose of this research, it was assumed that the continued successes of SMEs might further be improved if their knowledge sharing practices are placed on a sound footing. This assumption is line with the views expressed by Antoncic and Omerzel (2008:1184), namely that the management of knowledge assets may be critical to provide small companies with new tools with which to survive, grow and maintain a sustainable competitive advantage. Because knowledge has become one of the most important driving forces for business success, companies are becoming more knowledge-centred, focusing more on hiring 'minds' rather than 'hands' to facilitate the increasing need for leveraging knowledge (Wong 2005:261). From the above-mentioned statements, it is clear that knowledge is the one asset with which a

company can distinguish itself from its competitors. This also implies that knowledge, although intangible, is being treated as a resource and therefore as a means of improving and maintaining competitive advantage. The objective of this research is therefore to determine the nature and extent of SMEs' knowledge-sharing practices in the Western Cape Province. If these sharing practices could be identified and nurtured, any particular SME could be in a better position to gain competitive advantage over its competitors.

Research methodology

The research conducted was qualitative in nature and a case study approach was followed. Ten small and medium enterprises were studied and interviews were conducted for data collection purposes with a selected number of participants from the consulting civil engineering industry. Stead and Struwig (2001:8) believe that this method of research is not used often enough as it entails an in-depth study of a small number of situations or cases. However, its main purpose is to provide a complete description and understanding of the matter that is studied, notwithstanding the small number of people involved. These authors (2001:8) also state that three important factors normally are identified in this type of study, namely:

• features that are common to all cases in the general group
• features that are not common to all cases, but are common to certain subgroups
• features that are unique to specific cases.

In this regard, it was argued that the case study approach should provide the researcher with a clear understanding of the current status of knowledge-producing processes within the enterprise. Both illustrative and experimental case study approaches were used amongst small and larger enterprises in order to determine the extent to which knowledge practices were adopted within SMEs and the potential contribution of these practices to improving competitive advantage. In this way, the researchers could perhaps create a clearer picture of the status of knowledge sharing in SMEs.

The civil engineering sector was chosen for the purposes of this study because it is characterised as a highly specialised, knowledge-intensive and project-based industry within the Western Cape. Maintaining competitive advantage in this regard is therefore of the utmost importance in this category of enterprises. After careful consideration, 10 SMEs from the civil engineering sector in the Western Cape were selected. An initial pilot study was conducted with three small and medium-sized companies in the construction and consulting engineering field to establish the validity of the questionnaire that had been created in view of establishing the nature of knowledge sharing. However, it was decided to limit the research to only the consulting civil engineering sector as the two spheres of engineering (constructing and consulting) have quite different work practices. More information regarding the companies interviewed, their core business and the number of employees in each is listed in Table 1.

TABLE 1: List of consulting engineering companies interviewed.

Name	Core business	Number of years in existence	Number of employees
Company A	Consulting civil engineers (including structural engineering)	4 years (since 2006)	2 Professional engineers and technologists 2 Administrative personnel 1 Student (doing in-service training)
Company B	Consulting civil engineer consultants (including structural engineering)	5 years (since 2005)	2 Professional engineers 2 Technicians and draughtsmen 2 Technologists 1 Administrative personnel
Company C	Consulting civil engineers and project managers	8 years (since 2003)	5 Professional technologists 1 Human resource practitioner 2 Administrative assistants
Company D	Consulting civil engineers	5.5 years (since 2005)	2 Professional technologists 5 Technicians 2 CAD operators 1 Administrative assistant
Company E	Consulting civil engineers	7 years (since 2003)	3 Professional engineers 1 Technologist (BTech student) 2 Administrative personnel
Company F	Consulting engineers (civil, electrical, structural, traffic engineering and GIS applications)	11 years (since 1999)	52 Civil and electrical engineers and technologists 17 Engineering CAD operators and technicians 9 Administrative officers
Company G	Consulting civil engineers	15 years (since 1995)	80 Staff, comprising: Professional engineers and technologists, technicians and CAD operators, and administration support staff
Company H	Multidisciplinary consulting engineers	25 years (since 1985)	3 Administrative personnel 8 Technical staff, plus a number of consultants
Company I	Consulting civil engineers	7 years (since 2003)	1 Professional engineer 2 Technicians 2 Trainee technicians 4 Site supervisors
Company J	Consulting civil engineers	22 years (since 1988)	2 Professional engineers 5 Technicians 14 Draughtsmen 5 Administrative personnel

CAD, computer-aided design; GIS, geographic information system.

As mentioned above, in-depth interviews were conducted with the owners, directors and senior staff of selected SMEs. All interviews were manually recorded and a case study was written for each SME. The structured questionnaire (see Appendix Interview Questionnaire) was designed under the following broad categories:

- Section A: Biographical and company information, including organisational structure and outline of employees. This was needed to determine the type of company, as well as the categories of staff according to professional, technical and administrative abilities.
- Section B: Knowledge and information sharing practices. This was necessary to establish, *inter alia*, what challenges the various companies' face, their modes of communication with staff, whether there was a culture of trust amongst management and employees to facilitate the sharing of knowledge, training and mentoring, and whether succession-planning measures were in place.
- Section C: Information needs and knowledge sources. This was important for establishing the companies' information needs and information retrieval techniques.
- Section D: Management of knowledge and acquisition of external information. Answers to questions in this section would identify, *inter alia*, whether there were alliances in place with partners to gain external knowledge and expertise, the type of organisational structure used by the companies, the use of various storage and retrieval techniques, the use of information technology and information systems, the companies' research and development activities, the extent of their face-to-face communication and social networking practices, and any affiliations to professional bodies.

- Section E: The level of competitive advantage (CA). This included information on what sets these companies apart from their competitors, their strategy with regard to achieving CA, their efforts to increase market share, efficiency and gain CA, who their competitors are and whether they knew what their competitors were up to, who their customers are, and the extent to which they valued their customers.
- Section F: The combination of knowledge management and competitive advantage practices. Similarly, information about the combination of these practices was needed to identify if and how company knowledge was managed, whether the company promoted a KM-friendly environment, organisational practices with regard to KM, whether they knew what type of marketing activities rival companies undertook with regard to their increasing CA, what they did to increase their own CA, and how they used their knowledge to gain CA.

Some questions from previous prominent KM studies were extracted and modified for the purposes of this study, for example, those undertaken by authors such as Kok, Van Brakel and Van der Walt (2004), Snyman and Van der Berg (2003) and Uit Beijerse (1999, 2000) (see Appendix Examples of previous knowledge management studies that have been undertaken).

The next section briefly discusses the current status of KM implementation in SMEs globally, thereafter the methodology of this is described in more detail and the results of the current research are interpreted.

Brief overview of knowledge management in small and medium enterprises

It is common knowledge that KM was originally mostly practiced in larger enterprises, with specific foci on issues such as culture, networking, and the development of organisational and technological infrastructures to accommodate KM initiatives, especially in large multinational environments. Awazu and Desouza (2006:40) assert that SMEs knowingly or unknowingly manage knowledge intuitively in the right way, that is, the humanistic way, whilst Furu, Salojarvi and Sveiby (2005:104) contend that although KM is practiced in small companies, SME managers do not necessarily know it as such, or call it knowledge management. Similarly, Uit Beijerse's (2000:175) study on 12 innovative small companies in the Netherlands found no less than 79 different KM activities in these businesses. According to the same source, this was owing to the fact that SMEs have emerged as a business paradigm in today's knowledge economy. However, SME successes, and ultimately their growth, will determine to what extent they manage their knowledge work and thus knowledge sharing.

According to a recent study, many SME managers in German-speaking countries have come to realise and appreciate that the inventiveness and uniqueness of each of their knowledge workers would lead to customer satisfaction, as well as the success of the SME (Fink & Ploder 2009:37). Although these SMEs were often cash-strapped and did not have enough capital to invest in KM initiatives, it was necessary for them that their knowledge was leveraged optimally in order to achieve most of the goals of the enterprise. Fink and Ploder's (2009) research also emphasises the importance of capturing individual and organisational knowledge, which could result in gaining CA in SMEs, predominantly because human capital is the source of creativity in enterprises. Consequently, it is also imperative that a typical small enterprise's implicit or tacit knowledge should be converted to explicit formats in order to perform, store and retrieve functions to enhance organisational value (Bozbura 2007:210). In order to achieve this, enterprises should invest in their employees by means of training and mentoring. In other words, for KM to be successful, employees optimally should share both tacit and explicit knowledge and information within the organisational memory base. Tacit knowledge, which is regarded as a key ingredient of socially constructed knowledge, is primarily captured by means of informational discussions in whichever formats. Because this knowledge resides within the minds of people and is therefore difficult to formalise, transfer or spread, it cannot be thought of or argued about in the same way as explicit knowledge. Thus, it seems less complicated to apply KM processes in small and medium companies because it is easier to capture tacit knowledge in less formalised (small) environments such as SMEs.

In his research on KM practices in Turkish SMEs, Bozbura (2007:211) emphasises the importance of capturing and acquiring knowledge, which is gained by arranging and managing an organisation's relationship with its customers, shareholders, suppliers, rivals, the state, the official institutions, society, and so on. His research reveals that their success can be attributed to four factors:

- training and mentoring of employees
- policies and strategies of KM
- knowledge capturing and acquisition from outside
- effects of organisational culture.

Empirical evidence from research conducted by Chen et al. (2006:20) should also be taken in account. This research was undertaken amongst British SMEs in the service sector to identify their needs and practices regarding inter-organisational knowledge transfer. It showed that external knowledge was of paramount importance for SMEs. Their research also showed that customers had the biggest impact on SMEs and thus it is imperative for SMEs to develop and maintain good customer relationship management practices. Holding regular meetings with main customers and suppliers, obtaining advice from counterparts in other organisations and dealing with complaints, as well as engaging in social and electronic networking, are some of the ways in which inter-organisational knowledge transfer can take place in SMEs.

Massa and Testa (2008:2) state that although information and data management are important aspects of KM, the latter involves broader issues, such as the creation of processes and behaviours that allow people to transform information within the organisation to enable them to create and share knowledge. Therefore, it is imperative that KM in SMEs should also include people, process, technology and culture.

Du Plessis's research (2008:61–66) on the impact of communities of practice (CoPs) as vehicles for knowledge sharing in SMEs revealed that CoPs can be an effective KM tool for SMEs. Du Plessis (2008) defines CoPs as groups of people who work together with the aim of achieving specific goals by means of creating, sharing and leveraging information. Although these groups of people are often from different backgrounds, they can work together towards achieving a common goal, using their knowledge, skills and abilities to achieve this. They also share a common concern or passion for what they do and each one brings unique skills to the CoP, which are then shared amongst members of the community. These members do not necessarily work together on a daily basis, but they benefit and find value in their regular meetings and interactions. They share information, insight and advice, explore new ideas and often act as sounding boards for one another. CoPs can be either technologically advanced, for example, they may use particular management systems, or they could be simplistic in nature, such as a group of like-minded people discussing a work-related problem, or seeking a solution with minimal or no use of technology. Some of the points extracted from Du Plessis's (2008:61–66) research focus on knowledge sharing and how CoPs can impact on SMEs in this regard, for example, (1) CoPs can assist in managing the knowledge sharing life cycle and (2) CoPs can serve as vehicles to combat knowledge loss.

Du Plessis's research shows the enormous impact that CoPs can have on SMEs, emphasising the fact that knowledge is a definite factor for CA within SMEs. In this research project, the researchers therefore also aimed to establish whether they could assist with the creation, sharing and leveraging of knowledge in these smaller communities, as well as whether they could assist these communities to cope with knowledge losses when employees retire or leave the organisation. These and other research findings are discussed below.

Findings, analysis and interpretation
Knowledge and information sharing practices (Interview questions B1–6)

As mentioned above, SMEs in general face a number of financial and other challenges. This also emerged during the interviews (see Appendix Interview Questionnaire for the specific questions in this regard), with the three biggest challenges seeming to be the following:

Attracting good quality staff and staff retention

It was apparent that staff retention is always a challenge in any small business environment as many employees were often lost to larger companies who offered higher salaries and more benefits, which SMEs found difficult to match. Qualified engineers seemed to start their careers in small businesses, but were often lured away by the salaries offered by larger organisations. Some engineers often specialised in a particular area and once they gained enough experience, they moved on to larger organisations. A large portion of respondents cited access to finance as another challenge for SMEs.

Finance

Fierce competition was identified as a predominant factor for SMEs during the past 5 years (and earlier), as many enterprises tendered at substantially lower prices, which made it difficult for others to compete. It was therefore important for them to distinguish themselves as being preferred providers in the industry, not only in terms of the prices that they offered for their services, but also in terms of having expert knowledge and using this knowledge to their competitive advantage.

The findings highlighted the importance of creating a culture in which the sharing of knowledge is encouraged, supported and promoted by management. Although informally approached, a definite culture of sharing and trust amongst management and staff was found amongst the companies within this study and, in this way, the sharing of knowledge, both tacit and explicit, was facilitated, for example, by means of hands-on training, focused staff discussion and debriefing sessions. The findings also showed the importance of converting tacit knowledge into explicit knowledge in order for it to have added value. This ensured that if a skilled person

retires or leaves the company, some of those skills would remain with the company. One of the ways in which tacit knowledge was shared was by means of informal debriefings and the less formalised structure of SMEs provided unique platforms where these informal discussions could take place. Additionally, the findings emphasised the importance of these companies' knowledge assets, which included their past projects, processes and procedures, competitor information and drawings that were captured and retained in the corporate memory, such as within databases, portals and digital libraries, to facilitate the retrieval thereof. In this way, these knowledge assets could be used and leveraged to the companies' advantage. Training of staff and mentoring were distinguishing factors that contributed to the effective management of the SMEs and enabled their staff to work together as a cohesive unit in which staff felt appreciated and valued. In this way, staff performance was enhanced, which ensured that an enterprises' strategic objectives were realised, which could eventually lead to gaining CA. From our research it is clear that most SMEs definitely implement KM processes, albeit in an informal and very intuitive basis.

In terms of information and knowledge sharing practices, it can therefore be concluded that:

- Some of the major challenges faced by SMEs are, (1) attracting good quality staff, (2) retaining staff and (3) finance.
- SMEs were generally well managed, which was largely owing to the more relaxed and informal atmosphere that is prevalent within them. SMEs consisted of cohesive, well organised teams that worked together as a single unit.
- There was a culture of trust amongst management and staff that facilitated the sharing of knowledge. Platforms were created where staff could come together to share tacit knowledge. These included hands-on training on site and dedicated weekly report back sessions.
- There was an effective flow of communication between management and staff.
- If a highly skilled employee were to leave their employ, it was not always seen as a total loss, as there were measures in place to cope with such a loss. This was due to the fact that most of the knowledge resided with the owner or director and was also transferred to others within the company by means of mentoring and hands-on training. Some enterprises had joint ventures with other companies; hence, they could tap into the resources of their competitors. Two of the companies (Companies D and H) were multidisciplinary, which meant that they had experts in all the engineering spheres and the loss of a skilled staff member was easily absorbed.
- Knowledge was shared, even in the absence of a formal policy. This proved that there was a definite culture of sharing and trust amongst management and staff.
- Succession planning was a problem, however, as only a few respondents (Companies D, F and J) had identified senior staff as likely succession candidates, but there were no formal measures in place.

Information needs and knowledge sources (Interview question C1)

Respondents were asked about their information needs and knowledge sources, as well as how often they had to search for information in order to establish the extent of their explicit knowledge base. All respondents stressed that their information needs were industry-specific. In other words, they worked according to SABS-approved standards and specifications. They all stated that whilst the Internet was their main source of information with regard to their projects, they often referred to their clients' standard documents for information and guidelines, for example, the Provincial Government of the Western Cape, which is their biggest client, has its own design guidelines. Companies C, D and F obtained information from their own digital libraries, which they have built up over a period of time, for example, Company E was a member of the American Society of Mechanical Engineering and had access to this society's library. Other sources of information were civil engineering journals and magazines – for example, the *International Journal of Green Energy* or *Engineering News* – engineering textbooks for referencing, and product manuals. Companies A and G also cited other specialists in the industry (engineers and academics) as sources of information.

All respondents stated that they do not have to search for information on a regular basis, but when they did, their first port of call was the Internet. They were seldom bombarded with loads of information as their information needs were industry-specific and they often found what they are looking for without having to conduct lengthy searches. Thereafter, they would consult other sources such as digital libraries, manuals, engineering journals and textbooks, as well as experts who have the relevant experience from within industry.

Companies C and D had intranet access to a document management system where pro-forma documents, templates, policy guidelines and other information regarding projects were stored. Others (Companies C, D and F) had built up internal traditional and digital libraries over the years, which served as a good source of information. Information in this regard was stored in a manner that facilitated easy retrieval.

Therefore, from the above it is clear that:

- The information requirements of various companies were basic because they worked according to approved SABS standards and specifications.
- Most of their information could be retrieved from their own paper collections and digital libraries, as well as learning from the knowledge of experts within the industry itself.

Management of knowledge and acquisition of external information (Interview questions D1–7)

Although indirectly applied, it was clear from the interviews that information and knowledge per se was seen as a very important driving force for business success. The acquisition of external information, as well as the storage and dissemination of internally generated information, was important to the SMEs interviewed. The attendance of conferences, forums and seminars created a platform where staff could network and collaborate with peers and other experts in the field. At these platforms, people from diverse business backgrounds were able to meet, make initial contact and extend their own networks. External information was also gained from conferences arranged by major manufacturers. Attendees were then exposed to the latest market trends in engineering and this could lead to further collaboration with manufacturers. It was found that the senior staff members, especially, would arrange not only formal but also informal meetings or workshops to provide feedback (knowledge sharing) of what they acquired at these conferences. The findings also highlighted the importance of networking in a competitive market. If these networks, which consisted of people with specialised skills and expertise, could be nurtured, it could facilitate the dissemination of tacit, as well as explicit, knowledge and ultimately could enhance or support CA for a particular small or medium enterprise.

To summarise:

- External information and knowledge (explicit and tacit) was gained through conference, seminar and forum attendance, where staff networked and collaborated with peers and other experts in the field. The majority of companies – except for Companies A and D –indicated that their staff attend conferences or seminars at least twice a year.
- Companies F, G and H indicated that was imperative for them to maintain their membership of professional bodies such as the Engineering Council of South Africa. There is a rewards system in place whereby members are awarded a number of points for attending conferences and seminars, as well as for attending training courses and mentoring of students.It was vitally important for companies to determine the nature of the information and knowledge that they need in an effort to gain and maintain CA. Typical information and knowledge acquiring needs that were identified were, *inter alia*, about dams and multi-storey structures, geometrics technology, and road design.

The level of competitive advantage (Interview questions E1–8)

All respondents had special knowledge and skills that could provide them with a competitive edge, which is an important aspect for their survival in this highly competitive field. They all strive to provide their clients with expert service and personal attention. Owners and directors of the companies had diverse backgrounds in the fields of business and academia and this reflected in their company strategy, as their staff and competitors were able to tap into their vast fields of knowledge and expertise. Because of the small and intimate nature of the consulting civil engineering field, and combined with the fact that they are well known amongst their peers, they were often seen as the preferred service provider in the field by both the City of Cape Town and private clients.

From the findings, it can be deduced that the implementation of KM processes could lead to CA and, in the case of the SMEs that were interviewed, we found that their expert knowledge and skills gave them a competitive edge. Because of the diverse backgrounds of owners and directors of the companies, not only in the field of business, but also in terms of academia, they often possessed expert knowledge and other consulting companies would consult with them or tap into their expertise. Owing to the fact that the consulting engineering field is small and they were well known amongst their peers for their expertise, they were often preferred service providers. This is important for their survival in this highly competitive field. They had also established themselves as preferred providers in the industry and this was owing to the fact that they had established strategies to achieve and maintain their CA. This could be further enhanced through effective marketing, which was lacking in SMEs.

In terms of CA, therefore:

- All respondents had special knowledge and skills that, if constantly developed, would provide them with a competitive advantage.
- They all had established strategies to achieve and maintain CA.
- All respondents indicated that they had achieved some or all of their objectives. For example, an important objective of Companies F and G was the employment of historically disadvantaged individuals.
- Many believed that they could still achieve more in order to gain and maintain CA.
- A concern was that few respondents engaged in any formal marketing activities. Companies B and G were the only companies that engaged in some form of marketing. Reasons cited for the lack of marketing included lack of time and lack of finances. They all agreed that it was a priority and placed it on their list of priorities for 2011.

The combination of knowledge management and competitive advantage practices (Interview questions F1–4)

Because the engineering sector was regarded as being highly project-based, it was important for information and knowledge to be managed in a way that could favour the CA of a particular enterprise. In other words, information and knowledge should be captured and stored in a way that would simplify retrieval and dissemination, especially if they had to refer to previous but similar projects. It was also an imperative for such information and knowledge to be accessible to everyone in the company. It was evident from the findings that sound information and knowledge sharing processes were not yet in place with regard to the majority of enterprises interviewed. It was also clear that not many avenues were utilised to capture and share tacit knowledge. As an example, only one company (Company J) had a paper-based site instruction book where experiences and ideas could be recorded and stored for future use. No electronic means to share knowledge (for example a company network)

was utilised by any of the enterprises. Some of the other means of sharing tacit knowledge was through hands-on training, but was not made explicit. This is largely a result of the fact that no formal KM policy was in place in any of the enterprises. The recording of valuable information was found to be vitally important and could help to preserve the companies' expertise, especially in view of the fact that staff retention is one of main the problems experienced by SMEs. This is also important because succession planning does not seem to be a priority amongst SMEs.

In order to remain competitive, it is important for companies to know what their competitors are doing. Owing to a lack of marketing activities in almost all of the companies that were interviewed, few of them knew, in detail, what their competitors do to stay ahead in the field. Companies E and J were involved in joint ventures with their competitors and, to this extent, they had some knowledge of what others in the industry were doing. The consulting civil engineering field is close-knit and because they compete amongst themselves and not with large companies, the only knowledge they had about one another concerned tender prices. In other words, they were able to estimate which company had tendered at what price. Even so, this information was often obtained through the 'grapevine' or via notices in the local newspaper, which could be attributed to the fact that not much research was undertaken regarding their competitors' operations.

The above findings show that although it is important for companies to know how their competitors operate in order for them to improve their services, their efforts to stay abreast of this information were not that impressive. Improvements in this regard could be achieved through effective marketing or by, for example, appointing a dedicated staff member to browse or scan news sources for competitor achievements. The civil engineering field is fairly small in the Western Cape and it is important for companies to have that special feature that sets them apart from their competitors and which ultimately ensures them a competitive advantage in the field. When questioned about this, respondents mentioned the following features or strong points, which 'set them apart from their competitors':

- The company strategy and good reputation of completing projects within the required timeframe. In other words, they were well known for their track record in terms of service delivery.
- Their specialty in terms of different focus areas, namely structural and civil engineering, water supply and storm water design, transportation, sewer design, or storm water traffic.
- The fact that they operated in silos. This means that specialists in their specific fields operated independently in groups, separately from everyone else in the company.
- Their good relationship with local authorities and other companies in the field.
- Their multidisciplinary approach in incorporating all spheres of civil engineering, which gave them a niche in the market.
- The vast knowledge and experience of the owners and directors of the enterprises.

The majority of respondents agreed that they had the right people in the company in order to achieve CA. The majority of Company H's staff comprised consultants who also had other priorities and, as such, their time was divided between their company and other companies. Some therefore preferred to employ retired consultants who would be able to give their full attention to the company. Many cited their staff as one of their most important organisational assets. Coupled with this, the expert knowledge of both the owners and staff of SMEs played a prominent role in achieving and maintaining CA. When questioned about the ways and means in which their knowledge contributed to their CA, some of the answers the companies provided were as follows:

- Their vast experience in working for local government, as well as municipalities, gave them good knowledge of government processes and procedures, particularly because the City of Cape Town is their largest client.
- The extensive personal knowledge and experience of directors in areas of business and academia was a major factor. This knowledge was shared and disseminated throughout the company though hands-on training and mentoring, making it easy for the enterprise to operate in the absence of the director or owner when he or she is away for any length of time. The director of Company F stated that he often shared his expertise with competitors and did not see this as a threat to his own business, as the sharing of knowledge served to strengthen the engineering sector as a whole.
- Many companies 'grew their own timber' – this meant that students who did their in-service training at the company were often offered a full-time position. Such staff members would have been mentored by the owner or director and were therefore able to plough their skills back into the company. In this way their expertise was grown in-house, which also ensured that most of the work was done in-house. In addition, this process allowed for tacit knowledge to pass from owner or director to staff member.
- Their various areas of expertise, which allowed them to establish a niche in the market, were major competitive tools that made them preferred providers in the industry.

Conclusion

Results from the research show that most SMEs do not have formal policies or procedures in place to align their strategic objectives. Also, although a number of KM practices came to the fore, no formal information and knowledge sharing practices exist as yet. However, it was also found that good but informal, or rather unstructured, communication means exist between management and staff. The sharing of information and knowledge (both tacit and explicit) was encouraged by means of dedicated forums and hands-on training and there was a definite culture of trust amongst management and staff, which facilitated the sharing of tacit knowledge. It was clear that the SMEs that were interviewed actively used information technology to capture, store and disseminate knowledge, which they could then use to achieve and maintain CA. All of the companies had measures in place whereby knowledge was captured and stored to

simplify retrieval thereof, whether tacit or explicit. However, none of the companies that were interviewed already made use of Web-based or social networking tools in order to share information and knowledge effectively. When interviewed, some respondents acknowledged the importance of these tools and the fact that they would be an important vehicle to facilitate better knowledge sharing in SMEs; SMEs could benefit from the establishment of social networking.

The research also indicated that competitive advantage stems from a company's unique knowledge warehouse. The management of such a unique knowledge base, therefore, has the potential to make enterprises more competitive and profitable. The combination of competitiveness and profitability can lead to high-margin niche markets. However, in order to achieve and maintain CA, companies should distinguish themselves not only in terms of the service that they offer, but also in terms of the type of information at their disposal. In order to achieve this they should have a distinct information and knowledge policy in place.

Further research is necessary to establish how modern knowledge sharing approaches and technologies can best be implemented in the typical small and/or medium enterprise. The availability of the Internet will have a profound impact on the way in which these enterprises can share their tacit and explicit knowledge.

References

Akinwumi, O. & Olawale, F., 2010, 'The determinants of access to trade credit by new SMEs in South Africa', *African Journal of Business Management* 4(13), 2763–2770, viewed 17 January 2011 from, http://www.academicjournals.org/AJBM

Antoncic, B. & Omerzel, D.G., 2008, 'Critical entrepreneur knowledge dimensions for the SME performance', *Industrial Management & Data Systems* 108(9), 1182–1199, viewed 18 March 2011, from http://www.emeraldinsight.com/10.1108/02635570810914883

Awazu, Y. & Desouza, K.C., 2006, 'Knowledge management at SMEs: Five peculiarities', *Journal of Knowledge Management* 10(1), 32–43, viewed 02 June 2009, from http://www.emeraldinsight.com/10.1108/13673270610650085

Berry, A., Von Blottnitz, M., Cassim R., Kesper, A., Rajaratnam, B. & Van Seventer, D.E., 2002, *The economics of SMMEs in South Africa in trade and industrial policy strategies*, viewed 19 November 2008, from http://www.tips.org.za/files/506.pdf

Bozbura, F.T., 2007, 'Knowledge management practices in Turkish SMEs', *Journal of Enterprise Information Management* 20(2), 209–221, viewed 02 June 2009, from http://www.emeraldinsight.com/10.1108/17410390710725788; http://dx.doi.org/10.1108/17410390710725788

Chen, S., Duan, Y., Edwards, J.S. & Lethaney, B., 2006, 'Toward understanding inter-organizational knowledge transfer needs in SMEs: Insight from a UK investigation', *Journal of knowledge management* 10(3), 6–23, viewed 02 June 2009 from, http://www.emeraldinsignt.com/10.1108/13673270610670821; http://dx.doi.org/10.1108/13673270610670821

Du Plessis, M., 2008, 'The strategic drivers and objectives of communities of practice as vehicles for knowledge management in small and medium enterprises', *International Journal of Information Management* 28(1), 61–67, viewed 08 April 2011, from http://www.elsevier.com/locate/ijinfomgt; http://dx.doi.org/10.1016/j.ijinfomgt.2007.05.002

Fink, K. & Ploder, C., 2009, 'Balanced system for knowledge process management in SMEs', *Journal of Enterprise Information Management* 22(1/2), 36–50, viewed 02 June 2009, from http://www.emeraldinsight.com/Insight/viewContentItem.do;jsessionid=4C39A55B2; http://dx.doi.org/10.1108/17410390910922813

Furu, P., Salojarvi, S. & Sveiby, K.E., 2005, 'Knowledge management and growth in Finnish SMEs', *Journal of Knowledge Management* 9(2), 103–122, viewed 02 June 2009, from http://www.emeraldinsight.com/10.1108/13673270510590254

Kok, J.A., Van Brakel, P.A. & Van der Walt, C., 2004, 'Knowledge sharing via enterprise intranets – Asking the right questions', *South African Journal of Information Management* 6(2), viewed 23 March 2007, from http://www.sajim.co.za/default.asp?to=peer3vol6nr4

Massa, S. & Testa, S., 2008, 'A knowledge management approach to organizational competitive advantage: Evidence from the food sector', *European Management Journal* 27(2), 129–141, viewed 26 June 2009, from http://www.elsevier.com/locate/emj

Snyman, M.M.M. & Van der Berg, H., 2003, 'Managing tacit knowledge in the corporate environment: Communities of practice', *South African Journal of Information Management* 5(4), viewed 23 March 2007, from http://www.sajim.co.za/default.asp?to=peer3vol5nr4

South Africa business guidebook 2004–2005, 2006, 'Small, medium & micro enterprises (SMMEs)', 9th edn., pp. 241–243, 3SMedia, viewed 24 July 2006, from http://www.journals.co.za/ej/ejour_ws_sabg.html

South African Government, 1996, *National Small Business Act No. 102 of 1996*, South African Government, Pretoria, viewed 26 June 2009, from http://www.info.gov.za/view/DownloadFileAction?id=70848

South African Government, 2009, *Together doing more and better – Medium term strategic framework: A framework to guide Government's programme in the electoral mandate period 2009–2014*, The South African Presidency, Pretoria, viewed 15 September 2011, from http://www.thepresidency.gov.za/docs/pcsa/planning/mtsf_july09.pdf

Stead, G.B. & Struwig, F.W., 2001, *Planning, designing and reporting research*, Maskew Miller Longman, Cape Town.

Uit Beijerse, R.P., 1999, 'Questions in knowledge management: Defining and conceptualising a phenomenon', *Journal of Knowledge Management* 3(2), 94–109, viewed 10 June 2009, from http://www.emeraldinsight.com/Insight/viewContainer.do?containerType=Issue&containerId=16017

Uit Beijerse, R.P., 2000, 'Knowledge management in small and medium-sized companies: Knowledge management for entrepreneurs', *Journal of Knowledge Management* 4(2), 162–179, viewed 02 June 2009, from http://www.emeraldinsight.com./10.1108/13673270010372297

Wong, K.Y., 2005, 'Critical success factors for implementing knowledge management in small and medium enterprises', *Journal of Industrial Management & Data Systems* 105(3), 261–279, viewed 01 June 2009, from http://www.emeraldinsight.com/0263-5577.htm

APPENDIX

Interview questionnaire

Section A: Biographical and company information

1. Name of organisation:
   Physical address:
   Core business of organisation:
   Number of years in existence:
2. Name of Owner, Director, Chief Executive Officer and/or Chief Information Officer:
   Number of people working in the organisation:
   Categories of staff (e.g. professional, administrative, technical, etc.):

Section B: Knowledge and information sharing practices

1. Research shows that small and medium-sized enterprises (SMEs) face many challenges, especially in terms of access to finance and attracting and retaining good quality staff. What challenges, if any, does your organisation face?
2. How do you generally communicate with your employees? Do new employees attend an induction session?
3. What do you do to encourage workers to communicate and share knowledge and ideas?
4. If a highly skilled individual should leave your employ, is it a total loss to your company or do you have measures in place to ensure that experienced staff transfer their knowledge to others?
5. How is knowledge and experience shared? What do you do to encourage workers to communicate and share knowledge and ideas?
6. Do you provide training and mentoring for new staff members who join the organisation? If so, how is this done?

Section C: Information needs and knowledge sources

1. Where do you obtain any required information from? How often do you search for information?

Section D: Management of knowledge and acquisition of external information

1. Do your staff members attend conferences, seminars and forums where they meet and network with peers or competitors?
2. Do you ever consult your competitors or do they (i.e. your competitors) consult you for advice in terms of sharing knowledge?
3. Do you make use of Facebook or Twitter to communicate and share ideas with your colleagues inside and outside of the company?
4. How are staff members encouraged to develop and implement new ideas or express their opinions? What does the company do to make it comfortable for workers to share knowledge?
5. Most of our knowledge is stored in our brains. Nevertheless, how do you store additional knowledge, for example, printed knowledge (i.e. explicit knowledge) such as reports and policies? Do you make use of databases or knowledge repositories?
6. We are often faced with an overload of information in the world today. How do you filter through masses of information in order to get to the right information to ensure effective decision-making?
7. Do you ever determine what knowledge your company requires in order to realise the company strategy?

Section E: The level of competitive advantage

1. What makes your company special?
2. Do you believe that your company can achieve more in order to gain competitive advantage over competitors?
3. Do you believe that you have the right people in your organisation to achieve a competitive advantage?
4. We know that you have expert knowledge – does this knowledge (and/or the sharing of it) play a role in your achieving a competitive advantage over your competitors?
5. Do you conduct regular market surveys and/or research to find out what the market and customers want?
6. Who are your customers and how important are they to you?
7. What would you consider to be your most important organisational asset or assets?
8. What does your organisation strive to achieve and have you achieved it?

Section F: The combination of knowledge management and competitive advantage practices

1. Because the engineering field is regarded as being project-based, how do you record and transfer knowledge from one project to another? How is this information captured for future purposes? Where is it located and how can it help to make future decisions?
2. Do you have any knowledge of what your competitors are doing in order to stay ahead and maintain a competitive edge over you?
3. Would you say that your unique knowledge gives you a competitive advantage over your competitors? If so, how?
4. Where do you see yourself and/or your company in 5 years time?

Examples of previous knowledge management studies that have been undertaken.

Source of previous knowledge management study	Questions asked
Uit Beijerse (1999)	**Strategic questions:** 1. Does the management of the organisation know what kind of market activities competing companies undertake with regard to the development of knowledge? 2. Does the management of the organisation know what the core competencies of the organisation are in terms of knowledge assets? 3. Does the management of the organisation have a long-term vision about knowledge, which will be required in future? Given this, does the management of the organisation actively try to build a collective ambition regarding this? 4. Does the management of the organisation formulate a short-term and medium-term strategy with regard to the acquisition, sharing and evaluation of knowledge? Given this, has the management formulated a knowledge policy? **Organisational questions:** 1. Does the organisation have a knowledge management-friendly organisational structure that facilitates the acquirement, sharing and evaluation of knowledge between (knowledge) workers? 2. Does the organisation have a knowledge management-friendly organisational culture that motivates the acquisition, sharing and evaluation of knowledge between (knowledge) workers? 3. Is the style of management within the organisation such that it stimulates sharing and evaluation of knowledge amongst (knowledge) workers? 4. Is there some kind of integrating knowledge infrastructure within the organisation, which secures the necessary continuing steps to determine knowledge gaps, develop and buy knowledge, share knowledge and evaluate knowledge? **Instrumental questions:** 1. Are there instruments within the organisation, which are specifically aimed at the determination of the difference between available and required knowledge? 2. Are there instruments within the organisation, which are specifically aimed at the development of knowledge based on the determination of the knowledge gap? 3. Are there instruments available with which the use of knowledge is (constantly) monitored?
Uit Beijerse (2000)	1. Have you ever heard of knowledge management? 2. Would you say that knowledge is one of your most important competitive factors? 3. Do you ever determine what knowledge your company requires in order to realise your company strategy? 4. Do you ever determine what knowledge is present in your company and in the heads of your employees? 5. Have you ever been occupied with the external acquisition of knowledge for your company processes? 6. Do you occupy yourself with developing knowledge with regard to your company?
Snyman and Van den Berg (2003)	1. Have you become more aware of the importance of knowledge management and the necessity to share (and capture) knowledge since implementation of the community of practice? 2. Have you benefited from the discussions held in the community of practice? 3. Do you participate in the community of practice by sharing your own knowledge on a specific topic? 4. Would you like to have access to information previously acquired through the community of practice?
Kok, Van Brakel and Van der Walt (2004)	1. How often do you share your experience of knowing where to find information with other members of staff via the Internet? 2. How often do you share your experience of knowing who to ask for help amongst other members of staff via the Internet? 3. How often do you share your experience of knowing how to resolve a problem with other members of staff via the intranet? 4. What improvements do you believe can be made to the intranet to make knowledge sharing easier for daily work, projects, departmental information and company information? 5. How easily do you locate information on the intranet that is relevant to your work? 6. How easy is it to publish on the intranet? 7. What type of incentives do you receive in return for your knowledge sharing on the intranet (award and recognition, monetary – part of annual bonus scheme, promotion opportunities, training or educational opportunities, funding for travel and attendance of conferences)? 8. Do you receive the right level of training to participate effectively in knowledge-sharing initiatives on the intranet? 9. Do new employees attend an induction session on how to use the intranet? 10. To what extent does sharing your knowledge via the intranet create new business opportunities? 11. To what extent do new ideas for knowledge management initiatives come from all departments? 12. To what extent do new ideas for knowledge management initiatives come from one department?

Note: For more information, please see the full reference list of the article: Mohsam, F. & Van Brakel, P.A., 2011, 'Information and knowledge sharing trends of small and medium-sized enterprises in the Western Cape, South Africa', *SA Journal of Information Management* 13(1), Art. #462, 10 pages. doi: http://dx.doi.org/10.4102/sajim.v13i1.462

3

Analysing lawyers' attitude towards knowledge sharing

Authors:
Wole M. Olatokun[1]
Isioma N. Elueze[1]

Affiliations:
[1]Africa Regional Centre for Information Science (ARCIS), University of Ibadan, Nigeria

Correspondence to:
Wole Olatokun

Email:
woleabbeyolatokun@yahoo.co.uk

Postal address:
PO Box 22133, University of Ibadan, Nigeria

Objectives: The study examined and identified the factors that affect lawyers' attitudes to knowledge sharing, and their knowledge sharing behaviour. Specifically, it investigated the relationship between the salient beliefs affecting the knowledge sharing attitude of lawyers', and applied a modified version of the Theory of Reasoned Action (TRA) in the knowledge sharing context, to predict how these factors affect their knowledge sharing behaviour.

Method: A field survey of 273 lawyers was carried out, using questionnaire for data collection. Collected data on all variables were structured into grouped frequency distributions. Principal Component Factor Analysis was applied to reduce the constructs and Simple Regression was applied to test the hypotheses. These were tested at 0.05% level of significance.

Results: Results showed that expected associations and contributions were the major determinants of lawyers' attitudes towards knowledge sharing. Expected reward was not significantly related to lawyers' attitudes towards knowledge sharing. A positive attitude towards knowledge sharing was found to lead to a positive intention to share knowledge, although a positive intention to share knowledge did not significantly predict a positive knowledge sharing behaviour. The level of Information Technology (IT) usage was also found to significantly affect the knowledge sharing behaviour of lawyers'.

Conclusion: It was recommended that law firms in the study area should deploy more IT infrastructure and services that encourage effective knowledge sharing amongst lawyers.

Introduction

The acquisition, application, and leveraging of knowledge are important for organisations to achieve success. As the 21st century unfolds, many people regard the strategic management of knowledge resources as one of the key factors for sustainable competitive advantage. In particular, knowledge sharing is perceived to be the most essential process for knowledge management (Bock & Kim 2002). Grant (1996) regards knowledge as the most strategically important resource that an organisation possesses. It forms a very important part of an organisation's core competence and it is needed to combine other production factors effectively to achieve set goals (King & Iyoha 2008). Knowledge management comprises a range of practices applied by organisations to identify, create, represent, distribute and enable them to adopt what they know and how they know it, and these practices are tied to organisational objectives and goals. It is therefore imperative for workers in an organisation to have a constructive attitude to sharing knowledge in order for the organisation to be successful.

Lawyers are knowledge workers who engage in different types of knowledge intensive activities (Ojo & Grand 2011). Today the legal profession faces great challenges and lawyers are permanently being flooded with new information, such as frequent changes in legislation and new court decisions, amongst many other changes (Schulz & Klugmann 2005). Knowledge sharing in law firms is the process of distributing know-how relevant to legal practice and the success of the law firm. The theme of knowledge sharing in law firms has been discussed in some knowledge management literature that tends to highlight factors that affect knowledge sharing activity. Of these, 'attitude' has been cited as a major factor. Davenport (1997) argued that sharing knowledge is often unnatural, stating that people will not share their knowledge, and think their own knowledge is valuable and important. Some factors that could influence a person's willingness to share knowledge, have been identified including trust, promotion, incentives, rewards, motivation, relationships, incentive systems, culture, top management support, senior leadership, contribution, association, and other factors. Bircham (2003) considered that a recipient may not be willing to accept shared knowledge from others, owing to a lack of trust of the source individual. The recipient's attitude may also be influenced by how effectively knowledge has been articulated by the sender.

Attitudes affect people in everything they do and reflect what they are hence, it is a determining factor of the behaviour of people. Also, it provides people with a framework within which to interpret the world and integrate new experiences, as noted by Ogunmoye (2008). Thus, by understanding an individual's attitude towards something, one can predict with high precision his or her overall pattern of behaviour to the object. Ogunmoye also noted that according to Aiken (2000), attitude is a learned disposition that determines a positive or negative response to a specific object, situation, institution, or a person. Therefore, attitude reflects what the individual is and, hence, it is a determining factor of the individual's attitude, and provides people with a framework within which to interpret the world and integrate new experiences (Ogunmoye 2008).

Often, attitude influences how workers interact. Argote and Ingram (2000) suggested that organisational knowledge resides in the interactions between individuals and, therefore, forms the basis of competitive advantage. It has also been noted that the future, survival or existence of any individual, organisation, society or group of people will be determined by their ability to manage and share knowledge wisely, or their effective application of knowledge, which is an essential and precious global resource that is an embodiment of human intellectual capital and technology. Knowledge management is a key law firm business driver. The typical law firm knowledge management vision is to achieve market differentiation through leveraging its knowledge (Global Law Firm Knowledge Management Survey Report 2002). A positive attitude to knowledge sharing by workers of a law organisation would help the law organisation identify its weaknesses and strengths. Senior management in many organisations understand the importance of knowledge sharing amongst their employees and are, thus, eager to introduce knowledge management paradigms (Bock & Kim 2002). Law is a knowledge intensive industry. Fundamentally, the business of lawyers is the sale of their knowledge (Gottschalk, Brekke & Pedersen 2005). Law organisations increasingly recognise the value of knowledge sharing and if they must capitalise on the knowledge they possess, they must understand how knowledge is created, shared, and applied within the organisation. Knowledge exists and is shared at different levels in organisations (Ipe 2003). Creating and fostering a culture of knowledge sharing is, in practice, one of the most difficult tasks when introducing a Knowledge Management system into a law firm (Eiseman 2007). According to King and Iyoha (2008):

> We discovered that in Nigeria, most companies do not appreciate the importance of managing an organisation's knowledge; neither do they know the importance of expanding the organisation's knowledge base through knowledge sharing. They fail to understand the importance of knowledge sharing to sustaining an organisation's competitive advantage. (p. 9)

This study investigated the attitude of lawyers in some selected law firms in Ibadan, a Nigerian metropolis, towards knowledge sharing using the Theory of Reasoned Action model (TRA) (Azjen & Fishbein 1980). The theory states that attitude towards a behaviour is a precursor to an individual's intention towards performing a behaviour (Bock & Kim 2002). In the context of this study, it implies that if a worker has a favorable attitude towards sharing his or her knowledge with other workers, there is a high possibility that he or she will share available knowledge. A less favorable attitude may result in little or no knowledge being shared. As a result of the TRA having been successfully applied in some earlier studies on knowledge sharing (Bock & Kim 2002; Ryu, Hee-Ho & Han 2003; Gottschalk et al. 2005), the model is considered fit to guide the study. Expected reward, expected contribution, and expected association were determinants of the attitude of workers towards knowledge sharing, whilst attitude was a determinant of the workers' intention to share knowledge.

Literature review
Knowledge sharing in organisations

It has become a common activity within organisations to apply a variety of means to properly disseminate relevant information within their firms, in order to integrate all parts of the workforce in actualising the organisation's vision (Senge 2007). Methods, including brainstorming sessions, PowerPoint presentations and storytelling have all been part of a list of methods applied in different ways to share knowledge within the organisation. Chua (2003) defines knowledge sharing as the process by which individuals collectively and iteratively refine a thought, an idea or a suggestion in the light of their experiences. Similarly, according to Ipe (2003:340) the sharing of an individual's knowledge is imperative to the 'creation, dissemination, and management of knowledge at all other levels within an organisation'. An organisation's ability to effectively leverage its knowledge is highly dependent on its people, who actually create, share, and apply the knowledge. Leveraging knowledge is only possible when people can share their knowledge and build on the knowledge of others. Knowledge sharing is basically the act of making knowledge available to others within the organisation. Knowledge sharing between individuals is the process by which knowledge held by an individual is converted into a form that can be understood, absorbed, and applied by other individuals, that contributes to both individual and organisational learning (Ipe 2003). Knowledge sharing is important because it provides a link between the individual and the organisation by moving knowledge that resides with individuals to the organisational level, where it is converted into economic and competitive value for the organisation (Hendriks 1999). The voluntary act of an individual sharing his or her knowledge contributes to knowledge distribution, and the process of sharing may result in knowledge acquisition by other individuals within the organisation (Ipe 2003). Knowledge sharing between individuals, thus, results in individual learning, which in turn may contribute to organisational learning (Turner & Minonne 2010). Understanding the process of knowledge sharing between individuals is one step toward a better understanding of knowledge sharing as a whole in organisations.

Knowledge sharing is the capturing, storing and dissemination of information using appropriate media to further the development of employees and enhance the work processes. Knowledge sharing could be undertaken in many ways. It could be a mere discussion with a colleague or capturing and reusing experienced based knowledge residing within the organisation. In so doing this makes knowledge accessible to other employees. Knowledge sharing enables new knowledge to be created and also translated into innovative technologies and processes (Joseph, Firestone & McElroy 2005). The ability to share knowledge between organisational units and departments contributes immensely to the performance of the organisation (Hendriks 2005). The process, of exchanging ideas, information and, consequently, knowledge, enables organisations to increase thier knowledge base. The reasons why organisations encourage knowledge sharing stems from the fact that much of the knowledge of organisations is controlled at the level of the individual employee (Hendriks 2005). Individuals utilise their knowledge in the course of carrying out their duties at work (Joseph *et al.* 2005). An organisation is bound to lose knowledge if the individual possessing it leaves the organisation, and if the organisation has not facilitated the individual sharing their knowledge with other employees (Gupta 2000). But, if the employee remains with the organisation, the organisation may not utilise the knowledge of this employee unless there are opportunities for them to share this knowledge with others in the organisation (Gupta 2000). It is worthwhile, therefore, for organisations to create an atmosphere of sharing to ensure that knowledge remains within it, notwithstanding the resignation of an employee. The individual employees must work together, share ideas, information and knowledge in order to achieve organisational aims and objectives. Organisations must understand the needs and wants of their employees to understand what triggers employees' attitude to share knowledge, their intention to share knowledge and their overall knowledge sharing behaviour. It could be promotion, job security, meeting personal needs, attending training and courses, for example. By understanding these factors organisations will further improve the knowledge sharing capabilities of their employees. Ethnicity, employee age, educational level, employee ethics, corporate culture, trust, management commitment, involvement in the organisation and an individual's perception of the organisation, have been identified in various literature as criteria that affect an employee's willingness to share knowledge in knowledge intensive organisations. Other criteria are rewards, leadership, resources provided, job title, tenure, organisational climate, contributions, power, organisational politics and IT support.

Knowledge sharing in law firms

Gottschalk *et al.* (2005), in their study of the *Incentives for Knowledge Sharing through Information Technology*, carried out in two law firms in Norway, noted that a lawyer's attitude towards their own contribution in an organisation, was the factor that most predicted their share of knowledge, followed by their attitude towards rewards. The attitude towards associations and perceived management commitment was observed to be of less importance to a lawyer's knowledge sharing behaviour in the law firm. They also noted that, on average, a lawyer's willingness to share their knowledge with colleagues was influenced by their perception of their ability to contribute to the organisation.

Gottschalk *et al.* (2005) observed that perceived management commitment did not influence knowledge sharing amongst the workers in the law firms. They also noted that user satisfaction and user-friendly systems were very important when trying to motivate lawyers to apply and share knowledge via an IT system, and that lawyers did not share knowledge, publish documents, reports and other useful information on the intranet, because it was too time consuming and complicated. Ojo and Grand (2011), in their study carried out to investigate the extent of IT acceptance and application of knowledge management in Botswana law organisations, established that more than half of the lawyers in Botswana use IT moderately for knowledge sharing. They revealed that most of the individual law knowledge workers use IT for knowledge management activities at a moderate to high level, for a variety of knowledge management activities in Botswana law organisations. These activities were knowledge seeking and documentation, knowledge organising and knowledge sharing. They proposed that their finding, that IT is under utilised for knowledge sharing than it should be, represented that time and effort expended on knowledge sharing was not adequately recognised and rewarded in most Botswana law organisations.

Research model

This study adopts the Theory of Reason Action (TRA) as proposed by Bock and Kim (2002). The theory describes the psychological processes that mediate observed relations between human attitudes and behaviour. It employs the variables attitude, social influence and intention to predict behaviour in specific contexts. TRA is based on the premise that intention is the main determinant of a person's actions or actual behaviour. Two constructs influence a person's behavioural intention: his or her attitude toward a particular behaviour and the subjective norm or social pressure exerted on him or her to carry out a behaviour or not. In TRA the beliefs and evaluations affecting an individual's attitude refer to what they think about the consequences that could arise from their behaviour as well as the personal evaluation of the desirability of these consequences. It proposes that intention to perform a particular behaviour is influenced by an individual's attitude toward performing the behaviour and the subjective norm held by the individual. Attitude toward behaviour is defined as 'an individual's positive or negative feelings about performing the target behaviour' (Ajzen & Fishbein 1980:216) and subjective norm is defined as 'the person's perception that most people who are important to him think he should not perform the behaviour in question' (Ajzen & Fishbein 1980:302). The theory proposes that behavioural and normative beliefs are the ultimate sources of an individual's attributes and norms. The TRA was designed to explain human behaviour in general; it could be applied to a wide variety of contexts. Agbonlahor (2005, citing Venkatesh, Morris, Davis & Davis 2003) described TRA as 'one of the most fundamental and influential theories of human behaviour'. Also, the theory has been employed to predict a wide range of behaviours in diverse areas such as family planning, consumer behaviour, voting in American and British elections and an individual's acceptance of technology (Davis, Bagozzi & Warshaw 1992). According to TRA, a person's performance of a specified behaviour is determined by their behhavioural intention to perform the behaviour. The intention is jointly determined by the person's attitude and subjective norm concerning the behaviour in question. A person's attitude towards a behaviour is determined by his beliefs about the consequences of performing the behaviour. A particularly helpful aspect of TRA is that it assumes all other factors influence behaviour by influencing attitude. Based on this, TRA can be a useful model for explaining the knowledge sharing behaviour in organisations. This study adopts TRA as re-modelled by (Bock & Kim 2002). There are three factors (see Figure 1) that influence an employee's attitude towards knowledge sharing and their selected belief that they act as a facilitator to knowledge sharing. These factors are:

- expected reward
- expected contribution
- expected association amongst employees.

Based on the research model, the following hypotheses are formulated, that there is no significant relationship between:

1. 'expected rewards' and the attitude of lawyers towards knowledge sharing
2. 'expected associations' and the attitude of lawyers towards knowledge sharing
3. 'expected contribution' of lawyers to the organisation and their attitude towards knowledge sharing
4. the attitude of lawyers in Ibadan metropolis towards knowledge sharing and their intention to share knowledge
5. the intention of lawyers to share knowledge and their knowledge sharing behaviour
6. the level of IT usage of the lawyers in Ibadan metropolis and their knowledge sharing behaviour.

Method

The study utilised a survey design. The population comprised all lawyers and legal practitioners in all the registered law firms in the city of Ibadan, a Nigerian municipality. The total population of registered law firms in the city, as compiled by the Business Registration Unit of the Oyo state Ministry of Bureau and Commerce as of March, 2011, was obtained. The sample frame comprised all lawyers in selected law firms. The estimated average number of lawyers working in each law firm in Ibadan was given as $84/29 = 2.89$, which was approximately equal to three lawyers in each law firm. Given an average of three lawyers in each law firm in Ibadan, and given the number of law firms in Ibadan as 193, the sample frame was approximately 579 lawyers from which 289 (50%) were selected as a sample, using simple random sampling technique.

Data collection

Data were collected using a structured questionnaire which was divided into five sections. Section A collected demographic data on each of the respondents. Section B elicited information about the respondent's knowledge sharing behaviour, whilst section C collected data about the respondent's intention to share knowledge. Section D collected data on the respondent's beliefs whilst section E collected data on the respondent's attitude to knowledge sharing. For specific variables in the questionnaire, data were collected on these according to the criteria below.

Knowledge sharing behaviour

The knowledge sharing behaviour of the lawyers was collected by measuring how frequently they shared knowledge or knowledge sources with other lawyers. A 4–point Likert scale was developed to measure these opinions from:

- 1 ('never')
- 2 ('seldom')
- 3 ('occasionally')
- 4 ('frequently').

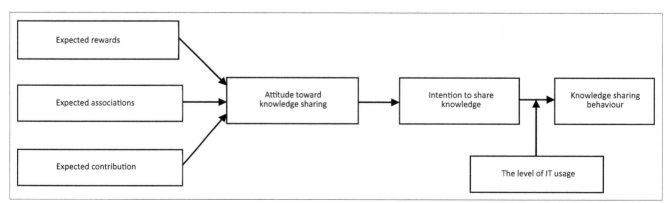

Source: Adapted from Bock, G.W. & Kim, Y.G. 2002, 'Breaking the Myths of Rewards: An Exploratory Study of Attitudes about Knowledge Sharing', *Information Resource Management Journal* 15(2), 14–21. http://dx.doi.org/10.4018/irmj.2002040102

FIGURE 1: Theory of Reasoned Action.

Level of Information Technology usage

To measure the level of usage of Information Technology (IT) services for knowledge sharing, a 4–point Likert scale was developed, from:

- 1 ('never')
- 2 ('seldom')
- 3 ('occasionally')
- 4 ('frequently').

This was intended to measure how frequently the lawyers used listed IT services to share knowledge with other lawyers.

Intention to share knowledge

To establish the intention of the lawyers to share knowledge, questions about their general intention to share knowledge with other lawyers were asked. A 5–point Likert scale was developed to measure these opinions from 1 ('strongly disagree') to 5 ('strongly agree').

Expected rewards, expected associations and expected contribution

To ascertain the individual lawyer's opinion about factors that may affect their knowledge sharing, questions were asked on their beliefs, with the following possibilities:

- of receiving rewards in return for knowledge sharing
- of changes in relationship between the lawyer and colleagues
- of the firm's improvement in its performance, as a result of the lawyer's knowledge sharing.

A 5–point Likert scale was developed to measure their responses ranging from 1 ('strongly disagree') to 5 ('strongly agree').

Attitude toward knowledge sharing

To measure the attitude of lawyers towards knowledge sharing, questions were asked about their general attitude to knowledge sharing. A 5–point Likert scale was also developed to measure their response ranging from 1 ('strongly disagree') to 5 ('strongly agree').

Background information

The demographic characteristics on which data were collected include gender, age, highest educational qualification, and length of service.

Instrument validation, administration and data analysis

Face and content validity of the instrument was carried out by researchers in the area of knowledge sharing. They thoroughly reviewed the content of the questionnaire, and the extent to which it was likely to measure the variables. It was also given to a judge of a customary court in Abuja (Nigerian Federal Capital Territory) and three other legal practitioners working in law firms in Lagos (Nigeria's commerical capital) for face validation, after which some adjustments were made to the constructs in the questionnaire. A total of 300 (numbered 001–300) copies were distributed to the lawyers

in the month of May 2011. The respondents were very busy, and the major challenge experienced during the fieldwork was getting them to complete the questionnaires on time. In some cases between two and seven repeated visits were made to some law firms before the completed questionnaires could be retrieved. Out of the 300 copies administered, 281 were collected. Of these, 11 were not useable for analyses for not being properly completed. Hence, a total of 273 copies were used for data analyses.

The data collected were reduced, summarised, coded and analysed using the Statistical Package for Social Science (SPSS) software. Frequency distribution tables were generated for all the variables. The variables used to measure intention to share knowledge and the individual's beliefs and attitude to share knowledge, were recoded using a 5–point Likert scale. These were recoded as: (1 = strongly disagree) + (2 = disagree) = (1 = disagree), (3 = undecided) = (2 = undecided) and (4 = strongly agree) + (5 = agree) = (3 = agree).

Principal component factor analysis was used to perform dimension reduction on all the constructs that made up each variable. This was performed to determine the highest loading factor, that is the constructs that are contributing the most to the variable and will best measure the variables; intention to share knowledge, the individual's beliefs and attitude to share knowledge. The aim was to bring out the few parsimonious variables that could absorb the others. Regression analysis was used to establish relationships between the independent variables and dependent variables, as stated in hypotheses 1 to hypotheses 5. The hypotheses were tested at 0.05% level of significance.

Results
Demographic characteristics of the respondents

Males accounted for 67.8% of the respondents, whilst 32.2% were females. The largest proportion of respondents was within the age group of 21–30 years. Respondents with a degree of masters in law accounted for 22.7.4%, 13.6% had a first degree in law and 57.9% had a bachelor of law degree from the Nigerian Law School. The length of service, of respondents working in the law firm, ranged from one year to 33 years, with a mean number of years of 5.98.

Knowledge sharing behaviour

The results for the knowledge sharing behaviour of the lawyers, and their use of information technology services to share knowledge, showed that many indicated sharing the following frequently: records of court proceedings (66.7%), judicial authorities (68.5%), statutory authorities (67.4%), case law (65.6%), law reports (65.8%), citations (51.3%), legal trends (46.9%), and expertise based on formal education and training (48.0%), whilst legislative developments in law and practice notes were shared occasionally, at (44.7%) and (42.1%) respectively. The frequency of the use of information technology services to share knowledge by the lawyers was scrutinised. Results showed that most respondents reported that they occasionally share their knowledge with other lawyers with the use of email (31.1%). However, they never shared knowledge with other lawyers via intranet (39.2%), online forums (44.0%), wikis (62.3%), knowledge repositories (31.9%) or through blogs (65.6%), whilst they often shared knowledge with (Global System for Mobile Communication (GSM) services (71.4%).

Principal component analysis of knowledge sharing behaviour

In order to simplify the analysis, data reduction tests were carried out on the constructs by carrying out principal factor component analysis tests, and by computing these to form a single variable called knowledge sharing behaviour. Table 1 shows a summary of the tests' results. Principal component factor analysis was applied to assess the underlying structure for the 11 knowledge sources. The Kaiser Mayer Olkin and Bartlett's test of sphericity is significant ($p = 0.000 < 0.05$) for all the factors. This indicates that the correlation matrix between the constructs is not an identity matrix, and the correlations between variables are therefore not all zero, thus permitting the reduction of the variable, either by the extraction or computing. Also, the determinant of correlation matrix (0.004 > 0.001) indicates that the analysis was possible.

Judicial authorities had the highest mean value of 3.610, with a standard deviation of 0.711, and had the highest loading factor of 0.868 with an Eigenvalue of 5.499. Relevant statutory authorities had the second highest mean value of 3.600 with a standard deviation of 0.662 and the second highest loading factor of 0.853. Expertise based on formal education and training had the second-to-lowest mean value of 3.210, which is a standard deviation of 0.927, but had the third highest loading factor of 0.812. Altogether these three constructs explained 74.788% of the total variance contributed by the 11 factors, and had a cumulative Eigenvalue of 8.226 out of the initial Eigenvalue of 1.0 allocated to each construct. Thus, they were computed to form a single variable to represent the higher variable knowledge sharing behaviour.

Principal component analysis of intention to share knowledge

To assess the respondents' intention to share knowledge, principal component factor analysis was also applied to examine the structure of the five identified constructs used to measure the parent variable (see Table 2).

Two components were extracted; 'I will share my knowledge with anyone in the firm if it is helpful to the law firm', and 'I intend to share my knowledge with other members in the firm more frequently in the future' had mean values of 2.870 and 2.820, and loading factors of 0.836 and 0.787 respectively. They accounted for 60.885% of the total variance explained by the five constructs, with Eigenvalues of 2.032 and 1.743. This indicated that these two factors, when computed, were sufficient to represent the variable intention to share knowledge.

Principal component analysis of the individual's beliefs

Principal component analysis was also used to reduce the constructs for the variables' expected rewards, expected associations and expected contribution into a few parsimonious constructs. The factor loading of the variables are presented in Table 3. To assess the individual's beliefs, which were factors identified as influencing the lawyers intentions to share knowledge, principal components factor analysis was applied to examine the structure of the thirteen constructs, which had already been grouped into three factors, namely, (1) expected rewards, (2) expected associations and (3) expected contribution. With $p = 0.000$, the Kaiser Mayer Olkin and Bartlett test of sphericity is significant at $p < 0.05$. Also, the determinant of correlation matrix gives values (0.374, 0.267 and 0.310 respectively for each variable) that are greater than 0.001 for all the three groups, indicating that the analysis is possible.

From the results in Table 3, the first factor of 'expected rewards', 'I will receive monetary rewards in return for KS' had a mean of 1.580 and a standard deviation of 0.841. 'I will receive additional points for promotion in return for my KS' had the second highest mean value of 1.870 and a standard deviation of 0.906, whilst 'I will receive an award, an honor or educational opportunity in return for my KS' had the highest

TABLE 1: Principal component analysis of knowledge sharing behaviour.

Knowledge sharing behaviour	Mean	SD	Factor 1
Knowledge sources			
Records of court proceedings	3.570	0.711	0.610
Judicial authorities	3.610	0.662	**0.868**
Relevant statutory authorities	3.600	0.664	**0.853**
Case law generally	3.560	0.716	0.782
Relevant law reports	3.570	0.689	0.712
Legislative developments in the law	3.290	0.764	0.699
Relevant case notes	3.250	0.843	0.772
Citations	3.320	0.841	0.780
Practice notes	3.010	0.955	0.705
Legal trends	3.260	0.856	0.734
Expertise based on education and training	3.210	0.927	**0.812**
Analysis			
Determinant of correlation matrix	-	-	0.004
KMO and Bartlett's test (significance level)	-	-	0.000

SD, standard deviation.
Figures in bold were the highest loading factors.

TABLE 2: Principal component analysis of intention to share knowledge.

Intention to share knowledge	Mean	SD	Factors 1
I will share my knowledge with more members in the law firm	2.900	0.340	0.696
I will always provide my knowledge at the request of other members of the law firm	2.920	0.333	0.764
I intend to share my knowledge with other members in the firm more frequently in the future	2.820	0.510	**0.787**
I try to share my knowledge with other members of the firm in an effective way	2.930	0.295	0.706
I will share my knowledge with anyone in the firm if it is helpful to the law firm	2.870	0.456	**0.836**
Determinant of correlation matrix	-	-	0.562
KMO and Bartlett's test (signifcance level)	-	-	0.000

SD, standard deviation.
Figures in bold were the highest loading factors.

mean of 1.950 and a standard deviation of 0.904. In addition, 'I will receive additional points for promotion in return for my KS' had the highest loading factor of 0.899 and the highest proportion of variance in the observation (69.372%). It also had an Eigenvalue of 2.081, which means that it absorbed the effect of two constructs, indicating that this variable was sufficient to represent the first group, 'expected rewards'.

'Expected associations' was the second construct; the first factor was 'KS would strengthen the tie between existing members and myself in the firm' which had a mean of 2.810, standard deviation of 0.503, and the highest loading factor of 0.803 and accounted for 53.476% of the total variance explained. It also had an Eigenvalue of 2.674. 'Knowledge sharing would get me well-acquainted with new members in the firm' had a mean value of 2.790, a standard deviation of 0.541 and the second best loading factor of 0.788, and it explains 16.697% of the total variation. 'Knowledge sharing would expand the scope of my associations with other members in the firm' had a mean of 2.830 and the third highest loading factor of 0.783. Together these three constructs accounted for a cumulative total variance of 91.296% and 4.1 of the cumulative Eigenvalues for all the factors. Thus, the three constructs were computed to obtain the variable expected associations. Although 'KS would create strong relationships with colleagues who have common interests in the firm' had the highest mean of 2.880 and the lowest standard deviation of 0.416, it also had the lowest loading factor of 0.513, and contributed the least to the total variance explained and had the lowest Eigenvalue (8.704% and 0.435 respectively).

The next factor was 'expected contribution'. 'KS would help other members in the firm to solve problems', 'KS would improve work processes in the law firm' and 'KS would increase the productivity in the firm' had equal mean scores of

2.950, with standard deviation values of 0.260, 0.221 and 0.230 respectively. 'KS would increase the productivity in the firm' had the highest loading factor of 0.803 with an Eigenvalue of 2.374, followed by 'KS would improve work processes in the law firm', which had a loading factor of 0.787, then 'KS would help the law firm to achieve its organisational objectives', with a loading factor of 0.716. Together, the total variance explained by these three constructs was 82.203%, indicating that computing the three variables was sufficient to represent the third group and variable expected contributions.

Principal component analysis of attitude towards knowledge sharing

Principal component factor analysis was applied to determine the potential variable that was used to represent and measure the variable attitude towards knowledge sharing. Constructs used to measure the variable include 'Knowledge sharing is good', 'Knowledge sharing is harmful', 'Knowledge sharing is an enjoyable experience', 'Knowledge sharing is valuable to me', and 'Knowledge sharing is a wise move' as shown in Table 4.

The Kaiser Mayer Olkin and Bartlett's test of sphericity was significant and was given a value of $p = 0.000$ for the factors, indicating that the correlation matrix was not an identity matrix justifying the reduction. Also, the determinant of correlation matrix gave a value = 0.284 that was greater than 0.001 for the group, indicating that the analysis could be carried out. The results in Table 4 showed that 'Knowledge sharing is good' had the highest mean score of 2.900, whilst 'Knowledge sharing is harmful' had the lowest mean score of 1.180. However, 'Knowledge sharing is a wise move' had the highest loading factor of 0.826, with an Eigenvalue of 2.592 that accounted for 51.835% of the total variance explained. Four constructs with the highest loading factors, which

TABLE 3: Principal components analysis of the individual's beliefs.

The individual's beliefs	Mean	SD	Factors (Communalities)		
			1	2	3
Expected rewards					
I will receive monetary rewards in return for KS	1.580	0.841	0.733	-	-
I will receive additional points for promotion in return for my KS	1.870	0.906	**0.899**	-	-
I will receive an award, an honor or educational opportunity in return for my KS	1.950	0.904	0.857	-	-
Expected associations					
KS would strengthen the tie between existing members and myself in the firm	2.810	0.503	-	**0.803**	-
KS would get me well-acquainted with new members in the firm	2.790	0.541	-	0.788	-
KS would expand the scope of my associations with other members in the firm	2.830	0.481	-	0.783	-
KS would draw smooth cooperation from outstanding colleagues in the future	2.800	0.528	-	0.730	-
KS would create strong relationships with colleagues who have common interests in the firm	2.880	0.416	-	0.513	-
Expected contribution					
KS would help other members in the firm to solve problems	2.950	0.260	-	-	0.608
KS would create new business opportunities for the firm	2.700	0.598	-	-	0.477
KS would improve work processes in the law firm	2.950	0.221	-	-	0.787
KS would increase the productivity in the firm	2.950	0.230	-	-	**0.803**
KS sharing would help the law firm to achieve its organisational objectives	2.920	0.317	-	-	0.716
Analysis					
Determinant of correlation matrix			0.374	0.267	0.310
KMO and Bartlett's test (signifcance level)			0.000	0.000	0.000

SD, standard deviation.
Figures in bold were the highest loading factors.

accounted for 92.090% of the total variance explained, were computed to arrive at the final variable attitude towards knowledge sharing.

Test of hypotheses

Table 5 presents the regression analysis for the test of hypotheses.

- **Hypothesis 1:** There is no significant relationship between expected rewards and the attitude of the lawyers towards knowledge sharing.

The results in Table 5 showed a positive and very weak correlation ($r = 0.058$). The result also indicated no significance ($p > 0.05$) in the relationship between expected rewards and attitudes towards knowledge sharing. Therefore, the null hypothesis is not rejected, that is there is no significant relationship between the lawyers' expected rewards and attitude towards knowledge sharing.

- **Hypothesis 2:** There is no significant relationship between expected associations and lawyers' attitudes towards knowledge sharing.

As shown in Table 5, the relationship showed a positive and strong correlation ($r = 0.540$). It also indicates a positive and significant slope (B = 0.363; $p = 0.000 < 0.05$). Hence, the null hypothesis is rejected, implying that there is a relationship with expected associations of lawyers in Ibadan and their attitude to sharing knowledge.

- **Hypothesis 3:** There is no significant relationship between the lawyers' expected contributions to the law firm and their attitudes towards knowledge sharing.

Table 5 showed that the expected contribution is significantly related ($r = 0.478$; $p < 0.05$) with the attitude towards knowledge sharing, of lawyers in the Ibadan metropolis. Therefore, the null hypothesis is rejected, meaning that there is a significant relationship between expected contributions

TABLE 4: Principal component analysis of attitude towards knowledge sharing.

Attitude towards Knowledge Sharing	Mean	SD	Factor 1
Knowledge sharing is good	2.900	0.349	**0.754**
Knowledge sharing is harmful	1.180	0.496	**0.447**
Knowledge sharing is an enjoyable experience	2.880	0.365	**0.763**
Knowledge sharing is valuable to me	2.870	0.389	**0.747**
Knowledge sharing is a wise move	2.880	0.348	**0.826**
Determinant	-	-	0.284
KMO and Bartlett's test (sig level)	-	-	0.000

SD, standard deviation.
Figures in bold were the highest loading factors.

and attitudes towards knowledge sharing amongst lawyers in the Ibadan metropolis.

- **Hypothesis 4:** There is no significant relationship between the attitude of the lawyers towards knowledge sharing and their intention to share knowledge.

The results in Table 5 showed that attitude towards knowledge sharing gave a positive correlation ($r = 0.156$) with the intention to share knowledge, which was significant, at $p < 0.05$. Therefore, the null hypothesis is rejected. This means that there is a significant relationship between the lawyers' attitudes towards knowledge sharing and their intention to share knowledge.

- **Hypothesis 5:** There is no significant relationship between the lawyers' intentions to share knowledge and their knowledge sharing behaviour.

From Table 5, the relationship between the intention to share knowledge and knowledge sharing behaviour is not significant ($r = 0.084$; $p = 0.165 > 0.05$). Therefore, the null hypothesis is thus accepted. This implies that there is no significant relationship between intention to share knowledge and the knowledge sharing behaviour of lawyers.

- **Hypothesis 6:** There is no significant relationship between the level of IT services usage by the lawyers and their knowledge sharing behaviour.

TABLE 5: Regression analysis on the test of hypotheses.

Model	Unstandardised coefficients		Standardised coefficients		
	B	SE	Beta	t	Sig.
Expected rewards and attitude towards knowledge sharing					
1. (Constant)	2.842	0.046	-	62.365	.000
Expected Rewards	0.022	0.023	0.058	0.954	0.341
Expected association and attitude towards knowledge sharing					
1. (Constant)	1.863	0.097	-	19.104	.000
Expected assosciations	0.363	0.034	0.54	10.573	.000
Expected contribution and attitude towards knowledge sharing					
1. (Constant)	0.937	0.218	-	4.306	.000
Expected contribution	0.661	0.074	0.478	8.965	.000
Attitude towards knowledge sharing and intention to share knowledge					
1. (Constant)	2.384	0.188	-	12.703	.000
Attitude towards KS	0.168	0.065	0.156	2.597	0.01
Intention to share knowledge and knowledge sharing behaviour					
1. (Constant)	0.792	0.104	-	7.609	.000
Intention to share knowledge	0.05	0.036	0.084	1.394	0.165
Level of IT services usage and knowledge sharing behaviour					
1. (Constant)	0.764	0.044	-	17.417	.000
Level of IT services usage	0.055	0.014	0.239	4.053	.000

B, coefficients represent the *independent* contributions of each independent variable to the prediction of the dependent variable; SE, standard error; Beta, coefficients reflect effects for standardised predictors; *t*, *t*-value measure the relative strength of prediction; Sig., significance.

Regression results in Table 5 showed that the relationship between the level of IT services usage and knowledge sharing behaviour of lawyers in the Ibadan metropolis showed a positive correlation (0.239), which was significant at $p < 0.05$. Therefore, the null hypothesis was rejected.

Summary of results from test of hypotheses

The summary from the results of the hypotheses test showed that the null hypotheses tested for hypothesis one and hypothesis five were not rejected, and were thus supported. Table 6 also shows that the null hypothesis 2, hypothesis 3, hypothesis 4 and hypothesis 6 were supported. These were tested for the following purposes, namely to establish:

- the relationship between expected associations and attitude towards knowledge sharing
- the expected contributions and attitude towards knowledge sharing
- the attitude towards knowledge sharing and actual knowledge sharing behaviour
- the level of IT use and actual knowledge sharing behaviour.

Structural model results

Figure 2 presents the results of the study based on the research model adopted. It shows that expected associations had the greatest influence on the lawyers' attitudes towards knowledge sharing.

Discussion of findings
Expected rewards

An interesting finding in this study is the expected rewards variable, as this is a factor that affects knowledge sharing amongst lawyers in the surveyed law firms. Although King and Iyoha (2008) emphasised that there had to be something that motivated the employees willingness to share their knowledge for the benefit of the organisation, stating that if the employees were not motivated, their knowledge may never be shared with others. This study discovered that expected reward was not one of the factors that motivated lawyers in Ibadan to share their knowledge within their law firms. King

TABLE 6: Hypothesis results summary.

Structural path	Standardised coefficients	Hypothesis testing
Expected rewards → Attitude to KS	0.058	Not supported
Expected associations → Attitude to KS	0.540***	Supported
Expected contributions → Attitude to KS	0.478***	Supported
Attitude to KS → Intention to KS	0.156**	Supported
Intention to KS → Actual KS behaviour	0.084	Not supported
Level of IT usage → Actual KS behaviour	0.239***	Supported

KS, knowledge sharing.
*$p < 0.05$; **$p < 0.01$; ***$p < 0.001$

and Iyoha noted that workers willingly shared knowledge with the hope of getting rewards either from the person they are sharing their knowledge with or from the organisation. But this study observed no significant relationship between expected rewards and attitudes towards knowledge sharing behaviour of the lawyers. Gottschalk et al. (2005) established that rewards had a significant impact on knowledge sharing. The framework of Sanghani (2009) also emphasised providing incentives and rewards for knowledge sharing, whilst Ipe (2003) acknowledged the effect of rewards and incentives as a contributing factor that may influence employees' attitudes to share knowledge within an organisation. He also noted that a way to motivate people to capture knowledge is to reward them for doing so, by providing the knowledge sharers with some compensation for sharing their knowledge. The findings of this study, concerning rewards, did not agree with all these propositions about the relationship between the effect of rewards and knowledge sharing amongst lawyers in Ibadan. It did however concur with the findings of Bock and Kim (2002) that the employees' beliefs about expected rewards were negatively related to their attitudes to knowledge sharing. Bock and Kim tried to find a reasonable explanation for this by insisting that rewards have a punitive effect that break off relations and may undermine intrinsic motivation.

Expected associations

Gottschalk et al. (2005) observed that lawyers' attitudes towards associations were of less importance to their knowledge sharing behaviour in the law firm. This study however showed a positive and strong relationship between

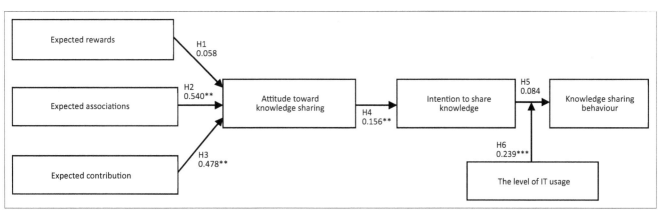

*$p < 0.05$; **$p < 0.01$; ***$p < 0.001$

FIGURE 2: Structural model results.

expected associations of lawyers in Ibadan and their attitude to sharing knowledge. Knowledge as power is demonstrated in the increasing value attributed to individuals who possess the right kind of knowledge. If individuals perceive that power comes from the knowledge they possess, it is likely to lead to knowledge hoarding instead of knowledge sharing (Hendriks 2005). One of the external factors that influenced the motivation to share knowledge, as identified by (Ipe 2003), was the relationship between the sender and the recipient. It was noted that lawyers in Ibadan have a positive attitude towards knowledge sharing, who considered that it may strengthen the relationship between themselves and other lawyers, thus supporting Ipe's 2003 proposition.

Expected contribution

Gottschalk *et al.* (2005), in their study of the *Incentives for Knowledge Sharing through Information Technology*, noted that lawyers' attitudes towards their own contribution were the factors that mostly predicted their knowledge sharing behaviour. They also noted that, on average, a lawyer's willingness to share their knowledge with others in a law firm was influenced by their perception of their ability to contribute to the organisation by sharing that knowledge. This study corroborates this finding, as its results established that the expected contribution was significantly related with the attitude of lawyers in the Ibadan metropolis, towards their knowledge sharing. This finding also corresponds to the definition of knowledge sharing within the organisation given by many researchers. For instance, knowledge sharing between individuals is the process by which knowledge held by an individual is converted into a form that can be understood, absorbed, and used by other individuals, and that contributes to both individual and organisational learning (Ipe 2003). Knowledge sharing is important because it provides a link between the individual and the organisation by moving knowledge that resides with individuals to the organisational level, where it is converted into economic and competitive value for the organisation (Hendriks 1999). The voluntary act of sharing knowledge by an individual contributes to knowledge distribution, and the process of sharing may result in knowledge acquisition by other individuals within the organisation (Ipe 2003). Knowledge sharing between individuals, thus, results in individual learning, which in turn may contribute to organisational learning (Turner & Minonne 2010). The ability to share knowledge, between organisational units and departments, contributes immensely to the performance of the organisation (Hendriks 2005). Thus, the motivation of workers for knowledge sharing is to exchange ideas, information and consequently knowledge to enable organisations to increase their knowledge base, improve work processes, increase productivity and help them achieve their objectives.

Attitude towards knowledge sharing

Results showed that there was a significant relationship between the attitudes of lawyers towards knowledge sharing and their intention to share knowledge. This finding agrees with Bock and Kim (2002) who found that attitudes towards knowledge sharing had a significant influence on behaviour intention. This also corroborates the finding of Ellahi and Mushtaq (2011) that confirmed that the attitudes of bloggers, towards knowledge sharing, significantly affected their intention to share knowledge in blogs. Also, the proposition of the TRA, that intention to perform behaviour is influenced by an individual's attitude toward performing the behaviour, was confirmed as attitudes towards knowledge sharing gave a positive and significant correlation with the intention to share knowledge amongst lawyers in the law firms surveyed.

Intention to share knowledge

This study determined that there was no significant relationship between the intention to share knowledge and the knowledge sharing behaviour of lawyers in the Ibadan metropolis. This deviated from the findings of Ellahi and Mushtag (2011) that the intention to share knowledge was positively related with actual knowledge sharing behaviour in blogs. Their study confirmed that one unit increase in intention to knowledge sharing will increase 0.90 units in actual knowledge sharing behaviour. The intention of bloggers, to share their knowledge, was a strong predictor of their actual knowledge sharing in blogs. The findings of this study also disagreed with the findings of Bock and Kim (2002) that an individual's actual knowledge sharing behaviour is highly correlated with the behavioural intention to share knowledge. The positive influences of attitude and intention on behaviour are, additionally, confirmed in the knowledge sharing context. It also disagreed with the TRA, based on the premise that intention is the main determinant of a person's actions or actual behaviour. This premise was not supported by the findings of this study.

Level of Information Technology usage for knowledge sharing

The relationship between the level of Information Technology (IT) services usage and knowledge sharing behaviour, of lawyers in the Ibadan metropolis, showed a positive correlation, which was significant. Ojo and Grand (2009) established that more than half of the lawyers in Botswana select IT moderately for knowledge sharing. Sanghani (2009) emphasised the importance of information technology for knowledge sharing, and noted that proper knowledge sharing was unthinkable without the appropriate technology, stating that Information Systems help the organisation manage and leverage knowledge systematically and actively. It should be noted however that only email and GSM services were being used by most of the lawyers in the Ibadan metropolis for knowledge sharing. The other IT services listed were either not being used at all or were being used by very few of them. This finding agreed with Gottschalk *et al.* (2005) that user satisfaction and user-friendly systems were very important when attempting to motivate lawyers to use and share knowledge via an IT system.

Implications and future studies

This study contributes to the prevailing literature, providing empirical data on the knowledge sharing attitudes of lawyers in the Ibadan metropolis. Whilst expected associations and expected contributions were related to the lawyers' attitudes to knowledge sharing, expected rewards was not. It is recommended that law firms in Ibadan should incorporate avenues for knowledge sharing amongst lawyers, which may be routine or periodical. Regular conferences could be organised to espouse recent developments in the legal profession and opportunities given to lawyers to share ideas. Provision should be made for organisational knowledge repositories, where knowledge sources may be stored and consulted when needed. IT infrastructure and services that encourage effective knowledge sharing may, additionally, be adopted. Only Global System for Mobile communication services and email were predominantly used by the lawyers for knowledge sharing, out of a variety of IT services available that could encourage effective knowledge sharing. Law firms are also encouraged to send their lawyers for occasional relevant training. Further studies may be carried out to unravel other factors that could influence knowledge sharing, apart from those investigated in this study. Also, the influence of socio-demographic factors on knowledge sharing could be determined. It may also be necessary to measure the level of IT usage with more diverse types of Information System for knowledge sharing, in respect to other professions, and other research models of knowledge sharing could be applied to carry out future studies.

Acknowledgements

Competing interests

The authors declare that they have no financial or personal relationship(s) which may have inappropriately influenced them in writing this paper.

Authors' contributions

W.M.O. (University of Ibadan) was involved in the design and data analysis aspects of the study and wrote the manuscript. I.N.E. (University of Ibadan), was involved in the design and was responsible for data collection and analysis.

References

Agbonlahor, R.O., 2005, 'Utilisation and Attitude of Higher Institution lecturers in Nigerian Universities towards Information Technology, Doctoral degree, Dept. of Information Science, Africa Regional Centre for Information Science, University of Ibadan, Nigeria.

Aiken, L.R. (2000). *Psychological Testing and Assessment*, 10th edn., Allyn and Bacon, Boston, MA.

Ajzen, I. & Fishbein, M., 1980, *Understanding attitudes and predicting social behaviour*, Prentice-Hall, Englewood Cliffs, NJ.

Argote, L. & Ingram, P. 2000, 'Knowledge transfer: A basis for competitive advantage in firms', *Organizational Behaviour and Human Decision Processes* 82(1), 150–169. http://dx.doi.org/10.1006/obhd.2000.2893

Bircham, H., 2003, 'The impact of question structure when sharing knowledge', *Electronic Journal of Knowledge Management* 1(2), 17–24.

Bock, G.W. & Kim, Y.G., 2002, 'Breaking the Myths of Rewards: An Exploratory Study of Attitudes about Knowledge Sharing', *Information Resource Management Journal* 15(2), 14–21. http://dx.doi.org/10.4018/irmj.2002040102

Chua, A. 2003, 'Knowledge Management System Architecture: A Bridge Between Knowledge Management Consultants and Technologists', *International Journal of Information Management* (24)1, 87–98.

Davenport, T.H. & Prusak, L., 1998, *Working Knowledge: How Organizations Manage What They Know*, Harvard Business School Press, Boston, MA.

Davis, F.D., Bagozzi, R.P. & Warshaw, P.R., 1992, Extrinsic and Intrinsic Motivation to Use Computers in the Workplace, *Journal of Applied Social Psychology* 22, 1111–1132. http://dx.doi.org/10.1111/j.1559-1816.1992.tb00945.x

Eiseman, J., 2007, 'Creating Intranet Applications for Knowledge Sharing within Law Firms', *Law and Technology Resources for Legal Professionals*, viewed 16 February 2011, from http://www.llrx.com/authors/1099

Ellahi, A.A. & Mushtaq, R., 2011, 'Probing Factors Affecting Knowledge Sharing Behaviour of Pakistani Bloggers', *The Electronic Journal on Information Systems in Developing Countries* 45(6), 1–14.

Global Law Firm Knowledge Management Survey Report, 2002, viewed 17 February 2011, from http://www.virtuallawjournal.net/?nodeid=32&lang=en

Gottschalk, P., Brekke, K. & Pedersen, H.C., 2005, 'Incentives for Knowledge Sharing through Information Technology in Law Firms' in *Virtual Law Journal*, viewed 17 February 2011, from http://www.virtuallawjournal.net/?nodeid=32&lang=en

Grant, R.B., 1996, 'Towards a knowledge-based theory of the firm', *Strategic Management Journal*, vol. 17 (Winter Special Issue), 109–122.

Gupta, A.K., & Govindarajan, V., 2000, 'Knowledge flows within multinational corporations' *Strategic Management Journal* 21, 473–496. http://dx.doi.org/10.1002/(SICI)1097-0266(200004)21:4<473::AID-SMJ84>3.0.CO;2-I

Hendriks, P., 1999, 'Why share knowledge? The influence of ICT on the motivation for knowledge sharing', *Knowledge and Process Management*, 6(2), 91–100 http://dx.doi.org/10.1002/(SICI)1099-1441(199906)6:2<91::AID-KPM54>3.0.CO;2-M

Hendriks, P.H.J., 2005, 'Book Review: Knowledge Management in Organizations: A Critical Introduction', *Management Learning* 36(4), 535–553, viewed 12 December 2011, from http://mlq.sagepub.com/content/36/4/535

Ipe, M., 2003, 'Knowledge Sharing in Organizations: A Conceptual Framework', *Human Resource Development Review* 2(4), 337–359, viewed 12 July 2011 from, http://hrd.sagepub.com/content/2/4/337

Joseph, M., Firestone, J.M. & McElroy, M.W., 2005, 'Doing Knowledge Management', *The Learning Organization Journal* 12(2), viewed 24 September 2010, from http://www.emeraldinsight.com/10.1108/0969647051

King, O.A. & Iyoha, G.E., 2008, 'Improving knowledge sharing capabilities of organizations: a case study of ReStral Nigeria Limited', Masters thesis, Blekinge Institute of Technology, Sweden.

Ojo, R.R. & Grand, B., 2011, 'An Analysis of the Extent of IT Acceptance and Use for Knowledge Management in Botswana Law Organizations', *Infotrends: An International Journal of Information and Knowledge Management* 1(1), 27–37.

Ogunmoye, E.M., 2008, 'A Survey of the Attitude of Students towards Online Education in South-Western Nigerian Universities', Masters project, Africa Regional Centre for Information Science, University of Ibadan, Nigeria.

Ryu, S., Hee-Ho, S. & Han, I., 2003, 'Knowledge sharing behaviour of physicians in hospitals', *Expert Systems with Applications* 25, 113–122. http://dx.doi.org/10.1016/S0957-4174(03)00011-3

Sanghani, P., 2009, 'Knowledge Management Implementation: Holistic Framework Based on Indian Study', *Association for Information Systems (AIS) Electronic Library (AISeL)*, viewed 18 August 2011, from http://aisel.aisnet.org/pacis2009/69

Schulz, M. & Klugmann, M. (2005), 'Creating a culture of knowledge sharing in law firms', *Professional Knowledge Management*, vol. 3782, pp. 386–391, Lecture Notes Artificial Intelligence (LNAI) Series, Springer Verlag, Berlin.

Senge, P., 2007, 'On sharing knowledge', *The Gurteen Knowledge*, viewed 14 November 2010, from http://www.gurteen.com/gurteen/gurteen.nsf/id/X00035A9E/

Turner, G. & Minonne, C., 2010, 'Measuring the Effects of Knowledge Management Practices', *Electronic Journal of Knowledge Management* 8(1), 161–170, viewed 12 December 2010, from www.ejkm com

Venkatesh, V., Morris, M.G., Davis, G.B. & Davis, E.D., 2003, 'User acceptance of information technology: Towards a unified view', *MIS Quarterly* 27(3), 425–478.

4

Corporate websites in Africa: Has online investor relations communication improved during the past four years? Evidence from Egypt, Kenya, Morocco, Nigeria and Tunisia

Authors:
Roelof Baard[1]
George Nel[1]

Affiliations:
[1]Department of Accounting, University of Stellenbosch, South Africa

Correspondence to:
Roelof Baard

Email:
rbaard@sun.ac.za

Postal address:
Private Bag X1, Matieland 7602, South Africa

Background: Investors require detailed financial and nonfinancial information to evaluate investments. This information is available in various forms (e.g. hard copies, published media, broker and investment consultants and corporate websites). Corporate websites have the potential to be both a one-stop-shop for investor needs and an efficient cost-effective medium for companies to communicate with investors. As previous research (Baard & Nel 2006) showed unacceptable low levels of Internet presence in selected African countries compared to other international companies, including companies in South Africa, a follow-up study was undertaken. An improvement was expected given the rapid increase in Internet users, improvements in infrastructure, the arrival of wireless access technologies and lower tariffs.

Objectives: The objectives of this study were to measure the availability of corporate websites and dedicated investor relations (IR) sections; to evaluate the content of IR information communicated and to compare findings with previous research.

Method: For ease of comparison this study has evaluated the same 40 companies in each of the countries, namely Egypt, Kenya, Morocco, Nigeria and Tunisia that were evaluated in the 2006 study. A number of steps were taken to find the websites after which all the working websites were screened and evaluated against a checklist of international best practices.

Results: Although improvements were apparent, 19% of the companies in the study still do not have websites, 20% do not supply financial information on websites and a significant number of companies do not optimally utilise websites according to international best practices.

Conclusion: Notwithstanding improvements, a significant number of companies do not optimally utilise their corporate websites to communicate to investors. Possible reasons were discussed (e.g. necessary skills, available technology and cost), but it was concluded that companies are probably either negligent, do not regard it as important to communicate information to investors via corporate websites, or do not realise the benefits of communicating company information in this manner.

Introduction

According to the 2009 World Bank Annual Report 50.9% of the population in Africa are living on less than $1.25 a day. It is regularly argued that increased foreign direct investments (FDI) are required to fight poverty. One type of FDI comprises investment by investors in existing companies. To evaluate such a potential investment, investors require detailed financial and nonfinancial information. This information is available in various forms (e.g. hard copies, published media, broker and investment consultants and corporate websites).

Corporate websites as an information source could potentially, if optimally used, have advantages for both investors and companies. For investors they could be an easy, quick, cheap, complete and up-to-date source of information that is readily available. For companies it will reduce the cost of and the time required for distributing information and will enable them to communicate with previously unidentified potential investors (FASB 2000).

Makinson Cowell in 2000 found that up to 75% of institutional investors review corporate websites before meeting a company's management. More recent research by the US Securities and Exchange Commission (SEC 2008) has found that 5% of retail investors said they completely rely on information from the Internet, 25% said they regularly relied on it to guide their investment decisions, and 26% said they rely on it a little. Investors who accessed information over the Internet to guide their investment decisions were asked where they go on the internet to get that information. The most often mentioned sources were individual company websites (38%) and financial investment information websites (24%; SEC 2008).

The SEC research showed that 21% of retail investors use websites as an information source. One possible reason for the discrepancy between the Makinson Cowell (2000) and the SEC (2008) research could be that retail investors will in general be more dependant on broker and investment consultants as information source compared to institutional investors.

On 01 August 2008 the SEC issued a document to provide guidance to companies regarding the use of company websites under the exchange act. In this document, the SEC states:

> we have reached the point where the availability of information in electronic form – whether on EDGAR or a company website – is the superior method of providing company information to most investors, as compared to other method.

(Harrington & Badian 2009, p. 25)

According to Robert Seberger, president of Investor Relations Marketing, the 'Big Four' components of corporate websites are investor relations (IR), public relations, employment and 'about us' information (Investor Relations Marketing 2006). Marston (1996) defines IR as the link between a company and the financial community by which information for evaluating the company is provided to the financial community (investors). Given this definition of IR, it is clear that investors will be particularly interested in the IR section when visiting a corporate website.

A study undertaken into the top 100 companies in the USA in 2000 revealed that 99 had websites and 93 made provision for investor relations (FASB 2000). A study by Allam and Lymer (2002), on the 50 largest companies in the USA, UK, Canada, Australia and Hong Kong, concluded that 99.6%[1] of these companies had websites and 100% of the companies with websites had investor relations sections.

According to research by Venter (2002), 85 of the top 100 companies in South Africa had active websites and 83 of the 85 companies had some form of investor relations or a financial information web page. Research by Loxton (2003) and Nel (2004) showed similar results. Baard and Nel (2006) showed that the 40 largest companies in South Africa all had working websites with a dedicated IR section in 2006. This, however, was not representative of the rest of Africa, as this research also showed that only 133 (67%) of the largest 200 companies in Egypt, Kenya, Morocco, Nigeria and Tunisia had working websites in 2006. Of these 133 companies with working websites, only 38 had a dedicated IR section and only 57 supplied some financial information (Baard & Nel 2006). Of the 38 companies with dedicated IR sections only

30 supplied financial information. Of the 200 companies investigated only 87 (44%) therefore supplied financial information.

More recent research by Africanir (2010) showed that 329 (77%) of 427 companies investigated in 10 African countries (Ghana, Mauritius, Malawi, Nigeria, Namibia, Kenya, Uganda, Tanzania, Zambia and Zimbabwe) had corporate websites. Only 128 (30%) of the 427 companies showed financial information.

Although the percentage of companies with corporate websites according to the Africanir research in 2010 was 10% higher compared to the 2006 research by Baard and Nel, the percentage of companies that actually display online financial information was 14% lower in the 2010 research (30% compared to 44%). It should however be noted that the 2006 research is not comparable with the 2010 research for the following reasons:

- Difference in market capitalisation of companies included in the 2006 research compared to the 2010 research. In the 2010 research, 60% of companies had a market capitalisation of less than $50 million compared to 22.5% of companies in the 2006 research.
- Internet presence of countries included in the 2006 research compared to the 2010 research. The 5 countries included in the 2006 research represent around 60% of internet users in Africa compared to the 10 countries from the 2010 research that represent around 32% (Internet World Stats 2010).

Although the Internet penetration rate in Africa was only 6.8% in 2009, compared to 26% for the world, it has improved from 2.6% (2005) to 4% (2006) and to 6.8% in 2009. Internet users in Africa increased from 22 million in 2006 to 67 million in 2009 (Business wire 2006; Internet World Stats 2010).

Given the rapid increase in Internet users, improvements in infrastructure, the arrival of wireless access technologies, lower tariffs and the absence of comparable research after 2007 a follow-up study of the 2006/2007 researches was undertaken.

Following the 2006 study, Baard and Nel (2007) developed a checklist based on previously published best practices (Investor Relations Society 2006) to evaluate the actual content of the IR information communicated via corporate websites. The IR sections of the aforementioned 38 companies were evaluated and compared with the 40 largest companies in South Africa. Although not all the companies evaluated from South Africa supplied all the information required by best practices, the South African companies scored considerably higher in all categories, compared to their Egyptian, Kenyan, Moroccan, Nigerian and Tunisian counterparts. Because the 40 largest companies in South Africa in 2006/2007 all had corporate websites with dedicated investor relation's sections and that their content mostly complied with best practices, this follow-up study only focused on the 40 largest companies in Egypt, Kenya, Morocco, Nigeria and Tunisia.

1.The study conducted was in total on 250 of which 249 had websites.

The objectives of this study were to:

- measure the availability of corporate websites
- measure the availability of a dedicated IR section on corporate websites
- evaluate the content of investor relations information communicated via corporate websites against a checklist of best practice guidelines for the content thereof
- compare the availability and content of IR sections against 2006/2007 findings.

Gathering the data

Selection of companies

For ease of comparison this study has evaluated the same 40 companies in each of the countries, namely Egypt, Kenya, Morocco, Nigeria and Tunisia that were evaluated in the 2006 study. The companies evaluated in the 2006/2007 study were selected as follows: Firstly, the largest 1000 African companies were sorted according to market capitalisation to establish the largest 200 companies in Africa. In view of the fact that South African companies represented 52% of the 200 largest companies in Africa, South African companies were removed from this list to avoid skewing of results toward South Africa. After removing South African companies, only Egypt, Kenya, Morocco, Nigeria and Tunisia were found to have more than 10 companies each in the top 200. The 40 largest companies in each of the countries (Egypt, Kenya, Morocco, Nigeria, South Africa and Tunisia) were subsequently selected (Baard & Nel 2006).

The checklist

To achieve objectives three and four, this study used the same checklist that was developed and used in the 2007 (Baard & Nel) study. The contents of the checklist will be discussed in the following section.

Company information

This entails information about the company from an investment perspective. Suggested ways to provide this information include an 'About us' section, detailed fact books or short one- to two-page fact sheets and management profiles (e.g. interviews, speeches and videos to explain the company, its strategy and the management's vision).

Financial data

Investors need financial data to quantify the expected returns and risks of an investment in a company. Although financial data primarily consist of the annual report (all the financial statements, director's and auditor's report), best practices include 14 key points to consider for the inclusion of financial data. These key points include:

- an archive of annual reports
- key financial ratios
- relevant information on main intangibles (including those not shown on the balance sheet) dividend history
- share price history
- financial presentations
- key performance indicators (both financial and nonfinancial).

Relevant news

The purpose of relevant news is to keep investors up to date with news about the company, its strategy and operating environment. It is regarded as important to have a central point of access to all news releases about the company.

Shareholder information

Best practice proposes a dedicated shareholder information section. This section should provide information on shareholder meetings; important dates for shareholders; contact details of company advisors; and share price movements and announcements. It should also facilitate shareholder administration, either by online management of shareholder information or by providing the information and relevant documentation for investors to download.

To enable current and potential investors to obtain information about the company or its shares, contact details for the investor relations officer or team responsible for shareholder communication should also be provided.

Bondholder information

Companies should provide clear information on their corporate debt situation and should include information such as credit ratings, terms of banking covenants and contact details for investors with queries relating to the debt situation.

Corporate governance

Directors manage companies on behalf of shareholders. Corporate governance gives information on how a company is managed. According to the Investor Relations Society's best practice guidelines, a corporate website should reflect the importance of corporate governance for investors by identifying this in the main investor index. Websites should therefore provide a section dedicated to corporate governance (Investor Relations Society 2006).

This section should include information about the company (such as its strategy, vision, products and services that it supplies and current changes), its directors (biographical details, appointment, remuneration, and their interest in the company and share transactions) and the audit committee.

Corporate responsibility

The corporate website should contain information about the company's corporate responsibility policies and data. Corporate responsibility includes all environmental, social, health and safety issues and the management of risks across the company.

Possible information that could be supplied includes details of individual(s) responsible for such policies, internal arrangements for implementation of these policies, a statement of specific policies (such as energy consumption, recycling of waste, carbon dioxide emissions, etc.) and policy objectives (e.g. maximum carbon dioxide emissions per annum).

Methodology followed in gathering the data

Availability of corporate websites (first objective)

A number of steps were taken to find the websites. The list of names of the relevant companies in the different countries was obtained and the first step was to enter the company names from the list into two search engines, namely Google (http://www.google.com) and Yahoo (http://www.yahoo.com). Only the first 50 results from each search engine were evaluated. If the URL of the company website was displayed in the first 50 results, the site was visited to gather the required information. When a technical error occurred, for instance if the site was under construction or there was a failure to access the site, that site was visited again on the following day to gather the required information.

When a particular company website could not be found on the first 50 results from any of the two search engines, certain websites containing company profiles and corporate information of various companies were used to try and find the company websites. The usage of these websites was made difficult in that some of these websites would only supply the relevant company information at a price, for instance (http://www.mbendi.co.za). There are websites that were used to find the company websites that did supply the information at no cost, to help find company websites that are not promoted on the first 50 results from the two search engines. These websites are (http://www.business.com) and (http://goliath.ecnext.com).

Availability of dedicated investor relations sections (second objective)

The working corporate websites that were found were subsequently screened for Investor Relations. When no Investor Relations section could be found, the websites were screened for any other financial information (e.g. financial statements).

Evaluating the content of investor relation information communicated (third objective)

The content presented on websites of companies offering dedicated investor relations sections were evaluated using the discussed checklist. Given the magnitude of the present study (200 companies were investigated); it was decided to only investigate the content of IR information that was communicated by corporate websites that had dedicated IR sections (69 companies). This study was also based on the underlying assumption that companies with dedicated IR sections on their corporate websites would on average communicate better with investors via their websites and therefore comply better with best practices.

Time spent to evaluate IR sections was limited to 15 minutes per company. The rationale behind this was that important information should be easily available and at first glance to users of corporate websites. If specific information could not be found, the search facility, if available, was used.

Although all the websites of the companies investigated in this section have investor relations sections and all the information included in the checklist was of an investor relations nature, it is not a best practice to group all investor relations communication under the investor relations section. To complete the checklist, both the dedicated investor relations section and the remainder of the corporate website were therefore investigated.

Best practice guidelines for content suggest a central point for relevant news and dedicated sections for shareholder information, corporate governance and corporate responsibility. The corporate websites of companies in this section that did not have dedicated sections for the items of information listed earlier were also screened for the availability of bits and pieces of such information, either under the investor relations section or in the remainder of the website including annual reports.

During the evaluation it was accepted that different companies, and especially different countries, would use different terminology for the different elements investigated. The following are examples of different names used for the different elements of the checklist:

- Company information: About us
- Relevant news: Media centre, news, news and media, pressroom
- Shareholder information: Equity shareholders, shares, share information
- Bondholder information: Credit rating, debt investors
- Corporate responsibility: Sustainability, sustainability reports, sustainable development, global reporting initiative, corporate social investment, social, policies, corporate citizenship.

It should also be noted that the quality and completeness of the information supplied was not evaluated in this study. As discussed, shareholder information should, for example, include information about shareholder meetings, important dates for shareholders, contact details of company advisors and share price movements and announcements. It should also facilitate shareholder administration, either through online management of shareholder information or by providing the information and relevant documentation for investors to download. If a company supplied only one element of shareholder information, for example, share price movements, it was taken that shareholder information was supplied and the checklist was marked.

Results

The availability of corporate websites (first and fourth objective)

In the 2006 study only 67% of the 200 companies investigated had working websites. Although this position has increased to 81% (see Table 1) it is still very disappointing for the following reasons:

- The companies evaluated were the top 40 companies in each country and the average market capitalisation of companies with no websites were over $350 million in 2006/2007
- The relatively low cost of developing and managing a corporate website
- The Internet presence of the countries involved, as they are all amongst the top ten internet companies in Africa and represent around 60% of all internet users in Africa.

Availability of dedicated investor relations sections (second and fourth objective)

As anticipated from the reported increase in working corporate websites, the number of websites with dedicated IR sections increased accordingly. It should be noted however, that 44% of the websites now have a dedicated IR section compared to 29% in 2006 (see Table 2). As a result, the percentage of websites that presented no IR section but some financial information decreased from 43% to 36%. An alarming 20% of all companies with working websites still do not supply any financial information on their websites.

Evaluating the content of communicated investor relations information (third and forth objective)

It is evident from Table 3 that the dedicated IR sections of companies evaluated in 2010 improved in all categories (except for financial reports – archive) after the 2007 study. It should be noted that 69 companies were evaluated in 2010, compared to the 38 evaluated in 2007, these being the companies that had dedicated IR sections on their corporate

websites in the respective studies. The results of each section in Table 3 are briefly discussed in the section after Table 3.[2]

Company information

In 2010, all companies communicated information about themselves on their corporate websites compared to 92% in 2007. This is mainly performed by means of an 'About Us' section on the corporate website, where various kinds of information about the company are communicated.

Financial Data: Annual reports and archive

Although 93% of the companies supplied financial statements on their corporate websites and nearly all of this information is available under the IR section, which represents an 18% improvement since 2007, the percentage of companies that supplied archive financial reports as well as the average archive years for which these reports were supplied decreased from 2007 to 2010. In total, five companies with dedicated investor relations sections have not supplied annual reports on their corporate websites. Nineteen companies (28%) are not supplying any archive annual reports on their corporate websites. This is not satisfactory, as one would expect that a listed company would at least have its annual report and archive of annual reports available to investors on the corporate website.

Relevant news

Three companies (4%) did not communicate any relevant company news, compared to 2007 when 10.5% (4 companies)

2.It must be noted that the information on the corporate websites of nine Tunisian companies was only available in French.

TABLE 1: Availability of corporate websites.

Availability	Year	Countries											
		Egypt		Kenya		Morocco		Nigeria		Tunisia		Total	
		n	%	n	%	n	%	n	%	n	%	N	%
Working website	2006	25	62.50	28	70.00	30	75.00	32	80.00	18	5.00	133	67.00
		30	77.00	35	88.00	30	79.00	34	89.00	29	73.00	158	81.00
No website	2006	7	17.50	11	27.50	6	15.00	6	15.00	22	55.00	52	26.00
	2010	4	10.00	4	10.00	5	13.00	2	5.00	10	25.00	25	13.00
Failed to access	2006	6	15.00	1	2.50	4	10.00	1	2.50	-	-	12	6.00
	2010	4	10.00	-	-	1	3.00	2	5.00	-	-	7	4.00
Under construction	2006	2	5.00	-	-	-	-	1	2.50	-	-	3	2.00
	2010	1	3.00	1	2.00	2	5.00	-	-	1	3.00	5	3.00

n, Given as means of number.
N, Given as means of total number.

TABLE 2: Provision for investor relations on existing working corporate websites.

Investor relations	Year	Countries											
		Egypt		Kenya		Morocco		Nigeria		Tunisia		Total	
		n	%	n	%	n	%	n	%	n	%	N	%
Investor relations section	2006	14	56.00	8	28.50	6	20.00	9	28.00	1	6.00	38	29.00
	2010	19	63.00	17	49.00	12	40.00	21	62.00	-	-	69	44.00
No investor relations section, but some financial information is supplied	2006	3	12.00	15	53.50	17	57.00	14	44.00	8	44.00	57	43.00
	2010	2	7.00	14	40.00	14	47.00	9	26.00	18	62.00	57	36.00
No investor relations section and no financial information	2006	8	32.00	5	18.00	7	23.00	9	28.00	9	50.00	38	29.00
	2010	9	30.00	4	11.00	4	13.00	4	12.00	11	38.00	32	20.00

n, Given as means of number.
N, Given as means of total number.

TABLE 3: Investor relations information communicated evaluated against the checklist.

Investor relations information	Years			
	2007		2010	
	n	%	*n*	%
Company information	35	92	69	100
Dedicated section – About us	35	-	69	-
Financial – Annual reports	30	79	64	93
Dedicated section[a]	29	-	61	-
Remainder of website	1	-	3	-
Financial – Reports archive	-	-	-	-
Annual reports – Archive	29	76	50	72
Archive – Years	4.4	-	4.1	-
Relevant news	34	89	66	96
Dedicated section	32	-	64	-
Remainder of website	2	-	2	-
Shareholder information	27	71	56	81
Dedicated section	26	-	54	-
Website	1	-	2	-
Bondholder information	9	24	19	28
Dedicated section	9	-	15	-
Website	0	-	4	-
Corporate governance	32	84	68	99
Dedicated section	15	-	31	-
Remainder of website	17	-	37	-
Corporate responsibility	21	55	58	84
Dedicated section	18	-	54	-
Remainder of website	3	-	4	-

n, Given as means of number.
[a], Dedicated section implies that information was communicated through either a dedicated section or under the investor relations section.

did not comply with this best practice. The current study found that 64 companies (out of 66 that do supply relevant news) communicate relevant company news via a central point (93%) on the corporate website, giving the investor easy access to relevant news about the particular company.

Shareholder information

The overall number of companies that supplied shareholder information has improved by 14% from 71% in 2007 to 81% in 2010. This means that 13 companies (19%) with investor relations sections are not communicating any shareholder information. In 2010, 78% of the evaluated companies supplied shareholder information, either under a dedicated section or under the investor relations section, compared to 68% in 2007. The remaining companies communicate shareholder information by supplying bits and pieces of information in various sections of their corporate websites, making it harder for the investor to find the required information.

Bondholder information

Although the availability of bondholder information increased slightly, from 24% in 2007 to 28% in 2010, it is still very low. Some bondholder information, for example debt ratios, can be calculated from annual reports, but other types of bondholder information, for example credit ratings, must be supplied specifically. The study found that, when companies do communicate bondholder information, it is mainly available under the investor relations section of the corporate website.

Corporate governance

Although nearly all companies (with the exception of one) supply this information, only 45% of companies have supplied the information under a dedicated IR or corporate governance section. The remaining 55% supplied the information through the rest of the website, resulting in information being scattered, making it harder for the investor to find the required corporate governance information. The overall number of companies that supplied corporate governance information has also improved, from 84% in 2007 to 99% in 2010.

Corporate responsibility

Companies that supply corporate responsibility information have increased significantly, from 55% in 2007 to 84% in 2010. The companies that do communicate this type of information mostly have a dedicated section for it on their corporate websites. Nearly 93% of the companies supply the information under a dedicated section. This is still much better compared to 55% of corporate governance information that is scattered around the website.

Conclusion

To evaluate an investment, investors require detailed financial and nonfinancial information. Although this information is available from various sources, corporate websites have some definitive advantages compared to more traditional source of information. Corporate websites are however not only about investment information, but also cater for the information needs of existing and potential clients and employees. In order to enable investors to obtain the relevant information that they need from corporate websites best practise website guidelines recommend a dedicated IR section that will act as a one-stop-shop for all investor needs.

As an absolute minimum, each company should have a corporate website to start with. This study found that only 81% of the companies investigated currently had working websites, compared to 67% in 2006. This result is surprising, as these companies are the top 40 companies in five of the larger economies in Africa. Of the 81% of companies with corporate websites, only 80% made use of a dedicated IR section or provided scattered financial information without a dedicated IR section. If someone would therefore be interested in investing in the top 40 companies in each of Egypt, Nigeria, Morocco, Kenya and Tunisia, relevant online financial information would only be found for 126 or 63% of the 200 companies. The remaining 74 or 37% of the companies will either have no corporate website or no relevant information on their corporate websites to assist investors. Furthermore, of the companies with dedicated IR sections on their corporate websites, five and nineteen respectively do not supply annual reports or archive annual reports. Given the importance of annual reports to investors, it is unacceptable for companies, and especially companies of the size investigated in this study, not to supply annual reports on their websites.

Having a corporate website or, even better, a dedicated IR section, does not necessarily guarantee that the corporate website will contain all the relevant information that the investor needs. Best practices that have been developed ensure that IR information communicated to investors contains at least the following information:

- company information
- financial data
- relevant news
- shareholder information
- bondholder information
- information on corporate governance and corporate responsibility.

Although the availability of this information has improved drastically since 2007, information on corporate governance is still not supplied under a dedicated section, as prescribed by best practices. In the case of 55% of the companies, corporate governance information is scattered through the website, which makes it very hard for the investor to find the required information. It is not only much more user friendly to have all relevant information gathered under one heading; it also decreases the risk of investors missing important pieces of information.

Notwithstanding the aforementioned improvements, a significant number of companies still do not optimally utilise their corporate websites to communicate to investors.

Possible reasons for the disappointing results recorded could involve a lack of the necessary skills or of available technology to develop and manage corporate websites. Companies may also have the perception that African investors, especially, do not use the Internet to find company information before making decisions. These reasons, however, may no longer be relevant, given the increase in Internet users and bandwidth availability over the past decade.

Cost cannot be a limiting factor (Baard & Nel 2006) as the average market capitalisation of the companies with no corporate websites reported in the study was in excess of $350 million. The costs associated with developing and hosting a corporate website is low compared to the perceived benefits of having a corporate website that communicates all the relevant information. A corporate website allows a company to communicate company information in a manner that is far cheaper, more flexible and more immediate than conventional communication media, like hard copies of information or the printed media.

The only remaining reasons that the authors of this study are able to offer for these poor results from companies in terms of information communicated, are that these companies are either negligent, do not regard it as important to communicate information to investors via corporate websites, or do not realise the benefits of communicating company information in this manner.

The AIC (Africa Investor Relations) sponsors annual online investor relations awards to reward pioneers in this field in Africa. As legislation and regulation in most African capital markets are not as strict as those in other markets and corporate liability not as high, progressive investor relations practices are not as prevalent. According to the AIC there is currently an enormous potential in Africa to build an online relationship and communications with investors (Online investor relations awards 2009). The winner in the category, best online IR programme 2009, was African Sun Limited.

Further research should be conducted to determine the reason(s) for the lack of corporate websites and compliance by companies with best practices of communicating information via corporate websites. Similar research as conducted by the SEC on the use of investors of the internet and more specific corporate websites would also be useful in the future development of capital markets in Africa. A recent post on an AIC Blog reads as follows: 'I read a study by the SEC on US investors and it got me thinking how none of the African markets have anything similar' (AIC Blog 2010).

References

AIC Blog, 2010, *Brief profile of US investors and Africa,* viewed 01 February 2010, from http://www.africanir.com/2010/01/01/brief-profile-of-us-investors-and-africa/

Africanir, 2010, *IR research: profiling sub-Saharan small caps,* viewed 01 March 2010, from http://www.africanir.com/2010/02/07/ir-research-profiling-sub-saharan small-caps/

Allam, A. & Lymer, A., 2002, 'Developments in Internet financial reporting: review and analysis across five developed countries', in *Birmingham Business School,* viewed 30 September 2003, from http://business.bham.ac.uk/bbs/static/page983.htm

Baard, R.S. & Nel, G.F., 2006, 'Using corporate websites to market to investors in Africa', *South African Journal of Information Management* 8(3), viewed 01 November 2009, from http://www.sajim.co.za

Baard, R.S. & Nel, G.F., 2007, 'Do corporate Web sites in Africa communicate investor information according to best practice guidelines?' *South African Journal of Information Management* 9(3), viewed 01 November 2009, from http://www.sajim.co.za

Business Wire, 2006, *Internet penetration in Africa reached 4 % in 2006, up from 2.6% on the previous* year, viewed 01 February 2010, from http://findarticles.com/p/articles/mi_m0EIN/is_2006_May_8/ai_n16347551/

FASB, 2006, *Electronic distribution of business reporting information: Financial Accounting Standards Board,* viewed 01 March 2006, from http://www.fasb.org/brrp/brrp1.shtml

Harrington, G. & Badian, L., 2009, *Corporate websites: Best practices for website disclosure,* MZ Bulletin, viewed March 2010, from http://www.google.com/url?sa=t&.source=web&cd=8&ved=0CEIQFjAH&url=http%3A%2F%2Farnoldporterllp.com%2Fresources%2Fdocuments%2FArnold%26PorterLLP_MZBulletin_2009.pdf&rct=j&q=%22corporate%20websites%3A%20best%20practices%22%20harrington&ei=iJ14TeSBIpSq8QPcxc3EBA&usg=AFQjCNGxiQ7M2xivgUc-1D9u1tfSA7QepQ&cad=rja

Internet World Stats, 2010, *Internet World Stats,* viewed 01 February 2010, from http://www.internetworldstats.com/stats.htm

Investor Relations Marketing, 2006, *Investor Relations Website Design,* viewed 01 March 2006, from http://www.investorrelationsmarketing.com

Investor Relations Society, 2006, viewed 01 May 2007, from http://www.ir-soc.org.uk

Investor Relations Society, 2006, *Website guidelines: Setting the standard for best practice in investor communications,* viewed 01 May 2007, from http://www.irsoc.org.uk/index.asp?pageid=87

Jones, D., 2008, *SEC survey a reality check on retail investor web use,* viewed 01 February 2010, from http://www.irwebreport.com/daily/2008/08/06/sec-survey-a-reality-check-on-retail-investor-web-use/

Loxton, L., 2003, 'Beleggersverhoudinge op die Internet: 'n Ondersoek in Suid-Afrika' [Investor relationships on the Internet: a Study in South Africa], *Meditari* 11, 81–93, viewed 30 March 2010, from *http://www.meditari.org.za/docs/2003/81_93.pdf*

Makinson Cowell, 2000, *Investor Relations Websites Expectation and Reality,* viewed 01 June 2006, from http://www.makinson-cowell.co.uk/mc/publications/

Marston, C., 1996, 'The organisation of the Investor Relations Function by Large UK Quoted Companies', *Omega* 24(4), 477–488. doi:10.1016/0305-0483(96)00015-1

Nel, G.F., 2004, 'Future of financial reporting on the Internet', *South African Journal of Information Management* June 2004, viewed 01 February 2006, from http://www.sajim.co.za.

Online investors relations awards, 2009, viewed 01 February 2010, from http://www.africanir.com/2010/01/30/2009-online-investor-relations-awards-2/

Securities and Exchange Commission, 2008, *SEC Report,* viewed March 2010, from http://www.sec.gov/comments/s7-28-07/s72807-142-phone.pdf

Venter, J.M.P., 2002, 'A survey of current online reporting practices in South Africa', *Meditari* 10, 209–225, viewed March 2010, from http://www.meditari.org.za/docs/2002/Venter - Meditari 2002 _15_.pdf

World Bank, 2009, *Annual Report,* viewed 01 November 2009, from http://www.worldbank.org/

5

Social media and mobile communications adoption patterns of South African civil society organisations

Authors:
Kiru Pillay[1]
Manoj S. Maharaj[1]

Affiliations:
[1]School of Management, Information Technology and Governance, University of KwaZulu-Natal, South Africa

Correspondence to:
Manoj Maharaj

Email:
maharajms@gmail.com

Postal address:
Private Bag X54001, Durban 4000, South Africa

Background: The resurgence of civil society has largely been attributed to the sector's ability to exploit new interactive technologies and its ability to adapt its communication and mobilisation strategies.

Objectives: This study focuses on how South African civil society organisations (CSOs) deploy Web 2.0 services and technologies for social advocacy and the context of this technology use.

Whilst the literature points to many studies relating to the use of the Internet for advocacy, it also suggests that the role and impact of emerging technologies have not been studied in any detail in CSOs. Such studies have the potential to provide new perspectives to current theoretical frameworks and also to add to the discourse around the use of emerging technologies for advocacy.

Method: A survey of South African CSOs explored the level of knowledge of social media services and revealed which services in particular were being adopted.

Results: The key findings that emerged were that the sector has a low level of knowledge of social media services and an accompanying low level of adoption. These are partly explained by factors such as macro-economic policies and low levels of Internet penetration and ICT readiness.

Conclusion: Further research to determine why certain social media services have been embraced more willingly than others and an analysis of the patterns of adoption to determine any underlying significance or relationships is necessary. An analysis of how CSOs build their advocacy capabilities by appropriating social media and how they thus provide alternate discourses and agendas would be instructive.

Introduction

The 2011 uprising in the Middle East, which started with the self-immolation of a single protester in Tunisia, has had profound worldwide sociopolitical ramifications. Social upheaval has not been confined to the Arab world, with riots in Greece aimed at government-introduced austerity measures, the *Los indignados* (The outraged) in Spain, civil unrest in other parts of Europe as the Euro crisis deepened and reached levels of contagion not seen since the Great Depression (Huffington 2011) and the Occupy Movement leading protests against the currency crisis and corporate greed in many of the world's major cities. Much of the success of the protests has been attributed to a young restive population with access to social media tools (Huffington 2011; Zakaria 2011).

Social media has also been successfully embraced by established civil society organisations with Greenpeace, for example, deploying social media services like YouTube and Facebook to successfully target large corporations like Nestle, McDonalds and even social networking giant Facebook itself in various campaigns aimed at changing corporate behaviour (Greenpeace 2006, 2010a, 2010b).

Civil society, technology and Web 2.0

The collective actions of civil society are a result of communication between different civil society actors, which in turn produce alternative discourses and oppositional debates in the public sphere (Fuchs 2008). These communications have always been achieved by a variety of media including brochures, leaflets and newsletters, all with the intention of gaining access to greater numbers of people within the organisation and in the public domain (Van de Donk *et al.* 2004).

Towards the end of the 1980s, civil society organisations began adopting computer-mediated communications strategies, with the Internet in particular being used to disseminate information.

This Internet-enabled activism is situated in the broader context of the revival of participatory politics that took place in the 1960s and 1970s (Chadwick 2009). Whilst these Internet-based technologies provide a platform for communication between like-minded organisations, they also facilitate diverse views, which are necessary to embrace a wider audience (Tandon 2000). It has long been recognised that the Internet and digital communication networks have the ability to circumvent barriers that may exist to collective action; they expand the mobilisation capacity of organisations across cultural and national levels (Hara & Shachaf 2008): Nugroho and Tampubolon (2008) credit the Internet and other advances in information technology with the current reinvention of the global civil society. The attractiveness of Internet technologies lies in its distributed, decentralised and relatively cheap and easily deployable architecture, which matches the organisational and political logic of global civil society networks (Deibert & Rohozinski 2008).

The emergence of a new set of interactive technologies, under the umbrella term of Web 2.0 (or social media), has resulted in a significant increase in Internet-driven campaigning (Castells 2009). Civil society now has the ability to advance their agenda through these technologies, to the extent that some commentators contend that the balance of power between governments and their citizens has shifted, largely due to the use of social media (Gapper 2009; Hara & Shachaf 2008). There are numerous open-standards websites and technologies (also referred to as services) that encapsulate the Web 2.0 concept; the Pew Research Center (2011) describes Web 2.0 as:

> an umbrella term that is used to refer to a new era of Web-enabled applications that are built around user-generated or user-manipulated content, such as wikis, blogs, podcasts, and social networking sites. (n.p.)

South African civil society

The history of South African civil society is characterised by two distinct periods. The first dates back to the early 1980s when there was a prodigious growth in civil society rooted in the protests against apartheid. The second phase dates to the post-democracy years from 1994 onwards when civil society, faced with different challenges and also new opportunities, changed fundamentally (Habib 2003). Prior to 1994 the majority of South African civil society organisations (CSOs) shared common cause with the dominant exiled liberation movements; post 1994, with the advent of democracy, civil society began to adopt more 'traditional' civil society-type activities and sought to place citizens' interests on the government's agenda (Ranchod 2007). The new democratic political environment has also resulted in the formation of many new social movements united against government's macro-economic policies, which they believe will further entrench poverty and inequality in South Africa.

Contextualising the research problem

The resurgence of civil society has been attributed to the sector's ability to exploit new emerging interactive technologies, and its ability to adapt its communication and mobilisation strategies in the emerging technological paradigm (Anheier, Glasius & Kaldor 2001; Castells 2004). Increased technological innovation has also given rise to distinctly new types of CSOs that can only exist in a digitally connected world. Ushahidi (2011) and Avaaz (2011) for example have embraced technology as the cornerstone of their strategy, and Garrett (2006) contends that they will gradually eclipse traditional CSOs. Traditional CSOs are increasingly considering how the structure, culture and operations of their organisations need to embrace the new technological paradigm.

South African civil society has been well researched in the recent past (Freedom House 2011; Habib 2003; Ranchod 2007) and research into the adoption of information and communication technologies (ICTs) in South African CSOs has also been well represented. In particular, two surveys, one in 2007 and the other in 2009, on the adoption of ICTs and the Internet by civil society were undertaken by a non-governmental organisation, the Southern African NGO Network (SANGONeT) in conjunction with the Internet research house World Wide Worx (2009). Whilst there has been research into the adoption of social media in international CSOs (MobileActive 2010; NTEN 2010, 2011a, 2011b), no published research into the adoption of social media in South African civil society has been undertaken to date. This study explores the extent to which South African CSOs deploy social media services and in particular identifies which services are being appropriated.

Research methodology

A survey, designed to evaluate the levels of knowledge and adoption of Web 2.0 services and targeting South African civil society organisations, was conducted between May 2011 and June 2011. The results of the survey painted a picture of the levels of knowledge and extent of adoption of Web 2.0 services across South African CSOs. The survey targeted South African CSOs whose details are stored in a database of South African CSOs maintained by the non-government organisation SANGONeT (2011). At the time of the survey 1712 organisations were eligible for this research (i.e. operational CSOs with an Internet presence and a valid email address). The contact persons listed on the organisations' websites were targeted by the survey and they were requested to either complete the survey or forward it to the relevant person in the organisation who could provide the requested information. At the end of the survey 122 responses were received and analysed, which represented 7% of the target population.

The theoretical framework underpinning this study is the diffusion of innovations (Rogers 2003), the use of which in the study of technology adoption has been established in research, in particular by Nugroho's (2007) study into the effects of Internet adoption in Indonesian civil society. Diffusion of Innovations provides a rigorous approach to theories of social change (Wejnert 2002) and also provides a theoretical framework for the identification and understanding of the constructs that impact the adoption of Web 2.0 in CSOs.

Analysis of results: Web 2.0 knowledge in South African civil society organisations

Figure 1 depicts the levels of knowledge regarding the use of Web 2.0 services as reported by respondents from South African CSOs. The original responses to this question were on a scale of one to five, with one representing 'not at all knowledgeable' and five meaning 'very knowledgeable'. The responses received were then grouped as follows: ones and twos were recorded under the heading 'a little knowledgeable'; threes were recorded as 'somewhat knowledgeable'; fours and fives were recorded as 'fairly knowledgeable'.

In response to the question on the levels of knowledge with regard to specific Web 2.0 services, respondents indicated 'fairly knowledgeable' for the following services: 55.4% for social networks, 43.3% for photos and multimedia sharing and 51.2% for messenger applications. The respondents indicated 'a little knowledge' for the following services: 73.6% for both social bookmarking and podcasts, 53.7% for both blogging and microblogging and 83.5% for data mashups.

Web 2.0 adoption in South African civil society

Figure 2 illustrates the extent and timelines of individual social media services adoption, with respondents reporting their organisations having adopted social media services as follows[1]:

- Social networks (82.4%)
- Photos and multimedia sharing (58.8%)
- Messenger applications (63%)
- Creating and maintaining of blogs (44.9%)
- Microblogging (43.7%)
- Wikis (42.4%)
- RSS feeds (44.6%)

Respondents reported the following services as having not been adopted within their organisations: social bookmarking (76.5%), downloading and the publishing of podcasts (60.8% and 72% respectively) and data mashups (71.2%). Respondents reported almost evenly on their organisations either having adopted blogging services (50%) or not having adopted this service (44.9%).

Table 1 illustrates the relationship between the adoption of social media services and the levels of knowledge regarding these services. Generally there is a strong correlation between knowledge and adoption rates of services. Only one service, the monitoring of the blogosphere, does not reveal a strong relationship, with 46.2% of respondents indicating being fairly

knowledgeable but with only 19.3% of respondents indicating that their organisations have adopted the service.

Rogers's (2003) diffusion of innovation framework, and specifically the attributes of relative advantage, compatibility, complexity, trialability and observability, can be used to begin to understand the emerging adoption patterns exhibited by South African CSOs. Compatibility for example, which is based on an organisation's need to adopt, explains why with 80% of online users in South Africa having a Facebook account (World Wide Worx 2011), it becomes incumbent on CSOs to adopt social networking in order to exploit this channel of communication and to potentially reach a larger audience.

Complexity – or the degree of difficulty in understanding and ultimately using an innovation – provides a possible explanation for the low adoption rates of data mashups (11%). Mashups are complex in that they have to aggregate various different types of data sources (e.g. databases and legacy systems). Furthermore, mashups are generally programmed by developers or have to be developed using a mashup development tool. Additionally, emerging technologies change constantly, which in turn means that CSOs have to engage with these technologies in an ongoing process of discovery and learning.

In a survey conducted by the Nonprofit Technology Network (NTEN 2010), it emerged that CSOs lack the trained staff required to improve the use of social networks, with 74.1% of respondents indicating a need to know 'which tools are useful for what' and 44.4% indicating a need for training in how these tools work.

Trialability is the ability to experiment with an innovation prior to any decision to adopt or reject it. Social networking and photos and multimedia sharing were cited by 82.4% and

Table 1: Adoption of Web 2.0 services reflect civil society organisations' knowledge of services.

Social media service	Cumulative adoption (%)	Fairly and somewhat knowledgeable (%)
Social networks (e.g. Facebook, MySpace)	82.4	81
Social bookmarking (e.g. del.icio.us, Social Marker)	16	26.5
Downloading of podcasts (e.g. Juice, iTunes)	29.2	26.4
Publishing of podcasts (e.g. Podcaster, PodProducer)	17.8	26.4
Photos and multimedia sharing (e.g. Flickr, YouTube)	58.8	68.3
Creating and maintaining own blogs (e.g. Blogger, WordPress)	44.9	46.2
Monitoring the blogosphere (e.g. Technorati)	19.3	46.2
Microblogging (e.g. Twitter, Tumblr)	43.7	46.3
Wikis (e.g. Wikipedia)	42.4	59.5
RSS feeds (e.g. FeedReader, Google Reader)	44.6	52.1
Data mashups (e.g. Ushahidi)	11	16.6
Messenger applications (e.g. MXit, Skype)	63	66.9

1. Adoption of services is reported by aggregating the responses from the following response categories: 'approximately three months ago', 'approximately six months ago' and 'approximately one year or more ago'.

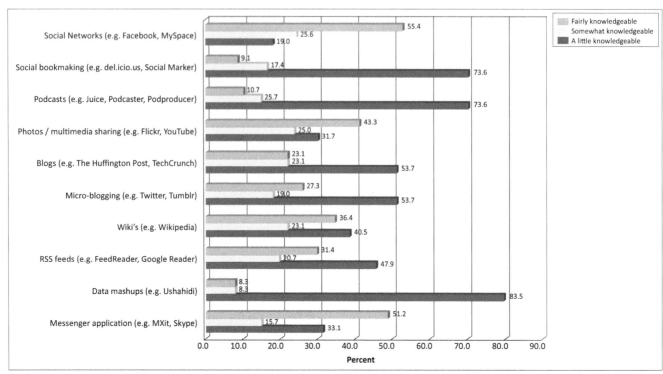

FIGURE 1: Knowledge of social media services in South African civil society organisations.

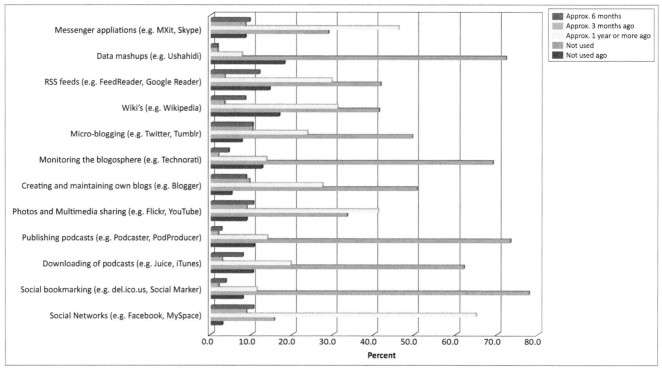

FIGURE 2: Social media service adoption in South African civil society organisations.

58.8% of respondents respectively as having been adopted by their organisations. Both these services can be discontinued fairly easily: Facebook in particular has evolved some fairly mature and well-defined steps for users wishing to discontinue their service.

The penetration rate for cellular phones in South Africa is fast approaching 100% of the adult population; this may be one possible reason why messenger applications and social networks are cited as having being adopted by a large percentage of CSOs (63% and 82.4% respectively). In a survey conducted by the European Network and Information Security Agency (ENISA), it was found that users who access Facebook via their mobile devices were approximately 50% more active on their Facebook accounts than non-mobile users (ENISA 2010), illustrating an increasing level of online activity on cellular phones. A study conducted by the University of Cape Town into digital media usage on cellular phones amongst urban youth found that 93% of youth surveyed access the Internet on their mobile devices (Kreutzer 2009). A report by the United Nations Children's Fund (UNICEF 2011) states that Internet access via the mobile network has already significantly influenced South African society through the wide-scale adoption of mobile-based applications such as MXit.

The use of photographs and imagery has always been an important tool in the arsenal of CSOs; Doyle (2007) states that photographs provide a discourse on 'visual truth' and effectively communicate the reality on the ground. This is supported by the research, which saw 58.8% of respondents indicating the adoption of photos and multimedia sharing services within their organisations.

Social networking in South Africa civil society organisations

The impact of social networking sites (not exclusively Facebook) in South African CSOs is depicted in Figure 3. Respondents reported that 37.8% of organisations have attracted at least 1000 visitors to their social networking sites. The Internet research organisation Socialbakers (2011) estimates that there were approximately 4 511 220 Facebook users in South Africa as at January 2012, which implies that South African CSOs had managed to attract just 0.02% of South African Facebook users to their sites. Only 2.5% of organisations have managed to attract more than 50 000 users to their social network sites.

Extent of Web 2.0 use

Figure 4 depicts the extent of usage of social media amongst South African CSOs as shown by respondents' answers to the survey question: 'Where would you place your organisation with respect to engaging with Web 2.0 social media?' Of the responses received, 21.5% of respondents reported using Web 2.0 services in almost all aspects of their work. There is an almost equal split between organisations using Web 2.0 in some aspects of their work (35.5%) and those who use it in only a few aspects of their work (33.1%). Respondents

indicated that 10% of their organisations do not engage with social media in any aspects of their work.

Social media adoption on a mobile platform

Mobile phones have become woven into the fabric of society; Columbia University's Earth Institute describes mobile phones as 'the single most transformative tool for development' (The Economist 24 September 2009:n.p.). In addition to being a useful tool in itself, mobile technology provides platforms for social media and offers great potential to communication independent of space and time (Wu & Unhelkar 2010). According to ENISA (2010) approximately 65 million people accessed Facebook via their mobile phones in 2009, whilst Facebook reported this number rose to more than 500 million in 2013 (Facebook 2013).

Figure 5 illustrates the cellular phone usage amongst South African CSOs. Whilst the responses were on a scale of one to five with one meaning low usage and five meaning high usage, these categories were aggregated and reported on as follows: ones and twos were recorded as 'less than average', threes were recorded as 'average' and fours and fives were recorded as 'above average'; 66.1% of respondents rated their organisations' usage of cellular phones as 'above average' for standard usage (i.e. making calls and texting), whilst 47.9% indicated an 'above average' usage for advanced use (i.e. connecting to the Web, accessing emails, etc.).

Development of a mobile platform

The development of mobile platforms amongst CSOs is illustrated in Figure 6. With respect to organisational plans to migrate websites and social media services to a mobile platform, respondents reported as follows: 43.8% reported no organisational plans to migrate, 30.6% of organisations were reported as currently in the process of developing mobile platforms and 18% had plans to do so within the next 12 months. Cumulatively, 48.6% of organisations were reported as either currently in the process of migrating to a mobile platform or planning to migrate in the next 12 months.

A report sponsored by a United Nations foundation and the Vodafone Group Foundation (Kinkade & Verclas 2008) found that whilst mobile phones were still used most extensively

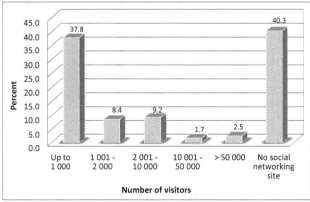

FIGURE 3: Number of visitors to civil society organisations social networking sites.

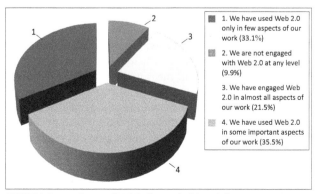

FIGURE 4: Extent of usage of Web 2.0 by South African civil society organisations.

for making voice calls and for text messaging, many civil society members use their mobile phones in other ways, including: taking and distributing photos and videos (39%), gathering and transmitting data (28%) and multimedia messaging (27%). Additionally, 8% of respondents reported using their devices for more complex activities like analysing data, whilst 10% used them for mapping purposes.

Summary: Knowledge and adoption of social media

What emerges from the data is a sector with an overall low level of knowledge of social media services and an accompanying low level of adoption. The majority of South African CSOs have little knowledge of many social media services; in particular, services like social bookmarking, blogging, microblogging, podcasts and mashups are relatively unknown. Organisations did have knowledge of social networks, photos and multimedia sharing and messenger applications and, not surprisingly, these are the services that have been adopted by South African CSOs (i.e. knowledge mirrors adoption).

Understanding social media usage data in South Africa

The link between emerging technologies and the wealth of nations, based on accounting models that link these technologies to productivity, has been well established (International Telecommunications Union 2009). Emerging technologies play a prominent role in creating sustainable growth in competitive economies, by helping to modernise these economies and improving living conditions. They also remain crucial not only for enhancing the possibility of innovation and long-term competitiveness of developed countries, but also for encouraging fundamental structural changes to the economy, improving efficiency and also for reducing the digital, economic and social divisions that exist in middle-income countries and developing countries (Greenhill 2011). Dutta, Mia and Geiger (2011) contend that ICTs, particularly social media and mobile phone applications, offer innovative and sophisticated communication channels that enable new types of social relationships.

Social networking adoption versus gross domestic product per Capita

The Pew Research Centre's Global Attitudes Project (Pew Research Center 2011) states that the number of adults who have a presence on social networking sites is partly related to Internet penetration rates, which in turn is influenced by the wealth of a country as measured by the gross domestic product (GDP). Similarly, the use of one particular social media service (i.e. social networking to explain adoption rates) draws upon arguments advanced by Memmi (2010), which states that social networking is a typical example of social media services.

The scatter graph (Figure 7), using 2012 GDP and social networking usage values that include South Africa,

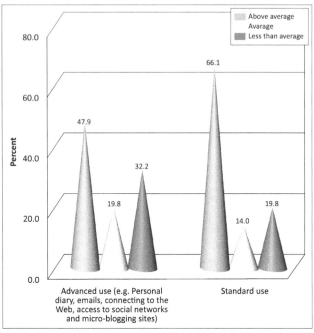

FIGURE 5: Mobile phone usage by South African civil society organisations.

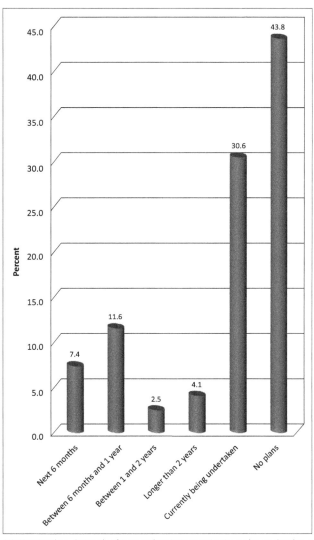

FIGURE 6: When do South African civil society organisations plan to develop a mobile platform?

illustrates the correlation between a country's GDP and the level of social networking adoption amongst the population. Amongst the countries surveyed, not only does the United States of America (USA) have the highest GDP per capita, but it also has one of the highest adult social networking populations. Pakistan and India in contrast have two of the lowest GDPs per capita and correspondingly they also have the lowest number of social networking users.

If one notes that social networking sites (like Facebook, LinkedIn, etc.) are a typical example of the broader social media umbrella of services (Memmi 2010), then the scatter graph is an indication of social media usage versus GDP (and not just social networking versus GDP). It must also be remembered that whilst there are many niche social networking sites that focus on specific issues or are popular in specific countries (e.g. MySpace for music and entertainment, LinkedIn for professional networking, Orkut in India and Brazil, Skyrock in France, VKontakte in Russia and Cyworld in South Korea, Rigby 2008), Facebook is the most popular social networking platform in South Africa. Plotting South Africa's GDP per capita along the X-axis and Facebook usage along the Y-axis reveals a point on the graph that lies below the regression line, implying that South African social media adoption should actually be higher with respect to its GDP per capita.

Social media adoption and network readiness

The network readiness index is a widely accepted measure that is used to evaluate an economy's readiness to leverage technological innovation for increased competitiveness; it does this by measuring the degree to which a country's economic infrastructure is conducive to ICT development and diffusion (Dutta & Mia 2011). South Africa is rated as fairly stable and is placed 70 overall out of a total of 144 countries, with notable strengths in the quality of its market, its regulatory environments and capacity for innovation, amongst others. On a less positive note, individual preparation and uptake of ICT remain very weak, at 113th and 95th respectively (Bilbao-Osorio, Dutta & Lanvin 2013). This is attributed, in part, to the very high access costs to ICT: South Africa has high subscription rates for monthly residential fixed-line, fixed broadband Internet and mobile cellular connections. Government readiness also remains poor and there has been little success in promoting ICT within government itself.

Social media adoption versus Internet usage

The Internet and the applications riding on high-speed broadband networks provide a unique and cost-effective way for economies to enhance national competitiveness and to rise above physical and geographic constraints. A report by the Pew Research Centre (2011) indicates that social networking adoption is largely determined by the overall Internet penetration rate of a country. South Africa's Internet penetration is estimated at around 41% of the population (Broadband Commission 2013). This relatively low Internet

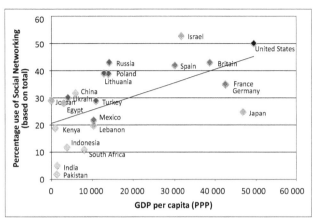

Source: Adapted from Pew Research Center, 2011, *Web 2.0*, viewed 26 November 2012, from http://www.pewinternet.org/topics/Web-20.aspx (including South Africa with 2012 figures)

FIGURE 7: The GDP per capita (PPP) and use of social networking.

penetration rate is a significant factor in the low adoption rate of social media.

Conclusion

This study explored the extent to which South African CSOs adopt and deploy social media services and in particular explored the adoption patterns of individual services.

The picture that emerges is that whilst the respondents were strongly positive about the impact of social media on their organisations, there is in fact a low level of adoption of these services. The study reveals a sector slowly awakening to the potential of social media.

Whilst computers and ICTs in general have become integral in South African CSOs the impact of social media is less obvious and many organisations exhibit a low level of knowledge and associated low levels of adoption. It must be cautioned that social media is a bundle of services and not one particular technology or innovation and it is therefore more difficult to qualify the adoption and the emergent patterns of adoption. This study has speculated on why certain social media services are regarded more favourably by CSOs, which is a topic for future research. It must be noted that individual services that have been adopted are generally adopted by a significant majority of organisations. The converse is also true for those services being less well adopted. Low adoption rates can be related to the difficulty of use of the service.

The role of cellular phones as a platform for social media services may also help to explain adoption rates as certain services are ideally suited to the mobile platform and others less so. Instant messaging applications, like MXit for example, are ideally suited to a mobile platform, whilst data mashup services require larger displays to be truly useful. A significant proportion of organisations utilise cellular phones for fairly advanced purposes (like accessing the Internet) as compared to simply using them for making calls and sending and receiving the ubiquitous SMSs. Given the high penetration rate of cellular phones in South Africa this is not unexpected. Cellular phones have the potential to become the single most transformative tool for development. Their ability to eliminate the boundaries of time and space is always going to be a vital tool in the arsenal of civil society in order to propagate alternative discourses, stimulate debate and change perceptions and attitudes.

Factors that affect the uptake of social media were also presented and what remains to be seen is what happens going forward both within the sector and in South Africa generally.

Acknowledgements

Competing interests

The authors declare that they have no financial or personal relationship(s) that may have inappropriately influenced them in writing this article.

Authors' contributions

This article arose out of the PhD research of K.P. (University of KwaZulu-Natal) under the supervision of M.S.M. (University of KwaZulu-Natal).

References

Anheier, H., Glasius, M. & Kaldor, M., 2001. 'Introducing global civil society', in H. Anheier, M. Glasius & M. Kaldor (eds.), *Global civil society*, pp. 3–22, Oxford University Press, Oxford.

Avaaz, 2011, *The world in action*, viewed 10 September 2013, from http://www.avaaz.org/en/about.php

Bilbao-Osorio, B., Dutta, S. & Lanvin, B., 2013, *The global information technology report 2013: Growth and Jobs in a hyperconnected world*, World Economic Forum, Geneva, Switzerland.

Broadband Commission, 2013, *The state of broadband 2013: Universalizing broadband*, Author, Geneva, Switzerland.

Castells, M., 2004, *The information age: Economy, society and culture*, vol. 2, Blackwell Publishing, New York.

Castells, M., 2009, *Communication power*, Oxford University Press, Oxford.

Chadwick, A., 2009, 'Web 2.0: New challenges for the study of e-democracy in an era of informational exuberance', *I/S: A Journal of Law and Policy for the Information Society* 5(1), 9–41.

Deibert, R., & Rohozinski, R., 2008, 'Good for liberty, bad for security? Global civil society and the securitization of the Internet', in R. Deibert, J. Palfrey, R. Rohozinski & J. Zittrain (eds.), *Access denied: The practice and policy of global Internet filtering*, pp. 123–150, The MIT Press, Cambridge.

Doyle, J., 2007, 'Picturing the clima(c)tic: Greenpeace and the representational politics of climate change communication', *Science as Culture* 16(2), 129–150. http://dx.doi.org/10.1080/09505430701368938

Dutta, S. & Mia, I., 2011, *The global information technology report 2010–2011*, World Economic Forum, Geneva, Switzerland.

Dutta, S., Mia, I. & Geiger, T. 2011. *The global information technology report 2010–2011*, World Economic Forum, Geneva, Switzerland.

ENISA, 2010, *Online as soon as it happens*, Author, Crete, Greece.

Facebook, 2013, *Newsroom: Facebook's latest news, announcements and media resources*, viewed 29 December 2012, from http://newsroom.fb.com/content/default.aspx?NewsAreaId=22

Freedom House, 2011, *Freedom on the net 2011: A global assessment of internet and digital media*, United Nations Democracy Fund, Washington, D.C.

Fuchs, C., 2008, *Internet and society: Social theory in the information age*, Routledge, New York.

Gapper, J., 2009, *Technology is for revolution (and repression)*, viewed 27 July 2011, from http://www.ft.com/intl/cms/s/0/4386d188-5cfe-11de-9d42-00144feabdc0.html#axzz1qyLdo6BA

Garrett, K., 2006. 'Protest in an information society: A review of literature on social movements and new ICTs', *Information, Communication and Society* 9(9), 202–224. http://dx.doi.org/10.1080/13691180600630773

Greenhill, R., 2011, *The global information technology report 2010–2011*, World Economic Forum, Geneva, Switzerland.

Greenpeace, 2006, *McVictory: Victory as fast food giant pledges to help protect the Amazon*, viewed 25 April 2013, from http://www.greenpeace.org/international/en/news/features/McVictory-200706/

Greenpeace, 2010a, *Nestlé - Kit-Kat*, viewed 16 July 2013, from http://www.youtube.com/watch?feature=endscreen&NR=1&v=OE0--1R_d8Y

Greenpeace, 2010b, *Unfriend coal*, viewed 19 May 2012m from http://www.greenpeace.org/usa/en/multimedia/videos/Facebook-Unfriend-Coal/

Habib, A., 2003, State-civil society relations in post-apartheid South Africa, paper presented at an Anthropology and Development Studies seminar, Rand Afrikaans University, Johannesburg.

Hara, N. & Shachaf, P., 2008, 'Online peace movement organizations: A comparative analysis', in I. Chen & T. Kidd (eds.), *Social information technology: Connection society and cultural issues*, pp. 52–67, Idea Group, Hershey. http://dx.doi.org/10.4018/978-1-59904-774-4.ch004

Huffington, A., 2011, *Lessons from Spain: 'Los Indignados,' Occupy Wall Street, and the failure of the status quo*, viewed 27 July 2013, from http://www.huffingtonpost.com/arianna-huffington/spain-indignados-protests_b_1029640.html

International Telecommunications Union, 2009, *Measuring the information society*, Geneva, Switzerland.

Kinkade, S. & Verclas, K.M., 2008, *Wireless technologies for social change: Trends in mobile use by NGOs*, UN Foundation-Vodaphone Group Foundation Partnership, Washington D.C./Berkshire.

Kreutzer, T., 2009, *Generation mobile: Online and digital media usage on mobile phones among low-income urban youth in South Africa*, University of Cape Town Center for Film and Media Studies, Cape Town.

Memmi, D., 2010, 'Sociology of virtual communities and social software design', in S. Murugesan (ed.), *Web 2.0, 3.0, and X.0: Technologies, business, and social applications*, vol. 2, pp. 790–803, Information Science Reference, New York.

MobileActive, 2010, *Nonprofit text messaging benchmarks*, viewed March 2010, from http://www.slideshare.net/blueeyepathrec/nonprofit-text-messaging-benchmarks-study-2010-1

'Mobile marvels: A special report on telecoms in emerging markets', *The Economist*, 24 September, 2009, n.p.

NTEN, 2010, *Nonprofit social network benchmark report*, viewed 01 April 2011, from http://www.nten.org/blog/2010/04/20/2010-nonprofit-social-network-benchmark-report

NTEN, 2011a, *3rd annual nonprofit social network benchmark report*, viewed 12 October 2011, from http://www.nonprofitsocialnetworksurvey.com/download.php

NTEN, 2011b, *2011 nonprofit communications trends report … and what it all means for your good cause*, viewed 01 November 2011, from http://www.nonprofitmarketingguide.com/resources/book/2011-nonprofit-communications-trends/

Nugroho, Y., 2007, 'Does the Internet transform civil society? The case of civil society organisations in Indonesia', PhD thesis, Faculty of Humanities, University of Manchester.

Nugroho, Y. & Tampubolon, G., 2008, 'Network dynamics in the transition to democracy: Mapping global networks of contemporary Indonesian civil society', *Sociological Research Online* 13(5).

Pew Research Center, 2011, *Web 2.0*, viewed 26 November 2012, from http://www.pewinternet.org/topics/Web-20.aspx

Ranchod, K., 2007, 'State-civil society relations in South Africa: Some lessons from engagement', *Policy: Issues and Actors* 20(7), 1–23.

Rigby, B., 2008, *Mobilizing generation 2.0: A practical guide to using Web 2.0*, Jossey-Bass, San Francisco.

Rogers, E.M., 2003, *Diffusion of innovations*, The Free Press, A division of Simon & Schuster, New York.

SANGONeT, 2011, *About SANGONeT*, viewed 31 October 2011, from http://www.ngopulse.org/about.

Socialbakers, 2011, *Heart of Social Media Statistics*, viewed 28 December 2011, from http://www.socialbakers.com.

Tandon, R., 2000, 'Riding high or nosediving: Development NGOs in the new millennium', *Development in Practice* 10(3/4), 319–329. http://dx.doi.org/10.1080/09614520050116488

UNICEF, 2011, *What's your 'ASLR' to do you wanna go private*, Author, New York.

Ushahidi, 2011, *Ushahidi*, viewed 29 September 2012 from http://www.ushahidi.com

Van de Donk, W., Loader, B., Nixon, P. & Rucht, D., 2004,' Social movements and ICTs', in W. van de Donk, B. Loader, P. Nixon & D. Rucht (eds.), *Cyberprotest: New media, citizens and social movements*, pp. 1–25, Routledge, London.

Wejnert, B., 2002, 'Integrating models of diffusion of innovations: A conceptual framework', *Annual Review of Sociology 28*, 297–326. http://dx.doi.org/10.1146/annurev.soc.28.110601.141051

World Wide Worx, 2009, *The state of ICTs in the South African NGO Sector*, Johannesburg.

World Wide Worx, 2011, *The South African social media landscape 2011*, Author, Johannesburg.

Wu, M.C. & Unhelkar, B., 2010, 'Mobile service orientated architecture (MSOA) for Business in the Web 2.0 era', in S. Murugesan (ed.), *Web 2.0, 3.0, and X.0: Technologies, business and social applications*, vol. 1, pp. 178–191, Information Science Reference, New York.

Zakaria, F., 2011, 'The people vs. Putin', *Time Magazine*, 26 December, p. 32.

6

A survey of online social networking used to support health awareness campaigns in the City of Johannesburg metropolitan municipality

Authors:
Karin Eloff[1]
Cornelius J. Niemand[1]

Affiliations:
[1]Centre for Information and Knowledge Management, University of Johannesburg, South Africa

Correspondence to:
Cornelius Niemand

Email:
corn@uj.ac.za

Postal address:
PO Box 524, Auckland Park 2006, South Africa

Background: The Department of Health (DoH) at the City of Johannesburg metropolitan municipality in South Africa develops various health awareness campaigns aimed at creating awareness of general health risks within the Johannesburg area. According to staff members of the DoH, the resources utilised in the current campaigns fail to reach a sufficiently broad audience and the campaigns struggle to deliver the intended messages. Furthermore, the development and implementation of campaigns are time consuming and costly.

Objectives: This research focused on how online social networking (OSN) can support health awareness campaigns for the DoH in the Johannesburg region. OSN may be regarded as a tool that will assist the DoH to reach a wider audience, send health-related messages and provide a two-way communication channel.

Method: The research used an exploratory research design with a purposive non-probability sample. A survey was used as the data collection instrument. Statistical analysis was performed on the data obtained from the surveys.

Results: The results indicate that the DoH can benefit from the use of OSN in health promotion campaigns. The benefits include, but are not limited to, an increase in engagement with the target market, ease of use and reach within the specified audience.

Conclusion: Although there are numerous advantages associated with the integration of OSN by the DoH, the DoH needs to develop training and development programmes for OSN to encourage its use by DoH staff members. The main aim of the programmes is to create internal OSN capabilities to support the OSN strategy.

Introduction

According to Smith (2011), online social networking (OSN) is 'one of the greatest innovations in the Internet today. The Internet provides the means for information dissemination, selling products and playing games'.

Glenn (2013) postulates that the use of OSN by Internet users has greatly increased over the last decade. The most popular, according to the Glenn (2013), may include, but are not limited to, Facebook, Twitter, MySpace and LinkedIn. According to various studies including Smith (2011) and Tau (2011:10) users of OSN identify them as a tool to reach wide audiences, broadcast a message, communicate with relatives and build relationships and connect with people.

A number of not-for-profit organisations and government agencies worldwide have started to implement OSN to share information and knowledge and communicate with their target market utilising the digital channels created by OSN. The Centre of Disease Control (CDC) is an example of a health-related department in the United States of America that makes use of OSN to promote awareness about current health promotion campaigns. The CDC recognises both advantages, including an increase in engagement with the target market, ease of use and reach, and disadvantages, including costs and time constraints with regard to use of OSN. The CDC has developed a toolkit to promote the use of online social networking. This toolkit provides guidance regarding OSN and lessons on how participation in and incorporation of OSN into government agencies to promote health promotion campaigns, can be achieved (Brodalski *et al.* 2011).

The Department of Health (DoH) at the City of Johannesburg metropolitan municipality in South Africa is continuously developing various kinds of health promotion campaigns that differ depending on the health requirement in the particular region. The present techniques that the DoH utilises include face-to-face interaction, information sessions, education and communication materials such as pamphlets and posters and other vocal and print media that can include press releases and radio broadcasts. The DoH made use of OSN sites in previous non–health-related campaigns such as the FIFA World Cup™ in 2010. These OSN sites were utilised to communicate and share information and knowledge regarding the events taking place during the World Cup. After the implementation of OSN throughout the World Cup, the DoH considered making use of OSN sites more extensively for health awareness promotion (Tau 2011:105–106).

Taking the aforesaid into consideration, the main objective of this study was to investigate:

- The extent to which OSN supports information sharing within health awareness promotion campaigns by the DoH.
- The types of social media channels that are currently being utilised by the DoH.
- Possible OSN sites or channels that could be implemented by the DoH.

The literature reviewed (with specific emphasis on the reports generated by the CDC in the United States of America) suggests that the DoH can achieve a variety of benefits by incorporating OSN into its communication strategy; the benefits include an increase in engagement with the target market, ease of use and reach from the implementation of OSN to promote current health promotion campaigns. However, within the DoH context, campaign managers lack practical experience in the use of OSN tools and are therefore not able to recognise the benefits that OSN holds for current health promotion campaigns.

Literature review

The development of the Internet and Web

To grasp the full extent of the use and integration of online social networking (OSN) within the new digital economy a brief overview of the development of the Internet and the Web is needed.

An earlier 'birthday' for the Internet may hark back to 1972, when the first connection was opened between the Advanced Research Project Agency Network (ARPANET) and another network, ALOHAnet in Hawaii, or even to 1969, when the first four nodes of ARPANET were connected to each other, or to the meeting of the Association of Computing Machinery in 1967, when Larry Roberts read the first public paper describing the ARPANET design. It is possible to go back even further, though, to Paul Baran's work on robust networks for research and development in the mid-1960s, or (albeit less convincingly) to the launch of Sputnik in 1957, which led to the convening of the Advanced Research Projects Agency (Thomas 1999:682).

Taking the aforesaid into consideration and according to Mowery (2002), however, the history of the Internet's development should ideally be divided into three phases (see Table 1).

TABLE 1: The history of the Internet.

Time period	Critical developments
1960–1985	Invention of digital packet-switching and associated standards and protocols Birth of Internet self-governance institutions
1986–1995	Growth of NSFNET and parallel private infrastructure Growth in installed base of PCs and local area networks
1996– the present	Diffusion of the World Wide Web Privatisation of the Internet infrastructure and commercialisation of the Internet content

NSFNET, The National Science Foundation Network; PCs, personal computers

Thus, it can be said that the Internet is a large network of networks; in other words, the Internet is a maze of phones and cable lines, satellites and network cables that interconnects computers around the world, thereby creating a global network through which any computer can communicate with any other computer, as long as they are both connected to the Internet.

Many people use the terms 'Internet' and 'Web' interchangeably, whilst they are, in fact, not even synonymous. The Internet and the Web are two separate, yet related, entities. The Word Wide Web, commonly referred to as 'the Web', can be seen as the multimedia section of the Internet, as it allows the individual surfer to explore a seemingly unlimited worldwide digital 'Web' of information, expanding by tens of thousands of websites each day. The Web presents the user with a way in which to represent information on the Internet. Information resources are located by using a uniform resource locator. This is an information-sharing model that is built on top of the Internet. The Web, therefore, needs the Internet, and not vice versa. The Web uses the hypertext transfer protocol to share information across the Internet. The Web also uses browsers, such as Internet Explorer, to access Web documents called 'Web pages', which are linked via hyperlinks. Web documents can also contain graphics, sound, text and video (Webopedia 2002).

Online social networking

According to Taprial and Kanwar (2012), OSN refers to 'the media that allows one to be social, or get social online by sharing content, news, photos etc. with other people'.

The Internet has directly influenced the way that people perform their daily activities over the past decade. Out of all online users, 90% are actively involved in some type of OSN site (Taprial & Kanwar 2012). OSN is not only a tool that is utilised by individuals for personal use but also by both profit and not-for-profit organisations for marketing purposes and as a business tool (for recruitment, communication and brand-building exercises). According to Lusted (2011), there are numerous advantages and challenges when making use of OSN sites. Advantages that organisations can gain from the implementation of OSN in general include increased communication and collaboration, improved education in terms of the topic at hand and building relationships. Furthermore, OSN assists with the broadcasting of messages over a large geographical area and allows participation to occur. There are also potential challenges involved in the implementation of OSN. These challenges include privacy issues, lack of understanding of the OSN tools and features and having a negative impact on staff productivity.

Furthermore, staff in general are generally resistant to change and will therefore not immediately be on board with adjustments to their routine activities. OSN sites can also be very time consuming for staff to update and maintain and to respond to messages sent via OSN sites (Lusted 2011). Bearing in mind the management of potential challenges, OSN has several advantages for health promotion campaigns within the DoH.

Statement of the problem

This study investigated the potential usage of OSN by the DoH as part of health promotion campaigns. OSN is a cost-effective tool that can reach a large target audience in a short period of time. The tools used by the DoH to share knowledge regarding campaigns were identified and the most unsuccessful tools were assessed. In addition, the research identified reasons why the DoH is currently not making use of OSN to promote current health promotion campaigns.

Research design

Sample

This study utilised a purposive sample. The objective of the study was to determine the use of OSN in the promotion of health campaigns by the DoH. The gathering of data was done by firstly identifying the respondents' knowledge regarding the definition of the concept, secondly recognising the respondents' awareness in terms of the benefits of OSN and finally determining their active involvement in OSN in both a personal and a professional environment. In order for the purposive sample to be successful, the respondents selected were managers of health promotion campaigns run by the DoH for the reason that they had direct involvement in the development of health promotion campaigns.

The DoH consists of two main sub-divisions, namely the central health department and the regional health department. It is the responsibility of the central health department to develop and implement health promotion campaigns. The central health department has five sub-units, namely management support, primary health care, public health, HIV/AIDS and environmental health units.

A total of 30 questionnaires were sent to the respondents. Of the 30 questionnaires, 18 legible and complete questionnaires were returned, which resulted in a 60% response rate. Of the 18 completed questionnaires one questionnaire was completed by each of these sub-units together with three questionnaires by the regional health department. The campaign managers of the following campaigns also completed a questionnaire: HIV/AIDS, TB, malaria, teenage pregnancy, suicide prevention and early childhood education centres.

Data collection instrument

The questionnaire utilised as the data collection instrument was developed with the main intention of evaluating the extent to which managers utilise OSN in the promotion of health campaigns by the DoH. The questionnaire included both closed-ended questions and multi-option questions. The questionnaire firstly focused on how the respondents fit into the DoH in terms of education and experience gained in the specific field of health promotion campaigns. In addition, it also focused on gathering general information regarding the tools utilised in health promotion campaigns and how successful these tools were in reaching the desired objectives.

The questionnaire then focused on each respondent's knowledge regarding OSN as well as the amount of time the respondents spend on OSN. A further goal of the questionnaire was to ascertain the benefits that OSN can hold for health promotion campaigns.

Data analysis and results

Statistical analysis was performed on the data obtained from the questionnaire. This identified the utilisation of OSN inside health promotion campaigns and the number of respondents actively involved in OSN, together with the average time spent on OSN in both a personal and a professional capacity. Furthermore statistical analysis, utilising statistical analysis tools, assisted with the identification of the respondents' opinions in terms of the possible effectiveness of OSN in health promotion campaigns and the percentage of time spent inside the DoH by respondents when working on health promotion campaigns.

Results

Figure 1 indicates that 56% of the respondents have a postgraduate qualification in a health-related field. The results indicated that 14% of the respondents have worked in a health-related institution for more than six years.

The DoH currently makes use of pamphlets, posters, print media releases including newspapers and magazines and vocal media releases including radio stations, TV, door-to-door campaigns, banners, health talks, fun runs and talk clinics to share knowledge of the health promotion campaigns. Figure 2 depicts that 78% of the respondents agreed that the different media mechanisms were successfully implemented, whereas 11% believed that that was not the case.

According to the respondents, pamphlets and media releases were the two most unsuccessful media that are currently implemented to promote health promotion campaigns.

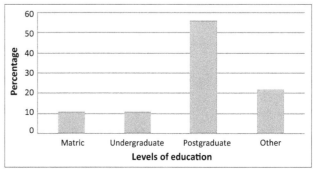

FIGURE 1: Educational levels.

Figure 3 provides a clear illustration of the reasons for current tools being unsuccessful. The majority of the respondents (56%) selected a lack in physical storage space as the main reason for the current tools being unsuccessful; 33% of the respondents believed that current tools are ineffective in reaching the target audience, 22% stated that current tools are not cost effective, 33% of the respondents believed that current tools are not able to share the message clearly and 38% believed a lack in interaction made them unsuccessful.

All participants indicated that they did know what OSN was. Respondents had to select from a list which OSN tools they recognised. None of the respondents selected all the OSN tools. A large portion of the respondents indicated Facebook, Twitter and MySpace as OSN tools. Respondents disregarded the following as OSN tools: blogs, wikis, LinkedIn and discussion groups.

Figure 4 displays reasons that OSN can possibly be successful in health promotion campaigns. The majority of

the respondents (61%) stated that reaching a wider audience is the key reason for success, 61% also believed that OSN can allow health promotion campaigns to share information more easily, 28% believed that OSN is a cost-effective option, 17% selected uncomplicated as an option and the other 17% believed that OSN will allow health promotion campaigns to focus on a narrower target market.

Discussion of the findings

The results indicate that the majority of respondents are highly educated in their specific health field. The majority of the respondents are not only educated but have also completed six or more years in a health-related field and therefore have gained a sufficient amount of experience.

Each individual health promotion campaign has its own target market that the campaign managers focus on. Each campaign focuses on both men and women. It is therefore important to select the most appropriate tool to promote the health promotion campaigns for both men and women. The DoH presently makes use of pamphlets, posters, print media releases and vocal media releases to promote current health promotion campaigns. Some of these media, for example door-to-door campaigns, are more effective in comparison with other media, such as pamphlets. It is important to evaluate which of these media are the most unsuccessful and could be replaced with an OSN tool. Pamphlets and media releases have been identified by the respondents as being the most unsuccessful. Some of the possible reasons include a lack of physical storage space, ineffective reach within the target audience, high expenses, lack of understanding by the community for the reason of it only being a one-directional communication channel, lack of interaction and other reasons such as citizens being illiterate or not understanding the language in which the pamphlets and media releases are presented.

Pamphlets and media releases can be eliminated and the DoH could rather implement OSN tools to promote current health campaigns. OSN sites provide a variety of features for users. Some OSN sites such as Facebook allow for a two-way communication channel through which users can interact with one another. Other OSN sites such as YouTube provide the opportunity for users to share a message with videos in order to assist users who are not computer literate, allowing the intended message to be more easily understood.

The results indicated that the respondents were aware of the concept of OSN but it is clear that these respondents are not fully aware of the different OSN tools. This may be the major reason why the respondents have not implemented OSN to share knowledge regarding health promotion campaigns. There is a lack in understanding of what online social media are and the online social media tools that could be utilised to share knowledge. It is essential for the health promotion campaign managers to be actively involved with different OSN tools to identify and recognise the benefits they can hold for a health promotion campaign as well as to recognise the challenges of OSN.

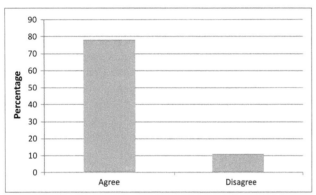

FIGURE 2: Current media successfully implemented.

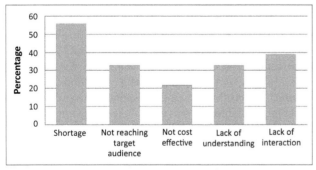

FIGURE 3: Reasons for current media being unsuccessful.

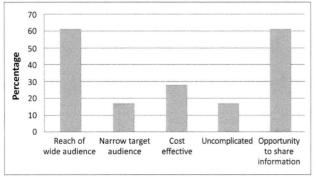

FIGURE 4: Reasons online social networking can possibly be successful in health promotion campaigns.

Online social networking does not need any physical storage space because it occurs via the Internet; it is utilised today by millions of users worldwide. OSN is also inexpensive but requires suitable staff to make updates. OSN makes a two-way communication process possible and if any misunderstandings do occur questions may be received and answered; it is also possible to conduct the communication process in more than one language.

Together with all the advantages, like it being an inexpensive communication channel, there are also some restrictions that can limit the DoH in implementing OSN tools. Some of these limitations can include a lack of Internet access, computer illiteracy and a lack of education.

Recommendations

An online social media strategy (OSMS) is suggested for the DoH, allowing OSN sites to be implemented and managed effectively and efficiently. The OSMS consists of the following four steps: planning, managing, implementing and feedback.

In the planning stage management will need to identify the problem at hand. The problem, for example, can be that current traditional media being utilised to promote health promotion campaigns are ineffective.

The second stage of the OSMS is the management of the problem. This stage focuses on the development of a few solutions. It is essential to list all the possible solutions together with the possible risks and the probability that these risks might occur in the near future. Identifying the risks together with their probabilities will assist the DoH to select the most appropriate solutions. There are a variety of solutions that the DoH can implement in order to eliminate media releases and posters as a current tool and replace these with OSN. In order for the DoH to successfully implement OSN to promote current health promotion campaigns, a few actions are recommended. These actions can include the development of training and development programmes to improve involvement from higher management and create awareness of the various OSN tools. The training and development programmes can educate the staff inside the DoH regarding the OSN tools and how these tools can be incorporated into health promotion campaigns in order to increase the success rate. Staff should be encouraged, after undergoing intensive training and education in the OSN tools, to test and implement the most appropriate tool. Creating awareness of the benefits of OSN tools will allow campaign managers to be encouraged and to experiment with these tools in different scenarios within different target markets.

The third step of the OSMS is based on the implementation of the selected solution, that is a specific OSN channel for a specific target market. Once the solution has been selected, a pilot event should be created. The pilot event will identify any potential problem areas associated with the selected channel of communication utilised for the specific target market. Once all problem areas have been identified and rectified, the utilisation of the solution may be replicated to other campaigns.

Feedback is the final stage and focuses mainly on the success of the OSN site. The feedback can be received from both staff inside the organisation and citizens making use of OSN to receive information regarding health promotion campaigns. Staff can provide feedback on a variety of aspects, including the physical usage of the OSN site (via various analytical tools like Google Analytics), the target audience that has been reached and the awareness that has been created. The OSMS, if implemented correctly and successfully, can assist the DoH to share information effectively in health promotion campaigns.

Limitations of the study

This study is limited to only managers of certain health promotion campaigns inside the DoH and not all the campaigns that are currently in place. The sample of the respondents meant that the study focused on top and middle managers' knowledge and experience gained in terms of OSN and information sharing.

Conclusion

The DoH is currently still utilising traditional media to share knowledge about health promotion campaigns. Some of these traditional media, with specific reference to pamphlets, are less effective than others, such as door-to-door campaigns. There are a variety of OSN sites available that can assist the DoH to share information about its health promotion campaigns.

The results of the study suggest that respondents lack practical experience in the use of OSN and therefore are incapable of identifying the benefits of OSN for health promotion campaigns.

It would be beneficial for the DoH to develop an OSN training and development programme. This programme will assist the staff in learning more about OSN tools and features together with the ability to select the most appropriate OSN sites for each specific health promotion campaign. This training and development programme should also motivate and highlight the importance of the use of OSN. An online social media strategy is recommended as it will allow the DoH to implement OSN more efficiently and effectively in four basic steps.

A suggestion for further research is to identify the specific OSN sites that are to be utilised to reach specific target markets. Health promotion managers have to know what the needs for each individual location are and how knowledge can be effectively shared with a specific target market. It is therefore essential to be able to identify which tools for health promotion campaigns are the most appropriate in specific locations.

Acknowledgements

Competing interests

The authors declare that they have no financial or personal relationship(s) that may have inappropriately influenced them in writing this article.

Authors' contributions

C.J.N. (University of Johannesburg) was the study leader and K.E. (University of Johannesburg), the student. Both authors made equal contributions in terms of the writing and analysis of this article.

References

Brodalski, D., Brink, H., Curtis, J., Diaz, S., Schindelar, J., Shannon, C. *et al.*, 2011, 'The Health Communicators social media toolkit', in *The health communicator's social media toolkit*, viewed 10 December 2012, from http://www.cdc.gov/socialmedia/tools/guidelines/pdf/socialmediatoolkit_bm.pdf

Glenn, D., 2013, 'Social media use has more than tripled among internet users 65 and older, study finds', *SocialTimes*, viewed 03 October 2013, from http://socialtimes.com/72-percent-of-online-adults-on-social-networks-pew-study_b133578

Lusted, M.A., 2011, *Social networking: MySpace, Facebook and Twitter*, ABDO Publishing Company, North Mankato.

Mowery, D.C., 2002, 'Is the Internet a US invention? An economic and technological history of computer networking', in *druid*, viewed 11 November 2013, from http://www.druid.dk/conferences/nw/paper1/movery.pdf

Smith, B., 2011, 'The great importance of social networking', in *Sooper Articles*, viewed 12 November 2012, from http://www.sooperarticles.com/internet-articles/spam-articles/great-importance-social-networking-300688.html

Taprial, V. & Kanwar, P., 2012, *Understanding social media*, Ventus Publishing, London.

Tau, M.P., 2011, *Joburg 2040: Growth and development strategy*, City of Johannesburg, Johannesburg.

Thomas, G., 1999, 'Shaping cyberspace – interpreting and transforming the internet', *Research Policy* 28, 681–698.

Webopdia, 2002, *The difference between the Internet and the world wide web*, viewed 11 November 2013, from http://www.webopedia.com/DidYouKnow/Internet/2002/Web_vs_Internet.asp

7

Evaluation of management information systems: A study at a further education and training college

Authors:
Mariette Visser[1]
Judy van Biljon[2]
Marlien Herselman[3]

Affiliations:
[1]Human Sciences Research Council (HSRC), Pretoria, South Africa

[2]School of Computing, College of Science, Engineering and Technology, University of South Africa, South Africa

[3]Council for Scientific and Industrial Research (CSIR), Pretoria, South Africa

Correspondence to:
Mariette Visser

Email:
mmvisser@hsrc.ac.za

Postal address:
Private Bag X41, Pretoria 0001, South Africa

Background: Management information systems (MIS) are pivotal in the efficient and effective running of Further Education and Training (FET) colleges. Therefore, the evaluation of MIS success is an essential spoke in the wheel of FET college success. Based on an extensive literature review it was concluded that no MIS success evaluation model for FET colleges in South Africa exists.

Objectives: The main objective was to propose a MIS evaluation model and evaluation tool (questionnaire), and verify the model empirically by evaluating the MIS at a selected FET college. The supporting objectives were firstly, to identify the most appropriate MIS evaluation models from literature. Secondly, to propose a MIS evaluation model for FET colleges based on the literature. Thirdly, to develop the evaluation tool (questionnaire) based on these models. Fourthly, to capture and analyse data from one FET college, in order to evaluate the performance of the MIS at the college. The final supporting objective was to evaluate the proposed model by triangulating the findings from the survey with the findings from the interviews.

Method: The proposed MIS evaluation model is based on the integration of three existing MIS evaluation models. The evaluation tool was developed by combining four empirically tested questionnaires that capture the constructs in the underlying models. A survey and semi-structured interviews were used as data collection methods. The statistical tests for consistency, scale reliability (Cronbach's alpha) and unidimensionality (Principal Component Analysis) were applied to explore the constructs in the model.

Results: Results from the empirical testing of the newly designed evaluation tool were used to refine the initial model. The qualitative data capturing and analysis added value in explaining and contextualising the quantitative findings.

Conclusion: The main contribution is the *SA-FETMIS success model and evaluation tool* which managers can use to evaluate the MIS at an educational institution. The novelty of the research lies in using a mixed methods approach where previous MIS success evaluation studies mainly used quantitative methods.

Introduction

The South African National Department of Education has committed to the establishment of a standardised business management information system in all public FET colleges that will enable colleges to monitor and account for all their administrative business processes which include student administration, academic administration, financial administration, human resource management and development and asset management (Department of Education 2008; Department of Higher Education and Training 2011). The monitoring and evaluation of key success indicators is not only essential for the management of a specific FET college, but is also of critical importance for the Department of Higher Education and Training (DHET) to evaluate its own successes. The problem is that no documented evaluation model or tool to evaluate the success of MIS at public FET colleges in SA could be found. Therefore, there is a need to design and develop such an evaluation model and tool which can be used by managers of FET colleges as well as by DHET to ensure that all the systems at all colleges adhere to the same principles of evaluation.

This study constructed a conceptual framework that informs the design of an IS evaluation tool by using the knowledge and trends in the field of information systems evaluation and taking into account the requirements of the South African policy with regard to the administration and functioning of public FET colleges.

Reviewing information systems evaluation models

Evaluation research applies social science procedures to assess the conceptualisation, design, implementation and utility of social intervention programmes (Rossi & Freeman in Babbie & Mouton 2001:335). Furthermore, evaluation studies have three main purposes, namely, (1) to judge merit or worth, (2) to improve programmes and (3) to generate knowledge (Lange & Luescher 2003).

Table 1 provides a synthesised overview of IS success evaluation theories and the models based on the theories. From the table it can be observed that the following theories have been used:

- the theory of reasoned action
- the theory of planned behaviour
- the theory of beliefs and attitudes
- the behavioural theory of the firm and the mathematical theory of communications.

Based on those theories, the models proposed to evaluate the performance of IS are:

- the DeLone and McLean IS success model (D&M IS Success Model)
- the Technology Acceptance Model (TAM)
- the Task-Technology Fit model (TTF)
- the End User Computing Satisfaction model (EUCS).

Many researchers in the field of IS evaluation have conducted empirical studies based on portions, combinations or extensions of these models (Chow 2004; Gable, Sedara & Chan 2008; Ifinedo, Rapp, Ifinedo & Sundberg 2010; Ong, Day & Hsu 2009; Palmius 2007; Petter & Mclean 2009; Rai, Lang

& Welker 2002; Seddon 1997). As illustrated in Table 1, IS evaluation models are based on either one or a combination of theories. This raised the question: which model, extension or combination will be suitable for this study? The following eight models were considered in more detail to make an informed decision in this regard:

- Technology Acceptance Model (TAM) with its extensions (TAM2, UTAUT, TAM3)
- the Wixom and Todd model
- the Task-Technology Fit (TTF) model
- the Original DeLone and McLean (D&M) IS Success model
- the Updated DeLone and McLean (D&M) IS Success model
- the Model of User Satisfaction
- the Re-specified Model of IS success
- the End-user Computing Satisfaction model (EUCS).

Three models, namely, the Original D&M IS Success model, the Updated D&M IS Success model and the End-user Computing Satisfaction model were selected as most appropriate and integrated to develop the proposed conceptual model for this study. The selection was based on criteria for the evaluation of theories and models in the Information Systems discipline, namely, importance, level, novelty, parsimony and falsifiability (Weber 2012). The selected models are now discussed in more detail to show why they are deemed to meet these criteria.

TABLE 1: Synthesised overview of information systems success evaluation models and their underlying theoretical frameworks.

Year (theory developed)	Theory developed by	Theory	Name of the model based on theory	Model abbreviation	Model developed by	Year (Model developed)
1934	LaPiere, R.T. – Evidence in the literature of the link between attitudes and behaviours (Lapiere 1934)	Led to the formulation of the theories of reasoned action and planned behaviour	-	-	-	-
1949	Shannon and Weaver (Shannon & Weaver 1949)	Mathematical Theory of Communications	Expanded Shannon & Weaver's theory by extending the 'effectiveness level' into three categories	Expanded Mathematical Theory of Communications	Mason, R.O.	1978
1963	Cyert and March	Behavioural Theory of the Firm	Development of a Tool for Measuring and Analyzing Computer User Satisfaction (Bailey & Pearson 1983)	CUS	Bailey, J.E. Pearson, S.W.	1983
			The Measurement of End-User Computing Satisfaction (Doll & Torkzadeh 1988)	EUCS	Doll, W.J. Torkzadeh, G.	1988
		Integration of the two concept theories 'Beliefs and attitudes about the system' and 'Beliefs and attitudes about using the system'	Integration of the User Satisfaction literature and the Technology Acceptance Model (Wixom & Todd 2005)	Integration of User Satisfaction (US) and TAM	Wixom, B.H. Todd, P.A.	2005
1975	Fishbein and Ajzen (Fishbein & Ajzen 1975)	Theory of Reasoned Action, Theory of Planned Behaviour	Technology Acceptance Model (Davis et al. 1989)	TAM	Davis F.D. Bagozzi R.P. Warshaw P.R.	1989
			Technology Acceptance Model 2 (Venkatesh & Davis 2000)	TAM2	Venkatesh, V. Davis, F.D.	2000
			Unified Theory of Acceptance and Use of Technology (Venkatesh et al. 2003)	UTAUT	Venkatesh, V. Morris, M.G. Davis, F.D. Davis, G.B.	2003
			Technology Acceptance Model 3 (Venkatesh & Bala 2008)	TAM3	Venkatesh, V. Bala, H.	2008
			Task Technology Fit Model (Goodhue & Thompson 1995)	TTF Model	Goodhue, D.L. Thompson, R.L.	1995
			TAM/TTF Model with Computer Self-Efficacy (Dishaw et al. 2002)	Combined TAM/TTF Model	Dishaw, M.T., Strong, D.M., Bandy, D.B.	2002
1978	Mason (Mason 1978)	Expanded Mathematical Theory of Communications	DeLone and McLean IS Success Model (Delone & Mclean 1992)	D&M IS Success Model	DeLone, W.H. McLean, E.R	1992
			Extension of the DeLone and McLean IS Success Model combined with the Technology Acceptance Model (Seddon & Kiew 1996)	Extended D&M IS Success Model combined with TAM	Seddon, P.B. Kiew, M. Y	1996
			Respecification and extension of the DeLone and McLean Model of IS Success (Seddon 1997)	Partial behaviour model of IS Use	Seddon, P. B.	1997
			Updated DeLone and McLean IS Success Model (Delone & Mclean 2003)	Updated D&M IS Success Model	DeLone, W.H. McLean, E.R	2003

The original D&M taxonomy was based on Richard Mason's modification of Shannon and Weaver's (1949) mathematical theory of communications which identified three levels of information:

- the technical level (accuracy and efficiency of the system that produces it)
- the semantic level (its ability to transfer the intended message)
- the effectiveness level (its impact on the receiver) (Shannon & Weaver 1949).

Mason (1978) adapted this theory for IS and expanded the effectiveness level into three categories:

1. receipt of information
2. influence on the recipient
3. influence on the system.

The original DeLone and McLean (D&M) IS Success model identified six variables of success, namely:

- system quality
- information quality
- use
- user satisfaction
- individual impact
- organisational impact.

'System quality' was equivalent to the technical level of communication, whilst information quality was equivalent to the semantic level of communication. The other four variables were mapped to Mason's subcategories of the effectiveness level. 'Use' related to Mason's receipt of information; 'user satisfaction' and 'individual impact' were associated with the information's influence on the recipient and 'organisational impact' was the influence of the information on the system. Figure 1 shows the Original D&M IS Success model.

Based on further research the Original D&M Success model was updated to the model shown in Figure 2. The new model was modified so that quality included information, system and service quality. Therefore a key addition in the updated model was the inclusion of service quality (Delone & Mclean 2003). DeLone and McLean also recommended assigning different weights to system quality, information quality and service quality, depending on the context and application of the model (Delone & Mclean 2003).

Doll and Torkzadeh (1988) investigated end-user computing satisfaction by contrasting traditional versus end-user computing environments and reported on the development of an instrument which merges ease of use and information product items to measure the satisfaction of users who directly interact with the computer for a specific application.

Figure 3 provides an illustration of the model, a list of questions used and the identified underlying factors or components of end-user computing satisfaction acquired by factor analysis (content, accuracy, format, ease of use and timeliness).

Having considered the Original D&M IS Success model, the D&M Updated IS Success model and the End-user Computing Satisfaction model in more detail, the criteria

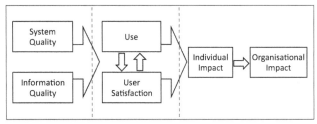

Source: DeLone, W. & McLean, E., 1992, 'Information Systems success: The quest for the dependent variable', *Information Systems Research* 3(1), 36 D&M, DeLone and McLean.

FIGURE 1: Original D&M IS Success model.

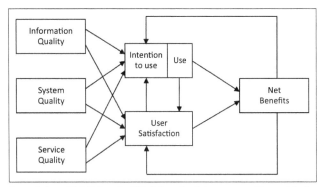

Source: DeLone, W. & McLean, E., 1992, 'Information Systems success: The quest for the dependent variable', *Information Systems Research* 3(1), 36 D&M, DeLone and McLean.

FIGURE 2: D&M Updated IS Success model.

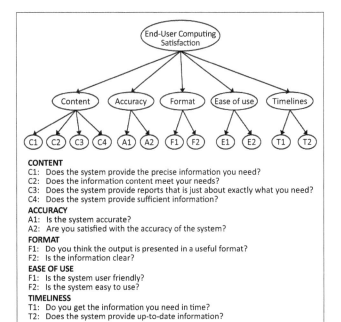

CONTENT
C1: Does the system provide the precise information you need?
C2: Does the information content meet your needs?
C3: Does the system provide reports that is just about exactly what you need?
C4: Does the system provide sufficient information?
ACCURACY
A1: Is the system accurate?
A2: Are you satisfied with the accuracy of the system?
FORMAT
F1: Do you think the output is presented in a useful format?
F2: Is the information clear?
EASE OF USE
F1: Is the system user friendly?
F2: Is the system easy to use?
TIMELINESS
T1: Do you get the information you need in time?
T2: Does the system provide up-to-date information?

Source: Doll, W.J. & Torkzadeh, G., 1988, 'The measurement of End-User Computing Satisfaction', *MIS Quarterly* 12(2), 259–274

FIGURE 3: A model for measuring end-user computing satisfaction.

for selecting these models based on the criteria proposed by Weber (2012) are now discussed:

- **Importance:** All 3 models can be considered as important based on the importance of their focal phenomenon (as depicted in Figure 1, Figure 2 and Figure 3) for MIS evaluation. Furthermore, the models have all been applied and cited.

- **Level:** All three models are based on macro-level theories that cover a broad range of phenomena with a high level of generality. However, the constructs are defined precisely enough to allow empirical testing.
- **Falsifiability:** The specification of constructs and the relationships between the constructs make it possible to do empirical testing that may disconfirm the theory.
- **Novelty:** The Original D&M IS Success model was novel in the sense that it proposed novel relationships between the constructs. The Updated D&M IS Success model was novel in proposing new constructs (i.e. service quality). The End-user Computing Satisfaction model was novel in focusing on the end-user.
- **Parsimony:** All three models have been subjected to quantitative analysis to ensure that the constructs satisfy internal validity without any redundancy.

Furthermore, Rai, Lang and Welker (2002) compared the original D&M model (1992) to the re-specified D&M IS Success model created by Seddon (1997) and found that the original model outperformed the Seddon model. Sedera, Gable and Chan (2004) tested several IS success models, including the D&M and Seddon models, against empirical data and determined that the D&M model provided the best fit for measuring enterprise systems success (Petter, DeLone & McLean 2008).

This provides further support for the importance of the D&M based models. The End-user Computing Satisfaction model was selected on the basis of two reasons:

- Firstly, because the broad concept of 'use' (or intention to use) as a measure of IS success only makes sense for voluntary or discretionary users as opposed to captive users, this construct (use) was omitted from the developed model.
- Secondly, the construct 'user satisfaction' as proposed in the initial D&M IS Success model was a concept without proposed effectiveness measures and, therefore, the established End-user Computing Satisfaction model was included to fill this void.

Having met the evaluation criteria stated, these models were selected for their fit to measuring MIS performance in an organisation, whilst models based on other theories such as the Diffusion of Innovation theory (Rogers 2003; Wejnert 2002) are geared towards explaining how, why and at what rate new ideas and technology spread through cultures and therefore includes user's personal decision to adopt an innovation.

In summary, the proposed theoretical model for this study, as depicted in Figure 4, comprises a combination of three models:

- the Original D&M IS Success model
- the Updated D&M IS Success model
- the End-user Computing Satisfaction model.

The Original D&M IS success model was adapted to include an additional construct 'service quality' which is part of the Updated D&M IS Success model. It was decided to omit the construct 'use' and extend the user satisfaction construct in the original D&M IS Success model by incorporating the End-user Computing Satisfaction model.

Research design

The proposed theoretical model was used to develop the evaluation tool (survey questionnaire) for evaluating the MIS of the selected public FET college. The quantitative data was gathered through a survey strategy by using the newly developed questionnaire and the qualitative data was gathered through semi-structured interviews with key stakeholders.

Population and sampling

Two sampling frames were involved in the study, namely the population of all public FET colleges (50 in total) and the population of MIS users at the selected public FET college. One public FET college (proposed to serve as a benchmark for the FET sector) was purposively sampled by applying the following criteria:

- The college should be one of the top performing public FET colleges.
- The college should be one of the public FET colleges in which the DHET has already implemented the new integrated MIS (there were three at the time).

The DHET is currently extending the implementation of this MIS to all public FET colleges and all staff members are obliged to use the system. The selected college, FET College X, (called FET College X according to the confidentiality agreement) has been purposefully selected on the bases of these criteria and also because this specific college was proposed by the head of the FET unit at the DHET (pers. comm., Interview 1, 03 March 2011).

The entire population of the second sampling frame, the total number of MIS users ($N = 163$ participants) at the selected public FET college participated in the survey, hence a 100% response rate was achieved.

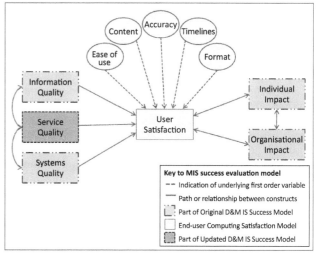

MIS, management information systems; D&M, Delone and McLean.

FIGURE 4: Proposed management information systems Success Evaluation Model.

Questionnaire design

The questionnaire used in this study (Visser 2011) consists of four sections that respectively cover questions on identification and consent, employment information, MIS evaluation, and personal information. The section in the questionnaire which investigates the evaluation of the MIS was developed by adapting and selecting questions from four standardised empirically tested questionnaires. That section consists of 42 items that were presented in a frequency-of-use Likert rating scale format in terms of which participants had to rate each item on a scale of 1 to 5, where 1 equals *almost never*; 2 equals *some of the time*; 3 equals *about half of the time*; 4 equals *most of the time*; and 5 equals *almost always*. Each MIS evaluation construct was generated by calculating the mean of the underlying items for each participant. The proposed conceptual model should therefore be studied in conjunction with the effectiveness measures included in the evaluation tool (questionnaire).

Data management and analysis

The quantitative data capturing, preliminary data cleaning and some of the exploratory data analysis was done with MS Access 2007. Further in-depth exploratory and inferential data analysis, which entailed the application of statistical techniques and procedures, was conducted with SPSS version 19. Additional mathematical calculations and graphical representations of the data were done with MS Excel 2007. Statistical techniques and tests that were applied on the data included: frequency tables, Principal Component Analysis (PCA), Pearson's Chi-square tests of statistical significance and Cronbach's alpha value.

Ethical clearance for the research was granted by the research ethical clearance committees of the Human Sciences Research Council and the University of South Africa.

Results and findings

This section presents the results of the study by firstly giving a brief description of the biographical characteristics of the users of the MIS at the college; secondly, motivating changes to the initial conceptual model, thirdly, providing summary results on the measurements of the different IS evaluation constructs and finally, providing summarised results on the triangulation of the qualitative and quantitative data analyses.

Profile of system users

The gender distribution of the respondents was almost equal with 58% (or 94 participants) being women and 42% (or 69 participants) men. Fifty-two per cent of the participants were lecturing staff, 37% support staff and 11% management staff.

The mean age of all participants was 35, with just over half the participants being younger than 35 years (56%). The average ages of support, lecturing and management staff was 31, 36 and 44 years respectively. More than half of the participants (57%) had a diploma or occupational certificate as their highest academic qualification. This is not surprising, because FET colleges focus primarily on offering vocational education.

Statistical analyses suggest changes to the initial conceptual model

The data analysis provided evidence for adaptations and extensions to the proposed theoretical model. Before each construct variable was calculated, tests for internal consistency and scale reliability (Cronbach's alpha) and unidimensionality (Principal Component Analysis (PCA) were done. Based on the results of the Principal Component Analyses which measure unidimensionality and the reliability statistic (as presented in Table 2 and discussed in the next section), the following changes to the initial conceptual model were suggested:

- The construct 'information quality' has two underlying components, namely, data quality and output quality
- The construct 'system quality' has two underlying components, namely, ease of access and ease of functioning
- The tests revealed that the construct 'user satisfaction' consists of three instead of five underlying components, namely, ease of use, content and format.

TABLE 2: Management information systems evaluation construct measurements and reliability statistic.

Success evaluation indicator or construct	Number of items	Reliability statistic (Cronbach's alpha)	Mean	Standard deviation	N
serq (Service quality)	5	0.934	3.76	.89	148
infq (Information quality)	11	0.943	3.71	.82	159
outpq (Output quality)	5	0.909	3.75	.82	158
dataq (Data quality)	6	0.922	3.67	.93	159
eucs (End-user computing satisfaction)	13	0.928	3.68	.77	162
for (Format)	5	0.909	3.75	.82	158
con (Content)	5	0.898	3.65	.92	160
eou (Ease of use)	3	0.765	3.64	.91	160
bmseval (Overall MIS evaluation)	41	0.981	3.61	.76	163
orgi (Organisational impact)	8	0.944	3.59	.96	156
sysq (System quality)	12	0.929	3.58	.80	161
eoa (Ease of access)	3	0.858	3.71	.93	158
eof (Ease of functioning)	9	0.915	3.52	.83	160
indi (Individual impact)	5	0.931	3.44	1.0	161

N, number; MIS, management information systems.

Each construct as depicted in the conceptual model was evaluated by using the ratings of all the MIS users on a number of items and were calculated as follows (the total variance of the sample explained as well as the number of items used in calculating the variable are given):

- **Individual impact** (*indi*) explains 78.5% based on the mean of five items.
- **Information quality** (*infq*) explains 74.5% based on the mean of eleven items.
- **System quality** (sysq) explains 66.0% based on the mean of twelve items.
- **Service quality** (*serq*) explains 79.4% based on the mean of five items.
- **Organisational impact** (*orgi*) explains 72.3% based on the mean of eight items.

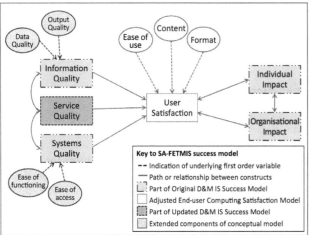

D&M, DeLone and McLean.

FIGURE 5: Conceptual model for evaluation of management information systems performance at public Further Education and Training College X – *The SA-FETMIS success model.*

- **End-user computing satisfaction** (*eucs*) explains 73.7% based on the mean of thirteen items.
- **Overall IS performance** (*bmseval*) explains 80.8% and was created by calculating the mean of 41 items that contributed to creating *indi, infq, sysq, serq, orgi* and *eucs*.

The adapted and extended *SA-FETMIS success model* is depicted in Figure 5.

Service providers received highest scores

Table 2 provides the mean scores (evaluation measurements) calculated for each construct in the adapted conceptual model. The main MIS evaluation constructs have been shaded in Table 2. The other variables, which have not been shaded, are constructs that underlie the main constructs. The main constructs are sorted in descending order according to the mean scores.

The overall mean of the performance of the MIS (*bmseval*) was calculated at 3.61, suggesting that the system users were satisfied with the system between half of the time and almost always. This is an indication that there is room for improvement in the overall performance of the system. The scores of the other evaluation indicators provide more detail on the specific aspects of the MIS that need improvement.

In summary, Figure 6 depicts the evaluation profile of FET College X on all evaluation constructs that were measured and shows that the quality of the services rendered is highly valued.

As can be seen in Figure 6, all constructs (dimensions) of the MIS have been rated between 3.76 (the highest value) and 3.44 (the lowest value), showing a relatively similar average of performance on all aspects of the system. This trend indicates that further differentiated analysis with regard to

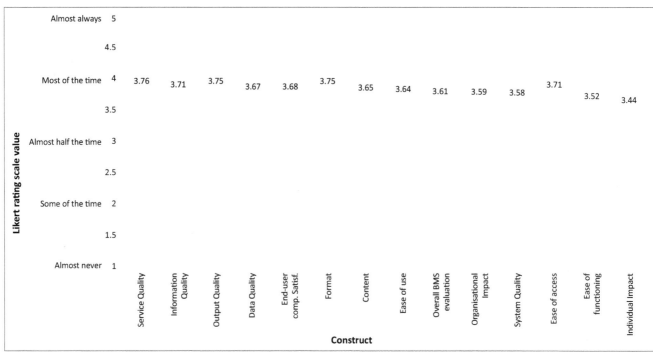

FIGURE 6: Evaluation profile of the management information systems at public Further Education and Training College X.

TABLE 3: Triangulation of quantitative and qualitative data with regard to evaluation constructs.

Construct	Quantitative	Qualitative
Service quality (*serq* with mean score of 3.76)	The highest mean of the main constructs, showing that the users were almost always satisfied with the services rendered by the internal and external service providers.	Interviewees had conflicting opinions about the quality of the service provided by the corporate unit (internally) and the external service provider. On the positive side, respondents felt that service providers were experienced, reliable, had up-to-date facilities and provided quality training. Concerns were raised about turnover times for some queries and requests.
Information quality (*infq* with mean score of 3.71)	The second highest score compared to the other main constructs and comprises two underlying constructs, namely, *data quality* (3.67) and *output quality* (3.75). Provide evidence that the respondents perceived the output to be readily usable, easy to understand, clear and well-formatted.	The interviewees were in agreement that the system is extremely valuable with regard to the information that it contains and the outputs that it produces. They reported that outputs from the system's report-generating options play an important role in quality assurance at the college. Respondents believed that the system contained important key information but that the data was not always accurate and up to date.
End-user computing satisfaction (eucs with mean score of 3.68)	The underlying component *format* (*for* with mean score of 3.75) contributed most to end-user computing satisfaction (*eucs*). The measurement of *content* (*con* with mean score of 3.65) and *ease of use* (*eou* with mean score of 3.64) showed these two underlying components had a negative effect on the measurement of *eucs*.	Interviewees reported that the system is easy to learn and use. They were satisfied with the information contained in the system and felt that the formats of the outputs were useful and a huge improvement compared to the former manual system. However, they did mention that the accuracy and timeliness of the output reports could be improved. Although the format of the reports were clear and easy to read and understand the content needed updating in some instances.
Organisational impact (*orgi* with mean score of 3.59)	Compared to the six main constructs, *orgi* received the third lowest score and included items such as overall productivity improvement, improved outcomes and outputs, increased capacity to manage a growing volume of activity, improved business processes and cost effectiveness.	The unanimous perception was that the organisation is benefiting from the presence of the system. All interviewees from various positions and ranks reported that the system is an excellent asset and contributes to productivity at the college, especially with regard to the monitoring and evaluation of different functions by means of the reports generated by the system. It was reported that the class lists of marks generated by the system, enable lecturers to inspect and monitor student performance easier than in the past. Support staff reported that the direct reporting functionality of the system is a tremendous improvement over the former manual system. Managers benefited from having an overall picture of the data, which could be extracted from the system in an instant.
Systems quality (*sysq* with mean score of 3.58)	Received the second lowest mean of all main constructs. Included items such as: access to information; data integration and consistency; necessary features and functions; network and internet availability.	At the time of the survey, all interviewees' perceptions of the system were very positive. The general perception was that when they were introduced to the system it felt as if they had to go through too many screens and options to achieve a task, but after they became familiar with the system it no longer felt difficult or time consuming.
Individual impact (*indi* with mean score of 3.44)	*Indi* had the lowest mean score, i.e. the MIS had the lowest impact (compared to other success measures) on the *development, productivity, efficiency and effectiveness of the users*, meaning the presence of the system did not have a high influence on users' individual capabilities and job effectiveness.	Interviewees voiced differing perceptions about the impact of the system on their individual capabilities and effectiveness in their job. They revealed that perceptions of high impact on individual's capabilities and effectiveness might be linked to the extent to which the user is using the system and the position of the staff member at the college. Support staff reported a high impact on their personal development, productivity and effectiveness in their job, whilst lecturing staff reported the contrary. It was noted that support staff were using the system extensively in their daily tasks, that the majority of staff are in possession of an International Computer Drivers Licence (ICDL) qualification and are highly computer proficient. College management encouraged enhancement of computer skills.

different groups or staff characteristics (rank, demography, job description, etc.) needs to be done to investigate differences between ratings within and between groups. It also shows in general that attention should be given to all aspects in order to move the performance of the system to the next level where the system performs well most of the time in all aspects or dimensions tested.

Triangulation results

As noted, the quantitative findings were triangulated with findings from seven semi-structured interviews held with system users which include lecturers, administrators, an IT manager, an MIS manager and two external stakeholders.

The qualitative data was analysed using thematic analysis. The findings related to the constructs from the model as explicated in Table 2 and Figure 5 are now discussed in Table 3.

Triangulation of the quantitative and qualitative findings as in Table 3 can be summarised as follows:

- The MIS is usable provided training is given before use.
- Although the construct 'organisational impact' received an average rate in the quantitative data analysis, interviewees unanimously applaud the system as a valuable asset to the college.
- The system adds much value to the management of the college in terms of monitoring and evaluation of key indicators suggesting satisfaction with information quality and quality of the format of output reports.

- The MIS is perceived to have a high impact on individual development and performance of staff who use the system more extensively (administrators) than those who use the system less extensively (lecturers).
- Data triangulation confirms the need for more systematic data quality control procedures at the college.

Conclusion

This study proposed an IS evaluation model and developed a tool based on extant models and tools and empirically tested the proposed model and tool by evaluating the performance of the MIS at public FET college X. A mixed methods approach was used which distinguished this study from previous research in IS evaluation where only quantitative methods were applied. The quantitative data was used to test the proposed model, including the composition of the constructs. The qualitative findings were triangulated with the quantitative to explain and contextualise the quantitative findings and make sense from a management perspective. This paper makes a theoretical contribution by presenting the *SA-FETMIS success model* supported by the survey tool for evaluating MIS performance at a public FET college. The changes clearly reflect the FET context. For example the construct 'information quality' is decomposed into two underlying components, namely, data quality and output quality which resonate with the focus on reporting, as evident from the qualitative findings. The construct 'system quality' has two underlying components, namely, ease of access and ease of functioning which reflects infrastructural issues. Having user satisfaction presented by three instead of five underlying components adds to the parsimony of the model.

The practical contribution lies in the usefulness of the model and tool on organisational and managerial levels where managers can apply the *SA-FETMIS* for MIS success evaluation. Further testing is needed to validate the *SA-FETMIS success model* and verify the general applicability of the model in measuring MIS performance at educational institutions.

Acknowledgements

We wish to thank the CEO and staff of public FET College X for their support and extensive contribution to the study, the University of South Africa and the HSRC for financial support of the study.

Competing interests

The authors declare that they have no financial or personal relationship(s) which may have inappropriately influenced them in writing this paper.

Authors' contributions

The study was conducted as part of the master's degree requirements of M.V. (HSRC). J.v.B (University of South Africa) acted as the supervisor and M.H. (CSIR) as the joint supervisor for the study.

References

Babbie, E. & Mouton, J., 2001, *The practice of social research*, Oxford University Press, Cape Town.

Bailey, J.E. & Pearson, S.W., 1983, 'Development of a tool for measuring and analysing computer user satisfaction', *Management Science* 29(5), 530–545. http://dx.doi.org/10.1287/mnsc.29.5.530

Chow, W.S., 2004, 'An exploratory study of the success factors for extranet adoption in E-supply chain', *Journal of Global Information Management* 12(4), 60. http://dx.doi.org/10.4018/jgim.2004010104

Davis, F.D., Bagozzi, R.P. & Warshaw, P.R., 1989, 'User acceptance of computer technology: A comparison of two theoretical models', *Management Science* 35, 982–1003. http://dx.doi.org/10.1287/mnsc.35.8.982

DeLone, W. & McLean, E., 1992, 'Information Systems success: The quest for the dependent variable', *Information Systems Research* 3(1), 36. http://dx.doi.org/10.1287/isre.3.1.60

DeLone, W.H. & McLean, E.R., 2003, 'The DeLone and McLean model of Information Systems Success: A ten-year update', *Journal of Management Information Systems* 19(4), 9–30.

Department of Education, 2008, *National Plan for Further Education and Training Colleges in South Africa*, Department of Education, Pretoria.

Department of Higher Education and Training, 2011, *Revised Strategic Plan, 2010/11 – 2014/15, and operational plans for the 2011/12 finacial year*, Department of Higher Education and Training, Pretoria.

Dishaw, M.T., Strong, D.M. & Bandy, D.B., 2002, 'Extending the Task-Technology Fit Model with self-efficacy constructs', *Human-Computer Interaction Studies in MIS, Eighth Americas Conference on Information Systems*, viewed 21 May 2011, from http://sigs.aisnet.org/SIGHCI/amcis02_minitrack/RIP/Dishaw.pdf

Doll, W.J. & Torkzadeh, G., 1988, 'The measurement of End-User Computing Satisfaction', *MIS Quarterly* 12(2), 259–274. http://dx.doi.org/10.2307/248851

Fishbein, M. & Ajzen, I., 1975, *Belief, attitude, intention, and behavior: An introduction to theory and research*, Addison-Wesley, Reading, MA.

Gable, G.G., Sedera, D. & Chan, T., 2008, 'Re-conceptualizing Information System Success: The IS-Impact Measurement Model', *Journal of the Association for Information Systems* 9(7), 377–408.

Goodhue, D.L. & Thompson, R.L., 1995, 'Task-Technology Fit and Individual Performance', *MIS Quarterly* 19(2), 213–236. http://dx.doi.org/10.2307/249689

Ifinedo, P., Rapp, B., Ifinedo, A. & Sundberg, K., 2010, 'Relationships among ERP post-implementation success constructs: An analysis at the organizational level', *Computers in Human Behavior* 26, 1136–1148. http://dx.doi.org/10.1016/j.chb.2010.03.020

Lange, L. & Luescher, T.M., 2003, 'A monitoring and evaluation system for South African higher education: Conceptual, methodological and practical concerns', *South African Journal of Higher Education* 17(3), 82–89.

Lapiere, R.T., 1934, 'Attitudes vs. actions', *Social Forces* 13, 230–237. http://dx.doi.org/10.2307/2570339

Mason, R.O., 1978, 'Measuring information output: A communication systems approach', *Information and Management* 1(4), 219–234. http://dx.doi.org/10.1016/0378-7206(78)90028-9

Ong, C.S., Day, M.Y. & Hsu, W.L., 2009, 'The measurement of user satisfaction with question answering systems', *Information & Management* 46, 397–403. http://dx.doi.org/10.1016/j.im.2009.07.004

Palmius, J., 2007, Criteria for measuring and comparing information systems, *proceedings of the 30th Information Systems Research Seminar in Scandinavia IRIS 2007*, Murikka, Tampere, Finland, August, 11–14, 2007, n.p.

Petter, S., DeLone, W. & McLean, E.R., 2008, 'Measuring information systems success: Models, dimensions, measures, and interrelationships', *European Journal of Information Systems* 17, 236–263. http://dx.doi.org/10.1057/ejis.2008.15

Petter, S. & Mclean, E.R., 2009, 'A meta-analytic assessment of the DeLone and McLean IS Success Model: An examination of IS success at the individual level', *Information & Management* 46(3), 159–166. http://dx.doi.org/10.1016/j.im.2008.12.006

Rai, A., Lang, S.S. & Welker, R.B., 2002, 'Assessing the validity of IS Success Models: An empirical test and theoretical analysis', *Information Systems Research* 13(1), 50–69. http://dx.doi.org/10.1287/isre.13.1.50.96

Rogers, E.M., 2003, *Diffusion of innovations*, 5th edn., Free Press, New York, NY.

Seddon, P.B., 1997, 'A respecification and extension of the DeLone and McLean Model of IS Success', *Information Systems Research* 8(3), 240–253. http://dx.doi.org/10.1287/isre.8.3.240

Seddon, P.B. & Kiew, M.Y., 1996, 'A partial test and development of DeLone and McLean's Model of IS Success', *Australian Journal of Information Systems* 4(1), 90–109.

Sedera, D., Gable, G.G. & Chan, T., 2004, A factor and structural equation analysis of the Enterprise Systems Success Measurement Model, *Proceedings Americas Conference on Information Systems*, New York, USA.

Shannon, C.E. & Weaver, W., 1949, *The Mathematical Theory of Communication*, University of Illinois Press, Urbana, IL.

Venkatesh, V. & Bala, H., 2008, 'Technology Acceptance Model 3 and a research agenda on interventions', *Decision Sciences* 39, 273–315. http://dx.doi.org/10.1111/j.1540-5915.2008.00192.x

Venkatesh, V. & Davis, F.D., 2000, 'A theoretical extension of the Technology Acceptance Model: Four longitudinal field studies', *Management Science* 46, 186–204. http://dx.doi.org/10.1287/mnsc.46.2.186.11926

Venkatesh, V., Morris, M.G., Davis, F.D. & Davis, G.B., 2003, 'User acceptance of Information Technology: Toward a unified view', *MIS Quarterly* 27, 425–478.

Visser, M.M., 2011, *Towards developing an evaluation tool for business management information systems' success at public Further Education and Training (FET) colleges in South Africa*, MSc thesis, University of South Africa, South Africa.

Weber, R., 2012, 'Evaluating and developing theories in the Information Systems discipline', *Journal of the Association for Information Systems* 13(1), 1–30.

Wejnert, B., 2002, 'Integrating models of diffusion of innovations: A conceptual framework'', *Annual Review of Sociology (Annual Reviews)* 28, 297–306. http://dx.doi.org/10.1146/annurev.soc.28.110601.141051

Wixom, B.H. & Todd, P.A., 2005, 'A theoretical integration of user satisfaction and technology acceptance', *Information Systems Research* 16(1), 85–102. http://dx.doi.org/10.1287/isre.1050.0042

8

Absorptive capacity: Relevancy for large and small enterprises

Authors:
Joshua R. Ndiege[1]
Marlien E. Herselman[1,2]
Stephen V. Flowerday[1]

Affiliations:
[1]Department of Information Systems, University of Fort Hare, South Africa

[2]Mereka Institute, CSIR, Pretoria, South Africa

Correspondence to:
Joshua Ndiege

Email:
joshuarumo@yahoo.com

Postal address:
PO Box 7426, East London 5200, South Africa

Background: Over the years, there has been a growing interest in organisational research in the absorptive capacity (AC) construct, but only a few theoretical and empirical studies on this topic have been carried out over the last decade. However, a number of scholars and practitioners have continued to cite AC as a significant factor in determining the success or failure of organisations. With the dramatic changes in business environments, there has been a growing rise in the use of knowledge by organisations to help improve and maintain their competitiveness and consequently their survival. AC is a fundamental element that helps organisations to gain competitive advantage by producing commercial products or services through the transformation of knowledge.

Objective: The purpose of this article is thus to provide a review of the literature on this subject with the aim of finding out how both large and small enterprises stand to benefit from AC. We intend to affirm that, by successfully carrying out a learning process that is characterised by the exploration and exploitation of external knowledge and the organisation's current knowledge base, organisations can realise competitive advantage irrespective of their size.

Method: In the literature search, three approaches were employed, namely academic databases, online search engines and a review of references of related studies which led to more relevant articles and works whose references were further reviewed and analysed. Content analysis was done on all collected articles for quality appraisal and synthesis, the results of which we present as discussions on various sections of this paper leading to answering of our study objective. Only peer-reviewed articles were used.

Results: Our findings reveal that, irrespective of the organisation's size, it can benefit significantly from AC. The study further reveal that AC is a strong predictor of an organisation's performance and hence a strategic asset for the organisation. Organisations with high AC are able to learn how to utilise new knowledge within their processes and come up with changes that improve their competitive advantage.

Conclusion: We submit that, because AC is a strong predictor of an organisation's performance, it is imperative that the necessary measures are taken to improve the levels of AC for all firms, irrespective of their size.

Introduction

Over the years, there has been a growing interest in organisational research in the absorptive capacity (AC) construct (Lane, Koka & Pathak 2006; Daghfous 2004). However, few theoretical and empirical studies were carried out on AC over the last decade (Bergh & Lim 2008; Chen 2004; Cockburn & Henderson 1998; Cohen & Levinthal 1990; Deed 2001; Gray 2006; Waalkens, Jorna & Postma 2004; Zahra & George 2002). A number of scholars and practitioners have continued to cite AC as a significant factor in determining whether an organisation is able to acquire and make use of external knowledge to their advantage (Bergh & Lim 2008; Lenox & King 2004; Harrington & Guimaraes 2005). With the dramatic changes in the business environment as a result of technological advancements, increased competition and market globalisation, amongst others, there has been a growing rise in the use of knowledge by organisations to help improve and maintain their competitiveness and consequently their survival (Scarbrough 2008; Higgins & Aspinall 2011; Cuervo-cazurra & Annique 2010; Uretsky 2001).

The primary objective of this article is to address the following question through a review of relevant literature: *How can both large and small enterprises benefit from absorptive capacity?* Methodologically, in conducting this study, we adopted Fink's (2005:3) definition of a research literature review in which he defines it as a 'systematic, explicit and reproducible method for identifying, evaluating and synthesising the existing body of completed and recorded work produced by researchers, scholars, and practitioners.' Guided by this definition, we made use of three approaches to the literature search in conducting the literature review for this study. Firstly, we made use of several academic databases such as Academic Publications eJournal, Academic Search and the Directory of Open Access Journal. Relevant keywords like absorptive capacity, knowledge management, organisations, SMEs and small business were used in the search. Secondly, we made use of online search engines. In doing so, the same keywords as in the academic database were employed in various combinations. The use of Boolean operators was employed in both cases to take particular advantage of the instruments. Finally, we collected and reviewed the references of related studies. Such reviews led to more relevant articles and works whose references were further reviewed and analysed. Content analysis was done on all collected articles for quality appraisal and synthesis (Okoli & Schabram 2010), the results of which we present as discussions on various sections of this paper leading to answering of our study objective. We believe that with this approach, the product of this study is scientific and hence reproducible.

The remainder of this paper is structured as follows: In the next section, we present the meaning of the AC construct, after which the various levels of AC are presented. We then provide a discussion on AC and organisational performance. Thereafter a presentation is made on AC within small enterprises. We finally draw conclusions on how the study addresses our objective and make recommendations for future research directions in this area.

Understanding absorptive capacity

A number of studies have been carried out around the AC construct in organisation restructuring (Bergh & Lim, 2008), information technology (Bi, Yu, Chen & Qi 2009; Haro-Dominguez, Arias-Aranda, Llorens-Montes & Moreno 2007; Harrington & Guimaraes 2005), knowledge management (Saghali & Allahverdi 2011; Chen 2004; Tsai & Wu 2011), service and product innovation (Melkas, Uotila & Kallio 2010; Nieto & Quevedo 2005; Stock, Greis& Fisher 2001), organisational learning (Sun & Anderson 2010) and business performance (Francalanci & Morabito 2008).

The term AC was originally coined by Cohen and Levinthal (1990) in the field of business strategy. The term is used to refer to the acquisition of new knowledge and the use of this knowledge to improve the organisation's competitiveness (Lane et al. 2006; Daghfous 2004; Cohen & Levinthal 1990). Cohen and Levinthal (1990:128) define AC as the organisation's ability to 'recognize the value of new information, assimilate it, and apply it to commercial ends'. Varied definitions of AC were provided by different researchers since the 1990s. Table 1 provides a summary of some of these definitions.

From Table 1, it is clear that there is no straightfoward empirical measure of AC. Lane, Koka & Pathak (2006) submit that this has not only led to minimal research on how AC is developed; it has equally resulted in problems with comparing research results.

TABLE 1: Definitions of Absorptive Capacity (own).

Definition	Author(s)
Ability to recognise the value of new external knowledge, assimilate it and apply it to commercial ends	Cohen and Levinthal (1990)
A set of skills needed to deal with tacit part of transferred knowledge and the need to transform this knowledge	Mowery and Oxley (1995)
Ability to learn and solve problems	Kim (1997)
Ability of an organisation to learn from another	Lane and Lubatkin (1998)
Includes evaluation, acquisition, integration, and the commercial utilisation of new external knowledge	Van Den Bosch et al. (1999)
A set of an organisation's routines and processes used to acquire, assimilate, transform and exploit knowledge	Zahra and George (2002)
Organisation's ability to learn and act on scientific findings and technological activities outside its limit	Sun and Anderson (2010)

Source: Authors' own data

It is also clear from the various definitions of AC (Table 1) that the construct is a multi-dimensional concept that consists of different skills as well as dimensions. Cohen and Levinthal (1990) aptly put it that the AC of an organisation is understood in terms of:

> the structure of communication between the external environment and the organization, as well as among the the subunits of the organization, and also the character and distribution of expertise within the organization. (p. 132)

They further observed that AC is largely influenced by the organisation's level of prior related knowledge. That is, without prior related knowledge, an organisation will not have the capability to learn from the new information gleaned from the external environment. Individuals with diverse knowledge within the organisation enhance the chance that the incoming knowledge will relate to the existing knowledge base within the organisation (Chen 2004). In its lowest level, Cohen and Levinthal (1990) view prior related knowledge to include basic abilities or even sometimes just shared language. However, it can also mean being in touch with current scientific or technological trends in a given field.

AC is a vital connection between external knowledge, the organisation's performance and its capacity to innovate (Volberda, Foss & Lyles 2010). AC allows organisations to identify new opportunities and integrate these opportunities with the existing knowledge base within their organisations.

From the preceding discussions and the definitions from various authors as presented in Table 1, it can be concluded that AC is the learning ability that organisations develop to identify external information and knowledge that is important to them, to internalise and to customise it to meet and suit their specific needs and consequently to take advantage of it for the good of the organisation. Two components thus clearly emerge in what constitute AC: communication channels within and across the organisation and the common knowledge that is shared within the organisation.

We consider Zahra and George's (2002) definition of AC to be more accurate since it takes into account the manifestation of the various processes that an organisation would go through to change new knowledge into knowledge that is valuable for application by the organisation. Further, this definition largely takes into account various elements mentioned by other authors in their definition of the AC construct (Table 1). As presented in Table 1, however, most researchers have abstracted AC into mainly two dimensions, namely external knowledge acquisition and internal knowledge dissemination. Zahra and George (2002) have included more discrete dimensions of the AC construct in their definition by decomposing it into four different dimensions:

- **Acquisition:** The ability of an organisation to locate, identify, evaluate and acquire outside knowledge regarded as essential for the survival of the organisation.
- **Assimilation:** The capability of the organisation to analyse, classify, process, interpret and eventually internalise and comprehend the external knowledge through its own routines. The members of the organisation need to interpret and understand the external knowledge to be able to assimilate and benefit from it.
- **Transformation:** The ability of the organisation to internalise and convert the newly acquired and assimilated knowledge. It is the capacity of the organisation to bring together the existing knowledge with the newly acquired knowledge. The result is a new cognitive composition derived from apparently dissimilar sets of knowledge.
- **Exploitation:** The capacity of the organisation to bring together knowledge acquired, assimilated and transformed for application and use in the organisation. This is considered as a strategic dimension for the organisation since it produces the outcomes following the effort to acquire, assimilate and transform knowledge. It is the development of routines that will take advantage of the knowledge for the betterment of the organisation.

Zahra and George (2002) classify the acquisition and assimilation dimensions as potential AC and transformation and exploitation as realised AC. They submit that potential AC is the ability of an organisation to acquire new external knowledge and assimilate it. Conversely, realised AC is the ability of an organisation to transform the external knowledge and exploit it. Whilst the two concepts (potential AC and realised AC) are closely related, they do refer to different kinds of practices. Potential AC is about learning practices whilst realised AC is concerned with operating practices (Zahra & George 2002). Figure 1 is used to illustrate the AC construct as reconceptualised by Zahra and George (2002).

Zahra and George (2002) observe that it is imperative that these dimensions of AC are managed for an organisation to realise greater performance. Their exposition sufficiently captures the various facets of the AC construct and has been widely accepted by several researchers (Francalanci & Morabito 2008; Chen 2004; Daghfous 2004; Haro-Dominguez et al. 2007; Harrington & Guimaraes 2005; Lenox & King 2004; Jansen, Van den Bosch & Volberda 2005).

Brokel and Binder (2007) observe that there are two kinds of knowledge transfers, namely intended and unintended. When individuals deliberately seek knowledge, the transfer is considered intended. Conversely, when actors 'stumble

upon' knowledge, the transfer is considered unintended. Brokel and Binder's view of knowledge transfer is in agreement with Ronde and Hussler's (2005) findings in their study of knowledge flows. The study revealed that deliberate knowledge flows have a significant influence on innovation. It is important for organisations not to allow knowledge transfer to take place as a mere coincidence. There needs to be a deliberate initiative by organisations to put in place structures that will facilitate the flow of valuable external knowledge to the organisation.

Levels of absorptive capacity

AC has been considered as a multilevel construct that can be found at different levels like the national, industry, inter-organisation, a whole organisation, inter-organisation units, organisation units and individual levels (Lane et al. 2006; Daghfous 2004; Bergh & Lim 2008; Cohen & Levinthal 1990; Minbaeva, Pedersen & Bjorkman 2003). Cohen and Levinthal (1990) argue that an organisation's AC depends on the AC of its individual members. This does agree with the general notion that organisational knowledge ultimately exist in the members of the organisation (Felin & Hesterly 2007). Since knowledge within organisations is possessed by individuals, it is imperative that the organisation establishes structures necessary for sharing this knowledge to enable the optimal

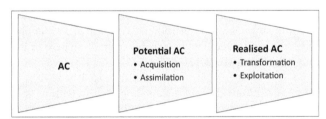

Source: Adapted from Zahra, S. & George, G., 2002, 'Absorptive Capacity: A Review, reconceptualization, and extension', *Academy of Management Review* 27(2), 185–203.
AC, apsorptive capacity.

FIGURE 1: Absorptive Capacity Construct.

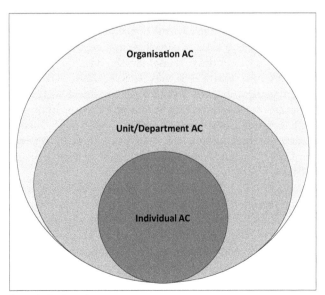

Source: Authors' own data.
AC, apsorptive capacity.

FIGURE 2: An Organisation's Levels of Absorptive Capacity (own).

utilisation thereof within the organisation. However, Malhotra, Gosain, and El Saw (2005) caution that the AC of an organisation is not just a summation of the employees' AC, but it is the collaboration amongst employees that will bring about the exploitation of new external knowledge, thereby producing successful change.

By decomposing the organisation into individual units and the units to employees within it, we can argue that an organisation's AC is determined by the AC of its individual units and the units' AC consequently is influenced by individuals within them (Minbaeva *et al.* 2003). Figure 2 illustrates this inter-relationship.

Absorptive capacity in an organisation cannot occur without individual AC (Cohen & Levinthal 1990), yet individual AC does not equal the organisation's AC. Therefore, to advance the understanding of an organisation's AC, insights into individual AC is important (Volberda *et al.* 2010). Employees who play a role in the identification, assimilation, application and dissemination of new knowledge are critical for the success of the organisation. For this reason, it is important for organisations to be keen on nurturing the AC of its individual members. The presence and richness of the structures of knowledge flow within the organisation's units and/or departments will determine the success of knowledge transfer within it. The position of an individual within the organisation's overall network of knowledge flow is also instrumental in determining the individual's ability to acquire and assimilate knowledge from elsewhere in the network (Tsai & Wu 2011).

Communication channels extending both within and outside of the organisation need to be well developed. A communication channel is the means by which information is transferred from one point to another within a social system (Easterby-Smith & Lyles 2005:123). Therefore, such channels are critical to AC as they are instrumental in enhancing knowledge flow to and within the organisation. Managers within the organisation have the responsibility of developing their organisation's AC by directly providing information to individuals within the organisation who have the potential to adopt new practices (Lenox & King 2004). They also need to ensure that the prevailing environment within the organisation is conducive for the discovery, assimilation and exploitation of valuable practices. The transfer of knowledge within the organisation can take place through internal seminars, brochures and demonstrations (Lenox & King 2004).

An organisation's AC does not only rely on its interface with external environments, but knowledge transfer within and across the organisation's subunits is also critical. Therefore, to understand the source of an organisation's AC, it is imperative to focus on the communication structures between the organisation and the external environment, as well as amongst the organisation's subunits, the character of expertise and their distribution within the organisation.

A number of studies have indicated that an organisation's ability to acquire, assimilate, transform and exploit new knowledge is a critical element in ensuring that it has a sustained competitive advantage. In the next section, the literature review on AC and its effect on the organisation's performance are presented.

Absorptive capacity and organisational performance

With the substantial uncertainty created by constant changes in the market such as changing preferences of customers, diminishing industry boundaries, changing demographics and social values, emerging competition, new technological advancements and other developments, organisations need to respond swiftly and decisively by making significant changes to their core business practices to avoid the risk of decline or failure. Central to the organisation's ability to respond effectively to market demands is a well developed AC.

Previous studies (Becker & Peters 2000; Bergh & Lim 2008; Chen 2004; Daghfous 2004; Gray 2006; Holmqvist 2003 and Saghali & Allahverdi 2011) have underscored the significant role played by knowledge and organisational learning in enhancing competitive advantage. By exploitation, organisations are able to learn how to improve their capabilities, make use of their present knowledge base and pay attention to existing activities in current domains (Holmqvist 2003). Furthermore, through knowledge routinisation and refinement, exploitation is able to help organisations realise reliability in experience (Holmqvist 2004). An organisation should be able to recognise, anticipate and consequently take action in response to market shifts or new technological developments in a manner that is superior to its competitors.

Whereas organisations that engage in exploitation make use of and enhance their competence, they can also put their energy into the exploration and pursuit of new competence. Exploration for an organisation involves searching for new routines and discovering new ways to businesses, processes, products and technology (Bi *et al.* 2009). Wiklund and Shepherd (2003) posit that knowledge-based resources have a direct positive influence on an organisation's performance. Darroch (2005) also discovered that organisations with a sound knowledge base and that manage such a resource well make more efficient use of their resources, are better performers and are more innovative.

To adapt to the increasingly competitive and constantly changing business environment, organisations need to develop their AC and exploit it to ensure a sustained competitive advantage. With this, organisations are able to renew themselves by exploiting their current competence and exploring new competence by developing or improving their potential and realised AC. With poor mechanisms for the acquisition, assimilation, transformation and exploitation of knowledge, organisations will more likely develop lethargy than responsiveness to market shifts.

A number of studies have been carried out indicating the connection between AC and organisations' performance. These empirical findings indicate the significant role played by AC in fostering organisation's performance as indicated in Table 2.

Organisations with a high AC are always better performers than those with a low AC (Deed 2001; Easterby-Smith & Lyles 2005; Haro-Dominguez et al. 2007; Melkas et al. 2010). However, the capabilities of an organisation are disadvantaged by a fixed knowledge base, inflexible capabilities and managerial perceptions that are path-dependent (Tripsas & Gavetti 2000). Because of this, such organisations do not often succeed in recognising and absorbing valuable external knowledge, resulting in stagnation in their growth and eventually an inability to survive in the highly competitive market environment. The AC of an organisation determines its ability to explore and exploit both external knowledge and its existing knowledge base. As a result, AC is a fundamental element that helps organisations to gain competitive advantage by producing a commercial product or service through the transformation of knowledge.

In their study, Teece, Pisano and Shuen (1997) submit that organisations that operate in environments with technological opportunities can benefit more if they have high levels of AC. With technological innovations constantly gaining momentum in the present era, organisations cannot afford to be caught napping. They need to be alive to the realities of these advancements and be ready and willing to exploit them to improve their business. However, the presence of technological opportunities in a given field does not imply that all organisations in that field are necessarily affected with the same level of intensity. The extent to which organisations exploit such opportunities will largely be influenced by the knowledge and the capacities they have at their disposal. Organisations that pose a critical mass of knowledge and have the capacity to absorb are the ones that are able to exploit technological opportunities (Nieto & Quevedo 2005). Therefore, the presence of AC is critical in organisations' efforts to exploit the pool of technological opportunities in their domain.

By comparison to large organisations, small enterprises have received less attention in AC research. In the following section, the literature review with regard to AC within small enterprises is presented.

Absorptive capacity within small enterprises

We begin by defining small enterprises and differentiating them from large organisations. Various indicators have been used to define small enterprises across the world. Research

TABLE 2: Effects of absorptive capacity (AC) on organisations (own).

The effect of AC on an organisation	Illustrative reference
Innovative performance; exploration or exploitation; new product development	Cohen and Levinthal (1990); Tsai (2001); Van Wijk, Van den Bosch and Volberda (2001); Stock et al. (2001) and Melkas et al. (2010)
Expectation formation; reactive or proactive strategy formation	Cohen and Levinthal (1990) and Van Den Bosch et al. (1999)
Information systems integration; IT success	Francalanci and Morabito (2008) and Harrington and Guimaraes (2005)
Information quality	Melkas et al. (2010)

Source: Authors' own data

TABLE 3: United Kingdom's definition of small enterprises.

Criteria	Small Firm	Medium Firm
Turnover	Not more than £2.8 million	Not more than £11.2 million
Balance sheet	Not more than £1.4 million	Not more than £5.6 million
Employees	Not more than 50	Not more than 250

Source: Adapted from Deakins, D., 1999, Entrepreneurship and Small Firms, 2nd edn., McGraw-Hill, London.

TABLE 4: European Union's definition of small enterprises.

Criteria	Micro	Small	Medium
Maximum employee	9	49	249
Maximum turnover	-	€7 million	€40 million
Maximum balance sheet	-	€5 million	€27 million

Source: Adapted from Burns, P., 2001, Entrepreneurship and Small Business, Palgrave, New York.

TABLE 5: Small Business Administration of the United States of America's definition of small enterprises.

Criteria	Very Small	Small	Medium	Large
Number of employees	Less than 20	20–99	100–499	Over 500

Source: Adapted from Megginson, L., Byrd, M. & Megginson, W., 2008, Small Business Management: An Entrepreneur's Guidebook, 4th edn., McGraw-Hill, New York.

TABLE 6: Republic of Tanzania's definition of small enterprises.

Criteria	Micro	Small	Medium	Large
Number of employees	Less than 5	5–49	50–99	Over 100
Capital investment (In millions)	Tsh. 5	Tsh. 200	Tsh. 800	Above Tsh. 800

Source: Adapted from Ngasongwa, J., 2002, Ministry of Industry and Trade, Republic of Tanzania, viewed 27 June 2010, from http://www.tanzania.go.tz/pdf/smepolicy.pdf

TABLE 7: World Bank's definition of small enterprises.

Criteria	Small	Medium
Number of employees	Up to 50	Up to 300
Total assets	Up to $3 million	Up to $15 million
Total sales	Up to $3 million	Up to $15 million

Source: Adapted from International Finance Group, 2012, SME Definition, viewed 13 July 2010, from http://www.ifc.org/sme/html/sme_definitions.html

and literature have also highlighted the definitional problems of small enterprises. There is no generally accepted or agreed upon definition for the term small enterprise (Culkin & Smith 2000). Organisations vary in size, location, nature of business, financial performance, maturity and management. These variations make it impossible for various researchers to agree on an objective measure to apply when defining small enterprises. Their definitions vary from country to country with different criteria used to classify them in order to address each country's political and economic purposes. Table 3 to Table 7 provide some examples in this regard.

From the definitions presented in Table 3 to Table 7, it is clear that the general indicators adopted for the definition of small enterprises are the number of employees, sales turnover and total assets. These variations in the definitions can make it difficult for researchers to compare different studies on small enterprises. In this study, therefore, any reference to small enterprises by other authors may range in its definition.

Despite being considered as the drivers of modern economies and thus always being indispensable, small enterprises still lack the proper and adequate application of modern concepts due to their small size (Ayyagari, Beck & Demirguc-Kunt 2007). Small enterprises often operate under challenging conditions and are further subjected to global pressures from large organisations and demands from customers. As a result, many of them remain unstable and vulnerable. In order to survive in the now highly competitive environment, small enterprises cannot afford to stagnate. They have to be willing and ready to be open to new ideas, new ways of carrying out their operations, new equipments and tools. They should also develop and have the ability to absorb as well as benefit from better ideas, modern ways of performing their operations and current equipment and tools.

Small enterprises provide an interesting and unique context for the exploration of AC due to the unique characteristics that separate them from large organisations. For example, most of them have limited resources in terms of finance, expertise and time (Agbeibor 2006). Furthermore, they tend to rely heavily upon the motivation and the expertise of their owner or manager. However, small enterprises have always been considered to be critical for the growth and development of any economy. Because of this, they will always have a special economic role to play.

Since small enterprises are often dominated by their owners or managers (Ayyagari et al. 2007), their culture are easily influenced by the leadership style and personality of their owners or managers (Wong & Aspinwall 2004). For this reason, the commonly held view that these enterprises have a flexible and open culture should be treated with some caution (Wiesner, McDonald & Banham 2007). It can thus be argued that the small enterprise owner or manager plays a central role in ensuring that information flows within and from outside the organisation. Hence, the AC of small enterprises will most certainly be influenced by their owners' or managers' AC. In their study on small enterprises in Iran, Talebi and Tajeddin (2011) revealed that those enterprises whose owners or managers and employees had high levels of education as well as clear growth objectives had a better capacity to acquire, assimilate and make use of new knowledge.

Small enterprises can use AC for tactical as well as for strategic purposes (Egbu, Hari & Renukappa 2005; Gray 2006). For tactical purposes, they can use their AC to react to their internal processing needs by using it to revamp their processes. Conversely, strategically they can make use of their AC to create knowledge that can be exploited for strategic planning. A study by Francalanci and Morabito (2008) revealed that small enterprises' AC has a mediation effect on business performance as well as on the integration of information systems.

Some organisations have a higher capability to absorb, diffuse and utilise knowledge than others (Cohen & Levinthal 1990). Organisations with more flexible structures are believed to be associated with greater capacities for knowledge acquisition (Bergh & Lim 2008). Because of their small size, small enterprises are always considered as highly flexible (Levy & Powell 2000), and they can exploit this flexibility to their advantage by encouraging knowledge transfer processes through the promotion of openness by its employees towards new external stimuli. This can be achieved by promoting collaboration and the exchange of knowledge within the organisation.

With regard to culture, behaviour and structure, small enterprises differ considerably from large organisations. The regular trend in small enterprises are social informal networking (Egbu et al. 2005), a flat and uncomplicated structure that is primarily operations-oriented (Wong & Aspinwall 2004). Such features are certainly conducive for AC to flourish (Daghfous 2004). Furthermore, such environments can promote flexibility and adaptiveness which may help to overcome resistance to change and create a better alignment to environmental changes and influences (Wiesner et al. 2007). Wong and Aspinwall (2004), however, observe that workers within small enterprises are mainly generalists who perform a number of tasks with a minimal degree of specialisation. This is likely to lead to lack of deep knowledge. Yao, Othman, Abdalla, and Jing (2011) further observe that a number of employees within small enterprises are not willing to share their knowledge due to the lack of a sense of benefit for doing so or a lack of reward for such efforts.

Due to their small size and resource constraints, we can expect small enterprises to have low levels of AC, a less developed approach towards AC, a lack of awareness of the relevance of AC and no sound understanding of the processes of knowledge acquisition, assimilation, transformation and exploitation. Furthermore, those small enterprises that tend to practice elements of AC do so in an ad hoc manner and relegate such ventures to the category of luxury, with most preferring to adopt the 'wait and see' approach. That is, they wait for large organisations to venture before they take action (Serenko, Bontis & Hardie 2007). It is therefore imperative that understanding in this field is developed for small enterprises.

Conclusion

AC can be considered as the ability of an organisation to carry out successfully a learning process that is characterised by the exploration and exploitation of external knowledge and the organisation's current knowledge base in order to achieve a competitive advantage. AC is therefore a strong predictor of organisations' performance and hence a strategic asset for the organisation. Organisations with a high AC are able to learn how to utilise new knowledge within their processes and to come up with changes that improve their competitive advantage.

It was made clear from the literature presented in this study that, irrespective of an organisation's size, AC is a critical factor for success. Whilst large enterprises have adequate resources and well-established structures, they can exploit these to help improve and benefit from AC. Conversely, small enterprises can use their small size and flexibility to improve their AC as they can easily adjust and accommodate changes with far less effort than would large organisations. Further, with the turbulent business environment, no organisations can risk stagnation. They have to be able to adapt their practices constantly in the light of environmental changes. It will be an uphill battle if enterprises cannot 'listen' to environmental shifts or exploit new vital external information to enable them to strategically position themselves.

The literature review conducted in this study was instrumental in addressing our research question which was: *How can both large and small enterprises benefit from absorptive capacity?* The answer is that, through AC, organisations (whether large or small) can benefit in the following ways:

- use AC for new product development
- improve their strategies
- integrate their information systems
- react and adapt to market shifts
- position themselves to better respond to the needs of their customers
- create cohesion between members of the organisation
- better flow of information and/or communication within and out the organisation
- take advantage of external valuable information.

We use Table 8 below to summarise, at a high level, how the literature in this study was instrumental in answering our research question.

We conclude that organisations (whether large or small) need to have properly developed capabilities in external knowledge acquisition and assimilation and intra-organisational knowledge transformation and exploitation in order to sustain their competitiveness. AC is no longer a preserve for large organisations, but it has become highly relevant for small enterprises as well.

From the literature review conducted in this study, we propose certain future research directions in the next section.

Future research directions

A number of related areas were revealed in this study that could be exploited in order to extend the current research in this field.

TABLE 8: How the literature study addressed the research question (own).

Heading from the literature	Contribution to study objective	Illustrative reference
Understanding Absorptive Capacity (AC)	Understanding various elements of AC and how they are realised	Cohen and Levinthal (1990); Sun and Anderson (2010); Van Den Bosch *et al.* (1999); Volberda *et al.* (2010); Lane *et al.* (2006) and Zahra and George (2002)
Levels of Absorptive Capacity (AC)	Organisational units and workers' role in firm's AC and how they are potential beneficiaries	Bergh and Lim (2008); Cohen and Levinthal (1990); Daghfous (2004); Lane *et al.* (2006); Lenox and King (2004); Minbaeva *et al.* (2003) and Tsai and Wu (2011)
Absorptive Capacity and organisational performance (AC)	Overall benefit organisations would derive from AC	Cohen and Levinthal (1990); Harrington and Guimaraes (2005); Melkas *et al.* (2010); Nieto and Quevedo (2005); Stock *et al.* (2001); Tsai (2001) and Van Wijk *et al.* (2001)
Absorptive capacity within small enterprises (AC)	What makes small enterprises have low levels of AC and features about small enterprises that could make them exploit AC	Agbeibor (2006); Ayyagari *et al.* (2007); Serenko *et al.* (2007) Wiesner *et al.* (2007); Wong and Aspinwall (2004) and Yao *et al.* (2011)

Source: Authors' own data

- As observed by Murovec and Prodan (2009), Bergh and Lim (2008), Harrington and Guimaraes (2005) and Spithhoven *et al.* (2010), the subject of AC has not been adequately researched. Our study too found scanty literature on the subject. Therefore, there is still a strong need for further research into this area to confirm already produced empirical findings or to determine their generalisability and to reveal further new insights.

- Additionally there is a lack of a commonly agreed upon measurements for AC. It is important that further work be carried out particularly on the measurement of AC in order to reach a common stand or at least a largely acceptable measurement for the construct.

- We also found very few studies conducted in this field within the context of developing countries. It would be interesting to study AC within organisations in developing countries and compare this to those that have been carried out in developed countries. Such research would certainly reveal new insights in this field that would no doubt be of interest to the research community in the area.

Acknowledgements
Competing interests

The authors declare that they have no financial or personal relationship(s) which may have inappropriately influenced them in writing this paper.

Authors' contributions

J.N. (University of Fort Hare) wrote the article and contributed to the review, discussions on the results, implications and commented on the manuscript at all stages. M.E.H. (University of Fort Hare) contributed to the review, discussions on the results, implications and commented on the manuscript at all stages. S.V.F. (University of Fort Hare) contributed to the review, discussions on the results, implications and commented on the manuscript at all stages.

References

Agbeibor, J., 2006, 'Pro-poor economic growth: Role of small and medium size enterprises', *Journal of Asian Economics* 17(1), 35–40. http://dx.doi.org/10.1016/j.asieco.2006.01.005

Ayyagari, M., Beck, T. & Demirguc-Kunt, A., 2007, 'Small and medium enterprises across the Globe', *Small business Economics* 29, 415–434. http://dx.doi.org/10.1007/s11187-006-9002-5

Becker, W. & Peters, J., 2000, 'Technological opportunities, absorptive capacity and innovation', *Eighth International Joseph A. Schumpeter Society Conference.* Center for Research in Innovation and Competition (CRIC), Manchester, UK, June 28 – July 01, 2000, pp. 1–38.

Bergh, D.D., & Lim, E.N.-K., 2008, 'Learning how to restructure: Absorptive capacity and improvisational views of restructuring actions and performance', *Strategic Management Journal* 29(6), 593-616, viewed 15 January 2012, from http://onlinelibrary.wiley.com/doi/10.1002/smj.676/pdf

Bi, X., Yu, C., Chen, T. & Qi, X., 2009, 'Absorptive capacity: Enhancing the absorption of information technology', *Management and Service Science*, MASS '09 International Conference, Wuhan, China, September 20–22, 2009, pp. 1–4.

Brokel, T. & Binder, M., 2007, 'The regional dimensions of knowledge transfers - A behavioral approach', *Industry and Innovation* 14(2), 151–175. http://dx.doi.org/10.1080/13662710701252500

Burns, P., 2001, *Entrepreneurship and Small Business*, Palgrave, New York.

Chen, C.-J., 2004, 'The effects of knowledge attribute, allience characteristics, and absorptive capacity on knowledge transfer performance', *R & D Management* 34(3), 311–321. http://dx.doi.org/10.1111/j.1467-9310.2004.00341.x

Cockburn, I.M. & Henderson, R N., 1998, 'Absorptive capacity, coauthoring behaviour, and the organization of research in drug discovery', *Journal of Industrial Economics* 46(2), 157–182. http://dx.doi.org/10.1111/1467-6451.00067

Cohen, W.A. & Levinthal, D.A., 1990, 'Absorptive capacity: A new perspective on learning and innovation', *Administrative Science Quarterly* 39, 128–152. http://dx.doi.org/10.2307/2393553

Cuervo-cazurra, A. & Annique, U.C., 2010, 'Why some firms never invest in formal R & D', *Strategic Management Journal* 31(7), 759–779, viewed 22 November 2011, from http://onlinelibrary.wiley.com/doi/10.1002/smj.836/pdf

Culkin, N. & Smith, D, 2000, 'An emotional business: A guide to understanding the motivations of small business takers', *Qualitative Market Research: An International Journal* 3(3), 145–157.

Daghfous, A., 2004, 'Absorptive capacity and the implementation of knowledge-intensive best practices', *Society for Advancement of Management Journal,* Spring, 21–27.

Deakins, D., 1999, *Entrepreneurship and Small Firms,* 2nd edn., McGraw-Hill, London.

Deed, D.L., 2001, 'The role of R&D intensity, technical development, and absorptive capacity in creating entrepreneurial wealth in high technology start-ups', *Journal of Engineering and Technology Management* 18, 29–47. http://dx.doi.org/10.1016/S0923-4748(00)00032-1

Easterby-Smith, M. & Lyles, M.A., 2005, *The Blackwell handbook of organizational learning and knowledge management*, illustrated edn., Blackwell, Wiley.

Egbu, C.O., Hari, S., & Renukappa, S.H., 2005, 'Knowledge management for sustainable competitiveness in small and medium surveying practices', *Structural Survey* 23(1), 7–21. http://dx.doi.org/10.1108/02630800510586871

Felin, T. & Hesterly, W.S., 2007, 'The knowledge-based view, nested heterogeneity, and new value creation: Philosophical considerations on the locus of knowledge', *Academy of Management Review* 32, 195–218. http://dx.doi.org/10.5465/AMR.2007.23464020

Fink, A., 2005, *Conducting research literature reviews: From the internet to paper,* Sage Publications, Thousand Oaks.

Francalanci, C. & Morabito, V., 2008, 'IS integration and business performance: The mediation effect of organizational absorptive capacity in SMEs', *Journal of Information Technology* 23, 297–312. http://dx.doi.org/10.1057/jit.2008.18

Gray, C., 2006, 'Absorptive capacity, knowledge management and innovation in entrepreneurial small firms', *International Journal of Entrepreneurial Behavior & Research* 12(6), 345–360. http://dx.doi.org/10.1108/13552550610710144

Haro-Dominguez, M.D., Arias-Aranda, D., Llorens-Montes, F.J. & Moreno, A.R., 2007, 'The impact of absorptive capacity on technological acquisition engineering consulting company', *Technovation* 27(8), 417–425. http://dx.doi.org/10.1016/j.technovation.2007.04.003

Harrington, S.J. & Guimaraes, T., 2005, 'Corporate culture, absorptive capacity and IT success', *Organization and Management* 15(1), 39–63.

Higgins, D. & Aspinall, C., 2011, 'Learning to learn: a case for developing small firm owner/managers, *Journal of Small Business and Enterprise Development* 18(1), 43–57. http://dx.doi.org/10.1108/14626011111106424

Holmqvist, M., 2003, 'A dynamic model of intra - and interorganizational learning', *Organizational Studies* 24, 95–123. http://dx.doi.org/10.1177/0170840603024001684

Holmqvist, M., 2004, 'Experiential learning processes of exploitation and exploration', An empirical study of product development, *Organizational Science* 15, 70–81. http://dx.doi.org/10.1287/orsc.1030.0056

International Finance Group, 2012, *SME Definition,* viewed 13 July 2010, from http://www.ifc.org/sme/html/sme_definitions.html

Jansen, J.J., Van den Bosch, F.A. & Volberda, H.W., 2005, 'Managing potential and realized absorptive capacity: How do organizations antecedents matter?', *Academy of Management Journal* 48(6), 999–1015. http://dx.doi.org/10.5465/AMJ.2005.19573106

Kim, L., 1997, 'The dynamics of Samsung's technological learning in semiconductors', *California Management Review* 39, 86–100.

Lane, P.J. & Lubatkin, M., 1998, 'Relative absorptive capacity and interorganizational learning', *Strategic Management Journal* 19(5), 461–477, viewed 17 November 2011, from http://onlinelibrary.wiley.com/doi/10.1002/(SICI)10970266(199805)19:5%3C461::AID-SMJ953%3E3.0.CO;2-L/pdf, http://dx.doi.org/10.5465/AMR.2006.22527456

Lane, P. J., Koka, B. & Pathak, S., 2006, 'The reification of absorptive capacity: A critical review and rejuvenation of the construct', *Academy of Management Review* 31(4), 833–863.

Lenox, M. & King, A., 2004, 'Prospects for developing absorptive capacity through Internal Information Provision', *Strategic Management Journal* 25(4), 331–345, viewed 20 February 2012, from http://onlinelibrary.wiley.com/doi/10.1002/smj.379/pdf

Levy, M. & Powell, P., 2000, 'Information systems strategies for small and medium-sized enterprises: an organisational perspective', *Journal of Strategic Information Systems* 9(1), 63–84. http://dx.doi.org/10.1016/S0963-8687(00)00028-7

Malhotra, A., Gosain, S. & El Saw, O.A., 2005, 'Configuration in supply chains: Gearing for partner-enabled market knowledge creation', *MIS Quarterly* 29(1), 145–187.

Megginson, L., Byrd, M. & Megginson, W., 2008, *Small Business Management: An Entrepreneur's Guidebook*, 4th edn., McGraw-Hill, New York.

Melkas, H., Uotila, T. & Kallio, A., 2010, 'Information quality and absorptive capacity in service and product innovation proceses', *Interdisciplinary Journal of Information, Knowledge, and Management* 5, 357–373.

Minbaeva, D., Pedersen, T. & Bjorkman, I., 2003, 'MNC knowledge transfer, subsidiary absorptive capacity, and HRM', *Journal of International Business Studies* 34(6), 586–599. http://dx.doi.org/10.1057/palgrave.jibs.8400056

Mowery, D.C. & Oxley, J.E., 1995, 'Inward technology transfer and competitiveness: The role of national innovation systems', *Cambridge Journal of Economics* 19, 67–93.

Murovec, N. & Prodan, I., 2009, 'Absorptive capacity, its determinants, and influence on innovation output: Cross-cultural validation of the structural model', *Technovation* 29, 859–872. http://dx.doi.org/10.1016/j.technovation.2009.05.010

Nalo, S. (2008, February Tuesday), Launch of MSME Case Studies – 2008, Ministry of Industrialisation, Nairobi, Kenya.

Ngasongwa, J., 2002, *Ministry of Industry and Trade, Republic of Tanzania*, viewed 27 June 2010, from http://www.tanzania.go.tz/pdf/smepolicy.pdf

Nieto, M. & Quevedo, P., 2005, 'Absorptive capacity, technological opportunity, knowledge spillovers, and innovative effort', *Technovation* 25(10), 1141–1157. http://dx.doi.org/10.1016/j.technovation.2004.05.001

Okoli, C. & Schabram, K., 2010, 'A guide to conducting a systematic literature review of information system research', *Sprouts: Working Papers on Information Systems* 10(26), 1–51

Ronde, P. & Hussler, C., 2005, 'Innovation in regions: What does really matter?', *Research Policy* 34(8), 1150–1172. http://dx.doi.org/10.1016/j.respol.2005.03.011

Saghali, A. & Allahverdi, S., 2011, The intervening role of organizational dynamic routines: Absorptive capacity and knowledge management perspective. *2011 International Conference on Economics and Finance Research*, Singapore, February 26–28, 2011, pp. 354–358.

Scarbrough, H., 2008, *The evolution of business knowledge* (illustrated edn.), Oxford University Press, New York.

Serenko, A., Bontis, N. & Hardie, T., 2007, 'Organizational size and knowledge flow: A proposed theoretical link', *Journal of Intellectual Capital* 8(4), 610–627. http://dx.doi.org/10.1108/14691930710830783

Spithoven, A., Clarysse, B. & Knockaert, M., 2010, 'Building absorptive capacity to organize inbound open innovation in traditional industries', *Technovation* 30(2), 130–141. http://dx.doi.org/10.1016/j.technovation.2009.08.004

Stock, G.N., Greis, N.P. & Fisher, W.A., 2001, 'Absorptive capacity and new product development', *The Journal of High Technology Management Research* 12(1), 77–91.

Sun, P.Y. & Anderson, M.H., 2010, 'An examination of the relationship between absorptive capacity and orgnizational learning, and proposed integration', *International Journal of Management Reviews* 12(2), 130–150. http://dx.doi.org/10.1111/j.1468-2370.2008.00256.x

Talebi, K. & Tajeddin, M., 2011, 'The adoption of new and innovative knowledge b small and medium enterprises of Iran: Opportunities and constraints for growth', *African Journal of Business Management* 5(1), 39–49, viewed 10 February 2012, from http://www.academicjournals.org/AJBM

Teece, D.J., Pisano, G. & Shuen, A., 1997, 'Dynamic capabilities and strategic management', *Strategic Management Journal* 18(7), 509–533. http://dx.doi.org/10.1002/(SICI)1097-0266(199708)18:7<509::AID-SMJ882>3.0.CO;2-Z

Tripsas, M. & Gavetti, G., 2000, 'Capabilities, cognition and inertia: Evidence from digital imaging', *Strategic Management Journal ,* 21(10/11), 1147–1162, viewed 22 February 2012, from http://onlinelibrary.wiley.com/doi/10.1002/1097-0266(200010/11)21:10/11%3C1147::AID-SMJ128%3E3.0.CO;2-R/pdf

Tsai, W., 2001, 'Knowledge transfer in intraorganizational networks: effects of networks position and absorptive capacity on business unit innovation and performance', *Academy of Management Journal* 44(5), 996–1004. http://dx.doi.org/10.2307/3069443

Tsai, Y.C. & Wu, C.S., 2011, 'The effect of interpartner resource alignment and absorptive capacity on knowledge transfer performance', *African Journal of Business Management* 5(26), 10434–10445, viewed 23 February 2012, from, http://www.academicjournals.org/AJBM

Uretsky, M., 2001, 'Preparing for the real knowledge organization', *Journal of Organizational Excellence* 21(1), 87–93. http://dx.doi.org/10.1002/npr.1122

Van den Bosch, F.A., Volberda, H.W. & De Boer, M., 1999, 'Coevolution of firm absorptive capacity and knowledge environment: Organizational forms and combinative capabilities', *Organization Science* 10(5), 551–568. http://dx.doi.org/10.1287/orsc.10.5.551

Van Wijk, R., Van den Bosch, F.A. & Volberda, H.W., 2001, The impact of the depth and breadth of knowledge absorbed on levels of exploration and exploitation. *Insights into knowledge transfer*, BPS Division, Washington DC.

Volberda, H.W., Foss, N. & Lyles, M.A., 2010, 'Absorbing the concept of absorptive capacity - How to realize its potential in the organization field', *Organization Science* 21, 1–21. http://dx.doi.org/10.1287/orsc.1090.0503

Waalkens, J., Jorna, R. & Postma, T., 2004, 'Absorptive capacity of knowledge intensive business services: The case of architectural and engineering SMEs', *Frontiers of e-Business Research 1*, 444–458, Tampere University, Tampere.

Wiesner, R., McDonald, J. & Banham, H.C., 2007, 'Australian small and medium sized enterprises (SMEs): A study of high performance managment practices', *Journal of Management and Organization* 13(3), 227–248. http://dx.doi.org/10.5172/jmo.2007.13.3.227

Wiklund, J. & Shepherd, D., 2003, 'Knowledge-based resources, entrepreneurial orientation, and the performance of small and medium-sized businesses', *Strategic Management Journal* 24(13), 1307–1314. http://dx.doi.org/10.1002/smj.360

Wong, K.Y. & Aspinwall, E., 2004, 'An empirical study of the important factors for knowledge management adoption in SME sector', *Journal of Knowledge Management* 9(3), 64–82. http://dx.doi.org/10.1108/13673270510602773

Yao, L., Othman, A., Abdalla, A.N. & Jing, W., 2011, 'A novel sensemaking model of effective knowledge management within SMEs', *African Journal of Business Management* 5(11), 4423–4431.

Zahra, S. & George, G., 2002, 'Absorptive Capacity: A Review, reconceptualization, and extension', *Academy of Management Review* 27(2), 185–203.

9

What drives Web 2.0 adoption in South African civil society organisations

Authors:
Kiru Pillay[1]
Manoj S. Maharaj[1]

Affiliations:
[1]School of Management, Information Technology and Governance, University of KwaZulu-Natal, South Africa

Correspondence to:
Manoj Maharaj

Email:
maharajms@gmail.com

Postal address:
Private Bag X54001, Durban 4000, South Africa

Background: The impact and consequences of social media adoption on society are only just being realised and studied in detail; consequently, there is no universal agreement as to the reasons for the adoption of these services. Even understanding why some social media services are popular remains to some extent elusive. The practical use of Web 2.0 does not provide any answers either with, for example, a noticeable difference in the way social media was strategically used by Barack Obama and Mitch Romney in the lead-up to the 2009 American elections. However, recent studies that have focused on social media adoption within specific sectors have begun to shed some light on these emerging adoption patterns; two studies in particular are illustrative: a 2012 study on the newspaper sector and a study on social media adoption and e-government.

Objectives: This study investigates why South African civil society organisations (CSOs) adopt Web 2.0 services and the perceived and actual benefits of such adoption.

Method: A survey questionnaire was sent to 1712 South African CSOs listed in the Prodder database to explore why certain social media services were adopted and the perceived benefits thereof.

Results: Internal reasons for the adoption of social media services by South African CSOs coalesce around organisational visibility and access to information. External reasons focus on organisations needing to become more relevant and more connected to like-minded organisations and initiatives.

Conclusion: The pervasiveness of Web 2.0 technologies makes it inevitable that CSOs will have to restructure themselves to remain relevant.

Introduction

Even a cursory glance at newspapers, magazines or the television is sufficient for even a casual observer to notice the amount of reporting relating to Web 2.0 social media. Social media has broken stories about terrorist attacks in India, a shark attack off the West Coast of South Africa and was extensively exploited during the Arab Spring uprisings. It has become the constant companion of high-profile personalities and also of a large majority of the online population. Facebook, the world's largest online social network, has approximately one billion users, which is exceeded only by the populations of China and India. The microblogging site Twitter recorded tweets at the rate of 25 088 per second during the screening of an anime movie in December 2011 (Akimoto 2011); social networking companies are amongst the fastest growing and social networking sites are regularly cited as the most searched for and viewed sites on the Internet (Most Popular Websites 2013).

The pervasiveness of social media has created a universal system of cooperation and collaboration encapsulated in a socially connected Web that supports, equally, all users' capacity to generate content. The ubiquitous nature of social media is what makes the Internet a strategic imperative in public-led socio-political campaigns. Social media has become an important tool in the arsenal of civil society organisations (CSOs) and indeed much of the success of a new resurgent civil society appears to be its ability to adopt and exploit new emerging technologies (Anheier, Glasius & Kaldor 2001; Castells 2004).

This study follows that path as it tries to explore and explain why South African CSOs adopt social media and what perceptions have characterised the reason for adoption, be it from internal or external perspectives. The benefits of and barriers to adoption are also explored. The diffusion of innovations theory (Rogers 2003) underpins the study and provides a theoretical framework for the identification and understanding of the constructs that impact the adoption of Web 2.0 in CSOs. The diffusion framework argues that it is individual perception of the attributes of an innovation that affects adoption and not necessarily attributes defined by experts (Rogers 2003).

Background

Civil society is those formal groups that facilitate the engagement of citizens in activities that exist and operate outside of government (Etling, Faris & Palfrey 2010). From its Latin and Greek origins of *societas civilis* and *politike koinona* respectively, the term civil society has come to mean a 'political society' (Anheier *et al.* 2001), which emphasises the central role of citizens in institutional and policy development (Kaldor 2003). Civil society is made up of various global networks of organisations, movements, institutions and behaviours that exist between governments, the markets and the family (Glasius 2002; Kaldor 2003).

Van de Donk *et al.* (2004) point out that civil society communications have always been accompanied by a variety of media, including brochures, leaflets and newsletters, with the intention of gaining access to greater numbers of people within the organisation and in the public domain. A resurgence of civil society has been attributed to the sector's ability to exploit new emerging interactive technologies and its ability to adapt its communication and mobilisation strategies in the emerging technological paradigm (Anheier *et al.* 2001; Castells 2004). Communication, both internal and external, is core to the effectiveness of civil society; it is this centrality of communications that promotes the adoption of technology by CSOs. As Internet usage and mobile telephone usage increase, so does the ability of CSOs to develop their network structures and strengthen their capacity to connect with organisations around the world. It suggests that there is a virtual cycle between the network society and civil society.

Research methodology

A survey, which was designed to evaluate reasons why CSOs adopt Web 2.0 services, was conducted between May and June 2011. The survey was developed using the Google Docs® toolset, which created an online version of the survey. A Microsoft Word® version was also developed and respondents could complete either.

The population of South African CSOs is most comprehensively embodied in the Prodder database, which is maintained and administered by the non-government organisation, SANGONeT, whose stated function revolves around delivering Information and Communications Technology (ICT)-related services to the broader civil society sector (SANGONeT 2011). Organisational information (organisation name, website address, legal status, contact persons' email addresses and telephone numbers) was extracted from the database and validated to eliminate all organisations that either did not have an email address listed or did not have a valid email address (emails being returned as undeliverable). The eventual population of the study was the remaining 1712 organisations. The contact persons listed on the organisation's website were targeted by the survey and they were requested to either complete the survey or forward it to the relevant person in the organisation who could provide the requested information.

During the course of the survey, three reminders were sent: the first was sent a week after the survey was initially distributed, the second a week later and the third two weeks later. The final responses received included 105 online and 17 Microsoft Word® documents, giving a total of 122, which was statistically adequate.

What drives Web 2.0 adoption in South African civil service organisations

Internal reasons for Web 2.0 adoption amongst South African civil service organisations

The internal reasons for the adoption of social media services in South African CSOs are illustrated in Figure 1. This analysis is in response to the question 'How important are Web 2.0 services to your organisation from an internal management perspective?' The responses were on a scale of one to five, with one signifying 'very unimportant' and five signifying 'very important'. The raw data was coded and aggregated and reported on as follows: one and two were grouped together as 'unimportant', three was coded as 'somewhat important' and four and five were aggregated as 'important'.

Over three-quarters (76%) of CSOs believe that Web 2.0 is important firstly to ensure that the organisation becomes well known (visibility) and secondly as an avenue to access information (information intensity). The need to adapt to new technology was rated as important by 61.2% of respondents. The ability to reduce communication and back-office costs was cited by 57% of respondents and, 56.2% cited the capacity of Web 2.0 to achieve organisational missions and goals. Web 2.0's usefulness in building expertise in ICTs was cited by 54.5% of respondents.

The power to gather information (or information intensity) is a strategic imperative for CSOs. The Internet has made countless information sources available, which has given CSOs a whole new world of intelligence and data-gathering capabilities (Surman & Reilly 2003). Additionally, the new collaborative technologies that define Web 2.0 give CSOs the ability to tap into the zeitgeist of their supporters (Rigby 2008). Competition amongst CSOs makes it imperative for CSOs to remain relevant, which means being 'in sync' with their main constituency of supporters and donors.

In support of the need for organisations to become more visible (chosen by 76% of respondents), Yang (2009) argues that online activists have begun to adopt marketing strategies to promote both their organisations and their causes. Activism no longer has the image of the scruffy children of the 1960s; rather, activists are now more likely to be full-time employees of advocacy organisations, possibly with a scientific background and very likely with a post-graduate degree in the field of politics or business.

There was overwhelming positivity about Web 2.0's importance; only a small number of CSOs considered social media as unimportant from an internal management perspective. The largest of this minority, 24.8%, consider social media as unimportant for capacity building. The factor analysis shows that there was no overlapping of variables, which indicates no mixing of factors for this question.

External reasons for Web 2.0 adoption

Civil society is made up of various global networks of organisations, movements, institutions and behaviours that exist between governments, the markets and the family (Glasius 2002; Kaldor 2003). They work at all levels of society and they work on the principle of broad involvement, which serves to develop the capacity for advocacy and activism at all levels (Keane 1995; Naidoo 2010). With the revolution in communication technologies transforming the world into the much-touted 'global village' (McLuhan 2011) social movements and social actions are also subject to the formal and informal rules of globalisation and are increasingly influenced by happenings in distant places (Della Porto & Kriesi 2009). The implication of all of this is that CSOs must have a strong outward focus, which, as Edwards (2004) states, must create a space for citizens and other like-minded CSOs to influence state processes and policy.

The importance attached to social media from an external perspective is depicted in Figure 2. This analysis is in response to the question 'Indicate how important you think Web 2.0 services are to your organisation from an internal management perspective'. The responses were on a scale of one to five, with one signifying 'very unimportant' and five signifying 'very important'. The raw data was coded and aggregated and reported on as follows: one and two

were grouped together as 'unimportant'; three was coded as 'somewhat important' and four and five were aggregated as 'important'.

Table 1 shows a cumulative percentage for the categories of 'somewhat unimportant' and 'important'.

A large number of the external reasons for Web 2.0 adoption were deemed important by a majority of respondents, including:

- To widen the influence on society (86%).
- To provide knowledge to beneficiaries (86%).
- To enable, empower and network (90.9%).
- To cooperate and collaborate with other organisations (87.6%).
- To disseminate information (88.4%).
- To get a wider perspective and share knowledge (90.9%).
- To gather information and knowledge (90%).
- To reduce environmental waste and travel (85.1%).

The majority of respondents were positive towards Web 2.0 as an external enabler. The largest negative factor relates to using Web 2.0 services to compete with other organisations: 28.1% of respondents rated this as unimportant. Only 47.9% of respondents saw Web 2.0's ability to accumulate bargaining power for advocacy as an important factor. When combined with the category 'somewhat important', this percentage rises to 72.7%, with the remaining respondents (27.3%) rating this as unimportant.

Factor analysis

Factor analysis revealed a grouping of social media services along two components; Table 2 illustrates component one

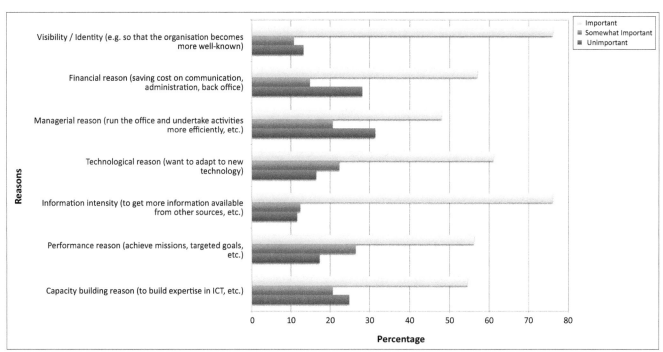

ICT, information and communications technology; PCs, personal computers.

FIGURE 1: Internal reasons for Web 2.0 adoption amongst South African civil society organisations.

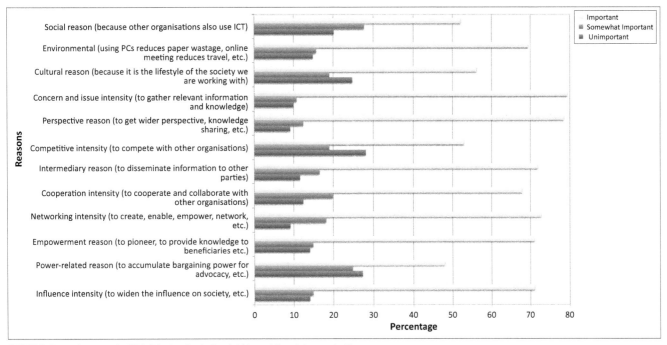

FIGURE 2: External reasons for Web 2.0 adoption in South African civil society organisations.

TABLE 1: External reasons for Web 2.0 adoption in South African civil society organisations.

External reasons for Web 2.0 adoption	Unimportant (%)	Important (%)
Influence intensity (to widen the influence on society, etc.)	14.0	86.0
Power-related reason (to accumulate bargaining power for advocacy, etc.)	27.3	72.7
Empowerment reason (to pioneer, to provide knowledge to beneficiaries, etc.)	14.0	86.0
Networking intensity (to create, enable, empower, network, etc.)	9.1	90.9
Cooperation intensity (to cooperate and collaborate with other organisations)	12.4	87.6
Intermediary reason (to disseminate information to other parties)	11.6	88.4
Competitive intensity (to compete with other organisations)	28.1	71.9
Perspective reason (to get wider perspective, knowledge sharing, etc.)	9.1	90.9
Concern and issue intensity (to gather relevant information and knowledge, etc.)	9.9	90.0
Cultural reason (because it is the lifestyle of the society we are working with)	24.8	75.2
Environmental (using PCs reduces paper wastage, online meeting reduces travel, etc.)	14.9	85.1
Social reason (because other organisations also use ICT)	20.2	79.8

ICT, Information and Communications Technology.

and component two factors, cross-tabulated against the external reasons for social media adoption.

The component two factors with a value over 0.5 are social, environmental, cultural, concern and issue intensity, perspective and competitive intensity. The remaining reasons fall under component one.

The majority of the component one factors over 0.5 appear to relate to 'outward facing' reasons, for example dissemination of information, collaboration with other organisations, empowerment and networking, provision of knowledge, widened influence on society and accumulation of advocacy

power. Tandon (2000) argues that emerging interactive technologies provide a communications platform between different types of local and international organisations that span a variety of interests, including religious, the labour movement, NGOs and diasporic groups, which provides some support for the 'outward facing' hypothesis that this section proposes.

In contrast, some of the component two factors over 0.5 are more organisationally 'inward facing,' for example: reducing wastage, increasing online meeting, reducing travel, gathering information, following trends set by other organisations and reflecting the society within which the organisation operates.

TABLE 2: Factor analysis.

External reasons for social media adoption	Component 1	Component 2
Social reason (because other organisations also use ICT)	0.186	0.788
Environmental (using PCs reduces paper wastage, online meeting reduces travel, etc.)	0.378	0.758
Cultural reason (because it is the lifestyle of the society we are working with)	0.285	0.791
Concern and issue intensity (to gather relevant information and knowledge)	0.540	0.690
Perspective reason (to get wider perspective, knowledge sharing, etc.)	0.579	0.655
Competitive intensity (to compete with other organisations)	0.325	0.681
Intermediary reason (to disseminate information to other parties)	0.817	0.398
Cooperation intensity (to cooperate and collaborate with other organisations)	0.798	0.387
Networking intensity (to create, enable, empower, network, etc.)	0.796	0.347
Empowerment reason (to pioneer, to provide knowledge to beneficiaries, etc.)	0.798	0.363
Power-related reason (to accumulate bargaining power for advocacy, etc.)	0.780	0.192
Influence intensity (to widen the influence on society, etc.)	0.828	0.351

PCs, personal computers; ICT, Information and Communications Technology.

Functions of Web 2.0 usage in South African civil society

The inescapability of social media has resulted in a significant increase in Internet-driven campaigning. These emerging technologies give CSOs the ability to advance their own agendas; organisational websites, blogs and email help in the mobilisation and coordination, not only of activists, but also of ordinary people who may have an interest in certain issues (Hara & Shachaf 2008). In a *Financial Times* article, Gapper (2009) argues that the balance of power between governments and citizens has fundamentally changed due largely to the ubiquity of social media, which helps CSOs to recruit, communicate, campaign and fundraise. This section analyses the functions for which Web 2.0 is used in South African CSOs as illustrated in Figure 3. The question asked

in which areas – marketing, market research, fundraising or campaigning – each of the listed Web 2.0 services was used.

Social networking is the most used service with just over 78% of respondents indicating their organisations adopting it for the following purposes: campaigning (25.2%), fundraising (7.8%), promotion of the brand (40.9%) and market research (4.3%). Perhaps surprisingly, fundraising via social networks garnered support from just 7.8% of CSOs. Photos and multimedia sharing and messenger applications followed in terms of usage with 59.6% and 58.4% of organisations using them for the one or more of the listed activities. The maintaining of organisational blogs (45.4%), microblogging (45.8%) and wikis (44.6%) were the next most utilised services.

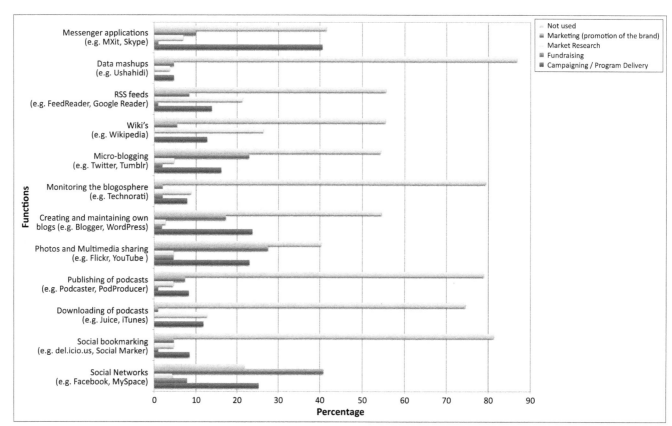

FIGURE 3: Functions of Web 2.0 usage in South African civil society organisations.

TABLE 3: Cumulative adoption versus cumulative areas of usage.

Social media services	Level of knowledge (fairly and somewhat knowledgeable) (%)	Cumulative adoption – three months or more ago (%)	Cumulative usage across all areas (e.g. marketing, research, etc.) (%)
Social networks (e.g. Facebook, MySpace)	81.0	82.4	78.2
Social bookmarking (e.g. del.icio.us, Social Marker)	26.5	16.0	18.7
Downloading of podcasts (e.g. Juice, iTunes)	26.4	29.2	25.4
Publishing of podcasts (e.g. Podcaster, PodProducer)	-	17.8	21.1
Photos and multimedia sharing (e.g. Flickr, YouTube)	68.3	58.8	59.6
Creating and maintaining own blogs (e.g. Blogger, WordPress)	46.2	44.9	45.4
Monitoring the blogosphere (e.g. Technorati)	-	19.3	12.8
Microblogging (e.g. Twitter, Tumblr)	46.3	43.7	45.8
Wikis (e.g. Wikipedia)	59.5	42.4	44.6
RSS feeds (e.g. FeedReader, Google Reader)	52.1	44.6	30.5
Data mashups (e.g. Ushahidi)	16.6	11.0	13.2
Messenger applications (e.g. MXit, Skype)	66.9	63.0	58.4

Table 3 summarises data on levels of knowledge about social media services, adoption rates and data with respect to the functions of social media usage.

As can be expected, there is a high degree of correlation between levels of knowledge, adoption and usage. For example, 81% of respondents indicated being knowledgeable about social networks; 82.4% of organisations had adopted social networks at least more than three months ago, with 78.2% using them for either campaigning and program delivery, fundraising, market research or promotion of the brand. Similar patterns emerged for all of the other services. Internationally, CSOs are using social networks as a tool for program delivery, marketing, customer support, fundraising and market research, and looking forward, the goal of these CSOs is to use social networking sites to engage members and grow membership (NTEN 2010).

Benefits and barriers

This section analyses the benefits of and barriers to Web 2.0 deployment in South African civil society. The questions from the survey that informed this analysis are: 'In what way has your organisation benefited from its use of Web 2.0 social media?' and 'What difficulties has your organisation experienced in deploying Web 2.0 services?'.

Benefits of social media adoption

Social media provide a cheap, flexible, ubiquitous and distributed medium that has given opposition movements the ability to mount challenges on various fronts. Shirky (2010) argues that one way to look at social media is as a long-term tool that has the ability to strengthen civil society and to provide alternate discourses in the public sphere. Figure 4 illustrates the benefits experienced by CSOs with regard to social media services.

The biggest benefits of social media to South African CSOs are performance reasons (55.5%), building wider networks (52.5%), and better communications of ideas with other organisations (48.3%). The common theme that emerges from these responses is one of communication and networking, which, taken together, have an average of 52%. Fundraising (32.8%) and opinion building (38.1%) were the other areas where some benefit was realised. Social media does not assist organisations to save costs or assist in the management of the with 41.9% indicating little benefit, or save costs with 43.6% indicating little benefit.

Paradoxically, whilst respondents see the benefit of social media in building wider networks with other organisations (52.5%), this does not extend to actually undertaking collaborative projects with other CSOs (40.2% of respondents saw little benefit in this). There were an almost equal proportion of respondents that saw either some benefit or little benefit in using social media for campaigning and opinion building (38.1% vs 35.6%). The factor analysis shows that there was no overlapping of variables, which indicates no mixing of factors for this question.

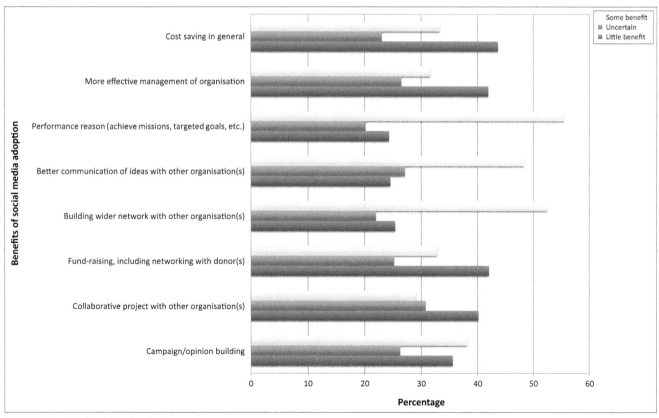

FIGURE 4: Benefits of social media adoption.

In the responses to the usage of social media, just under 8% of respondents indicated that they used social media for fundraising, whilst in response to the benefits of social media, 32.8% of respondents believed that social media has 'some benefit' in respect of fundraising. This is a case of expected benefits not equating to actual usage. One possible reason for this is that whilst social media may be a viable channel for fundraising, there is still a lot of hesitancy amongst South Africans in general for online financial transacting. In a study conducted by MasterCard (Polity.org.za 2012), 51% of South Africa's online population conduct online financial transactions. Of the people who have access to the Internet but who do not conduct online transactions, just over 50% cite online security as the reason for not transacting online. Fundraising online requires transmitting personal financial information and would be subject to the same security concerns cited above.

Barriers to the deployment of social media

Many CSOs, due to their reliance on external funding, exist in an environment of constant economic uncertainty. Additionally, emerging technologies change constantly, which in turn means that engaging with these technologies becomes an ongoing process of discovery and learning. These technologies also bring about a permanent change to the way the organisation communicates and collaborates. All of these factors make it difficult for these organisations to effectively run campaigns in the face of a lack of information, tools and skills.

In a survey conducted by the Nonprofit Technology Network (NTEN 2009), it was reported that CSOs required more time and more trained staff in order to improve their use of social networks. A large percentage of respondents (74.1%) indicated a need to know 'which tools are useful for what' and 44.4% indicated a need for training in how these tools work.

This section analyses the barriers to the deployment of social media in South African CSOs and the responses are illustrated in Table 4.

Thirty-six respondents (or 30%) cite the 'lack of skilled human resources' as the biggest barrier to deploying social media. The only other significant barrier identified was a 'lack of money', which was chosen by 19 (16%) organisations. The remaining barriers that were listed in the survey were insignificantly represented in the sample.

TABLE 4: Barriers to deploying social media.

Barriers to the deployment of social media	*f*	%
Lack of infrastructure	6	5.0
Lack of skilled human resources; Lack of infrastructure	6	5.0
Lack of money; Lack of skilled human resources	7	5.9
Lack of money; Lack of skilled human resources;- Lack of infrastructure	7	5.9
Internal policy, management	8	6.7
Lack of money	19	16.0
Lack of skilled human resources	36	30.3

f, frequency.

Perceived attributes and attitudes towards Web 2.0

This section looks at the results of the attitudes and perceptions of CSO respondents towards Web 2.0 social media.

Perceptions on the use of Web 2.0 in South African civil society

Figure 5 interrogates the responses to the question relating to the impact of social media on CSOs. Respondent perceptions of social media were as follows:

- Has a positive influence on the organisations relationships with other CSOs (52.9%).
- Helps the organisations gain a wider perspective towards issues and concerns (55.5%).
- Increases dialogue with supporters (54.6%).

The ratio of agreement to disagreement for the above statements is approximately two to one. The statements that relate to gaining 'a wider perspective towards issues and concerns' and 'increasing dialogue with supporters' are related to the benefits experienced by CSOs, that is: better communication of ideas with the public, better communication of ideas with other organisations and the ability to build wider networks with other organisations.

The first statement, that social media 'has assisted in the performance of the internal management of the organisation', reflects overall neutrality: there are as many respondents who agreed with the statement as there are those who disagreed. The factor analysis shows that there was no overlapping of variables, which indicates no mixing of factors for this question.

Increased dialogue with supporters is an important consideration for CSOs. The Internet, and in particular the World Wide Web, has given civil society more power to craft their public image thereby 'altering the landscape of protest' (Owens & Palmer 2003). Social movements also run the risk of alienating their supporter base by defining campaigns based on what will resonate with the media and other global publics (Mann 2008).

Impact of Web 2.0

This section establishes the areas within which civil society operates and where social media has had a positive impact (Figure 6).

All of the statements have positive responses except for those relating to internal staff development. However, the strength of the agreement is moderate when compared to the (high) levels of uncertainty for each statement. For example, comparing levels of agreement to levels of being unsure reveals the following: 55% versus 30% for development initiatives, 53.8% versus 28.6% for training and 57.5% versus 30% for advocacy. Internal staff development had an equal

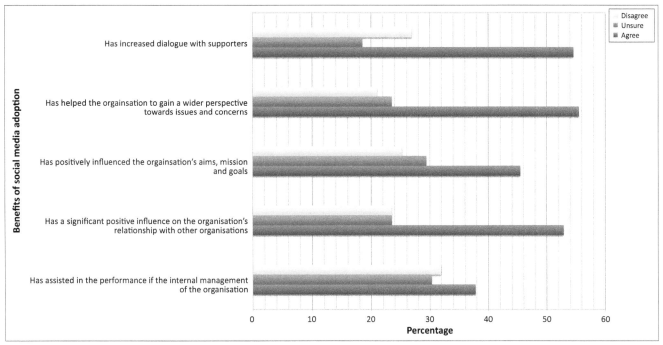

FIGURE 5: Perceptions on the use of Web 2.0.

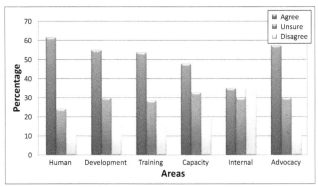

FIGURE 6: Areas of impact of Web 2.0.

split between those who agreed and those who disagreed. The factor analysis shows that there was no overlapping of variables, which indicates no mixing of factors for this question.

If social networking sites are a typical example of a Web 2.0 service, as argued by Memmi (2010), then, internationally, civil society sentiment towards social media is very positive: four out of five (80%) of organisations indicate that they find their social networking efforts valuable (NTEN 2010).

Conclusion

Two surveys (one in 2007 and the other in 2009) into the adoption of ICTs by CSOs have shown that South African civil society has, by and large, enthusiastically embraced technology and that ICTs have become integral to civil society's effective functioning (World Wide Worx 2009). With regard to social media services, internal reasons for adoption coalesce around organisational visibility and access to information. External reasons focus on organisations needing to become more relevant and more connected to like-

minded organisations and initiatives. The main reason for the deployment of social media by CSOs mirrors the external reason for adoption: promotion of the organisational brand.

The adopting of emerging technologies and innovation, and the planning and management thereof is almost always a complex and complicated exercise; new sets of knowledge competencies have to merge with the organisation's existing capabilities. In the case of civil society, add to this mix the emergence of new flexible and adaptable online CSOs all vying for the same set of supporters and you have a situation that makes it imperative for organisations to re-evaluate the very core of their values. Whilst social media adoption patterns, reasons for adoption and benefits, and barriers experienced are only just beginning to be explored, what is certain is that the pervasiveness of these technologies ensures the inevitability that organisations will have to restructure and reorientate themselves to remain relevant in a new emerging technology paradigm.

Acknowledgements

Competing interests

The authors declare that they have no financial or personal relationship(s) that may have inappropriately influenced them in writing this article.

Authors' contributions

M.S.M. (University of KwaZulu-Natal) supervised K.P. (University of KwaZulu-Natal) for his PhD.

References

Akimoto, A. 2011, 'The year when Japan went global over social networking', *The Japan Times*, viewed 28 December 2011, from http://www.japantimes.co.jp/text/nc20111221aa.html

Anheier, H., Glasius, M. & Kaldor, M., 2001, 'Introducing global civil society', in H. Anheier, M. Glasius & M. Kaldor (eds.), *Global civil society*, pp. 3–22, Oxford University Press, Oxford.

Castells, M., 2004, *The information age: Economy, society and culture*, vol. II, Blackwell Publishing, New York, NY.

Della Porto, D. & Kriesi, H., 2009, 'Social movements in a globalizing world: An introduction', in D. Della Porto, H. Kriesi & D. Rucht (eds.), *Social movements in a globalizing world*, pp. 3–22, Palgrave Macmillan, New York.

Edwards, M., 2004, *Civil society*, Cambridge Polity, Cambridge.

Etling, B., Faris, R. & Palfrey, J., 2010, 'Political change in the digital age: The fragility and promise of online organizing', *SAIS Review* 30(2), 37–49.

Gapper, J., 2009, 'Technology is for revolution (and repression)', *Financial Times*, viewed 27 July 2011, from http://www.ft.com/intl/cms/s/0/4386d188-5cfe-11de-9d42-00144feabdc0.html#axzz1qyLdo6BA

Glasius, M., 2002, *Global civil society yearbook 2002*, London School of Economics, London.

Hara, N. & Shachaf, P., 2008, 'Online peace movement organizations: A comparative analysis', in I. Chen & T. Kidd (eds.), *Social information technology: Connection society and cultural issues*, pp. 52–67, Idea Group, Hershey.

Kaldor, M., 2003, 'Civil society and accountability', *Journal of Human Development* 4(1), 5–27.

Keane, J., 1995, 'Structural transformations of the public sphere', *Communication Review* 1(1), 1–22.

McLuhan, M., 2011, *The Gutenberg galaxy – The making of typographic man*, University of Toronto Press, Toronto.

Mann, A., 2008, 'Spaces for talk: Information and communication technologies (ICTs) and genuine dialogue in an international advocacy movement', *Asian Social Science* 4(10), 3–13.

Memmi, D., 2010, 'Sociology of virtual communities and social software design', in S. Murugesan (ed.), *Web 2.0, 3.0, and X.0: Technologies, business, and social applications*, vol. II, pp. 790–803, Information Science Reference, New York.

Most Popular Websites, 2013, '25 March 25', in *Most popular*, viewed 25 March 2012, from http://mostpopularwebsites.net/

Naidoo, K., 2010, 'Boiling point: Can citizen action save the world', *Development Dialogue* 54, 1–200.

Nonprofit Technology Network (NTEN), 2009, *Common knowledge and the port (2009) Nonprofit social network survey*, viewed 30 July, 2009, from http://www.nonprofitsocialnetworksurvey. com

NTEN, 2010, *Nonprofit social network benchmark report*, viewed 01 April 2011, from http://www.nten.org/blog/2010/04/20/2010-nonprofit-social-network-benchmark-report

Owens, L. & Palmer, L., 2003, 'Making the news: Anarchist counter-public relations on the World Wide Web', *Critical Studies in Media Communication* 20(4), 335–361.

Polity.org.za, 2012, *MasterCard*, viewed 12 January 2012, from http://www.polity.org.za/article/south-africas-online-shopping-on-the-rise-2011-09-26

Rigby, B., 2008, *Mobilizing generation 2.0: A practical guide to using Web 2.0*, Jossey-Bass, San Francisco.

Rogers, E.M., 2003, *Diffusion of innovations*, The Free Press, A division of Simon & Schuster, New York.

SANGONeT, 2011, *About* SANGONeT, viewed 31 October 2011, from http://www.ngopulse.org/about

Shirky, C., 2010, *SXSW: South by southwest*, viewed 15 March 2011, from http://schedule.sxsw.com/2011/events/event_IAP000246

Surman, M. & Reilly, K., 2003, *Appropriating the Internet for social change: Towards the strategic use of networked technologies by transnational civil society organizations*, Social Sciences Research Council, Information Technology and International Cooperation Program, New York.

Tandon, R., 2000, 'Riding high or nosediving: Development NGOs in the new millennium', *Development in Practice* 10(3/4), 319–329.

Van de Donk, W., Loader, B., Nixon, P. & Rucht, D., 2004, 'Social movements and ICTs', in W. van de Donk, B. Loader, P. Nixon & D. Rucht (eds.), *Cyberprotest: New media, citizens and social movements*, pp. 1–25, Routledge, London.

World Wide Worx, 2009, *The state of ICTs in the South African NGO sector*, Author, Johannesburg.

Yang, G., 2009, *The power of the Internet in China*, Columbia University Press, New York.

10

An exploration of the role of records management in corporate governance in South Africa

Authors:
Mpho Ngoepe[1]
Patrick Ngulube[2]

Affiliations:
[1]Department of Information
Science, University of South
Africa, South Africa

[2]School of Interdisciplinary
Research and Graduate
Studies, University of South
Africa, South Africa

Correspondence to:
Patrick Ngulube

Email:
ngulup@unisa.ac.za

Postal address:
PO Box 392, Pretoria 0003,
South Africa

Background: Corporate governance maybe approached through several functions such as auditing, an internal audit committee, information management, compliance, corporate citizenship and risk management. However, most organisations, including governmental bodies, regularly exclude records management from the criteria for a good corporate-governance infrastructure. Proper records management could be the backbone of establishing good corporate governance.

Objectives: Utilising the King report III on corporate governance as a framework, this quantitative study explores the role of records management in corporate governance in governmental bodies of South Africa.

Method: Report data were collected through questionnaires directed to records managers and auditors in governmental bodies, as well as interviews with purposively selected auditors from the Auditor-General of South Africa. Data were analysed using various analytical tools and through written descriptions, numerical summarisations and tables.

Results: The study revealed that records management is not regarded as an essential component for corporate governance. Records management is only discussed as a footnote; as a result it is a forgotten function with no consequences in government administration in South Africa. The study further revealed that most governmental bodies have established internal audit units and audit committees. However, records-management professionals were excluded from such committees.

Conclusion: The study concludes by arguing that if records management is removed as a footnote of the public-sector operations and placed in the centre of operational concern, it will undoubtedly make a meaningful contribution to good corporate governance.

Introduction and background to the study

Barac (2001) describes corporate governance as the structures, processes, cultures and systems that stimulate the successful operation of organisations. It is the process by which the owners and creditors of an organisation exert control and require accountability for the resources entrusted to the organisation. For an organisation to be accountable and transparent, a number of corporate-governance components such as internal audit, an audit committee, internal controls and a records-management programme need to be put in place. A close working relationship between these structures can improve the effectiveness of corporate governance (Rezaee 2010:48). However, records management is often excluded from components of corporate governance as it is demonstrated in the results of this study.

Records management is a corporate function that has the potential to support corporate governance if its principles are appropriately implemented. Willis (2005:86) contends that many organisations are primarily focusing on corporate governance, and as a result, 'records management is an increasingly important preoccupation'. The link between recorded information and corporate governance is widely acknowledged. The International Records Management Trust (IRMT) (1999:64) posits that corporate governance is supported by three functions, namely, auditing, accounting and information management. The King report III on corporate governance in South Africa also acknowledges a link between good governance, compliance with the law and information management (Institute of Directors in Southern Africa [IoDSA] 2009:1). For example, in terms of clause 5.6 of the King report III, recorded information is the most important asset of an organisation as it is the evidence of business activities. According to Australia National Audit Office (2003), records management is a key component of any organisation's corporate governance and is critical to its accountability and transparency. Akotia (1996:9) similarly argues that the first and last stages of the budgetary cycle, accountability and auditing, are dependent upon effective records management.

However, the relationship between record-keeping and corporate governance has not been explored in much depth by scholars (Willis 2005:86). This sentiment is echoed by Isa (2009:iii) when he points out that the records-management community claims that records have to be preserved for accountability, but they rarely explore the role records play in corporate governance. Moreover, the contribution of records management to corporate governance is often not recognised by other professions and management (IRMT 1999:65). Isa (2009) is of the view that:

> In an age where corporate governance and accountability is a global agenda, it is imperative for the records management professionals to do self-introspection of their role in order to change the perception by other professions about records management's contribution towards achieving organisational goals in a highly regulated and compliance-bound environment in both the public and private sectors. (p. iii)

This article discusses records management in relationship to components that support good corporate-governance processes (i.e. auditing and audit committee) in the public sector of South Africa. It is essential to explore the relationship between records management and corporate governance in order for organisations to benefit from the synergy of their integration (Isa 2009:3–4). Nowadays, few areas in any sector are receiving as much attention as corporate governance. However, 'many efforts to strengthen financial controls have failed because the fundamental structures needed to underpin them are often overlooked, that is, record-keeping' (IRMT 2001). Records management may utilise the growing interest in corporate governance to leverage its low status by joining the ranks of corporate governance. It is hoped that this study will contribute to the records-management literature by providing empirical evidence concerning the nexus between records management and corporate governance. Insight gained from this study would be useful for governmental bodies to be more transparent and accountable. This study is guided by Chapters Three (Audit Committees) and Seven (Internal Audit) of the King report III (IoDSA 2009) on corporate governance in South Africa.

When conceptualising this study, chapter four (The governance of risk) of the King report III was deliberately excluded as the study would have been too broad to handle. Instead, the study focuses on examining the role of records management in supporting other elements of corporate governance such as internal audit and audit committee. With regard to chapter five (Governance of information technology) of the King report III, only clause 5.6, which deals with information assets, was included. It is hoped that this study will stimulate further research that embrace the other areas of corporate governance.

Background on corporate governance framework

The concept corporate governance was formally introduced world-wide in the 1980s as a result of the separation of ownership from management (Dandago 2009:94). However, it existed in some form from time immemorial. In the histories of the earliest civilisations, before the art of recording could have been known, corporate governance through auditing took place orally. The steward in charge of the cattle, goods and other forms of wealth would, from time to time, produce to his master the wealth with which he was entrusted and give account of his stewardship, reciting from memory the goods and cattle acquired, those disposed of and those still in his possession. The master would listen to that recital of the steward's transactions and question him thereon. The master was the listener, or auditor. This explains the derivation of the word auditing from the Latin word (audiré, which is 'to listen'), which acquired a secondary meaning: 'One who satisfies himself as to the truth of accountability of another' (Dandago 2009:95). This also manifests in the book of Luke 16:1 in the Bible when Jesus told his disciples about the parable of the shrewd manager who was summoned by his master to orally account for his management activities. In the end, the manager lost his job as he could not account.

In the modern world, because of the global financial crisis, various corporate failures such as the collapse of Enron and WorldCom and, locally in South Africa, the collapse of Saambou, Fedsure, Fidentia and Regal Bank and the public concern over the apparent lack of effective boards and management, the importance of corporate governance in both the public and private sectors has been increasingly acknowledged (Mallin 2010:2; Moloi & Barac 2009:49; Truter 2007:1). These factors have contributed to the explosion of interest in corporate governance. Improving corporate governance is now receiving significant attention from almost every sector of society (Rezaee 2010:48). Many private and public-sector organisations worldwide view corporate governance as a business imperative (Truter 2007:1).

Many governance frameworks have been developed around the globe to guide the implementation of best governance practices. These include the combined code on corporate governance in the United Kingdom (UK), Malaysia code on corporate governance, criteria for controls in canada and committee of sponsoring organisation internal control – integrated framework in the United States of America (USA) (Mallin 2010:2). However, the framework to be applied in this study is based on the governance model for South Africa as set out in the King report III (IoDSA 2009).

Corporate governance framework in South Africa

Whilst many organisations around the globe have embraced good governance for many years, it was only in 1994 that the King report on corporate governance, which is regarded as a seminal work on corporate governance in South Africa, was issued (Jackson & Stent 2010; Moloi & Barac 2009:49). The report was a consequence of the establishment of a Committee on Corporate Governance in 1992. The Committee was formed under the auspices of the Institute of Directors in Southern Africa (IoDSA) (Mallin 2010:2). Chaired by Mervyn King, the committee produced the King report on Corporate Governance late in 1994. The King report Committee was similar to the notion of the Cadbury committee in the United Kingdom (UK) but with wider terms of reference (Naidoo 2009:32). Unlike the Cadbury Committee, which was disbanded on completion of its mandate, the King Committee continued to exist after completing its first report.

As a result, when the need to update the King report I arose due to globalisation in the area of corporate governance, the growth of information and communication technology (ICT) and e-commerce together with legislative developments in South Africa, it was imperative to draw upon the expertise of the committee. Significant corporate failures such as Enron and the demise of South African companies such as Regal Bank added momentum and urgency to the drafting of the King report II in 2002 (Moloi & Barac 2009:49). The third report on corporate governance in South Africa became necessary because of the new *Companies Act, (Act No. 7 of 2008)* and changes in international governance trends (IoDSA 2009:5). Launched on 01 September 2009 by the institute of directors, the King report III officially came into effect on 01 March 2010. It heralded a new era in which risk management, internal auditing and recorded information were regarded as important. The King report III has nine chapters. Chapters 3, 4, 5 and 7 are relevant to this study as they deal with an audit committee, risk management, information management and internal auditing. Furthermore, the chapters provide valuable guidance on how the various processes can be integrated.

The King report III (IoDSA 2009) recognises the importance of including information as an integral part of corporate governance as information is regarded as an enabler of business. In terms of the King report III, people responsible for organisational governance must be able to rely on competent and trustworthy internal resources, capable of accurately assessing the effectiveness of the processes in place to manage and mitigate risks (Institute of internal auditors 2009:1). The King report III applies to all private and public entities in South Africa. The principles contained in the King report III were, therefore, drafted so that they can be applied by every entity and, in doing so, achieve good governance across the entire economic spectrum in South Africa (Prinsloo & Pieterse 2009:53).

A shortcoming of the King report III (IoDSA 2009) is that much emphasis has been placed on information technology (IT) as if the concept embraces all information-management matters. Even though the emphasis of the King report III is more on information-communication technology (ICT) than the other branches of information management, there is a strong link between this framework and other theories of records management. The King report III draws the attention to this imperative in chapter 5, clause 6, which deals with management of information assets: 'The board should ensure that information assets are managed effectively.' Essentially, the King report III stresses that an organisation's information is in itself a company asset. Thus, the company's directors are accountable for strategically managing and protecting this information asset to extract optimum value as they should be

doing with any other company asset. The onus is thus on the company's directors to ensure that governance information is supported by efficient and effective records management. It all comes down to the basics of having a proper records-management system in place as it (records management) is the bedrock of information management in organisations and is fundamental to good business practice.

Problem statement

Despite the importance of recorded information in corporate governance and the availability of governance models in many countries, IRMT (1999:64) and Palmer (2000:63) bewail the fact that records management tends to be excluded from components of corporate governance such as auditing and risk management. Records management is often not regarded as essential for good governance by senior management in either the public or private sector. Isa (2009:148) postulates that an integrated records-management and corporate-governance approach is not yet being practised in the public sector world-wide, hence this study attempted to fathom the relationship between records management and corporate governance. Together, records management and other components of corporate governance provide the layer of control that is essential to ensure transparency, accountability and good governance for organisations. Ironically, research shows that some areas of public administration are reluctant to embrace the contribution that records management can make to corporate governance (Australian National Audit Office 2003:21; Isa 2009:133). When a records-management system breaks down, the consequences for corporate governance are serious. Typical symptoms, according to IRMT (1999), include the following:

- Monitoring systems are inadequate and information is difficult to access.
- Votes ledgers are not kept properly and an important tool for expenditure control is lost.
- Accounts are not produced on time, rendering them of limited value for expenditure control and monitoring. (p. 65)

Research purpose and objectives

The general purpose of this study was to explore the relationship between records management and corporate governance in the public sector of South Africa with a view to entrench the culture of good corporate governance. The specific research objectives were to:

- Investigate the relationship between records management and internal auditing in governmental bodies of South Africa.
- Establish whether governmental bodies in South Africa have set up functioning internal-audit committees that include records-management practitioners.
- Investigate the role of leadership in records management and corporate governance in governmental bodies of South Africa.
- Investigate the availability of systems to manage information assets.

Research methodology

In order to explore relationship between records management and corporate governance in the public sector of South Africa, this study relied on a quantitative approach and triangulated data-collection methods in order to enhance the validity of the findings. This study utilised a self-administered questionnaire directed to records managers and internal auditors of governmental bodies in South Africa as the principal instrument for data collection. Data collected via questionnaires were supplemented through interviews with purposively selected external auditors of governmental bodies at the Auditor-General of South Africa's office.

The population of the study consisted of governmental bodies in South Africa (national departments, provincial departments, municipalities and statutory bodies). The stakeholder database of the Auditor-General of South Africa, which listed 283 municipalities, 37 national government departments, 108 provincial government departments in all nine provinces and 30 constitutional bodies or public entities, was used as a sampling frame. The population was divided into strata of municipalities, national departments, provincial departments and public entities to ensure that it is representative. Municipalities and provincial departments were further grouped into sub-strata according to their respective provinces. Since the population was large, sampling was conducted to ensure that the final sample size was manageable.

Though it is at times presumed that, when determining the size of a sample, a 10% sample should be fine in most cases (Seaberg 1988; Grinnell & Williams 1990 cited in Ngulube 2005), this study utilised a mathematical formula, which is based on sampling theory, for determining sample size. In this regard, a Raosoft sample size calculator (Raosoft 2012) was used to calculate the sample size at a margin error of 95%. As a result, a proportional sample size of 37% (171) was taken from the population. In other words, the sample in each stratum was taken in proportion to the size of the stratum (see Table 1 for the sampling proportion). The advantage with proportional stratified sampling is that it makes possible the representativeness of a particular segment of the population (Singleton & Straits 2010:183). For each governmental body selected in the sample, the participants consisted of either a records manager or an internal auditor who was assigned to complete the questionnaire.

Data collected via questionnaires were supplemented with telephonic interviews conducted with four purposively selected auditors from the Auditor-General of South Africa (AGSA).

TABLE 1: Stratified proportional sampling.

Stratum	Elements in population	%	Proportional sampling
Municipalities	283	37	105
National departments	37	37	14
Provincial departments	10	37	40
Statutory bodies	30	37	12
Total	-	-	171

Data analysis and findings of the study

This section analyses and presents the results of the data obtained via questionnaires and interviews. Data analysis is a key aspect of any research, and it helps with drawing conclusions and generalisations from the data as it relates to a problem statement (Creswell 2009:152). Of the 171 questionnaires distributed, only 94 were returned, representing a 55% response rate. Quantitative data from questionnaires were analysed, using different analytical tools and computer software such as Microsoft Excel® Spreadsheet and PHstat to produce the graphs. Qualitative data from interview results were analysed manually and used to substantiate numerical data. Results are presented through written descriptions, numerical summarisations and tables. The results are presented according to research objectives outlined in Section 4. It is worth mentioning that the data presented in this study do not reveal the identity of any individual or institution that participated in this study as anonymity was promised during data collection.

Availability and composition of audit committees in governmental bodies

The purpose of this study objective was to examine the establishment and composition of audit committees in the public sector and to investigate the involvement of records managers in the committees. Chapter 3 of King report III (IoDSA 2009) recommends that organisations should ensure that they establish effective and independent audit committees. The audit committee fulfils a vital role in corporate governance. Amongst other things, they ensure the integrity of integrated reporting and internal financial controls.

According to Ferreira (2007:4), in order to ensure that organisations increase good corporate governance, a well-functioning audit committee should be in place. Ferreira (2007) defines an audit committee as:

> standing committee of the management created to provide an oversight function on behalf of the management with regard to financial reporting process, internal control, risk management, auditing and governance process. (p. 27)

The King report III (IoDSA 2009) recommends the establishment of an audit committee for the private and public sectors. Principle 3.1 of the King report III calls for the board or management to ensure that the organisation has an effective and independent audit committee (IoDSA 2009). The role of the audit committee is to function as an independent advisory body to the municipal councils, accounting officers, chief information officers, directors, board members, political office-bearers, et cetera on matters relating to risk management, accounting policies, internal controls and audits.

Findings are presented according to the following sub-themes:

- the availability of audit committees
- the composition and skills of audit committees.

The availability of audit committees

The respondents were asked whether their organisations had established audit committees. Results reflect that 77.7% (73) indicated that their organisations had established audit committees as compared with 22.3% (21) that did not. As illustrated in Table 2, a study by Sigidi (2012) indicated that 254 (91%) of 278 municipalities had established audit committees by March 2012.

The composition and skills of audit committee members

According to Ferreira (2007:98), the actual size of the audit committee depends on the size and complexity of the organisation. The King report III (IoDSA 2009) recommends that the audit committee should consist of at least three members. In this study, it was discovered that the number of the audit-committee members in governmental bodies ranged from three to eighteen. However, some respondents indicated that not all people who attended the audit committee meetings were members. Of the 94 respondents, only 10 indicated that records management was represented in the audit committee through the head of information technology (IT).

However, none indicated that a member of the records-management team was part of the audit committee. The respondents indicated that they did not think that records-management issues were addressed in the audit committee meetings, as compared to auditing, risk management, supply-chain management and IT. Others argued that audit-committee members in their organisations just glorify the committee as there is no value added. They further indicated that audit-committee members had minimal knowledge of records management. This supports Ferreira (2007:90)'s argument that, in South Africa, many audit-committee members lack the necessary skills, knowledge and experience to perform their duties optimally. Even authors such as Isa (2009:133) and Janse van Rensburg and Coetzee (2010:29) share sentiments that many audit-committee members do not possess the necessary skills, knowledge and experience to act as audit-committee members in either the public or private sector.

The relationship between records management and internal audit

The need to keep records is partly determined by the necessity to meet internal and external audit requirements. These records are significant because they summarise operations and set out policies. Such records have to do with the receipt, transfer, payment, adjustments or encumbrance of funds which may need to be retained to meet audit requirements. The internal audit function plays a critical role in corporate governance by providing a wide spectrum of assurance. It is the in-house resource for the accurate and objective assessment and assurance of information as reliable and trustworthy. The internal audit function may be outsourced if the organisation requires assistance to develop its internal capacity and the management has determined that this is feasible or cost-effective.

De Jager (2006:3) points out that the internal audit function in South Africa has grown significantly as a result of the release of the King report III (IoDSA 2009). Internal auditing plays an important role in any country's public sector and, in particular, in organisations' corporate governance, internal control structure, risk management and financial reporting (Janse van Rensburg & Coetzee 2010:29).

The questionnaire sought to establish whether governmental bodies in South Africa had established internal audit units. It is believed that effective internal audit units may prepare governmental bodies to be ready for external auditors. Result show that 74.5% (70) had internal audit units as compared to 25.5% (24) which did not have. Those that did not have an internal audit unit were mainly provincial government departments and indicated that the Premier's offices had a transversal role in internal auditing for provinces. In this regard, the internal audit unit in the Premier's Office was responsible for the entire province. However, others did indicate that the internal audit function was outsourced in their organisations.

In support of the finding above, in a study by Sigidi (2012) as reflected in Table 3, it was found that 220 of 278 municipalities have established internal audit units.

It is assumed that a close working relationship between records management and internal auditing can improve the effectiveness of corporate governance. However, this relationship has not been established in most governmental bodies. Respondents indicated that records management and auditing did not always work hand in glove. Although respondents indicated that records management is a

TABLE 2: The establishment of audit committee in municipalities (N = 278).

South African Province	Total number of municipalities	Number of municipalities with audit committees	%
Eastern Cape	45	43	96
Free State	24	19	79
Gauteng	12	12	100
KwaZulu-Natal	61	59	97
Limpopo	30	29	97
Mpumalanga	21	20	95
Northern Cape	32	24	75
North West	23	20	87
Western Cape	30	28	93
Total	**278**	**254**	**91**

TABLE 3: The establishment of internal-audit units in municipalities (N = 278).

South African Province	Total number of municipalities	Number of municipalities with internal audit units	%
Eastern Cape	45	30	67
Free State	24	24	100
Gauteng	12	9	75
KwaZulu-Natal	61	61	100
Limpopo	30	30	100
Mpumalanga	21	20	95
Northern Cape	32	9	28
North West	23	14	61
Western Cape	30	23	77
Total	**278**	**220**	**79**

vital ingredient in the success of auditing, the majority of respondents 72.3% (68) indicated that the scope of internal auditing in their organisations did not include records management. Reports by the internal audit unit can provide the organisation with a key source of information on the entity's performance. Despite the availability of internal audit units, governmental bodies continued to receive negative audit results from the Auditor-General of South Africa (AGSA).

Results of interviews with AGSA indicate that the major contributors to negative audit opinions in governmental bodies is a lack of supporting evidence (records) for financial statement items and a lack of knowledge amongst finance staff to properly deal with accounting issues. A respondent from AGSA indicated that an audit can only be conducted if the auditee has proper records that are available for viewing and that supports the balances and transactions disclosed in the annual financial statements. According to the respondents, the records that are mostly required for the audit by AGSA include invoices supporting expenditure, memo's or approvals by relevant officials to procure the expenditure, journal vouchers substantiating entries passed in books, trial balances and general ledger of the entity, salary advices and payment evidence.

The role of leadership in corporate governance and records management

Adequate leadership involvement and oversight that will set the tone at the top of the institution and create an environment conducive to good corporate governance and service delivery is vital. If key officials such as heads of departments, chief financial officers, chief executive officers and municipal managers support corporate governance and are available during the audits to deal with audit-related matters and clear these in timely manner, it will go a long way towards assisting the organisations. It will also go a long way towards avoiding qualifications in auditing because they (leadership) can gain earlier notices of audit findings to take corrective action before the final conclusions leading to the audit opinion.

When asked about the role of leadership in corporate governance and records management, only 85% (80) of the respondents indicated that leadership was supposed to play a monitoring and oversight role, which did in reality not happen. This, according to respondents, would ensure that information is made available during the auditing cycle to ensure effective corporate governance. The respondents emphasised that the visibility of leadership was also of outmost importance as it may contribute to audit outcomes. The respondents indicated that the availability and visibility of leadership during the audit cycle would ensure that records are retrieved by relevant officials when requested by auditors. As well, leadership will be able to see the value of records management for the auditing process. As a result, leadership may then support records-management programmes in their organisation.

This role was confirmed by respondents from AGSA as they felt that leadership was supposed to be available to discuss any matter that auditors bring to their attention. In this way, leadership would be able to address queries before it became too late.

The availability of systems to manage information assets

According to clause 35 of the King Report III (IoDSA 2009), information management encompasses:

- The protection of information (information security).
- Management of information (information management).
- the protection of personal information processed by companies (information privacy).
- The King report III views information contained in records as the most important information assets as they are evidence of business activities. Therefore, there is a requirement in terms of clause 37 for the board to ensure that there are systems in place for the management of records. (n.p.)

The availability of a records-management unit in governmental bodies goes a long way towards helping with the implementation of policies and securing information assets. It is essential to manage the transactions, information and knowledge necessary to sustain an organisation. In this regard, records can easily be retrieved when requested by auditors or whoever seeks information. The study also sought to establish whether governmental bodies had established records management programmes. Results revealed that 83% (78) of respondents had records-management units as compared to 17% (16) that did not have any. Those that did not have records-management units indicated that records management were the responsibility of each unit and in some cases of records creators. In this regard, it was not clear from the respondents whether records were protected against destruction or unauthorised access. However, those with established programmes indicated that only records-management staff had access to the storage, and other staff members could access records on request.

With regard to the level of records managers in the organisation, it was depressing to note that 39.4% (37) of respondents indicated that their organisation did not have a records manager whereas 20.2% (19) indicated that the records manager was at a junior level, 26.6% (25) indicated a manager at middle-management level and only 8.5% (8) indicated that they have a records manager at senior management level. No governmental body had a records manager at top-management level. This partly explains why records-management professionals were not invited to audit-committee meetings as indicated by respondents.

Discussion of the results

The results of the study revealed that most governmental bodies (70%) have established internal audit units. This is almost in line with the results of a survey by Sigidi (2012) that found that 79% of municipalities in South Africa had established internal audit functions. This indicates the increasing recognition of the internal-audit function in the public sector in South Africa. However, it would seem that the establishment of internal-audit functions in most governmental bodies was just for ceremonial and compliance purposes as governmental bodies continue to experience problems such as negative audit results. The results indicate that records management could play an enabling role in auditing process. For example, auditors rely on records to support their findings. Therefore, records management supports the entire accounting function as the beginning of accounting cycle starts with the creation of a record. However, it is clear from the results that records-management and auditing units did not always work in unison as the majority of respondents indicated that the scope of internal auditing in their organisations did not include records management.

The study also found that most governmental bodies did establish audit committees. Not surprisingly, records management was not represented in the audit committees in most governmental bodies. In cases where it was represented, it was through IT officials who did not have enough background information about records management. The assumption is that the lack of expertise is related to the fact that most records managers in governmental bodies were at middle-management and junior levels. Therefore, records managers were not invited to audit-committee meetings as in most instances, only senior managers and higher were required to attend. As a result, there is a possibility that records-management risks were not addressed in these meetings. This study also revealed the failure of individual committee members to contribute to committees due to a lack of knowledge, especially in information management. Instead of records management being a standing item on the agenda of audit-committee meetings, the function did not feature anywhere as indicated by the respondents.

The results indicate that the leadership has a supportive and oversight role to play in records management and corporate governance. However, this was not the case in most governmental bodies. It would seem that leadership always shifts this responsibility to junior staff members. Perusal of AGSA reports revealed that governmental bodies that achieved good corporate governance had the following in common:

- the commitment and single-minded intention of their leadership to lead and set the right tone from the top
- basic internal controls in place
- daily, monthly and quarterly reconciliations of financial records
- a working partnership between leadership, internal audit and audit committees that ensured effective oversight.

Conclusion and recommendations

It is clear from the results that the absence of proper record-keeping partly contributes to negative audit results and impacts negatively on the auditing process. Records management, just like internal audit, plays an integral role in good corporate governance. Auditors ascertain the quality of organisations' operations by relying on records to verify their findings. Therefore, well-managed records provide the framework for the management of all other resources. Unless records are managed as part of the monitoring process, the objective of the system is not achieved, and the control mechanism fails to inform (Akotia 1996:7). Public records, if managed well, have the potential to provide a meaningful resource by which both the executive and civil-service machinery can present themselves as honest, well-meaning and accountable.

It would seem from the study that many public organisations in South Africa still regard corporate governance as a compliance issue. Organisations need to recognise that corporate governance has a pivotal role to play in attracting foreign direct investment and in ensuring that organisations are sustainable. Compelling organisations to comply with the King Report III (IoDSA 2009) is not enough. If organisations commit themselves to good corporate governance and if leadership set the right tone, it may augur very well for the country's future. As Isa (2009:133) would attest, if records management is integrated with other governance components, it will break its narrow roots and become an even more valued function of general management.

This study calls for records management practitioners to work together with other disciplines (stakeholders) such as auditors, risk managers and IT professionals. The scope of internal audit should also include records management. For records management to contribute positively to corporate governance, this study recommends that records management should be a standing item at audit-committee meetings. In that way, records-management issues may be identified and addressed before the external auditors arrive at the organisation to do their audit. Furthermore, records-management professionals should form part of internal audit committees. Audit-committee members should also be inducted in records management and made aware of the legislation that regulates records management in governmental bodies and its potential contribution to good corporate governance. Audit committee can also play a role in overseeing internal audit to ensure that all corporate-governance components are monitored. Also, audit committees may provide an interface between management and external auditors. The overall role of audit committees could be to ask relevant questions about the overall corporate-governance process. The committee should be aware that IT does not constitute information management, but it is an enabler and a component within information management. AGSA could establish a partnership with the National Archives and Records Service of South Africa, which has a regulatory role to manage records in the public sector of South Africa. In this regard, as Bhana (2008) would attest, AGSA can play a role in reporting cases of poor records management in government institutions to the National Archives, which may in turn assist the affected institutions in setting up proper records-management programmes. Furthermore, AGSA could also test specifically for compliance of key aspects of the applicable legislation pertaining to records management. Finally, the King Committee should consider the revision of chapter five of the King Report III to explicitly include the management of records.

Acknowledgement

Competing interests

The authors declare that they have no financial or personal relationship(s) that may have inappropriately influenced them in writing this article.

Authors' contributions

P.N. (University of South Africa) was the project leader, and M.N. (University of South Africa) conceptualised the research, collected and analysed data and compiled the article in collaboration with P.N. (University of South Africa).

References

Akotia, P., 1996, 'The management of public sector financial records: The implications for good government', University of Ghana, Legon, viewed 10 January 2012, from http://www.acarm.org/documents/financial.pdf

Australian National Audit Office, 2003, 'Record keeping in large Commonwealth organisations', Australian National Audit Office, Canberra, viewed 11 February 2012, from www.anao.gov.au/uploads/documents/2003-04_Audit_Report_7.pdf

Bhana, P., 2008, 'The contribution of proper record-keeping towards auditing and risk mitigation: Auditor-General of South Africa's perspective', paper presented at the 3rd Annual General Meeting of the South African Records Management Forum, Midrand, South Africa, 10–11 November', viewed 15 June 2013, from http://www.khunkhwane.co.za/uploads/The%20Contribution%20of%20Proper%20Records%20Keeping%20towards%20auditing%20and%20risk%20mitigation%20%20Auditor%20General%20Perspective.pdf

Barac, K., 2001, 'Corporate governance in the public sector', Auditing SA, viewed 28 February 2012, from http://www.saiga.co.za/publications-auditingsa.htm

Creswell, J.W., 2009, Research design: Qualitative, quantitative, and mixed methods approaches, Sage Publications, Thousand Oaks.

Dandago, K.L. (ed.), 2009, Advanced accounting theory and practice, Adonis & Abbey, London.

De Jager, H., 2006, 'Editorial: Auditor-general', Auditing SA, Summer, 1–3, viewed 15 January 2012, from http://www.saiga.co.za/documents/publications/summer%202006-7/01%20Editorial%20-%20herman%20de%20jager.pdf

Ferreira, I., 2007, 'The role of internal auditors in the professional development of audit committee members', Masters of Commerce Dissertation, Dept. of Auditing, University of South Africa, Pretoria.

Institute of Directors in Southern Africa (IoDSA), 2009, King report on corporate governance for South Africa, Institute of Directors in Southern Africa, Sandton.

Institute of Internal Auditors, 2009, 'A new level of audit committee involvement', Tone at the top 44, 1–3.

International Records Management Trust (IRMT), 1999, Managing financial records, International Records Management Trust, London, viewed 27 January 2012, from www.irmt.org/documents/educ...sector.../IRMT_financial_recs.doc

International Records Management Trust (IRMT), 2001, Principles and practices in managing financial records: A reference model and assessment tool, International Records Management Trust, London.

Isa, A.M., 2009, 'Records management and the accountability of governance', PhD thesis, Humanities Advanced Technology and Information Institute, University of Glasgow, Glasgow, viewed 13 April 2012, from http://theses.gla.ac.uk/1421/

Jackson, R D.C. & Stent, W.J., 2010, Auditing notes for South African students, 7th edn., LexisNexis, Durban.

Janse van Rensburg, C. & Coetzee, P., 2010/11, 'The internal audit capability model endorsed by South African public sector legislation and guidance', Auditing SA, Summer, 29–31.

Mallin, C.A., 2010, Corporate governance, 3rd edn., Oxford University Press, Oxford.

Moloi, T. & Barac, K., 2009, 'Corporate governance compliance reporting in the annual reports of listed South African companies', Auditing SA, Summer, 49–51.

Naidoo, R., 2009, Corporate governance: an essential guide for South African companies, 2nd edn., LexisNexis, Durban.

Ngulube, P., 2005, 'Research procedures used by Master of Information Studies students at the University of Natal in the period 1982 to 2002 with special reference to their sampling techniques and survey response rates: A methodological discourse', International Information and Library Review 37(2), 127–143. http://dx.doi.org/10.1016/j.iilr.2005.04.002

Palmer, M., 2000, 'Records management and accountability versus corruption, fraud and maladministration', Records Management Journal 10(2), 61–72. http://dx.doi.org/10.1108/EUM0000000007256

Prinsloo, P. & Pieterse, L, 2009, 'King III in the public sector', Auditing SA, Summer, 53–56.

Raosoft, 2012, Sampling calculator, viewed 03 May 2012, from http://www.raosoft.com/samplesize.html

Republic of South Africa, 1999, Public Finance Management Act, No 1 of 1999, viewed 12 April 2012, from http://www.info.gov.za/view/DownloadFileAction?id=70577

Rezaee, Z., 2010, 'The importance of internal audit opinions', Internal Auditors, April, 47–50.

Seaberg, J.R., 1988, 'Utilizing sampling procedures', in R.M. Grinnell (ed.), Social work research and evaluation, 3rd edn., pp. 240–259, Peacock, Itasca.

Sigidi, M., 2012, 'Operation clean audit for 2014', paper presented at the Auditor-General of South Africa's records management seminar, Kempton Park, South Africa, 20 April.

Singleton, R.A. & Straits, B.C., 2010, Approaches to social research, 5th edn., Oxford University Press, New York.

Truter, M., 2007, 'Implementation of enterprise risk management as a tool for improving corporate governance within the public sector', MBL Dissertation, Dept. of Business Leadership, University of South Africa, Midrand.

Willis, A., 2005, 'Corporate governance and management of information and records', Records Management Journal 15(2), 86–97. http://dx.doi.org/10.1108/09565690510614238

11

Proposing a competitive intelligence (CI) framework for Public Service departments to enhance service delivery

Author:
Nisha Sewdass[1]

Affiliation:
[1]Department of Information Science, University of Pretoria, South Africa

Correspondence to:
Nisha Sewdass

Email:
nisha.sewdass@up.ac.za

Postal address:
Private Bag X20, Hatfield, Pretoria 0028, South Africa

Background: The aim of public service departments in South Africa is to improve service delivery through the transformation and improvement of human resources and the improvement of service delivery practices. Furthermore, it is important for the public service sector in South Africa to improve the quality of its service delivery, not only by comparing its performance with other sectors within South Africa but also by positioning itself amongst the best in the world. This can be achieved by benchmarking with other global industries and by implementing the most recent competitive intelligence strategies, tools and techniques. The environment of the public service organisations consists of competitive forces that impact the functioning of these organisations.

Objectives: This article focuses on proposing competitive intelligence-related strategies, tools and techniques for gathering and analysing information in the public service departments in South Africa in order to enhance service delivery.

Method: The study was qualitative in nature and was divided into two components, namely, (1) theoretical – through an extensive review of the literature and (2) empirical – an ethnographic study at the chosen public service department, the Department of Home Affairs (DHA). Ethnographic interviews with management-level staff, focus groups and document analysis were used to obtain adequate information to determine the current state of public service delivery in South Africa.

Results: The results of the study was the development of a new competitive intelligence-related framework for gathering and analysing information, and it represents a formal and systematic process of informing managers in public service departments about critical issues that these departments face or are likely to experience in future.

Conclusion: The strategic planning tools and techniques of this framework will fill the gap that exists in public service departments. Once this framework has been implemented, it could assist these departments to improve service delivery to its citizens.

Introduction

The aim of public service departments in most countries is to lead the modernisation of the public service by assisting government departments to implement their management policies, systems and structural solutions within a generally applicable framework of norms and standards in order to improve service delivery (National Treasury 2004). Furthermore, public service departments exist to serve the needs of the citizens of the country, and all citizens have the right to expect high-quality public services that meet their needs. The aim of public service departments in South Africa is to improve service delivery through the transformation and improvement of human resources and the improvement of service-delivery practices.

Public service organisations need to perform types of strategic planning activities similar to their private-sector counterparts. These activities include environmental analysis, resource analysis, goal formulation, strategy formulation and organisational or systems design. For the organisations to accomplish these activities, they require a vast amount of internal and external data, and this data have to be analysed in terms of its objectiveness and quality. This task is best carried out by the competitive intelligence (CI) function (Wagner 2003:70).

It is important for the public service sector in South Africa to improve the quality of its service delivery, not only by comparing its performance with other sectors within South Africa but also by positioning itself amongst the best in the world. This can be achieved by benchmarking with other global industries and by implementing the most recent CI strategies, tools and techniques.

Lenz and Engledow (1986:329) suggest that the 'essential character of organisational environments may be changing in ways that require new modes of thought and analysis'. The authors further indicate that mounting pressure is placed on senior-level managers and corporate staff in organisations to develop better methods for assessing the organisations' environments. Various models for environmental analysis that could assist organisations in strategic decision making have been identified and could be used by all types of organisations. It further relates to the environment of the organisation which consists of competitive forces that impact on the functioning of the organisation.

In light of the above, this article focuses on a proposed CI framework for gathering and analysing information in the public service departments in South Africa in order to enhance service delivery.

Background to the study

In South Africa, the public service departments have undergone significant changes in order to rectify the injustices of the past. These changes have meant that several processes which have rationalised functions, structures, legislation and resources have been adopted. Despite much progress, it is noticed that government does not have sufficient capacity to deliver and sustain a quality service to its citizens (Khumalo 2003:20–24). Many weaknesses exist within service departments and the customers very rarely, if at all, experience the 'Wow Effect' after visiting these departments for service. The public service departments are the sole suppliers or providers of certain products or services that the citizens need. They have no direct competition, and they usually do not close down, nor do they depend on the customer for their survival. As a result, one sees little emphasis on improving customer relations or service delivery. Even when service-delivery initiatives are implemented in these departments, they usually fail to show any benefit since there is no motivation to change the way things are done. This means that the customer is left with poor service and very little bargaining power for better or more effective service from these departments.

Public service organisations are structured and operate quite differently from private-sector organisations. The key difference, with respect to CI implementation, is the lack of profit motivation in the public sector. Public Services are structured to be bureaucracies with a budget that is drawn down to provide a specific service. Management incentives and rewards tend to be related more to budget management and budget size than to organisational effectiveness (Wagner 2003:71).

The public services are characterised by the intangibility of services and the existence of multiple service objectives. The consumer, or user, has little influence on the organisation because the organisation is often a local monopoly and user payments are not a primary source of funds. These organisations sometimes fail to analyse their competitive position in terms of funds, staff, other resources and even users. This is largely because they do not utilise the basic concepts of strategic management. Often they are unable to plan strategically because they lack a clear definition of the

service organisation's mission and goals (Greenberg 1982:81). This provides more of a motivation for the public services to implement the techniques practiced by businesses such as CI.

Because a study of this nature has not been done in public service departments and because of the fact that very little has been written about CI in public service or non-profit organisations, the results from this study should fill the gaps that exist in this area not only in South Africa but globally.

The Department of Home Affairs is one of the largest public service departments, and it was selected as it is the one public service departments that every citizen is reliant upon, from 'birth to death'. They hold a monopoly over the services that they offer, and citizens are compelled by law to utilise these services in order to ensure that proper public administration is practiced in the country. The results obtained from this study, however, will be applicable in all public service departments in South Africa.

The statement of the problem

This article forms part of a larger study that focused on ascertaining how competitive intelligence tools and techniques could be implemented in public service departments in South Africa to enhance the delivery of services. For the purpose of this paper, the focus will be on one of the aims of the study, namely, designing a CI-related framework for gathering and analysing information that can be used in all public service departments in South Africa to improve service delivery.

Related literature

Since CI is a relatively new management concept, it is necessary to ensure that an accurate understanding and definition of CI is obtained. Several terms such as Business Intelligence, Competitor Intelligence and even Industrial Espionage are found in literature to express the concept of CI. The basis of CI is knowing the difference between information and intelligence. Executives usually have to read through several reports and proposals before making decisions, and it is often found that they are overwhelmed with information and lack intelligence that will enable them to make more efficient decisions. Therefore, it can be said that companies that are able to turn information into intelligence will succeed.

A comprehensive definition of CI is 'the legal collection and analysis of information regarding the capabilities, vulnerabilities, and intensions of business competitors conducted by using "open sources" and ethical inquiry,' (SCIP 2008).

Kahaner (1997:12–14) eloquently discusses what the new world of CI is by showing how companies efficiently, systematically and economically collect information; then they analyse and use it to make decisions. This understanding can assist the decision makers in the public sector in making more informed decisions concerning the improvement of the quality of services offered to citizens.

CI is about differentiating between catching up and breaking out of an industry and then positioning oneself beyond best practices to invent new practices. It is about understanding the difference between 'getting better' and 'getting different' and then learning how to get different in ways that will stun and thrill customers. It is towards this that the Public Services in South Africa should strive. Hamel (2000) discussed these issues as well as the challenges that many companies, such as the Public Services, face in reinventing themselves not just in times of crisis but continually. He also provides an understanding of how companies can continue to grow and thrive in ever-changing turbulent times such as the situation in South Africa at present.

It is important for managers to understand the landscape within which the service sector finds itself. This will allow them to be better able to realise the contribution that they can make within this competitive landscape and to realise how they can benefit from a variety of strategic and tactical actions that are well suited for the service sector (Rodie & Martin 2001:19). Furthermore, such an understanding would provide managers with the reasons why the service sector should adopt an entrepreneurial attitude to improve its performance. This attitude is essential in order to provide sufficient background for commitment to the CI process in this sector.

Public service departments and other non-profit-making organisations also go through strategic planning processes regularly, just as their profit-making counterparts do. To improve the efficacy of the strategic planning process, the CI process can assist in collecting the necessary information to support decisions (Horne & Parks 2004:36). Whilst it must be acknowledged that CI alone is not the answer, it can and does provide external background and fundamental perspectives that can complement the traditional inward focus that Public Services usually have. This, then, can become a valuable tool for enhancing the quality of services delivered.

Competitive Intelligence (CI) has become increasingly important for organisations in the private sector, or profit-making organisations, because the level and intensity of competition has increased in recent years. CI helps organisations in the business environment to understand and respond to their competitors and the competitive environment (Horne & Parks 2004:33). This increase in the level and intensity of competition has also affected the public sector or non-profit-making organisations such as public service departments.

Whilst it can be argued that CI is of limited value or importance to public-sector organisations since there is a lack of profit motivation in this sector, and the functioning and structure of these organisations differ from the private-sector organisations to which CI principles are usually applied, it is believed that public sector organisations are becoming more like traditional profit-making organisations. Given the current economic environment within which these organisations function, the increased scrutiny in the operations of these organisations, the increased level of accountability placed on them and the new and improved service delivery options that are now available to these organisations, it is suggested that CI can benefit these organisations on a similar level as it does private-sector organisations (Horne & Parks 2004:36).

CI has the ability to justify its existence in profit-making organisations with regard to profit margins:

> It can improve the organisation's short term profits by improving the quality of tactical decisions and can increase its long term value by guiding management to make superior strategic decisions that increase shareholder value. (Wagner 2003:70)

This author further points out that CI fits within the operations of public-sector organisations only if it maximises value for the organisation's stakeholders. This refers to improving the quality of life of the general public or specific targeted demographic groups.

Research methodology

This study was qualitative in nature and was divided into two components:

- theoretical – through an extensive review of the literature
- empirical – the ethnographic study conducted at the chosen public service department, namely the Department of Home Affairs (DHA).

A comprehensive literature review or document analysis was conducted to identify the current state of service delivery in public services departments in South Africa, particularly in the Department of Home Affairs. The literature review also assisted the researcher in providing a better understanding of Competitive Intelligence, its functioning and its benefits for organisations in general and, more specifically, for its applicability in public service departments.

Ethnographic interviews with management-level staff, focus groups and document analysis were also used to obtain adequate information to determine the current state of public service delivery in South Africa. These tools have ensured that scientific methods have been followed and that the results obtained from the study will have meaning and value.

CI tools that were developed in a previous study by Clarke (2001:230–235) were then adapted for their usefulness in the Public Service. Whilst these CI tools are useful in business environments, the researcher adapted them for use in this instance. Benchmarking was used for this purpose to determine the best practices and tools used for CI in other service-providing organisations. This helped the researcher to select the most appropriate tools that can be used in the public service departments to improve the delivery of services. In the final stage of the study, a new CI-related framework for gathering and analysing information that can enhance the quality of service delivery was developed by theoretical and strategic means.

It is the assumption of the researcher that, if this framework is implemented, it could assist the departments to improve service delivery to its citizens.

It was essential to firstly identify the various form of competition that public service departments encounter before an appropriate CI framework could be designed to address these forms of competition.

Competitive realities at the Department of Home Affairs

Diversity of competition is most prominent in the Service Sector organisations such as the Department of Home Affairs (DHA), and the competition can be 'anything and everything' that will turn the customer away from an organisation's services (Sawyer 2002:7).

Table 1 provides a summary of the competitive realities identified from the findings of the empirical study at the DHA, and it also indicates some of the phenomena uncovered in each of these forms of competition. These are also indicated within the broader themes which determined the empirical study at the DHA. These themes can also be regarded as the forms of competition that the DHA experiences.

Greenberg (1982:86) suggests that, 'once an organisation has considered the various areas in which it competes for resources and users and identifies its competitors, it must decide on its strategy'. Furthermore, when resources are limited and scarce in the environment, the organisation with the most effective competitive strategies usually survives. This makes essential the identification of the most appropriate tools and techniques so that it can afford the DHA a competitive advantage.

Competitive Intelligence (CI) tools and techniques for the Department of Home Affairs

The present global environment is confronted with constant change and development as a result of technological innovations and new business developments. Access to information is also increasing, leading to information overload in certain instances. This means that it is increasingly necessary for organisations (and individuals) to have the tools, strategies, techniques and models as well as the skills needed to manage this vast amount of information. Tools for gathering, sorting and analysing information so that it can be converted into actionable intelligence are required to assist CI practitioners in accomplishing their tasks. It is also important to note that, whilst several tools, techniques, and strategies are identified in the literature (Fleisher & Bensoussan 2003; Gieskes 2001:76–79; Marceau & Sawka 2001:160–163; Sandman 2000:69–95), each organisation has to select appropriate tools, techniques and strategies to suit

TABLE 1: Summary of competitive realities at the Department of Home Affairs (DHA).

Competition	Phenomenon identified at the DHA
Strategy (Vision, mission, strategic intent)	• No common vision embraced by all staff • No clear understanding of vision and mission statements • Broad mission statement • No commitment & personal effort from workforce to achieve strategic intent
Structure (Job redesign, restructuring, flow of information)	• Bureaucratic hierarchical structure • Structures increases number of reporting levels • Span of control deviates between departments • Fragmented flow of information
Business processes (Service-delivery activities)	• Civic services – core activity for the DHA • Immigration services • Support services • Poor or lack of financial services and proper financial analysis
Language and communication codes	• Doubtful communication channels • Poor interpersonal communication of managers • Job-related information not communicated to staff • Classification of documents not suitable for sharing and use by all staff • Grapevine ignored as communication tool
Internal policies and procedures	• Some policies are out-dated and no longer relevant • Lack of policies for many areas • Limited input from individuals in policy formulation
Organisational culture	• Weak and unhealthy organisational culture • Lack of sustained organisational culture • No dominant corporate culture visible • 'Hoarding culture' – no sharing and trust amongst staff
Interaction patterns	• Socialising between departments non-existent • Silo functioning of departments – no interaction • Lack of skills transfer due to poor interaction • Lateral interaction between managers • Large quantities of documents, reports, et cetra not utilised by staff – no sharing of information resources
Turnaround programmes	• Too many turnaround programmes • No benefits from previous turnaround programmes • New initiatives identified by turnaround programme • 'Quick wins' identified and attended to
Left field competition	• Sudden changes in demand from DHA • Labour costs for use of consultants • Scarce-skills competition • Competition from third-party service providers • World economic and financial fluctuations • Identity theft • Repositioning the image of the DHA

their unique environment and needs. In certain instances, a range of CI tools may be used in an organisation to ensure that information (intelligence) reaches the users in a form that they can assimilate easily and quickly.

Fleisher & Bensoussan (2003:xviii, 12, 20) state that the analysis of collected information requires creativity and technical knowledge, intuition, models and frameworks. They have discussed over four dozen techniques, tools and frameworks that organisations can utilise in order to obtain the CI that is needed. However, the authors have cautioned against the use of these formal methods as a means of taking 'superficial shortcuts' to management decision making. They also indicate that, whilst these techniques are available and have been used by organisations for many years, there is no one right analytical tool that can solve the problems of every organisation.

The complexity and depth of the analysis and, subsequently, the tools and techniques that will be chosen are dependent on the business situation and the needs of the organisation.

Furthermore, no method will by itself be able to provide all the answers that decision makers need to improve their competitiveness. Therefore, it is advised that appropriate methods be chosen for use in specific situations, and a combination of methods may be more beneficial to obtain optimal results. CI practitioners should guard against repeatedly choosing the same method and tools that they are familiar with. Apart from compromising the quality of the outcome, it can also give the competitor an idea of the organisation's strategic plans especially if they are aware of the techniques or tools on which the organisation consistently relies.

It should also be noted that many tools, techniques and models applicable for CI use are actually the traditional business or managerial tools, techniques and models that have been used in organisations for strategic planning and management decision making. They are based on solid research that has been conducted and are usually backed up by theory but on their own may not be adequate for CI purposes. However, they are flexible enough and with slight modifications and adjustments, creativity and innovative thinking, they can be used successfully in CI activities.

Specific tools and techniques are chosen depending upon various factors such as CI needs, time constraints, financial constraints, staffing limitations, data availability and relative priorities of data (McGonagle & Vella 1993).

The CI tools and techniques all have certain strengths and weaknesses, and it is essential for the managers to be aware of these aspects before using the tools and techniques. This will help them to determine the quality of the intelligence that is obtained. It will also assist them to choose the right combination of tools and techniques to use so that useful intelligence is gained as opposed to using all the tools and techniques that have more limitations than benefits and may not adequately address the needs of the user.

In order to assess the adequacy of CI analysis tools and techniques, Fleisher & Bensoussan (2007:80) developed a unique concept for analysis known as the FAROUT approach. This approach can be used as a guide for the manager to determine which tools and techniques are appropriate for a specific situation. The FAROUT approach is 'based on the premise that for analytical output to be insightful, intelligent, and valuable to business decision makers, it needs to meet a number of common characteristics' (Fleisher & Bensoussan 2007:80). A profile of the strengths and weakness of each tool and technique is also provided that can assist the manager to make an informed choice out of the myriad of tools and techniques that are available.

A 5-point scale is also used to rate the tools and techniques. An assessment of analysis techniques using the FAROUT scheme is indicated in Table 2. By using this means of selecting and using the tools and techniques, the managers can rest assured that the quality of the output will be high and that they will be in a position to make decisions with confidence.

CI is regarded as a tool for decision makers, and in order to support the decision-making process, CI tools and techniques are used to transform the complex data and information into simplified, meaningful intelligence. This usually involves analysis of the data, where tools and techniques of analysis are used. As already established in the ethnographic study (Table 1), the DHA possesses a large quantity of documents, reports and project material that hold very valuable information, but they lack the ability to analyse the information and use it to make informed decisions. Hence, the tools and techniques that are chosen for the DHA can be regarded as CI analysis tools.

Competitive Intelligence (CI) framework for gathering and analysing information at the Department of Home Affairs

Whilst several tools and techniques are available for managers to use, it is important to note that no single tool or technique is able to address the complex situations at the Department of Home Affairs (DHA). Furthermore, some tools and techniques can be used in several situations for a more integrated and linked view of issues. Hence a combination of tools and techniques has been decided upon for the DHA. The CI framework for gathering and analysing information at the DHA is reflected in Figure 1, and it represents a formal and systematic means for informing managers about critical issues that the DHA faces or is likely to experience in future.

TABLE 2: FAROUT elements and assessment scheme.

Element	Rating	5-point rating scale
Future orientation	1	Model's output is not future-oriented. It may be too anchored in the past or present
	5	Model is highly future-focussed
Accuracy	1	The level of accuracy for outputs using this model is low
	5	The requirements of the model leads to the generation of highly accurate outputs
Resource-efficiency	1	Model requires a large volume of data and financial and human resources, and it is low in efficacy
	5	Techniques are highly efficient in their use of resources and in deriving desired outputs from new inputs
Objectivity	1	Specific tool provides a low level of objectivity due to the presence of biases and mind-sets in its application
	5	Potential for bias can be minimised
Usefulness	1	Application of a tool delivers less useful output and requires additional work by or on behalf of a decision maker
	5	Tool provides a high level of valued output without requiring additional effort by the decision maker
Timeliness	1	Tool requires a great deal of time to complete well
	5	Tool takes little time to successfully complete

Source: Adapted from Fleisher, C.S. & Bensoussan, B.E., 2007, *Business and competitive analysis: effective applications of new and classic methods*, FT Press, Upper Saddle River.

Three levels have been chosen for the framework, and each level focuses on an important form of analysis that can be beneficial for decision making mainly at the different levels in an organisation. These levels can be identified as:

- **Strategic level**: The first level represents analysis of information that can assist the DHA at the strategic decision-making level. This level also provides a framework within which other levels (tactical & operational levels) of intelligence collection and analysis take place, and it assists the organisation in identifying important trends and patterns that emerge in its environment as well as the threats and opportunities available to the organisation (Fleisher & Bensoussan 2007:27). In the framework, Figure 1, this level is represented as the environmental analysis.
- **Tactical level:** Level two represents the analysis of information that can assist mainly in tactical decision making at the organisation, and it also supports the strategic level. According to Fleisher & Bensoussan (2007:27), a symbiotic relationship exists between the strategic and tactical levels of intelligence analysis. This level is represented by the service-business analysis, evolutionary analysis and financial analysis in Figure 1.
- **Operational level:** The third level of the framework represents the operational level of information analysis, and it focuses on the actual delivery of services to the customers at the DHA. The tools used here are mainly to identify customers' needs, behaviour analysis and the forms of competition that affect the provision of services to the customer. This level is, therefore, represented as customer analysis and competition analysis in Figure 1.

Whilst several tools and techniques are available for organisations to use at each of the levels, it should be noted that these tools and techniques were not originally designed with service-sector organisations in mind. However, some of these tools and techniques can still be adapted and used successfully to address the problems that the DHA experiences and these have been selected from the array of tools and represented in the framework. After identifying the various forms of competition at the DHA, care was taken to identify only those tools and techniques that would be able to assist the DHA to outsmart these forms of competition in order to enhance its service delivery.

The tools for the framework have been divided into several elements in order to inform managers of their focus in each category and to make it easy for the model to be used in any other service sector. Furthermore, the elements of the framework are sequential in nature, commencing with a broad *environmental analysis* of the environment in which the DHA operates. The focus then moves to a *service-business analysis* where the DHA is analysed in relation to its operating environment.

At this level, two elements of serious concern to the DHA have been identified separately, and they should be analysed concurrently with the service business to benefit the organisations' overall operations. These elements are the *financial analysis* and the *evolutionary analysis*.

The financial analysis is non-existent, and the DHA's financial situation is in dire straits (Table 1). The evolutionary analysis focuses mainly on the left field competition. The separation of these two elements from the rest of the service-business analysis serves to highlight the level of importance and priority of these analyses for the DHA. In the context of a public service organisation, financial analysis requires a keen accounting of the resources used and investments made. It also needs to look at the efficiency and effectiveness by which financial resources are being utilised. Unlike a Private Sector organisation, which has the benefit of GAAP (generally accepted accounting principles), financial ratio and statement analysis (FRSA), a Public Sector service context is more akin to the work done by management accountants who attempt to make internal and time-based comparisons of the efficiency and effectiveness of financial resources.

Once the DHA has a better understanding of its position and operations in its industry, that is the public service sector, it is essential for it to analyse both its *competition* and its *customers* before it can develop and implement strategic decisions for the organisation. Once again the competition and customers are the most crucial elements of any service organisation, and the DHA exists to provide a service to customers. The fact that the organisation has dedicated so little attention to these elements warrants them being part of the framework as it is believed that, if these elements are not sufficiently addressed at the decision-making stage, service delivery will not be improved (Fogli 2006; Parasuraman, Zeithaml & Berry 1994). The first element to be investigated here is the environmental analysis.

Environmental analysis

The DHA has to understand the environment, or market, in which it operates if it intends to position itself for success within that environment. Several groups and organisations in the external environment in which the DHA works will have to be monitored, either directly or indirectly, for changes in their needs, perceptions and preferences. Furthermore, trends and changes in regulatory and political authorities need to be monitored and analysed as these influence the operations of the DHA. Any form of competition from its funding authorities and its customers should also be monitored and analysed.

Milliken (1987:135) indicated that there are different types of uncertainty about the environment that organisations experience when they try to make sense of and respond to conditions in the external environment. This uncertainty about the environment can be as a result of the individual's lack of understanding of how the components of the environment might be changing or the inter-relationships that exist between these components in the environment. This uncertainty about the environment could lead to poor strategic planning and resource allocation. Hence environmental analysis is essential to provide this form of understanding for decision makers in an organisation.

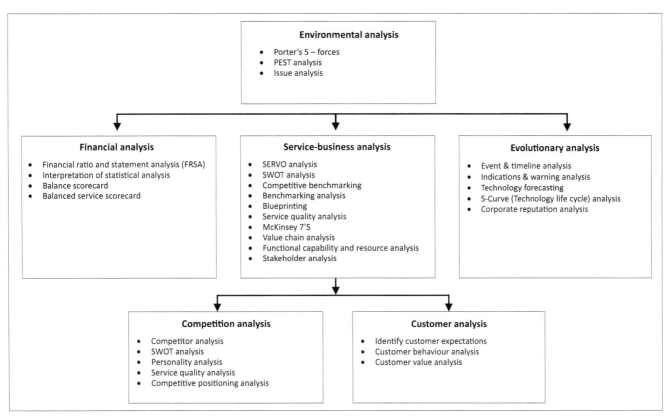

Source: Adapted from Clarke, D.E., 2001, 'Competitive intelligence in service industries', in C.S. Fleisher & D.L. Blenkhorn (eds.), *Managing frontiers in competitive intelligence,* pp. 223–237, Quorum Books, Westport, Connecticut.

FIGURE 1: Competitive Intelligence (CI) framework for gathering and analysing information at the Department of Home Affairs (DHA).

As stated by Clarke (2001:232), the competitive analysis should be able to identify which resources are scarce and what untapped opportunities exist, as this is where sustainable competitive advantages can be created. Hence the tools identified to assist the DHA for these purposes are *PEST analysis, Porter's 5-forces model* and *Issue analysis*. The PEST analysis focuses on the political, economic, social and technological climate of the DHA. Porter's 5-forces model can be used together with the PEST analysis for a more comprehensive understanding of the environment and the relationships and dynamics that exist in its market environment. Whilst it may be argued that Porter's 5-forces model was designed mainly to assist the profit-seeking industries where the delivery of products to customers is important, the researcher believes that this model can also assist service-sector organisations such as the DHA. The DHA functions within the broader environment: Suppliers of specific products, resources and services come from this environment, and they are usually the same suppliers as for the profit-making industries. The end-product of DHA may be intangible (services), but the delivery of these services is reliant on several other aspects in order for it to be effective and efficient. Hence, using Porter's 5-forces analysis will provide the DHA with a better understanding of its industry environment.

Issue analysis can assist the DHA to become more aware of the changes in its environment and to be proactive, participating in policy developments that impact on its operations. The lack of sound policies and procedures that have been identified at the DHA (Table 1) can be addressed by this analysis.

In addition, these tools and techniques can assist the DHA to understand its environment better and, in doing so, align its strategic objective and planning with that of its industry environment. Once a thorough understanding of the environment in which DHA operates has been established, it will have to analyse its own service-business environment.

Service-business analysis

According to Sandman (2000:78), it is not possible for an organisation to understand its competitors unless it first understands its own organisation and its service business. Furthermore, this form of analysis will focus on the organisation's internal environment and identify those forces that operate inside the organisation with specific implications for managing organisational performance (Fleisher & Bensoussan 2003:275). The organisation will also be in a position to ascertain its degree of fit between the service organisation and its competitive environment by making use of tools such as the *SERVO analysis.* Beyond this, the DHA needs to examine its internal strengths, weaknesses, opportunities and threats, and this can be identified by a *SWOT analysis.* However, this cannot be done in isolation and will therefore require input through *benchmarking* with other service organisations within the government, private sector and even with other organisations that offer the same or similar services, although it may be in very different environments. Such an organisation would be the Home Office in the UK, whose operations and mandate is the same as that of the DHA. *Competitive benchmarking* helps to analyse the performance of the DHA against the best-in-class, and the DHA will be able to set targets to exceed the performance of the competition and to pay attention to the skills and competencies that will be required to do this.

Whilst benchmarking is an outward focus, *blueprinting* has more of an inward focus that can assist the DHA to communicate the details of its services from beginning to end (Clarke 2001:234). This can be useful for DHA managers and staff as it will help to identify service gaps that can be detrimental to the operations of the organisation's performance. It is further essential to analyse the quality of services offered, and the *service quality analysis* is useful for service-providing organisations such as the DHA. This analysis will provide useful information to decide whether the DHA is providing the quality of service that meets the expectations of its customers.

Having already identified the changes that the DHA is undergoing as a result of the Turnaround Programme (Table 1) and the forms of competition experienced as a result, the *McKinsey 7 S analysis* has been included in the framework to facilitate the process of strategy implementation within this context. The McKinsey 7 S model will allow the DHA to realise the interrelationships that are necessary between structure, strategy, systems, style, staff, skills and shared values within the DHA, and it will assist in the design and restructure of the organisation. It will also assist in determining how the organisational design of the DHA will impact on service delivery and whether the systems and processes in place will be able to support the strategic needs of the organisation.

The *value chain analysis* can also assist the DHA in its organisational design as it can provide valuable insight about the activities that add the greatest value to the organisation and need to be controlled and protected. It also assists in identifying the activities that add no value and need to be discontinued. There will also be activities that add little value, and concerning these, consideration is needed as to whether they should be made more efficient, be outsourced or stopped completely (Sandman 2000:93). Value chain analysis can identify core competencies that are required by the DHA to achieve its desired results.

Once these core competencies have been identified, *functional capability and resource analysis* can be used by the management of the DHA to analyse its internal tangible and intangible assets, along with its core capabilities, to determine whether these assets are valuable resources that are capable of providing the organisation with a competitive advantage. This resource-based view to sustained competitive advantage is also confirmed by Barney (1991:99). He states that organisations' resources have the potential to generate competitive advantage for the organisation. Organisations and managers should therefore obtain a

better understanding of how resources can impact the long-term success of the organisation, and this should be taken into consideration during the strategic planning initiatives of the organisation.

Wagner (2003:77) states that, 'because of the nature of public organisations, it is important to consider the opinions of all key stakeholders, or "publics", when evaluating the distinctiveness of resources'. In addition, public organisations with strong cultures can easily lose sight of public opinion and rely too heavily on internal, often biased, opinions. Therefore, *stakeholder analysis* is an important tool for the DHA. It can provide insight into those stakeholders who are valuable to the DHA and assist management to allocate resources appropriately to manage its stakeholders. It can also be used to motivate for additional funds to service the needs of these stakeholders.

Financial analysis

The first financial analysis tool is the *financial ratio and statement analysis* (FRSA) which provides managers with an understanding of the organisation's competitive performance. Ratios are used to assess the current performance, examine business trends, evaluate business strategies and monitor progress (Fleisher & Bensoussan 2003:400).

These authors further indicate that FRSA is an extremely helpful information overload tool as it can transform large quantities of disjointed financial data into manageable and meaningful outputs, and it connects the several pieces of financial data into one integrated analysis. DHA will find this tool useful as it does not have a system that integrates all its financial data.

Another financial tool that can be useful is the *interpretation of statistical analysis* which enables a simple description of complex situations and can provide predictive insights (Fleisher & Bensoussan 2007:417). This tool provides systematic and objective methods for examining financial and other forms of research data and for obtaining valuable information from an organisation's operations and activities. This is vital for the DHA which operates in a highly political environment where each manager tries to obtain the largest share of the resources, based on their political affiliation rather than actual performance. Decision making can also be supplemented by objective statistical data which can then be used to motivate for additional funding and resources.

Whilst these tools for financial analysis can be beneficial for the DHA, it should be noted that these tools will require the skills and competencies of financial accountants and managers. Since the DHA does not, currently, have these skills and competencies available internally, it will have to seek the services of outside financial consultants and management accounts until staff with these competencies and skills have been acquired.

The *balanced scorecard* uses performance measures to track and adjust business strategy. Together with the financial perspective, the balanced scorecard forces managers to incorporate the customer perspective, operations and the organisation's innovation and learning ability (Have, Have & Stevens 2003:12). It makes it possible to ascertain financial consequences of non-financial measures that can impact the long-term financial success of the organisation. With the lack of skilled and competent staff to conduct a financial analysis at the DHA, this tool will be valuable as it does not require extensive financial knowledge, although it does produce data that can be used for financial assessment. Furthermore, the balanced scorecard encourages the establishment of tangible objectives and measures that are linked to the mission, vision and strategy of the organisation. The problems relating to the vision, mission and strategy of DHA can be addressed with this tool.

A modification to the balanced scorecard is a *balanced service scorecard* which 'helps to identify opportunities to increase value realisation and predicting the expected performance in the future with some confidence' (Tyagi & Gupta 2008). The service scorecard can also assist the DHA in its organisational structuring as it makes the organisational structure more visible and acceptable to all employees in the organisation. Top-level leadership is responsible for the implementation of service scorecards, and this leadership is critical for the organisation to achieve its objectives as it inspires employees to excel and improve their performance. This tool will therefore be useful to the DHA to encourage strong leadership and improved performance of its staff, especially at the level of senior management.

This leads to another service-level analysis that was identified as valuable for the DHA: evolutionary analysis.

Evolutionary analysis

As a result of the fundamental changes, redesign, restructuring and turbulence that the DHA has gone through with its previous Turnaround Programmes and the present Turnaround Programme, tools for evolutionary analysis were deemed necessary to assist management to react appropriately and to make difficult decisions that arise amidst these situations. These tools will also prepare the DHA to react to the left field competition that it encounters.

The first evolutionary tool suggested is therefore the *event and timeline analysis* which is a group of related techniques that display events sequentially in a visual manner. When conducted systematically, it can uncover important trends about the organisation's competitive environment and serve an early-warning function (Fleisher & Bensoussan 2007:343). These authors suggest that this tool is best used when an organisation is dealing with a large number of discrete events that transpire over a long period of time or are otherwise obscured.

Another tool that can serve as an early-warning sign for decision makers is the *indications and warning analysis*. This tool can assist in reducing the element of surprise, uncertainty and risk, and it alerts managers well in advance of a situation arising, thereby allowing them to take the necessary action to counteract the impact of the situation. This tool can assist the DHA to address the sudden changes in demand. This tool will also afford the DHA the opportunity to become proactive in its decision making and enhance its innovative capacity.

The culture of innovation and frequent changes in technology has challenged DHA to keep up with these developments in all its operations and activities. The lack of internal IT capacity in the DHA also means that the existing technology is not used optimally and has not been upgraded to meet the changes in its operations. Hence *the technology forecasting* and *S-Curve (technology life cycle) analysis* has been included in the framework as these tools can provide information about the changes and development in technology. It will also assist the DHA in recognising the limits of its existing technology and in making decisions about what new technology to acquire that may assist in transforming and enhancing its processes, operations, resource allocation and budgeting, communication and flow of information within the organisation. This tool can assist in creating a positive image and in positioning the DHA in a more favourable manner. Whilst these tools are created by organisations to deal with their specific requirements, the DHA can still utilise these tools on condition that they have been created by other organisations who are dealing with similar technological contexts. This can be done either by purchasing, outsourcing or borrowing and adapting the model to suit its own specific needs.

Corporate reputation analysis will be another useful tool for the DHA as it will be able to identify the organisation's image amongst its key stakeholders and enable managers to improve its relations with its stakeholders in future (Fleisher & Bensoussan 2007:275). Having knowledge of its reputation and image is also important for the DHA as this can impact on its funding, support from its customers and employees. It can also assist the DHA in repositioning its already tainted image as identified in Table 1. Another way for the DHA to determine the exact nature of its reputation and image would be to conduct an analysis of its customers. Use of this tool also allows the DHA to compare itself with other public service agencies, some of which will compete with it for talented staff, for resources from the political centre and/or for time in the positive media spotlight.

Customer analysis

DHA has an important goal of ensuring that it delivers quality services to its customers. Hence, it needs to understand and *identify the customers' expectations* of the services that it offers in order to make sure that it delivers according to these expectations. Furthermore, *customer behaviour analysis* would assist the DHA to create a profile of its customers' behaviour and then strategise to meet and exceed the desires and expectation of its customers. These tools are necessary for the DHA especially since it is experiencing problems in this regard as noted in Table 1. Using these tools will ensure that the DHA responds to the needs of its customers and that its services are provided impartially, equitably and without bias.

Conducting a *customer value analysis* will complement the two tools already identified. Customer value analysis comprises of several tools and techniques that can assist the DHA better to understand its customers, competitors and markets (Fleisher & Bensoussan 2003:180). Understanding customer expectations can also be important for competitor analysis as the provider that can best meet the expectations of the customer will win their support.

Competition analysis

In order to survive in the competitive environment within which the DHA is situated, *competitor analysis* is an important tool that provides a comprehensive picture of the strengths and weaknesses of current and potential competitors (Fleisher & Bensoussan 2003:144). It helps to create a profile of the competitor, and this is useful for the DHA to adopt more confident, aggressive and proactive measures to outsmart the competitors and also to help managers to identify the kinds of resources, skills and competencies that the DHA needs to remain competitive.

A tool that is closely related to competitor analysis and that reduces the threats posed by the competition is the *SWOT analysis.* This is suggested for the DHA as it can assist in developing a profile of the competitors. This tool can be used, together with the competitor analysis, to obtain an enhanced profile of the competitors.

Personality analysis is a tool that provides a more qualitative type of information that may help to explain how a competitor perceives itself and how it may react in a particular situation (Cook & Cook 2000:129). It also provides an understanding of the competitor's corporate culture, values and past strategies. This is important for developing strategies that will counteract the reaction of the competitor before it can impact the organisation, and it will be able to assist in strategic planning. This can also be focused internally on the DHA itself to obtain a better understanding of how decisions makers and the decision-making groups within the organisation react to certain types of contexts or situations.

Service quality analysis is another competitor analysis tool that may be useful for the DHA to analyse the quality of its competitors' and its own service. Having an idea of the quality of the competitors' service can assist the DHA in implementing certain measures and activities that can ensure that they exceed the quality of the competitors and thereby remain the organisation of choice for the customers. It can also contribute towards its competitive positioning in the environment.

According to Fleisher & Bensoussan (2007:103), *competitive positioning analysis* enables an organisation to make strategic

plans in relation to its current competitive position whilst also providing information about the organisations' competitors. This tool requires research and exploration in specific areas to obtain accurate information on the organisation's competitive positioning, and this process enhances the research capability of the organisation. The information is used for strategic planning and the management of the organisation, and this will benefit the DHA since it will provide useful information about the reputation and image of the organisation. Organisations with a better competitive position in the environment are likely to attract more valuable stakeholders, partners, employees and alliances, which can assist the organisation successfully to achieve its goals. The DHA needs to attract more valuable stakeholders, partners, employees and alliances as it does experience a serious problem in terms of scarcity skills and senior-management capabilities. Perhaps a positive competitive positioning will assist the DHA in attracting and retaining professional skills that are lacking.

This CI framework for gathering and analysing information will fill the gap that exists at the DHA in terms of its tools and techniques for strategic planning. It will assist the organisation in moving away from strategic planning that is merely a paper exercise based on monthly reports and 'gut feel' to a more evidence-based, factual process of strategic planning that involves thorough analysis and is based on a structured, systematic and reliable process. It will enable the DHA to identify and respond to the competitive forces that bedevil its operations and hamper service delivery. Table 3 provides a brief summary of the CI objectives of each tool and technique suggested in the CI Framework for the DHA, and this table is intended to be a quick guide to the managers and decision makers.

Assessing the adequacy of the tools and techniques suggested for use at the Department of Home Affairs

In order to make decisions based on the intelligence gained from using the CI tools and techniques, the management team needs to be sure that the intelligence is accurate and as far as possible provides an unbiased and authoritative account of reality. They also need to feel comfortable with the tools and techniques chosen for each situation and have confidence that it will provide the intelligence that is needed for the desired outcomes of the DHA. Furthermore, management has to know that the intelligence obtained from using these tools and techniques can and will be used to add value to the organisation.

There may be some situations where more than one tool or technique or a combination of several tools and techniques may have to be used in order to obtain the desired result. The selection of these tools will depend on the managers' skills and analysis competencies. At the DHA, there is already a shortage of skilled and competent senior-management staff. Therefore, some guidance and assurance about the tools and

TABLE 3: Competitive Intelligence (CI) objectives of each tool and technique suggested in the Competitve Intelligence (CI) framework for the Department of Home Affairs (DHA).

CI Tool	CI Objectives
Environmental analysis	
Porter's 5-Forces	• Identifies strengths and competitive rivalry facing the service sector • Determine the five fundamental competitive forces that impact the service sector
PEST analysis	• Identifies the political, economic, social and technological issues affecting the service sector
Issue analysis	• Enables the anticipation of changes in the external environment in order for organisations to become proactive and participate in public policy development
Service-business analysis	
SERVO analysis	• Analyses of the DHA's management preferences, resources, strategies and capabilities, and how these elements fit with the environment
SWOT analysis	• Identifies the DHA's strengths, weaknesses, opportunities and threats
Competitive benchmarking Benchmarking analysis	• Identifies similar organisational processes in other industries and improve standards and processes to that of the best in the business
Blueprinting	• Develops a process blueprint to identify every aspect of the DHA's operations
Service quality analysis	• Analyses the quality of service provided by the DHA to its customers
McKinsey 7'S	• Facilitates the process of strategy implementation within the context of organisational change that the DHA is currently undergoing
Value chain analysis	• Identifies activities that add the greatest value to the DHA and need to be controlled and protected • Identifies core competencies that are required by the DHA to accomplish its desired results
Functional capability and resource analysis	• Analyses the DHA's internal tangible and intangible assets and core capabilities to determine if these assets are valuable resources that are capable of giving the organisation a competitive advantage
Stakeholder analysis	• Provides insight into those stakeholders that are valuable to the DHA and assist management to allocate resources appropriately to manage its stakeholders
Financial analysis	
Financial ratio and statement analysis (FRSA)	• Analysis tool which provides managers with an understanding of the organisation's competitive performance by means of ratios
Interpretation of statistical analysis	• Systematic and objective methods for examining financial data and for obtaining valuable information from an organisation's operations and activities
Balance scorecard	• Uses performance measures to track and adjust business strategy
Evolutionary analysis	
Event & timeline analysis	• Group of related techniques that display events sequentially in a visual manner to uncover important trends about the organisation's competitive environment and serves as an early warning function
Indications & warning analysis	• Analyses the elements of surprise, uncertainty and risk and alerts managers well in advance of a situation transpiring thereby allowing them to take the necessary actions to counteract the impact of the situation
Technology forecasting S-Curve (Technology life cycle) analysis	• Analyses the changes and development in technology and assists the DHA to recognise the limits of its existing technology and make decisions about what new technology to acquire
Corporate reputation analysis	• Identifies the organisation's image amongst its key stakeholders and enable managers to improve its relations with its stakeholders in the future
Customer analysis	
Identify customer expectations	• Identifies customer expectations of the services that it offers in order to make sure that it delivers according to these expectations.
Customer behaviour analysis	• Identifies and creates a profile of behaviour of the DHA's customers and then strategise to meet and exceed the desires and expectation of its customers
Customer value analysis	• Analysis comprises of several tools and techniques that can assist the DHA better to understand its customer's, competitors and markets
Competition analysis	
Competitor analysis	• Analyses and provides a comprehensive picture of the strengths and weaknesses of current and potential competitors
SWOT analysis	• Analyses and develops a profile of the competitor and can be used together with the competitor analysis to obtain an enhanced profile of the competitor
Personality analysis	• Provides qualitative information that may help to explain how a competitor perceives itself and how it may react in a particular situation
Service quality analysis	• Analyses its competitors' and its own service quality
Competitive positioning	• Enables an organisation to make strategic plans in relation to its current competitive position and it also provides information about the organisations' competitors

Source: Authors' own data

techniques are essential as this will assist even the most doubtful and unskilled manager to make a decision about the selection of tools and techniques that are adequate for use in a specific situation or to obtain specific intelligence.

In the light of this, the FAROUT approach as discussed above was used to access the adequacy of the CI tools and techniques selected for the DHA. The output of every tool and technique that was chosen for the DHA was assessed according to the six elements of the FAROUT approach as reflected in Table 2. The assessment scheme and the profile of the strengths and weaknesses of each tool and technique were carefully examined. This was to ensure that the tools and techniques reflected in the CI framework for gathering and analysing information at the DHA (Figure 1) are indeed useful for addressing the specific situations that the DHA needs to address through their use. In certain cases where the tool has had a low rating, another tool of a higher rating and with greater strengths was selected in order to complement the first, weaker tool. Therefore, suggestions for the selection of tools can be noticed for each element in the framework.

It is also important to note that it is not feasible for an organisation to make use of all these tools and techniques simultaneously to address it needs. Some of these tools and techniques are usually used by organisations prior to strategic planning, on an on-going basis or as-needed for specific aspects or projects at hand. Some tools are required to be used for decision making, and when major decisions need to be taken, they can prove to be very useful. However, in the case of the DHA, where it was identified in the ethnographic study that not many tools and techniques were used to assist in strategic planning, restructuring, decision making and new projects, it is suggested that the organisation make every effort to use all these tools and techniques during the next planning phase. The planning phases usually come a year ahead of the announcement of its strategic plans and objectives. These tools and techniques should be used to try to rectify the current problems and challenges that the DHA experiences in terms of its service delivery.

Future research

The findings and the development of the CI framework for gathering and analysing information for public service departments has led to the following areas that need further investigation:

- The CI framework that has been reflected in Figure 1 needs to be tested in the DHA and other public service departments. It will be interesting to investigate what the situation will be with regard to service delivery after these tools and techniques have been implemented. This can be studied by means of longitudinal evaluative research method where pre and post-testing can be done.
- The opinions and perceptions of customers' and employees should be investigated after these tools have been implemented in the DHA to determine whether the service delivery has improved and to determine whether the CI tools have been useful for Public services departments in South Africa.
- The positive outcomes of enhanced service delivery by public service departments, such as political, technological and socio-economic advantages, should be investigated.

Conclusion

This article focussed on CI tools and techniques that have been identified as suitable for use in the DHA in order to

improve service delivery. The discussion commenced with an overview of the competitive realities that exist at the DHA, and this provided a basis for identifying and suggesting several tools and techniques that were depicted in a CI framework for gathering and analysing information in the DHA.

The CI framework for gathering and analysing information at the DHA is reflected in Figure 1, and it represents a formal and systematic means for informing managers about critical issues that the DHA faces or is likely to experience in the future. The tools for the framework have been divided into several elements in order to inform managers of their focus in each category and to make it easy for the model to be used in any other service sector. These elements are: environmental analysis, service-business analysis, financial analysis, evolutionary analysis, customer analysis and competition analysis. This framework will fill the gap that exists at the DHA as far as its strategic planning tools and techniques are concerned.

It should be noted that not all the tools and techniques indicated in the CI framework for the DHA can be used by the organisation at once. However, a selection can be made from these tools and techniques to respond to the competitive forces that bedevil the operations and service delivery as indicated in Table 1. It is further suggested that the DHA could consider starting with the tools and techniques in the customer analysis and evolutionary analysis categories as these tools will be able to assist the department to immediately attend to the poor reputation and customer service with which it has been plagued.

Whilst it is difficult to motivate and justify the implementation of CI activities in the public service sector mainly because of the lack of an easily quantifiable outcomes measure, it was found that the Public Services have several stakeholders who are involved in the operations of the departments, and these stakeholders can view the outcomes measure from varying perspectives. This can be regarded as an ideal motivation and opportunity for CI to be implemented so that it can add value to the functioning of public service. CI activities, in this case, can ensure that appropriate, accurate and actionable intelligence is made available for the organisation to meet its challenges.

Acknowledgements

Competing interests

The author declares that she has no financial or personal relationship(s) which may have inappropriately influenced her in writing this paper.

References

Barney, J., 1991, 'Firm resources and sustained competitive advantage', *Journal of Management* 17(1), 99–120. http://dx.doi.org/10.1177/014920639101700108

Clarke, D.E., 2001, 'Competitive intelligence in service industries', in C.S. Fleisher & D.L. Blenkhorn (eds.), *Managing frontiers in competitive intelligence*, pp. 223–237, Quorum Books, Westport, Connecticut.

Cook, M. & Cook, C., 2000, *Competitive Intelligence: create an intelligent organization and compete to win,* Kogan Page, London.

Fleisher, C.S. & Bensoussan, B.E., 2003, *Strategic and competitive analysis: methods and techniques for analyzing business competition*, Prentice Hall, Upper Saddle River.

Fleisher, C.S. & Bensoussan, B.E., 2007, *Business and competitive analysis: effective applications of new and classic methods*, FT Press, Upper Saddle River.

Fogli, L. (ed.), 2006, *Customer service delivery: research and best practices*, Jossey-Bass, San Franscisco.

Gieskes, H., 2001, 'Competitive Intelligence at Lexis-Nexis', in J.E. Prescott & S.H. Miller (eds.), *Proven strategies in Competitive Intelligence: lessons from the trenches,* pp. 69–82, John Wiley & Sons, New York.

Greenberg, E., 1982, 'Competing for scarce resources', *Journal of Business Strategy* 2(3), 1–87.

Hamel, G., 2000, *Leading the revolution*, Harvard Business School Publishing, Boston.

Have, S.T., Have, W.T. & Stevens, F., 2003, *Key management models: the management tools and practices that will improve your business*, Financial Times Prentice Hall, London.

Horne, M. & Parks, T., 2004, 'Implementing competitive intelligence in a non-profit environment', *Competitive Intelligence Magazine* 7(1), 33–36.

Kahaner, L., 1997, *Competitive intelligence: how to gather, analyse, and use information to move your business to the top*, Touchstone, New York.

Khumalo, F., 2003, 'Government strategy to enhance service delivery institutions', *Service Delivery Review* 2(1), 20–24.

Lenz, R.T. & Engledow, J.L., 1986, 'Environmental analysis: the applicability of current theory', *Strategic Management Journal* 7, 329–346. http://dx.doi.org/10.1002/smj.4250070404

McGonagle, J.J. & Vella, C.M., 1993, *Outsmarting the competition: practical approaches to finding and outsmarting the competition*, McGraw-Hill, London.

Marceau, S. & Sawka, K., 2001, 'Developing a world-class CI program in telecoms', in J.E. Prescott & S.H. Miller (eds.), *Proven strategies in Competitive Intelligence: lessons from the trenches,* pp. 148–167, John Wiley & Sons, New York.

Milliken, F.J., 1987, 'Three types of perceived uncertainty about the environment: state, effect, and response uncertainty', *Academy of Management Review* 12(1), 133–143.

National Treasury, 2004, *Medium term budget policy statement*, Government Printer, Pretoria.

Parasuramen, A., Zeithaml, V.A. & Berry, L.L., 1994, 'Alternative scales for measuring service quality: a comparative assessment based on psychometric and diagnostic criteria', *Journal of Retailing* 70(3), 201–230. http://dx.doi.org/10.1016/0022-4359(94)90033-7

Rodie, A.R. & Martin, C.L., 2001, 'Competing in the service sector: the entrepreneurial challenge', *International Journal of Entrepreneurial Behaviour & Research* 7(1), 5–21. http://dx.doi.org/10.1108/13552550110385718

Sandman, M.A., 2000, 'Analytical models and techniques', in J. Miller and the Business Intelligence Braintrust (eds.), *Millennium intelligence: understanding and conducting Competitive Intelligence in the digital age*, pp. 69–95, Cyber Age Books, Medford.

Sawyer, D.C., 2002, *Smart services: competitive information strategies, solutions and success stories for service businesses,* Information Today, Medford.

SCIP, 2008, *Society for Competitive Intelligence Professionals*, viewed 17 June 2008, from http://www.scip.org

Tyagi, R.K. & Gupta, P., 2008, *A complete and balanced service scorecard: creating value through sustained performance improvement*, FT Press, Upper Saddle River.

Wagner, R.B., 2003, 'Can competitive intelligence be effectively applied to public-sector organizations?', in C.S. Fleisher & D.L. Blenkhorn (eds.), *Controversies in competitive intelligence: the enduring issues*, pp. 70–82, Praeger, Westport.

12

From conceptualisation to commercialisation: The Gradnet story

Authors:
Zenia Barnard[1]
Chris Rensleigh[1]

Affiliations:
[1]Department of
Information and Knowledge
Management, University of
Johannesburg, South Africa

Correspondence to:
Zenia Barnard

Email:
zenia@zeniabarnard.com

Postal address:
PO Box 524, Auckland Park
2006, South Africa

Background: A very small percentage of all the research generated by universities is commercialised. The article is a case study of the transformation from action research to a spin-off company. It looks at the practical implications of such a transformation.

Objectives: The aim of this article is to provide a holistic view of what the process entailed to leap from academic research to the commercialisation of the research into a company as was the case for Gradnet.

Method: A case-study approach was used to document the conceptualisation and development of the research-based, spin-off company, Gradnet. This includes the background of the original research that formed the basis of the innovation process.

Results: It was found that the commercialisation process of academic research is not necessarily a natural process for the researcher in the absence of an appropriate supporting infrastructure.

Conclusion: All academic disciplines have the potential for establishing commercially viable research projects. This potential should be actively explored and pursued by the institution.

Introduction

During the post-apartheid era, the higher education landscape in South Africa has been changing rapidly and drastically. The merger of the Rand Afrikaans University (RAU) and the Technikon Witwatersrand (TWR) was a trying and challenging event. Preparation for the merger started with the announcement of the merger in June 2002 (Department of Education 2002), but practical challenges began to be addressed in earnestness in early 2004 as the date for the merger was set for January 2005. One of the challenges of this merger was the communication with and information dissemination to graduates (also known as alumni) from both institutions.

Many educational institutions strive to forge strong and loyal bonds with their alumni for purposes of fundraising, community engagement, networking opportunities and career advancement (Barnard, Rensleigh & Niemann 2005). This relationship building often takes years to reap mutually beneficial rewards for all participating parties and provide a 'return on relationship' (Gummeson 2004) for all the stakeholders who invested in it. A merger could prove fatal to the established loyalty bonds which were formed over many years of relationship building by the merging institutions as alumni may feel threatened and alienated by the loss of institutional identity and the consequent loss of their own educational identity. In the case under consideration, a lack of timeous and efficient communication to these alumni was a further instigator of the perceived threat as information dissemination through the grapevine filled the communication vacuum that was created by the uncertainty of the merging institutions. A very real need arose to create and maintain cost and time-efficient communication channels and content to these external affinity groups that could convey to them the continued institutional integrity and new brand identity of the merged institution. The purpose of such a move would have been to establish a new loyalty to the new brand by means of continued and sustainable involvement between alumni and institution (to be called the University of Johannesburg [UJ]).

It was also necessary to present to the alumni of both merging institutions benefits of and incentives for involvement as the new brand would have no impact in terms of loyalty and allegiance from their point of view. Generation X alumni has an increasing attitude of 'what's in it for me' with regard to institutional involvement, and higher education institutions have to find innovative and novel ways of proving the value of involvement to the new generation alumni (Yrle, Hartman & Payne 2005). It was also accepted that alumni would be hesitant to donate funds to a new institution to which they felt no affinity. Therefore a new approach was needed to engage them in a meaningful and sustainable way.

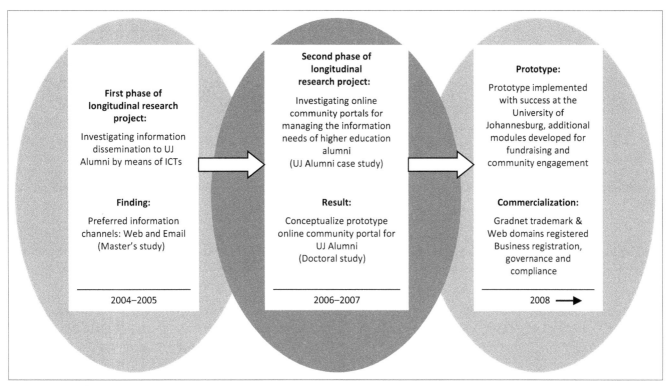

FIGURE 1: Phases of the longitudinal research project.

This article is a case study of the conceptualisation and development of a research-based, spin-off company, Gradnet, which entails the development of an academic research project into a commercialised entity (Barnard & Rensleigh 2013). The article will focus on two phases of a longitudinal study as well as on the prototype and commercialisation process (see Figure 1).

The research that shaped the innovation

Innovation usually arises as a result of a felt need to improve the status quo and identify more opportunities for resource generation (Barnard & Van der Merwe 2014). During the pre-merger years of the University of Johannesburg, the need arose to create a different and improved vehicle for communication and interaction between the then Rand Afrikaans University and its alumni stakeholder group. Electronic communication such as emails and the World Wide Web was still a novelty for the majority of the public in South Africa, and in addition to that, the digital divide was an element to be reckoned with. The communication systems used by the higher education institutions during that time period was limited mostly to postal services. These services had obvious disadvantages: The mail was slow to reach its destination and was often returned to sender due to the outdated postal address information of the university databases. The cost (with regard to financial and human resources) of printing and mailing was disproportionately high in comparison to the benefit gained by this form of communication.

At the time, the creator of Gradnet was employed as the Head of Alumni Relations at one of the pre-merger institutions. The limited number of staff members in this office, the annually increasing number of graduates from the institution that needed to be added and managed on the alumni database, as well as a limited budget to engage with alumni were catalysts in the innovation process that commenced in 2003. The employee wanted to conduct research into the most effective ways of engaging with alumni that would save money, time and resources for the institution. However, a core objective was to convince alumni to be more supportive of the activities of the institution, especially since the institution was facing a difficult and much-contested merger. Action needed to be taken if the sense of alienation within the alumni stakeholder groups from both pre-merger institutions were to be transcended. The employee decided to enrol for a Master's degree in Information Science at the institution to conduct formalised research for the purposes as set out above.

According to the Workers' Compensation Board (n.d.), research is an attempt by careful enquiry, experimentation, study, observation, analysis and recording to:

• discover new facts, knowledge and information
• develop new interpretations of facts, knowledge or information
• discover new means of applying existing knowledge.

Rowley (2004) lists the essential criteria for good research. It has to:

• add to existing knowledge
• have a clear purpose or research question
• be objective and reliable

- address the issues of access (to people, organisations, data, etc.) politics (internal) and ethical conduct (with regard to privacy, confidentiality and transparency).

The rapid development of information and communication technology (ICT) is a factor that needs to be borne in mind in terms of research time and time to application. An innovative and active research model is necessary to accommodate this ever-changing, fast-evolving environment (Wieringa & Morali 2012) in a holistic manner (Flood 2010). Action research is such a research paradigm, comprising a powerful combination of research and action that proceed parallel to each other as Rowley (2004) argues:

> … action research depends upon a collaborative problem-solving relationship between the researcher and the client with the aim of both solving a problem, and generating new knowledge. An action researcher working inside an organisation has two roles: that of employee and that of researcher. (p. 209)

Feurer and Chaharbaghi (1995:4) and Flood (2010) state that, when adopting the action research approach, the researcher has a number of objectives with regard to the understanding and improvement of current practices, the enhancement of the problem-solving capacities of the practitioners with whom the researcher collaborates and the advancement of knowledge about the practice itself. These objectives imply that the outcomes of the research are highly organisation-specific, which is an appropriate approach for research-strategy formulation and implementation in dynamic environments (Feurer & Chaharbaghi 1995) such as the founding of UJ. The action research cycle is, therefore, important in order to determine the outcomes, that is, whether the original diagnosis was correct and whether or not the appropriate action was taken.

First phase of the longitudinal study

Due to the practical nature of the research topic, it was decided to follow an applied action research approach by which a useful, real-world solution to a problem is devised. The implementation of the research results into something workable was the main aim of this type of approach and falls under Pasteur's quadrant of use-inspired research (Stokes 1997). Quantitative empirical research is the underpinning of this approach and can be compared to market research (including a feasibility study) in the context of a commercialisation process. Barnard *et al.* (2005) endorse the principle that market research, and matching value offerings to clients' needs, form the basis of a solid ideas-to-market and profitable enterprise. In addition, applied research focuses on an experimental investigation which makes use of existing knowledge for new applications or for improving upon existing applications in a significant way. It is directed at meeting specific needs by gaining comprehensive knowledge and understanding of the application, allowing for the solving of imminent problems (Stokes 1997:3). For this purpose, applied research on its own can be too 'slow' to accommodate the dynamic, ever-changing and fast-evolving Web environment. Consequently, an innovative and active

research model is necessary such as a combination of applied and action research. Such a research approach can form the foundation for an innovation process as it seeks to determine or measure the gap between the status quo and the ideal circumstances for realising advancement objectives in a timeous manner (Barnard & Rensleigh 2013).

The first phase of the longitudinal study took 11 months to complete (Barnard 2004). This phase of the research project aimed to determine whether the alumni stakeholder group wanted to have contact with the institution, and if so, what the preferred channels and frequency of information dissemination would be. This study investigated the different information and communication channels available to reach the alumni target audience and determined which ones would be best suited to fill both the management needs of the institution and the benefits needs of the alumni. By means of self-selecting, purposeful and convenient sampling, a broad feedback scope was created that provided a clear indication of the needs and wants of the target audience. To ensure equal representation of the different alumni affinity groups, stratified sampling was used to sample the target-group population, namely the alumni of the University of Johannesburg, into homogenous groups. A sample of 600 alumni was randomly selected from the alumni databases of the RAU and the TWR according to the specified strata, namely the institution where they have graduated, gender and age. In addition, the different information-communication technologies available to disseminate information to the target audience were investigated and compared. The empirical study was done by compiling a questionnaire about the specific needs of alumni regarding the reception of information. These questions were designed in accordance with the literature study that was done within the theoretical context of the research. The questionnaire consisted of three relevant sections, namely biographical information, information and communication media and technology, and relationship building. An integrated, multi-disciplinary approach was necessary to create a holistic picture of the multifaceted profiles of the research subjects. Only close-ended questions were included in the questionnaire with scaled options from which participants could select the most appropriate alternative. A telephonic survey was done over 22 days to gather the empirical data. The decision to gather the data via telephonic interviews was made because of the quick response times associated with this method as well as the thorough manner in which the questionnaire could be completed. Of the total number of the sample population approached, 99.7% were willing to participate. Only two (0.3%) of the respondents were not willing to participate, either because of time constraints or because of a lack of interest.

Second phase of the longitudinal study

When it was established by Barnard (2004) that the online community portals would be the most effective information and communication technology to engage the alumni target audience, the second phase of the longitudinal study was formalised in the form of a doctoral thesis. This phase aimed to determine the extent to which Web-portal technology and online communities could be successfully utilised by the alumni offices of higher education institutions in South Africa, using the University of Johannesburg as a case study. Furthermore, the phase aimed to create information sharing with and amongst its alumni affinity groups in order to build and maintain valuable relationships, networks and partnerships with them (Barnard 2007). Again, very specific sub-questions were formulated that had practical significance for an application strategy.

Both quantitative and qualitative approaches were taken with the second phase of the research project. As part of the quantitative study, an empirical survey was conducted amongst the 'new' (post-merger) alumni of the University of Johannesburg to determine their information needs with regard an online community portal and the content required for such a community Web model. A total number of 10 380 questionnaires was distributed over 17 days to graduates of the University of Johannesburg at the graduation ceremonies, thereby making it a self-selecting, purposeful and convenient sample. The questionnaire consisted of four sections, namely biographical information, online activities, alumni information services and alumni community needs. The final sample group, namely those who thoroughly completed the questionnaire, came to a total number of 1139 participants.

In order to establish what the impact of this research project could be on the wider alumni audiences of South African higher education institutions, qualitative research was conducted as a second component of the empirical research. This consisted of a discussion forum that was hosted by the UJ Alumni Relations Office to which all the management representatives for Alumni Relations and Fundraising of all the state-subsidised tertiary institutions in South Africa were invited. The objective of these discussions was primarily to test their opinions on the use of Web technology (such as online community portals) for meeting the needs of their alumni target audience. Of the 17 institutions that were invited, the total number of participants for this empirical phase came to 14 institutions, with 35 representatives attending. The need for knowledge sharing was determined when the representatives called for a consortium to be established as a result of the discussions.

Development of a prototype

The research findings provided an indication of the business processes that should be in place to enable the UJ Alumni Relations Department to have a successful information management strategy for optimal relationship management of its alumni stakeholder group. The results of the survey, combined with the results from the discussion forum, were used as the blueprint for the design of a fully functional prototype for an online community portal relevant to higher education alumni. The theoretical framework was set to determine the make-up, context, need and value of an online community portal for higher education alumni. In addition,

a gap analysis outlined the current (at the time) state of involvement and information requirements of the alumni stakeholders and the institution versus the 'to be' state that needs to be developed to meet those requirements and manage the information flow amongst alumni stakeholders more effectively. The functionality of the prototype had the potential of promoting not only business-to-business (B2B) and business-to-consumer (B2C) interaction but also consumer-to-consume (C2C) interaction. It also had the potential of exploiting the possibility of human-resource placements through career services, amongst other income-generating services. The aim at this stage was not to commercialise the research but to share knowledge and possibly transfer technology to other institutions in South Africa who were faced with similar challenges.

As with managing any project, planning, organising, implementing, controlling and evaluating are critical to the overall success of the execution. An overall objective is necessary to guide the development of the project from launch to end. Van Brakel (2003) outlines a portal-development strategy in eight steps, which were used as guideline in the development of a portal strategy for the UJ alumni's online community portal. The development of the prototype of the alumni's online community portal was funded by the UJ Alumni Association and formed part of the second phase of the longitudinal study. It was built using a Microsoft platform, namely ASP.Net 2.0 as the Web application platform, which was a secure and stable platform that allowed for interactive functionality. Microsoft SQL server 2000 was the database platform. This prototype was a fully functional core-system that was implemented at the University of Johannesburg's Alumni Office. The doctoral thesis was published by Barnard (2007), and it includes screen shots of the completed prototype. The prototype was implemented with success at the University of Johannesburg, and additional modules for fundraising and community engagement were added for use in these sectors.

The commercialisation process

The demand from the tertiary institutions that participated in the qualitative research to obtain a solution for their institutions led to the establishment of a spin-off company to make the technology available on a bigger scale (Barnard & Rensleigh 2008). From a business point of view, this segment of the research was, correspondingly, a needs analysis of the potential clients of the end product as they would be able to utilise the solution to their own advantage and to that of their alumni (clients).

At this point the intention to commercialise the product started to emerge. A research-based spin-off (Conceicao, Fontes & Calapez 2012) is a company that is established by a public research institution, has an equity investment from the public sector or university or has the university or employee of the public sector as the (co-)founders (Barnard 2011). With government subsidies decreasing and students struggling to pay fees, more and more higher education institutions realise the value of applying their research output in generating (third-stream) income for the institution. Conceicao *et al.* (2012) emphasise that the process of transforming research into spin-offs can provide an avenue for generating significant income for institutions. Commercialisation is the process of introducing a new product or production method to the market (Lam 2011). After the new product or production method has been developed, it will be officially launched into the market by means of a sales and marketing strategy (Barnard 2011).

Technology transfer transpires after the commercialisation process (Rasmussen, Mosey & Wright 2014). According to Souder, Nashar and Padmanathan (1990) and Ramanathan (1994), this is the process of moving technology from one entity to another. The transfer of the technology is seen to be successful if the receiving party – or transferee – can use the technology effectively and eventually integrate it into its own core activities (Ramanathan 1994). Bozeman (2000) and Rasmussen *et al.* (2014) point out that moving this technology can include know-how, technical knowledge or physical assets. The movement of technology from laboratory to industry and from one application to another domain can also be seen as technology transfer (Phillips 2002). Innovation is fundamental to successful commercialisation and technology transfer as it is the catalyst to growth and the element that provides a competitive advantage to enterprises. Universities, which are hubs for research and development, are receiving more consideration as producers of innovation (Rasmussen *et al.* 2014).

The Gradnet trademark was registered, and the acquisition process for the relevant web domains was underway. The services of a patent attorney were acquired to execute the legal documentation and processes with regard to the trademark and copyright. In addition, a fiduciary company was appointed to perform the necessary business registration, governance and compliance procedures.

Value proposition of Gradnet

Gradnet showed potential for generating third-stream revenue (meaning income sources from any other means than from student fees and government subsidies) from partnerships and product offerings. This was possible due to the dual nature of the system: Primarily it could be used as a database management, administrative and communication tool by the institution, but equally important, it could be used as an interactive communication platform for the alumni affinity groups and individuals who wanted to network with each other. The portal could be brand customised according to any participating institution's specifications, providing institutions with the freedom and opportunity to enhance and advance their own institutional brand via the portal offering. The value-added modules that were offered via the portal would be designed and developed on a continuous basis to address the pertinent needs and challenges of the business and educational sectors by offering relevant and sustainable solutions, services, products and functionality.

The public would gain access to an updated feed of participating institutional news, events, research output and partnership opportunities via the main web domain, www.gradnet.com, whilst the academic application would provide e-learning opportunities, journal articles, research and fundraising databases to institutional stakeholders. The administrative application made provision for the secure capturing, storing and retrieving of data, statistical reports, content management and stakeholder segmentation for improved relationship marketing. The commercial application included a CV compiler and e-recruitment, qualification authentication and online shops, although this application was at first not a primary focus of the portal.

The mission of Gradnet was to create an optimal online collaborative environment for higher education institutions and their stakeholders that would: (1) promote networking, brand loyalty and lifelong learning (in support of an organisation's intellectual capital, business intelligence and knowledge sharing) and (2) create unique value propositions and mutually beneficial partnerships (Barnard 2011). To achieve this mission, it was important to provide the technology at no cost to participating institutions as this would provide equal opportunities to all institutions to capitalise on the revenue model. This split-revenue model consisted of an instant click-through split in profit whenever transactions occurred via the system. A three-way split in profit was proposed between the participating institution, the service provider (whose core business was the provision of products and services) and Gradnet. It was a medium to long-term profit plan for Gradnet, but it would be well worth it according to income projections. This would also enable the participating institutions to benefit from the centrally developed functionalities that would be deployed to all users as and when they were made available. Gradnet would take on the responsibility for continued research and development whilst institutions would provide the users to the system (Barnard 2011).

To enable a stable, scalable and cost-effective structure for the Gradnet portal going forward, the founder started to investigate different options before taking the leap to production. Projections of the marketing and business plan indicated that the amount of active users on the system could reach significant numbers. These growth projections secured seed funding for the first five years. The vastness of the projected growth potential would require a very reliable and stable platform base. Due to the high cost of using and developing on a Microsoft platform, meetings were set up with the Google team in South Africa.

At the time, Google was establishing itself as a strong global competitor for Microsoft with its various Google Apps offerings. The founder was invited to the Google London office for detailed discussions about the possibilities of migrating Gradnet onto the Google platform. The availability of the Google Apps for Education was an excellent match that complimented the Gradnet mission, and the contracts were finalised with Google for the secure and scalable storage of all data on the Google servers (i.e. The Cloud) whilst embedding the Google Education Applications within the Gradnet framework (Barnard 2011). Google guaranteed a much more flexible and cost-effective offering than did Microsoft as well as a 99% uptime of their servers. It was a leap of faith from Gradnet's side as operating businesses from the Cloud were still considered very novel and bold at the time, but it was worth the risk as it enabled Gradnet to provide the portal at no charge to participating institutions in support of its mission.

The benefits of Gradnet for institutions included the following:

- collaborative knowledge sharing
- the creation and execution of partnership opportunities
- the recruitment and headhunting of graduates for company vacancies
- supporting the institutional value-chain concept
- managing customer relationships (CRM) more effectively through improved information management in tertiary institutions.

A major benefit of Gradnet was that, the more institutions participated in the network, the bigger their potential became to generate third-stream revenue as a result of the shared-revenue model, which was made possible by embedding the PayPal system into the portal (Barnard 2011).

The PayPal e-commerce engine enabled the proposed split in profit sharing by providing an instant transaction-split functionality that made every transaction transparent to all partners. PayPal was at the core of the payment system with the custom-designed Gradnet billing and invoicing system as well as the custom-built, shop-front functionalities running alongside it. The objective was to provide a secure online-transaction space with minimal risk to all participants. This was also communicated frequently to the institutions via the marketing presentations. End users worldwide are familiar with the PayPal brand and perceive it as a safe place to store their personal financial information. First National Bank is the institution that brought PayPal to South Africa. Companies would be able to sell discounted merchandise to the Gradnet end users via the Gradnet Online Mall with a secure and well-known e-commerce engine. The principles underlining the commercialisation of Gradnet were to provide IT infrastructure to institutions as a tool to motivate more engagement from stakeholders. Therefore, the more active users that joined, the more valuable Gradnet would become, irrespective of actual annual turnover from sales. Financial value would therefore be derived from participation and not from selling off IT infrastructure (Barnard 2011).

In terms of human resources, a support team needed to be appointed to assist with the implementation, training and help desk of Gradnet. Because of the web-based nature of the product and enterprise, implementation did not require on-site implementation, but training institutional

users to navigate the system optimally was required as well as a fulltime help desk to answer calls for assistance from institutional users. A training manual, which was used as a central guideline document that would assist with the training of users, was therefore written. This was also published on the Help-Desk website for easy reference. Although the system was very user friendly, the manual and website provided step-by-step schedules on how to apply the different functionalities of the system and provided an overview of the navigation structure of the functionalities.

The handling of end users' biographical data was an important aspect in terms of security and access. During marketing presentations, it was emphasised that all data would be handled to comply with the national Information Security Act. Compliance to this guarantee was core to the ethical business approach of Gradnet.

The actual launch of the Gradnet brand and beta website and services in 2010 was a showcase of all the mentioned aspects to the public and interested parties. A regional representative of Google was the guest speaker at the event, which was held at a five-star hotel in Sandton, South Africa. This was done to create clout and credibility for the newly established brand. The speaker addressed the audience as an authority on Cloud computing and referenced Gradnet as a prime example of an innovative company who was pioneering and embracing new technology. After the conclusion of the formalities at the event, guests could move amongst the mounted plasma screens in the conference venue and 'test-drive' the functionalities that formed part of the system. It must be emphasised that the marketing, branding and positioning of an end-product that is being taken to the market is central to a successful commercialisation process.

Following her exit strategy from Gradnet in 2012 with the selling of the Gradnet Holdings companies, the founder can look back at valuable lessons learnt and priceless experience assimilated that form the basis for generating and sharing knowledge in future.

Lessons learnt

Making the transition from researcher to managing director of a company is a leap by any measure. On paper, a research project can look simple and fairly straightforward, but aspects such as the business plan, legal framework, funding, technology transfer, operations, finances, marketing and brand management are challenges that need to be dealt with swiftly and timeously (Barnard 2011). Good timing is a critical factor in taking a concept from idea to market. If a research project shows potential to be commercialised and both the institution and the researcher are serious about pursuing this course of action, researchers need to know that no research findings are to be published prior to registering the patents and trademarks of that innovation. The moment that research findings or methodology is published, they become public property. If anyone reads the published work and files a patent based on that information, the researcher will not be able to defend the innovation and secure the patent afterwards. Careful planning is therefore required when embarking on a commercialisation trajectory for a research project. Similarly, when research collaboration takes place across institutions, it is important to clearly document the contributions in detail as the project unfolds. Meticulous logging and documentation of collaboration might be a difficult and tedious task, but not doing so can eventually lead to legal action that has the potential of destroying the momentum and potential of commercialisation.

When a researcher is publishing results under the name of, or in co-operation with, an educational institution, it is important to be aware of the intellectual property policy of that institution. This policy should provide guidelines as to what the initial legal framework would be for setting up the company and shareholding structures. However, it is an acceptable and advisable practice that form should follow function, and therefore, structuring the business side of things should only commence once there is a clear business plan on the table. The business plan should be as comprehensive as possible, keeping in mind that it is a flexible document that should be regarded as a frame of reference, a tactical and strategic guide, for all business endeavours on the short, medium and long-term. The business plan is the central component to secure the funding for the commercialisation process and to document the shared vision comprising the objectives and projections of the enterprise.

Sufficient funding is arguably the most crucial executor of the commercialisation process. Due to a lack of funding, start-up companies can fail even before they have been properly launched. Innovators and entrepreneurs can have the best of ideas, but without funding, their ideas are dead in the water. When a researcher at a university comes up with a commercially viable project or idea, the institutional commercialisation office usually assists with the sourcing of funds. Agreements should be drafted to determine and formalise the exchange. Usually inventors dilute their initial shareholding in exchange for funding, and this becomes an ongoing process for every fundraising round that the business requires in future. If the institution is not interested in pursuing the commercialisation avenue for a specific research project, the Intellectual Property and Commercialisation Policy of the institution should make provision for that by assigning to the researcher full ownership of intellectual property and the freedom to commercialise. Again, documenting these agreements and sessions are crucial to prevent any future legal disputes. These session agreements with regard to the intellectual property should be regarded as the foundations of the commercialisation process. Acquiring the assistance of experienced intellectual property attorneys is highly recommended.

Company structures should be set up in accordance with the legal requirements of the specific country's regulations and the funding agreements. Determining and establishing the company structure is another important element to be finalised before business transactions can commence. A board of directors, who will govern the company going forward, needs to be appointed or elected. If the founder or the inventor of the company is not trained or experienced in business management, they need to do a crash course in taking on this responsibility themselves. Alternatively, employ someone with business management experience. Occasionally the funders of the business will insist on employing their own CEO or Managing Director to take control of the business aspects of the innovation (Barnard 2011). This will leave room for the founder to continue with research and development activities in the continuous improvement of the innovation. Often the founder will be involved with the marketing strategy of the innovation in order to provide more credibility and gravitas when addressing the target audience and demonstrating functionalities.

One of the most expensive exercises for an Internet company is the registration of its brand trademarks and patents internationally. Different countries have different regulations, and this could be a very complex route to follow. An easier and more cost-effective route for brand management would be to register all the web domains (especially the primary ones such as .com, .net, .info, .org) of the Internet company's brand as soon as possible as this gives a professional and international 'ownership' to the brand. However, this will not prohibit other companies from registering the brand trademark in foreign countries. Owning all the web domains for that brand can make it very difficult for other companies to do business online using that brand name. Nevertheless, if an Internet company wants to open offices or shops in different foreign countries, it would have to go the route of registering the brand trademark and patents in those specific jurisdictions.

When looking at the complex legal and regulatory framework that accompanied the commercialisation process of Gradnet, it is recommended that researchers and universities appoint a fiduciary company to handle these terms of reference. Many universities in South Africa do not have the necessary skills and hands-on approach that is needed in the business environment. The red tape usually associated with the university milieu is more than often not conducive to quick and efficient decision-making that is an especially critical requirement in a start-up business environment. Running a business successfully requires a fast-pace assertiveness that will ensure a competitive edge for the company.

Conclusion

One of the greatest discoveries made during the innovation process of Gradnet was the interdisciplinary nature of action research. In a tumultuous modern world, it is impossible to ignore the many grey areas that are constantly identified as 'falling through the cracks' of the academic and managerial silos that many universities and companies have constructed. It is especially those overlapping areas that can provide the key to unlocking new knowledge and innovative solutions to universal challenges. Multi-layered partnerships and strategic collaboration play a significant role in the innovations of the present and the future.

Another observation is the lack of an integrated and streamlined approach at many South African universities with regard to their commercialisation activities. The University of Stellenbosch serves as a prime example of an institution that is getting it right. Other institutions can look at this institution for mentorship and guidance for their own commercialisation endeavours. There should be stronger collaboration between public universities and government institutions such as TIA (Technological Innovation Agency) and the IDC (Industrial Development Corporation) in order to identify viable research projects and secure seed funding for these innovations.

In conclusion, it must be noted that all academic disciplines have the potential for establishing commercially viable research projects. It is a common misperception that only the 'hard-core' sciences have the potential of commercialisation and technology transfer. This is not the case as the global landscape poses many challenges that need resolving. If an applied action research approach is followed in any academic discipline, it could render practical solutions to address those challenges while at the same time provide an enterprise opportunity to the innovators. Looking for these opportunities is where entrepreneurship starts.

Acknowledgements

Competing interests

The authors declare that they have no financial or personal relationships which may have inappropriately influenced them in writing this article.

Authors' contributions

Z.B. (University of Johannesburg) conducted the research as part of a PhD postgraduate study under the supervision of C.R. (University of Johannesburg).

References

Barnard, Z., 2004, 'Information dissemination to alumni of the University of Johannesburg', MA dissertation, Dept. of Information and Knowledge Management, University of Johannesburg.

Barnard, Z., 2007, 'Online community portals for managing the information needs of alumni of the South African higher education sector to enable valuable networking: A University of Johannesburg Alumni case study', PhD thesis, Dept. Information and Knowledge Management, University of Johannesburg.

Barnard, Z., 2011, 'Technology transfer in support of sustainable development', Ideas to Market Seminar of the Research Institute for Innovation & Sustainability (RIIS), 25 October 2011, Pretoria, South Africa.

Barnard, Z. & Rensleigh, C., 2008, 'Investigating online community portals for enhanced alumni networking: A case study of the University of Johannesburg Alumni', *The Electronic Library* 26(1), 433–445. http://dx.doi.org/10.1108/02640470810893710

Barnard, Z. & Rensleigh, C., 2013, 'From conceptualization to commercialization: Case study of a web-based research spinoff', *Proceedings of the 15th annual conference on World Wide Web applications*, 10–13 September 2013, Cape Town, South Africa.

Barnard, Z., Rensleigh, C. & Niemann, I., 2005, 'Investigating ICTs for relationship marketing targeting alumni of the University of Johannesburg', *International Journal of Technology, Knowledge and Society* 1(6), 103–114.

Barnard, Z. & Van der Merwe, D., 2014, 'From local imperative to global significance: The University of Johannesburg scenario', *The Business and Management Review* 4(4), 309–320. *Proceedings of the International Conference on Business and Economic Development (ICBED)*, 24–25 March 2014, New York.

Bozeman, B., 2000, 'Technology transfer and public policy: A review of research and theory', *Research Policy* 29, 627–655. http://dx.doi.org/10.1016/S0048-7333(99)00093-1

Conceicao, O., Fontes, M. & Calapez, T., 2012, 'The commercialisation decisions of research-based spin-off: Targeting the market for technologies', *Technovation* 32(1), 43–56. http://dx.doi.org/10.1016/j.technovation.2011.07.009

Department of Education, 2002, 'Government notice: Transformation and restructuring: A new institutional landscape for higher education', *Government Gazette* 23549(855), Pretoria.

Feurer, R. & Chaharbaghi, K., 1995, 'Researching strategy formulation and implementation in dynamic environments', *Benchmarking for Quality Management & Technology* 2(4), 15–26. http://dx.doi.org/10.1108/14635779510102829

Flood, R.L., 2010, 'The relationship of 'systems thinking' to action research', *Systemic Practice and Action Research* 23(4), 269–284. http://dx.doi.org/10.1007/s11213-010-9169-1

Gummeson, E., 2004, 'Return on relationships (ROR): The value of relationship marketing and CRM in business-to-business contexts', *Journal of Business & Industrial Marketing* 19(2), 136–148. http://dx.doi.org/10.1108/08858620410524016

Lam, A., 2011, 'What motivates academic scientists to engage in research commercialization: "Gold", "ribbon" or "puzzle"?', *Research Policy* 40(10), 1354–1368. http://dx.doi.org/10.1016/j.respol.2011.09.002

Phillips, R.G., 2002, 'Technology business incubators: How effective as technology transfer mechanisms?', *Technology in Society* 24, 299–316. http://dx.doi.org/10.1016/S0160-791X(02)00010-6

Ramanathan, K., 1994, 'The polytropic components of manufacturing technology', *Technological Forecasting & Social Change* 46, 221–258. http://dx.doi.org/10.1016/0040-1625(94)90003-5

Rasmussen, E., Mosey, S. & Wright, M., 2014, 'The influence of university departments on the evolution of entrepreneurial competencies in spin-off ventures', *Research Policy* 43(1), 92–106. http://dx.doi.org/10.1016/j.respol.2013.06.007

Rowley, J., 2004, 'Researching people and organizations', *Library Management* 25(4/5), 208–214. http://dx.doi.org/10.1108/01435120410533792

Souder, W.E., Nashar, A.S. & Padmanathan, V., 1990, 'A guide to the best technology-transfer practices', *Journal of Technology Transfer* 15(1/2), 5–16. http://dx.doi.org/10.1007/BF02377652

Stokes, D.E., 1997, *Pasteur's quadrant: Basic science and technological innovation*, Brookings Institution Press, Washington.

Van Brakel, P., 2003, 'Information portals: A strategy for importing external content', *The Electronic Library* 21(6), 591–600. http://dx.doi.org/10.1108/02640470310509153

Wieringa, R. & Morali, A., 2012, *Technical action research as a validation method in information systems design science, lecture notes in Computer Science, 7286,* University of Twente, The Netherlands.

Workers' Compensation Board (WCB), n.d., 'Research definitions', viewed 01 September 2004, from http://www.wcb.ab.ca/research/definitions

Yrle, A.C., Hartman, S.J. & Payne, D.M., 2005, 'Generation X: Acceptance of others and teamwork implications', *Team Performance Management* 11(5/6), 188–199. http://dx.doi.org/10.1108/13527590510617765

13

Data protection laws and privacy on Facebook

Authors:
Phillip Nyoni[1]
Mthulisi Velempini[2]

Affiliation:
[1]Department of Information Systems, North-West University, South Africa

[2]Department of Computer Science, University of Limpopo, South Africa

Correspondence to:
Mthulisi Velempini

Email:
mvelempini@gmail.com

Postal address:
Private Bag X1106,
Sovenga 0727, South Africa

Background: Social networks have changed the way people communicate. Business processes and social interactions revolve more in the cyber space. However, as these cyber technologies advance, users become more exposed to privacy threats. Regulatory frameworks and legal instruments currently lacking a strong cyber presence are required, for the protection of users.

Objectives: There is need to explore and evaluate the extent to which users are exposed to vulnerabilities and threats in the context of the existing protection laws and policies. Furthermore, to investigate how the existing legal instruments can be enhanced to better protect users.

Method: This article evaluates and analyses these privacy challenges from a legalistic point of view. The study is focused on the South African Facebook users. Poll information gathered from the profile pages of users at North-West University was analysed. A short survey was also conducted to validate the poll results. Descriptive statistics, including measures of central tendency and measures of spread, have been used to present the data. In addition, a combination of tabulated and graphical description data was also summarised in a meaningful way.

Results: The results clearly show that the legal frameworks and laws are still evolving and that they are not adequately drafted to deal with specific cyber violation of privacy.

Conclusion: This highlights the need to review legal instruments on a regular basis with wider consultation with users in an endeavour to develop a robust and an enforceable legal framework. A proactive legal framework would be the ideal approach unfortunately; law is reactive to cyber-crimes.

Introduction

The content of Web 2.0 is largely user generated and site owners and operators are not fully in control of the content rendered by their sites (Mansfield-Devine 2008). Unfortunately, the user generated content may be used in ways for which it was not originally intended. It is important to note that social media generates a lot of personal information on individual profiles. Furthermore, third party applications that facilitate the exchange of information have the ability to access profile information for individuals and associate it with their identities (Gartrell, Han & Beach 2008).

Social networking websites (for example Facebook and Twitter) have gained popularity in recent years. Facebook alone has grown to 1.28 billion users who spend a considerable time on social networks each day (Digital Insights 2014). These sites are part of the larger trend of websites whose content is user generated. Social media users are increasingly concerned about what personal information they may reveal when online and how it can be used. Of concern are third party organisations that derive revenue from personal information collected on websites (Gartrell *et al.* 2008).

Most users are concerned about their privacy, which they feel is under threat more than ever, given the advances in technology. Databases and Internet records containing private data such as financial statements, medical records and mobile calls do exist. Interestingly users have no knowledge of the existence of multiple data stores of their personal information, who is able to access them and how the information is used. They also do not have control over these data stores (Gartrell *et al.* 2008). This lack of awareness of what information is stored about users and how it is used has led many users to question Facebook's approach to privacy.

This research seeks to examine the data protection laws that are designed to help secure the privacy of users in South Africa. Given the risk of disclosing personal information online, users need to be made aware of the policies and legal instruments that have been drafted to protect them. The awareness will give users a safer social network experience. The article also examines possible areas where these laws can be reconfigured and enhanced to better protect users, whilst enabling the owners of these sites to continue providing their services in an optimal and secure manner.

The article is organised into the following sections: a literature review on privacy, social networks and the law and data protection laws applied in different regions in the world. It then discusses the methodology employed to gather data from profile pages of students of North-West University and how this data were analysed. A combination of graphical description as well as tabulated description with statistical analysis is also presented. The article concludes with guidelines and recommendations.

Related work

Privacy, social networks and the law

According to the Information Security Group of Africa (2011) privacy is, 'the appropriateness of the use of personal information and depends on a number of factors such as context, regulatory requirements, the individual's expectations as well as the right of an individual to control how their personal information is used or processed'. Privacy therefore concerns the control individuals have over information relating to them. This control is linked to users' ability to decide on the amount of visibility and online presence.

Privacy can also be viewed as informational self-determination – the right to determine who accesses one's personal data. This interpretation is widespread in Europe (Stahl 2000). Self-determination can be wielded in various ways, for example users can be granted the right (through legal channels) to know when their personal information is collected, the right to decide how their information may be used, for what purposes and by who. The right to decide on information release is the right that many online users lack. Thus, privacy will exist when the usage, release and circulation of personal information can be controlled (Information Security Group of Africa 2011).

A different perspective is that privacy is in fact a form of property. If personal information can be treated as property, then privacy issues can be reduced to more established (intellectual) property laws (Spinello 2000). If it is treated as a form of property, users should be entitled to legal rights to privacy. It is a means of generating value for not only the generators of information, but also those who collect and sell it to other parties. Using this metaphor, it becomes clear that it requires legal protection in the form of comprehensive legislation from the public sector regulators (policymakers and advocates) and the private sector regulators (businesses and consumers) (Spinello 2000).

Various countries have implemented varying degrees of privacy legislation, which has been designed to control how companies access and utilise information about potential customers. America has had a relatively business-friendly, minimal intervention approach encouraging organisations to provide self-regulated privacy protections. By contrast, the European Union has taken a pro-consumer approach with tough regulations banning the use of personal information until consent is received from users (Turner & Dasgupta 2003). Each approach has its benefits and drawbacks. For example, letting the service providers self-regulate will allow for innovation amongst the competing companies with the users rewarding the site operators with best protection privacy laws. Meanwhile, having the government intervening might be necessary given the fact that outside regulators often have better understanding of what constitutes abuse and privacy violation than the companies within the ecosystem. The ultimate aim of either approach is the effective mitigation of privacy issues, which promotes increased user participation, thus improving revenue for online business initiatives and facilitating future growth in the international e-commerce market place.

Some sectors of the online community, however, challenge the involvement of government, arguing that privacy is the sole responsibility of users. The understanding is that users willingly enter into agreements and contracts with companies for the protection of their data (Smith 2004). It is unfortunate that users do not read extensive and comprehensive agreements. This means that individuals would have to possess a greater awareness of and appreciation for personal data. If one considers Smith's (2004) argument, it is evident that he is advocating for users to ensure that their personal information is managed effectively by service providers. Users are therefore expected to lobby individual companies that provide weaker protection mechanisms.

The activities of users can be easily tracked online without the awareness or permission of users, thereby violating the privacy rights of users. Depending on how this information is used, it can later damage or ruin one's reputation, costing one employment or a political office (Warren 2008). Therefore, getting users personally involved in the protection of their privacy is vital in ensuring that violations can be quickly dealt with.

Although there are laws designed to protect the privacy of individuals, many individuals risk their privacy by willingly posting personal and damaging information online (Warren 2008). Research to date has shown that privacy is the responsibility of individuals (Fogel & Nehmad 2009), whilst others are of the view that privacy is the responsibility of companies (Mishra 2008).

Privacy legislation

The Internet is a disruptive technology that has brought about many challenges. One of those challenges has been the protection of privacy, which is generally accepted as one of the main issues of computer and information ethics (Stahl 2000). New technologies raise a number of issues for privacy protection. Whilst participating in online communities (social networks) it is possible for individual users' actions to be tracked without the users' awareness or permission and this presents a threat to the very principles of freedom and openness that the Internet was founded on (Stahl 2000).

Facebook currently operates under its own set of terms and conditions. This means that without sufficient oversight the ecosystem can become very toxic with many dangers for users to watch out for. Facebook attempts to inform its users about changes in its privacy policies, but most users find it difficult and time consuming to read and understand privacy policies. It is even more difficult to figure out how to request that the use of one's personal information be restricted. Privacy concerns are making consumers nervous about going online, but current privacy policies for sites tend to be so long and difficult to understand that consumers rarely read them (Mishra 2008). This is when government legislation becomes necessary: when site operators can no longer effectively ensure user privacy.

The most pervasive individual Web privacy concerns stem from the secondary use of information, defined as personal information collected for one purpose and used, subsequently, for a different purpose (Mishra 2008). According to a report by Mishra (2008):

1. Users are more willing to provide personal information when they are not identified.
2. Some information is more sensitive than others.
3. The most important factor is whether or not the information will be shared with other companies. Users dislike unsolicited communications and any form of automatic data transfer (n.p.).

The privacy challenge has been sensitised by privacy advocates lobbying governments for user protection. They have also established protection laws and regulations in an endeavour to address the privacy challenge. However, the philosophical concepts of privacy, which are not easy to identify yet are fundamental, remain a challenge in drafting privacy-related legal instruments (Stahl 2000). These concepts have been alluded to previously as viewing privacy as property or informational self-determination. However, there are a clear set of common activities that are undoubtedly privacy invasions:

1. The collection and analysis of user data without the user's knowledge, consent or authorisation.
2. Employing of user data in a way other than for which it was intended or authorised.
3. Disclosing, sending or sharing user data without the user's knowledge and permission.

Given all these possible privacy violations, most users want to be informed about what information is being collected, how it will be used and whether the information will be used for the express intent only. Users are less likely to perceive business practices as privacy invasive when they perceive that information is collected in the context of an existing relationship, is relevant to the transaction and will be used

to draw reliable and valid inferences and that they have the ability to control its future use (Baker 1991).

Development of data protection legislation in the United States of America

Privacy has been recognised as an important issue affecting business and users and its significance has continued to escalate as the value of information continues to grow. The United States (US) government is encouraged to take responsibility in protecting users from corporate abuse by enforcing appropriate legislative instruments (Mishra 2008).

Privacy legislation in the US had its beginnings in Congressional hearings held in the 1970s, in which privacy advocates sought to ban credit bureaus from using centralised computer databases, leading to the recognition that both organisations and users have responsibilities regarding information collection and use (Mishra 2008). Since 1973, fair information practice principles have served as the basis for establishing and evaluating US privacy laws and practices.

These principles consist of:

1. notice and awareness
2. choice and consent
3. access and participation
4. integrity and security
5. enforcement and redress.

There is general consensus that organisational privacy policies should reflect these principles. Privacy violations that still occur today prove though that this is not always the case. The US has had a relatively business-friendly, minimal intervention approach encouraging organisations to provide self-regulated privacy protections (Turner & Dasgupta 2003). This may explain why most social media sites are not held accountable for violations as they are registered companies in the US. This is changing however as the US government seeks to secure the homeland through the mass surveillance of its citizens and tracking of their online communications (Craig & Ludloff 2011).

Development of data protection legislation in the European Union

During the early 1980s the Organisation for Economic Cooperation and Development (OECD), issued guidelines similar to the ones the United States produced on the protection of privacy and trans-border flows of personal data (Mishra 2008). The OECD guidelines are the current best-practice global standard for privacy protection and are the recommended model for legislation in member countries. Although not legally binding, the guidelines are recognised by all OECD members, especially the European Union (EU) and the US. They are implemented, however, differently by individual members, suggesting that privacy views differ between countries (Turner & Dasgupta 2003).

As the EU developed their privacy legislation in 1995, they produced their own legal document – the Directive on Data Privacy. It places the responsibility only on companies and organisations, which should seek permission before using personal information for any purpose. The EU has taken a pro-user approach with tough regulations banning the use of personal information until consent is received from users (Turner & Dasgupta 2003). EU directives that are based on the OECD guidelines have been noted to be stricter and more comprehensive with respect to privacy than in the US (Mishra 2008).

The EU is restricting the operation of US companies unless they fall in line with the EU guidelines and it is estimated that 90% of US companies have not addressed the EU directive. An example of one of the directives is that companies are required to inform customers when they plan to sell their personal information to other firms (Kruck *et al.* 2002). Hence the occasional lawsuits for antitrust in the EU against search engines like Google. These suits show that it is indeed possible to charge large corporations such as Google or Facebook for any violation their business practices are causing within the country or region they are operating in.

Development of data protection legislation in South Africa

As mentioned before, in Europe, modern privacy legislation has been maturing since 1981, with the establishment of the Convention for the Protection of Individuals. In the US the approach that informed the establishment of privacy legislation followed a more disparate path. The foundation of commerce in the US is based on the laissez-faire principle (a free-flowing private transactional engagement, without state intervention) and, as such, the various states in the US regulate themselves independently (Information Security Group of Africa 2011).

In South Africa, a new *Act* was signed into law on 26th November 2013 and it is officially known as the *Protection of Personal Information Act* (PoPI). This law protects individuals as it prosecutes organisations and third parties that fail to secure private and personal information such as identity and contact details (Ministry of Justice and Constitutional Development 2013).

The PoPI has been created to enable global commerce and cross-jurisdictional information flow. In order to understand and appreciate the boundaries of the right of privacy and to balance privacy with other competing rights in the Constitution of South Africa, it is important to place privacy in the economic and political context in which personal information is used (Ministry of Justice and Constitutional Development 2013).

Protection of Personal Information Act
Background
The PoPI seeks to give effect to the right to privacy as explained in the Constitution by introducing measures to make sure that all organisations working within South Africa process personal information in a fair, responsible and secure manner (Ministry of Justice and Constitutional Development 2013). It requires that personal information be processed in line with the following guidelines:

1. Accountability.
2. Purpose specification.
3. Security safeguards.
4. Data subject participation (KPMG 2009).

The Act seeks to protect privacy by:

1. Protecting personal information processed by public and private bodies.
2. Ensuring the implementation of information protection principles as minimum requirements for the processing of personal information.
3. Providing for the establishment of an information protection regulator.
4. Providing for the issuing of codes of conducts.
5. Providing for the rights of persons regarding unsolicited electronic communications and automated decision-making (Information Security Group of Africa 2011).

The tenets of the *Act* will help to protect user privacy in various ways. For example, the establishment of an information protection regulator is most welcome. This will ensure that service providers will be held accountable for any data privacy violations. The efficacy of the regulator will depend on how swift it can respond to complaints and the compliance measures it will administer (Ministry of Justice and Constitutional Development 2013).

Impact of PoPI

Facebook already operates in territories where data protection laws are established but has since spread to territories where its operations and its privacy implementations are not regulated (KPMG 2009). With the introduction of PoPI, Facebook will be held accountable as much as it is in the US and the United Kingdom. According to the core principles of PoPI, there must be reasonable processing of personal information in a manner that is consistent with the guidelines set out in the *Act*. The *Act* also applies to third parties that store and process information (KPMG 2009).

The effectiveness of PoPI in the social media has not been investigated. It is envisioned that its effectiveness will be subjected to public scrutiny by the research community in the near future. Its introduction has generated a lot of interest in social networks and security. However, the *Act* is still new, having been signed into law on 26 November 2013, and to date there are no cases that have been prosecuted under it.

Framework

This study utilised the mixed-method approach to data collection. This approach was chosen as it allowed for the subject matter to be viewed from a variety of angles. The participants were drawn from the students pursuing their studies at North-West University (NWU) who have liked the official NWU Facebook page. Facebook was chosen as a representative social network site largely because it commands a huge following. It is the largest social media site with 1.2 billion users (as of 2014), a number which is steadily growing (Digital Insights 2014).

Profile page polling

The profile pages of each participant were compared against a set checklist that covers different aspects of the users' activities on the social media platform that are sensitive in nature. These sensitive activities may be violated in the absence of privacy laws. In total, 357 user profiles were targeted for this study based on the convenience sample. Data collection took over two months as each page required on average 15 minutes to analyse and evaluate.

The sample population was selected from the students who have liked the official NWU Mafikeng campus Facebook page, which had 5701 likes from students, lecturers and other stakeholders from the university community when the data was gathered.

Every user on the social networking website Facebook has a profile page containing the user's personal information. The sensitive data were gathered from these profile pages. Each of the 357 user profiles on Facebook was scrolled through by the researcher using a framework that acted as a checklist to assess each user's privacy awareness. This data are in the public domain and in this work the names of users are not used for ethical reasons. Furthermore, this research has an ethical clearance certificate.

It took on average 15 minutes to gather basic user information such as name, address and place of work. The framework was filled in, matching the observed data (which was freely available over the public domain – Facebook). Each profile would have data covering the individual's likes, friends, location information and activities, which were recorded using the framework. This process was repeated for each participating user.

The sample size of 357 users was used based on a number that has been obtained from suggested sample sizes (Krejcie & Morgan 1970). Convenience sampling was used here due to the accessibility and proximity of the target population. All participants were currently enrolled at the university and have their personal data available on Facebook.

Survey

Furthermore, a short survey was developed based on the questions used in the poll to confirm the results of the framework – the checklist instrument. The survey was based on convenience sampling in which students who were willing to participate were targeted for a quick response. The survey had seven questions and was distributed to 70 participants;

it was designed to support and confirm the findings of the main research instrument, the checklist.

Data instrument

The checklist framework was utilised to profile users by capturing their details on Facebook. It was designed to cover the privacy and data protection concepts of the research. The survey utilised a short questionnaire with questions that covered data protection and the awareness of users regarding legislation protecting them online.

Results
Demographics

Figure 1 shows the gender composition of the sample population which was chosen for this study.

It was observed that 55% (n = 198) of the participants were female whilst 45% (n = 159) were male (see Figure 1). The most common age represented was between 18 and 25 (n = 214), as depicted in Figure 2. This was expected considering that the majority of students in the sample population were undergraduate students.

As shown in Figure 2, young people are the most vulnerable age group as they are the most active group on Facebook. This

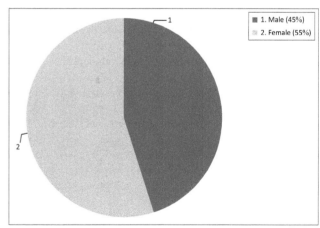

FIGURE 1: User gender.

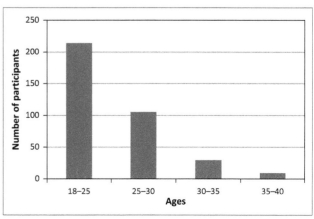

FIGURE 2: Ages of participants.

means that on a more regular basis they are creating personal information about their location, movements, activities and who they spend time with. This sensitive information is publicly available and can be violated by criminal elements and third parties (Gartrell *et al.* 2008).

Users' personal information and self-disclosure

Availability of user details

Figure 3 shows that of the users polled for this study, 67% (*n* = 240) have partially available sensitive information (name, email address or contact numbers) online whilst 33% (*n* = 117) have their full details available (name, email address, contact numbers, address, high school, status, etc.). This is largely because Facebook does not protect personal information of users. The main objective of Facebook is to encourage users to find friends and view other users' profiles.

The fact that most users have their data partially available on Facebook (name and email address or contact numbers) is an indication that Facebook aims to make personal information publicly available (Warren 2008). It is unfortunate that this may result in privacy violations. Furthermore, some users who want to interact only with their friends on Facebook, run the risk of having their posts seen by users who are outside their circle of friends, given the connectedness of Facebook. This violates the privacy of such individuals. On the other hand, some users could use this information for malicious purposes.

Sharing of geo-location

Interestingly, according to the findings of this study, Table 1 illustrates that 31% of Facebook users (*n* = 110) often share their geo-location information with friends on Facebook. The geo-location information ranges from destinations visited, restaurants visited, holiday trips, hotels and accompanying friends. This is based on the level of trust these users have with their friends on the social network. As a result such sensitive information is shared publicly at one's own risk. This can lead to users being targeted by criminals who track their activities via social networks (Blair 2011). The remaining 44% of the sample population (*n* = 157) occasionally share limited geo-location information, such as country or city visited,

without sharing the specific location like hotel, with the sole purpose of alerting their friends of their visits. Many users access Facebook on mobile platforms, where location sharing is a by-product of posting anything on Facebook (Clooke 2013). Location information can also be shared without the consent of a user. Only 25% of this sample do not share their location on Facebook. These could be desktop users or users who deactivated the geo-location feature on Facebook.

Method of access

According to the findings demonstrated in Figure 4, 57% (*n* = 205) of users access Facebook using desktop computers and 43% (*n* = 152) use mobile devices (smartphones or tablets) to access Facebook.

This generation of users prefer to log onto Facebook and 'inbox' (send messages) each other in order to communicate, with the added advantage of being able to share multimedia such as photographs, audio and video (Mourer 2014). Unfortunately, some multimedia data contain sensitive information such as physical addresses and vehicle registration numbers.

According to this study 43% of the users access their profiles through their smartphones. This could explain why their geo-location is automatically updated and loaded onto Facebook as metadata. Most smartphone operating systems now incorporate GPS software that allows smartphone owners to share their location with apps like Facebook Messenger. Whilst these apps inform users that this is how they work, most users may not be aware of how this makes them vulnerable. If a user goes online and posts a comment or uploads a picture, their location becomes a part of that post or upload. If the user simply feels like checking in (a term Facebook uses for those who wish to simply state where

TABLE 1: Sharing of geo-location.

Frequency of geo-location sharing	User %
Often	31 (110 users)
Sometimes	44 (157 users)
Never	25 (90 users)

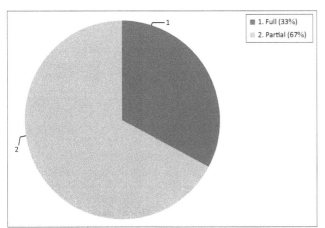

FIGURE 3: Availability of user details.

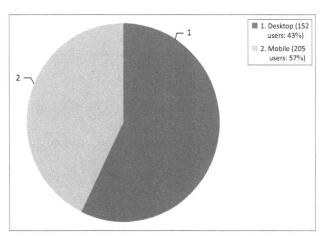

FIGURE 4: Method of access.

they are) then they can do so and the information will be seen by other Facebook users as a post (Clooke 2013).

The availability of geo-location enables third parties to package location-specific commercial advertisement and deliver them to target users (Clooke 2013). However, this can be perceived as annoying and an invasion of one's privacy. Checking in on social media creates a picture based on a user's activities online over a given period of time. These footprints render one traceable (Clooke 2013). As mentioned earlier, criminals can take advantage of the information the social media provide them with (Blair 2011).

Frequency of user tagging

Figure 5, shows the frequency of uploaded photographs that are tagged on Facebook by the study's sample population; 65% (*n* = 233) of the tagging is done by other users whilst 14% (*n* = 49) is done by friends. Tagging a friend avails the information of the tagged user to friends of the tagging user, who are not necessarily friends with the tagged user.

Survey

The survey consisted of questions focusing on the privacy awareness of the users about the PoPI, what violations they

have faced on Facebook as well as the features of Facebook they would like to see protected. The study surveyed 70 respondents who participated in an online survey. Figure 6 shows that 57 of users (81%) do not know there was such an *Act* (PoPI) dedicated to personal information protection in South Africa. These users were under the impression that they were simply communicating online with no need to have their privacy protected by the law. Only 19% (13) were aware of the *Act* but were unsure if it was applicable to Facebook and other social media. The *Act* is still new and may not be as well publicised as would be desirable.

One of the most frequent violations that the surveyed users experience on Facebook is strangers or other Facebook users who have no relationship with a particular user writing on their wall. In Figure 7, 40 (57%) users stated that this has happened to them, whilst 22 (31%) users said they had been tagged in something they did not approve of or found offensive on their Facebook walls, which could be viewed by anyone. Figure 7 also shows that 20 (28%) users claimed someone had uploaded something they did not approve of without prior consultation. Finally, 10 (14%) users stated that they had never encountered any of these violations.

In Figure 8, not surprisingly, when asked which feature they believed would benefit the most from improvement on Facebook, users stated that they would like to see their news feed improve. According to the survey, 60 (85%) users would like to have control of what they see from other users as well as what

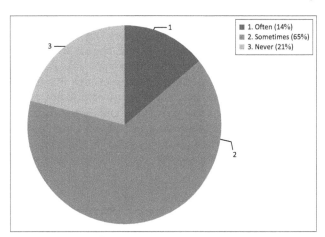
FIGURE 5: Frequency of user tagging.

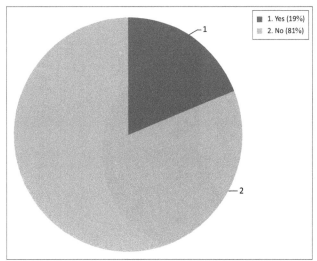
FIGURE 6: User awareness of PoPI.

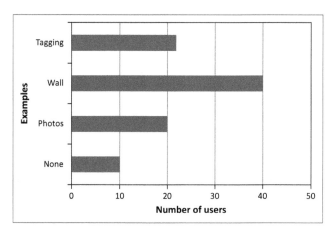
FIGURE 7: Examples of violations of user privacy.

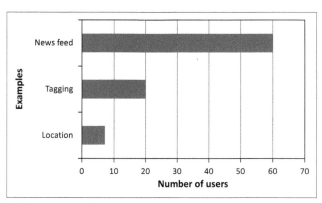
FIGURE 8: Features to be improved upon.

other users see from them via the news feed feature on Facebook. The general account settings of Facebook enable users to control shared information; however, the findings suggest that users require more protection. Furthermore, 20 (28%) respondents would improve the way users can be tagged in unsavoury material on Facebook whilst only 7 (10%) respondents were concerned with location information sharing, which they want changed on Facebook. The poor responses on geo-location information shows that users lack security awareness of how sharing sensitive information and geo-location information impacts negatively on their online presence.

Summary of findings
Privacy

The study reveals that users do not always choose to set their profiles to private when they first register with Facebook. This is because users are not that knowledgeable and also lack awareness. This is consistent with the findings in Figure 8: 86% of respondents (60 news feed respondents including geo-location and tagging respondents) were not aware of the controls that can assist them to regulate their privacy such as picking who can post on their wall, tag them in a photograph or share their location with others without their knowledge. Most user data is partially available on user profiles, a situation that can be exploited by criminal elements. Anyone masquerading as one of the user's friends can access this sensitive data by logging on and searching for this data. Users have less privacy protection on the Internet and this has an influence on the way these sites should be run. Based on these findings, privacy could be achieved through training and awareness on how to fully utilise privacy settings on social media. Users must be taught the different techniques to secure their personal information (Warren 2008).

Users also have experienced different kinds of violations that have infringed on their privacy online. These have ranged from people writing on their walls (reports of unwanted attention, insults or abuse) to being tagged in photographs that are questionable and which may project the user in a negative way (lewd, violent or racist images). Privacy controls (Facebook 2014), if properly taken advantage of, could mitigate some of these violations, but from these findings, it is clear that most users are still unaware of the necessity of the tools to protect themselves (Mourer 2014). This lack of safety consciousness was highlighted in a study by Hoadley *et al.* (2010). The researchers noted that service providers needed to develop privacy enhancing features that are easy to use for the average user. This study has found that most users are not protecting their data, thereby allowing anonymous people on Facebook to access their sensitive data. Users regard the sharing of personal information online to be low risk; therefore, they are not motivated to change their online behaviour (Hoadley *et al.* 2010).

User personal information and self-disclosure

It is easier to view other users' information on Facebook and this makes it possible for those with malicious intent to get hold of sensitive data. The greatest challenge users face is the perception of individuals in a group of friends that they cannot be attacked. However, there is a possibility that they will be attacked. The information that users willingly supply is highly valuable. Attackers are after one's username and password and they do not hesitate to mine Facebook to access such credentials (Fogel & Nehmad 2009).

Attackers have figured out that people hardly change their usernames and passwords, so if they can figure out what their credentials are on Facebook, it is likely they could be the same as the ones used for banking. This is a basic form of social engineering as potential attackers make use of information such as a birthday, pet's name, husband's name, girlfriend's name or high school name, which are the most common types of passwords or security questions used to recover an online account (Fogel & Nehmad 2009).

Geo-location sharing and tagging

To a skilled and seasoned social engineer, location sharing is integral in tracking the movements and establishing patterns of an individual (Blair 2011). This information is quite easy to obtain from the profiles of users. A number of social networks attacks are possible given the high level of trust people place in these sites. In fact, a survey done in 2011 in the United Kingdom revealed that 50 cases of burglary succeeded because the perpetrators relied on social media sites like Facebook in planning their crimes and that location information was useful in their operations (Blair 2011).

The sharing of geo-location makes users vulnerable as they can be tracked. A log of an individual's movements and activities can be created by a potential attacker who can recognise patterns in the user's activities and thereafter plan break-ins when users are not at their place of residence (Blair 2011) with full knowledge when they would be back home. Timing and time management is crucial in any operation.

Most users enjoy sharing their photos with their friends and selected individuals in their news feed or wall posts. The challenge with being tagged is that users can be tagged in some offensive material that might be racist, xenophobic or graphic in nature. These images are then seen by all the friends of their friends as fresh updates on their news feed, thereby bypassing any controls set by the first user. This is an undesirable outcome of tagging. Fortunately Facebook allows users to untag themselves from such images; however, they cannot delete the copies of such images that may have been downloaded on many servers across the globe (Alcorn 2012).

Users often tag each other in photographs on Facebook. Some of the images users are tagged in can leave undesirable impressions on those who view them on their news feed. Facebook has also introduced face-recognition software that can automatically pick up users in images and tag them. Some of these new features from Facebook have met resistance from the user base as they are seen to be clear violations of their privacy. Facebook simply wishes to enable a more efficient service that allows users who know each other to share their experiences with their friends online, but the risk is that users may end up losing their privacy. The need for efficiency may inadvertently create security risks which tend to be unforeseen by the over-eager developers behind these sites. The concept of being tagged in a photograph that you have not consented to is simply a violation of one's privacy. Hopefully this will be considered by service providers when they develop their sites (Alcorn 2012).

Legal issues

Users are not aware of the new legislation, the PoPI, which seeks to defend their rights to privacy. This could be due to a broad disinterest or inability to understand what the *Act* entails. Interestingly, we are migrating more and more to cyberspace and this will necessitate the development of comprehensive and user-friendly privacy legislation to support safety on these websites (Information Security Group of Africa 2011).

South Africa has developed security legislation such as the PoPI as it was necessary to keep up with the pace of technology and e-commerce. There has been a need for separate and more adequate legislation on data protection. The *Act*, however, is not conclusive and does not adequately cover data that is generated on social media sites. There may be a need for tailor-made legislation to help solve any grey areas regarding the application of laws and the description of specific violations (Information Security Group of Africa 2011). There has been a provision within the *Act* for the establishment of an information regulator who has jurisdiction throughout the republic. This board may be able to take up the issues of social media privacy as privacy violations are reported to the regulator. However, it has to be represented and well informed. Unfortunately, the world is lagging behind in cyber security. The design of protection laws is largely reactive instead of being proactive.

There is limited research on the effectiveness of this new PoPI in South Africa. Reports on the application of privacy laws across the world are widely available online. For example, Google was fined 150 000 Euros in France as they violated privacy laws when they failed to inform users regarding the use of personal data (Bodoni 2014). However, this is not the case in South Africa. These cases, however, serve as a benchmark for how PoPI can penalise those who infringe privacy rights. It is possible for the government to hold Facebook accountable as much as the Europeans do and other nations of the world (China, for example, is strict when dealing with Google). This will force the government to be proactive and continue to police the operations of Internet-based companies.

Conclusion

This article has sought to assess how new data protection laws in South Africa affect user behaviour on social media

(Facebook in particular). As can be seen in Figure 6, many users (81%) indicated that they were not aware of the new PoPI and how it is supposed to protect their privacy rights online. Highlights from the findings also show that users still post sensitive personal information on their profiles that can be used to track their movements, location and activities by interested parties. The majority of users believe that information posted on their Facebook profiles is not viewable by anyone outside of their social spheres on Facebook. The study has revealed that there is more than enough information available in the public domain about a user, which can be used to profile and track a user's online habits (Warren 2008).

The new *Act* is likely to face a number of challenges since many Internet-based companies operate outside the jurisdiction of South Africa. It is not easy to see an immediate solution to this challenge of policing international digital cyberspace. A central problem is that behaviour on the Web cannot be controlled. This has traditionally been seen as a good thing. Also it is difficult to reach international consensus on Web privacy because the concept of privacy is heavily dependent on widely variable cultural and political issues (Mishra 2008). For example, the self-regulatory approach adopted by the US is in direct contrast with the government-mandated approach adopted by the EU. This has to do with the region-specific attitudes towards state intervention in online activity (Information Security Group of Africa 2011).

Governments in general lag behind in the creation of privacy protection laws. This is caused by lengthy processes which involve the consultation of industry specialists, practitioners, advocates and users in designing appropriate laws for data protection (Mishra 2008). Furthermore, policymakers lack the expertise to enact such laws. As a result, various international countries have implemented varying degrees of privacy legislations (such as the OECD guidelines), which have been designed to control how companies access and utilise information on potential customers (Information Security Group of Africa 2011). Unfortunately, cyber technology is dynamic, fluid and transnational. The laws are largely reactive to abuses and privacy violations.

There is also a need to enforce privacy laws to deter companies from violating the privacy of users. On the other hand, the challenge of getting users to be proactive about their privacy may be the key to gaining success in this area. Future work may explore the crafting of global privacy laws which are in tandem with national laws designed to police the activities of companies whilst protecting users. User security awareness also requires special attention.

Acknowledgements
Competing interests

The authors declare that they have no financial or personal relationships that may have inappropriately influenced them in writing this article.

Author's contributions

P.N. (North-West University) was responsible for research design, investigation and also wrote the manuscript. M.V. (University of Limpopo) was the project leader and editor of the manuscript.

References

Alcorn, A., 2012, *Facebook really needs more sophisticated privacy controls*, viewed 18 June 2014, from http://www.makeuseof.com/tag/facebook-sophisticated-privacy-controls-opinion/

Baker, J., 1991, 'Personal Information and Privacy', in *Proceedings of the first conference on computers, freedom, and privacy*, pp. 42–45, IEEE Computer Society Press, Los Alamitos. http://dx.doi.org/10.1109/CCFP.1991.664754

Blair, K., 2011, *New survey: Burglars use social media to plan crimes*, viewed 18 June 2014, from http://socialtimes.com/new-survery-burglars-use-social-media-to-plan-crimes_b79475

Bodoni, S., 2014, *Google fined maximum French penalty for privacy violations*, viewed 30 January 2014, from http://www.bloomberg.com/news/2014-01-08/google-fined-maximum-french-penalty-for-privacy-violations.html

Clooke, R., 2013, *Facing the risks of location sharing*, viewed 18 June 2014, from http://www.mobilesecurity.com/articles/526-facing-the-risks-of-location-sharing#sthash.gO0eDEGi.dpuf

Craig, T. & Ludloff, M., 2011, Privacy and big data, O'Reilly Media, Sebastopol.

Digital Insights, 2014, *Social media statistics for 2014*, viewed 23 March 2015, from www.adweek.com/socialtimes/files/2014/06/social-media-statistics-2014.htm

Facebook, 2014, *Privacy policy of Facebook*, viewed 25 March 2015, from www.facebook.com/policies/privacy/basic/?ref_component

Fogel, J. & Nehmad, E., 2009, 'Internet social network communities: Risk taking, trust, and privacy concerns', *Computers in Human Behavior* 25(1), 153–160. http://dx.doi.org/10.1016/j.chb.2008.08.006

Gartrell, M., Han, R. & Beach, A., 2008, *Solutions to security and privacy issues in mobile social networking*, University of Colorado, Boulder.

Hoadley, C., Xu, H., Lee, J. & Rosson, M., 2010, 'Privacy as information access and illusory control: The case of the Facebook news feed privacy outcry', *Journal of Electronic Commerce Research and Applications* 9(1), 50–60. http://dx.doi.org/10.1016/j.elerap.2009.05.001

Information Security Group of Africa, 2011, *Revealing privacy in South Africa: What you need to know*, Information Security Group of Africa, Pretoria, South Africa.

KPMG, 2009, *Information privacy & financial institutions: White paper*, KPMG, Pretoria, South Africa.

Krejcie, R.V. & Morgan, D.W., 1970, 'Determining sample size for research activities', *Journal of Educational and Psychological Measurement* 30, 607–610.

Kruck, S.E., Gottovi, D., Moghadami, F., Broom, R. & Forcht, K.A., 2002, 'Protecting personal privacy on the Internet', *Information Management & Security* 10(2), 77–84. http://dx.doi.org/10.1108/09685220210424140

Mansfield-Devine, S., 2008, 'Anti-social networking: Exploiting the trusting environment of Web 2.0', *Network Security* 11, 4–7. http://dx.doi.org/10.1016/S1353-4858(08)70127-2

Ministry of Justice and Constitutional Development, 2013, *Protection of Personal Information Act, No. 4 of 2013*, Parliament of South Africa, Pretoria, South Africa.

Mishra, A., 2008, *Web privacy: Issues, legislations and technological challenges*, IGI Global, Hershey. http://dx.doi.org/10.4018/978-1-59904-804-8.ch001

Mourer, K., 2014, *Texting to surpass phone calls for business communication*, viewed 18 June 2014, from http://www.icmi.com/Resources/Mobile/2014/03/Texting-to-Surpass-Phone-Calls-for-Business-Communication

Smith, H., 2004, 'Information privacy and its management', *MIS Quarterly Executive* 3(4), 201–213.

Spinello, R., 2000, *Cyber-ethics: Morality and law in cyberspace*, Jones and Bartlett, London.

Stahl, B.C., 2000, *The impact of the UK Human Rights Act 1998 on privacy protection in the workplace*, IGI Global, Hershey.

Turner, E.C. & Dasgupta, S., 2003, 'Privacy on the web: An examination of user concerns, technology, and implications for business organisations and individuals', *Journal of Information System Management* 20(1), 8–18. http://dx.doi.org/10.1201/1078/43203.20.1.20031201/40079.2

Warren, J., 2008, *Self-imposed violations of privacy in virtual communities*, University of Texas, San Antonio.

14

Knowledge-management practices at selected banks in South Africa

Authors:
Joel Chigada[1]
Patrick Ngulube[2]

Affiliations:
[1]Department of Information Science, University of South Africa, South Africa

[2]School of Interdisciplinary Research and Postgraduate Studies, University of South Africa, South Africa

Correspondence to:
Patrick Ngulube

Email:
ngulup@unisa.ac.za

Postal address:
PO Box 392, Pretoria 0003, South Africa

Background: Effective knowledge organisations (EKO) create dynamic capabilities through the acquisition, creation, sharing and retention of knowledge. These EKOs are designed to enable an organisation to improve best practices in business. As knowledge is different from other organisational resources, decision-makers ought to understand the importance of knowledge to an organisation. In order to fully utilise knowledge-management (KM) practices and to enhance efficiency, management should appreciate and understand the importance of KM. A proper understanding of KM will add value to organisational knowledge.

Objective: This study focused on investigating the knowledge-management practices at selected banks in South Africa. The objective was to establish the extent to which selected banks had implemented knowledge-management practices such as the acquisition, sharing and retention of knowledge.

Method: Quantitative and qualitative data for this study were collected through the use of a multi-methods approach. Data were collected from middle and senior managers through the use of questionnaires and an interview protocol. All usable quantitative data were analysed using Survey Monkey and Microsoft Excel 2010 whilst thematic analysis was used to extract detailed, rich and complex data accounts from interviews.

Results: Though the study revealed the presence of KM practices at selected banks, KM concepts were not universally understood, thus impeding the organisation-wide implementation of KM practices. Knowledge-management practices were only discussed as a footnote because no formal policies existed to add value to KM initiatives.

Conclusion: The study concludes that organisations such as banks should perform a knowledge inventory. Knowledge inventories will become handy during the process of developing KM policies and practices for integrating work processes, collaborating and sharing (including the efficient use of knowledge technology platforms) and developing an enabling institutional culture.

Introduction and background to the study

As pointed out by (Gaffoor & Cloete 2010:1), 'Knowledge management (KM) has become a focal point for debates on mechanisms to assist firms in acquiring a greater competitive edge in the emerging global information economy'. This means that organisations – big and small, global and domestic – are channelling their focus on knowledge assets as strategies for competitive advantage. Knowledge tools and systems are being developed to give an organisation a competitive edge. Fowler and Pryke (2003) defines KM as follows:

> ... an established management approach that is successfully applied across corporate sectors by methodically creating, sharing, preserving and optimally applying the extensive knowledge present in the organisation, to better achieve organisational objectives. (p. 254)

The above definition captures fundamental issues that are used in discussing KM practices in this study. In this regard, Cong and Pandya (2003) suggest the following:

> ... any given control mechanism has the capacity to affect both the nature and flow of knowledge in a firm by the manner in which the firm processes particular attributes of knowledge. (p. 27)

The South African banking environment is characterised by intense competition, thus compelling the players to use strategies and create knowledge assets that are difficult to imitate. For an institution to remain competitive and relevant in a knowledge environment, there are opportunities to create, own, protect and use commercial and industrial knowledge assets which are difficult to copy. The South African banking industry comprises four commercial banks, namely ABSA, FNB, Nedbank and Standard Bank whilst the other banks focus on unsecured lending (personal loans). FNB and Nedbank were selected for this study for the following reasons:

- FNB was chosen because it is the second largest South African commercial bank (after ABSA) in terms of staff complement, assets and branch network (Moneyweb 2012).
- Nedbank was selected because the first author was formerly employed by the bank. This means that permission to conduct a study on Nedbank was already granted, and recruiting participants for the study was relatively easy.

Selecting one bank would have sufficed, but because a comparative approach is utilised in this study, it is of paramount importance to extrapolate different research issues. If two or more cases show to be supporting the same theory, replication can be claimed, and the greater the number of case studies that show replication, the greater the rigour with which theory has been established (Rowley 2002).

The banking customers' ever-changing tastes and preferences require banks to proactively improvise products, exit projects and product lines that can drag down the business and engage in others that maximise the growth potential as radical market shifts threaten to put the bank's business with the wrong product. By rapidly exploiting and applying fragmented internal and external knowledge, a bank can reliably detect emerging windows of opportunity before competition takes the market by surprise. This study investigated the extent to which selected banks in South Africa have implemented KM practices such as the acquisition, sharing and retention of knowledge.

Literature review

The literature review was used to establish how other scholars investigated the same problem. The purpose of reviewing a variety of scholarly thinking was to look at what other scholars have done in areas that are similar or have a relationship to this study (Leedy & Omrod 2005:64). To gain a better understanding of KM practices, it is important to define the area of interest. In Sarrafzadeh, Martin and Hazeri (2006), KM practices are defined '... as the way ideas are translated into action in the process accomplishing specific goals'. Branin (2003:25) opines that 'KM practices include the understanding of KM, knowledge generation, acquisition, organisation, storage, transfer, sharing and retention'. However, Singh (2007) argues as follows:

> Information professionals need to develop the capabilities to survive in knowledge based society, there is need for organisations such as banks to invest in information and knowledge architectures to produce more knowledge. Investments can be in the form of databases systems, patents and tacit knowledge which when fully utilised in the organisation can produce streamlined processes and high quality services and products. (pp. 177–178)

These outputs from a knowledge-based organisation should add value to the organisation as well as provide value for customers.

Knowledge acquisition

Pacharapha and Ractham (2012) define knowledge acquisition as the process of the development and creation of insight, skill and relationships. For knowledge to be acquired, '... there should be willingness and ability of a recipient to acquire and use knowledge are crucial elements' (Gupta & Govindarajan 2000; Ragsdell 2009). During the process of knowledge acquisition, it is important that both source and recipient should be willing to share. There are three motivational drivers that should be taken into consideration: '... attitude towards knowledge sharing, cost and benefit, subjective norms and organisational climate and perceived value of knowledge' (Ford & Staples 2006:14). Knowledge acquisition envisages learning from others through interaction between recipient and source. Nonaka and Takeuchi (1995) opine that the SECI (socialisation, externalisation, combination, and internalisation) and *ba* models play important roles in knowledge acquisition through interaction and collaboration with other individual systems. In knowledge-intensive institutions such as banks, enabling environments are envisaged that allow different departments or individuals to acquire insight, skill and relationships. Management should counter the silo mentality and allow departments to share information, notwithstanding the privacy and secrecy policies of banks. Training and development programmes inherent in banks should pave ways for knowledge acquisition, which is consistent with the SECI and *ba* models.

Knowledge sharing

KM practices help organisations to refocus on using knowledge that exists already by '... creating an environment for innovation rather than limiting themselves to best practice solutions only' (Laudon & Laudon 2012:245). Turban, Mclean and Wetherbe (2004) define knowledge sharing:

> ... as the wilful application and transfer of one or more person's ideas, insights, solutions and knowledge to another person(s), either directly or via an intermediary, such as a computer-based system. (p. 412)

The definition by Turban *et al.* (2004) illustrates that organisations should have systems in place that help the process of knowledge sharing. A good example of such systems would be computer-based systems because of its speed, ability to store large volumes of information and retrieval capabilities. Knowledge sharing enables organisations such as banks to converge towards '... knowledge portals rather than separate silos of knowledge' (Moneyweb 2013). Knowledge sharing occurs during induction (of new employees) or when employees quit the organisation. Knowledgeable and experienced employees who possess knowledge should be willing to share it. Knowledge shared by individuals and by a community of practice becomes organisational knowledge.

Knowledge may be shared during seminars, conferences, team-building exercises, written reports, performance appraisals and conventional programmes where employees make suggestions. Discussion fora give people opportunities to share personal experiences about a particular event. Seminars and conferences are ideal platforms for 'shy' or 'less vocal' employees to talk freely and openly with their colleagues. Platforms for knowledge sharing should make the communication process easier for different categories of employees. Sentiments or opinions expressed during seminars or conferences should not be used as personal attacks, and managers should not use these events to settle personal scores. Knowledge sharing can encounter challenges such as a lack of time, a lack of experience and a lack of visible rewards for sharing knowledge.

Knowledge retention

Kim (2005:37) defines knowledge retention '… as all systems and activities that capture and preserve knowledge and allow it to remain in the organisational system once introduced'. Management needs to put in place strategies for retaining organisational knowledge before it is lost. The knowledge and expertise of employees should be retained before they leave the organisation. In the absence of knowledge retention strategies, organisations lose tacit knowledge when employees leave for other organisations or due to other forms of attrition. Nonaka and Takeuchi (1995) state that 80% of knowledge lies in the brains of people who possess know-how, secrets and personal skill that will never be shared if no one works on it. This is consistent with Polanyi's (1962) view that '… we know more than we can tell'. In Polanyi's (1962) view, one person may have much knowledge but may not be able to say much about that knowledge. There are employees who carry large volumes of knowledge (tacit knowledge) in their heads, but they may not be prepared to or the environment may limit them from saying much. Tiwana (2008:103) suggests that, in order to make better use of tacit knowledge, a way must be found for it to be transferred directly to one another, making it explicit so that it can be shared throughout the organisation. Individuals who are rich in tacit knowledge (experienced employees, retirees and other talented experts) constitute a wealth of intangible assets for the organisation (Nonaka & Takeuchi 1995).

Wamundila and Ngulube (2011) and Levy (2011) established that knowledge retention could be achieved through documentation and integrating knowledge back into the organisation with special emphasis on retaining best practices. To safeguard against a loss of knowledge, organisations need to devise ways of retaining employees' know-how and best practices so that knowledge can be passed on to future workers, and replacements who should regain the on-the-job knowledge that ex-employees spent years accumulating (Thilmany 2008). Wamundila and Ngulube (2011) posit that knowledge can be retained in an organisation through various strategies that may involve education, training, establishing communities of practice and professional networks, documenting the processes and using advanced technology to capture work processes. This knowledge has to be captured and stored in databases, documents, software and processes, products and services. The human-resources management

function of the banks plays a significant role to coordinate planning programmes for training and development as well as induction and succession. For these elements to work together, the prevailing organisational culture, 'as enabler' of KM, helps to facilitate synergy between the KM practices. There are barriers to implementing KM practices. These include a lack of employee interaction, the salience of value, a lack of KM policies, a lack of structural ties and the absence of KM enablers. These barriers require attention should an organisation plan to implement KM practices. Failure to pay attention can result in the failure of KM initiatives as evidenced by the low level of KM practices at selected banks.

Methodology

We used multiple methods in the study to improve the reliability and validity of the data collected, culminating in the collection of a rich set of data (triangulation). Multi-methods research was designed to guarantee the reliability and validity of quantitative measures (Romm & Ngulube in press). An embedded case-study design offered the opportunity to explore in depth the extent to which banks have implemented KM practices such as the acquisition, sharing and retention of knowledge. Embedded case studies are studies in which different levels or sources of data are collected (Yin 2003). According to Powell (1997:66), the population should be selected with great care, bearing in mind the selection criteria, the desired size and the parameters of the survey. In light of the above, We selected two commercial banks from the four commercial banks in South Africa (population) but then targeted middle managers and purposively selected senior-level managers from the population. The population of a study is the group about whom one wants to draw conclusions. In this case, it was all middle-level managers and purposively selected executive managers (Babbie 2010:111). The whole population (190) of middle-level managers was considered in the study whilst four senior executives were purposively selected to participate in face-to-face interviews. These were selected from the already-delineated sample perceived by the researchers to be key individuals who would give invaluable insight and more detailed answers to the research questions on KM policies.

Questionnaires were used to collect data from geographically dispersed participants whilst interview protocol and document analyses were ideal for collecting qualitative data. Questionnaires were distributed and received through Survey Monkey©, an online survey platform. A total of 190 questionnaires were distributed to middle-level managers at the selected banks. The questionnaire comprised open-ended questions that allowed the participants to give as much feedback as possible. A set of pre-designed, open-ended questions were used during the interview process to ask participants questions on KM policy issues that were not addressed in the survey.

All quantitative data were analysed using Survey Monkey© and Microsoft Excel© 2010 whilst thematic analysis was used to analyse qualitative data. Using the constant comparative method of analysis (Leedy & Ormrod 2010:145), we looked for emerging themes and recurring events and categorised them. The themes and patterns emerging from interviews and surveys were grouped together, making it easier to analyse the data. Braun and Clarke (2006:77) argue in this regard that '… thematic analysis can act as a core analytical method because of its flexibility with both interpretive and constructivist paradigms'.

Major findings and discussions

Of the 190 questionnaires distributed, 101 (53.15%) responses were received, which is consistent with the findings of Greenlaw and Brown-Wetty (2009). They (Greenlaw & Brown-Wetty 2009:467) established that '… a response rate of 51.58% from a web-based survey tool was higher than many responses rates of that type of survey as reported in literature'. This study achieved a response rate that was 1.57% rate higher than that of Greenlaw and Brown-Wetty. Of the 101 respondents who participated in the study, 58 (57.43%) were from Nedbank and 43 (42.57%) were from FNB. The gender characteristics of respondents were as follows: 39 (38.61%) male managers from Nedbank compared to 27 (26.73%) male managers from FNB, 19 (18.82%) female managers from Nedbank compared to 16 (15.84%) female managers from FNB. It was established that, in all gender categories, more respondents were from Nedbank. The findings of the study are presented in two sections, namely quantitative and qualitative.

Quantitative findings

Respondents were asked to indicate KM practices and to what extent their bank had implemented KM practices. All study participants indicated that the acquisition, sharing and retention of knowledge are practiced at their bank. The study established that selected banks use different KM practice though a few of these KM practices were indeed found to be similar. The study identified the following KM practices.

Departmental meetings and team-building sessions

The data in Table 1 show that 18.84% of the respondents believed that departmental meetings and team-building sessions were the most widely used KM practices at the selected banks. The study revealed that, during departmental meetings, employees were exposed to information pertaining to global trends in the banking industry such as credit-card fraud, systems to combat cyber-crime and rules from MasterCard and Visa International. Departmental meetings were used as platforms for discussing and highlighting challenges and opportunities in the South African banking industry. It was established that team-building sessions were platforms for fostering awareness of the team spirit and to reinforce commitment to the team's shared goals and objectives' (Jain 2011:6). The study established that team-building sessions were designed to encourage individual team members to cooperate in the team's work environment, interacting and integrating skills into a united effort so that each individual's goal achievement is connected to the greater overall team's goal achievement. This thinking is consistent with the views of Jain (2011), namely that tacit knowledge can be achieved through face-to-face meetings and electronic discussions. Nonaka and Takeuchi (1995) posit that tacit knowledge can be transmitted through social interactions between individuals.

Succession planning

Eleven (10.89%) of the respondents believed that succession plans enable selected banks to retain organisational knowledge. The study established that succession planning is designed to ensure the continued effective performance of selected banks by providing for the deployment and replacement of key people over time. Participants indicated that lateral transfer and redeployment are a common practice at selected banks. Though redeployment and lateral transfer are common, this study could not establish if the motive was in line with KM initiatives. 'Effective succession or talent-pool management concerns itself with building a series of feeder groups up and down the entire leadership pipeline or progression' (Noe et al. 2010:447). There is no guarantee that experienced employees will retire or spend the rest of their working life in one organisation. Hence, organisations engage in succession planning programmes to ensure that businesses survive into the future in the event of a loss in tacit knowledge. With the changing demographics of the global village, organisations lose key staff to competitors due to working conditions or opportunities presented by competitors (Hill 2010:276). When key staff resigns or retires, it becomes a challenge to replace the key staff if the organisation does not have contingency measures in place.

Internet and intranet

Respondents indicated that the intranet and Internet play a key role as evidenced by a response rate of 14.85%. Technology facilitates communication between management and employees as well as quick access to, the search for and the retrieval of information. Dewah (2011:106) posits that '… technology comprising collaborative computing tools, knowledge servers, enterprise knowledge portals, electronic document management systems, knowledge harvesting tools and search engines' are critical enablers of knowledge-management. This information-communication technology plays an important role in how banking processes and transactions are conducted. Jain (2011) opines that effective knowledge-management practices could be achieved by utilising the latest IT tools in order to capture, create, store, transfer, share, retrieve, maintain and update knowledge. The study established that employees at selected banks have email addresses and a laptop or a personal computer, justifying their arguments that information and knowledge was created and shared through the Internet and intranet.

Road shows

As shown in Table 1, 3.96% of the respondents stated that road shows were common at Nedbank. Kotler and Keller (2013) define a road show as follows:

> … a program comprising a series of marketing events that companies organise at multiple locations to generate interest

TABLE 1 Knowledge-management practices at selected banks.

Knowledge-management practices at selected banks	Nedbank (%)	FNB (%)	Total number of respondents (%)
Departmental meetings and team-building sessions	12 (11.89)	6 (5.95)	18 (18.84)
Succession planning	7 (6.93)	4 (3.96)	11 (10.89)
Use of the intranet and Internet	9 (8.91)	6 (5.94)	15 (14.85)
Road shows	4 (3.96)	-	4 (3.96)
Tea or lunch breaks	5 (4.95)	-	5 (4.95)
Seminars	3 (2.97)	-	3 (2.97)
Facebook, Wikis, Blogs and Twitter	6 (5.94)	2 (1.98)	8 (7.92)
Staff promotions/secondment	3 (2.97)	-	3 (2.97)
Mentorship	4 (3.96)	-	4 (3.96)
Project teams	5 (4.95)	3 (2.97)	8 (7.92)
Innovators campaign	-	7 (6.93)	7 (6.93)
Training centre	-	5 (4.95)	5 (4.95)
Extension of retirement age	-	3 (2.97)	3 (2.97)
Knowledge portals	-	3 (2.97)	3 (2.97)
Suggestion boxes	-	4 (3.96)	4 (3.96)
TOTAL	**58 (57.43)**	**43 (42.57)**	**101 (100)**

regarding a subject that they want to promote. It could about new products/services targeted at customers, new investment offerings targeted at investors, new social initiatives targeted at the community and so on. (p. 476)

These marketing events are usually conducted by the chief executive officer or managing executive of the bank in the case of Nedbank. They use the executive to add dignity and credibility to the roadshow as well as to attract high-profile individuals in society. The study revealed that road shows were conducted at Nedbank's regional head offices in Sandton, Pretoria, Polokwane, Cape Town and Durban, thus isolating other towns or cities.

Tea and lunch breaks

Tea and lunch breaks are platforms used to discuss social issues as evidenced by 4.95% of the respondents from Nedbank. Knowledge sharing platforms during tea or lunch breaks are not used at FNB as indicated in Table 1. During tea or lunch breaks, employees sometimes talk about work-related challenges and political and economic matters. These platforms enable employees to create and share knowledge and information. Social issues dominate tea and lunch breaks as friends want to 'catch-up' with weekend events.

Seminars

Nedbank respondents (2.97%) stated that seminars are environments where participants socialise and create and share knowledge with their colleagues. This finding is consistent with Nonaka and Konno (1998) who state that knowledge is shared within a contextualised space, called *ba*, which is a Japanese word roughly meaning 'place'. This designates a specific time and place where interactions between individuals take place. Employees should be given platforms to interact face-to-face, such as conferences meetings, so as to share a common understanding through shared language and narratives across networks. Trust also increases the incentive to exchange knowledge, and norms of reciprocity facilitate the transfer of novel information and tacit knowledge (Sheriff & Sheriff 2008).

Interactive communication channels

Interactive communication channels are tools such as emails, short message services, Facebook, WhatsApp, Twitter, Blogs, Wikis and BlackBerry messaging that handle, store, locate, distribute, receive and communicate tacit and explicit knowledge through social networks amongst people in possession of knowledge. Eight (7.92%) respondents confirmed the use of interactive communication channels at selected banks. Dewah (2011) posits that the adaptive-structuration theory draws some links between individuals and organisational learning due to the key concepts that address aspects of group interaction with technology. Organisational learning is regarded as a continuous phenomenon emerging from the social interactions and practices of individuals (Ryu, Kim & Chaudhury 2005). With the advent of interactive communication technology such as wikis, blogs, Facebook and Twitter, to name but a few, individuals are exposed to new information and knowledge.

Staff promotions and secondment

The study established that knowledge retention is achieved through the use of staff promotions and secondment as evidenced by 2.97% of respondents from Nedbank. Participants from FNB did not indicate the use of staff promotions and secondment as a knowledge retention practice. The study established that staff were promoted on the basis of years of experience, opportunities that arose due staff attrition and as part of Nedbank's succession planning policy. However, it was not clear if staff promotions were in any way aligned to knowledge-management initiatives.

Mentorship

The subject expert or experienced employee transfers tacit knowledge to the inexperienced employee (Nonaka 1995). Mentorship entails the pairing of an experienced member of staff with an inexperienced or new employee in order to assist the new employee in acquiring new knowledge

(Beazley, Boenisch & Harden 2002). During mentoring and apprenticeship training, senior or experienced managers transfer their knowledge, wisdom, specific insights and skills to their juniors within a short space of time so that, when the experienced employees leave the organisation, the organisation's practices, knowledge, history, stories and culture are preserved. The evidence (3.96%) shown in Table 1 indicates that mentorship programmes are used as a practice for the creation, sharing and retention of knowledge at Nedbank.

Project teams

The study found that selected banks have assembled groups of individuals to perform activities that contribute toward achieving a common task-related goal. The study established that product development, systems development, marketing campaigns and training and development projects are managed by project teams consisting of skilled workers from the same or different function areas. Eight (7.92%) of the respondents indicated that assignments or tasks at the selected banks are managed by retirees or experienced employees. They provide critical skills and experience to mentor junior and less-experienced employees, thus allowing senior employees to share knowledge and experiences during project management.

Innovators campaign

Seven (6.93%) of the respondents (from FNB) stated that the innovators campaign is a great success story for knowledge-creation and sharing because FNB's success is attributable to rewards and incentives awarded for innovation. The website Moneyweb (2012) reports on this matter as follows:

> First National Bank awarded R4 million in 2009 to winning ideas through its FNB Innovators initiative, in a bid to improve its service delivery and at the same time motivate staff to higher levels of excellence.
>
> The initiative identifies and rewards staff who display creative thinking and come up with innovations to ensure more efficient and effective systems and procedures. (n.p.)

In addition, the Steve campaign, eBucks and eWallet exemplify innovation initiatives at FNB, and individuals who came up with those concepts were rewarded for creative thinking. The study recorded that the innovators campaign is an important KM practice at FNB. This practice was not found at Nedbank.

Training centre

Results shown in Table 1 show that FNB has put in place KM practices such as training centres as indicated by 4.95% of the respondents. The study established that the FNB training centre is situated in the Sandton Business district, comprising 16 versatile conference venues, 3 boardrooms and a 140-seater auditorium and several breakaway rooms (First National Bank [FNB] 2011/12). The training centre is equipped with state of the art technology and facilities, and it offers an enabling environment for knowledge-creation and sharing (Nonaka & Takeuchi 1995).

Extension of retirement age

The risk of losing critical knowledge has a negative operational impact for organisations. This could be reduced by knowledge retention through capturing the organisations' individual tacit knowledge and subsequently transforming it into organisational knowledge and document processes. Critical knowledge in some of the banks' departments largely rests with people rather than in processes. When such people leave the bank, they take with them that critical knowledge. If the expertise of these senior or experienced people is not shared or transferred to the next employees, the potential to innovate is eroded, and the risk of unavoidable mistakes increases as these become a regular occurrence. It was established that the retirement age at FNB is not fixed to give both the employer and employee room for negotiation. Three (2.97%) respondents indicated that a policy on extending the retirement age exists at FNB whilst such a practice does not exist at Nedbank.

Other practices

The study recorded that knowledge portals (2.97%) and suggestion boxes (3.96%) are used for knowledge sharing at FNB, but there are no knowledge portals at Nedbank. Knowledge portals provide the infrastructure and enabling technology to support the creation, production, acquisition, aggregation, filtering, organisation, transmission, dissemination, usage and/or retention of knowledge. If the computer of today is a network, the desktop of today is a portal (FNB 2011/12). As suggested by Dewah (2011), organisations require ICTs that enable the acquisition, sharing, storage, retention and retrieval of organisational memory for future reuse. Knowledge portals become effective KM enablers if the systems are aligned to organisational KM policies. The study established that FNB's IT department is tasked to manage knowledge-related issues to reduce the cost of information publishing and distribution; to increase compliance with corporate standards, rules and processes for information storage and dissemination; to automate business processes such as price-quote generation or lead and forecast sharing and to preserve and leverage prior investments in back-end document management, enterprise resource planning (ERP) and data-warehousing systems (Moneyweb 2013). This study found that managers tend to conflate IT and KM, and this probably explains why the IT department was given these tasks. Both online and physical suggestion boxes are used as platforms for collecting and sharing information with customers and employees. Loyal customers send feedback on the quality of services delivered. The results are shown in Table 1.

The study noted that there are times when knowledge is relevant, and there are times when knowledge is not relevant. The point is that organisations need to use knowledge as soon as it becomes readily available. It was established that information use leads to knowledge-creation, which is possible if an organisation's management creates an enabling knowledge sharing culture. An environment that promotes knowledge acquisition is an environment where employees are provided with '… spaces for emerging relationships, which might be physical, virtual, or mental, providing a platform for advancing individual and/or collective knowledge' (Nonaka & Takeuchi 1995).

Qualitative findings

The knowledge assets of selected banks were found in places like databases, filing cabinets, Internet, intranet, extranets, annual reports and people's heads. The use of the intranet exposes staff to readily available information in order to acquire as much new knowledge as possible. Consequently, some relevant knowledge is acquired through bulletins posted on the intranet, but the veracity or relevance of the knowledge needs to be questioned. It was not clear whether management at selected banks are formally accepting and adopting knowledge as a strategic organisational asset. The banks' reports did not feature the KM practices in their mission statements or core philosophies. However, the FNB self-study of 2011 reveals that KM principles are in fact resident within the Information Technology Department. This finding is also complemented by Nedbank's self-study of 2011, which states that the Group Technology Shared Services (GTSS) is the custodian of knowledge practices. From this information, it is clear that banks misconstrue IT to be knowledge.

Patrick and Dotsika (2007) view knowledge sharing as the social interaction that involves the sharing of both the goal and the favourable outcome centred on problem solving. Platforms for knowledge sharing should then create opportunities for social interaction. The selected banks demonstrated a global presence on iTunes, U Blogs and social networking with the use of Facebook, Twitter, YouTube, WhatsApp and Blackberry Messaging (BBM). One observation from the study is that information-flow and Web 2.0 technology are used in banks as knowledge sharing tools. In addition, podcasts are included in iTunes to reach as many banking clients as possible. However, an interesting revelation was that the technology was created for customers, but employees have limited access to the use of such (Moneyweb 2012). In view of the selective use of Web 2.0 technology, employees felt marginalised in the process of knowledge sharing.

The process of keeping useful knowledge inside the banks and building organisational memory (OM) is documented in the selected banks' reports. This knowledge is preserved and kept in very safe places to ensure knowledge retention. It was established that KM awareness is limited as reflected in the following statement:

> … there did not appear to be a documented inventory of the banks' skills base, or evident records of succession planning, even if the banks' annual reports suggested that there were career development practices. (FNB 2011/12; Nedbank Group South Africa 2012)

The absence of documents to indicate the progress on implementing KM practices could possibly explain why the cultures prevailing at the selected banks were not in favour of knowledge retention. In the event of the loss of key staff in these banks, management would have to revert to contingency measures to mitigate the loss in tacit knowledge.

This study noted that knowledge acquisition is a sub-set of knowledge capture because the knowledge acquired at the selected banks came from such sources as individuals and their colleagues as well as the intranet, Internet, documents and databases (Mavodza & Ngulube 2011). One observation was that expert systems are used by organisations to acquire knowledge from experienced individuals before the expiry of that knowledge. Though the selected banks have platforms for the acquisition, creation, sharing and retention of knowledge, it was noted that some of the KM practices do not provide employees with opportunities for asking questions or making suggestions as pointed out by one survey respondent. It seems clear that each KM practice has strengths and weaknesses. Therefore, the use of complimentary practices would be ideal to compensate the weaknesses of some practices.

The data for this study was both quantitative and qualitative in nature. Therefore, I needed to combine the data (triangulation) to provide answers to the research questions. The depth, clarity, reliability, transferability and truthfulness of the research findings are enhanced when two sets of data are put together. It should be noted that quantitative data are represented in numerical and graphical format whilst qualitative data are more descriptive. It was important to combine quantitative and qualitative data to ensure that relevant data was collected to address the KM practices that were investigated in this study. When multiple research methodologies are used, challenges abound when one tries to combine divergent paradigms. The challenges include the following: It is possible to end up by not doing either type of research well, especially as this research was done by an individual (Fidel 2008). Both quantitative and qualitative findings show that the IT departments of the selected banks are mandated to run all KM initiatives, a notion whereby many people conflate IT into KM or whereby all KM practices are part of IT. Findings from both sets of data indicate that ICTs are paramount in the acquisition, sharing and retention of KM practices.

Organisational knowledge conversion theory (SECI Model)

The study noted that KM practices at selected banks are based on the organisational knowledge conversion theory, that is, the SECI model. The conversion of organisational knowledge rests on the premise that knowledge is converted from one state to another (Nonaka &Takeuchi 1995). In this way, critical knowledge can be retained in the organisation by either sharing it or preserving it in the archives, thus forming part of the organisational memory. Nonaka and Takeuchi (1995) opine that organisational knowledge conversion deals with the conversion of knowledge from tacit to tacit (socialisation), from tacit to explicit (externalisation), from explicit to tacit (internalisation) and from explicit to explicit (combination) knowledge.

Socialisation: This entails the process of sharing knowledge between experts, mentors and retirees from whom juniors and new entrants at work can learn and in the process create tacit knowledge such as technical skills that may be obtained through observation, imitation and practice (Nonaka & Takeuchi 1995). In the selected banks, socialisation (originating *ba*) occurred when banking employees had direct, physical, face-to-face experiences with banking clients. Much of the interaction was in the banking halls, specifically with tellers and enquiries counters. The selected banks also used different ICTs in their operations. This means that employees are provided with laptops, and personal computers are made available in the banking halls for customers with online access. The banks also provide guidance on the effective use of technological resources. The latter could be viewed as the starting-point of the knowledge-creation process. The use of PCs in the banking halls is designed for customer convenience and easy access to the Internet. This is a simple way of capturing customer knowledge.

The sharing of tacit knowledge also manifested itself in the card and IT divisions of the selected banks. The study also established that tacit knowledge is transferred to fellow employees in the card division regarding trends in the credit-card payment industry, asset finance and personal loans. Through emails, intranet, electronic bulletin boards, training and brainstorming activities, tacit knowledge is transferred from one employee to other employees. Computer technology makes it possible for the organisational knowledge to be spread across the entire organisation (Nemani 2010).

Externalisation: It refers to the process of articulating tacit knowledge in the form of explicit concepts such as metaphors and analogies (Nonaka & Takeuchi 1995). The study established that selected banks use automated processes as well as manual systems to externalise tacit knowledge into paper records (organisational memory and archival repositories) that are accessed by the employees for use (codification). Externalisation (interacting *ba*) in the selected banks is expressed through the building and management of a collection of knowledge that comes in a variety of formats and their associated technology (Nemani 2010). In the case of FNB, innovative teams excel in bringing new services or products on board whilst, at Nedbank, externalisation is triggered by dialogue, regular formal meetings and brainstorming sessions (*dashikai*).

Combination: This is the process of combining bodies of explicit knowledge. In the process of combination, explicit knowledge is systemised and refined by, for example, utilising information and communication technology and databases (Lwoga, Ngulube & Stilwell 2010; Nonaka & Takeuchi 1995). In the selected banks, explicit knowledge is transferred through emails, documents, meetings and conversations, and such knowledge leads to the generation of new knowledge (Nonaka & Takeuchi 1995). Because of strict security policies, employees in selected banks share their explicit knowledge with fellow professionals during

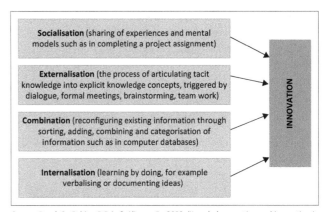

Source: Daud, S., Rahim, R.E.A. & Alimun, R., 2008, 'Knowledge creation and innovation in the classroom', *International Journal of Social Sciences* 3(1), 76.
FIGURE 1: SECI Model: Innovation in selected banks.

departmental and general meetings, through business cell phones and via emails.

Internalisation: It is the process of converting explicit knowledge to tacit knowledge and is closely related to learning by doing (Nonaka & Takeuchi 1995). In this study, archives and procedure manuals were identified as sources of technical knowledge that were acquired by employees and then used to solve some work-related problems. The card divisions of selected banks refer to merchant profiles to determine the levels of fraudulent transactions, merchant transactions and other queries. Innovation by bank staff who work in a modern information environment is subsequently reflected in the enhanced quality of service and innovative products provided. The SECI processes are depicted in Figure 1.

The study established that a culture that promotes the creation of new knowledge in the organisation is vital because this allows organisations to create new knowledge from shared and existing knowledge repositories. The new knowledge must be preserved and retained as knowledge assets in appropriate media. Albers (2009) states that an ideal knowledge-management culture is characterised by trust, openness, teamwork, collaboration, risk taking, common language, courage and learning. Stankosky (2005) states that people are rewarded and recognised for individual achievements, sharing knowledge and contributing to teamwork. This is possible in an environment where the culture of knowledge sharing is a common practice. The implication of a lack of open-mindedness concerning KM practices is that any attempt by the banks to encourage these KM features would be fruitless if they are not a part of the banks' knowledge sharing culture. It would not even matter if there were no proper IT platform to share information. It was established that reward systems could be used to create re-usable knowledge resources. Contributing towards a collection of re-usable knowledge resources, knowledge capture could, if put in place, start happening in a formal way (Dewah 2011).

It was noted that a lack of knowledge-management practices leads to high costs due to a loss of institutional memory, knowledge gaps and uninformed decisions. Managing knowledge in a bank can leverage efficiency across all of its services to customers through accessing the right information for making informed decisions and eliminating duplication of efforts. Baskerville and Dulipovici (2006; see Jain 2007) mention the following:

> ... one of the characteristics of the economic school of KM as incorporating the ability to be a learning organisation that enables creativity and in the process increases the value generation capacity of an organisation. (n.p.)

The study established that knowledge enhances organisational performance as shown by 21.78% of the surveys though the point was raised by 17.83% of the respondents that a combination of knowledge and business strategies enhances organisation performance. Surveys and interviews concurred that, in the knowledge economy, organisations leverage efficiency across departments, thus improving service delivery and processes. This was evidenced by 13.86% of the respondents who viewed KM as a solution to business problems whilst 11.88% of the respondents felt that KM enhances customer relationships. Building relationships with customers or suppliers is regarded as a competitive strategy (Kotler & Keller 2010, 2013).

Building long-term relationships with suppliers and customers will enable the selected banks to leverage such relationships for growth. Nine (8.91%) of the respondents stated that knowledge-management improves work processes whilst 6.93% of the respondents stated that KM improves product and services development – an important factor required to address the ever-changing tastes and needs of customers. An organisation that has technology and processes that produce products and services within a shorter space of time than competitors usually satisfies customers (Kotler & Keller 2010, 2013) – resulting in knowledge work.

Conclusions

KM practices in the banking situation should be actions aimed at improving the internal flow and use of information and knowledge, and banks can be a major participant in these activities. Examples of such practices include the creation of 'best practices', databases, regular training and development programmes as well as the encouragement and promotion of employee interaction within departments and between individual staff and departments (Nonaka & Takeuchi 1995). One issue that was observed was that departments operated in knowledge silos. In this regard, Nonaka and Takeuchi (1995) advocate for interaction between individuals or departments to share knowledge and information. KM practices need not be based on the preconception that an organisation can mandate people to share their knowledge. It is likely that individuals would be willing to share their knowledge because they want to, not because they have been told or coerced to do so. It was established that there are no stipulated practices at selected banks for the acquisition,

creation, sharing or retention of knowledge. However, the efforts that are made included staff meetings, team-building sessions, the use of Internet and intranets, succession planning, innovation campaigns, knowledge portals and project management teams.

The study established that knowledge at selected banks is not properly managed to facilitate the implementation of competitive KM practices for surviving in the knowledge economy. Being a dynamic competitive and information-intensive industry, bankers should possess skills that include the identification of knowledge needs, distinguishing knowledge-management from information management which can facilitate a broader and more inclusive KM initiative. This could result in the development of a KM framework for sharing institutional practices that include all employees – an important component of a KM strategy. From the findings presented in this study, it is recommended that the low level of KM practices at selected banks would be mitigated if there were clear KM policies and plans in place. From a structural perspective, it is recommended that the position of chief knowledge officer be established to formulate KM policies and drive all KM initiatives.

Acknowledgements

Competing interests

The authors declare that they have no financial or personal relationships which may have inappropriately influenced them in writing this article.

Authors' contributions

Both J.C. (University of South Africa) and P.N. (University of South Africa) conceptualised the study and then the first author did the research as part of his PhD study. Both authors were involved in writing up of the article and dealing with comments from the reviewers and the Editorial Board.

References

Albers, J.A., 2009, 'A practical approach to implementing knowledge management', *Journal of Knowledge Management Practice* 10(1), 1–8.

Babbie, E., 2010, *The practice of social research*, 12th edn., Wadsworth/Thompson, Southbank.

Baskerville, R. & Dulipovici, A., 2006, 'The theoretical foundations of knowledge management', *Knowledge Management Research and Practice* 4(2), 83–105. http://dx.doi.org/10.1057/palgrave.kmrp.8500090

Beazley, H., Boenisch, J. & Harden, D., 2002, *Continuity management: Preserving corporate knowledge and productivity when employees leave*, John Wiley and Sons, Hoboken.

Branin, J.J., 2003, 'Knowledge management in academic libraries: Building the knowledge bank at the Ohio State University', *Journal of Library Administration* 39(4), 1–56. http://dx.doi.org/10.1300/J111v39n04_05

Braun, V. & Clarke, V., 2006, 'Teaching thematic analysis: Overcoming challenges and developing strategies for effective learning', *The Psychologist* 26(2), 120–123.

Cong, X. & Pandya, K., 2003, 'Issues of KM in the public sector', *Electronic Journal of Knowledge Management* 1(2), 25–33.

Dewah, P., 2011, *Knowledge retention strategies in selected southern African public broadcasting corporations*, University of Fort Hare, East London.

Daud, S., Rahim, R.E.A. & Alimun, R., 2008, 'Knowledge creation and innovation in the classroom', *International Journal of Social Sciences* 3(1), 76.

Fidel, R., 2008, 'Are we there yet? Mixed methods research in library and information science', *Library and Information Science Research* 30, 265–272.

First National Bank, 2011/12, *Annual reports*, viewed 20 May 2013, from http://www.fnb.co.za/htm.pdf

Ford, D.P. & Staples, D.S., 2006, 'Perceived value of knowledge: The potential informer's perception', *Knowledge Management Research and Practice* 4, 3–16. http://dx.doi.org/10.1057/palgrave.kmrp.8500079

Fowler, A. & Pryke, J., 2003, 'KM in public service provision: the child support agency', *International Journal of Service Industry Management* 14(3), 254–28. http://dx.doi.org/10.1108/09564230310478828

Gaffoor, S. & Cloete, F., 2010, 'Knowledge management in local government: The case of Stellenbosch Municipality', *South African Journal of Information Management* 12(1).

Greenlaw, C. & Brown-Wetty, S., 2009, 'A comparison of web-based and paper-based survey methods: Testing assumptions of survey mode and response cost', *Evaluation Review* 33(5), 464–480. http://dx.doi.org/10.1177/0193841X09340214

Gupta, A.K. & Govindarajan, V., 2000, 'Knowledge flows within multinational corporations', *Strategic Management Journal* 1(21), 473–96. http://dx.doi.org/10.1002/(SICI)1097-0266(200004)21:4%3C473::AID-SMJ84%3E3.0.CO;2-I

Hill, C.W.L., 2010, *International business: Competing in the global marketplace*, 7th edn., McGraw Hill/Irwin, New York.

Jain, P., 2007, 'Knowledge management in e-government', *Journal of Knowledge Management Practice* 10(4), 1–10.

Jain, P., 2011, 'Personal knowledge management: The foundation of organisational knowledge management', *South African Journal of Libraries and Information Science* 77(1), 1–14. http://dx.doi.org/10.7553/77-1-62

Kim, M.P., 2005, *Knowledge retention enhances performance-based management*, viewed 28 February 2012, from http://www.dcma.mil/htm.pdf

Kotler, P. & Keller, K.L., 2010, *Marketing management*, 12th edn., Pearson Education Limited, Edinburgh Gate, Harlow, Essex.

Kotler, P. & Keller, K.L., 2013, *Marketing management*, 14th edn., Pearson Education Limited, Edinburgh Gate, Harlow, Essex.

Laudon, K.C. & Laudon, J.P., 2012, *Management information systems: Managing the digital firm*, 11th edn., Prentice Hall, Pearson Education, Upper Saddle River, New Jersey.

Leedy, P.D. & Omrod, J.E., 2005, *Practical research, planning and design*, 8th edn., Pearson Education International, Upper Saddle River, New Jersey.

Leedy, P.D. & Ormrod, J.E., 2010, *Practical research: Planning and design*, 9th edn., Pearson, Upper Saddle River.

Levy, M., 2011, 'Knowledge retention: Minimizing organizational business loss', *Journal of Knowledge Management* 15(4), 582–600. http://dx.doi.org/10.1108/13673271111151974

Lwoga, E.T., Ngulube, P. & Stilwell, C., 2010, 'Understanding indigenous knowledge: Bridging the knowledge gap through a knowledge creation model for agricultural development', *South African Journal of Information Management* 12(1), 436–438.

Moneyweb, 2012, *Information communication technologies in the banking industry in South Africa*, viewed 13 January 2014, from http://www.moneyweb.co.za/html

Moneyweb, 2013, *Modern banking*, viewed 11 February 2014, from http://www.moneyweb.co.za/html

Mavodza, J. & Ngulube, P., 2011, 'Exploring the use of knowledge management practices in an academic library in a changing information environment', *South African Journal of Libraries and Information Science* 77(1), 15–25. http://dx.doi.org/10.7553/77-1-63

Nedbank Group South Africa, 2012, *Annual report*, viewed 19 November 2012, from http://www.nedgroup.co.za/reports/html

Nemani, R.R., 2010, 'The role of computer technologies in knowledge acquisition', *Journal of Knowledge Management Practice* 11(3), 1–11.

Noe, R.A., Hollenbeck, J.R., Gerhart, B. & Wright, P.M., 2010, *Human resource management: Gaining a competitive advantage*, 8th edn., McGraw-Hill Irwin, New York.

Nonaka, I., 1995, 'A dynamic theory of organizational knowledge creation', *Journal of Organization Science* 5(1), 14–37. http://dx.doi.org/10.1287/orsc.5.1.14

Nonaka, I. & Konno, N., 1998, 'The concept of "Ba", building a foundation for knowledge creation', *California Management Review* 4(3), 40–54. http://dx.doi.org/10.2307/41165942

Nonaka, I. & Takeuchi, H., 1995, *The knowledge creating company: How Japanese companies create the dynamics of innovation*, Oxford Press, New York.

Pacharapha, T. & Ractham, V.V., 2012, 'Knowledge acquisition: The roles of perceived value of knowledge content and source', *Journal of Knowledge Management* 16(5), 724–739. http://dx.doi.org/10.1108/13673271211262772

Patrick, K. & Dotsika, F., 2007, 'Knowledge sharing: Developing from within', *The Learning Organisation* 14(5), 395–406, viewed 22 October 2013, from http://www.emeraldinsight.com/0969-6474.htm/

Polanyi, M., 1962, *Personal knowledge: Towards a post-critical philosophy*, University of Chicago Press, Chicago.

Powell, R., 1997, *Basic research for librarians*, 3rd edn., Ablex Publishing Corporation, London.

Ragsdell, G., 2009, 'Inhibitors and enhancers to knowledge sharing: Lessons from the voluntary sector', *Journal of Knowledge Management Practice* 10(1), 1–9.

Rowley, J., 2002, 'Using case studies in research', *Management Research News* 25(1), 16–27. http://dx.doi.org/10.1108/01409170210782990

Romm, N. & Ngulube, P. (in press), 'Mixed methods research', in E.R. Mathipa & G.T. Gumbo (eds.), *Addressing research challenges: Making headway for emerging researchers*.

Ryu, C., Kim, Y.J. & Chaudhury, A., 2005, 'Knowledge acquisition via three learning processes in enterprise information portals: Learning-by-investment, learning-by-doing, learning-from-others', *Management Information Systems Quarterly* 29(2), 245–278.

Sarrafzadeh, M., Martin, B. & Hazeri, A., 2006, 'Library information systems professionals and knowledge management: Some recent perspectives', *Journal of Library Management* 27(9), 621–635. http://dx.doi.org/10.1108/01435120610715527

Sheriff, K. & Sheriff, A.S., 2008, 'The social capital before you think knowledge transfer', in E.M. Jennex (ed.), *Current issues in knowledge management*, pp. 53–56, Hershey, New York. http://dx.doi.org/10.4018/978-1-59904-916-8.ch005

Singh, S.P., 2007, 'What are we managing: Knowledge or information?', *VINE: The Journal of Information and Knowledge Management Systems* 37(2), 169–179. http://dx.doi.org/10.1108/03055720710759946

Stankosky, M.A., 2005, 'Advances in knowledge management: University research toward an academic discipline', in M. Stankosky (ed.), *Creating the discipline of knowledge management: The latest in university research*, pp. 1–14, Butterworth-Heinemann, Burlington. http://dx.doi.org/10.1016/B978-0-7506-7878-0.50005-3

Thilmany, J., 2008, 'Passing on know-how: Knowledge retention strategies can keep employees workplace-acquired wisdom from walking out the door when they retire', *HR Magazine*, June, viewed 16 February 2013, from http://www.knowledgeharvesting.com/documents/HRM%20%20Passing%20n%20know-How.pdf/htm

Tiwana, A., 2008, *The knowledge management toolkit: Orchestrating IT, strategy and knowledge platforms*, 2nd edn., Prentice Hall, Upper Saddle River.

Turban, E., McLean, E. & Wetherbe, J., 2004, *Information technology for management: Transforming organizations in the digital economy*, 6th edn., John Wiley and Sons, New York.

Wamundila, S. & Ngulube, P., 2011, 'Enhancing knowledge retention in higher education: A case of the University of Zambia', *South African Journal of Information Management* 13(1), 439–448. http://dx.doi.org/10.4102/sajim.v13i1.439

Yin, R.K., 2003, *Case study research: Design and methods*', Sage, Thousand Oaks, California.

Young, R., 2010, *Knowledge management and innovation in a global knowledge economy. KM Egypt 2010, April 20–21*, Knowledge Associates International, London.

15

The password practices applied by South African online consumers: Perception versus reality

Authors:
Rika Butler[1]
Martin Butler[2]

Affiliations:
[1]School of Accountancy,
Stellenbosch University,
South Africa

[2]Business School,
Stellenbosch University,
South Africa

Correspondence to:
Rika Butler

Email:
rbutler@sun.ac.za

Postal address:
PO Box 3369, Matieland
7602, South Africa

Background: The ability to identify and authenticate users is regarded as the foundation of computer security. Although new authentication technologies are evolving, passwords are the most common method used to control access in most computer systems. Research suggests that a large portion of computer security password breaches are the result of poor user security behaviour. The password creation and management practices that online consumers apply have a direct effect on the level of computer security and are often targeted in attacks.

Objectives: The objective of this study was to investigate South African online consumers' computer password security practices and to determine whether consumers' perceptions regarding their password security ability is reflected in the password creation and management practices that they apply.

Method: A Web-based survey was designed to (1) determine online consumers' perceptions of their skills and competence in respect of computer password security and (2) determine the practices that South African online consumers apply when creating and managing passwords. The measures applied were then compared to (1) the users' perceptions about their computer password security abilities and (2) the results of international studies to determine agreement and inconsistencies.

Results: South African online consumers regard themselves as proficient password users. However, various instances of unsafe passwords practices were identified. The results of this South African study correspond with the results of various international studies confirming that challenges to ensure safe online transacting are in line with international challenges.

Conclusion: There is a disparity between South African online consumers' perceived ability regarding computer password security and the password creation and management practices that they apply.

Computer password systems and vulnerability

The use of computer systems on a daily basis has changed the way in which people conduct their lives as well as their business (Shaikh & Karjaluoto 2015:541). Computer systems are accessed from users' homes, their places of employment, as well as from anywhere that they are able to access the Internet. These systems are used for business purposes, to communicate and transact over the Internet as well as for a variety of entertainment-related activities.

Stallings (1995:213) describes the use of a password system as 'the front line of defence against intruders' within a computer security environment. Having to identify oneself uniquely by way of a password before being allowed to perform certain actions has become acceptable, understandable and even expected in order to ensure a secure environment (Weber *et al.* 2008:45).

In order to control access, whilst maintaining confidentiality and integrity, user identification and authentication are essential to ensure computer security (Conklin, Dietrich & Walz 2004:1). Although other user authentication systems, such as biometrics (using physical characteristics) and one-time PINs (using device ownership), are evolving, passwords as part of security and authentication systems remain one of the most cost effective and efficient methods to use (Campbell, Kleeman & Ma 2007:2; Tam, Glassman & Vandenwauver 2010:233).

Whilst the authentication of users is critical to control access, the authentication process remains problematic (Chiasson & Biddle 2007:1). Central to the challenges concerning user authentication are the different avenues of attack used to gain unauthorised access to computer systems. The various forms of attacks to which passwords are susceptible (Figure 1) can be classified into the following (Butler 2007:520; Campbell *et al.* 2007:3; Conklin *et al.* 2004:4;

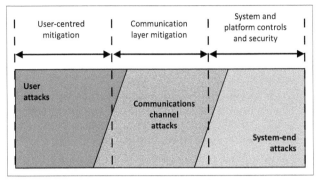

Source: Authors' own construct
FIGURE 1: Attacks to discover passwords can be aimed at various levels.

Florencio & Herley 2007:657; Notoatmodjo & Thomborson 2009:71; Tetri & Vuorinen 2013:1014):

- **System-end.** Technical or brute force attacks are launched to crack or guess the passwords of authorised users or exploit backdoors or known vulnerabilities in systems or the platforms that they use.
- **Communication channel.** Attacks on the communication channel over which passwords are transmitted by increasingly sophisticated technologies deployed at different layers of the network infrastructure.
- **User.** Attacks aimed directly at users to discover their passwords. Phishing and social engineering are increasingly popular methods of deceiving computer users into disclosing passwords.

To counter these attacks appropriate mitigation at the relevant level is necessary. Mitigation of system-end attacks should take place at the service provider level, as should mitigation of attacks on the communication channel (Butler & Butler 2014:151). However, collaboration with users of computer systems is also necessary to ensure secure transacting over networks (Figure 1). Taking cognisance of the work of Zviran and Haga (1999:164), who state that 'practically every penetration of a computer system at some stage relies on the attacker's ability to compromise a password', this research is aimed at the user level and the procedures applied (or not applied) by the computer user. According to Leach (2003:686), a large portion of the threats to passwords is the result of poor user security behaviour. When users do not select and manage passwords with care it may make those passwords easier to guess, discover or hack (Garrison 2008:70).

The responsibility of the computer user

Proper password practices refer to the execution of the policies and procedures that are used to ensure the security of passwords. Password practices encompass the measures applied when (Kothari *et al.* 2015):

- Choosing or creating passwords, which involves aspects such as the origin and composition of the password.
- Managing passwords once created (i.e. the practices relating to the safekeeping of passwords during the period of its use).

Garrison (2008:70) remarks that the 'burden' to choose a strong password (password creation) that is kept secure and confidential (password management), falls on the computer user. According to Tam *et al.* (2010:233) even the most sophisticated security system becomes useless if computer users do not apply proper password practices. Users applying proper practices when (1) creating and (2) managing passwords have a direct effect on the security of a particular computer system and the information contained in it. Although the practices of creating and managing passwords are clearly interdependent, they are viewed as distinct, yet sharing certain actions, for the purposes of this study.

Whilst certain password users may be proficient in the password creation and management practices that they apply, proper security measures and guidelines are often 'unknown, neglected, or avoided' by others (Notoatmodjo & Thomborson 2009:71). One of the reasons why many computer users apply unsafe password practices is because 'they may not know any better' due to a lack of appropriate knowledge, guidance and support (Furnell 2007:445). Researchers (Butler 2007:520; Conklin *et al.* 2004:5; Garrison 2008:70) support the argument that computer users are often ignorant and uninformed about secure password practices. Adams and Sasse (1999:42) found that ignorant users tend to 'make up their own rules' concerning passwords, which leads to the creation of 'weak' passwords or inadequate management of passwords (irrespective of whether they are 'weak' or 'strong').

However, whilst a lack of the necessary knowledge may be the reason why some computer users apply unsafe password practices, studies by Riley (2006), Tam *et al.* (2010) and Wessels and Steenkamp (2007) discovered that even users with the ability to distinguish between secure and insecure practices often don't apply these secure practices. This lack of application could stem from a lack of awareness of their vulnerability and the possible consequences related to their poor password behaviour (Gaw & Felten 2006:45).

Proper password selection entails selecting passwords that are difficult to guess but still memorable (Conklin *et al.* 2004:5; Stallings 1995:218). However, users rarely choose passwords that are both hard to guess and easy-to-remember (Yan *et al.* 2004:25). When users choose 'stronger' passwords, they are more difficult to remember and, conversely, easy-to-remember passwords are 'weaker'. This was confirmed by Zviran and Haga (1999:179), who commented on the correlation between users' difficulty with remembering passwords and password characteristics such as length, composition and lifetime – all factors that contribute to 'stronger' passwords. The conflict between convenience of remembering and security plays an important role in the quality of the passwords practices applied by computer users (Brown *et al.* 2004:650; Tam *et al.* 2010:242; Weber *et al.* 2008:46).

Florencio and Herley (2007:657) found that the average computer user has 25 password-protected accounts. As the use of password-protected systems increases, the usability of the passwords decease as human memory limitations place a strain on the memory of computer users who have to remember their numerous passwords to access these systems (Chiasson & Biddle 2007:1; Egelman *et al.* 2013). With more systems and services requiring users to identify and authenticate themselves online, the desire to select memorable passwords only increases as the number of passwords required increases. Even more disconcerting is the enforced lifetime policies and composition characteristics that in isolation (user and system) leads to stronger passwords, but at user level often leads to multiple uses of the same password (Egelman *et al.* 2013), thereby increasing risk.

Notoatmodjo and Thomborson (2009:71) refer to computer users suffering from 'password overload' and suggest that this is a major contributor to unsafe password practices. To deal with the memory challenge, users begin to devise their own methods (Adams & Sasse 1999:42), which often results in insecure password creation and management practices. Examples of such methods include: using short and weak passwords that are easy-to-remember, sharing passwords, writing down passwords and reusing passwords (Campbell *et al.* 2007:3).

Proper password practices

Since attacks on passwords can be aimed at cracking 'weak' passwords (resulting from poor password creation practices) as well as discovering or gaining access to all ('strong' and 'weak') passwords (the result of poor password management practice), it is imperative that proper password practices encompass both *creation* and *management*.

The most important criteria when *creating passwords* include the origin of the password, the characters used in its composition and the purpose of the password. Proper password creation practices include:

- **Using non-personal information:** Passwords should not use meaningful personal information such as the user's name, surname, nickname, date of birth, ID number, telephone number or any other aspect that may be associated with the user (Furnell *et al.* 2000:530).
- **Using uncommon information:** Passwords should not use words that can be found in dictionaries, acronyms or common permutations (Gehringer 2002:370).
- **Using a combination of characters:** Use a combination of uppercase and lowercase letters as well as numbers when creating passwords (Brown *et al.* 2004:650).
- **Ensuring sufficient length:** Passwords should be at least eight characters long (Garrison 2008:70).
- **Ensuring uniqueness:** Use unique passwords that are not used for other purposes (Gaw & Felten 2006:44).
- **Correlating complexity with risk:** Vary the complexity of the password to match the risk associated with its use (Brown *et al.* 2004:650).

Once users have selected a password, the *management of that password* should adhere to the following principles:

- **Single ownership:** Passwords should be kept secret and not be disclosed to or shared with other persons (Adams & Sasse 1999:41).
- **Regular changes:** Passwords should be changed regularly. The shorter the lifetime of a password, the better (Adams & Sasse 1999:41). However, although frequently changing passwords reduces the risk of undetected compromised passwords and reduces their predictability, it also hinders memorability (Zviran & Haga 1999:172).
- **Safekeeping:** Ensure proper safekeeping of passwords, including ensuring that passwords are not written down or stored in places where they could easily be discovered (Campbell, Ma & Kleeman 2011:379).
- **Single use:** Do not reuse previous passwords. When compromised in one (less secure) system, such passwords can be used to simultaneously access other systems (Gaw & Felten 2006:44).

A lack of knowledge of these password practices often leads to unsafe practices (Adams & Sasse 1999:42). However, computer users typically have different views about their skills and competence with regard to the password creation and management practices that they apply, which could contribute to users unknowingly applying improper practices (Chiasson & Biddle 2007:2).

Users' perceptions of password practices

Humans base their perceptions of performance (good or bad) on their preconceived general view about their own skills and abilities (Dunning *et al.* 2003:83; Ehrlinger & Dunning 2003:6). A phenomenon known as optimistic bias (or unrealistic optimism) often leads to an overestimation of one's own skills and competence (Weinstein 1980:806).

Covello (1983) extended the work of Weinstein for technological risk in particular and commented on the problem of overconfidence that 'leads people to believe that they are comparatively immune to common hazards'. In a similar vein, password users often overestimate their ability to create 'strong' passwords that are managed properly, whilst underestimating the potential risk associated with compromised passwords. This misconception about potential vulnerability results in poor password practices as many users believe that attackers will not be able to guess or discover their passwords (Chiasson & Biddle 2007:2).

Research objective

The objective of this study is to determine:

1. The extent to which proper password practices are applied by South African online consumers.
2. Any significant differences between the practices of South African online consumers when compared with international studies.

3. Whether consumers' perceived ability about their password practices correlates with the password practices that consumers apply.

Methodology

An online survey was designed to determine the password practices and perceived abilities from respondents for analysis. The survey instrument was refined via two iterations of pilot testing. The survey contained 43 questions which included both structured and open-ended questions. In order to ensure that users did not feel uncomfortable sharing potentially sensitive information, respondents were informed that they did not have to disclose any passwords, merely the practices that they use when creating and managing passwords. The survey was distributed to a database of online users from the authors' tertiary institution and snowball sampling was also applied. In spite of the assurances provided some respondents who were hesitant contacted the return address to confirm the validity of the study.

A total of 916 respondents began the survey. However, 101 respondents did not complete the survey. Excluding respondents not making use of social media or Internet banking, entrance barriers for the survey, the data set consisted of 737 responses for analysis.

The first data analysed were demographical information to determine a potential element of bias within the sample. Secondly, the practices that users apply when they select and manage passwords were analysed. These results, not detailed data, were then compared with one previous South African and multiple international studies.

To compare respondents' perceived versus actual ability a *perceived ability* score and *measured ability* score were calculated for each respondent. The perceived ability score was calculated based on respondents' self-reported ability, including their password-related knowledge. A measured ability score was calculated based on the password practices that respondents apply, as well as their ability to distinguish between different sets of passwords, varying in strength. Respondents were initially presented with a choice between two passwords from which the stronger password needed to be selected; this task increased in complexity to requiring respondents to arrange five different passwords in order of strength. After comparing the respondents' perceived ability with their measured ability, the respondents were classified as either unaware, overconfident, modest or proficient password users.

Demographics

The element of bias due to using snowball sampling was a concern. In order to express an opinion on the validity of the sample, the distribution of the gender, age and education of the respondents was compared to those of the South African Internet population. The gender distribution for

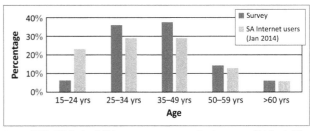

Source: IABSA, 2014b, *South African ecommerce report, effective measure/IAS South Africa Report – January 2014*, viewed 16 May 2014, from http://www.effectivemeasure.com/documents/South_Africa_Ecommerce_Report-Jan14.pdf

FIGURE 2: The age distribution of the respondents is in keeping with the South African online community.

South African online consumers is 51% female and 49% male (IABSA 2014a). This shows sufficient correlation with the survey distribution of 54% female and 46% male.

The age distribution of the sample and the South African online community (IABSA 2014b) was also compared (Figure 2). For the interval 15–24 years there is a significantly larger online population than that included in the survey. However, a significant portion of abandonment of the survey was within this younger demographic and consequently did not meet the criteria for inclusion. The age groups 25–34 and 35–49 years are both slightly over-represented, which is probably to be expected as a database of working graduates associated with the researchers' tertiary institution was used. The trend is nonetheless in line with national demographics.

The overall level of education of the respondents was quite high, with 196 respondents (21%) indicating their highest level of education as a bachelor's degree, 231 respondents (25%) an honours or postgraduate diploma, 157 (17%) a masters' degree and 30 a doctoral degree. When compared with the national demographics the postgraduate qualifications are slightly over-represented. This probably stems from the database of graduates to whom the survey was originally distributed. Even so the trend is in line with national demographics.

Based on the demographic comparison it is evident that the sample population is a reasonable, but far from perfect, fit to the South African online consumers. The slightly younger respondents are noted as well as higher than normal education levels. Although the interest in individual perceptions contrasted with reality is not influenced by any element of bias in the sample, no statistical correlation with international studies has been done. Although the researchers will present the findings as applicable to the South African online population, care must obviously be taken when extrapolating from this sample, due to an element of bias as indicated.

Online activities

Users were asked to provide an indication of their Internet experience as well as the extent of usage. Most of the respondents were experienced Internet users with 67% of

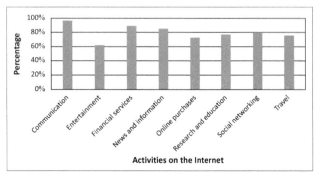

FIGURE 3: Respondents are active Internet users.

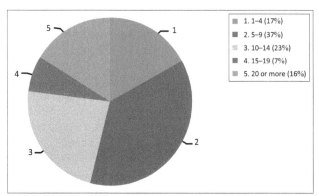

FIGURE 4: Number of Internet sites accessed that require passwords.

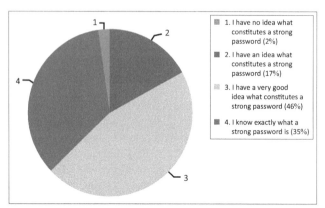

FIGURE 5: Respondents perceive that they possess the required knowledge to create strong passwords.

the respondents indicating that they have been using the Internet from the year 2000 or earlier. In response to their methods of access, most used laptop computers (84%) and mobile phones (82%). Their place of access was indicated as their residential home (90%), place of employment (83%) and always connected to the Internet via mobile access (50%). The extent of online activities indicated that 52% use the Internet equally for work and leisure, 31% mainly for work and 14% primarily for leisure.

In terms of different activities on the Internet respondents were provided with a set of choices compiled from various previous Internet surveys. The results (full sample, not only those using social media or Internet banking) show a diverse distribution of activities, with the most prevalent being communication (email, Skype, instant messaging) (96%), followed by financial services (89%) (Figure 3).

It is evident that all the respondents have been subjected to the creation and management of passwords when interacting on the Internet, as deduced from respondents when asked about the number of sites visited that require password authentication (Figure 4). A total of 83% of the respondents visit at least five sites requiring password authentication and 46% visit 10 or more sites.

The 16% of respondents who indicated 20 or more sites requiring authentication should have 20 or more passwords in the ideal situation where no passwords are reused. However, the more passwords users have, the greater the probability that they will not be used properly (Furnell 2005:10), as remembering the numerous passwords

can prove problematic. Studies (Gaw & Felten 2006:54; Notoatmodjo & Thomborson 2009:76) have shown that the reuse of passwords increases with the number of accounts or sites that require authentication.

Findings and discussion of results
Perceived ability concerning passwords

Respondents indicate that they perceive themselves to have the required skills and competence to create strong passwords and manage them properly. Respondents were rather confident about their ability to create strong passwords (Figure 5) with 'knew exactly' (35%) and 'very good idea' (46%) how to create strong passwords being selected by more than 80% of respondents. Only 3% of the respondents had 'no idea' what constitutes a strong password.

The trend of perceived ability amongst respondents was further evident with 78% of the respondents indicating that they are comfortable about their password creation practices and 76% who felt comfortable about the password management practices that they apply. Users' potential overconfidence in ability is further supported by a question prompting respondents about their relative online 'abilities' (whilst purposefully not defining ability) where a total of 63% rated their abilities as above average, 35.5% as average and only 1.5% below average.

Measured passwords creation and management practices

Despite users' perception that they were proficient in their ability to apply proper password practices, this study found that many respondents apply unsafe password creation and management practices.

Selecting passwords

The majority of the respondents considered both convenience and security when creating new passwords. However, 'ease of remembering' was regarded by more respondents as the most important consideration when compared with 'strength' of passwords being the foremost consideration.

Convenience-orientated practices that are used when creating new passwords include using personally meaningful words (61%), personally meaningful numbers or dates (45%) and personally meaningful combinations of letters (31%). Less popular, but still present, practices were letters sequential in the alphabet (3%), sequential numbers (10%), letters consecutive on keyboards (3%), numbers consecutive on keyboards (4%) and special characters or symbols consecutive on keyboards (4%).

These results correlate with international studies which found that users often compromise security by choosing passwords that contain information that is personally meaningful to the user in order to enhance their memorability (Zviran & Haga 1999:165). Tam *et al.* (2010:242) found that 36% of their respondents were willing to sacrifice security for the ease of remembering a password. Campbell *et al.* (2007:4) determined that even the enforcement of password composition guidelines and restrictions does not discourage users from using meaningful information to create passwords.

Brown *et al.* (2004:646) determined that 83% of passwords that the respondents to their study used were derived from information about themselves or those close to them (such as nicknames, relatives, friend, pet, meaningful dates and numbers). A study by Riley (2006) indicated that more than 50% of the respondents use personally meaningful words (such as names of children and pets) when creating passwords, whilst 55% indicated that they use personally meaningful numbers (such as telephone numbers and birth dates). Studies by both Campbell *et al.* (2007:7) and Wessels and Steenkamp (2007:13) indicated that 54% of the respondents choose passwords containing meaningful information or consisting of a combination of meaningful information.

Although all the respondents use lowercase letters, the usage of different character sets decreases with numbers (98%), uppercase (85%) and special characters (67%) in use. Brown *et al.* (2004:646) found that 36% of passwords contained only alphabetical characters, 36% were numeric and 25% of their respondents' passwords consisted of alphanumeric characters. Research by Zviran and Haga (1999:170) found that users tend to avoid non-alphanumeric characters in their passwords with more than 80% of the respondents preferring to use only alphabetical characters in their passwords. This is not the case for the sample population where only 33% do not use special characters.

In a study by Riley (2006), 8% used uppercase letters, 86% of the respondents used lowercase letters, whilst 57% reported that they use numbers or digits in the passwords that they create. In all instances the usage of combinations of character sets seems to indicate a higher degree of complexity than what was indicated by previous international research. This could be an indication of more modern controls (since Zviran and Haga's 1999 research) enforcing the use of these characters.

Risk awareness and impact on passwords

Although researchers advise that the complexity of a password be varied to match the purpose of the password, the study indicates that the 'perceived risk associated with a site' is not that important a consideration for users when creating new passwords. It was indicated as the most important consideration by 18% of the respondents and the second most important by 16%. When compared to 44% of the respondents who indicated that 'ease of remembering' the password was the most important consideration and 23% who indicated this as the second most important consideration, it is clear that, although it is considered, the purpose of the password is less important to users than choosing a password that is convenient to remember.

Riley (2006) found that nearly 60% of respondents do not vary the complexity of their passwords depending on the nature of the purpose of the password. This is contradicted by Florencio and Herley (2007:660), who state that users use passwords of varying strength, depending on the importance of the information related to the accounts that they aim to protect. Their research indicates that users tend to reuse weaker passwords at more websites as opposed to the reuse of stronger passwords. This practice is fairly common in users who are risk-conscious as they tend to use one stronger password for a single or limited number of high-risk authentications (e.g. Internet banking), but another less secure password or passwords for a combination of other sites and purposes.

Password sharing and safekeeping

One of the foundations of a password system is that passwords are kept secure. However, 52.1% of the respondents to the survey indicated that they have shared a password with another person. This password sharing culture is further strengthened by the fact that 51.7% of the respondents also indicated that they know the password to an account or system that is not their own. The results of the South African study correlates with a study by Teer, Kruck and Kruck (2007:109), who found that 53% of users intentionally share their password with another person. In their study, Tam *et al.* (2010:235) found that 42% of their respondents were willing to share their passwords with trusted persons, such as friends or family members.

Forgotten passwords and password mix-ups are common (Florencio & Herley 2007:663). Although 68% of the respondents to the survey indicated that they rely on their memory to remember their passwords, 82% of the respondents indicated that they have experienced trouble remembering a password. This is more than the results of a study by Brown *et al.* (2004:647), which found that 31% of respondents have forgotten and 23% have mixed up their passwords.

Gaw and Felten (2006:50) examined the methods used to store passwords and found that whilst the majority of the

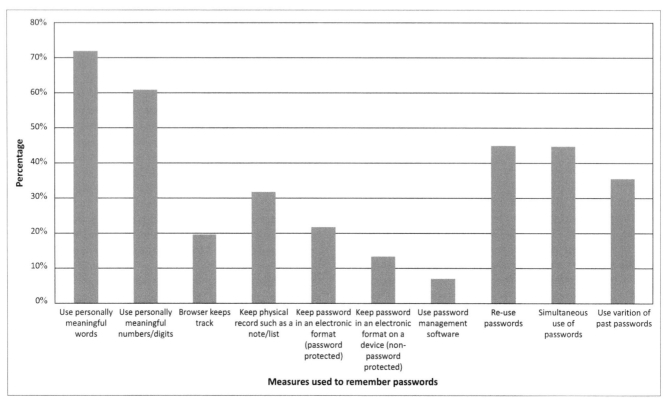

FIGURE 6: Respondents employ various practices to remember passwords.

respondents rely on their memory, respondents also applied other measures to remember and store their passwords. Figure 6 indicates the various practices that respondents use to help them remember their passwords.

Using meaningful words was indicated as the most popular technique (73%), followed by using meaningful numbers (62%). A rather significant number of respondents (19%) have designed their own measure, a protected electronic list of their passwords. This contrasts sharply with the least used method, namely password management software (6%), which provides the same, but a commercial and probably more secure concept. Two of the least secure measures, using a browser to help them keep track of their passwords (18%) and keeping a non-password-protected record (14%), are used by some users. However, when compared to previous studies, which indicated 55% (Brown *et al.* 2004:648) and 50% (Adams & Sasse 1999:42) who kept written records of their passwords, this figure is below the international trend.

Changing and reusing passwords

The requirement to change passwords regularly was tested for Internet banking, which is the highest risk activity performed by 93% of respondents. Although respondents are aware of the need to change passwords (45%), only 23% do actually regularly change their passwords. Of the respondents, 93 (13%) indicated that they have personally suffered a security breach in the past. Alarmingly, 13% of those who personally suffered breaches did not change their passwords. Password behaviour for Internet banking

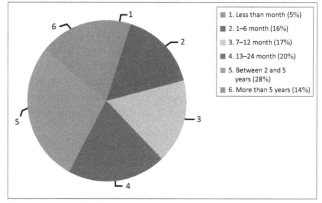

FIGURE 7: Internet banking passwords are not changed regularly.

users shows 64% of respondents have not changed their passwords in the last year and 42% not within the last two years (Figure 7).

Nearly 53% of the respondents to the Riley (2006) survey indicated that they do not change their passwords unless the system forces them to do so and Zviran and Haga (1999:172) found that nearly 80% of their respondents never changed their passwords. These findings are supported by Wessels and Steenkamp (2007:11), who found that 68% of the respondents never change their passwords if not forced to do so. Riley found that the average length of time users have maintained their primary personal use password was approximately two years and seven months.

An interesting dynamic emerges from the data and previous research. When users are not forced to change their passwords,

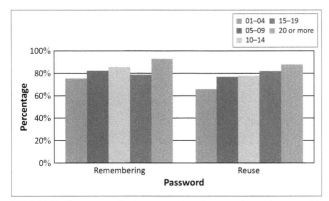

FIGURE 8: Problems remembering passwords and password reuse increase with the number of Internet sites accessed.

it rarely happens and creates a situation where passwords could potentially be reused, leading to less secure practices. However, forcing regular password changes lead to password overload and also contributes to poor password management practices. Another factor impacting practices is the total number of passwords required. Gaw and Felten (2006:54) found that the more accounts users have, the more likely they are to reuse their passwords. These researchers predict that password reuse rates will continue to rise over time, due to the pressure placed on the memories of users when they have more accounts (i.e. more passwords to remember).

Remembering passwords becomes an increasing challenge for users accessing more sites (Figure 8). Conversely, reuse of passwords also increases with the number of sites visited, confirming the conclusion of previous studies that more instances of authentication lead to weaker password creation and management practices. The data clearly indicates that users do not select unique passwords for all accounts and purposes. An alarming 75% of the respondents indicated that they reuse past passwords and 88% have simultaneously used a password for more than one purpose. Reusing passwords (43%), using the same password simultaneously (45%) and using a variation of a past password (35%) were indicated by the respondents as techniques used to help them with password overload.

Brown *et al.* (2004:647) determined that almost all the respondents reused passwords to gain access to at least one other account. In addition they found that 39% of the

respondents simultaneously used one password to gain access to more than one account or system and that nearly two out of three passwords chosen by users involved duplications. According to Riley (2006), 55% of the respondents indicated that they use the exact same password for more than one account 'very frequently' or 'always' and 33% use some form of variation of the same password for multiple accounts. Gaw and Felten (2006:44) found that the majority of their respondents reused their passwords at least twice. Studies by Riley as well as Florencio and Herley (2007) found that an increasing number of users have a set of predetermined passwords that they frequently use.

A study by Taiabul Haque, Wright and Scielzo (2014:873) found that users classify passwords into different levels according to the perceived importance of the site and vary their password practices based on this classification. The results of this study supports these research findings and indicate that South African users are more cautious regarding their Internet banking password. Whilst respondents are currently using their Internet banking passwords (20%) for access to other sites, 12% have reused their Internet banking password in the past, but have stopped this practice and 69% of users have never used their Internet banking password to access other sites.

Notoatmodjo and Thomborson (2009:76) found that 37% of their participants reused passwords for high importance accounts compared to 68% who reused passwords for less important accounts. This correlation between reuse and the importance of the password purpose was also evident from this South African study (Figure 8), indicating an element of risk awareness and different practices associated with different levels of perceived risk. However, the survey indicated a potential higher level of care when dealing with Internet banking passwords (69% have never used it for another purpose) compared to the international norm.

Summary of poor practices compared with international research

Most of the results and trends regarding poor password practices that were evident from this survey show consistency with international studies (Table 1). A major

TABLE 1: Comparison of summary of poor password practices evident from this study with international studies.

Poor password practice	Result of study for South African online consumers	Comparative international studies
Convenience and security trade-off	Convenience is more important than security of passwords for many users.	Tam *et al.* (2010:242); Zviran and Haga (1999:165).
Use personally meaningful information	Use of personally meaningful words, numbers, dates, as well as sequential letters and numbers, is prevalent.	Campbell *et al.* (2007:7); Riley (2006); Brown *et al.* (2004:646).
Composition of passwords	Despite the fact that only uppercase or lowercase or alphabetical or numerical letters are used (and not combinations), the South African trend seems better that the international norm.	Zviran and Haga (1999:170); Brown *et al.* (2004:646); Riley (2006).
Insufficient consideration of perceived risk	Only 18% considers perceived risk as the most important and 16% as the second most important aspect when creating new passwords.	Riley (2006); Notoatmodjo and Thomborson (2009:76).
Password sharing	A common practice reported by the majority of the respondents.	Teer *et al.* (2007:109); Tam *et al.* (2010:235).
Changing passwords regularly	Most respondents only change passwords when forced and previous passwords are still used for high-risk environments.	Riley (2006); Zviran and Haga (1999:172).
Reuse of passwords	88% have simultaneously used a password for more than one purpose and 20% are currently using their Internet banking password to access other sites.	Florencio and Herley (2007); Brown *et al.* (2004:647–648); Gaw and Felten (2006:44, 54).

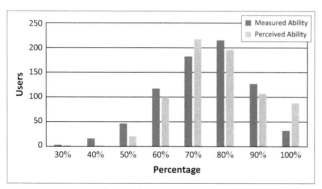

FIGURE 9: Comparison of respondents' perceived ability and measured ability.

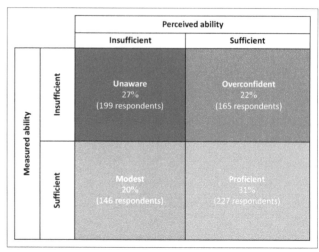

FIGURE 10: Classification of respondents as unaware, overconfident, modest or proficient after comparing their measured ability with their perceived ability.

difference observed between data in this study and previous international studies, was the extensive use of different combinations of character sets by South African consumers.

With results in line with international trends the focus moves to the final research objective, namely establishing whether users have an accurate self-awareness of their own ability (or inability) in respect of computer password security. Any change in behaviour commences with self-awareness. Hence, improving users' behaviour will require an accurate view of their existing knowledge regarding password-related matters.

Perceived ability versus measured ability

Although the majority of South African online consumers feel that they are proficient Internet users who are able to apply proper password practices, the results from the survey clearly indicate that users tend to apply unsafe password creation and management practices and are consequently not as skilled as they may perceive themselves to be.

Comparing measured ability scores and perceived ability scores

An interesting trend emerges from the comparison between users' measured ability and their perceived ability (Figure 9). For the first four intervals (<30%–60%), it seems that users underestimate their ability. Then an interesting reverse in the trend is evident in the last four intervals (70%–100%), where users mostly overestimate their perceived ability when compared to their measured ability. This poses an interesting question of whether looking at individual users' perceived ability and measured ability, rather than summarising this observed variance for the group as a whole, would provide a different view.

Classification of online consumers based on their password behaviour

Using a proficiency level of 70% for both perceived and measured ability, the responses of individual users were analysed and their ability was classified as either sufficient or insufficient. A matrix was used to plot users' perceived

online security abilities (sufficient or insufficient) compared to their measured ability (sufficient or insufficient). Based on this analysis respondents were divided into four different categories (Figure 10):

- **Unaware** – although they correctly perceive themselves as not being sufficiently capable, in this case ignorance is not necessarily bliss. The practices applied by these users could lead to compromised systems and resultant losses.
- **Overconfident** – users reported adequate ability, yet measured ability is not sufficient. By being overly optimistic about their abilities they are probably not that keen on improving their knowledge and as such could be the most vulnerable group.
- **Modest** – users that do not rate their own ability as sufficient, yet the measured ability indicates proficiency. On the plus side these users' lack of ability may lead to a very conservative approach, which could make them behave in a more secure manner.
- **Proficient** – the group of respondents that correctly assessed their perceived ability when compared with their measured ability. These users practice sufficiently secure password behaviour. The ideal state.

Although the sample variance when perceived and measured ability were compared (Figure 9) seems rather small, when viewed at an individual user level (Figure 10) it is clear that there is a pronounced lack of alignment between users' perceived ability and measured ability.

Conclusion

It is the 'burden' of the computer user to choose a strong password that is kept secure and confidential (Garrison 2008:70). Unfortunately, the results of this study identify and confirm some alarming facts about the extent to which users 'deal' with this burden. Disturbingly, it also raises a new concern about the lack of users' self-awareness about their computer password practices, which could hamper initiatives to improve system security.

Despite the fact that users' perceived ability indicated that they are able to create strong passwords and that strength was considered an important aspect when creating new passwords, this study found that respondents apply unsafe password creation practices. In addition, whilst respondents felt comfortable with the measures that they apply to keep their passwords safe, the use of insecure password management practices was evident.

The password practices applied by the South African respondents are fairly consistent with those observed by international studies. The main exceptions, both positive, are the clear difference in the usage of respondents' Internet banking passwords (exceeding international trends in terms of regular changes and reuse) as well as the use of a combination of different character sets, which are significantly higher than those indicated by international studies. It should be noted that the comparative studies are dated and that users' behaviour may change over time, for the better.

Optimistic bias was, however, very evident amongst South African online consumers when comparing their perceptions about their passwords creation and management practices with the password practices that they apply. For a significant number of respondents who indicated a level of comfort with their proficiency in terms of secure password behaviour, this confidence was not supported by their measured ability. This raises a rather serious concern about potential improvements in their behaviour since these users are unaware of the need to improve their password creation and management practices.

Clearly any effective measures aimed at improving the deficiencies in computer user password security identified by this research should take cognisance of the gap between users' perceptions and reality. Addressing this gap is paramount to improving computer password security. The process to address this problem should start by recognising that there are different challenges for different users (Figure 10). Uniform educational improvement programmes would therefore not be appropriate. Further research to shed light on the reasons for the lack of alignment between users' perceived and measured ability, as well as potential demographic factors that may relate to the poor alignment, is recommended.

Acknowledgements
Competing interests

The authors declare that they have no financial or personal relationships that may have inappropriately influenced them in writing this article.

Authors' contributions

M.B. (Stellenbosch University) and R.B. (Stellenbosch University) contributed equally to the research effort in terms of design, execution, analysis and publication.

References

Adams, A. & Sasse, M.A., 1999, 'Users are not the enemy', Communications of the ACM 42(12), 41–46. http://dx.doi.org/10.1145/322796.322806

Brown, A.S., Bracken, E., Zoccoli, S. & Douglas, K., 2004, 'Generating and remembering passwords', Applied Cognitive Psychology 18(6), 641–651. http://dx.doi.org/10.1002/acp.1014

Butler, R., 2007, 'A framework of anti-phishing measures aimed at protecting the online consumer's identity', The Electronic Library 25(5), 517–533. http://dx.doi.org/10.1108/02640470710829514

Butler, R. & Butler, M.J., 2014, 'An assessment of the human factors affecting the password performance of South African online consumers', in Proceedings of the Eighth International Symposium on Human Aspects of Information Security & Assurance (HAISA 2014), Plymouth, UK, July, pp. 150–161.

Campbell, J., Kleeman, D. & Ma, W., 2007, 'The good and not so good of enforcing passwords composition rules', Information Systems Security 16(1), 2–8.

Campbell, J., Ma, W. & Kleeman, D., 2011, 'Impact of restrictive composition policy on user password practices', Behaviour & Information Technology 30(3), 379–388. http://dx.doi.org/10.1080/10658980601051375

Chiasson, S. & Biddle, R., 2007, 'Issues in user authentication', CHI Workshop Security User Studies Methodologies and Best Practices, viewed 28 June 2014, from http://chorus.scs.carleton.ca/wp-content/papercite-data/pdf/chiasson2007issues-chiworkshop.pdf

Conklin, A., Dietrich, G. & Walz, D., 2004, 'Password-based authentication: A system perspective', in Proceedings of the 37th Annual Hawaii International Conference on System Sciences, Hawaii, January 5–8, 2004, pp. 1–10. http://dx.doi.org/10.1109/hicss.2004.1265412

Covello, T.V., 1983, 'The perception of technological risks: A literature review', Technological Forecasting and Social Change 23(4), 285–297. http://dx.doi.org/10.1016/0040-1625(83)90032-X

Dunning, D., Johnson, K., Ehrlinger, J. & Kruger, J., 2003, 'Why people fail to recognize their own incompetence', Current Directions in Psychological Science 12, 83–87. http://dx.doi.org/10.1111/1467-8721.01235

Egelman, S., Sotirakopoulos, A., Muslukhov, I., Beznosov, K. & Herley, C., 2013, 'Does my password go up to eleven? The impact of password meters on password selection', in Proceedings of the Conference on Human Factors in Computing Systems, Paris, France, May, 2013, pp. 2379–2388. http://dx.doi.org/10.1145/2470654.2481329

Ehrlinger, J. & Dunning, D., 2003, 'How chronic self-views influence (and potentially mislead) estimates of performance', Journal of Personality and Social Psychology 84(1), 5–17. http://dx.doi.org/10.1037/0022-3514.84.1.5

Florencio, D. & Herley, C., 2007, 'A large-scale study of Web password habits', in Proceedings of the 16th international conference on World Wide Web, Banff, Canada, May, 2007, pp. 657–666. http://dx.doi.org/10.1145/1242572.1242661

Furnell, S.M., 2005, 'Authenticating ourselves: Will we ever escape the password?', Network Security 3, 8–13. http://dx.doi.org/10.1016/S1353-4858(05)00212-6

Furnell, S.M., 2007, 'An assessment of website password practices', Computers and Security 26, 445–451. http://dx.doi.org/10.1016/j.cose.2007.09.001

Furnell, S.M., Dowland, P.S., Illingworth, H.M. & Reynolds, P.L., 2000, 'Authentication and supervision: A survey of user attitudes', Computers and Security 19, 529–539. http://dx.doi.org/10.1016/S0167-4048(00)06027-2

Garrison, C.P., 2008, 'An evaluation of passwords', CPA Journal, 70–71.

Gaw, S. & Felten, E.W., 2006, 'Password management strategies for online accounts', in Proceedings of the 2nd Symposium of Usable Privacy and Security, Pittsburgh, P.A., July, pp. 44–55. http://dx.doi.org/10.1145/1143120.1143127

Gehringer, E.F., 2002, 'Choosing passwords: Security and human factors', in Proceeding of the 2002 International Symposium on Technology and Society, Raleigh, N.C., June, pp. 369–373. http://dx.doi.org/10.1109/istas.2002.1013839

Interactive Advertising Bureau of South African (IABSA), 2014a, Effective measure data for January 2014, viewed 16 May 2014, from http://www.iabsa.net/research/effective-measure-data-for-january-2014

IABSA, 2014b, South African ecommerce report, effective measure/IAS South Africa Report – January 2014, viewed 16 May 2014, from http://www.effectivemeasure.com/documents/South_Africa_Ecommerce_Report-Jan14.pdf

Kothari, V., Blythe, J., Smith, S.W. & Koppel, R., 2015, 'Measuring the security impacts of password policies using cognitive behavioral agent-based modelling', in Proceedings of the 2015 Symposium and Bootcamp on the Science of Security, Urbana, I.L., April 2015, pp. 13–22.

Leach, J., 2003, 'Improving user security behaviour', Computers and Security 22(8), 685–692. http://dx.doi.org/10.1016/S0167-4048(03)00007-5

Notoatmodjo, G. & Thomborson, D., 2009, 'Passwords and perceptions', in Proceedings of the Australasian Information Security Conference (AISC2009), Wellington, January, 2009, Conferences in Research and Practice in Information Technology, 98, pp. 71–78.

Riley, S., 2006, 'Password security: What users know and what they actually do', Usability News 8(1), viewed 18 August 2012, from http://psychology.wichita.edu/surl/usabilitynews/81/Passwords.asp

Shaikh, A.A. & Karjaluoto, H., 2015, 'Making the most of information technology & systems usage: A literature review, framework and future research agenda', Computers in Human Behavior 49, 541–566. http://dx.doi.org/10.1016/j.chb.2015.03.059

Stallings, W., 1995, *Network and internetwork security principles and practice*, Prentice Hall, Englewood Cliffs.

Taiabul Haque, S.M., Wright, M. & Scielzo, S., 2014, 'Hierarchy of users' web passwords: Perceptions, practices and susceptibilities', *International Journal of Human-Computer Studies* 72(12), 860–874. http://dx.doi.org/10.1016/j.ijhcs.2014.07.007

Tam, L., Glassman, M. & Vandenwauver, M., 2010, 'The psychology of password management: A tradeoff between security and convenience', *Behaviour & Information Technology* 29(3), 233–244. http://dx.doi.org/10.1080/01449290903121386

Teer, F.P., Kruck, S.E. & Kruck, G.P., 2007, 'Empirical study of students' computer security practices/perceptions', *Journal of Computer Information Systems* 47(3), 105–110.

Tetri, P. & Vuorinen, J., 2013, 'Dissecting social engineering', *Behaviour and Information Technology* 32(10), 1014–1023. http://dx.doi.org/10.1080/014492 9X.2013.763860

Weber, J.E., Guster, D., Safanov, P. & Schmidt, M.B., 2008, 'Weak password security: An empirical study', *Information Security Journal: A Global Perspective* 17(1), 45–54.

Weinstein, N.D., 1980, 'Unrealistic optimism about future life events', *Journal of Personality and Social Psychology* 39, 806–820. http://dx.doi.org/10.1037/0022-3514.39.5.806

Wessels, P.L. & Steenkamp, L., 2007, 'Assessment of current practices in creating and using passwords as a control mechanism for information access', *South African Journal of Information Management* 9(2), 17 pages.

Yan, J., Blackwell, A., Anderson, R. & Grant, A., 2004, 'Password memorability and security: Empirical results', *Security and Privacy* 2(5), 25–31. http://dx.doi.org/10.1109/MSP.2004.81

Zviran, M. & Haga, W.J., 1999, 'Password security: An empirical study,' *Journal of Management Information Systems* 15(4), 161–185.

16

Enhancing knowledge retention in higher education: A case of the University of Zambia

Authors:
Sitali Wamundila[1]
Patrick Ngulube[2]

Affiliations:
[1]Department of Library and Information Science, University of Zambia, Zambia

[2]School of Graduate Studies, University of South Africa, South Africa

Correspondence to:
Patrick Ngulube

Email:
ngulup@unisa.ac.za

Postal address:
PO Box 392, UNISA 0003, South Africa

The purpose of this study was to investigate how knowledge retention may be enhanced at the University of Zambia (UNZA). A quantitative case study design employing a triangulation of data collection methods was used. Data were collected using interviews and questionnaires. Purposive sampling was used to determine participants for the interviews whilst stratified random sampling was employed to select the respondents for the questionnaire. The quantitative and qualitative data that was analysed using SPSS® indicates that UNZA lacked certain knowledge retention practices that might enable it to retain operational relevant knowledge. In view of the findings, the study recommends the adoption of a knowledge retention framework that could be embedded in UNZA's knowledge management policy.

Introduction

World economies are increasingly becoming knowledge-based (Association of Commonwealth Universities 2006; Loh *et al.* 2003; Maponya 2004). Knowledge is viewed as a strategic resource that offers a competitive advantage in organisations (Halawi, Aronson & McCarthy 2005). Although organisations have realised the value of knowledge, not many have actually started managing knowledge efficiently and effectively (Kruger & Snyman 2005). Managing knowledge for value creation in organisations is still a 'management concern' (Ngoc 2006). Despite the fact that other organisational operations such as 'marketing, finance, sales or even supply chain' are well mastered, road maps for effective management of knowledge are still being investigated (Perez-Soltero *et al.* 2006).

Managing knowledge entails knowledge identification, acquisition, development, sharing and distribution, utilization and retention (Probst, Raub & Romhardt 2000:30). Knowledge retention, which is the focus of this article, includes knowledge assessment, knowledge acquisition and knowledge transfer. The need to retain organisational knowledge is a well-known concern for most organisations including universities (UniSA 2007). It is widely recognised that the ability to retain organisational knowledge is a key characteristic for a successful organisation in the knowledge economy. The magnitude of the problem is apparent considering the volume of research efforts aimed at addressing knowledge retention within organisations (Davidson, Lepeak & Newman 2007).

Knowledge retention in universities

The core business of universities is to create, manage and transfer knowledge (Association of Commonwealth Universities 2006). However, according to Ratcliffe-Martin, Coakes and Sugden (2000) in Maponya (2004:8), universities fail to recognise the importance of knowledge as a strategic resource. As universities operate in the knowledge era they must focus on retaining their institutional knowledge both in the tacit and explicit format. For instance, the retention and management of knowledge enhances performance and may benefit universities by:

- facilitating better decision-making capabilities
- reducing 'product' development cycle time (i.e. curriculum development and research)
- improving academic and administrative services
- reducing costs
- preserving corporate memory
- combating staff turnover by facilitating knowledge capture and transfer (Kidwell, Vander Linde & Johnson 2000:31).

Corporate entities, including universities, are now initiating knowledge retention initiatives (Loh *et al.*, 2003; Kidwell, Vander Linde & Johnson 2000; MacGregor 2006). In the United Kingdom (UK), the University of Edinburgh is an example of an institution that has started knowledge retention initiatives (University of Edinburgh 2005). Threats of an aging workforce, shrinking talent pool and demographic changes partly explain the need for knowledge retention (DeLong

2008; MacGregor 2006; McQuade *et al.* 2007; Phaladi 2011). Similar knowledge retention-related problems also affect performance in many African universities (Association of Commonwealth Universities 2006).

Knowledge retention at the University of Zambia

The University of Zambia (UNZA) is no exception to the knowledge retention challenges mentioned which have been mentioned in the earlier section. A recent assessment by IOTA Consulting Services (2001) revealed the existence of the following operational problems related to knowledge retention:

- high staff turnover
- inability to retain experienced and qualified staff
- lack of explicit routines and procedure manuals
- lack of succession planning
- lack of sustained leadership
- ineffective information management.

The Bobby Bwalya Commission appointed in 1997 to investigate the operations of the university warned that:

> without significant attention being paid to the retention, motivation and commitment of critical staff in the university, quality in the core functions of the university would be in jeopardy.

(cited in IOTA Consultancy Services 2001:5)

Knowledge attrition through retirements and resignations result in the loss of tacit knowledge in any organisation which leads to lost potential for innovation and growth, decreased operational efficiency and effectiveness, and increased costs which in turn affect organisational performance (DeLong 2008; Purdum 2006; Sutherland & Jordaan 2004). In addition, employee mobility which is one of the trends observed in workers, including higher-education employees, in the knowledge economy is worrisome (Stovel & Bontis 2002; Sutherland & Jordaan 2004). Knowledge needs to be retained in organisations to support service delivery. In order to provide effective and efficient services, UNZA (2001) recognises that:

> in the era of information society and knowledge based economy...the world of work is being radically redefined, and the university has an obligation to respond to the challenges that this entails.

(UNZA 2001:11)

Although the importance of knowledge retention and management is addressed in the strategic plan of the university, our experience at UNZA clearly shows that very little effort is being made by the management to put in place procedures and processes that will ensure knowledge retention for the operational benefit of the university (UNZA 2001:11). For instance, there are no guidelines for managing knowledge in general and knowledge retention in particular.

Universities, like many other learning organisations have difficulty retaining knowledge (Jarrar 2002; Smith 2007). Managing knowledge systematically is fundamental to knowledge retention. Knowledge management (KM) techniques such as knowledge assessment, knowledge acquisition and knowledge transfer provide a useful framework for understanding knowledge retention processes in organisations (Tennessee Valley Authority 2005). The knowledge retention framework suggested by the Tennessee Valley Authority (2005) was instructive when investigating knowledge retention at UNZA.

The literature shows that drivers for knowledge loss in organisations include changing workforce demographics, employee turnover and mobility, and lack of documentation (Padilla 2006; Stovel & Bontis 2002). Failure to address these challenges leads to loss of operational relevant knowledge (Kruse 2003; McQuade *et al.* 2007; Padilla 2006; Scalzo 2006; Stovel & Bontis 2002). Based on this understanding, this research sought to find out if UNZA faced knowledge retention challenges with a view to developing a knowledge management framework to enhance knowledge retention at UNZA. The research questions that guided the study were the following:

- What tools of knowledge assessment are used at UNZA?
- What methods of knowledge acquisition are employed at UNZA?
- Which techniques of knowledge transfer are used at UNZA?
- What is being done regarding knowledge retention at UNZA?

Methodology

A case study design employing a triangulation of data collection instruments was used in this research. Case studies were used to study different knowledge management issues (Basu & Sengupta 2007; Nguyen, Smyth & Gable 2004; Tellis 1997). The data collection methods employed in this study were document review and a survey based on interviews as well as questionnaires. Thirteen senior management staff that were deemed to be relevant to the study were purposively selected for the interviews, whilst a questionnaire was used to collect data from a stratified random sample of 205 academics obtained from a database at the computer centre. One hundred and twenty-four, that is, 60% of the surveyed academics responded to the questionnaires that were sent out at the end of 2009.

Following the coding, the collected questionnaires were first checked for errors in responses as well as identifying unanswered questions before being entered into the SPSS® software. Within the survey, the open-ended questions involving qualitative data were content analysed and categorised. Data analysis was carried out after data entry for both closed and open-ended questions was complete. The Microsoft Word® computer package was used to transcribe the interview sessions. Content analysis was then applied where the researchers read all the thirteen transcripts in order to identify themes.

Results and discussions

The findings are presented in four major areas, namely, (1) knowledge assessment practices, (2) knowledge acquisition strategies, (3) knowledge transfer techniques and (4) knowledge retention processes at UNZA. The responses of the academics were similar to those of senior management. For that reason the results are lumped together in the discussion of the findings. The exceptions to the rule are a few cases where the findings from the interviews did not necessarily corroborate data from the completed questionnaires.

Knowledge assessment practices at the University of Zambia

Knowledge assessment is an initial stage in any knowledge management programme (Paramasivan 2003). It aims at understanding, establishing and ascertaining an organisation's capabilities and competencies in relation to tacit and explicit knowledge assets (Henczel 2000). Knowledge assessment is a well-known tool that serves as a source for operational knowledge, especially in organisations faced with knowledge loss challenges (Rothwell 2004). Authorities such as Henczel (2000), Hylton (2002) and Paramasivan (2003) argue that the lack of knowledge assessment as a knowledge retention tool undermines operational performance, as it would be difficult for an organisation to uncover and ascertain its operational strengths and weaknesses with regard to vital operational knowledge. Knowledge assessment practices include organisational capabilities assessment, workforce planning and knowledge auditing.

Organisational capabilities assessment

Organisational capability assessment involves the identification of documented operational processes, policies, work manuals and procedures (Consultas 2007; Rothwell 2004). The availability of documented operational processes, policies, work manuals or procedures serve as a source of operational knowledge for all, and especially for new individuals who may replace lost experienced and knowledgeable staff (Rothwell 2004).

In view of the aforementioned and in recognition of the variety of tasks carried out at UNZA, this study in both the survey and interviews looked for available documented processes, policies, work manuals and procedures (explicit knowledge assets). In the survey results, 17 (13.7%) respondents mentioned the availability of teaching practice manuals. Mention of manuals for functions such as consultancy, recruitment and training of staff was limited. Thus, the survey findings revealed that of the known documented processes, policies, work manuals and procedures, none of them covered core academic functions such as curriculum development, research and academic citizenship.

On the other hand, the results obtained through interviews indicated that work tasks at UNZA were not documented. However, there were some written general processes, policies and procedures, such as the following:

- some written policies, procedures and regulations covering some teaching tasks such as syllabuses, time table and assessment criteria for examinations
- a written but not yet wholly implemented policy on consultancy
- a written draft research policy that provides a general framework for conducting research
- some policies and procedures on some of the human resources functions such as training, recruitment and promotion of academic staff.

Considering the number of specialised units and tasks available at UNZA, the existing documented processes, policies, work manuals and procedures were not sufficiently representative of what could, potentially, be documented. Although a training policy was available, there was no comprehensive policy on recruitment or procedures on other human resources functions such as industrial relations, safety and health, and performance appraisal.

The researchers observed that whilst there were documented syllabuses, timetables and assessment criteria for examinations representing the core function of teaching, the actual teaching as a task was not documented. For instance, there was no documentation that defined teaching and its role at UNZA. Documentation on the student-lecturer relationship was also absent. In addition, there was no documentation that defined consultancy as a task at UNZA, that is, how to manage it and the value it added to knowledge creation at various levels.

The findings from the survey and interviews show that there is a paucity of documented processes, policies, work manuals and procedures at UNZA. The findings suggest that UNZA hardly knows its operational capability because of the limited documentation available on how work gets carried out in the various operations carried out at the institution. This in turn implies that there is no mechanism in place that provides a platform according to which operational knowledge within UNZA can be acquired, retained and leveraged in order to sustain effective and efficient operations.

The fact that 82 (66.1%) of the survey respondents agreed that it was important for UNZA to have documented processes, policies, work manuals and procedures for operations demonstrates the extent to which the respondents valued the need for documenting policies and processes. This affirmation on the importance of documented processes, policies, work manuals and procedures is in line with the advocacy for the creation of knowledge repositories for operational benefit by Kruse (2003) and Rothwell (2004).

Workforce planning

Workforce planning involves the management of an organisation's tacit knowledge base by ensuring the availability of employees with relevant experience, skills and knowledge at all times (American Public Power Association 2005). The findings on the assessment of tacit knowledge through workforce planning were obtained through interviews with heads of units and UNZA management. According to the findings, it was clear that workforce planning was not a formal recognised practice as only a few units undertook some uncoordinated workforce planning. The implication of this finding therefore is that UNZA currently does not have a system for identifying the tacit knowledge requirements for the effective and efficient undertaking of its operations.

Knowledge auditing

The third knowledge assessment tool that was investigated was knowledge auditing. According to Hylton (2002), knowledge auditing seeks to expose the available explicit and tacit knowledge resources of an organisation for operational benefit. Such exposure of knowledge resources usually culminates in knowledge inventories (Paramasivan 2003). According to the survey results, 62 (50%) respondents revealed that UNZA had no skills and competencies inventories whilst only 45 (36.3%) agreed that skills and competencies inventories were available at UNZA. Furthermore, 17 (13.7%) respondents did not have an opinion on the matter. With regard to the interview findings, only one interviewee claimed to have a skills and competencies inventory in his unit. These results, therefore, show that UNZA lacks skills and competencies inventories. This deficiency implies that it is difficult for UNZA to know the risks and opportunities associated with its current knowledge base (Hylton 2002; Paramasivan 2003).

Whilst many organisations are using documentation of work operations, workforce planning and knowledge auditing to assess organisational capabilities in ensuring effective and efficient operational performance (American Public Power Association 2005; Hylton 2002; Rothwell 2004; University of New England 2002), UNZA has no adequate knowledge assessment practices in place. It is thus difficult to retain operational knowledge in order to sustain performance in various operations at UNZA (Hylton 2002; Paramasivan 2003; Rothwell 2004).

Knowledge acquisition practices at the University of Zambia

Knowledge acquisition refers to the practices used by an organisation to possess knowledge (DeLong 2008; Man 2006). Knowledge acquisition practices include recruitment, training and development, brainstorming, expert systems, subject matter experts and after-action reviews (McCall 2006; Tsai & Lee 2006). With this understanding in mind, both the survey and interview data collection methods identified various knowledge acquisition practices existing at UNZA.

Recruitment

Recruitment as a knowledge acquisition technique involves the determination of an organisation's knowledge requirements and employing individuals deemed to possess such knowledge (DeLong 2008). The findings on the acquisition of tacit knowledge through recruitment of

individuals with the requisite knowledge were obtained through interviews. Two interviewees indicated that before recruitment was carried out, a needs assessment aimed at establishing gaps in the knowledge and skills of the staff was conducted. Pursuing recruitment in this manner has been recommended as a best practice (DeLong 2008). However, all the interviewees expressed concern over the freeze on recruitment and unfilled vacancies. Considering that 80% – 90% of corporate knowledge is tacit-based (Hylton 2002), this concern implies that UNZA's knowledge base is incomplete and it is therefore difficult to accomplish operations effectively and efficiently in the absence of the required operational knowledge.

Training and development

Training and development equips employees with relevant operational knowledge beneficial to organisational operations (Rowold 2007; Vermeulen 2002). The survey findings revealed that less than half of the academics (50 respondents or 40.3%) were professionally trained in the academic tasks of teaching, research (56 respondents or 45.2%), curriculum development (29 respondents or 23.4%), academic citizenship (28 respondents or 22.6%) and consultancy (23 respondents or 18.5%). As a result of these deficiencies, there was an overwhelming need for training in functions, policies and procedures of the university (111 respondents or 89.5%), teaching methodology (113 respondents or 91.1%), research methodology (110 respondents or 88.7%), curriculum development (107 respondents or 86.3%), and in school or departmental administration and management (93 respondents or 75%).

On the other hand, almost all the interviewees claimed to facilitate knowledge acquisition through training, although most of it was not operationally specific. For instance, core tasks such as teaching were not amongst those being undertaken. Thus, the results indicate that training and development aimed at the acquisition of job specific knowledge at UNZA was inadequate. The lack of training and development presupposes ineffective and inefficient performance in organisational operations (Vermeulen 2002).

Brainstorming

Brainstorming as a knowledge acquisition technique involves the generation of ideas by a group of people aiming at finding solutions for a given problem (Liou 1990). According to the survey findings, 76 (61.3%) respondents agreed that brainstorming was used at UNZA. Similar findings were established from the interviewees as most of them reported that most decisions in their units were achieved through consensus in meetings.

Subject matter experts

Subject matter experts are individuals considered knowledgeable in a given subject area (IBM Business Consulting Services 2003). According to the survey results, 101 (81.5%) respondents agreed that UNZA used subject matter experts as a tool for knowledge acquisition. The interview findings also firmly confirmed that subject matter experts constituted many of the operational committees at UNZA. This finding, therefore, indicates that in making operational decisions, UNZA placed value on subject matter experts as facilitators of knowledge acquisition.

Expert systems or knowledge bases

Expert systems or knowledge bases are computer-based repositories of explicit knowledge (IBM Business Consulting Services 2003). According to the survey findings, 86 (69.4%) respondents indicated that expert systems or knowledge bases were not in use at UNZA. Similarly, all interviewees stated that UNZA had no expert systems or knowledge bases. Based on these findings, one can conclude that UNZA does not use expert systems or knowledge bases for knowledge acquisition.

After-action reviews

The last knowledge acquisition technique considered in this study was after-action reviews. According to IBM Business Consulting Services (2003), the after-action review is an operational practice in which improvements on operations are made by making deliberate efforts to re-evaluate them. The survey findings indicate that the practice was not prevalent as only 17 (13.7%) respondents reported that after-action reviews were used very often, whilst 51 (41.1%) respondents indicated that after-action reviews were only used sometimes. All interviewees mentioned that their operations were reviewed at different forums such as the Board of Studies for academic units. Given these findings, one may conclude that after-action reviews as a knowledge acquisition practice are fairly common at UNZA.

Given the aforementioned discussion, it appears that UNZA is currently doing well in terms of knowledge acquisition practices such as brainstorming and subject matter experts. However, critical knowledge acquisition practices such as after-action reviews, recruitment and training, and development were generally not being implemented. Coupled with the nonavailability of knowledge bases or repositories, which employees could refer to when performing a given task this means that more is required to improve UNZA's capacity to acquire relevant operational knowledge if efficient and effective performance is to be achieved in operations.

Knowledge transfer practices at the University of Zambia

Knowledge transfer has been defined as an activity that facilitates knowledge flows in organisations (Bou-Llusar & Segarra-Cipres 2006). Knowledge acquisition is a tool for problem-solving and operational enhancement (McCall 2006). Such knowledge flows may involve interactions of individuals or making references to codified knowledge (Lochhead & Stephens 2004). Knowledge transfer practices include succession planning, communities of practice, knowledge repositories, mentoring, coaching, phased retirement, job rotation, storytelling and orientation (Butler & Roch-Tarry 2002; Gale 2007; Stovel & Bontis 2002).

Succession planning

As a common knowledge transfer technique, succession planning involves deliberate facilitation of knowledge flow amongst staff in order to avoid knowledge loss through attrition challenges (Butler & Roch-Tarry 2002). The survey findings show that 34 (27.4%) respondents indicated that succession planning was in existence at UNZA. However, interviewees indicated that succession planning, as a formal knowledge transfer technique did not exist. Given the importance placed on succession planning (Stovel & Bontis 2002), the findings clearly indicate that succession planning, as a knowledge transfer technique is underdeveloped.

Communities of practice

Communities of practice are formal or informal groupings of employees whose common goal is to share operational knowledge (Mngadi & Ngulube 2009). According to the survey findings, only 12 (9.7%) respondents agreed that communities of practice existed at UNZA. However, a crosscheck question that provided statements that defined communities of practice revealed that 62 (50%) respondents belonged to an informal grouping where they shared operational knowledge, whilst 60 (48.4%) were members of a formal grouping that shared operational knowledge. These survey findings were confirmed by the interview findings in which most interviewees indicated that many meetings were held in which various operational matters were discussed. Given these findings, one can safely argue that employees at UNZA shared knowledge amongst themselves at a large scale during the meetings. DeLong (2008), and Ngulube and Mngadi (2007) reached the same conclusion in their studies.

Knowledge repositories through documentation

Documenting relevant operational knowledge has been advocated in order to mitigate attrition challenges and aid in the learning period for new employees (IBM Consulting Services 2003). In this research the survey findings indicate that 39 (31.5%) respondents agreed that UNZA had knowledge repositories. Only 36 (29%) agreed that their schools or departments had operational policies, procedures, or work manuals located in a central place where each member of staff could easily access them. The interview results also show that UNZA lacked knowledge repositories. Given these results, it is clear that UNZA has insufficient knowledge repositories in which operational documentations are kept. The finding concurs with Padilla's (2006) assertion that most organisations do not document their operational relevant knowledge. Thus, UNZA's operational memory is inadequately documented.

Mentorship (formal and informal)

Mentorship is one way in which knowledge in an organisation may be transferred. According to Beazley, Boenisch and Harden (2002), mentoring involves the pairing of an experienced staff member with a novice in order to help the novice acquire competencies required for operational benefit. The survey results indicate that 97 (78.2%) respondents agreed that both formal and informal mentorship existed at UNZA. However, a further verification of this finding revealed that only 28 (22.6%) agreed with the statement that new employees in their departments were allocated a mentor. The interview results on the other hand revealed that no mentorship activities were in place except for the fact that each member of staff was encouraged to consult colleagues on various issues regarding operations. These findings therefore suggest that there might be some mentorship at UNZA, most of which would be informal. Such a situation shows a lack of commitment in ensuring that operational knowledge at UNZA is transferred amongst staff when compared to other universities that have formal mentorship programmes (University of Aberdeen 2006; University of Reading 2007).

Coaching

Related to mentorship, coaching involves the guiding and monitoring of a trainee's progress on training given in order to consolidate the trainee's operational relevant knowledge which enhances such a trainee's performance (University of Reading 2007). The survey results show that 78 (62.9%) respondents agreed that coaching existed at UNZA. However, the interview results indicate that no coaching is in place at UNZA. This finding is thus somewhat similar to the findings on mentorship, and as such one could argue that unofficial coaching of staff might be taking place. Thus, UNZA is missing an opportunity for transferring knowledge from experienced long-serving staff to young, new employees.

Phased retirement

Phased retirement is a range of employment arrangements that allow an employee who is approaching retirement, to continue working, usually with a reduced workload (Brainard 2002:1). In situations where the retirement of staff is identified as a driver for knowledge loss, phased retirement has been used to transfer knowledge amongst staff (Lochhead & Stephens 2004). This knowledge transfer technique is also common in universities (Gale 2007). A total of 75 (60.5%) respondents revealed that phased retirement existed at UNZA. This finding was further confirmed by 96 (77.4%) respondents who agreed that healthy eligible retirees at the age of 55 were often retained on contract conditions of service. However, not all support staff were retained on contract except for those identified to posses unique and exceptional skills and knowledge. These findings indicate that phased retirement is an existing practiced knowledge transfer technique at UNZA.

Orientation or induction

Orientation involves the initiation of staff to general and specific operational requirements in their roles (University of Reading 2007). With regard to the use of orientation as a knowledge transfer practice at UNZA, 49 (39.5%) respondents agreed that both general and specific orientation existed at UNZA. This finding is also in line with most interviewees who were of the opinion that no formal orientation programmes were organised for their staff, especially for academic members of staff. This finding contradicts the fact that staff orientation at UNZA is a formal requirement for all staff as reported by the interviewee vested with the responsibility.

Job rotation

Rotation of staff in different roles is one of the methods used to transfer relevant operational knowledge (UNESCWA 2003). Based on the survey results, 75 (60.5%) respondents agreed that job rotation, as a knowledge transfer practice existed at UNZA. The interview results revealed that only nonacademic staff practiced job rotation. Overall, these results point to the fact that job rotation is a knowledge transfer technique used at UNZA. These findings therefore show that through exposure to different roles, UNZA is able to transfer some operational knowledge.

Storytelling

Stories may be helpful in sharing knowledge. They provide employees with an opportunity to pass on their knowledge to others. No wonder, narratives that constitute operational knowledge have been considered as knowledge transfer tools (Prusak 2001). The survey results show that storytelling is not widely used as a knowledge transfer practice at UNZA considering that only 17 (13.7%) respondents agreed that it existed. The interview results also revealed that it was difficult to tell if stories formed part of the knowledge transfer tools used by staff in their operations. These findings imply that storytelling as a knowledge transfer tool is lacking at UNZA. As such, the lack of storytelling as a knowledge transfer technique shows that UNZA's capacity to expose tacit knowledge for operation benefit is inadequate.

Knowledge retention at the University of Zambia

Both the survey and interview findings strongly established the existence of knowledge retention challenges such as retirements 73 (58.9%), resignations 80 (64.5%) and deaths 72 (58.9%). The interviewees also mentioned these knowledge loss challenges. The effects of these knowledge loss challenges include:

- disruption of services provided
- overworking available staff
- lack of effective and efficient operational continuity.

One hundred and nine (87.9%) of the surveyed respondents agreed that attrition challenges deprived UNZA of relevant operational knowledge whilst 69 (55.6%) of them held the view that UNZA had no knowledge preservation processes in place. The existing loss of operational knowledge and lack of knowledge preservation techniques at UNZA was also expressed by most interviewees.

The researchers also wished to verify whether UNZA required a knowledge retention policy. According to the survey findings, 111 (89.5%) respondents mentioned the need for a knowledge retention policy. The need to formulate knowledge retention policies is well documented (Kidwell, Vander Linde & Johnson 2003; UniSA 2007). Based on both the survey and interview findings, it could be argued that institutions of higher learning should have knowledge retention policies in order not to lose essential operational knowledge.

Recommendations and conclusions

At the beginning of the study, the researchers assumed that most organisations including UNZA were faced with the problem of knowledge loss and that proactive responses such as knowledge retention were required to handle the dilemma. The research findings established knowledge loss challenges arising from staff attrition challenges such as retirements and resignations. These knowledge retention challenges are regarded as a threat to operations (DeLong 2008; McQuade *et al.* 2007; Padilla 2006; Purdum 2006; Sutherland & Jordaan 2004).

The results show that a number of gaps existed in the current knowledge retention practices at UNZA. With regard to knowledge assessment as an integral dimension of knowledge retention, three techniques, namely organisational capabilities assessment, workforce planning and knowledge auditing, were investigated. The findings with regard to these techniques were not positive. It was clear that very few work processes and tasks were documented. Workforce planning was not practiced and skills and competency inventories were lacking.

With regard to the findings on knowledge acquisition as another knowledge retention strategy, the investigated practices revealed both positive and negative findings. Knowledge acquisition was supported in the form of generation of ideas, utilisation of expertise and reviews on operations. An observation made by the researchers was that all these knowledge acquisition practices usually take place in the form of meetings. Meetings are forums in which operational decisions are usually made by experts (Turban, Mclean & Wetherbe 2003). At UNZA, a number of committees that handle operational matters were found to exist. Yet there was no wide support for training and development, and the use of expert knowledge bases as knowledge acquisition practices. According to the literature, knowledge acquisition cannot take place in a situation where staff is not trained in operational tasks and where repositories for operational knowledge are lacking (IBM Business Consulting Services 2003; Rowold 2007; Tsai & Lee 2006; Vermeulen 2002).

The participation of staff in various meetings, job rotation, phased retirements and the retention of employees beyond their retirement age were some of the methods used for knowledge transfer at UNZA. In contrast, formal succession planning, coaching, knowledge repositories, storytelling, orientation, general and job specific training and mentorship were lacking at UNZA. Referring to succession planning, Butler and Roch-Tarry (2002) argue that the failure to identify talent, skills and competencies undermine knowledge management efforts in an organisation. We propose that UNZA consider the formulation of a well-coordinated and integrated approach for retaining operationally relevant knowledge.

Based on the findings, we suggest the knowledge retention framework (KRF) presented in Figure 1. KRF depicted in

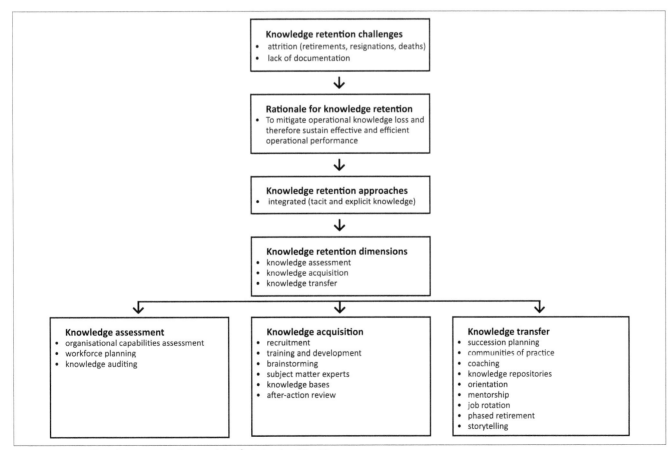

FIGURE 1: Proposed knowledge retention framework for the University of Zambia.

Figure 1 is based on the following:

- organisation's ability to identify knowledge retention challenges
- organisation's acknowledgement of a need and purpose for knowledge retention
- organisation's preparedness to integrate tacit and explicit knowledge
- organisation's understanding of the dimensions of knowledge retention which primarily encompasses knowledge assessment, acquisition and transfer.

Such a knowledge retention framework (as is shown in Figure 1) may help UNZA to enhance knowledge retention at the institution. If UNZA believes that such a framework would serve its interests, it should integrate the KRF into the institutional policies and the whole institution should take ownership of the policy, ideally under the guidance of a knowledge champion.

References

American Public Power Association, 2005, *Workforce planning for public power utilities: ensuring resources to meet projected needs*, viewed 01 June 2007, from http://www.appanet.org/files/PDFs/WorkForcePlanningforPublicPowerUtilities.pdf

Association of Commonwealth Universities, 2006, *Trends in academic recruitment and retention: a Commonwealth perspective*, in J. Kubler & C. DeLuca (authors), Association of Commonwealth Universities, London, UK.

Basu, B. & Sengupta K., 2007, 'Assessing success factors of knowledge management initiatives of academic institutions – a case of an Indian Business School', *The Electronic Journal of Knowledge Management* 5(3), 273–282, viewed 10 November 2007, from http://www.ejkm.com/volume5/issue3

Beazley, H., Boenisch, J. & Harden, D., 2002, *Continuity management: preserving corporate knowledge and productivity when employees leave*, John Wiley & Sons, Inc., Hoboken, NJ.

Bou-Llusar, C.J. & Segarra-Cipres, M., 2006, ' Strategic knowledge transfer and its implications for competitive advantage: an integrative conceptual framework', *Journal of Knowledge Management* 10(4), 100–112.

Brainard, K., 2002, *Phased retirement overview: summary of research and practices*, viewed 10 November 2007, from http://www.nasra.org/resources/Phased%20Retirement%20Overview.pdf

Butler, K. & Roche-Tarry, D., 2002, 'Succession planning: putting an organisation's knowledge at work', *Nature Biotechnology* 20, 201–202.

Consultas, 2007, *Process mapping and procedure development*, viewed 10 November 2007, from http://www.consultas.com.au/manage/ConsultasProcessMapping.pdf

Davidson, G., Lepeak, S. & Newman, E., 2007, *The impact of the aging workforce on public sector organisations and mission*, viewed 03 June 2007, from http://www.ipma-hr.org

DeLong, D., 2008, 'Knowledge loss prevention: five keys to decisions vis-à-vis an ageing workforce', *Inside Knowledge* 11(5), 15–19.

Gale, F.S., 2007, *Phased retirement*, viewed 22 October 2007, from http://www.workforce.com/section/02/feature/23/47/31/index.html

Halawi, A.L., Aronson, E.J. & McCarthy, V.R., 2005, 'Resource-based view of knowledge management for competitive advantage', *The Electronic Journal of Knowledge Management* 3(2), 75–86, viewed 22 October 2007, from http://www.ejkm.com/volume3/issue2

Henczel, S., 2000, 'The information audit as a first step towards effective knowledge management: an opportunity for the Special Librarian', *INSPEL* 34(3/4), 210–226, viewed 20 December 2005, from http://forge.fh-potsdam.de/~IFLA/INSPEL/00-3hesu.pdf

Hylton, A., 2002, *Measuring and assessing knowledge - value and the pivotal role of the knowledge audit*, viewed 12 September 2006, from http://www.providersedge.com/docs/km_articles/Measuring_&_Assessing_K-Value_&_Pivotal_Role_of_K-Audit.pdf

IBM Business Consulting Services, 2003, *Grey matter matters: preserving critical knowledge in the 21st century*, viewed 20 December 2005, from http://www-935.ibm.com/services/uk/igs/pdf/esr-grey-matter-matters.pdf

IOTA Consultancy Services, 2001, *Final report: staff and organisation audit at the University of Zambia*, IOTA Consultancy Services, Lusaka.

Jarrar, Y., 2002, 'Knowledge management: learning for organisational experience', *Managerial Auditing Journal* 17(6), 322–328.

Kidwell, J.J., Vander Linde, K.M., and Johnson, L.S., 2000, 'Applying corporate knowledge management practices in higher education', *Educause Quarterly* 23(4), 28–33.

Kruger, C.J. & Snyman, M.M.M., 2005, 'Principles and strategies for the effective management of knowledge', *Mousaion* 23(1), 62–80.

Kruse, S., 2003, 'Remembering as organisational memory', *Journal of Educational Administration* 41(4), 332–347.

Liou, Y., 1990, 'Knowledge acquisition: issues, techniques, and methodology', in *ACM Press*, viewed 04 April 2006, from http://www.acm.org

Lochhead, C. & Stephens, A., 2004, 'Employee retention, labour turnover and knowledge transfer: case studies from the Canadian plastics sector', in *Canadian Labour and Business Centre Report*, viewed 04 April 2006, from http://www.cpsc-ccsp.ca/PDFS/CPSC%20Final%20Report%20June28%20-%207%20case%20studies2%20oct%207%202004.pdf.

Loh, B., Tang, A., Menkhoff, T., Chay, Y. & Evers, H., 2003, *Applying knowledge management in university research*, viewed 03 August 2006, from http://www.uni-bonn.de/~hevers/papers/Loh-Tang-Menkhoff-Chay-Evers2003-new.pdf

MacGregor, D., 2006, 'So much for the senility gang', *Academic Matters: The Journal of Higher Education* (Spring), 17–18.

Man, T., 2006, 'Exploring the behavioural patterns of entrepreneurial learning: a competency approach', *Education & Training* 48(5), 309–321.

Maponya, M.P., 2004, *Knowledge management practices in academic libraries: a case study of the University of Natal, Pietermaritzburg libraries*, viewed 20 April 2006, from http://citeseerx.ist.psu.edu/viewdoc/summary?doi=10.1.1.137.8283

McCall, H., 2006, *Knowledge management system use and knowledge acquisition: some initial evidence*, viewed 03 February 2007, from http://mgt.ncsu.edu/pdfs/accounting/KMS-HLMcCall2-16-2006.pdf

McQuade, E., Sjoer, E., Fabian, P., Nascimento, J.C. & Schroeder, S., 2007, 'Will you miss me when I'm gone? A study of the potential loss of company knowledge and expertise as employees retire', *Journal of European Industrial Training* 31(9), 758–768.

Mngadi, B. & Ngulube, P., 2009, 'Utilization of communities of practice in the humanities at the Universities of KwaZulu-Natal and Zululand', *African Journal of Library, Archives and Information Science* 19(1), 1–12.

Ngoc, P., 2006, *An empirical study of knowledge transfer within Vietnam's IT companies*, viewed 10 February 2007, from http://diuf.unifr.ch/is/staff/ngoct/files/internal%20working%20paper-10-6.pdf

Nguyen, T., Smyth, R. & Gable, G., 2004, 'Knowledge management issues and practices: a case study of a professional services firm', in *ACIS 2004 Proceedings*, Paper 74, viewed 23 October 2007, from http://aisel.aisnet.org/acis2004/74

Padilla, R., 2006, *Baby Boomers sticking around longer?*, viewed 29 November 2006, from http://blogs.techrepublic.com.com/tech-manager/?cat=337

Paramasivan, T., 2003, 'Knowledge audit', in *The Chartered Accountant*, viewed 02 June 2007, from http://icai.org/resource_file/11294p498-506.pdf

Perez-Soltero, A., Barcelo-Valenzuela, M., Sanchez-Schmitz, G., Martin-Rubio, F. & Palma-Mendez, T. J., 2006, *Knowledge audit methodology with emphasis on core processes*, viewed 03 May 2007, from http://www.iseing.org/emcis/EMCIS2006/Proceedings/Contributions/C20/CRC/EMCIS%20KAMCP%20Final.pdf

Phaladi, M.P., 2011, 'Knowledge transfer and retention: the case of a public water utility in South Africa', Masters thesis, University of Stellenbosch, Stellenbosch.

Probst, G., Raub, S. & Romhardt, K., 2000, *Managing knowledge: building blocks for success*, John Wiley, London, UK.

Prusak, L., 2001, *Story: organisational perspective*, viewed 11 June 2007, from http://www.creatingthe21stcentury.org/Larry-I-overview.html

Purdum, T., 2006, *Workforce shortage: retaining knowledge and expertise*, viewed 20 November 2006, from http://www.cpsc-ccsp.ca/PDFS/Workforce%20Shortage.pdf

Rothwell, W., 2004, 'Knowledge transfer: 12 strategies for succession management', in *IPM-HR NEWS*, viewed 12 September 2007, from http://www.greenchameleon.com/uploads/12_Strategies_for_Succession_Management.pdf

Rowold, J., 2007, 'Individual influences on knowledge acquisition in a call centre training context in Germany', *International Journal of Training and Development* 11(1), 21–34.

Scalzo, N., 2006, 'Memory loss? Corporate knowledge and radical change', *Journal of Business Strategy* 27(4), 60–69.

Smith, L.D., 2007, *Standard process for knowledge retention*, viewed 18 April 2011, from http://www.levidsmith.com/papers/ie591_research_paper.pdf

Stovel, M., & Bontis, N., 2002, 'Voluntary turnover: knowledge management – friend or foe', *Journal of Intellectual Capital* 3(3), 303–322.

Sutherland, M., & Jordaan, W., 2004, 'Factors affecting the retention of knowledge workers', *SA Journal of Human Resource Management* 2(2), 55–64.

Tennessee Valley Authority, 2005, Knowledge *retention: preventing knowledge from walking out the door: an overview of processes and tools at the Tennessee Valley Authority*, viewed 02 October 2006, from http://www.tva.gov/knowledgeretention/pdf/overview.pdf#search=%22Tennessee%20valley%20Authority%20knowledge%20retention%22

Tellis, W., 1997, 'Introduction to case study', *The Qualitative Report* 3(2), viewed 3 July 2007, from http://www.scribd.com/doc/7129411/Tellis-W-1997-Introduction-to-Case-Study-the-Qualitative-Report-23

Tsai, M-T. & Lee, K-W., 2006, 'A study of knowledge internalisation from the perspective of learning cycle theory', *Journal of Knowledge Management* 10(3), 57–71.

Turban, E., Mclean, E. & Wetherbe, J., 2003, *Information technology for management: making connections for strategic advantage*, John Wiley and Sons Inc, New York, NY.

United Nations Economic and Social Commission for Western Asia, 2003, *Knowledge management methodology: an empirical approach in core sectors in ESCWA member countries*, viewed 12 June 2007, from http://www.landray.com.cn/Uploads/Knowledge/200710239172897611.pdf

University of Aberdeen, 2006, University of Aberdeen strategic plan 2002–2006, viewed 19 June 2007, from http://www.abdn.ac.uk/admin/docs/straplan2.doc

University of Edinburgh, 2005, *Knowledge management strategic plan*, viewed 19 June 2007, from http://www.kmstrategy.ed.ac.uk/KM_Strategy/PLAN-05-06/KM-Plan-05.pdf

University of New England, 2002, *Workforce planning*, viewed 20 May 2007, from http://www.une.edu.au/policies/pdf/workforceplanning.pdf

University of Reading, 2007, *Guidelines for the mentoring of new academic staff*, viewed 10 September 2007 from, http://www.reading.ac.uk/Handbooks/Teaching_and_Learning/mentors.html

University of South Australia, 2007, *Workforce demographics*, viewed 30 March 2007, from http://www.unisa.educ.au/hrm/resources/planning/demographic.asp

University of Zambia, 2001, *University of Zambia strategic plan 2002-2006*, UNZA, Lusaka.

Vermeulen, R., 2002, 'Narrowing the transfer gap: the advantages of "as if" situations in training', *Journal of European Industrial Training* 16(8), 366–374.

17

Conquering the digital divide: Botswana and South Korea digital divide status and interventions

Authors:
Nonofo C. Sedimo[1]
Kelvin J. Bwalya[2]
Tanya Du Plessis[3]

Affiliations:
[1]Department of Library and Information Studies, University of Botswana, Gaborone

[2]Center for Information and Knowledge Management, University of Johannesburg, South Africa

[3]Department of Information and Knowledge Management, University of Johannesburg, South Africa

Correspondence to:
Tanya du Plessis

Email:
tduplessis@uj.ac.za

Postal address:
PO Box 524, Auckland Park 2006, South Africa

Background: Botswana is putting in place initiatives towards establishing itself as a knowledge-based economy. Transformation from a resource-based to a knowledge-based economy is partly hinged on innovation, research and development capability, knowledge channels, and the funding of research and development activities.

Objectives: Bridging the digital divide and narrowing the intra-national divide brings about global information and communication technology (ICT) usage that translates into changing work patterns and eventually transformed economies. This article outlines the different interventions implemented in Botswana to bridge the divide. The South Korean experience in bridging the divide is discussed so as to serve as lessons on how to effectively bridge the divide to Botswana's initiatives.

Method: Using a mix of exploratory and empirical study, this article presents the findings on the status of ICT uptake in Botswana and investigates the level of the digital divide in the country.

Results: The results of the study show that the digital divide is much more evident in Botswana than in South Korea. South Korea has put in place robust strategic initiatives towards reducing the digital divide and this has largely transcended into its transformation into a full-fledged knowledge society.

Conclusion: This article is timely as it unearths the different pointers that may be utilised in policy formation and what interventions need to be taken at both the individual and national level to bridge the digital divide.

Introduction

The digital divide presents itself as a roadblock to socio-economic development in different regions and countries. With the presence of the digital divide, many opportunities offered by the digital revolution such as online job search, efficient information management (IM), online social networks and electronic mail systems cannot be accessed. At a national level, it is possible that a country may fail to benefit from the returns of the global socio-economic value chains if there are blatant levels of digital divide. In this article, the concept 'digital divide' refers to the difference in access and usage of information and communication technologies (ICTs), and correspondingly to information content and any socio-economic opportunities such as jobs, social inclusion and tribal and/or regional integration.

Understanding the extent of the digital divide is vital as access to ICTs is now commonly looked at as the *fons et origo* of contemporary innovation practices. There are basically two kinds of digital divide. The first kind is the 'vertical divide', which outlines the gap between users and non-users of information technology (IT). This is considered the first level of the divide and it presents the problem of unequal opportunity to efficient access of information resources. The second type of divide is the 'horizontal divide', which outlines the gap among IT users. This is correspondingly considered the second level of the divide and it presents the problem of social integration and inclusiveness. It is worth mentioning that the digital divide is a complicated phenomenon that hinges on many different factors (James 2009). This article investigates these two types of the divide at the intra-national level of Botswana.

Botswana has recognised that in order to compete favourably in the global economic value chains, it requires a national focus towards transforming from a resource-based economy to a knowledge-based economy (KBE). A KBE involves codification of knowledge (using knowledge engineering and knowledge management) in different socio-economic sectors with a view of differentiation towards a competitive edge. In a KBE all the measures of production and productivity as well as innovation are fueled by knowledge. A KBE is attained when a country effectively participates in the 'information society' where knowledge is utilised in all the socio-economic value chains. The attainment of a KBE entails that a country is going to be placed at a competitive edge in global business value chains. This recognition has been compounded by the following pronouncement in Vision 2016: 'Botswana aims to be a prosperous, productive and innovative society; an open democratic and accountable society; and an educated, informed society' (Hall & Lewin 2005:20).

Any aspiration to transform towards a KBE cannot be achieved without the efficient use of ICTs. Under the current dispensation of the Vision 2016, using different forms of ICTs is recognised as a major cornerstone towards achieving a competitive economy. Botswana's ICT sector development has ushered in a paradigm that promotes efficient information and knowledge management through the use of ICT platforms. This is a cardinal milestone towards establishing an economy where the emphasis is on the effectual management of knowledge despite economies of scale of production and other business management strategies, including six sigma, and despite earlier economics researchers' theories such as Frederick Winslow Taylor (1911–1915) in his theory of scientific management (Serrat 2010:139, 153, 163–165).

Transforming from a resource-based economy to a KBE requires an understanding of present economic and non-economic indicators of the digital divide. The economic indicators include the financial cost of acquiring access to ICT tools and platforms such as mobile phones, computers and the Internet. The non-economic indicators are divided into social, cultural and opportunity cost of not engaging in ICT usage, and technical indicators such as the level of individual ICT literacy skills and usability of the ICT platforms. To shed some light on these indicators, this article firstly presents background information on the phenomenon of the digital divide by providing more theoretical underpinnings, followed by the empirical study. Secondly, the different approaches in addressing the digital divide in Botswana and South Korea (henceforth, Korea) are presented respectively. This is followed by an analysis of the gaps in the status of the digital divide in Botswana and Korea to determine the lessons learnt from these experiences. Korea has been chosen to showcase how the massive integration of ICTs into various socio-economic value chains can improve the innovation potential of a nation. Currently, Korea is the leader of consumer electronics and e-Government development, and also occupies a top spot in Digital Opportunity Index (DOI) worldwide (UNDESA, 2010). It is thought that a closer look at Korea may serve as lessons to Botswana as it intends to bridge its massive digital divides.

By using the current socio-economic indicators, the two countries are not comparable. However, comparison is necessary as in 1966, when Botswana achieved its independence, both countries had socio-economic indicators that were within the range of comparison. Currently, both countries have a dedicated leadership that is committed to enabling all citizens to have equal access to information; both aim to participate effectively in the information society and reduce dependency on natural resources, and both have comparatively high literacy rates. Just like Korea with its limited natural resources, Botswana is also devising plans to diversify from over-dependence on diamonds to being innovative in various other sectors of the economy. This can be accentuated by its plans to establish the Botswana Innovation Hub (BIH) and the already established Botswana Productivity Center (BPC) to drive the national innovation and competitiveness agenda. In order for this to be achieved, access to information through global usage of ICTs such as computers and the Internet is desired. Korea's brilliance in emerging as a global leader in as far as broadband and Internet penetration is concerned can serve as a lesson to Botswana. It is not the intention of this paper to compare Korea and Botswana one-on-one but to highlight Korea's experience as a reference point for effective design of digital divide interventions.

Korea is a transitional economy that has higher Internet and broadband penetration rates than Botswana. In the not too distant past, Korea was a developing country with no tangible natural resources but with a promising human resource base. Botswana has a middle-income economy that is showing a lot of potential to bridge the massive digital divide gaps amongst its population so that it can later participate effectively in the information society. The economic prowess of Korea is hinged on the rigorous exploitation of consumer electronics (such as Samsung, LG electronics), the automobile industry (such as Hyundai, Daewoo, KIA) and the shipbuilding industry. Korea has a Gross Domestic Product (GDP) of $1338 trillion (Gambrill 2010), a literacy rate of 99%, a GDP per capita (purchasing power parity) of $20 000, a population of 48 520 835 (Kettani 2010) and a land surface area of 98 444 m^2 with over 443 000 km^2 of marine area and about 12 000 km of political borders defined by maritime boundaries. Botswana has a land area of approximately 582 000 km^2 (Mathuba 2003), a population of 1.99 million, a GDP of $15.2 billion and a GDP per capita of about $14 800.

Of the possible ICTs that may be utilised to access information resources, this study probed participants' access to computers and correspondingly the Internet. Access to the Internet through other convertible modes such as mobile phones was also considered. The study intended to investigate the vertical and horizontal divides, in other words, access to information through the Internet. The investigation of the extent of the digital divide also involved analysing the ICT policy and institutional frameworks, the tele-density, broadband and Internet penetration, and the actual access and usage of computers and the Internet. The study also contained an empirical part for Botswana in a view to probe and emphasise the actual status of the divide at the individual level.

Since Korea has achieved very high broadband and Internet penetration rates, it can be used as reference points when devising strategies for global ICT penetration and mitigating the extent of the digital divide. This article provides guidance on how policy should be framed, for the case of Botswana, by indicating which interventions have been implemented to encourage Internet penetration in Korea.

Background

Many researchers have investigated the impact of the digital divide and the value of information on different endeavors to transform economies into KBEs. In the contemporary world, information is viewed as a dematerialised economic entity and is correspondingly used as a measure of power (Bassey 2008). Information brings about convergence of a variety of social norms and the codification of information in a manner that it enables ideas to be shared easily and cheaply. This characteristic of information makes efficient management of information a prerequisite to establishing a KBE.

Countries with developed economies have shown that appropriate utilisation of ICTs in different socio-economic sectors comes with a 'leapfrog effect' in as far as development is concerned (Mansell 2001). The 'leapfrog effect' is a term that has been utilised in this context to show that effective and proper utilisation of ICTs may result in revolutionary or instantaneous rather than incremental effect (or ripple effect) on a country's development. Efficient use of ICTs in enterprises will translate into greater productivity (Bresnahan, Brynjolfsson & Hitt 1999). This efficient use of ICTs can only be ushered in when there is good political will to encourage proliferation of ICTs in all socio-economic sectors. The preceding comment was confirmed by James (2002) who posits that there is substantial evidence that emerging democracies such as South Africa and Brazil have leapfrogged in their adoption, synthesis, integration and application of digital technologies. This may point to the assertion that appropriate digital diffusion requires fertile ground for democratic development.

A lack of appropriate IM channels may limit information flow and therefore impact on productivity at both enterprise and individual levels. The World Bank Report (2000) suggests that disparities in the productivity levels may be attributed to poor telecommunications infrastructure and practices in most of the African states. An empirical case of this assertion is that of Zimbabwe and Botswana where 'areas with high levels of resources and skilled labour but with lower levels of telephony have fewer 'productivity enterprises' (Robison & Crenshaw 2000:5). This may not be exhaustive but presents a clue as to how ICT infrastructure plays an indirect role on impacting on economic growth. Effective utilisation of ICTs will enable enterprises to pursue blue oceans, viz 'the unserved market, where competitors are not yet structured and the market is relatively unknown' (Hollensen 2007; cf Kim & Mauborgne 2004; Burke, Van Stel & Thurik 2010:28). This is especially the case for countries with developing economies; ICTs will enable them to appropriately market their natural resources, which may culminate into an increase in foreign direct investment (FDI).

The digital divide negatively affects FDI (Fuchs & Horak 2008:109). Unequal access, adoption and usage of ICTs result in limited access to information resources. When this situation is evident, we say the digital divide exists. Researchers agree that 'digital divide' is the metaphor used to 'describe the perceived disadvantage of those who either are unable or do not choose to make use of information technologies in their daily life' (Cullen 2003:247). The digital divide has also been defined as 'the strikingly differential extent to which rich and poor countries are enjoying the benefits of information technology' (James 2003:25) and as 'the unequal distribution of computers, Internet connections, fax machines and so on between countries' (James 2003:23). James (2009:25) further describes the digital divide as the differentiation that comes about with benefits reaped from use of ICTs by both the rich and poor countries. Campbell (2001) simply defines the digital divide as a situation in which there is a clearly identified gap in the access or use of ICT platforms. This gap can be looked at as the 'haves' and 'have-nots' with reference to people with or without access to ICTs (Chon 2001; Cronin 2002). The digital divide, which presents itself as a gap between information haves and have-nots, is evident amongst different groups in the same country, referred to as 'intra-national digital divide'; and between countries, referred to as 'global digital divide' (Ono 2005). Wilson (2006:300) concludes that the digital divide is 'an inequality in access, distribution, and use of information and communication technologies between two or more populations'.

The digital divide is not only linked to Internet access but also to its usage attributes such as ease-of-use (usability) and overall benefit (Fuchs & Horak 2008). The Organisation for Economic Co-operation and Development (OECD 2004) posits that the digital divide includes factors such as education and literacy, income, ICT skills, marker structures, institutional frameworks, and competition. Apart from associating the digital divide with the provision of computer connections and the Internet, it also encompasses a complex array of factors such as human, digital, physical and social relationships (Warschauer 2001). Norris (2001) defines the digital divide as being multidimensional in nature. It includes different versions such as global, social and democratic digital divide. The International Telecommunications Union (ITU 2005:vii) ascertains that the digital divide highlights the uneven distribution and differences or gaps that exist in opportunities to access and the use of ICTs amongst diverse population groups, be they individuals, households, businesses, institutions or geographical areas.

Having defined the different aspects of the digital divide, it is necessary to show the levels of access and usage of Internet in Botswana as compared to different African countries. This is important to show how Botswana fares when compared to other countries with the same socio-economic conditions. Table 1 shows the ICT use and penetration status in three

TABLE 1: Internet users and population statistics for specific countries.

Africa	Population	Internet users		Penetration	%	
	(2009 Est.)	Dec. 2000	Latest data	(% population)	User growth	Total users in Africa
Angola	12 799 293	30 000	**550 000**	4.3	1733.30%	0.6
Botswana	1 990 876	15 000	**120 000**	6.0	700.00%	0.1
Burkina Faso	15 746 232	10 000	**140 000**	0.9	1300.00%	0.2

Source: Internet World Statistics, 2010, *Internet users and population statistics for specific countries*, viewed 16 August 2011, from www.internetworldstats.com
Note: The user growth data is for the period 2000-2009.

African countries, Angola, Botswana and Burkina Faso, and the growth in Internet users from 2000 to 2009 in each country.

From Table 1, it can be shown that Botswana has only 120 000 people actively using the Internet accounting for 0.1% of the total users in Africa. It is evident that Internet penetration has to increase for Botswana to fully participate in the knowledge economy, to model an information economy, or to develop into a knowledge-based economy.

In general, different models of the information and/or knowledge-based economies may be applied at the urban level to measure the intra-national digital divides, and between and within regions (Van der Meer & Van Winden 2003; Venturelli 2002). Using countries as the unit of analysis for the digital divide, the ITU (2006) carried out a study to ascertain the level of the digital divide between the countries with developed economies and those with developing economies. Table 2 shows the digital divide with reference to mobile phone subscription from 1998 to 2004 in two broad categories, namely, so-called 'developed' and 'developing' countries.

Table 2 presents a significant decrease, albeit in relative terms, with regard to the digital divide. This is in line with the prediction of Norris (2001), namely that with time, the digital divide would decrease as more and more people will have access to ICTs. This line of reasoning is premised on Moore's Law, viz, that the number of transistors on integrated circuits and hence processing power doubles every 18 months while the costs do not increase. Whether this reasoning holds true to Botswana and the digital divide is further investigated in the empirical study discussed in the next section.

The empirical part of the paper aims to show the proportion of people who may be 'information rich' versus those who may be 'information poor' in Botswana owing to their lack of efficient access and usage of ICTs. It is assumed that ICTs may facilitate access to essential information at any time and promote effective and informed decision-making, improve innovation and correspondingly promote competitiveness.

Empirical study

Botswana is currently putting in place initiatives towards establishing itself as a KBE (Hall & Lewin 2005:20). Transformation from a resource-based to a knowledge-based economy is partly based on innovation, research and development capability, knowledge channels, knowledge solutions, and the funding of research and development

activities (Serrat 2010). Narrowing the intranational digital divide brings about global information and communication technology usage that translates into changing work patterns and productivity growth. This section presents the findings of the empirical study on the status of ICT uptake in Botswana and investigates the level of the digital divide in the country.

In an attempt to understand the extent of the digital divide in Botswana, both a literature review and a document analysis were done. The literature and document analysis aimed at understanding the different interventions that have been done to bridge the digital divide. The empirical study aimed at understanding the actual divide at the individual level thereby investigating the vertical and the horizontal divides.

A questionnaire with both open and closed-ended questions was utilised in this study. This questionnaire was pilot-tested with 10 participants to establish its face validity, test its reliability and improve the clarity of the questions so that participants may comprehend it with ease (in conformance with Creswell 1994). It was important to establish the reliability of the data collection instrument so that errors and biases were eliminated as much as possible (Yin 2003). Measuring the validity of the questionnaire was important to make it possible for correct and authentic data to be collected and later appropriately subjected to correct empirical analysis (Luk 2009). Open-ended questions ensured that there were no restriction on how a respondent could answer questions and presented an opportunity where participants' opinions on probed phenomena could not be answered using pre-defined categories (Wilson 1996). Alternatively, closed-ended questions come with many options out of which a respondent is mandated to choose one or more of them relating to his or her experience about the phenomenon under investigation (Saunders *et al.* 2002).

The survey, conducted in 2010, was aimed at exploring the use of ICTs by citizens of Botswana. The study specifically aimed at understanding whether ICTs are being utilised to access essential information or utilised to ease peoples' daily activities. In so doing, the study wanted to understand the

TABLE 2: Digital Divide from 1998–2004.

Type of country	Mobile phone subscribers per 100 persons	
	1998	2004
Developed	24.6	76.8
Developing	1.9	18.8
Size of digital divide (relative terms)	12.9	4.1

Source: International Telecommunications Union, 2006, *Statistics, International Telecommunication Union*, viewed 02 September 2011, from www.itu.int/ITU-D/ict/statistics/

impact of ICT usage on some aspects of the digital divide. A random sampling technique was utilised in this research targeting people with different levels of education and exposure to ICTs.

To be included in the study, participants had to be at least 21 years old, have completed high school, and have potential and requisite ICT skills to effectively utilise ICTs in their daily endeavors. Out of this group, there were participants who chose not to utilise ICTs (non-users) because they thought the perceived value was low. These were compared with the participants that utilised ICTs thereby obtaining a subjective feeling of the extent of the divide (vertical divide). Amongst the active users, qualitative analysis of the difference functions for which they utilise ICTs was also subjectively measured (horizontal divide). Because of resource constraints, all the respondents were drawn from Gaborone. Over 50% of the respondents were women aged between 25 and 36 years old. This is important because it shows that the study employs gender inclusiveness.

The catchment area for the project was Gaborone (capital city of Botswana). Specifically, data was collected from faculty and students from the University of Botswana, workers from the Ministry of Education, Mascom Wireless Company, and the Botswana Council of Non-Governmental Organisations (BOCONGO). The study utilised a short questionnaire comprising only seven questions. The sample frame included 153 people. Eventually, a total of 119 people participated in the survey. Of these, 62 were women (52%) and 57 were men (48%). The study targeted individuals who utilise ICTs in their day-to-day activities. Prior to being involved in the study, potential participants were asked whether they have the necessary ICT literacy levels to potentially engage in ICT usage. The majority of the study was conducted at the University of Botswana where a total of 87 questionnaires were distributed to the respondents and only 61 (70% response rate) were included in the final analysis. At Mascom Wireless Company, 15 questionnaires were distributed and 14 (93% response rate) were returned for analysis. At the Ministry of Education, 46 questionnaires were distributed and 39 of them were returned for analysis (85% response rate), and at BOCONGO 6 questionnaires were distributed and 5 were returned for analysis (83% response rate).

The first question requested respondents to provide information on the frequency with which they use ICTs on a daily basis. The options were, 'Never', 'One to three times' and 'More than three times'. The majority of respondents, 83.5%, indicated that they use ICTs more than three times a day, whilst 6.5% of respondents mentioned their frequency of ICT usage between one to three times per day. Of the respondents, 10% indicated that they have the requisite ICT skills but do not use ICTs at all in their day-to-day activities at work apart from checking e-mails.

The second question requested respondents to provide information on their different uses of ICTs. Figure 1 illustrates respondents' reasons for using ICTs, with communication and data ranking the highest, followed by other uses such as work, entertainment, e-Commerce and school work.

The third question required respondents to provide information on the value that the use of ICTs adds to their daily routines. Respondents had to rank the value they experienced from using ICTs in terms of personal development, easy access to information, saving time, convenience, speed with which work is done and economical value. The results are shown in Figure 2. Respondents mostly perceived the value of using ICTs on a personal development level.

The next question expected respondents to specify if they preferred automating daily routines with the use of ICTs or not. Responses were limited to the options 'Yes' and 'No'. Only 10% of the respondents chose 'No', whilst 90% of the respondents said they preferred automating daily routines with the use of ICTs.

Question five requested respondents to specify whether the use of ICTs increases their access to personal and professional information. They had a choice to choose between 'Yes' and 'No'. In opting for 'No', respondents were also expected to give reasons for their choice. All the respondents chose 'Yes', thereby indicating that the use of ICTs is seen to positively facilitate access to personal and professional information.

Question six required respondents to indicate the challenges that they face when attempting to access ICTs. Respondents had the choice to select more than one option from the following list:

- low bandwidth
- lack of ICT skills
- lack of security
- high cost of ICTs
- lack of ICT resources
- operations failure.

The responses are presented in Figure 3, with low bandwidth and lack of ICT resources perceived by respondents as the two major challenges to accessing ICTs.

The answers to six of the seven questions asked indicate a high usage of ICTs, with the daily use of ICTs being the norm. This amplifies the fact that ICT are an important component in today's socio-economic environment. The majority of this survey's respondents use ICTs for communication and data manipulation. There was also a high indication that people use ICTs for work related purposes and entertainment. Most respondents perceived the use of ICTs as beneficial to their personal development. Other perceived advantages of ICT usage include that it helps save time, increases speed with which work is done and convenience. These factors can be translated to higher productivity levels. Despite this being the case, yet others still found ICTs not to be of any value preposition.

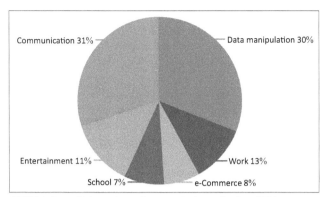

FIGURE 1: Uses of information and communication technology (ICTs).

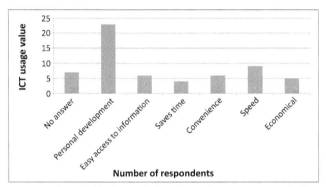

FIGURE 2: Value added by the use of information and communication technology (ICTs).

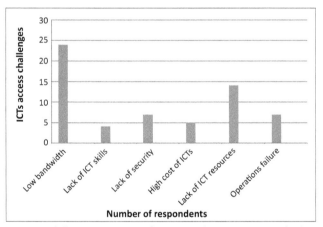

FIGURE 3: Challenges in accessing information and communication technology (ICTs).

The majority of respondents indicated that they would prefer to automate their daily routines with the use of ICTs. Those respondents who refrained from such automation cited reasons such as low ICT skills, and trust and usability issues as being the major challenges. All participants agreed that ICT usage facilitates information access and efficient management of personal and professional information. The general challenges that participants faced in accessing ICTs are associated with a lack of basic ICT skills on their part, unavailability of readily accessible ICT platforms, security, and operation failure issues. Specific notice should also be taken of the main challenges that were identified, namely, low bandwidth and lack of ICT resources.

Finally, the respondents were asked about their knowledge on the different digital divide interventions that are currently in place in Botswana. Respondents indicated that they had some knowledge on what the government is currently doing to address the ICT related challenges. However, respondents mostly do not know what the government is doing to address their problems in ICT usage. Most of the respondents recommended that in order for the government to leapfrog the campaign to bridge the digital divide, there is a need to look more into ICT education, lowering ICTs costs and improving electronic service delivery. There is also an outcry for industry revolution and the provision of ICTs resources. From these responses, it is clear that the intra-national divide is very evident in Botswana.

The status of the digital divide (demand side of ICT access) in Botswana, as presented earlier in the article, may reveal some gaps in the effectiveness of the various interventions put in place to address the divide. In the next section a discussion follows regarding the different interventions that have been established in both Botswana and Korea. This will allow us to identify the gaps in these different interventions (supply side of ICTs) and shed some light on what should be done in the case of Botswana with full consideration of the local context. As mentioned earlier in the article, there currently is no outright similarity between Korea and Botswana but this comparison is done to assess the impact of robust interventions in ICT access and usage promotion, and what impact this has on the overall digital divide. Botswana (with a GDP per capita of $57.97 in 1960) and Korea (with a GDP per capita of $156 in 1960) now have GDP per capitals of $13 100 and $30 200 respectively (CIA 2011). This massive growth of GDP in the case of Korea is attributed to the role of ICT on general economic growth and the increase in productivity and innovation amongst the different enterprises and businesses (Yoon, Na & Jung 2009). To compare the level of ICT adoption and the extent of the digital divide between Botswana and Korea, document analysis was done to establish what interventions have been done on the supply side to encourage global ICT access and usage and therefore reduce blatant intranational digital divides.

Botswana and Korea digital divide status and interventions

Botswana

The status of Internet adoption in Botswana can be established by assessing the latest figures released by the ITU and the Botswana Telecommunications Company – BTA (which is soon to be replaced by the Botswana Communications Regulatory Authority (BOCRA). According to the ITU (2009), there were 120 000 Internet users as of September 2009 in Botswana. This represents 6% of Botswana's population which stands at 2 065 000 (US Census Bureau 2011). Considering the size of the country at 581 730 km², Botswana is sparsely populated. The ITU (2009) further ascertains that there were only 15 000 Internet users in Botswana in the year 2000 representing 0.3% of the population at that time. Looking at this precedence of growth in Internet users, it is evident that it is quite likely that the number of Internet users will keep growing.

The BTA Annual report for 2010 (BTA 2010) puts the number of fixed line telephony subscribers in Botswana at 136 593 users, whereas the number of mobile telephony subscribers is 2 339 029 users (this is because most of the subscribers would have more than two SIM cards from different mobile telecommunication service providers). Tele-density for fixed telephony subscribers is 8% whereas that for mobile subscribers is 105%. Over the years, the growth of the fixed-line and mobile subscribers in Botswana has grown tremendously, from 150 000 in 1997 to about 1 800 000 subscribers in 2009, according to the BTA Annual Report (2009).

Botswana has a fairly developed ICT infrastructure (Isaacs 2007). This robust ICT infrastructure has led telecommunications service providers to offer adequately advanced services. The three mobile operators, Mascom Wireless, Orange Botswana, and BeMobile (subsidiary of the fixed-line monopoly operator, BTC, i.e. the Botswana Telecommunications Company) provide different ICT services such as 3G mobile, WiMAX, and bundling with fixed-line (ADSL) services. With the increase in mobile technology adoption, these services can help a myriad of ICT applications (such as e-Government, e-Learning, and e-Commerce) reach the marginal individuals in all corners of the country. In some instances, the ICT infrastructure is under-utilised with considerable disparity in the access to ICTs between the rural and urban areas. This can partly be attributed to the unreliable power supply, high cost of computers and computer gadgetry, lack of appropriate ICT skills and lack of local content on the Internet that would generate interest of the general citizenry (Isaacs 2007).

Hall and Lewin (2005:86) have outlined the importance of affluent policy in the efforts by the Botswana government towards the proliferation of ICT adoption and usage. Botswana has three main ICT policy cornerstones.

- To create an enabling environment for growth of ICT in the country.
- To provide universal service and access to information and communications facilities in the country with, for example, an Internet access point in every village.
- To make Botswana into a regional ICT hub so as to make the country's services sector globally competitive.

Apart from the aforementioned policy cornerstones, Botswana has put in place strategic initiatives to bridge the divide at various levels of the socio-economic hierarchy. Some of the pronounced initiatives that have been put in place will now be listed (Keakopa & Bwalya 2010).

- The Maitlamo ICT policy was launched in 2005.
- The Universal Access (UA) and Universal Service (US) Policy aim to allow all citizens access ICT opportunities on equal basis.

- Foreseeable merging of the Tertiary Education Council and BOTA to push forward the Human Resource Development (HRD) strategy so as to usher in a competent human resource base to lead innovation strategies.
- Botswana Telecommunications Corporation (BTC) has successful completed the multi million Pula Trans-Kalahari fibre optic project (approximately 2000 km) for data, voice and electrical signal transmission.
- The BTC runs a rural communication programme that aims to connect 62 villages.
- The government has identified 3 Very Small Aperture Terminals (VSAT) sites comprising a Tele-Education Centre (learning Centre) at the University of Botswana (UB), a Tele-medicine Centre (Patient-end-terminal) at Nyangabgwe Referral Hospital in Northern District and a VVIP location at the office of the president.
- The BTC has a signatory status to three consortia that are intended to develop undersea optical fibre systems: the East Africa Submarine System (EASSY), to run alongside the eastern coast of Africa from Port Sudan through East African seaports down to Mtunzini in South Africa; the West Africa Festoon System (WAFS), intended to run alongside the western coast of Africa from Nigeria through Gabon and the DRC down to Angola, and possibly Namibia; and the Africa West Coast Cable (AWCC), proposed to run alongside the western coast of Africa from South Africa, Namibia through to the United Kingdom. It is anticipated that once these projects are completed, they will culminate into higher Internet and broadband penetration.
- The Nteletsa I & II project by BTC aims to supply, install commission, and carry out operation and maintenance of network infrastructure in rural areas of Botswana.
- Tele-centers such as Community Access Centers (CAC) – Kitsong – were initiated in 2006/07 to serve as a gateway to the Internet and access to other services in the rural areas.
- Large commitment has also been shown to encourage the use of ICTs in the public sector delivery frameworks in the form of electronic government (e-Government). To this effect, a participatory e-Government strategy meeting was convened to receive input in the working strategy document on e-Government roadmap from various stakeholders such as citizens, the private sector and the civil society.
- The Thuto.Net project strives to have enough computers linked to the Internet for all secondary and high schools, and later in primary schools in the country.
- The Ministry of Communication, Science and Technology launched a project known as i-Partnership aiming to empower government employees and unemployed youth to buy computers using government schemes.
- Recently, the Sesigo project has been implemented by the ACHAP together with co-operating partners to introduce the use of ICTs in public libraries.

All these projects are aimed at enhancing broadband connectivity and Internet penetration and therefore directly contributing to bridging the digital divide at the community, individual, and enterprise level in Botswana. The question however remains: are these interventions adequate given Botswana's vision to transform into a KBE? A look into the different interventions that have been put in place in the context of Korea may offer some comparative insights.

Korea

It is widely known that small countries such as Korea and Malaysia have shown impressive growth in ICT usage and innovation, and are therefore speedily delving towards establishing themselves as KBEs (Lee, O'Keefe & Yun 2003; Wong & Goh 2009). Massive deployment of ICTs in the various socio-economic frameworks was born out of the fact that Korea has limited natural resources and so it was necessary for it to move towards becoming a KBE for it to remain economical viable and competent. Korea has highly matured ICT penetration and currently boasts the world's highest per capita Internet and mobile penetration (Kang 2009), thanks to efforts dating back to the early 1990s. Lee, O'Keefe and Yun (2001) posit that Korea has a steadily privatised and fully liberalised ICT sector anchored on deregulated market principles.

Kang (2009) ascertains that Korea has kept intensifying its efforts to bridge the digital divide to put in place a people-oriented and inclusive information society. By 2005, over 12 million citizens had access to broadband Internet and over 72% of the population was regular Internet users (Kang 2009). Kang (2009) also mentions that in 2001, mobile phone subscribers per 10 000 persons were 2905 compared to 4427 in 2008. Within the same period, Internet banking subscribers constituted 1131 per 10 000 people and 4694 in 2008. This demonstrates that access to ICTs has kept growing at a significant rate, thanks to dedicated initiatives.

The different digital divide initiatives and interventions in Korea were made with public-private-partnership (PPP) frameworks. The PPP consisted of over 679 individual members from different sectors of the economy. Kang (2009) articulates some of the major interventions put in place by the PPP arrangements in Korea such as a high speed information infrastructure project (1997); the 'Cyber Korea 21' programme which focused on digital mobile migration and mobile Internet service (1999); the 'e-Korea Vision 2006' which laid the foundation of e-Government and initiated the world's first IMT-2000 service (third generation (3G) wireless technology for higher data rates between mobile phones and base antennas); the broadband convergence network (BcN) implementation plan (2004); and the u-Sensor network and IPv6 Master Plan. The digital convergence era started in 2005 and saw the launch of terrestrial and satellite digital multimedia broadcasting (DMB) services. In 2006, there was transition towards the ubiquitous world, cemented by establishing the 'u-Korea Master Plan', and the launch of commercial services such as BcN, WiBro, and HSDPA (Kang 2009). These interventions saw a surge in ICT access by ordinary citizens and the country being ranked top in the world by the Digital Opportunity Index

(DOI) criterion (Kang 2009). The Korean experience provides a case where utilisation of ICT in various socio-economic sectors such as in education was speedily adopted due to the cultural acceptance of the ICT phenomenon (Kim 2002). This positively impacted on the ICT diffusion process. Parents and pupils related to ICTs as a medium of education that had much potential for a promising future.

Because of the aforementioned interventions in promoting global broadband Internet access, Korea now leads the world in broadband Internet connections per capita and also has the highest WiFi hotspots per capita (currently at 55 000 hotspots nationwide). According to a technical report by Freedom House (2011:2), in 2009, Korea had an estimated 39.4 million Internet users and in 2010 had over 80% of the households accessing broadband Internet. As of December 2010, there were 50.8 million mobile phone subscribers with more than 56% of these able to access Internet from their mobile phones.

Larger Internet penetration and usage, together with higher broadband penetration has culminated into Korea being highly innovative and efficient in a variety of its enterprise and national productivity value chains. For example, Korea is the largest shipbuilder in the world and is also the world's leading memory chip producer - indicating its technological competence and expertise (Kang 2009).

Analysis of gaps and interventions

A critical look at the two exploratory studies reveals that Korea started putting in place strategic initiatives towards effective bridging of different kinds of digital divides from the early 1990s. The situation in Botswana is a bit different in that these initiatives are just being authored at the moment. This entails that the benefits of these initiatives are not to be expected now but for some time in the near future. Looking at the Korean case, it is evident that the PPPs had the intention to bridge the digital divide using multiple approaches considering the fact that the digital divide is a multi-dimensional phenomenon. Korea implemented over 31 e-Government projects and enacted over 101 laws (Noh 2009) to make sure the institutional, legal and regulatory frameworks were in place before they started talking about fully transcending towards KBE or reducing the divide that existed between the rural and urban areas.

Botswana, however, is following a pragmatic approach, which entails that it aims to put in place a firm ICT infrastructure and policy background that will pave the way for carrying out robust implementation of ICT projects. This in itself is good but there are still disparities on ICT access and usage at individual levels. The largely identified vertical and horizontal gaps amongst different individuals is largely caused by lack of appropriate and adequate awareness campaigns on the benefits of active usage of computers and accessing the Internet to take advantage of the different socio-economic opportunities. Another major reason why there are a lot of disparities in the usage of computers and the Internet is that individuals may not have requisite and adequate ICT skills to effectively engage in ICT usage. The situation in Botswana is different from Korea because Koreans have a vibrant and world-class education system where ICT education is introduced right from the inception of the primary education curriculum and promotion campaigns for the benefits of ICT are more than adequate. To potentially bridge the vertical and horizontal divide in the case of Botswana, there is a need to introduce compulsory ICTs education in the curriculum and robust campaigns on all the feasible national communication channels on the benefits of ICTs.

Amongst some of the main endeavors of countries shifting their economies towards KBEs, the Korean approach has shown to be one of the most plausible examples regardless of where it is implemented. Thus it seems as though Botswana can use the Korean approach in its initiatives towards a KBE.

In order to make sure that the digital divide is reduced, Botswana should first implement background strategic initiatives, such as:

- putting in place robust institutional, legal and regulatory frameworks
- erecting appropriate ICT infrastructures
- developing relevant ICT skills of ordinary people
- establishing different rigorous ICT task-forces
- conducting substantial awareness campaigns.

It is anticipated that the aforementioned initiatives will go a long way in Botswana's pursuit towards a KBE.

Conclusion

There are many efforts that have been devoted towards fighting the intra-national digital divide in Botswana. This article has outlined the different principles of the digital divide and what tentative strategies have been implemented in Botswana. The Korean case is considered a noteworthy example of bridging the digital divide. In comparison to the Korean case, gaps are evident between the strategic initiatives and the approach for bridging the divide in Botswana. One of the very first steps towards bridging the intranational divide in Botswana is that it should promote broadband communication. This is in conformance with the premise that countries such as Korea, Malaysia, and Singapore – having introduced broadband communication – have seen their ICT uptake and innovation grow exponentially. The introduction of broadband will transcend into global accessibility of ICTs in the case of Botswana.

With the aforementioned strategies in place, full-fledged efforts towards transcending into a KBE can be established. As the empirical study has shown, the intra-national digital divide is evident in Botswana and this needs to be addressed before ambitious projects of establishing itself as a regional hub or transforming into a KBE can be pursued.

Author acknowledgements

The authors would like to thank the Ministry of Education, Botswana, who provided funding to the student (Nonofo) to facilitate this research as an undergraduate project aimed to understand the extent of the digital divide in Botswana.

Author contributions

Nonofo Sedimo was responsible for collecting the data, doing the preliminary data analysis and preliminary draft of this paper. This paper is part of her undergraduate final project, which she completed with a distinction.

Author competing interest

We declare that we have no financial or personal relationship(s) that may have inappropriately influenced us in writing this paper.

Bwalya Kelvin was responsible for coordinating the overall research process and paper writing. Prof. Du Plessis is a PhD supervisor for Kelvin and was responsible for ensuring that this paper achieves the adequate scholar rigor it has attained and was responsible for supervising the overall revision process upon obtaining peer review comments.

References

Bassey, C., 2008, 'Digital Money in a Digitally Divided World: Nature, Challenges and Prospects of ePayment Systems in Africa', paper presented at the Workshop on Everyday Digital Money: Innovation in Money Cultures and Technologies, University of California, Irvine, CA, 18–19th September.

Bresnahan, T., Brynjolfsson, E. & Hitt, L.M., 1999, 'Information technology, workplace organization, and the demand for skilled labor: Firm-level evidence', Working Paper No. 7136, National Bureau of Economic Research, Cambridge, MA.

Botswana Telecommunications Authority, 2009, *Annual report 2009*, viewed 22 May 2010 from, http://www.crasa.org/download.php?doc=doc_pub_eng44.pdf

Botswana Telecommunications Authority, 2010, *Annual report of Botswana Telecommunications Authority (BTA)*, viewed 23 June 2011 from, www.crasa.org/download.php?doc=doc_pub_eng44.pdf

Burke, A., Van Stel, A. & Thurik, R., 2010, 'Blue Ocean vs Five Forces', *Harvard Business Review* 88(5), 28.

Campbell, D., 2001, 'Can the Digital Divide be Contained?', *International Labour Review* 140(2), 119–141. http://dx.doi.org/10.1111/j.1564-913X.2001.tb00217.x

Central Intelligence Agency, 2011, *The World Fact Book*, viewed 15 April 2011 from, https://www.cia.gov/library/publications/the-world-factbook/geos/bc.html.

Chon, K., 2001, 'The Future of the Internet Digital Divide', *Communications of the ACM* 44(3), 116. http://dx.doi.org/10.1145/365181.365231

Creswell, W.J., 1994, *Research design: Qualitative and quantitative approaches*, SAGE publications, London, UK.

Cronin, B., 2002, 'The Digital Divide', *Library Journal* 127(3).

Cullen, R., 2003, 'The Digital Divide; A Global and National Call to Action', *The Electronic Library* 21(3), 247–258. http://dx.doi.org/10.1108/02640470310480506

CWM, 2010, 'Second wave of sponsor, CRO growth hitting Asia-Pac', viewed 20 June 2011, from http://www.centerwatch.com/news-resources/sample/monthly/cwm1702_20100201_Cu0nLN.pdf

Freedom House, 2011, *South Korea*, viewed 12 October 2011, from www.freedomhouse.org/images/File/FotN/SouthKorea2011.pdf

Fuchs, C. & Horak, E., 2008, 'Africa and the digital divide', *Telematics and Informatics* 25(2), 99–116. http://dx.doi.org/10.1016/j.tele.2006.06.004

Gambrill, S., 2010, 'Second wave of sponsor, CRO growth hitting Asia-Pac', *The CenterWatch Monthly* 17(2), February, 6–12, viewed 20 June 2011, from http://www.centerwatch.com/news-resources/sample/monthly/cwm1702_20100201_Cu0nLN.pdf

Hall, R. & Lewin, D., 2005, 'A final report to the Botswana Telecommunications Authority: ICT policies and liberalization', viewed 17 May 2010, from www.bta.org.bw/pubs/final%20report%20%20-%20liberalisation.doc

Hollensen, S., 2007, *Global marketing: A decision oriented approach*, 4th edn., Prentice Hall, Englewood Cliffs, NJ.

Isaacs, S., 2007, *ICT in Education in Botswana, Survey of ICT and education in Africa: Botswana Country Report. Botswana – 1*, viewed 18 February 2010, from www.infodev.org.

International Telecommunication Union, 2005, 'Measuring Digital Opportunity', WSIS Thematic meeting on Multi-Stakeholder Partnerships for Bridging the Digital Divide, Korea, Seoul, 23–24th June.

International Telecommunications Union, 2006, *Statistics, International Telecommunication Union*, viewed 02 September 2011, from www.itu.int/ITU-D/ict/statistics/

International Telecommunications Union, 2009, *Botswana Internet Usage and Marketing Report*, viewed 11 January 2011, from www.internetworldstats.com/af/bw.htm.

Internet World Statistics, 2010, *Internet users and population statistics for specific countries*, viewed 16 August 2011, from www.internetworldstats.com

James, J., 2002, 'The digital divide between nations as international technological dualism', *International Journal of Development Studies* 1(2), 25–40.

James, J., 2003, *Bridging the Global Digital Divide*, Edward Elgar Publishing, Cheltenham, UK.

James, J., 2009, 'Measuring the global digital divide at the level of individuals', *Current Science commentary* 96(2), 25.

Kang, B-S., 2009, 'Bridging the Digital Divide between Urban and Rural Areas: Experience of the Republic of Korea', IDD/TP-09-07 (Version 1.0.), Technical paper, ESCAP, Bangkok.

Keakopa, M.S. & Bwalya, K.J., 2010, ,An Evaluation of ICT policy developments in Botswana', in E.E. Adomi (ed.), *Handbook of Research on Information Communication Technology: Trends, Issues and Advancements*, pp. 1–14, IGI Global, Hershey.

Kettani, H., 2010, '2010 World Muslim Population', *proceedings of the 8th Hawaii International Conference on Arts and Humanities*, Honolulu, Hawaii, January 12–16, 2010, viewed 24 June 2011 from www.pupr.edu/hkettani/papers/HICAH2010.pdf

Kim, H-S., 2002, 'Sociological Analysis of 2002 Digital Formation of Korea', paper presented at the 2002 International Conference on the Digital Divide: Technology & Politics in the Information Age, David C. Lam Institute for East-West Studies, Hong Kong Baptist University, 22–23 August.

Kim, W.C. & Mauborgne, R., 2004, 'Blue Ocean Strategy', *Harvard Business Review* 82(10), 76–84.

Lee, H., O'Keefe, R.M. & Yun, Y., 2003, 'The Growth of Broadband and Electronic Commerce in Korea: Contributing Factors', *The Information Society* 19(1), 81–95. http//dx.doi.org/10.1080/01972240309470

Luk, S.C.Y., 2009, 'The impact of leadership and stakeholders on the success/failure of e-government service: Using the case study of e-stamping service in Hong Kong', *Government Information Quarterly* 26, 594–604. http//dx.doi.org/10.1016/j.giq.2009.02.009

Mansell, R., 2001, 'Digital Opportunities and the Missing Link for Developing Countries', *Oxford Review of Economic Policy* 17(2), 282–295. http//dx.doi.org/10.1093/oxrep/17.2.282

Mathuba, B.M., 2003, 'Ministry of Lands and Housing – Botswana', paper presented at an International Workshop on Land Policies in Southern Africa, Berlin, Germany, 26–27 May, viewed 21 June 2011, from www.fes.de/in_afrika/studien/Land_Reform_Botswana_Botselo_Mathuba.pdf

Noh, Y.K., 2009, *ICT development in Korea*, viewed 19 May 2010, from www.tiaonline.org/gov_affairs/events/Young_Noh_Presentation.ppt

Norris, P., 2001, *Digital divide: civic engagement, information poverty and the Internet worldwide*, Cambridge University Press, Cambridge, UK.

Organisation for Economic Co-operation and Development (OECD), 2004, *Regulatory reform as a tool for bridging the Digital Divide*, OECD, Paris.

Ono, H., 2005, 'Digital Divide in East Asia: Evidence from Japan, South Korea and Singapore', Working Paper Series 26, The International Centre for the Study of East Asian Development, Kitakyushu.

Robison, K. & Crenshaw, E., 2000, 'Cyberspace and post-industrial transformations: A cross-national analysis of Internet development', paper presented at the Annual Meeting of the American Sociological Association, Washington, DC, 12–16th August.

Saunders, M., Lewis, P. & Thornhill, A., 2002, *Research methods for business students*, 3rd edn., Prentice Hall, Harlow, UK.

Serrat, O., 2010, *Knowledge solutions: tools, methods, and approaches to drive development forward and enhance its effects*, Asian Development Bank, Mandaluyong City.

United Nations Department of Economics and Social Affairs, 2010, *UN e-Government Survey: Leveraging e-government at a time of financial and economic crisis*, viewed 04 October 2010, from http://unpan1.un.org/intradoc/groups/public/documents/UN-DPADM/UNPAN038853.pdf

US Census Bureau, 2011, *International Data Base – Botswana*, viewed 19 June 2011, from www.census.gov/population/international/data/idb/country.php

Van der Meer, A. & Van Winden, A., 2003, 'E-governance in cities', *Regional Studies*, 37(4), 407–419. http//dx.doi.org/10.1080/0034340032000074433

Venturelli, S., 2002, 'Inventing e-regulation in the US, EU and East Asia', *Telematics and Informatics* 19(2), 69–90. http//dx.doi.org/10.1016/S0736-5853(01)00007-7

Warschauer, M., 2001, 'Language, identity and the Internet', in B. Kolko, L. Nakamura, G. Rodman (eds.), *Race in Cyberspace*, pp. 208–231, Routledge, New York, NY.

Wilson, E.J., 2006, *The Information Revolution and Developing Countries*, MIT Press, Cambridge, MA.

Wilson, M., 1996, 'Asking questions' in R. Sapsford & V. Jupp (eds.), *Data Collection and Analysis*, p. 94, Sage, London, UK.

Wong, C-Y. & Goh, K-L., 2009, 'Modeling the Self-Propagating Growth Function of Science and Technological Diffusion for Selected Asian Countries', *Computer Science and Information Technology, IEEE proceeding- IACSIT Advanced Management Science*, Riverview Hotel, Singapore, April 17–20, 2009, pp. 226–230.

World Bank Group, 2000, 'The networking revolution: Opportunities and challenges for developing countries', InfoDev Working Paper, Global Information and Communication Technologies Department, World Bank Group, Washington, DC., viewed 19 August 2011, from http://www.infodev.org/library/NetworkingRevolution.pdf

Yin, R., 2003, *Applications of Case Study Research*, Sage Publications, London, UK.

Yoon, C-H., Na, K-Y., & Jung, H-J., 2009, *The Role of ICT in Economic Growth of Korea: Productivity Changes across Industries since 1985*, viewed 15 April 2011, from http://www2.wiwi.hu-berlin.de/wt1/studying/past courses/W08-09/The_Role_of_ICT(seminar).pdf

eThekwini Municipality's intranet for augmenting knowledge–sharing in the organisation

Author:
Udo R. Averweg[1,2]

Affiliations:
[1]Graduate School of Business & Leadership, College of Law and Management Studies, University of KwaZulu-Natal, South Africa

[2]Information Services, eThekwini Municipality, Durban, South Africa

Correspondence to:
Udo Averweg

Email:
averwegu@durban.gov.za

Postal address:
PO Box 50612, Musgrave Road 4062, South Africa

Background: The age of technology, where information and knowledge perform important roles in the organisational context, creates an opportunity for local government organisations (such as metropolitan municipalities) in South Africa to support knowledge–sharing. One such technology that supports knowledge–sharing is an intranet. If an intranet is not effectively managed, knowledge–sharing in an organisation shall not be augmented.

Objective: To investigate whether or not an intranet augments knowledge–sharing in the selected organisation of eThekwini Municipality.

Methods: In this study a quantitative research approach was adopted.

Results: The results of this survey suggest that firstly the intranet appears to be at a medium maturity level; secondly, whilst there is information sharing, the intranet does not appear to be effective as a knowledge–sharing structure; and thirdly there appears to be scope for improvement of the content on the intranet. The implication thereof is that eThekwini Municipality's recently formed Municipal Institute of Learning (MILE) may be ideally poised to address the identified shortcomings.

Conclusion: Intranet technology plays an important role in an organisation by enabling the effective acquisition, sharing and presentation of knowledge. Because of this an intranet must be effectively managed to readily augment knowledge–sharing in the organisational context of local government organisations (such as metropolitan municipalities) in South Africa.

Introduction

The age of technology, where information and knowledge perform important roles in the organisational context, creates an opportunity for local government organisations (such as metropolitan municipalities) in South Africa to support these knowledge–sharing technologies. With an increase in the development of systems in organisations that support collaboration and knowledge–sharing, these systems and technologies (such as an intranet) provide access to greater amounts of information within the organisation. These technologies can overwhelm employees in an organisation and thus inhibit their use and therein their value. This inhibition might hamper the productivity of employees (or knowledge workers) and their ability to generate knowledge and requires the provision of requisite 'value–added' decision–making support for an organisation. It also reflects the need for an organisation to shift to an information and knowledge–sharing environment where 'retrieve' (i.e. employees actively search for and retrieve information) and not 'alert' (i.e. broadcasting or alerting of relevant information) is the predominant knowledge gathering technique, and employees are able to shape, to an extent, what is received and how it is received (Patrick & Dotsika 2007:396). The growth in knowledge work and knowledge workers, to support knowledge–sharing, requires the ability to find and access information and knowledge contained in an organisation's intranet.

An intranet is a powerful tool for communication and collaboration, that presents data and information and the means to create and share knowledge, in one easily accessible place (Sayed, Jabeur & Aref 2009:228). Such data and information can, for example, be located in a municipality's reports and documents. Lehaney, Clarke, Coakes and Jack (2004:238) suggest that these documents should be made available electronically and should be easily accessible from a single point of access. An intranet supports such an IT architecture and is therefore well–suited for the distribution of data and information of an organisation. Kord, Yaghoubi and Porbar (2011:95) suggest that an intranet can be used for the 'distribution of different aspects of information across the organization'.

An intranet 'can be regarded both as an information and strategic management tool' (Edenius & Borgerson 2003:124). The intranet, which is based on Web technology, can provide useful and people–inclusive knowledge management (KM) environments (Stenmark 2002). In such environments, an intranet can be tailored to suit and enhance an organisation's knowledge–sharing processes. Knowledge–sharing is usually a process through which knowledge is exchanged in an organisation.

Research objective

Information technology (IT) plays an important role in organisations to make effective the managing and sharing of knowledge. IT supports KM by facilitating quick searching, access to retrieval of information, which in turn encourages co-operation and communication between the employees in an organisation (Yeh, Lai & Ho 2006:799). If IT, such as an intranet, is not effectively managed, knowledge–sharing in an organisation shall not be augmented. Investigating whether or not an intranet augments knowledge–sharing in a selected organisation in South Africa is the research objective of this paper. The research question is: To what extent does an organisation's existing intranet augment knowledge–sharing? This question is explored by selecting the metropolitan municipality of eThekwini Municipality as the field of application.

Background to the research

There is a call for the adoption of new processes in South African municipalities which will improve their effective functionality (Gaffoor & Cloete 2010:1). Practices in the workplace will need to enable managers to promote managing knowledge and knowledge–sharing to enable the municipal organisation to adopt the role of a knowledge–based organisation. For example, one of eThekwini Municipality's programs is to create 'an environment to enable knowledge acquisition, sharing and preservation …' (EM 2008:301). Knowledge is the primary element of any business process because a tangible deliverable cannot be developed without adequate knowledge (Taylor 2007:20). There is thus a related need to evaluate existing processes (e.g. benefits and content areas of an intranet) to ensure that they enable knowledge–sharing in the organisation.

Hahn and Subramani (2000:302) indicate that knowledge–sharing and KM initiatives in organisations are increasingly becoming important as organisations make significant IT investments in deploying KM systems. Such organisations include metropolitan municipalities in South Africa. Furthermore most KM initiatives rely on IT as an important enabler (Alavi & Leidner 2011). Given these investments and their enablement with IT, it therefore seems appropriate to investigate whether or not the intranet in the selected organisation (eThekwini Municipality) augments knowledge–sharing between its employees. In this study the views of employees (knowledge workers or end users of the intranet) will be distilled from the findings of the Ask Africa Report (2006). The 'views of the end users are … important' (Skok & Kalmanovitch 2005:736).

Intranets

Intranets create a common foundation for communication and information sharing. Sayed *et al.* (2009:229) note that knowledge–sharing can be significantly augmented by the use of the intranet when dealing with organisational communication (e.g. virtual meetings, chats, email transactions, conferencing, official memoranda, etc.). Examples of official memoranda include reports and documents. Brelade and Harman (2003); suggest intranets can be used on a 'push' basis, where information is presented to employees, and on a 'pull' basis, where employees may seek out and retrieve information for themselves. Nowadays the 'push' and 'pull' terms are more commonly referred to as 'alerting' and 'retrieving' information. These mechanisms are described as follows:

- The 'alerting' basis is when it is important that certain material is presented to employees at their workstation. It ensures that no other function takes place until all the information is correctly accessed.
- The 'retrieving' basis is when employees decide when to pull information from the intranet website they wish to view.

Information contained on the intranet website could, for example, be policy documents. A standard internet browser provides a seamless experience when accessing and viewing information and knowledge pages on an intranet.

The mode of intranet utilisation depends upon the complexities and maturity of the intranet (Masrek, Karim & Hussein 2008:90). Intranet maturity can be identified as low, medium or high (Gartner Group, Inc. 1996; Casselberry *et al.* 1996 cited in Masrek, Karim & Hussein 2008:90). Low maturity signifies that information is published on the intranet and the information flow is uni-directional. Medium maturity signifies that the intranet is used for collaboration purposes, such as for sharing information and for conducting organisational interaction between employees. High maturity signifies that the intranet serves as a common user interface to back–end applications, and five different modes of utilisation are possible: publishing, transacting, interacting, searching and recording (Damsgaard & Scheepers 1999). Whilst this maturity classification is useful, it is noted that this is a view of information dissemination only, and does not concern (tacit) knowledge.

Knowledge–sharing

The intranet facilitates internal communication and knowledge–sharing (Zhang & Wang 2008:465). Knowledge–sharing is a key component of KM systems (Alavi & Leidner 2001), however, knowledge–sharing is not well defined in the associated literature partially because this research area has not been very active (Bechina & Bommen 2006). Lee (2001) suggests that knowledge–sharing refers to processes of transferring or disseminating knowledge from one person, group, or organisation to another. Bartol and Srivastava (2002) define knowledge–sharing as individuals sharing organisational–relevant information, ideas, suggestions and expertise with one another. Knowledge–sharing is understood as the exchange of knowledge between and amongst individuals, and within and amongst teams, organisational units and organisations (King 2006). Employees are a key source of knowledge that is owned and managed by an organisation, as the employees create, acquire and share knowledge. IT is a fundamental enabler in the implementation of KM to store, organise and disseminate knowledge and aid in externalising and socialising knowledge. KM offers local government organisations the benefit of decision–making and efficiency (Gaffoor & Cloete 2010:6).

With the advent of Web 2.0 technologies (e.g. social networks, blogs, wikis, tagging 'folksonomy', etc.), these can bring change to organisational communication, and information and knowledge processes. One difference between a traditional knowledge–sharing approach and that of Web 2.0 technologies is that, as transactional costs to information sharing with the advent of Web 2.0 have dropped, new ways of knowledge–sharing have become more prevalent and practical on a larger scale (Tapscott & Williams 2006; Shirky 2008). However, when adopting this in a municipal environment, one's assumption is that knowledge–sharing, using Web 2.0 technologies, is an effective means of collaboration (Paroutis & Al Saleh 2009). Another assumption is that a knowledge–sharing culture is part of an organisation's culture.

To describe how an intranet can facilitate knowledge–sharing, Stenmark (2002) developed a model that described intranet utilisation to support KM. Stenmark's model suggests that the intranet as a knowledge–sharing environment should be seen from three perspectives: information, awareness and communication (Masrek *et al.* 2008:92). Masrek *et al.* (2008) indicates that of these three the information perspective explains that the intranet gives employees access to both structured and unstructured information in the form of databases and documents. For the awareness perspective, users of the intranet are kept well–informed and connected to information and fellow employees in the organisation. The communication perspective enables employees to collectively interpret available information by supporting a variety of channels for negotiations and conversation. When an employee collaborates with fellow employees, who share their objectives, the common context for knowledge–sharing will then exist.

eThekwini Municipality

Environment

eThekwini Municipality, a metropolitan municipality in the City of Durban, South Africa, comprises six clusters or service units (Office of the City Manager, Treasury, Governance, Sustainable Development and City Enterprises, Corporate and Human Resources and Health, Safety and Social Services) and employs approximately 18 000 employees. eThekwini Municipality has some 6000 networked desktops (personal computers, thin clients and laptops), and electronic communication (i.e. email) takes place via Novell's GroupWise (Client version 7.0.3). A total of 6654[1] GroupWise account holders exist in eThekwini Municipality. However,

the maximum number of concurrent users (i.e. employees using GroupWise) who can access eThekwini Municipality's intranet is 6000. Currently (as at 05 July 2011) there are 3534 Internet account holders utilising either Microsoft Internet Explorer or Netscape Navigator Web browsers.

Municipal Institute of Learning (MILE)

In a study of KM in a selected South African municipality (Stellenbosch), Gaffoor and Cloete (2010:6) recommend a separate KM division which will result in the municipality's ability to better utilise and disseminate knowledge – this is a basic condition for other local government organisations. During 2009, eThekwini Municipality initiated the formation of the first municipal–driven Institute of Learning. During the 2009 to 2010 financial year, the setup for the Municipal Institute of Learning (MILE) was completed (EM 2010:225). MILE's function forms part of eThekwini Municipality's KM strategy to position the City of Durban as a Centre of Learning (www.MILE.org.za). From this website, one of the strategic objectives of MILE is to 'co-ordinate the internal knowledge management agenda within the eThekwini Municipality'.

From the www.MILE.org.za website, the approach to the KM agenda in the eThekwini Municipality is comprised of four key elements that:

1. build systems to improve internal access to information – to allow employees easy access to information;
2. co-ordinate policy – all new policies must agree with existing policies and all approved policies must be accessible to all employees;
3. create an enabling KM organisational culture – institute mechanisms that assist in moving from tacit to explicit knowledge and focus on projects that allow effective knowledge transfer to facilitate succession planning; and
4. document and share innovations and good practice – encourage clusters or service units to document lessons learnt.

Research methodology

Every major organisational process should be regularly evaluated and the evaluation should be purposeful and completed (Debowski 2006:274). One method of data collection is a survey. In a survey, email is useful for data collection purposes. Debowski (2006:277) suggests that survey 'evaluations take a number of forms ... and may be conducted via telephone, email our mailouts' and '... data should be gathered by electronic means ...' and this '... is an increasingly useful quantitative data collection strategy, as it is non-invasive and low cost'. In this study, the means used to distribute the survey was email because it is non-invasive and the purpose and benefits of an email survey justified the cost.

Data collection

The data, selected to evaluate eThekwini Municipality's intranet, were collected by an independent research

---

1.From a count taken during survey period in 2006.

company, Ask Africa, thus, secondary data were used in the author's survey. The rationale for using secondary data was that:

- it was considered relevant to the author's study
- there were savings of time and money by using available data rather than collecting original data.

Whilst there are benefits to using secondary data, their general shortcomings are acknowledged:

- the author ensured that terms used in the Ask Africa Report (2006) were not compromised when used in the author's research;
- whilst it is possible that there may have been measurement errors with the Ask Africa data collection, it was decided that a 'good' level of accuracy existed with these collected (secondary) data – the raw and data scores were made available to the author for verification purposes;
- the author acknowledges that he has 'vested interests' in consulting Ask Africa's collected data but considered that these interests were not significant (or biased) for his research purposes; and
- the data collection by Ask Africa coincided with the timescale of the author's research so these collected data were not out–of–date for the author's research purposes.

The commonly utilised Internet browser in eThekwini Municipality is Microsoft Internet Explorer. On 13 June 2006 eThekwini Municipality employees were selected by email invitation from the Communications Department – to participate in an online intranet survey. The survey instrument comprised questions where respondents could give feedback in a Likert-scale format. The aim of this survey was 'to identify areas where the intranet may need improvements' and 'to allow positive user experiences to be obtained'. eThekwini Municipality employees who expressed an interest in participating in this survey received questions online. This survey was emailed by Ask Africa's research partner (MicroIces) to each eThekwini Municipality employee. The data collation process was handled by Ask Africa. The data used in this research were sourced and distilled from the eThekwini Municipality Intranet Research Report, (July 2006) compiled by Ask Africa. The reported findings inform this study.

One hundred and fifty email invitations were sent to eThekwini Municipality employees and 39 responses were received. This represents 26% of the total number of employees who originally expressed interest in participating in the survey. Whilst this is a relatively small sample, Debowski (2006:274) suggests that response 'rates as low as 20% may still provide some sense of the issues'.

Data analysis

Extracted from the eThekwini Municipality Intranet Research Report (Ask Africa 2006), the results were analysed and presented. From the 39 responses received during the survey, the intranet user experience classification is reflected in Table 1.

From Table 1, it is seen that the majority of respondents (34) were non-beginner intranet users. This is important because Intermediate and Advanced users comprised 87% of the survey sample and they could therefore give meaningful perspectives during the survey period.

In Table 2, the ranking in ascending order of Strongly Agree or Agree responses to 'benefits the intranet holds' are reflected.

From Table 2, the greatest perceived benefit that the intranet holds is for employees to use it is as a platform to share and access inter-departmental (i.e. clusters or service units) information. This suggests that information sharing (explicit knowledge) as opposed to 'knowledge' sharing is taking place and this sharing implies that the information flow between employees is multi-directional. From the discussion in Section 2.1, the intranet is therefore no longer at a low maturity stage because the information flow would have been uni-directional. There is evidence of relatively high sharing and accessing of inter-departmental information (87%) and also of employees conducting organisational interaction (81%). This suggests that the intranet is used for collaborative information purposes and the intranet therefore appears to be at a medium maturity stage. Since only 50% of respondents agree that the intranet is necessary to perform daily work functions (which may include back–end applications for daily work functions by employees), this implies that the intranet has not yet reached a high maturity stage.

Information sharing of relevant information, ideas, suggestions and expertise between employees appears to

TABLE 1: Intranet user experience classification.

User classification	Tally and Percentage of Respondents (n = 39)	
	Tally	%
Beginner	5	13
Intermediate	25	64
Advanced	9	23

Adapted from eThekwini Municipality Intranet Research Report compiled by Ask Africa, 2006, *eThekwini Municipality Intranet Research Report*, Unpublished report, 1–72, July.

TABLE 2: Ranking in ascending order of Strongly Agree or Agree responses to 'benefits the intranet holds'.

Statement	Percentage of Respondents (n = 19)		
	Strongly Agree/ Agree	Neutral	Disagree
Useful platform to share and access inter-departmental information	87	9	4
The intranet is an effective way to conduct organisational interaction	81	14	5
Quickest focal point to disseminate and get organisational communication	77	14	9
Enhances departmental communication	72	5	24
Helps the organisation improve its service to customers	65	15	20
Helps with productivity	63	14	23
Using the intranet is necessary for employees to perform daily work functions	50	5	45

Adapted from eThekwini Municipality Intranet Research Report compiled by Ask Africa, 2006, *eThekwini Municipality Intranet Research Report*, Unpublished report, 1–72, July.

be evident in eThekwini Municipality's intranet but there is limited evidence to support that the intranet is effective towards knowledge–sharing. For example, Gaffoor and Cloete (2010:6) suggest that there is a need to extract information (such as lessons learned and best practices to follow) from reports and documents. Such tacit knowledge contained in reports and documents will augment knowledge–sharing, and this process will be beneficial to the eThekwini Municipality. However, from the author's survey, it should be noted that the perceived benefit does not explicitly indicate whether or not there is a sharing of tacit knowledge in eThekwini Municipality or if eThekwini Municipality's intranet is effective towards knowledge–sharing. Nevertheless it is argued that this perceived benefit will serve to augment key element 1 and element 4 discussed in Section 3.2.

The second highest reported perceived benefit was as 'an effective way to conduct organisational interaction'. This includes virtual maps, chats and email transactions. When employees engage in collaborative work with fellow employees in different clusters or service units and between different hierarchical levels that share their objectives, the context of knowledge–sharing exists. Mechanisms may need to be instituted to assist in moving from tacit to explicit knowledge in different clusters or service units and between different hierarchical levels. This second highest reported perceived benefit will then serve to augment key element 3 discussed in Section 3.2.

The ranking, in ascending order, of Strongly Agree or Agree responses to the content of the intranet is reflected in Table 3.

From Tables 2 and Table 3, it appears that the surveyed respondents generally considered the intranet to hold benefits but that the contents of the intranet requires improvement for information seeking. This will enable an employee to search for and find the required explicit knowledge, retrieve it and then relate it to his existing knowledge. This suggests that whilst the information on the intranet website is generally seen to be reliable, the regular updating of content

TABLE 3: Ranking, in ascending order, of Strongly Agree or Agree responses to the content of the intranet.

Statement	Percentage of Respondents (*n* = 18)		
	Strongly Agree/ Agree	Neutral	Disagree
The information and content on the website is relevant	63	11	26
The information on the website is reliable	61	17	22
Overall I am happy with the quality of content on the website	57	14	29
I am happy with the quality of the search process	57	14	33
The content on the site is regularly updated	53	11	38
There is a high likelihood of finding information I am looking for even though I do not know where to find it	52	10	38

Adapted from the eThekwini Municipality Intranet Research Report compiled by Ask Africa, 2006, *eThekwini Municipality Intranet Research Report*, Unpublished report, 1–72, July.

and finding information that an employee is looking for needs to be improved (Ask Africa 2006:45). For an intranet to be of 'real value' to employees, the contents should be relevant, reliable, accurate, informative and up to date. In order to augment knowledge–sharing, employees need the ability to share organisationally relevant information with one another. An important use of most intranets is to find reports and documents (e.g. policy documents) that 'point' to employees who have knowledge and expertise. By finding the information, this may result in the creation of knowledge and move it from tacit to explicit knowledge. This will serve to augment key element 2 discussed in Section 3.2. Furthermore there will be a common context that allows a growth spiral as knowledge moves amongst fellow employees (and also in communities of practice [CoP]), and between groups of employees in different organisational levels in eThekwini Municipality.

- The summary of the survey results is as follows:
- the eThekwini Municipality's intranet appears to be at a medium maturity level;
- whilst there is information sharing using the intranet, the intranet does not appear to be effective towards knowledge–sharing
- there appears to be scope for improvement to the intranet content areas.

One initiative which may serve to address the shortcomings in facilitating knowledge–sharing utilising eThekwini Municipality's intranet, is the recently formed MILE which was established subsequent to the intranet online survey. MILE may be ideally poised to address the identified intranet shortcomings. Gaffoor and Cloete (2010:6) recommend that a KM division (i.e. in the case of eThekwini Municipality – MILE) should not only be responsible for the technological aspects of KM but in order 'to take advantage of opportunities for innovation' should establish CoP within the municipality. Such CoP can be established on eThekwini Municipality's intranet. Whilst the survey results suggest that the intranet augments four key elements (1–4 in Section 3.2), further investigation is required. This may be one avenue for future research. A second avenue for future research may be to gauge whether or not Web 2.0 technologies are likely to influence collaboration and knowledge–sharing processes (and activities) in eThekwini Municipality's intranet.

Conclusion

An intranet should be tailored to suit and enhance an organisation's knowledge–sharing processes through its 'alerting' and 'retrieving' mechanisms. Because IT plays an important role enabling the effective acquisition, sharing and presentation of knowledge, an intranet must be effectively managed to readily augment knowledge–sharing. In the case of eThekwini Municipality's intranet, whilst there is information sharing, the intranet appears to augment limited knowledge–sharing. With the recent formation of MILE to create an enabling KM organisational culture, mechanisms may soon be instituted to assist it to move from tacit to explicit knowledge. This will generate knowledge to support knowledge–sharing, and employees will thereby utilise eThekwini Municipality's intranet more effectively.

Acknowledgements
Competing interests

The author declares that he has no financial or personal relationship(s) which may have inappropriately influenced him in writing this paper.

References

Alavi, M. & Leidner, D.E., 2001, 'Review: Knowledge Management and Knowledge Management Systems: Conceptual Foundations and Research Issues', *MIS Quarterly*, 25(1), 107–136. http://dx.doi.org/10.2307/3250961

Ask Africa, 2006, *eThekwini Municipality Intranet Research Report*, Unpublished report, 1–72, July.

Bartol, K.M. & Srivastava, A., 2002, 'Encouraging Knowledge Sharing: The Role of Organizational Rewards', *Journal of Leadership and Organizational Studies* 9(1), 64–76. http://dx.doi.org/10.1177/107179190200900105

Bechina, A.A. & Bommen, T., 2006, 'Knowledge sharing practices: Analysis of a global Scandinavian consulting company', *The Electronic Journal of Management* 4(2), 109–116.

Brelade, S. & Harman, C., 2003, *Knowledge Management – The Systems Dimension*, Thorogood, London.

Damsgaard, J. & Scheepers, R., 1999, 'Power, influence and intranet implementation: a safari of South African organizations', *Information Technology & People* 12(4), 333–358. http://dx.doi.org/10.1108/09593849910301630

Debowski, S., 2006. *Knowledge Management*, John Wiley & Sons, Milton, Queensland.

Edenius, M. & Borgerson, J., 2003, 'To manage knowledge by intranet', *Journal of Knowledge Management* 7(5), 124–136. http://dx.doi.org/10.1108/13673270310505430

eThekwini Municipality (EM), 2008, *Annual Report 2007/8*, Durban, South Africa.

eThekwini Municipality (EM), 2010, *Annual Report 2009/10*, Durban, South Africa.

Gaffoor, S. & Cloete, F., 2010, 'Knowledge management in local government: The case of Stellenbosch Municipality', *SA Journal of Information Management* 12(1), Art. #422, 7 pages. http://doi.org/10.4102/sajim.v12i1.422

Gartner Group, Inc., 1996, 'Developing a powerful corporate intranet: Issues Challenges and Solutions', *Gartner Letter Special Report*, Gartner Group, Stamford.

Hahn, J. & Subramani, M.R., 2000, 'A framework of knowledge management systems: issues and challenges for theory and practice', in *Proceedings of the twenty–first international conference on Information Systems*, Brisbane, Australia, December 10–13, 2000, pp. 302–312.

King, W.R., 2006, 'Knowledge Sharing', *Encyclopedia of Knowledge Management*, 493–498, Idea Group Inc, Hershey.

Kord, B., Yaghoubi, N.M. & Porbar, A.Q., 2011, 'A Review on Intranet Acceptance in the Organization: An Empirical Research', *European Journal of Scientific Research* 49(1), 95–102.

Lee, J.N., 2001, 'The impact of knowledge sharing, organizational capability and partnership quality on IS outsourcing success', *Information & Management* 38(5), 323–335. http://dx.doi.org/10.1016/S0378-7206(00)00074-4

Lehaney, B., Clarke, S., Coakes, E. & Jack, G., 2004, *Beyond Knowledge Management*, Idea Group Inc, Hershey.

Masrek, M.N., Karim, N.S.A. & Hussein, R., 2008, 'The effect of organizational and individual characteristics on corporate intranet utilizations', *Information Management & Computer Security* 16(2), 89–112. http://dx.doi.org/10.1108/09685220810879591

Paroutis, P. & Al Saleh, A., 2009, 'Determinants of knowledge sharing using Web 2.0 technologies', *Journal of Knowledge Management* 13(4), 52–63. http://dx.doi.org/10.1108/13673270910971824

Patrick, K. & Dotsika, F., 2007, 'Knowledge sharing: developing from within', *The Learning Organization* 14(5), 395–406. http://dx.doi.org/10.1108/09696470710762628

Sayed, B.T., Jabeur, N. & Aref, M., 2009, 'An Archetype to Sustain Knowledge Management Systems through Intranet', *International Journal of Social Sciences* 4(4), 228–232.

Shirky, C., 2008, *Here comes everybody: The power of organizing without organizations*. Penguin, New York.

Skok, W. & Kalmanovitch, C., 2005, 'Evaluating the role and effectiveness of an intranet in facilitating knowledge management: a case study at Surrey County Council', *Information & Management* 42, 731–744. http://dx.doi.org/10.1016/j.im.2004.04.008

Stenmark, D., 2002, 'Information vs. knowledge: The role of intranet in knowledge management', in *Proceedings of the 35th Hawaii International Conference on System Sciences (HICSS-35)*, Hawaii, USA, January 07–10, 2002, pp. 1–10.

Tapscott, D. & Williams, A.D., 2006, *Wikinomics: How mass collaboration changes everything*, Portfolio, New York.

Taylor, L., 2007, *Knowledge, Information and the Business Process: Revolutionary Thinking or Common Sense?* Chandos, Oxford.

Yeh, Y., Lai, S. & Ho, C., 2006, 'Knowledge management enablers: A case study', *Industrial Management & Data Systems* 106(6), 793–810. http://dx.doi.org/10.1108/02635570610671489

Zhang, R. & Wang, J., 2008, 'The Role of Intranet in Enterprise Knowledge Management', in *Proceedings 2008 International Conference on Multimedia, Information Technology and its Applications (MITA2008)*, Chiang Mai, Thailand, July 03–05, 2008.

19

Applying geographic information systems to delineate residential suburbs and summarise data based on individual parcel attributes

Authors:
Stefan A. Sinske[1]
Heinz E. Jacobs[1]

Affiliations:
[1]Department of Civil Engineering, University of Stellenbosch, South Africa

Correspondence to:
Heinz Jacobs

Email:
hejacobs@sun.ac.za

Postal address:
Private Bag X1, Matieland
7602, South Africa

Background: Information aggregation to suburb level is of interest to engineers and urban planners. Readily available suburb boundaries do not always correspond to the suburb names recorded for individual properties in different data bases and unwanted errors are inherent. This mismatch of suburb names at different spatial scales poses a particular problem to analysts. As part of a parallel research project into the development of a robust guideline for suburb-based water demand analyses it was necessary to evaluate a large number of suburbs in terms of various attributes, one of which was the total suburb area.

Objectives: Suburb boundaries were needed to assess the total suburb area. The objective of this research was to develop a novel geographic information system (GIS) application to delineate suburbs with boundaries corresponding to information contained in another data base comprising individual property records. The suburb boundaries derived in this manner may not relate to municipal boundaries, or sociopolitical boundaries, nor do they have to. The fundamentally correct suburb boundary would be the one encompassing what is perceived to be the suburb based on the suburb name in a particular data base that also contains other interesting attributes, such as water use, of individual properties.

Method: The ArcGIS environment was used to delineate suburbs by means of triangulated irregular network (TIN) modelling. Boundaries for suburbs with predominantly residential land use were created that included all residential properties according to the suburb name field as recorded in the treasury system. Other vacant areas were also included so as to obtain the total suburb area. The methodology was developed to assist research in the field of potable water services, but the method presented could be applied to other services that require management of information at suburb level.

Results: This article illustrates how a tedious task of suburb delineation could be automated in the GIS environment. The tool prevents subjective results that would be prone to error. The automated procedure described could effectively delineate a large number of predominantly residential suburbs in a relatively short time span and produce repeatable results. A reasonable outline could only be obtained if a sufficient number of parcels in the area contained the same suburb name. Functionality was added to the tool so that a limit could be set for this purpose. The default was that if more than 20% of the records were erroneous it was considered impractical to delineate a suburb. The derived suburb boundaries correspond to useful information in other data bases and would thus enable more effective management of the information.

Conclusion: A novel procedure to delineate suburb boundaries in the GIS environment was illustrated in this article. Information at two different spatial scales, namely, individual consumers and suburbs, could be married for the purpose of further research into suburban attributes. The tool was applied as part of a parallel research project to delineate 468 suburbs in this manner, results of which were submitted for publication elsewhere.

Introduction

Background

Engineers are regularly faced with the challenge of effective information management in an effort to ensure municipal service delivery to communities, preceded by appropriate planning studies. Water services are generally seen as one of the most crucial municipal services in terms of human survival and public health. This research focuses on potable water supply and, in particular, on methods to deal with water consumption information at the planning stage, where crude estimates of water demand are required. Jacobs and Fair (2012) addressed information management as it pertains to water consumption data and concluded by identifying geographical information systems as a key to the next level of increasing information processing capacity.

The application of geographic information system (GIS) tools in engineering and research into their effective application is not new. Research has been presented of GIS application in various engineering disciplines, such as public transport management (Dondo & Rivett 2004), sewer system analysis (Sinske & Zietsman 2002), river flood plain modelling (Yang, Townsend & Daneshfar 2006) and water master planning (Vorster *et al.* 1995).

Urban development and water demand estimates

Greenfield land is defined as undeveloped land used for agriculture, landscape design or to evolve naturally. These areas of land are usually agricultural or amenity properties being considered for urban development (Wikipedia 2012a). The engineer responsible for planning water services would need to estimate the water requirement of the potential future land users. The eventual land use could for example be residential, commercial or industrial.

Various methods are available for estimating residential water demand in South Africa, with a comprehensive review provided by Jacobs (2008). The most recent publications in this regard were by Van Zyl, Ilemobade & Van Zyl (2008) and Jacobs, Geustyn, Loubser and Van Der Merwe (2004). Further discussion of these water demand estimation methods is beyond the scope of this text; suffice it to say that all the available local methods for estimating water demand are based on the size of individual residential plots. Households living on larger plots use more water per day than those on smaller plots.

Motivation

Greenfield land development studies require planners to make estimates of water use and other service-related variables on a relatively large spatial scale, for example, at suburb level. Details of the expected development at a small spatial scale (individual plots) is often limited at this early stage of planning because of the inherent uncertainties involved in urban development. It would thus make sense to apply a robust method to estimate the water demand for the planned suburb based on the total suburb area only. The delineated area would ultimately include all the roads, parks, public open spaces and private properties, despite much of this not requiring water supply per se.

Research problem: Suburbs, suburb names and suburb boundaries

A suburb is generally defined as a residential area existing as part of a city or within commuting distance of a city. The word is derived from the Latin terms *sub* [under] and *urbs* [city]. Most suburbs have a name and a physical boundary delineating the outer perimeter. There may be exceptions where the line between different suburbs has become blurred over time with no clear distinction between them. In such cases it would be impossible to delineate suburbs by drawing a boundary around it. In an attempt to match individual addresses, Coetzee and Rademeyer (2009) reported that address matching may be complicated by an incomplete or inaccurate input address that includes an incorrect suburb name. These mismatch problems were noted to be the result of ambiguities originating from uncertainties regarding suburb and/or place name boundaries in that study. Coetzee and Bishop (2009) investigated national address databases and compared two different approaches for harvesting data.

It may not seem clear at first why it would be important to create suburb boundaries as presented in this article. Formerly created suburb boundaries in the required format would certainly be available. The problem is that this may not necessarily be true for each suburb and, even if it were, the information does not necessarily link up between different data sets as desired for a particular research project. For example, predefined suburb boundaries were found to be dissociated in some instances from suburb names for individual plots in the treasury data base.

As part of a parallel research project into the development of a robust guideline for suburb-based water demand analyses (Jacobs, Sinske & Scheepers in press) it was necessary to evaluate a large number of suburbs in terms of various attributes, one of which was the total suburb area. An automated method was needed to delineate suburbs in order to obtain the total suburb area. The derived suburb boundaries needed to correspond to the available water use information for individual consumers stored in the treasury data base. The suburb boundaries derived in this manner may not relate to municipal boundaries or sociopolitical boundaries, nor do they have to. The fundamentally 'correct suburb boundary' would be the one encompassing all properties with the suburb name in a particular data base. Such a boundary may not exist nor may available boundaries be associated with the database to be analysed; it thus needs to be created.

Overview

This article describes a novel procedure that was developed for this purpose. The initial steps of this research involved a review of a geographic information system (GIS) in other fields of engineering in order to assess the potential application in this study. In developing the semi-automatic method to delineate suburb boundaries using GIS it was necessary to extend the available commercial GIS product functions. The conceptual development and subsequent procedures to delineate suburbs for the purpose of obtaining the total suburb area are described in this article with a particular focus on information management. The technical findings regarding water consumption based on suburb areas derived in this manner were reported elsewhere (Jacobs *et al.* in press).

Information management with a geographic information system
Geospatial data handling ability

Wikipedia (2012b) describes GIS as any information system that integrates, stores, edits, analyses, shares and displays geographic information for informing decision-making. GIS is a computer system that handles the location and attributes of geographically referenced data (Obermeyer & Pinto 1994; Chang 2010). The ability of GIS to process geospatial data distinguishes GIS from other information systems and makes it a valuable tool for engineers in the field of urban services such as water, sewer, gas, electricity and telephone networks. GIS is also valuable in terms of transport planning, as well as in the fields of urban and regional planning (Burrough & McDonnell 1998; Maguire 1992; Obermeyer & Pinto 1994; Shekhar & Chawla 2003; Chang 2010). Some of these GIS applications are discussed below.

Application of a geographic information system in municipal service delivery

The spatial database, graphical display capabilities and internal programming language of a GIS were identified as excellent building blocks for a spatial information system in the public transport services planning field (Dondo & Rivet 2004). The ability of GIS to combine various layers of information can, for example, be deployed in sewer-system analysis. Census enumerator areas (e.g. to derive residential sewage production) and land use area information (for business and industrial sewage production) can be selected graphically from respective layers and be allocated to manholes where the wastewater would enter the system. An analysis run can then directly be performed within the GIS via an embedded programme. Results can be displayed as thematic maps (Sinske & Zietsman 2002). Sinske and Zietsman (2004) reported a GIS-based spatial decision support system for pipe-break susceptibility analysis of municipal water distribution systems. Beuken *et al.* (2010) researched the potential of using GIS for the analysis and management of water distribution networks and pointed out several successful GIS implementations at Dutch water companies.

It is apparent that GIS has found wide application in the field of engineering services, including water and planning. None of the applications addressed the need to match information at different spatial scales and delineate suburbs or any other similar area described by polygons as described in this text.

Complex modelling in a geographic information system

In most of the above applications the standard GIS functionality of an available commercial product was extended with internal programming languages to perform complex modelling. The following software programs were deployed in this study:

- The widely used ArcGIS Desktop 10.0 software package (licence type ArcInfo) from ESRI was used as GIS platform. ArcMap, which is the central application of ArcGIS, was used as the main spatial viewer. File management tasks were performed with ArcCatalog and spatial analyses with ArcToolbox, both part of the ArcGIS Desktop and accessed via ArcMap (ESRI 2010).
- ArcScene is a 3D visualisation application and part of ArcGIS, and was used in conjunction with the 3D Analyst tools of ArcToolbox to perform complex surface modelling for the suburb delineation process. The 3D

Analyst extension of ArcGIS is a system requirement for the above.
- The end results were finalised via ModelBuilder, which is part of ArcGIS.

Suburb delineation using a geographic information system

Definition of a geographic information system parcels and features

In real estate terms, a lot or plot is a tract or parcel of land owned or meant to be owned by an owner or owners. Some countries use the terminology 'parcel of real property' whilst others use 'immovable property', meaning practically the same thing. Each property is described by a polygon in GIS, commonly referred to as a parcel. In between the parcels are other areas of land and interesting geographic features with spatial attributes that may be recorded in the GIS data base as well (some may also be irrelevant parcels). In addition to the parcel polygons the data base may contain point features (e.g. a beacon or centre point of a parcel) and also line features (e.g. a small water canal or hiking route). The most basic type of polygon would be a triangle. Each parcel has a unique GIS-code with associated information for it stored in the corresponding data base.

Chang (2010) defines a feature as any representation of a real-world object on a GIS-map; it could be any shape. In ArcGIS, a feature class stores spatial features of the same geometric type (i.e. point, line, polygon, etc.), same attributes (i.e. common set of attributes) and the same spatial reference (i.e. common mapping co-ordinate system). In the above context, for example, all the parcels addressed by the delineation procedure would be stored in a feature class. Feature classes again are stored in an ArcGIS geodatabase as either standalone or grouped in a feature dataset. These terms are applicable to this study as defined below.

Description of the research problem in terms of a geographic information system polygons

The research problem is firstly explained in terms of GIS terminology before moving on to presentation of the automated procedure for suburb delineation. This description is presented by considering a hypothetical example and uses water consumption as a desired attribute aggregated to suburb level. The suburb name and the number of houses used in this section are completely irrelevant and did not form part of this or further research work with the suburb delineation tool presented in this article. The name Suburb A and the 500 plots (approximately) were simply chosen to clearly illustrate the research problem and the devised method to delineate suburbs. The actual method could be applied to any real suburb or any number of real suburbs in a given area.

The treasury data base would contain information for each of these 500 consumers or residences. Each would have a water meter read monthly, with data stored in the treasury data base. Each consumer's property would be described by numerous fields in the data base. One of these fields would be the suburb name field with the entry: Suburb A. The town planner would be able to provide an independent GIS data base describing the cadastral layout of the town - this could be seen as a map of the town showing all the properties. This GIS data base typically contains the suburb name and land use for each property in separate data fields. The suburb name in the GIS data base would not always match up with the suburb name in the treasury data base.

In between these 500 parcels comprising residential plots would also be vacant areas that would typically represent roads, parks or public open spaces, but these would not typically be flagged with the suburb name. These vacant areas are often not specifically captured as parcel polygons. It would be obvious to the reader that all the parcels, roads and other vacant areas in between the parcels should actually be part of Suburb A if the total suburb area needs to be considered.

Readily available up-to-date polygons (in GIS format) depicting suburbs in the desired fashion are unfortunately seldom available. Boundary and name changes over time, particularly after local political change in the mid–1990s, resulted in lacunae. This was true for boundaries at the provincial level to suburb and ward level. Another problem was that of duplicate suburb names, for example, a study that would encompass the entire country and where the same suburb name would be found in different cities. The suburb boundary matching desired attributes and encompassing all spaces in between plots could easily and quickly be generated by the method reported in this study, producing repeatable results.

This suburb delineation could be done by hand, in other words by clicking with a mouse around the plots to create a single polygon for the suburb. Such a task would become tedious, subjective and prone to error when repeated for hundreds of suburbs. This article presents an automated procedure that could delineate a suburb and would produce repeatable results. A reasonable outline could, of course, only be obtained if a sufficient number of parcels in the area contained the same suburb name (and same spelling) in the data base. Functionality was added to the tool so that a limit could be set for this purpose. The default was that if more than 20% of the records were erroneous it was considered impractical to delineate a suburb.

Triangulated irregular network modelling

The novel GIS method to delineate suburbs boundaries is based on triangulated irregular network (TIN) terrain modelling. A TIN is a set of adjacent (i.e. connected), continuous and non-overlapping triangles constructed by triangulating irregularly spaced nodes or observation points. These points are vertices with x, y and z co-ordinates. The principles of TIN are described in more detail by Burrough (1986) and Chang (2010). The TIN model, with its network of triangles in the form a sheet, or so-called mesh, is ideal for terrain representation and modelling (Burrough & McDonnell 1998).

Different methods of interpolation are available to form these triangles. The most widely used is called Delaunay triangulation and is implemented in the ArcGIS software suite (ESRI 2010). This triangulation method ensures that all sample points are connected with their two nearest neighbours to form triangles as equiangular or compact as possible. In this manner, it is possible to avoid the formation of too many unwanted sharp, long and skinny triangles (ESRI 2010; Chang 2010; Li & Ai 2010). A finished TIN comprises three types of geometric objects, namely, (1) triangles (facets), (2) points (nodes) and (3) lines (edges). Elevation data is stored at the nodes, whereas slope and aspect data are stored for each facet and remain constant over the facet (Chang 2010). Most GIS software packages implement TIN because one of their data structures and have the ability to export the abovementioned individual components of the TIN as separate polygon, point and line features for further analysis. Apart from TIN, most GIS also implement the grid structure for terrain modelling. One of the biggest advantages of the TIN model over the grid model is the flexibility of TIN to model more detail at certain locations (i.e. terrain specific source data such as roads, rivers, lakes and parcels can be incorporated in the triangulation process). Only high-resolution grids can show these detailed features, but this would not be an optimal solution with regard to data storage because the cell size (which is constant for the grid) will have to be defined as very small over the whole study area (Burrough 1986; Burrough & McDonnell 1998; Chang 2010).

A TIN data model can also be used to represent and model two dimensional (2D) surfaces, as is the case with this research. Li and Ai (2010) discussed the application of Delaunay TIN to detect various spatial and structural characteristics hidden in 2D geometry data (i.e. a type of spatial data mining application). They also pointed out an important aspect of Delaunay TIN, namely, that the triangle element can play two roles: either the component of the polygon feature or the bridge between neighbouring objects. Triangles playing the bridging role are distributed on the principle of 'nearest connection' of Delaunay TIN. Hereby, the neighbourhood relationship is presented by only one triangle no matter how far between these objects, which is a useful characteristic for spatial neighbourhood analysis.

The suburb delineation process presented in this article is also a 2D TIN application based on the abovementioned dual role of the Delaunay TIN triangle. This means that some triangles will be used to cover the entire area of parcels in the suburbs (i.e. TIN triangles located on parcels) and others will span the empty space between parcels (i.e. a TIN triangle located in the empty space bridging the gap between two other TIN triangles located on parcels). The method can delineate a large amount of suburb boundaries all at once and can be executed in ArcGIS via ten geoprocessing steps (Figure 1).

The suburb delineation process requires spatially referenced parcel data as an input, with attribute data fields containing the suburb name and land use. The land use description data is not relevant at this stage. An ArcGIS file geodatabase (.gdb) can now be created in ArcCatalog (Step 1 of Figure 1)

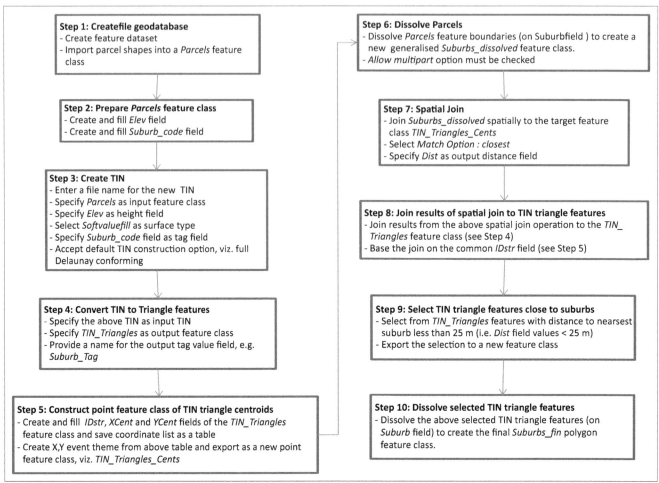

FIGURE 1: Suburb delineation procedure.

and the shapefile, containing the parcels, could be imported as feature class within a new feature dataset. The feature dataset provides a logical structure (almost like a file folder) wherein feature classes can be grouped together. The ArcGIS file geodatabase with unlimited storage space was chosen instead of the ArcGIS personal geodatabase, which has a storage limit of 2GB.

The elevation field (in the *Parcels* feature class) can be filled with any constant elevation value (such as e.g. 1 m) for all parcels (Step 2 of Figure 1) because the TIN will be used for 2D analysis only. The suburb code in the *Parcels* feature class (Step 2 of Figure 1) must be a unique integer code for each suburb name. The TIN model can best be created in the ArcScene environment with the *Create TIN* tool (Step 3 of Figure 1), accessible from the integrated ArcToolbox (note, the 3D Analyst extension of ArcGIS is required). The 2D TIN model will be built based on the parcel vertices, which all have the abovementioned 1 m spot height allocated. Important is to set the surface type to *Softvaluefill*. This will ensure that the parcel boundaries will be enforced in the triangulation as breaklines (i.e. TIN triangle edges will not cross the parcel boundaries [Figure 2a]). Furthermore, the TIN triangles inside these parcel polygons will hereby be attributed (i.e. filled) with the corresponding suburb code tag value (for cross-reference checking). These TIN triangles

can now be extracted from the TIN model and saved as a new polygon feature class (Step 4 of Figure 1) via the ArcToolbox conversion tool *TIN Triangle*.

Geoprocessing

A series of geoprocessing steps (Step 5 to Step 8 of Figure 1) are now required to determine the name of the closest suburb and corresponding distance for each TIN triangle. The latter is measured from the geometric centroid of the triangle (Step 5 of Figure 1) to the closest parcel edge in the suburb. This can be accomplished in ArcMap via the *Calculate Geometry* function in combination with the *Spatial Join* and *Dissolve* tools (accessible from the integrated ArcToolbox). The dissolve operation based on the suburb name (Step 6 of Figure 1) merges all individual parcels in a suburb into one multipart suburb polygon, in order to improve the spatial join operation time (Step 7 of Figure 1). This temporary suburb polygon is only used in the spatial join operation. The spatial join results include the name of the closest suburb and the corresponding distance and can now be joined to the TIN triangle features (Step 8 of Figure 1) for further queries and analyses.

The distance to the nearest suburb can be queried (Step 9 of Figure 1) to obtain a selection of TIN triangles close to suburbs. A TIN triangle can be regarded as close to a suburb when it is either completely within a suburb parcel (distance will then be zero) or within approximately 25 m from a suburb parcel. The latter scenario is when the TIN triangle is located in a street or in a nearby unidentified (vacant) land use area either somewhere in the interior of the suburb or in the outer border regions between suburbs. The abovementioned distance selection process will assign in these border regions approximately half of the TIN triangles to the one suburb and half to the other (i.e. they slot together almost like a jigsaw puzzle [Figure 2b]).

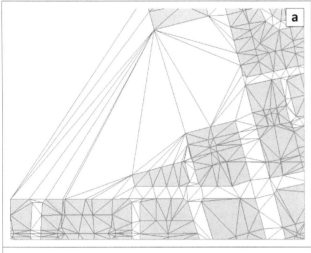

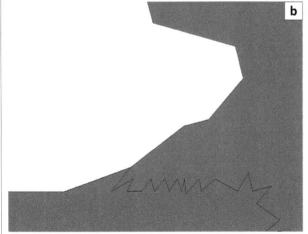

FIGURE 2: Transforming (a) individual parcels to (b) suburb areas using a triangulated irregular network (TIN).

Final selection for suburb polygons

The invalid long and skinny TIN triangles located in the undefined land use areas on the edges of a suburb (as the result of the TIN interpolation process) will also mostly all be filtered out by the distance selection process. Some smaller ones may be missed by the process and can afterwards be wiped manually for 'aesthetic' reasons. For the suburb area calculation, however, they are insignificant and could remain in the system.

The final selection of TIN triangles can now be dissolved (Step 10 of Figure 1) based on the suburb names from the above spatial join results in order to obtain the final delineated suburb polygons. It can be recalled that this boundary does not need to match up to any other boundary - it needs to delineate the outer edge of a number of plots that were flagged in a given data base as being part of this suburb, plus all spaces in between.

Data summary output

Prior to the analysis, the land uses in the suburbs need to be identified according to the types, namely, residential, open space, business, industrial, et cetera. The land use information must be summarised per suburb in order for the model to extract the predominantly residential suburbs. The summarisation process is illustrated in Figure 3.

Composite land use information needs to be summarised per suburb (Step 1 inFigure 3) by generating a summary table on the *Parcels* feature class. This can be accomplished in ArcMap with the integrated ArcToolbox function *Summary Statistics* and specify the *Suburb* and *Land_use* fields as the two *Case* fields on which the summary should be based. The resultant summary would contain the various information required as output in multiple suburb records and could be linked with the *Suburbs* feature class (containing the final delineated suburb boundaries) via a one-to-many relationship. This type of relationship would, however, make further processing by the model unnecessarily complex.

A simpler link could be accomplished in ArcMap by selecting and exporting from the composite table the abovementioned land uses into separate tables and consecutively joining them (i.e. one-to-one relationship) with the *Suburbs* feature

Step 1: Summarise composite land use info per suburb
- Generate summary table on *Parcels* feature class based on combination of *Suburb* and *Land_use* fields

Step 2: Extract single land use per suburb
- Select and export separately from the above composite table the following land uses: residential, open space, institutional, business and industrial
- Note, the five output tables now contain one record per suburb with the specific land use info summarised accordingly.

Step 3: Join summary tables to *Suburbs* feature class
- Join consecutively the above land use summary tables to the *Suburbs_fin* feature class (i.e. the final output from the flowchart of Figure 1)
- Join also water demand table to the above *Suburbs_fin* feature class
- finally export as new feature class *Suburbs_fin1*

Step 4: Finalise fields structure of *Suburbs* feauture class
- Rename *Suburbs_fin1* fields to be compatible with the *finalise end results* ModelBuilder™ model

FIGURE 3: Land use summarisation.

class (Step 2 and Step 3 of Figure 3). The *Suburbs* feature class now contains one record per suburb with the land use information contained in separate fields, which is ideal for further processing. The procedure checks that the number of parcels per suburb deviate less than 20% from the number of parcels as recorded for the corresponding suburb in the treasury database. Suburbs with more than 20% deviation in number of parcels are excluded from the selection because in these cases there are obvious fundamental differences in the suburb boundaries between the two data sets and the delineated suburb would not be considered valid for the purpose of deriving its total area.

Conclusion and future research needs

This article illustrates how a tedious task of suburb delineation could be automated in the GIS environment. The article shows how information at two different spatial scales, namely, (1) individual consumers and (2) suburbs, could be married for the purpose of further research into suburban attributes. The suburb boundaries obtained from the system also encompass the vacant areas and roads (in between the parcels). The automated procedure employed built-in logic to enable the selection of predominantly residential suburbs and to derive the total suburb area. The tool was employed as part of a parallel research project into suburban water demand to delineate 468 suburbs in this manner, results of which were submitted for publication elsewhere (Jacobs *et al.* in press).

The GIS based information system presented in this article could further be improved by implementing the following possible enhancements:

- The semi-automatic suburb delineation process and the land use summarisation process could be implemented directly as models in the ModelBuilder environment, subsequently reducing the analysis time.
- The invalid (long and skinny) TIN triangles located on the edges of the suburb after the TIN interpolation process add inaccuracies to the suburb delineation procedure in some cases. An improved selection of TIN triangles could be obtained with almost no invalid triangles on the suburb edges by reducing the threshold settings. Only a few valid triangles located on wide roads and traffic circles would be wrongly missed by this finer threshold. The distance threshold cannot be reduced significantly for study areas containing suburbs with many unidentified (vacant) land areas (i.e. those not captured as parcels) because these vacant areas would then wrongly be excluded from the suburb area calculation.

Acknowledgements

The authors would like to acknowledge the University of Stellenbosch for the grant towards a two-year post-doctoral fellowship held by one of the authors without which this research would not have been possible. The authors also appreciate input from the various role players who provided information for the purpose of this research.

Competing interests

The authors declare that they have no financial or personal relationship(s) which may have inappropriately influenced them in writing this paper.

Authors' contributions

H.E.J. (University of Stellenbosch) instigated this research, selected the journal and handled editorial matters. The GIS applications were developed by S.A.S. (University of Stellenbosch). Both authors contributed equally to the text in this manuscript.

References

Beuken, R.H.S., Van Daal, K.H.A., Pieterse-Quirijns, E.J. & Zoutendijk, F.J.M., 2010, 'The use of GIS for analysis of water distribution networks', in J. Boxall & C. Maksimovic (eds.), *Proceedings of the 10th International Conference on Computing and Control for the Water Industry, CCWI 2009 – 'Integrating water systems'*, Sheffield, UK, September 01–03, 2009, pp. 93–98.

Burrough, P.A., 1986, *Principles of geographical information systems for land resources assessment*, Oxford University Press, Oxford.

Burrough, P.A. & McDonnell, R.A., 1998, *Principles of geographical information systems*, Oxford University Press, Oxford.

Chang, K.T., 2010, *Introduction to geographic information systems*, 5th edn., McGraw-Hill, New York.

Coetzee, S. & Bishop, J., 2009, 'Address databases for national SDI: Comparing the novel data grid approach to data harvesting and federated databases', *International Journal of Geographic Information Science* 23(9), 1179–1209. http://dx.doi.org/10.1080/13658810802084806

Coetzee, S. & Rademeyer, I.M., 2009, 'Testing the spatial adjacency match of the Intiendo address matching tool for geocoding of addresses with misleading suburb or place names', *In-proceedings International Cartography Conference*, Santiago, Chile, November 15–21, 2009, n.p.

Dondo, C. & Rivett, U., 2004, 'Spatial information systems in managing public transport information', *South African Journal of Information Management* 6(2), 8 pages.

ESRI, 2010, *ArcGIS Desktop Help*, Environmental Systems Research Institute, Redlands, CA.

Jacobs, H.E., Sinske, S.A & Scheepers, H.M., in press, article submitted for peer review and possible publication to *Urban Water Journal*, submitted September 2012.

Jacobs, H.E., 2008, 'Chronologiese oorsig van Suid-Afrikaanse riglyne vir residensiële gemiddelde jaarlikse waterverbruik met erfgrootte as onafhanklike veranderlike: Navorsings- en oorsigartikel', *Suid-Afrikaanse Tydskrif vir Natuurwetenskap en Tegnologie* 27(4), 240–265.

Jacobs, H.E., 2008, 'Residential water information management', *South African Journal of Information Management* 10(3), 12 pages.

Jacobs, H.E. & Fair, K.A., 2012, 'A tool to increase information-processing capacity for consumer water meter data', *South African Journal of Information Management* 14(1), 7 pages.

Jacobs, H.E., Geustyn, L.C., Loubser, B.F. & Van Der Merwe, B., 2004, 'Estimating residential water demand in southern Africa', *Journal of South African Institution of Civil Engineering* 46(4), 2–13.

Li, J. & Ai, T., 2010, 'A triangulated spatial model for detection of spatial characteristics of GIS data', in Y. Wang (ed.), *Proceedings of the 2010 IEEE International Conference on Progress in Informatics and Computing, PIC 2010*, Shanghai, China, 10–12 December 2010, IEEE, Washington, DC, pp. 155–159.

Maguire, D.J., 1992, An overview and definition of GIS, in D.J. Maguire, M.F. Goodchild, & D.W. Rhind (eds.), *Geographical information systems: Principles and applications*, Vol.1, pp. 9–20, Longman, New York.

Obermeyer, N.J. & Pinto, J.K., 1994, *Managing geographic information systems*, The Guilford Press, New York.

Shekhar, S. & Chawla, S., 2003, *Spatial databases: A tour*, Pearson Education, Inc., Upper Saddle River, NJ.

Sinske, S.A. & Zietsman, H.L., 2002, 'Sewer-system analysis with the aid of a geographical information system', *Water SA* 28(3), 243–248. http://dx.doi.org/10.4314/wsa.v28i3.4891

Sinske, S.A. & Zietsman, H.L., 2004, 'A spatial decision support system for pipe-break susceptibility analysis of municipal water distribution systems', *Water SA* 30(1), 71–79. http://dx.doi.org/10.4314/wsa.v30i1.5029

Van Zyl, H.J., Ilemobade, A.A., & Van Zyl, J.E., 2008, 'An improved area-based guideline for domestic water demand estimation in South Africa', *Water SA* 34(3), 381–392.

Vorster, J., Geustyn, L.C., Loubser, B.F., Tanner, A. & Wall, K., 1995, 'A strategy and master plan for water supply, storage and distribution in the East Rand region', *Journal of South African Institution of Civil Engineering* 37(2), 1–5.

Wikipedia, 2012a, 'Greenfield land', viewed 22 August 2012, from http://en.wikipedia.org/wiki/Greenfield_land

Wikipedia, 2012b, 'GIS', viewed 22 August 2012, from http://en.wikipedia.org/wiki/GIS

Yang, J., Townsend R.D. & Daneshfar, B., 2006, 'Applying the HEC-RAS model and GIS techniques in river network floodplain delineation', *Canadian Journal of Civil Engineering* 33(1), 19–28. http://dx.doi.org/10.1139/l05-102

20

The Information Warfare Life Cycle Model

Authors:
Brett van Niekerk[1]
Manoj S. Maharaj[1]

Affiliations:
[1]School of Information
Systems and Technology,
University of KwaZulu-Natal,
South Africa

Correspondence to:
Brett van Niekerk

Email:
vanniekerkb@ukzn.ac.za

Postal address:
University Road, M-Block,
Westville Campus, Durban
4000, South Africa

Information warfare (IW) is a dynamic and developing concept, which constitutes a number of disciplines. This paper aims to develop a life cycle model for information warfare that is applicable to all of the constituent disciplines. The model aims to be scalable and applicable to civilian and military incidents where information warfare tactics are employed. Existing information warfare models are discussed, and a new model is developed from the common aspects of these existing models. The proposed model is then applied to a variety of incidents to test its applicability and scalability. The proposed model is shown to be applicable to multiple disciplines of information warfare and is scalable, thus meeting the objectives of the model.

Introduction

Information warfare is a construct that was brought to prominence by the United States Department of Defence in the 1990s (Kopp 2000:31). The concept of information warfare brings together a number of disciplines that revolve around information and information systems; a number of these disciplines have existed since antiquity; however, the rapid evolution of information and communications technology has made them more prominent in a globalised society. Information warfare is a dynamic and developing concept, and is still prone to changes and debates; consequently there is no coherence in the definitions, constructs, or models. However, it is clear that information warfare is a global phenomenon. The implementation of information warfare may be hindered by the lack of a standardised taxonomy or nomenclature (Armistead 2010:109). The purpose of this article is to develop a life cycle framework for information warfare that incorporates the common aspects of the various disciplines, is scalable, and may be applied to both the civilian and military domains where information warfare tactics are employed. By doing so, it is intended that the existing models are related and brought together in a single framework in an attempt to further standardise the information warfare concept in a global context. This model forms the second step and consists of consolidating the various levels of models into a single framework. The first step was submitted in a companion paper, which compares the variations of individual models (Van Niekerk & Maharaj in press). For the purposes of this paper, the background will provide the information relevant to the proposed model.

Information Warfare

This section provides the background theory to information warfare and presents the models previously proposed to describe aspects of Information Warfare (IW). Existing models and frameworks to describe IW cycles are then presented and discussed.

Background

Information Warfare can be defined as:

> offensive and defensive operations against information resources of a 'win-lose' nature. It is conducted because information resources have value to people. Offensive operations aim to increase this value for the offence while decreasing it for the defence. Defensive operations seek to counter potential losses in value.
>
> (Denning 1999:21)

From the aforementioned definition it can be seen that the use of IW is an attempt to gain an advantage over a competitor or adversary by either leveraging one's own information resources or denying the opponent the ability to fully leverage their information resources. The first definition mentions that information warfare can be conducted in the physical, information and cognitive domains; this illustrates that information warfare may include traditional physical destruction of information-related resources and may also target the human mind.

Six functional areas or 'pillars' of IW have been identified (Brazzoli 2007:221):

- Command and control warfare entails actions to preserve the ability to command your own forces whilst hindering the adversary's similar capabilities. In a corporate environment it would refer to the management of employees and departments.

- Intelligence based warfare entails the ability to gather and process intelligence, and disseminate it to the relevant end-users whilst disrupting similar capabilities of the adversary.
- Information infrastructure warfare entails protecting the information infrastructure (and those infrastructures upon which it is dependant) whilst exploiting those of an adversary.
- Psychological operations entail influencing a target audience to ultimately behave in a manner favourable to your objectives and countering attempts to influence the audience against those objectives.
- Network warfare entails preserving the use of the information networks whilst exploiting those of an adversary or degrading their networks.
- Electronic warfare entails preserving the availability of the electro-magnetic spectrum for one's own use whilst degrading the ability of an adversary to utilise it. This has far greater applicability to the military environment than the corporate sphere.

A seventh pillar has been proposed by some researchers and has been adopted by India (Chatterji 2008:10); this is 'economic IW'. Chatterji describes this as a blockade of economic information, where a competing nation would be starved of external information relevant to its economy. Economic and industrial espionage may also form part of economic IW.

The 'CIA Triad' model (Denning 1998:41; Waltz 1998:22) describes three attributes of information and the supporting information infrastructures that need to be preserved:

- Confidentiality – only those who have the required authority or clearance may gain access to sensitive information or knowledge of the functioning, operations or characteristics of infrastructures.
- Integrity – only authorised persons should be able to alter information or systems settings that could affect the infrastructure, and the authenticity of the information and alterations should be ensured.
- Availability – the information and its supporting infrastructure should be available when required.

There are extensions to this model; however, those are more applicable to information security in general and are not relevant to the information warfare discussion presented in this paper.

To counter the 'CIA Triad' there are three main strategies that may be used to attack information and the supporting infrastructure. Waltz (1998:23), Borden (1999), Hutchinson and Warren (2001:3), and the United States Air Force (1998:9) all provide similar models, with variations in the terms used and sometimes there is a sub-division of the strategies. The three strategies and some of their sub-divisions are:

- deny, disrupt or degrade access to information, or destroy the information
- steal, exploit or intercept the information
- corrupt the information by modifying the contents, inserting additional false information (fabrication), altering the context in which the information is viewed

and changing the perceptions of people towards the information.

Existing Information Warfare models and frameworks

This section presents selected existing models and frameworks from which the proposed IW Life Cycle Model may be generated. Two models describing IW in general are discussed, followed by the Message Flow Model for psychological operations and a discussion of a proposed framework for network warfare.

General Information Warfare models

Ventre (2009:276) contends that many confrontations over computer networks and the Internet are a result of tense political situations; and proposes a model shown in Figure 1. Whilst it was developed specifically for the case of politically motivated cyber-attacks it can be used to model any incident where an IW attack has occurred. Some context results in potential adversaries and motivations, which may result in an IW attack. This has ramifications for the target, which will react in an attempt to recover and gain protection from current and future attacks. Any reaction of the target, and any active retaliation, will result in the overall context being influenced.

The disciplines and capabilities relevant to information warfare may be employed outside the traditional military command and control target set (Wik 2002:617). Figure 2 illustrates a process for information warfare developed from this. Once the operations have been planned, the available 'weapons' are applied to the target set: primarily infrastructure and systems which modern society revolves around, such as communications systems, the mass media and other infrastructures in society (Wik 2002:617). The attack on these target sets will create affects that impact on humans themselves, altering or creating new thought

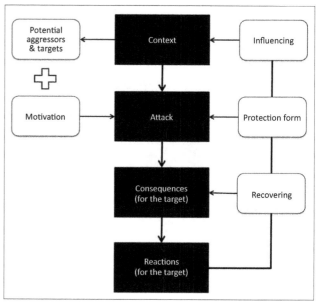

Source: Adapted from Ventre, D., 2009, *Information warfare*, ISTE, London, UK.
FIGURE 1: Information warfare cycle.

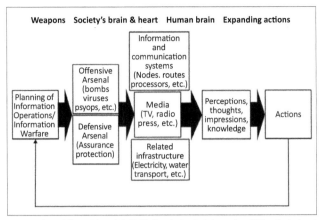

Source: Adapted from Wik, M.W., 2002, 'Revolution in Information Affairs: Tactical and Strategic Implications of Information Warfare and Information Operations', in A. Jones, G.L. Kovacich & P.G. Luzwick (eds.), *Global information warfare*, pp. 579–628, Auerbach Publications, Boca Raton/London/New York.

FIGURE 2: The Information Operations Process.

processes and ultimately actions and re-actions. This model is a detailed version the attack, consequences and reaction blocks in Figure 1.

Psychological operations: The Message Flow Model

The model for psychological operations proposed by Cox (1997:42) takes the form of a message flow, which is illustrated Figure 3. The message will be constructed in such a way that it coerces, deters or provides incentives to the target audience with regards to a specific behaviour or action (Cox 1997:42). The sender delivers the message via an instrument of power, such as the mass media or pamphlets, which results in a phenomenon that can be observed, interpreted and internalised by the target audience. The target audience react according to whether they support or oppose the message; the sender then re-evaluates the message by assessing this reaction (Cox 1997:42).

Network warfare

Veerasamy and Eloff (2008:100) proposed a network warfare framework; this can be seen in Figure 4. The framework includes factors that may constrain the use of network warfare and the intended target set. The syntactic level denotes the structured organisation of the networks, and the semantic level denotes the meaning of the received data (Veerasamy & Eloff 2008:103) and could be seen as

related to the cognitive domain as it involves trust. Many of the principles contained in the framework are standard information security principles that should be internal to any organisation. Important concepts are covered under the 'approach' block: the defensive approaches may be preventative, where it is attempted to secure vulnerabilities to prevent an attack; the detective approach attempts to detect when an attack is occurring to take measures to mitigate the effects; and the reactive approach will focus on recovering from the attack once it has occurred. Generally, a combination of all three strategies is employed in what is known as 'defence-in-depth'.

Proposed Information Warfare Life Cycle Model

This section presents the proposed Information Warfare (IW) Life Cycle Model, which is illustrated in Figure 5. The model was generated by identifying common aspects from the models discussed in the earlier sections. The objective of generating this model is to create one that is scalable for various 'sized' incidents, has a mix of high-level concepts and detail to adequately describe the incident and is applicable to various forms of IW which may be distinct from each other, such as psychological operations and electronic warfare.

Through a review of the available literature, four models were identified which describe IW incidents or actions, as opposed to the models that described IW structures or attributes (presented in the background section). It appears that attempts to relate the IW structures and attributes to broader contexts and actual operational planning is limited to the four models identified; this corresponds to the claim by Armistead (2010:63) that there is still a disconnect between the technical issues and the broader context.

From Figures 1 to Figures 4, it can be seen that there are common aspects: there is some context to the IW operations, which includes an aggressor with a motivation to attack a target. Some planning is required for the operations, which include some restrictions, limitations and other considerations that may affect the operation and target selection. The attack commences against a target set, using offensive techniques and tools, whilst the target defends and protects against the attack with associated tools and techniques. The attack

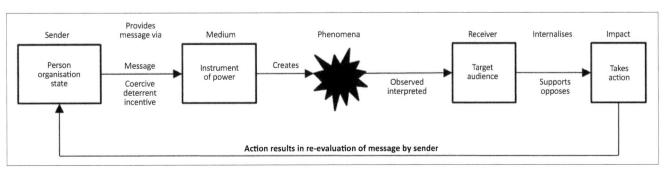

Source: Adapted from Cox, L.-V., 1997, *Planning for psychological operations: a proposal*, Air Command and Staff College, Maxwell Air Force Base, Montgomery, Alabama, and Ramluckan, T., & van Niekerk, B., 2009, 'The Terrorism/Mass Media Symbiosys', *Journal of Information Warfare* 8(2), 1–12.

FIGURE 3: Message Flow Diagram.

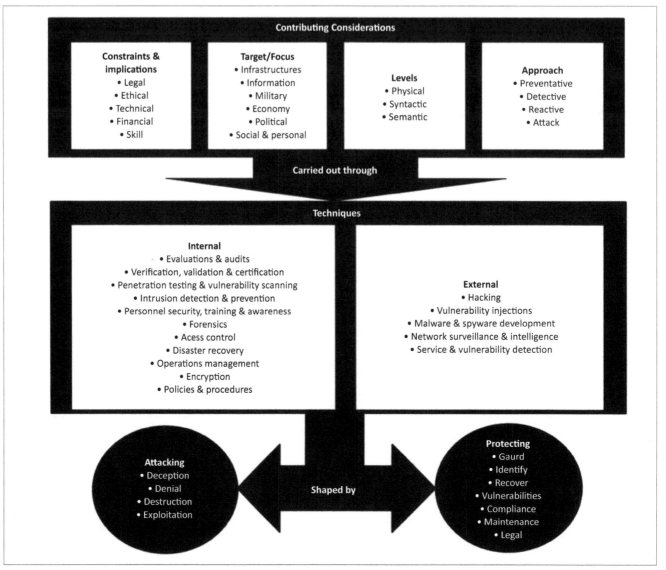

Source: Adapted from Veerasamy, N. & Eloff, J., 2008, 'Understanding the Elementary Considerations in a Network Warfare Environment: An Introductory Framework', in *Proceedings of the Workshop on ICT uses in Warfare and the Safegarding of Peace*, pp. 95–108, CSIR, Pretoria.

FIGURE 4: Network Warfare Framework.

will result in some phenomena that will have an impact on the target set which has consequences for the society; this results in a reaction by the members of the target, their allies and observers. The reaction will by necessity constitute a bolstering of defences and an attempted recovery from the attack. The reactions and ability of the target to defend itself will result in a re-evaluation of the attack by the aggressor, and there will be some influence on the overall context. This may result in the initial target becoming the aggressor and retaliating against their attacker.

As many detailed models may overlap with multiple high-level concepts, a dual-layered cycle was developed. The high-level cycle contains the basic blocks of the IW life cycle the context, attack and defence, the consequences, reactions, recovery and influence on the context. This is overlaid with a more detailed cycle, which shows the applicability to multiple high-level concepts; for example the planning of operations would be performed with consideration to

the current context and may be conducted for both attack and defence. The 'Attack' block contains multiple detailed constructs:

- the possible target set
- the functional areas that may be employed
- the offensive tactics
- the tools with which to conduct them.

The 'Defend and Protect' block similarly has the defensive techniques and tools. The society block overlaps four high-level concepts:

1. attack
2. defence
3. consequences
4. recovery.

The impact on society results in an impact on humans, who react; this results in the feedback to the 'Recovery', 'Defence' and 'Influence' blocks.

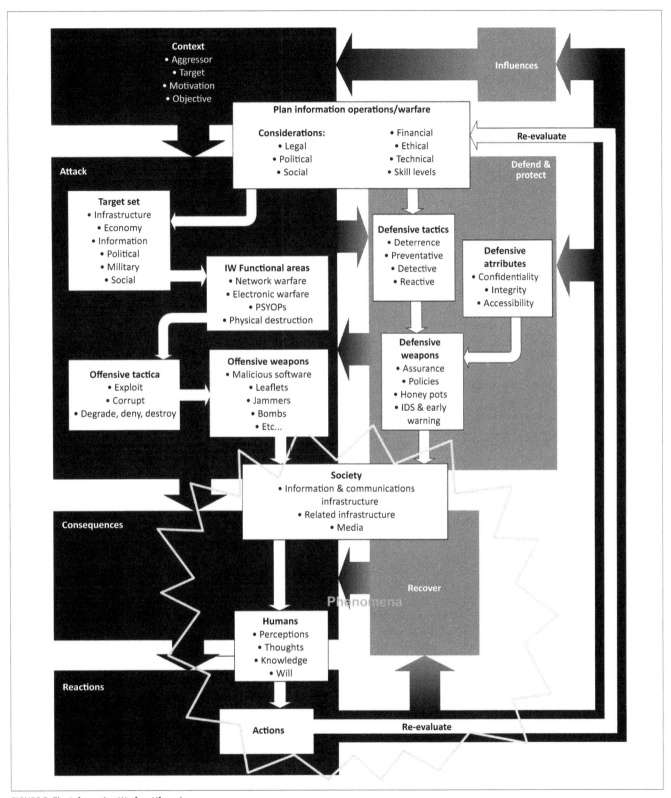

FIGURE 5: The Information Warfare Life cycle.

According to Armistead (2010:63), there is still a need to relate the issues surrounding many aspects of information operations and IW to broader contextual issues; the retention of the context block and the considerations in the planning block is an attempt to address that. These two blocks were drawn from the 'context' block proposed by Ventre (presented in Figure 1), the 'planning' block proposed by Wik (presented in Figure 2) and the consideration proposed by Veerasamy and Eloff (presented in Figure 4). The individual contexts and considerations will be unique to each incident or situation and also for each national or organisational outlook. As a result, an in-depth discussion of such considerations is beyond the scope of this paper.

Application of the Information Warfare Life Cycle Model

This section illustrates the application of the proposed Information Warfare (IW) Life Cycle Model to historical and current examples of IW incidents. The following sections each focus on a specific incident; each incident falls within a different functional area of IW. These sections will provide a brief background to the incident and then apply the IW Life Cycle to the incident. As IW is a global phenomenon, the incidents will not be restricted to any one region or nation.

Estonia: Cyber-based attack on infrastructure

The background provided for this incident is a summary of the following sources: Landler and Markoff (2007), Rolski (2007), Germain (2008), and StrategyPage.com (2010b). The Estonian government decided to relocate a war memorial from the Second World War which also honoured Russian soldiers; many Ethnic Russians took offence to the relocation and the Estonian Embassy was attacked amidst street riots. On 26 and 27 April 2007, the signs of a distributed denial of service (DDoS) attack from botnets were becoming apparent; a few days later several newspaper websites were brought down. Estonia raised suspicion of Russian government involvement or backing in the attacks, which was denied. Defensive preparations began and many Internet service providers (ISPs) aided in blocking the traffic relating to the attacks. Prior to a public holiday celebrating the Soviet victory in the Second World War, additional defensive preparations were made; on 09 and 10 May 2007 a severe DDoS attack hit Estonia, the major bank had to shut down its online services, losing over $1 million. The government websites and email systems were also targeted and badly affected. The attacks subsided on 16 May 2007. As a result of the attacks, a cyber-defence centre was established in Estonia, and NATO members extended the alliance to include cyber-attacks.

The incident will now be analysed using the Life Cycle Model:

- **Context:** The aggressor(s) are ethnic Russians; the target is the Estonian Government; the motivation is to show political dissatisfaction and revenge for the relocation of a war memorial.
- **Attack:** Network warfare denial tactics were used against many websites; some psychological warfare was employed through network warfare by defacing government websites. Botnets were used to flood target websites with traffic.
- **Defence:** Initial defensive preparations by the Estonians were preventative; by requesting aid from international ISPs in blocking the denial-of-service traffic.
- **Consequences:** The impact of the initial attacks was relatively minor; a few newspaper websites were brought down. Later attacks managed to severely disrupt the major

Estonian bank's online services; and damages exceeded $1 million.
- **Reaction:** Initial reaction by the Estonians was to increase defensive preparations for future attacks. After the incident was concluded, a cyber-protection centre was established.
- **Influence of context:** The influence on the initial context was minimal; however, political tensions were raised as Russia was accused of participating or sanctioning the attacks. The attacks eventually subsided; the international impact was that several nations expanded war treaties to include cyber-attacks.

The Channel Dash: Electronic warfare operations

This is a summary of a description of the 'Channel Dash' by Radloff, quoted by Sikwane (2010). In 1942 three German capital ships and a number of destroyers were ordered to return to their home base from a port in France, which necessitated transit through the English Channel. The German forces incrementally increased noise jamming (electronic warfare) against British radar stations in order to mimic atmospheric disturbances; the British fell for the deception and reduced the gain of the radar stations, and the German warships were therefore able to transit the English Channel undetected. When the British realised the deception, it was too late to intercept the warships.

What follows is an analysis of the incident using the IW Life Cycle Model:

- **Context:** German warships were required to transit the English Channel; the German electronic warfare units were the aggressor, with the aim of disrupting the English radar stations. As this was a time of war, there was very little in terms of restrictions that could possibly effect planning, other than technical capability.
- **Attack:** German units broadcast signals in such a manner that the English radar appeared to be malfunctioning due to atmospheric interference. The Germans used electronic warfare jamming equipment to interfere (degrade) the functionality of the British radar systems in such a manner to deceive the radar operators to further reduce the radar capability.
- **Defence and consequence:** The English radar operators reduced the gain on the radar units to mitigate the effects of the German interference. The German warships were able to transit the English Channel with the English radar unable to fully detect them.
- **Recovery and reaction:** The British realised there was deception and returned the radars to their normal operating conditions; however, it was too late to intercept the warships.
- **Influence on context:** The Germans successfully completed their objective.

Somalia (Blackhawk Down): Psychological operations

United States (US) forces entered Somalia to assist the United Nations forces that were providing aid and were continuously being raided by the Somali militias; the US forces began targeting a specific warlord, Mohammed Farah Aidid. After a series of raids, the incident known as 'Black Hawk Down' occurred, where a US serviceman was captured and five killed in the skirmish (Adams 1998:67–75). Televised images of the bodies of the US servicemen were broadcast by CNN; the shock to the US public resulted in them successfully pressuring the government into withdrawing the remaining troops from Somalia (Adams 1998:74–75; Taylor 2002:24). The US government and public were completely unprepared for this type of attack; the incident and the withdrawal also resulted in negative media towards the US government, military command, and policies (Adams 1998:75–77).

What follows is an analysis of the incident using the IW Life Cycle Model:

- **Context:** United States servicemen had been involved in a skirmish infamously known as the 'Black Hawk Down' incident. Mohammed Farah Aidid (the Somali warlord) wished to drive US forces out of Somalia; his target was the US public.
- **Attack:** The bodies of US servicemen killed in the skirmish were dragged in front of CNN cameras to psychologically shock the US public (psychological operations); the mass media was the 'weapon' of choice. The planning was to affect the morale, will and society of the US public.
- **Defence:** This type of attack came as a surprise; consequently there was no defence. Once the images were released, there was nothing the United States of America could do to defend themselves from this attack. There was a reactive defence in terms of locating and extracting any servicemen held hostage before the withdrawal.
- **Consequences and reaction:** The US public were horrified by the images; and put pressure on the US government to withdraw from Somalia. This was eventually done; however, there was continuing negative media and reactions by the US public.
- **Influence on context:** The Somali warlord was able to effectively defeat the US forces through the strategic use of the media resulting in the withdrawal of the troops; the existing context in Somalia was therefore completely altered as well as the political context in the US.

Wikileaks incidents – cyber-based conflict

This is the most complex of the case studies as it comprises of a number of 'sub-incidents', where sets of compromised documents were released online by the Wikileaks, eventually provoking a retaliation by the US government, which in turn resulted in a series of cyber-based attacks and counter-attacks by the supporters of the different 'factions'. Whilst this is by no means a cyber-war between nation states, it can be seen as a cyber-conflict and has the characteristics that a major cyber-war may exhibit in terms of the action-reaction cycle of the main protagonists and their supporters.

Wikileaks attempts to make available information that is not usually accessible to the public, primarily on occurrences or activities that may be considered irregular, claiming to be advocating for greater transparency. Throughout the course of the year, there have been major releases of compromised documents that have targeted the US military and to some extent the government. Some of the releases received media attention from a number of media 'partners' across the world. The initial responses to the release of the war log documents only appeared to have been met with public condemnation and an internal investigation into the source of the leak; there did not appear to be any direct retaliation against Wikileaks. The release of the diplomatic cables was met by a far stronger reaction. The following is a chronological list of occurrences that contribute to this incident.

- In April 2010 a video of a US helicopter gunship firing on what turned out to be journalists was released (Bronstein 2010); however, there was debate around some claims that arose from the video (StrategyPage.com 2010a).
- In June 2010 a US intelligence analyst was arrested for releasing classified documents after a probe (Poulsen & Zetter 2010). He appears to have also taken the blame for later releases.
- In July 2010 Wikileaks released logs of the conflict in Afghanistan (Poulsen 2010).
- In October 2010 similar logs were released for the Iraq conflict (Stewart 2010).
- On 29 November 2010 Wikileaks released a series of diplomatic cables. A pro-US hacker conducted a DDoS attack against Wikileaks (Goodwins 2010).
- The US puts pressure to remove Wikileaks from the Internet domain registry, and block the financial accounts, notably PayPal, Visa, Mastercard, Amazon and a Swiss bank called Post Finance in a period from 04 to 08 December 2010. Most of the organisations do cancel the accounts and registrations (Walker 2010). Rape accusations also re-surfaced against Julian Assange and queries over some of Wikileaks finances are raised (Gilligan 2010).
- On 04 December 2010, the PayPal blog experiences a DDoS attack by a pro-Wikileaks group called Anonymous; on 06 December 2010 the main PayPal website and the website of the Swiss bank are attacked, and Anonymous's website is counterattacked (Walker 2010).
- On 07 December 2010 Anonymous attacks the website of Assange's prosecutors, EveryDNS (for delisting Wikileaks), a US Senate website, the lawyers of the rape accusers and the Swiss bank; there was a counter-attack against Anonymous which appears to be retaliation for the attack on the Senate website (Walker 2010).
- On 08 December 2010 Anonymous attacks the Mastercard, Visa and Paypal websites, the attack on the lawyer's website is ongoing, and Twitter disables Anonymous' account (Walker 2010).
- On the 09 December 2010 Amazon is attacked and the attack on PayPal continues; counter-attacks against Anonymous are also ongoing (Walker 2010).

The following is an application of the IW Life Cycle Model to the first iteration of the incident:

- **Context:** Wikileaks claims to promote transparency and may have been motivated to attempt to discredit the USA.

- **Attack:** Sensitive documents were obtained by an insider, breaching confidentiality of a sensitive intelligence network. Wikileaks release these documents in a number of batches, each release being publicised though the media and online; this appears to be a pseudo-psychological operation.
- **Defence and reaction:** The primary defence strategy appeared to be reactive. The initial response was to publicly denounce the releases. An internal investigation resulted in the arrest of the alleged source of the leak. The release of the diplomatic cables was met with a stronger reaction; a pro-US hacker conducted a DDoS attack against Wikileaks and a number of organisations were pressured into removing support for Wikileaks. These appear to be a combination of reactive and preventative measures.
- **Consequences and influence on context:** International society was impacted (and divided) in that a 'superpower' had been discredited and the source of the attacks was controversial; there is some support for both factions. The context became more politically heated and a number of vigilante groups became involved.

What follows is an application IW Life Cycle Model to the second iteration of the incident:

- **Context:** Wikileaks released a series of sensitive documents in an attempt to discredit the USA. Global opinion over the releases is divided. The USA attacks Wikileaks through diplomatic pressure and a vigilante group also targets Wikileaks.
- **Attack:** A vigilante hacker conducts a DDoS against Wikileaks to disrupt the ability to release the store of the diplomatic cables. The USA pressures various organisations to withdraw support from Wikileaks.
- **Defence:** Wikileaks reacted by trying to preserve the accessibility to the information; visitors were directed to the main website by the IP address; and many other websites that had managed to access the content made it available.
- **Consequences and influence on context:** The global community became more polarised into those who supported the USA and those who supported Wikileaks. Vigilantes began targeting organisations that submitted to US pressure and withdrew support and services from Wikileaks.

What follows is an application of the IW Life Cycle Model to the first iteration of the incident:

- **Context:** The USA reacted to the document releases by pressuring organisations to withdraw services and support of Wikileaks; and a vigilante had attacked the Wikileaks websites. As a result, a group of vigilante hackers counter-attacked the pro-USA hacker and the organisations that withdrew support.
- **Attack:** The vigilante hacker group known as Anonymous launched DDoS attacks against PayPal, Amazon, Visa, Mastercard, a Swiss bank and various other websites.
- **Defence:** The targeted organisations appear to have attempted to 'ride out' the DDoS attacks. The pro-US hacker counter-attacked Anonymous. Twitter disabled the Anonymous account.

- **Consequences and influence on context:** Many individuals were unable to use or access the websites targeted; this proved a source of frustration for them; this probably reduce support for the Anonymous group to some degree. A series of web-based DDoS attacks and counterattacks between pro-USA and pro-Wikileaks hackers resulted.

Summary

The IW Life Cycle Model was applied to five incidents of varying scale and with different focus areas that fall within information warfare. The model could describe each incident in sufficient detail (which is limited to the information available for the respective incident) for different functional areas of information warfare namely, (1) psychological operations, (2) network warfare, (3) electronic warfare and deception and (4) the Wikileaks incident that constitutes a number of functional areas. The model was capable of describing the incidents; and for larger and more complex incidents such as Wikileaks, was able to describe them through multiple iterations. The model therefore meets its objectives of being scalable, applicable to different functional areas, and providing both high-level and detailed descriptions of incidents.

Conclusion

Information warfare comprises a number of disciplines and the existing models that are used to describe incidents where information warfare tactics are employed are either specific to a discipline or of a high-level nature. The need for a standardised model of IW was identified. This paper proposes a scalable model that incorporates characteristics that are common amongst existing models; it was intended to exhibit both high-level and detailed concepts to accurately describe the life cycle of an information warfare incident. The objective of the model was to consolidate the various theories of which IW comprises into a single model. The proposed IW Life Cycle Model was applied to a number of historical and current incidents to illustrate its scalability and applicability to various disciplines. The model adequately described these incidents.

Acknowledgements

The first author has received grants from the South African Department of Defence and Armscor Ledger Program through the Cyber Defence Research Group at the Council for Scientific and Industrial Research, Defence, Peace, Safety and Security (CSIR-DPSS), and the University of KwaZulu-Natal for his PhD research, of which this paper forms part.

Authors' contributions

The first author provided the content as part of a PhD thesis. The second author is the PhD supervisor and provided fact checking and suggestions.

Author competing interests

The authors declare that they have no financial or personal relationship(s) which may have inappropriately influenced them in writing this paper.

References

Adams, J., 1998, *The next world war,* Arrow Books, London.

Armistead, L., 2010, *Information operations matters*, Potomac Books, Washington, DC.

Borden, A., 1999, 'What is information warfare?', in *Air & Space Power Journal*, viewed 02 July 2009, from http://www.airpower.maxwell.af.mil/airchronicles/cc/borden.html

Brazzoli, M. S., 2007, 'Future Prospects of Information Warfare and Particularly Psychological Operations', in L. le Roux (ed.), *South African Army Vision 2020*, pp. 217–232, Institute for Security Studies, Pretoria.

Bronstein, P., 2010, *The Wikileaks incident: how social media has changed warfare coverage*, The Huffington Post, viewed 07 April 2010, from: http://www.huffingtonpost.com/phil-bronstein/the-wikileaks-incident-ho_b_527788.html

Chatterji, S.K., 2008, 'An Overview of Information Operations in the Indian Army', *IOSphere,* special edition, 10–14.

Cox, L.-V., 1997, *Planning for psychological operations: a proposal,* Air Command and Staff College, Maxwell Air Force Base, Montgomery, Alabama.

Denning, D.E, 1999, *Information warfare and security,* Addison-Wesely, Boston, MA.

Germain, J.M., 2008, *The art of cyber warfare, part 1: the digital battlefield,* TechNewsWorld, viewed 01 September 2009, from http://www.technewsworld.com/story/The-Art-of-Cyber-Warfare-Part-1-The-Digital-Battlefield-62779.html

Gilligan, A., 2010, 'Now Wikileaks suffers its own leaks', in *The Telegraph*, viewed 13 December 2010, from http://www.telegraph.co.uk/news/worldnews/wikileaks/8196946/Now-Wikileaks-suffers-its-own-leaks.html

Goodwins, R., 2010, *Wikileaks shows US cyber intelligence at work, gets DDoS attack,* ZDNET, viewed 29 November 2010, from http://www.zdnet.co.uk/blogs/mixed-signals-10000051/wikileaks-shows-us-cyber-intelligence-at-work-gets-ddos-attack-10021175/

Hutchinson, B. & Warren, M., 2001, *Information warfare: corporate attack and defense in a digital world*, Butterworth Heinemann, Oxford/Auckland.

Kopp, C., 2000, 'A Fundamental Paradigm of Infowar', *Systems*, 31–38.

Landler, M. & Markoff, J., 2007, 'Digital fears emerge after data siege in estonia', in *The New York Times Online*, viewed 14 April 2010, from http://www.nytimes.com/2007/05/29/technology/29estonia.html?_r=1

Poulsen, K., 2010, *Wikileaks Releases Stunning Afghan War Logs - Is Iraq Next?,* Wired.com Threatlevel, viewed 26 July 2010, from http://www.wired.com/threatlevel/2010/07/wikileaks-afghan/

Poulsen, K. & Zetter, K., 2010, *U.S. intelligence analyst arrested in Wikileaks video probe*, Wired.com Threatlevel, viewed 07 June 2010, from http://www.wired.com/threatlevel/2010/06/leak/

Ramluckan, T., & van Niekerk, B., 2009, 'The Terrorism/Mass Media Symbiosys', *Journal of Information Warfare* 8(2), 1–12.

Rolski, T., 2007, 'Estonia: ground zero for World's first cyber war', in *ABC News*, viewed 23 September 2009, from http://abcnews.go.com/print?id=3184122

Sikwane, B., 2010, 'The art of hide and seek in warfare', in *Aardvark AOC*, viewed 29 December 2010, from http://aardvarkaoc.co.za/index_files/Page316.htm

Stewart, P., 2010, 'Pentagon braces for huge wikileaks dump on Iraq war', in *Yahoo News*, viewed 18 October 2010, from http://news.yahoo.com/s/nm/us_usa_iraq_leaks

StrategyPage.com, 2010a, *What was not said*, viewed 12 April 2010, from http://www.strategypage.com/htmw/htiw/articles/20100411.aspx

StrategyPage.com, 2010b, *The NATO cyber war agreement*, viewed 03 May 2010, from http://www.strategypage.com/htmw/htiw/articles/20100501.aspx

Taylor, P.M., 2002, 'Perception Management and the "War" Against Terrorism', *Journal of Information Warfare* 1(3), 16–29.

United States Air Force, 1998, *Information Operations*, (Air Force Doctrine Document 2–5), United States Air Force, Washington, DC.

Van Niekerk, B. & Maharaj, M.S., (in press), 'Relevance of Information Warfare Models to Critical Infrastructure Protection,' *Scientia Militaria.*

Veerasamy, N. & Eloff, J., 2008, 'Understanding the Elementary Considerations in a Network Warfare Environment: An Introductory Framework', in *Proceedings of the Workshop on ICT uses in Warfare and the Safegarding of Peace*, pp. 95–108, CSIR, Pretoria.

Ventre, D., 2009, *Information warfare*, ISTE, London, UK.

Walker, R., 2010, *A brief history of operation payback*, Salon.com, viewed 21 December 2010, from http://mobile.salon.com/news/feature/2010/12/09/Waltz, E., 1998, *Information warfare: principles and operations*, Artech House, Boston/London.

Wik, M.W., 2002, 'Revolution in Information Affairs: Tactical and Strategic Implications of Information Warfare and Information Operations', in A. Jones, G.L. Kovacich & P.G. Luzwick (eds.), *Global information warfare*, pp. 579–628, Auerbach Publications, Boca Raton/London/New York.

21

The role of process analysis and expert consultation in implementing an electronic medical record solution for multidrug-resistant tuberculosis

Authors:
Harsha Desai[1]
Rubeshan Perumal[2]
Rosemary Quiling[3]
Yashik Singh[4]

Affiliations:
[1]Department of Health Informatics, School of Nursing and Public Health, University of KwaZulu-Natal, South Africa

[2]Centre for the AIDS Programme of Research in South Africa (CAPRISA), University of KwaZulu-Natal, South Africa

[3]Discipline of Information Systems & Technology, School of Management, IT & Governance, College of Law & Management Studies, University of KwaZulu-Natal, Durban, South Africa

[4]Department of Telehealth, School of Nursing and Public Health, University of KwaZulu-Natal, Durban, South Africa

Correspondence to:
Rubeshan Perumal

Email:
rubeshanperumal@gmail.com

Postal address:
Centre for the AIDS Programme of Research in South Africa (CAPRISA), University of KwaZulu-Natal, Durban 4000, South Africa

In the title column on page 1, the names of two contributing authors to this article have been erroneously omitted. In addition, the order of the listed authors of this article has also been rearranged. The correct order list, affiliations, and authors' contributions of the article is provided below:

Authors:
Harsha Desai[1]
Rubeshan Perumal[2]
Rosemary Quiling[3]
Yashik Singh[4]

Affiliations:
[1]Department of Health Informatics, School of Nursing and Public Health, University of KwaZulu-Natal, South Africa

[2]Centre for the AIDS Programme of Research in South Africa (CAPRISA), University of KwaZulu-Natal, South Africa

[3]Discipline of Information Systems & Technology, School of Management, IT & Governance, College of Law & Management Studies, University of KwaZulu-Natal, Durban, South Africa

[4]Department of Telehealth, School of Nursing and Public Health, University of KwaZulu-Natal, Durban, South Africa

Authors' contributions:

R.P. (University of KwaZulu-Natal) and H.D. (University of KwaZulu-Natal) developed the concept for the study and conducted the process analysis. H.D. conducted the Delphi study. H.D. and R.P. analysed the data from both study phases, and contributed to the writing of this manuscript. R.Q. (University of KwaZulu-Natal) and Y.S. (University of KwaZulu-Natal) guided the design and write-up of the study.

in 2012), and is the only country with a growing incidence of TB (currently estimated at 1 new case per 100 persons) (WHO 2013). The total cost for treating MDR-TB is approximately 30 times more than that of drug-sensitive TB, and diverts resources away from managing a national TB programme (Tupasi *et al.* 2006; Resch *et al.* 2006; Uplekar & Lonnroth 2007). The South African National TB Control Programme provides local guidelines for the management of drug resistant tuberculosis, which is based on WHO recommendations. The current cure rate for MDR-TB in most developing countries is between 30–50%, and the second line drugs used to treat MDR-TB are poorly understood, difficult to administer, and have poor side effect profiles (Pooran *et al.* 2013; Resch *et al.* 2006; Tupasi *et al.* 2006; Uplekar & Lonnroth 2007). Whilst the initial response to the MDR-TB epidemic in South Africa mirrored the World Health Organisation guidelines in the provision of centralised inpatient care, the high burden of disease in this country rapidly made centralised care unsustainable. As an alternative to centralised care, KwaZulu-Natal has moved toward a decentralised model of care, with comparable outcomes (Loveday *et al.* 2012). Whilst tuberculosis is a curable infectious disease, successful treatment outcomes require both patient adherence and a functional health system. Health system factors have been demonstrated to significantly impact treatment outcomes, and may contribute to avoidable negative clinical outcomes (Loveday *et al.* 2008). Therefore, there exists the potential to improve how multidrug-resistant tuberculosis (MDR-TB) is diagnosed and treated, as a result of employing a process engineering intervention built into an electronic medical record system could be significant (Fraser *et al.* 2006). As a key component of the global public health response to MDR-TB, the WHO has recommended a complete migration to electronic data collection by 2015 (WHO 2013). In light of decentralised care, this would require a comprehensive electronic medical record system that is able to satisfy the data recording purposes of public health authorities as well as the clinical and operational needs of patients and their health care providers. The complexity of such an electronic medical record (EMR) system will require the collaboration of a number of key stakeholders, and specifically an iterative relationship between designers of the system and the end-users (Allen *et al.* 2007; Ammenwerth, Iller & Mahler 2006; Blaya, Holt & Fraser 2008; Clifford *et al.* 2008; Elske, Carola & Mahler 2006; Fraser *et al.* 2006; Gerntholtz, Van Heerden & Vine 2007).

Little research is available for healthcare process management both in South Africa and other developing countries. South African health care processes have been described as 'fundamentally broken' and, thus, research in this area is much needed (Gerntholtz, Van Heerden & Vine 2007). South Africa's boldest attempt to implement an EMR solution across all government hospitals in Limpopo failed in 1998. Healthcare workers were inadequately prepared and a lack of attention to the intent of processes and their unique application in South Africa appear to have played a role in this failure (Littlejohns, Wyatt & Garvican 2003).

Technology is a mechanism to enhance delivery; and one such technology is OpenMRS which has a specific module for management of MDR-TB programmes (Choi & Fraser n.d.; Seebregts *et al.* 2006). OpenMRS is one of the most widely used open source EMR solutions in Africa (Seebregts *et al.* 2006; Tierney *et al.* 2010). OpenMRS is designed using international standards (HL7, DICOM, and LOINC) for interfacing with other technologies and is designed for universal deployment. The OpenMRS MDR-TB module that is discussed in this study was developed to provide an intuitive 'front end' to support the treatment of MDR-TB for WHO sponsored projects. The module can be customised with some medium to high level computer skills for specific geographical or treatment requirements (Choi & Fraser n.d.). To date OpenMRS has been implemented in over 25 countries, these being mostly low income, and supports HIV and TB programmes. The OpenMRS MDR-TB module may be used as an electronic medical record solution, but may, in addition, provide the electronic framework for providing process engineering support to the critical MDR-TB clinical programme. The combination of a grounded process analysis tool, together with expert consultation, is a novel method for designing and optimising an EMR solution. This study aims to describe the role of process engineering and iterative consultation in shaping an EMR solution (OpenMRS) in the South African MDR-TB programme.

Methods

The study employed a qualitative two phase design. The first phase focused on the creation of process models based on the South African clinical guidelines and the OpenMRS MDR-TB module using Business Process Modelling Notation (BPMN). The procedures in the guidelines were translated into business processes (National Department of Health 2009). The tutorial from the OpenMRS MDR-TB module together with an out-of-the-box installation were used to create process models that represent how the health information system should be used to manage the data of patient's diagnosed with and treated for MDR-TB.

A business process model visually illustrates the sequence of tasks completed to achieve the organisations objective. Each task is detailed in a rectangular shape, starting with a verb to focus on the action taken. In order to achieve both a big picture and a detailed view of processes a process is divided into sub-processes. Each sub-process is then reconfigured into a process map. The process rules are represented by 'gateways' (a diamond shape symbol). The process is contained by a start point and end point marked by circle shapes at either end of the process. The starting point indicates the trigger that sets off the process and the end points indicates the attainment of the organisation's objective. BPMN is a well-used technique for illustrating process models in a simple and easily understandable manner. The process goal for each process is determined based on the understanding of the objective of the guideline. The process goal is used to evaluate whether or not each task in the process is contributing to the process goal. The process model and analysis was grounded in the

FITT (fit between individual task and technology) theoretical framework (Elske, Carola & Mahler 2006). This model explicitly looks at three dimensions and the relationship between each:

1. user and technology
2. task and technology
3. user and task.

Whilst the focus of the methodology is on the task and the technology fit, it aims to also consider the implications for users in terms of their fulfilment of tasks and use of technology.

The second phase of the study involved a two round Delphi study where experts in the clinical management of MDR-TB in South Africa, or the implementation of OpenMRS modules, were surveyed to assess the process analysis findings and to offer insights for the future design of EMR solutions in MDR-TB management. These experts were identified by creating a list of authors from the literature review conducted, and assessing their potential involvement based on the following criteria:

1. Published research related to OpenMRS deployment in Africa or South Africa in the past five years.
2. Member of the OpenMRS Implementers' Community for the past three years.
3. Published research related to TB or MDR-TB from a South African perspective in the past five years.
4. Currently or previously a clinician.
5. Availability of an email address.

An invitation was sent to 28 participants (11 Clinicians and 16 OpenMRS implementers) identified to participate in the study, requesting their participation. Seven participants responded, confirming their participation in the study within a two-week period (three clinicians and four OpenMRS implementers). Five of the seven participants who responded within two weeks of the request provided responses to the first and second rounds of the Delphi study. With the objectives of the study in mind, the collated responses from the first round were used to create questions for the second round. As no new responses arose in round two there was no need to conduct a third round. The opinions from the experts were analysed according to emergent themes. Thematic content analysis was used to determine the points of contention and consensus with regard to the value of process engineering when using OpenMRS to manage patient medical data. All analyses were collated and graphically presented using Microsoft Excel® and Microsoft Visio® respectively. Ethical approval was obtained from the University of KwaZulu-Natal Biomedical Research Ethics Committee (Ref: BE036/11).

Results

A detailed process model for the South African National Tuberculosis Control Programme reflects five core activities enclosed between the start and end points (Figure 1). The results of a detailed process analysis by core activity highlight various inefficiencies and gaps (Table 1). Some of these problems are related to the lack of integration of upstream processes with downstream processes. Break points refer to an activity with hand-offs between departments, people, systems or functions. With the 54 break points that were identified, steps need to be put in place to ensure that the transition at the break points are smooth to support optimal flow of the process. The second metric, Business Rules, directs an individual or machine through a different path depending on the condition that is met. During the analysis the applicability of the business rules were questioned and found to be relevant. The Gaps identified focused on identifying where the out-of-the-box instance of OpenMRS did not meet specific requirements in the South African context. This means that some customisation will be required. The Risks identified highlight potential weaknesses in the process. Finally the waste identified in the process highlighted the potential opportunities to streamline the process.

In the Delphi study five participants responded to both rounds in the study, and profiled themselves as spending their time doing research, implementing EMR solutions and performing clinical activities. All three clinicians in the group had knowledge of the South African clinical guidelines. Only one participant refrained from indicating their level of experience with EMR solutions, whilst two of the participants expressed 'some experience' and another two expressed a 'great deal of experience'. With the exception of the one participant who practices process analysis on a daily basis, all other participants had limited exposure to process analysis. One of the clinicians expressed an interest to learn process analysis. The majority (four out of five) of the participants regarded the alignment of process, technology and individual as 'important'. The participants' responses affirm the underlying principle of the FITT framework that has been used as a theoretical framework for the study (Chan & Kaufman 2010; Elske, Carola & Mahler 2006; Tsiknakis & Kouroubali 2009a; Tsiknakis & Kouroubali 2009b). On reviewing the participants' statements, a pattern emerged, that 80% of statements were related to either 'Process', 'Individual', or 'Technology'. The participants tended to use the terms from the FITT framework that were used in the questions. The remaining statements were then

TABLE 1: Summary of a process model of OpenMRS and the National tuberculosis guidelines.

Process analytics	Total instances of analytics identified
Break points: Errors that can occur during hand-offs between departments, people, systems and functions.	54
Business rules: Directions for healthcare workers or machines which are ambiguous or unnecessary.	2
Gaps: Functions or steps required by the clinical guideline but which cannot be captured or supported by OpenMRS.	12
Moments of truth: The interaction between the patient and the health care facility.	9
Risks: Errors that may occur that could prevent the flow of the process from successfully reaching its objective.	3
Wastes: The aversion of activities in the process that results in avoidable inefficiencies.	5

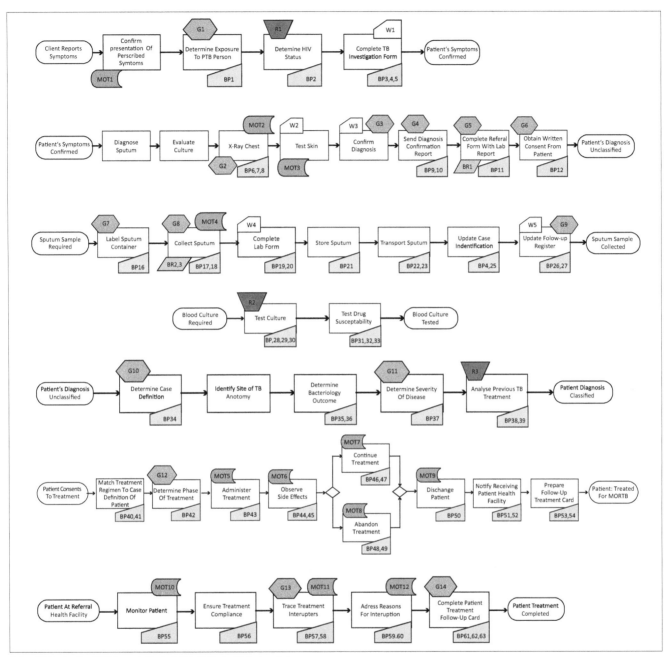

G, Gap; BP, Break point; MOT, Moment of truts; R, Risk; W, Waste; BR, Business Rule

FIGURE 1: Detailed process model for diagnosis and treatment of TB with process analytics at points of disjunction between the clinical guideline and OpenMRS.

TABLE 2: Contributions of process analytics by process analysis and by Delphi technique.

Contributions	Process analysis	Delphi study		
		Total	Clinical respondents	Medical informatics
Gaps	12	5	4	1
Process improvements	4	5	4	1
Synergies	-	11	-	-
Risks	7	3	2	1

reviewed to identify common themes, and two additional themes, namely 'collaboration' and 'capacity', were added. This illustrated that participants contributed new ideas to the process analysis as opposed to simply validating what they were presented with. Overall, the Delphi study demonstrated support for and affirmation of the process analysis findings (Table 2).

A summary of gaps identified in the process analysis is shown in Table 3. Delphi participants identified five unique gaps after final coding which were not identified in the process analysis phase (displayed in bold). This finding demonstrates the synergistic potential of process analysis, with an iterative consultation process, with stakeholders.

Wastes were stated as improvements, gaps or risks in the second round of the Delphi study and tested for agreement with the participants. In agreement with existing research, their responses show that two of the greatest inefficiencies in current non-EMR settings are the redundant capture of information and laborious data analysis (Clifford *et al.* 2008; Blaya, Holt & Fraser 2008; Gerntholtz *et al.* 2007; Vine 2007). As noted by a participant, it is important for an EMR solution to be customisable, 'The reality of the operational set up is that the care process is highly fluid'. Understanding the gap between the technology and the process is a critical exercise that must be conducted, to ensure that there are limited work-a-rounds once the hospital information system (HIS) implementation is completed. The gap analysis indicates there is a high concentration of gaps between the process and the technology.

A participant, who is an international OpenMRS implementer, highlighted that nine of the thirteen gaps between task and technology could be addressed by customisations. OpenMRS has been customised and integrated with other applications such as Chasqui in Peru, FrontlineSMS in Ghana and AMPATH in clinics in sub-Saharan Africa, and Google maps in Pakistan (Tierney *et al.* 2010; Staccini *et al.* 2000; Seerbregts *et al.* 2009; Seebregts *et al.* 2006; Frasier, May & Wanchoo 2008; Choi & Fraser n.d.; Blaya *et al.* 2007; Allen *et al.* 2007). Of the nine improvements proposed by participants, five of these

related to technology improvements (Figure 2). The figure further illustrates that the majority of the respondents agreed with the need for technology related improvements, with the exception of increased access to GeneXpert diagnostic technology. This was possibly because the South African Department of Health had announced its plans for a national roll-out of the technology just prior to this study, making such an improvement unnecessary. The technology has since been widely rolled out and enjoys the growing support of the medical and scientific community (Theron *et al.* 2013).

Given the growing use of technologies to support clinical decision making, it was not surprising that participants, particularly clinicians, made recommendations with regard to the need to integrate specialised technologies (Andersson, Hallberg & Timpka 2003; Isern & Moreno 2008; Terazzi *et al.* 1998). This is reinforced by the outcome in which the majority of participants responded positively to the technology improvement in OpenMRS regarding clinical decision making support to aid healthcare workers.

One of the greatest opportunities to enhance the OpenMRS system is to ensure that the processes that are supported by the system adequately provide relevant communication to stakeholders involved in the process. Quality improvement research highlights the need for effective communication amongst healthcare workers during the clinical care process, to support care co-ordination (Boston-Fleischhauer

TABLE 3: List of Gaps clustered according to themes.

Themes	Gap Identified
Gap between individual & technology	• The limited ability of healthcare workers to use computer technology to support clinical tasks.
Gap between capacity demand and capacity supply	• There are insufficient human resources available to support the clinical care of MDR-TB patients.
Gap between Technology & Process (based on out of the box OpenMRS MDR-TB module implementation)	• OpenMRS does not support the ability to track a sample group of patients.
	• There is limited integration of specialist technologies like Gene Expert to support the diagnosis process.
	• There is limited access to rapid and accurate diagnostic technologies.
	• OpenMRS does not support the ability to capture details about the exposure to TB unless taken in an unstructured textbox.
	• X-ray results can only be captured as part of a patient encounter and not as part of the MDR-TB diagnosis form within OpenMRS.
	• Lab results can only be captured once the diagnosis has been completed. This forces the healthcare worker to bridge the connection between the point at which the patient requires a test and when it is completed.
	• A disconnect occurs between the point at which the patient requires a test, and the test completion point, results in a record of the test that is only captured in OpenMRS after the test is completed. This results in the inability to capture the turn-around time of the lab results.
	• The system does not have the ability to send confirmation of the diagnosis to healthcare workers. This limits the speed at which healthcare workers can begin preparing the patient for treatment.
	• OpenMRS does not provide clinical protocols to instruct the healthcare worker on the procedure to collect sputum. This assumes that the healthcare worker has previous knowledge of the process.
	• OpenMRS does not allow the time the sputum sample is collected to be recorded.
	• OpenMRS does not have the ability to track patients' status through the diagnosis process and, therefore, no report can be created listing all patients who are still awaiting confirmation of diagnosis. This also results in delays in responding to queries on a patient's diagnosis status.
	• OpenMRS does not have the ability to capture the standardised case definition and allow healthcare providers to select the relevant option.
	• OpenMRS does not have the ability to capture the severity of the disease. This is important for informing treatment dosage.
	• OpenMRS does not allow for the phase of the treatment to be captured.
	• OpenMRS does not support the capturing of treatment compliance or treatment interruption on the part of the patient.

Unique gaps identified by the Delphi study shown in bold.
MDR-TB, multidrug-resistant tuberculosis.

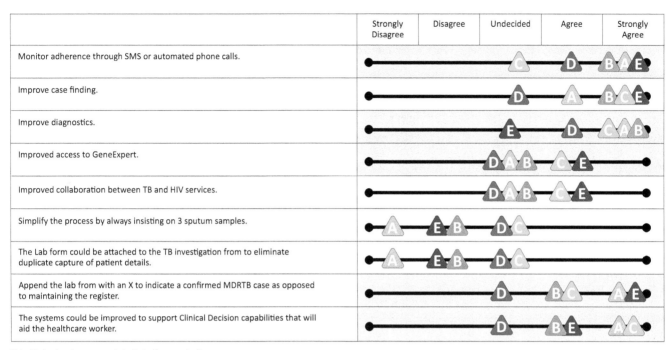

	Strongly Disagree	Disagree	Undecided	Agree	Strongly Agree
Monitor adherence through SMS or automated phone calls.			C	D	B A E
Improve case finding.			D	A	B C E
Improve diagnostics.			E	D	C A B
Improved access to GeneExpert.		D A B	C E		
Improved collaboration between TB and HIV services.		D A B	C E		
Simplify the process by always insisting on 3 sputum samples.	A	E B	D C		
The Lab form could be attached to the TB investigation from to eliminate duplicate capture of patient details.	A	E B	D C		
Append the lab from with an X to indicate a confirmed MDRTB case as opposed to maintaining the register.			D	B C	A E
The systems could be improved to support Clinical Decision capabilities that will aid the healthcare worker.			D	B E	A C

Note: Technology improvements indicated by grey shading.
FIGURE 2: Improvements identified and rated by participants.

2008; Taneva *et al.* 2010). Not all participants responded to statements relating to the need for the system to support communication, and responses varied widely. An individual's perspective on this issue may be dependent on the environment in which the participant operates.

The participants with OpenMRS implementation experience also contributed to the synergies identified, indicating that electronic monitoring systems could support patient treatment adherence. This is not surprising, as OpenMRS implementations in other African countries have already encountered such challenges and have worked on solutions, such as SMS reminders (Allen *et al.* 2007; Choi & Fraser n.d.).

Whilst there are numerous gaps highlighted in the out-of-the-box installation of the OpenMRS MDR-TB module, it does help to mitigate various identified risks and eliminate waste, making the diagnosis and treatment process of MDR-TB more efficient (see Table 1). However, it would be better if the gaps identified in the study were closed before an implementation is carried out. This might have been possible if the implementation was preceded by a process analysis with iterative consultation, as described in this study.

Five improvement opportunities were identified by participants, four of which were from a clinical perspective. One of the suggested process improvements (Simplify the process by always insisting on 3 sputum samples) to address the perceived waste in the system was not supported by the experts, possibly because new modalities of diagnosis, such as GeneXpert, no longer require multiple first contact sputum specimens.

According to the second round of the Delphi study the most frequently experienced risks were:

- Paper records that are more likely to be lost or corrupted than electronic records
- Long laboratory turn-around times that result in delayed treatment
- Unclear timing of integration of antiretroviral therapy
- Dependency on the patient providing the correct information
- The limited linkage of health records between health facilities
- Suboptimal patient adherence.

All of these risks may have a negative impact on clinical decisions made by providers.

Ten synergies were identified by four participants, three of whom are MDR-TB clinicians. One of the main themes that were stressed by participants is the collaboration of treatment facilities for HIV positive and MDR-TB patients. Some of the synergies that participants disagreed on were: electronic monitoring systems that do not require specialised data capturers, and separate clinic notes and registers and provision of isoniazid prophylaxis for all immune-compromised individuals, especially post-TB treatment. In contrast to the fact that most participants disagreed with the synergy to provide isoniazid prophylaxis to all immune-compromised individuals, especially post-TB treatment, all participants agreed with the comprehensive treatment of other opportunistic infections, including the provision of co-trimoxazole prophylaxis. The synergies that received the most agreement from participants were:

- Identification of delays, and the reasons for the delay, in initiating HIV treatment of MDR-TB patients. This is especially significant as recent data suggests that delayed initiation of treatment is a major challenge to the health system and is a significant contributor to morbidity and mortality in patients with MDR-TB (O'Donnell *et al.* 2009; Padayatchi *et al.* 2014).

- The provision of support to HIV and MDR-TB patients to adhere to their treatment programmes.
- One service provider focusing on treatment of both conditions.
- Ensuring that all TB facility attendees are offered an HIV test.

The synergies that received the most agreement from participants are supported by the growing support for the integration of TB and HIV programmes (Loveday & Zweigenthal 2011; Perumal, Padayatchi & Stiefvater 2009; Van Rie *et al.* 2013). Participants went so far as to suggest one service provider to support co-treatment, in keeping with the integration of TB and HIV care as a current major health systems priority (Loveday & Zweigenthal 2011; O'Donnell *et al.* 2009; Padayatchi *et al.* 2014; Perumal *et al.* 2009).

Discussion

The management of any medical condition is complex, and reflects the fluid interaction between the patient, healthcare provider, and the healthcare system. In the context of MDR-TB, an 'emerging' infectious disease entity, any attempt at introducing a meaningful electronic record solution must be mindful of the rapidly changing clinical practices. As new evidence emerges, clinical practices change to accrue the advantages of this new knowledge. An important example of this was the shift in the method of diagnosis of MDR-TB from a sputum culture based diagnosis, to a newer rapid diagnosis by nucleic acid amplification technology (Xpert technology).

In addition, new evidence which has demonstrated the substantial survival benefit, of integrating antiretroviral therapy early within MDR-TB treatment, would need rapid incorporation into an MDR-TB EMR solution that contributes to the 'process' of MDR-TB management (Loveday *et al.* 2012; O'Donnell *et al.* 2009; Padayatchi *et al.* 2014). The benefit of using an open-source EMR solution such as OpenMRS lies in the ability of a wide community of developers to be called upon to deal with gaps and the need for revising the existing version, as has been performed with the MDR-TB module in this setting. Whilst EMR implementers might attempt to remain abreast of clinical developments, regular iterative input from clinical experts may serve as a more pragmatic response to keeping an EMR both useful and relevant. The move from centralised care for MDR-TB patients to growing support for a decentralised model of care will further challenge an EMR solution for MDR-TB. Central services are well documented to be easier for the implementation of EMR solutions, whilst decentralised care, especially in rural, resource-constrained settings, presents significant challenges to the implementation of an EMR solution (Heeks 2006; Lapao *et al.* 2009; Littlejohns, Wyatt & Garvican 2003; Seebregts *et al.* 2006; Seerbregts *et al.* 2009; Tierney *et al.* 2010; Tsiknakis & Kouroubali 2009a). The responsiveness of a health informatics solution to such programmatic changes will be crucial for its sustainability, and will make iterative feedback (through methods such as the Delphi technique) essential to understand unique challenges that may emerge only once a programme is shifted to more rural and outlying settings. Clinical support for any EMR solution will only be possible if clinicians are in agreement that the EMR adds value to the process of MDR-TB management, and that the value added, in terms of existing advantages, matches its accuracy and relevance when placed in the context of prevailing clinical guidelines. This is the major potential benefit of including a process analysis approach to EMR design and development. Including stakeholders, particularly healthcare workers in an EMR system selection and design, may improve their openness to the technology and reduce resistance to change (Tierney *et al.* 2010).

In keeping with evidence from other settings, participants in this study identified the use of process analysis, in the development of clinical protocols, as the highest ranked advantage (Taneva *et al.* 2010). The second and third ranked advantages (The ability of healthcare workers to personally identify problems in the healthcare system, and the ability to identify operational health system factors which may negatively impact on clinical outcomes.) attested to the use of process engineering as a quality improvement tool. There is a growing trend in healthcare quality improvement programmes and research to promote healthcare workers to initiate improvement identification opportunities (Chassin *et al.* 2010; Martikainen, Korpela & Tiihonen 2014).

Conclusions

Process analysis and expert consultation may serve as important tools in the future design, implementation and monitoring of EMR solutions in a dynamic health care setting. Process analysis and expert consultation demonstrate good compatibility for providing insights to EMR implementation, and are complementary in their generation of information. The opportunity to utilise EMR solutions as a vehicle for enhancing programmatic function, by supporting clinical decision making and guiding processes, should be harnessed. This can be achieved through customisation in an expanding open development environment. Overall, the findings highlight the inefficiencies, risk and gaps in the current process and the need for an operational excellence intervention. The study demonstrated the value of process engineering with iterative expert consultation, toward developing a meaningful EMR solution consultation in a resource constrained, developing world context.

Acknowledgements

Competing interests

The authors declare that they have no financial or personal relationship(s) that may have inappropriately influenced them in writing this article.

Authors' contributions

R.P. (University of KwaZulu-Natal) and H.D. (University of KwaZulu-Natal) developed the concept for the study and conducted the process analysis. H.D. conducted the Delphi study. H.D. and R.P. analysed the data from both study phases, and contributed to the writing of this manuscript.

References

Allen, C., Jazayeri, D., Miranda, J., Biondich, P.G., Mamlin, B.W., Wolfe, B.A. *et al.*, 2007, 'Experience in implementing the OpenMRS medical record system to support HIV treatment in Rwanda', *Studies in Health Technology and Informatics* 129, 382–6.

Ammenwerth, E., Iller, C. & Mahler, C., 2006, 'IT-adoption and the interaction of task, technology and individuals: A fit framework and a case study', *BMC Medical Informatics Decision Making* 6, 3. http://dx.doi.org/10.1186/1472-6947-6-3

Andersson, A., Hallberg, N. & Timpka, T., 2003, 'A model for interpreting work and information management in process-oriented healthcare organisations', *International Journal of Medical Informatics* 72, 47–56. http://dx.doi.org/10.1016/j.ijmedinf.2003.09.001

Berg, M. & Toussaint, P., 2003, 'The mantra of modeling and the forgotten powers of paper: A sociotechnical view on the development of process-oriented ICT in health care', *International Journal of Medical Informatics* 69, 223–234. http://dx.doi.org/10.1016/S1386-5056(02)00178-8

Blaya, J., Holt, B. & Fraser, H.S., 2008, 'Evaluations of the Impact of eHealth Technologies in Developing Countries: A Systematic Review', *Working paper for Rockefeller eHealth Meeting*, Harvard-MIT Division of Health Sciences and Technology, Partners In Health, Division of Social Medicine and Health Inequalities, Cambridge, MA.

Blaya, J.A., Shin, S., Yagui, M.J., Yale, G., Suarez, C.Z., Asencios, L.L. *et al.*, 2007, 'A web-based laboratory information system to improve quality of care of tuberculosis patients in Peru: functional requirements, implementation and usage statistics', *BMC Medical Informatics Decision Making* 7, 33. http://dx.doi.org/10.1186/1472-6947-7-33

Blondal, K., 2007, 'Barriers to reaching the targets for tuberculosis control: multidrug-resistant tuberculosis', *Bull World Health Organzation* 85, 387–394.

Boston-Fleischhauer, C., 2008, 'Enhancing healthcare process design with human factors engineering and reliability science, part 2: Applying the knowledge to clinical documentation systems', *Journal of Nursing Administration* 38, 84–89. http://dx.doi.org/10.1097/01.NNA.0000295632.80345.3d

Chan, C.V. & Kaufman, D.R., 2010, 'A technology selection framework for supporting delivery of patient-oriented health interventions in developing countries', *Journal of Biomedical Informatics* 43, 300–306. http://dx.doi.org/10.1016/j.jbi.2009.09.006

Chassin, M.R., Loeb, J.M., Schmaltz, S.P. & Wachter, R.M., 2010, 'Accountability measures – using measurement to promote quality improvement', *New England Journal of Medicine* 363, 683–688. http://dx.doi.org/10.1056/NEJMsb1002320

Choi, S. & Fraser, H., n.d., *Developing Multidrug-resistant TB Systems Using OpenMRS*. Partner in Health, Harvard Medical school.

Clifford, G.D., Blaya, J.A., Hall-Clifford, R. & Fraser, H.S., 2008, 'Medical information systems: A foundation for healthcare technologies in developing countries', *BioMedical Engineering OnLine* 7.

Elske, A., Carola, I. & Mahler, C., 2006, 'IT - Adoption and the interaction of task, technology and individuals: a fit framework and a case study', *BMC Medical Informatics Decision Making* 6, 1472–6947.

Fraser, H.S., Blaya, J., Choi, S.S., Bonilla, C. & Jazayeri, D., 2006, 'Evaluating the impact and costs of deploying an electronic medical record system to support TB treatment in Peru', *AMIA Annual Symposium Proceedings*, 264–268.

Frasier, H., May, M.A. & Wanchoo, R., 2008, 'e-Health Rwanda Case Study', in *American Medical Informatics Association*, viewed 12 September 2014, from http://ehealth-connection.org/files/resources/Rwanda%20+%20Appendices.pdf

Gerntholtz, T., Van Heerden, M.V. & Vine, D.G., 2007, 'Electronic Medical Records – Why should you consider implementing an EMR?', *Continuing Medical Education* 25, 24–28.

Heeks, R., 2006, 'Health information systems: Failure, success and improvisation', *International Journal of Medical Informatics* 75, 125–137. http://dx.doi.org/10.1016/j.ijmedinf.2005.07.024

Isern, D. & Moreno, A., 2008, 'Computer-based execution of clinical guidelines: a review', *International Journal of Medical Informatics* 77, 787–808. http://dx.doi.org/10.1016/j.ijmedinf.2008.05.010

Lapao, L.V., Rebuge, A., Silva, M.M. & Gomes, R., 2009, 'ITIL Assessment in a healthcare environment: the role of IT governance at Hospital Sao Sebastiao', *Studies in Health Technology and Informatics* 150, 76–80.

Littlejohns, P., Wyatt, J.C. & Garvican, L., 2003, 'Evaluating computerised health information systems: Hard lessons still to be learn't', *Journal of Biomedical Informatics* 326, 860–865.

Loveday, M., Thomson, L., Chopra, M. & Ndlela, Z., 2008, 'A health systems assessment of the KwaZulu-Natal tuberculosis programme in the context of increasing drug resistance', *International Journal of Tuberculosis and Lung Disease* 12, 1042–1047.

Loveday, M., Wallengren, K., Voce, A., Margot, B., Reddy, T., Master, I., *et al.*, 2012, 'Comparing early treatment outcomes of MDR-TB in decentralised and centralised settings in KwaZulu-Natal, South Africa', *International Journal of Tuberculosis and Lung Disease* 16, 209–215. http://dx.doi.org/10.5588/ijtld.11.0401

Loveday, M. & Zweigenthal, V., 2011, 'TB and HIV integration: obstacles and possible solutions to implementation in South Africa', *Tropical Medicine & International Health* 16, 431–438. http://dx.doi.org/10.1111/j.1365-3156.2010.02721.x

Ludwicka, D.A. & Doucettea, J., 2009, 'Adopting electronic medical records in primary care: Lessons learned from health information systems implementation experience in seven countries', *International Journal of Medical Informatics* 78, 22–31. http://dx.doi.org/10.1016/j.ijmedinf.2008.06.005

Martikainen, S., Korpela, M. & Tiihonen, T., 2014, 'User participation in healthcare IT development: A developers' viewpoint in Finland', *International Journal of Medical Informatics* 83, 189–200. http://dx.doi.org/10.1016/j.ijmedinf.2013.12.003

National Department of Health, 2009, 'South African National Tuberculosis Guidelines', in HEALTH, Pretoria.

O'Donnell, M.R., Padayatchi, N., Master, I., Osburn, G., Robert, C. & Horsburgh, C.R., 2009, 'Improved Early Results for Patients with Extensively Drug Resistant Tuberculosis and HIV in South Africa', *International Journal Tuberculsosis Lung Disease* 13, 855–861.

Padayatchi, N., Abdool Karim, S.S., Naidoo, K., Grobler, A. & Friedland, G., 2014, 'Improved survival in multidrug-resistant tuberculosis patients receiving integrated tuberculosis and antiretroviral treatment in the SAPiT Trial', *International Journal of Tuberculosis and Lung Disease* 18, 147–154. http://dx.doi.org/10.5588/ijtld.13.0627

Perumal, R., Padayatchi, N. & Stiefvater, E., 2009, 'The whole is greater than the sum of the parts: recognising missed opportunities for an optimal response to the rapidly maturing TB-HIV co-epidemic in South Africa', *BMC Public Health* 9, 243. http://dx.doi.org/10.1186/1471-2458-9-243

Pooran, A., Pieterson, E., Davids, M., Theron, G. & Dheda, K., 2013, 'What is the cost of diagnosis and management of drug resistant tuberculosis in South Africa?', *PLoS One* 8, e54587. http://dx.doi.org/10.1371/journal.pone.0054587

Resch, S.C., Salomon, J.A., Murray, M. & Weinstein, M.C., 2006, 'Cost-effectiveness of treating multidrug-resistant tuberculosis', *PLoS Medicine* 3, e241. http://dx.doi.org/10.1371/journal.pmed.0030241

Seebregts, C., Mars, M., Fourie, C., Singh, Y. & Weyer, K., 2006, 'Inexpensive Open Source TB and HIV electronic medical record system (OpenMRS) in South Africa Collaborating Toward an EMR for Developing Countries', *Proceedings of the AMIA Symposium*. Washington DC. November 11–15.

Seebregts, C., Mamlin, B., Biondich, P., Fraser, H., Wolfe, B., Jazayeri, D., *et al.*, 2009, 'The OpenMRS implementers network', *International Journal of Medical Informatics* 78, 711–720. http://dx.doi.org/10.1016/j.ijmedinf.2008.09.005

Staccini, P., Joubert, M., Quaranta, J.F., Fieschi, D. & Fieschi, M., 2000, 'Integration of health care process analysis in the design of a clinical information system: applying to the blood transfusion process', *Proceedings of the AMIA Symposium* 824–828, California, November 4-8.

Taneva, S., Grote, G., Easty, A. & Plattner, B., 2010, 'Decoding the perioperative process breakdowns: a theoretical model and implications for system design', *International Journal of Medical Informatics* 79, 14–30. http://dx.doi.org/10.1016/j.ijmedinf.2009.10.001

Terazzi, A., Giordano, A. & Minuco, G., 1998, 'How can usability measurement affect the re-engineering process of clinical software procedures?', *International Journal of Medical Informatics* 52, 229–234. http://dx.doi.org/10.1016/S1386-5056(98)00141-5

Theron, G., Zijenah, L., Chanda, D., Clowes, P., Rachow, A., Lesosky, M. *et al.*, 2013, 'Feasibility, accuracy, and clinical effect of point-of-care Xpert MTB/RIF testing for tuberculosis in primary-care settings in Africa: a multicentre, randomised, controlled trial', *Lancet* 383, 424-435. http://dx.doi.org/10.1016/S0140-6736(13)62073-5

Tierney, W.M., Achieng, M., Baker, E., Bell, A., Biondich, P., Braitstein, P. *et al.*, 2010, 'Experience implementing electronic health records in three East African countries', *Studies in Health Technology and Informatics* 160, 371–375.

Tsiknakis, M. & Kouroubali, A., 2009a, 'Organizational factors affecting successful adoption of innovative eHealth services: a case study employing the FITT framework', *International Journal of Medical Informatics* 78, 39–52. http://dx.doi.org/10.1016/j.ijmedinf.2008.07.001

Tsiknakis, M. & Kouroubali, A., 2009b, 'Organizational factors affecting successful adoption of innovative eHealth services: A case study employing the FITT framework', *International Journal of Medical Informatics* 78, 39–52. http://dx.doi.org/10.1016/j.ijmedinf.2008.07.001

Tupasi, T.E., Gupta, R., Quelapio, M.I., Orillaza, R.B., Mira, N.R., Mangubat, N.V. *et al.*, 2006, 'Feasibility and cost-effectiveness of treating multidrug-resistant tuberculosis: a cohort study in the Philippines', *PLoS Medicine* 3, e352. http://dx.doi.org/10.1371/journal.pmed.0030352

Uplekar, M. & Lonnroth, K., 2007, 'MDR and XDR - the price of delaying engagement with all care providers for control of TB and TB/HIV', *Tropical Medicine & International Health* 12, 473–474. http://dx.doi.org/10.1097/01.qai.0000434954.65620.f3

Van Rie, A., Patel, M.R., Nana, M., Driessche, K.V., Tabala, M., Yotebieng, M. *et al.*, 2013, Integration and task-shifting for TB/HIV care and treatment in highly resource-scarce settings: one size may not fit all', *Journal of Acquired Immune Deficiency Syndromes* 65, e110–117. http://dx.doi.org/10.1097/01.qai.0000434954.65620.f3

Vine, D.G., 2007, 'Communicating between colleagues - pitfalls and practical solutions', *Continuing Medical Education* 25, 14–16.

World Health Organisation, 2013, 'Global Tuberculosis Report 2013', Geneva.

22

Convergence of functional areas in information operations

Author:
Brett van Niekerk[1]

Affiliation:
[1]School of Management, IT and Governance, University of KwaZulu-Natal, South Africa

Correspondence to:
Brett van Niekerk

Email:
brettvn@gmail.com

Postal address:
Private Bag X54001, Durban 4000, South Africa

Background: Contemporary technology and its rapid rise to a ubiquitous nature are affecting the way in which technology is used. This holds implications for military information operations and information warfare concepts as the previously separate functional areas are increasingly overlapping due to the increased convergence of information technology. Objective: The aim of the article is to illustrate the convergence of the functional areas of information operations through the use of reported examples and descriptive models.

Methods: A qualitative review and analysis of practitioner documents, academic publications, and other reports is conducted. The diverse views of this phenomenon are contrasted and discussed. The possible implications of the convergence and possible management techniques are proposed and discussed.

Results: There is strong opinion that the domains are not converging, however practice shows that there is an increasing overlap of operational considerations and organisational structure.

Conclusion: It is concluded that the domains are not converging, but the operations and management of the information operations functional areas may converge, and this has an impact across all functional areas that needs to be taken into consideration.

Introduction

Contemporary technology such as social media, the rapidly growing prevalence of wireless networking technology and the expanding capabilities of smart mobile devices result in what is termed as digital convergence. This has an impact on the military use of information technology, namely information operations (IO) and information warfare (IW), as the technology upon which the different functional areas are based converge and evolve. Through the use of examples and descriptive models, the convergence of the functional areas of information warfare and information operations is discussed.

An overview of information operations, information warfare and their constituent functional areas is provided, after which the existing relationship amongst the main functional areas is described through the use of generally accepted models of information technology and reviews of existing debates on the topic. The convergence through the prevalence of contemporary information technology is illustrated through the use of reported examples, and the implications of the convergence and management thereof are discussed.

Methodology

The convergence of information operations, in particular between electronic warfare and computer network operations, is being debated, mostly in practitioner forums. There is limited academic contribution to these debates, but it has been indicated that there is a need for academic models for information operations (Armistead 2010:108). This article aims to fill the gap by providing an academic perspective on the debate and by proposing an alternative model to those discussed previously.

The research takes an interpretivist stance in that the analysed documents that consider convergence in information operations are often authored by practitioners whose reasoning is not only intended to understand the concept but to actively participate in defining it. The approach taken is inductive, seeking to develop theory on the convergence amongst the functional areas in information operations. A qualitative document analysis of reports and examples, combined with logical argument, is used to derive on-going convergence and the potential impact thereof. Rouse and Dick (1994:51) illustrate the importance of qualitative research for information systems '... to capture holistic real-world answers to real-world problems in a way that is not possible in a quantitative context'. Publication databases and search engines were used to identify academic and practitioner publications and documents which consider the topics of interest. Search engines were used to identify relevant news reports that illustrate the existence of the concepts under discussion. A total of 11 academic or practitioner publications and 18 news reports were identified. All of these are considered in the article.

Functional areas in information operations

This section describes the various functional areas of information operations. The definition of IO and IW varies by country and organisation. Usually this reflects the specific strategy or focus that is employed. For this paper, two definitions will be considered. Denning (1999) defines IW as the following:

> … offensive and defensive operations against information resources of a 'win-lose' nature. It is conducted because information resources have value to people. Offensive operations aim to increase this value for the offence while decreasing it for the defence. Defensive operations seek to counter potential losses in value. (p. 21)

Brazzoli (2007) considers IW to be as follows:

> All actions taken to defend the military's information-based processes, information systems and communications networks and to destroy, neutralise or exploit the enemy's similar capabilities within the physical, information and cognitive domains. (p. 219)

These definitions highlight the value of information and that certain activities seek to change or maintain the current value or status of the information through activities relating to information assets and related infrastructure and systems. The notion of different domains is also raised: people or psychological, virtual and physical aspects of information. Whilst the military aspect is emphasised, Cronin and Crawford (1999) indicate that information operations can be applied to non-military situations, supporting the views considering information operations as an extension of IW to non-conflict scenarios (such as peacetime and periods of increased competition).

Computer network operations (also known as cyber-warfare) focus on computer networks and the Internet. It comprises of computer network exploitation (intelligence gathering), computer network attack, computer network defence and computer network support. In some instances, this is extended to include the protection of critical infrastructure from attacks through computer networks (Brazzoli 2007:221; Van Niekerk 2011:39–40). This functional area is the newest functional area and is yet to be fully established.

Electronic warfare (EW) focuses on the electromagnetic spectrum, comprising of electronic protection, electronic support and electronic attack. This most commonly includes the jamming, detection and interception of signals (Joint Chiefs of Staff 1998:II–5).

Psychological operations (PSYOP) are actions taken to influence a population's perceptions, attitudes and behaviour (Brazzoli 2007:221). PSYOP can be considered to be limited to military operational areas whereas strategic communication and propaganda can be considered to be of a larger scale, aimed at national or international audiences ranging from competition to conflict scenarios.

Other notable areas deal with intelligence gathering, command and control and the network support to operations and decision-making. It also includes data and audio and imagery communication via wired and wireless networks and infrastructure (Brazzoli 2007:221). This results in a shift from the traditional platform-centric operations and command and control to the network-centric form where information can be shared amongst platforms so that everyone has access to the same information. The intelligence process of gathering, analysing and disseminating data and information to support the decision-making process (command and control) is therefore key. Offensive operations attempt to disrupt these capabilities of the adversary, and defensive operations seek to maintain these capabilities in allied and own forces (Brazzoli 2007:221).

Porche et al. (2013:25–28) indicate that there are problems with the current definition and construction of IO: There is a lack of common vision ranging from too focussed to too broad. Many functional areas are treated as compartmentalised (Porche et al. 2013:24), and there is no explanation as to how it will act as a co-ordinating function or as to the relationships amongst the different functional areas. The next section describes the relationships between different functional areas of IO through the use of examples and positions advocated in documents.

Relationships amongst functional areas

There has been much debate regarding the relationship between EW, cyber-warfare and computer network operations and the implications of the various forms of terminology. Smith and Knight (2005:53) apply EW concepts to network security. This indicates a number of parallels between EW and cyber-warfare such as jamming and denial-of-service (DoS) or flares and honeypots.

A report by the US Government Accountability Office indicates that the two domains should be considered as separate (Chabrow 2012). Knowles (2013:48) proposes that cyber-space is a man-made physical environment, including telecommunication, data, networks and processors. In contrast, the electromagnetic spectrum is natural. Wireless communication is seen as the human exploitation of an existing natural space whereas cyber-space is a purely man-made construct. However, it can be argued that the physical components of the telecommunication and data networks that form cyber-space are based upon guided or radiated electromagnetic signals and therefore part of the electromagnetic spectrum (Clifford 2011:41; Hahn 2010: 44–46). Clifford (2011:41) argues that it is incorrect to say that cyber-space and the electromagnetic spectrum are equivalent due to the fact that they are based on similar physics. Some of the discussion revolves around terminology: Borque (2008:30–40) discusses whether cyber-operations are a combination of EW and computer network operations and concludes that EW and cyber-operations are separate. Cloud (2007:10–12) takes the contradictory view that cyber-operations entail a broader domain and include the electromagnetic spectrum, indicating that EW is a subset of cyber-operations.

The use of the psychological and cyber-domains is also related. The concept of hacktivism can be considered a combination of two areas: Activism can be seen as a form of psychological operation, and hactivism combines it with cyber-warfare concepts. Therefore website defacement can be described as cyber-enabled PSYOP. In some instances, the cyber-attack is meant to create the psychological impact such as the tactics used by the group Anonymous. The attack on the website of the South African Police Service was a cyber-attack with the intent to cause a psychological impact. It is reported that sensitive information on whistle-blowers was publicly released and that the attackers claimed that it was in retaliation for slow investigations in the Marikana mine shooting (Tubbs 2013). Anonymous Africa targeted a number of websites in Zimbabwe and South Africa with DoS attacks in protest against the Zimbabwean Government (Alfreds 2013; Daily News Correspondent 2013). There are reports of Israel hacking into phone voicemail systems to leave messages (StrategyPage.com 2009). This can be seen as an example of cyber-delivered PSYOP. There is also a possible relationship with EW and PSYOP in that radio or television broadcasts could be jammed to prevent them from being used to incite violence as happened in Rwanda (Van Niekerk & Maharaj 2009:6).

A number of espionage operations have been conducted over the Internet. These are cyber-attacks based on malicious, code-infecting targeted systems which then copy files onto a server from where the attackers can retrieve them. Major attacks of this type are the GhostNet cyber-espionage in 2009 and Red October, discovered in 2013 after an estimated five years of operation (Higgins 2013; Information Warfare Monitor 2009). In 2013, details surfaced of data-collection activities by US intelligence agencies that were monitoring telecommunications meta-data and online communications (Greenwald & MacAskill 2013). However the most recognised case is that of Wikileaks, a website which posts information from whistle-blowers online. The major releases which created both support and condemnation of the website internationally were the series of releases of US military information

BOX 1: Relationship of IW Areas to the OSI Model and IP Layers

OSI Layers	IP Layers	Functional Area
Application		PSYOPs, C2W
Presentation	Application	
Session		Network Warfare
Transport	Transport	
Network	Network	
Data-link	Data-link	
Physical	Physical	Electronic Warfare

TABLE 1: Proposed Layer Model for IW.

Layer	Functional area
Utility	C2W, PSYOPs
Grey area	
Connection	Network warfare
Grey area	
Access (wired and wireless)	Electronic warfare

Source: Maasdorp, F. & Du Plessis, W., 2012, 'Using a layered model to place EW in context within the informationsphere', *Proceedings of the 4th Workshop on ICT Uses in Warfare and the Safeguarding of Peace 2012 (IWSP 2012)*, 16 August 2012, Sandton, pp. 29–33.

and diplomatic cables (Gragido & Pirc 2011:193–195; Van Niekerk & Maharaj 2011:7–8). These incidents indicate a strong relationship between intelligence, counter-intelligence and cyber-space.

As EW targets primarily radiate the use of the EMS (but can conceivably have an effect on guided transmissions as directed-energy) and are concerned with the modulation and frequency of these transmissions, it is applicable to the physical layer of the OSI model and may extend to the data-link layer. As cyber-space is the interconnection of systems and networking, it can be considered to extend from the data-link layer to the presentation layer, and in some cases, it overlaps with the application layer. Other areas, such as PSYOP and command and control, occur at the application layer, as these are ultimately end-user functions where the key aspect is their presentation of information. The functional areas can similarly be mapped to the Internet Protocol (IP) layers as illustrated in Box 1.

Maasdorp and du Plessis (2012:29–33) propose another layered model to describe the relationship amongst the various aspects of IW and IO. This is shown in Table 1. Three layers are proposed: the utility layer, which is what humans will work with and consciously use; the connection layer, which is the logical connections of a network; and the access layer, which is the electromagnetic transport of analogue or digital bits. Overlap between the layers and their corresponding IW functional areas are allowed through the grey areas (Maasdorp & du Plessis 2012:29–33).

The convergence of functional areas through contemporary information technology

Contemporary technology such as the ubiquitous nature of mobile and wireless technology and social media are increasing the overlap amongst the domains and may therefore result in the convergence of IW functional areas.

The most discussed area for potential convergence is cyber-operations and EW, largely due to the evolution of wireless and mobile technology. Retired General Cartwright expressed views regarding the links between EW and cyber-operations (Freedberg 2013b), which are corroborated by reports that the development of new EW technology for the US Army is being complicated by the role of cyber-warfare and new attack methods. Chabrow (2012) also indicates that the management of EW is being complicated by the role and synergies with computer network operations. In conjunction with the development of the new EW systems, a new doctrine for cyber-electromagnetic operations is being developed (Freedberg 2013a), and a new training centre for the US Army is to incorporate aspects of cyber-operations, EW and other communications-related actions (Gould 2013). This culminated in a US Army doctrine for cyber-electromagnetic activities where such operations are seen as the overlap amongst cyber-space operations, electronic warfare and spectrum management operations (Department of the Army 2014:1–2). Similarly, the US Air Force is developing systems for 'spectrum warfare' which will cover EW, cyber-operations and other aspects. Some of the associated programs include research into 'net-enabled electronic warfare technologies' (Keller 2013). This indicates that the electromagnetic spectrum, traditionally the focus of EW, is now being related to computer networks. Another project is aimed at detecting cyber-attacks through the use of radio-frequency measurement and signals intelligence (Prince 2012). This can be seen as an intersection of intelligence, EW and cyber-operations.

Mobile technology, in particular smartphones and tablets, has integrated a number of forms of technology, which would previously have been separate tools for conducting espionage. They have integrated navigation, camera and video capture and the ability to transmit these wirelessly. They support Web browsing, have integrated social media connectivity and can function as a basic telephone in addition to having a variety of other applications. These include a hacking tool and a method for PSYOP message delivery (Van Niekerk & Maharaj 2012:4–7).

The mobile-phone infrastructure is different from traditional fixed-line communications where the data and voice channels are separate. With mobile phones, it is feasible that data-based attacks can impact the voice channels (Amoroso 2013:102). In addition, by targeting the wireless transmission using EW, both voice and data can be simultaneously disrupted or compromised. The introduction of voice over IP (VOIP) allows voice to be carried over the data networks. Many instant-messaging applications provide support for text, voice, video or a combination of these, which are transmitted over data networks. These forms of communication are susceptible to standard network attacks. Examples may include disruption by DoS and possible interception of and eavesdropping on communication.

TABLE 2: Mentions of areas converging.

Cyber-EW	Cyber-intelligence	Cyber-PSYOP	EW-PSYOP
12	4	7	1

TABLE 3: Sentiment regarding convergence.

Pro-convergence	Anti-convergence
6	4

Social media is a useful tool for PSYOP, and as it is cyber-based, it can be seen as a combination of these two as cyber-security concerns to protect the accounts used in such operations will also be relevant. The open nature of social media enables operators to gather intelligence on targeted individuals or groups to enable them conduct PSYOP on these targets (Van Niekerk 2012). Social media can be used on a large-scale in what can be called social IW by allowing groups to protest online with global support and organise and guide physical protests. Examples of this are the Arab Spring demonstrations and the related Occupy movement (Kamzi 2011; Madrigal 2011).

A number of cases discussed in this section will commonly be called convergence. However, Knowles (2013:48) suggests that convergence as a term is over-used and often misused and that sharing is a more appropriate term when discussing this phenomenon. The motivations for separate domains discussed in this section are largely limited to the domains. It is possible that the domains themselves remain separate, but the operations and management related to those domains converge. Therefore, the functional areas of IO can converge. Maasdorp and du Plessis (2012:32–33) support this view to an extent, indicating that there should at least be interaction between researchers and operators in the various fields to increase the efficiency and effectiveness of efforts. The increase in combined training for electronic warfare and cyber-operations indicates that there is a strong view that operations, or the management thereof, in these domains can be combined or integrated from a practical perspective.

Summary of convergence concepts regarding information operations

This section summarises the prior discussions regarding convergence. Table 2 illustrates the number of discussions related to the convergence between specific functional areas. As is evident, the focus is on cyber-operations and the electromagnetic spectrum. There is also some focus on the psychological aspects of cyber-operations, probably due to the number of hacktivist or propaganda-motivated cyber-attacks. The weakest overlap is between EW and PSYOP. Whilst there is some possible overlap between this two, the scope is very limited.

Table 3 illustrates the sentiment regarding convergence: Documents that take a pro-convergence perspective slightly outnumber those that take an anti-convergence perspective.

Implications of the convergence of functional areas in information operations

This section discusses the implications of the convergence of the functional areas of IO. These affects could be ethical, legal and operational and could affect the structuring of units or organisations and require specific management techniques.

The disruptive nature of networked communications

Whilst cyber-operations are still emerging and not yet fully established, they are having disruptive effects on previously established functional areas. The result of the shift to network-centric operations is a primary driver of convergence. This results in an upheaval of previously established functional areas. As was described above, computer network operations are complicating the management of EW, and this may also be the case for other functional areas such as PSYOPs. In addition to the other implications discussed below, specialists in many functional areas are required to adjust their thinking, and many may be dissatisfied with or resistant to some of the implications of convergence.

Legal and ethical considerations

The availability of information due to networked communication has increased drastically, and the open nature of social media has hastened this. A legal issue with conducting PYSOP on social media is that it may be difficult to restrict the operation to a specific target population due to its global availability. Therefore, it is highly likely that unintended audiences could access the content. This becomes problematic when there are legal restrictions on the population that is to be targeted. In addition, whilst a specific website may be for a specific nationality, it may be hosted in a different country that is off-limits. Therefore, targeting the audience of the webpage may fall into a grey area, legally speaking. The implications of this are that, when conducting cyber-enabled PSYOP, very careful legal analyses should be conducted to ensure that some legal boundary is not inadvertently crossed, which could result in severe embarrassment should a public outcry result.

The use of social media for mass influence or mass surveillance has additional ethical and legal concerns, particularly surrounding the misuse of these capabilities. An example is the use of social media by Pakistanis to threaten Indian citizens living in a particular area (Abbas 2012). These citizens then left the area in panic, causing a humanitarian crisis. Social media can be used to frame or misrepresent people as fake profiles can be created under names or legitimate profiles can be compromised with the specific goal of using these profiles to conduct misbehaviour for which the real person will then be blamed. Mass surveillance, legitimate or otherwise, has the real possibility of infringing on personal rights, particularly on privacy. The revelations that the US intelligence agencies were accessing a variety of communications resulted in a

massive international outcry (Leyden 2013; Vijayan 2013). The very revelations of the communication intercepts and the information released by Bradley Manning and Wikileaks (Gragido & Pirc 2011:192–195) fall within an ethical grey area. Their actions can be seen as a severe breach of security and irresponsible behaviour. However, their claimed motives and the views of their supporters are that this information is of public interest and illustrate governments' misuse of power. The releases were a form of IO in that the perpetrators were aiming to alter perceptions against the various governments and agencies. However, there seems to be an attitude that mass surveillance and cyber-espionage are allowable as long as you do not get caught: The US often complained about apparent Chinese incursion into their networks, and then the intercept revelations were made (Leyden 2013). French authorities are also showing anger. However, there are reports that they are involved in similar activities (Crowley 2013:12; Leyden 2013; Vijayan 2013). Many nations conduct espionage on competitors and allies alike (Crowley 2013:12), and the vast array of interconnected digital and telecommunications networks makes it easier to intercept or steal that information.

Legal jurisdiction over data and signals may become problematic. Data may cross multiple national boundaries between the sender and receiver, and with cloud computing, data may permanently reside outside of the owner's national borders. Likewise, radiated electromagnetic signals may cross national borders. These signals or data transfers may then be subjected to a wide variety of data or communication laws. If psychological or data attacks transit via a third nation, can this nation consider itself as under attack (when the attack is not aimed at it)? If this question can be answered, it still needs to be proved who the actual perpetrator is, as one of the problematic aspects of cyber-warfare is the difficulty of attribution (Liff 2012:412). This indicates that other attacks delivered through cyber-warfare tactics will probably be difficult to attribute. This perceived difficulty in attributing attacks may provide a feeling of invisibility and encourage activity which borders or crosses the line into being unethical whilst the perpetrators make the assumption that they will not be discovered.

Another issue with the difficulty of attribution is retaliation against an innocent party. This becomes more likely with the attacker actively framing a third party, hoping that the latter will get the blame. Should the retaliation against an attack be destructive in nature, it is imperative that the attribution information is accurate as this may inadvertently target innocent civilians whose system had been compromised by the attacker.

Organisational restructuring

In a business environment, Dennis and Durcikova (2012:109, 452) indicate that technological convergence of voice, video and data results in the audiovisual, IT and telecommunication departments of organisations merging to cope with the integrated technology. In a similar way, military units for PSYOP, EW, communication and cyber-warfare may find themselves strongly supporting each other, and joint-functionality IO cells may be formed for operations.

In a corporate setting, the corporate-communication and public-relations functions need to be concerned with the cyber-dimension in a more dynamic fashion. Not only do they need to run email communications to stakeholders and maintain traditional webpages, but they need to protect the organisation's image on social media. This entails an element of business intelligence where corporate-communication departments need to monitor the social media profiles run by them for negative comments. They also need to have intelligence on other potentially 'hostile' websites and profiles where disgruntled clients or employees could complain or behave in a manner damaging to the corporate image.

From an operational perspective, there is now a broader range of technology that need to be managed, integrated into operations and secured. Due to overlaps in domains and technology, the impact of operations may be broader than expected, and it may become difficult to contain operational effects. This then calls for improved business and competitive intelligence, particularly in the areas of assessing operational impacts. New committees may be required, or existing committees may need additional members with more or different specialities.

IO units or cells could therefore be comprised of a number of specialists working together, each of whom are experts in a specific area. Each specialist provides in-depth knowledge of their individual area. However, their expertise in other areas may be limited, and different views may cause conflict. An alternative is that the IO unit or cell is comprised of generalists who have grounding in multiple (or all) areas but are not necessarily experts in any. The generalists may be able to work together better due to common training and expertise. However, they may not have the depth of understanding that specialists would, potentially resulting in mistakes.

Porche *et al.* (2013) suggest separating the technical and psychological components in IO, and making commanders responsible for the integration of these when required. These authors indicate that the convergence of electronic warfare and cyber-operations requires personnel to have new specialities, pointing to a tendency to having generalists in technical areas (Porche *et al.* 2013:25). This will then effectively require two sets of specialists: those who deal with the technical aspects (cyber and EW) and those who deal with the psychological aspects (PSYOPs, strategic communications and public affairs). As the commanders are expected to be responsible for integration, they could then be considered as generalists.

Management techniques

The convergence of IO functional areas provides those with hostile intent with a variety of 'payloads' and delivery methods. At a strategic level, this may be managed to a certain degree by international policies and agreements. Operations including cyber and psychological aspects should be clarified in international law, particularly as it relates to armed conflict.

At the operational and tactical levels, the use of management information systems for command and control of cyber-operations and EW, such as the proposed systems described by Keller (2013) and the integrated cyber and electronic warfare system (Hatamoto 2013), will increase the efficiency of these operations by providing commanders with decision-support tools. These support systems can be utilised for both technical (EW and cyber) and psychologically based (including strategic communication) operations. These systems will necessitate efficient knowledge management and intelligence, which can be supported by the operations themselves (cyber-espionage and electronic intelligence) for data acquisition.

Training will need to be adjusted to cater for the converging operations. Those with technical skills will need to learn both EW and cyber-warfare concepts, as well as some of the psychological aspects of IO. The psychological operators will need to have combined training for PSYOP and more common public affairs practices with an introduction to the technical aspects, particularly the limitations regarding their use. The extent to which the cross-training is implemented will be determined by the structure of IO units and the extent to which they comprise of specialists or generalists as discussed above. Commanders, who will need to co-ordinate and ensure the integration of operations, will need to have extensive cross-training.

To ensure that operations do not cross any legal or ethical boundaries, legal advisors should be attached to IO cells or should advise commanders overseeing the activities.

Conclusion

IO consists of various functional areas, and a number of operational relationships exist amongst them. The overlaps are becoming larger due to the rapid uptake of wireless technology and social media. The article presented a qualitative document analysis to determine the nature of the convergence and the views thereof. There are many views on the convergence of functional areas in IO. Some strongly advocate that the cyber and electromagnetic domains should be kept separate. This article motivates that the domains can remain separate, but the operations and management thereof must be converging. This has management implications such as legal and ethical considerations for operations, organisational structure and training.

Acknowledgements

Competing interests

The authors declare that they have no financial or personal relationships which may have inappropriately influenced them in writing this article.

References

Abbas, M., 2012, 'Web 2.0: Pakistan's new weapon?', CIOL.com, 21 August, viewed 23 August 2012, from http://www.ciol.com/ciol/news/108402/web-pakistans-weapon

Alfreds, D., 2013, 'ANC admits website hack attack', News24, 14 June, viewed 17 June 2013, from http://www.news24.com/Technology/News/ANC-admits-website-hack-attack-20130614

Amoroso, E.G., 2013, Cyber attacks: Protecting national infrastructure, Elsevier, Waltham, M.A.

Armistead, L., 2010, Information operations matters, Potomac Books, Washington, D.C.

Borque, J., 2008, 'A (pragmatic) future for joint electronic warfare: Does EW + CNO = Cyber?', Journal of Electronic Defence 31(9), 30–40.

Brazzoli, M.S., 2007, 'Future prospects of information warfare and particularly psychological operations', in L. le Roux (ed.), South African army vision 2020, pp. 217–232, Institute for Security Studies, Pretoria.

Chabrow, E., 2012, 'Aligning electronic and cyber warfare', viewed 11 July 2012, from http://www.govinfosecurity.com/aligning-electronic-cyber-warfare-a-4930

Clifford, J., 2011, 'What electronic warriors should know about physics, language and concepts', Journal of Electronic Defense 34(3), 40–47.

Cloud, D.W., 2007, 'Integrated cyber defenses: Towards cyber defense doctrine', Master's dissertation, Naval Postgraduate School.

Cronin, B. & Crawford, H., 1999, 'Information warfare: Its application in military and civilian contexts', The Information Society 15(4), 257–263. http://dx.doi.org/10.1080/019722499128420

Crowley, M., 2013, 'Spy vs. spy', Time Magazine, 11 November, p. 12.

Daily News Correspondent, 2013, 'Hackers target Zimbabwe government', Independent Online, 14 June, viewed 14 June 2013, from http://www.iol.co.za/dailynews/news/hackers-target-zimbabwe-government-1.1532349#.UbtKI1EaKM8

Denning, D.E., 1999, Information warfare and security, Addison-Wesely, Boston.

Dennis, A. & Durcikova, A., 2012, Fundamentals of business data communications, 11th edn., Wiley, New York.

Department of the Army, 2014, Field Manual 3–38: Cyber electromagnetic activities, US Department of Defence, Washington, D.C.

Freedberg, S., 2013a, 'Army electronic warfare goes on the offensive: New tech awaits approval', 29 January, viewed 01 April 2013, from http://defense.aol.com/2013/01/29/army-electronic-warfare-new-tech/

Freedberg, S., 2013b, 'Gen. Hoss Cartwright talks immigration, cyber, China & Afghans with iPhones', 25 March, viewed 27 March 2013, from http://defense.aol.com/2013/03/25/gen-hoss-cartwright-talks-immigration-cyber-china-and-afghans-w/

Gould, J., 2013, 'New center, school to bring signals, cyber, EW together', Army Times, 25 June, viewed 07 September 2013, from http://www.armytimes.com/article/20130625/CAREERS/306250002/New-center-school-bring-signals-cyber-EW-together

Gragido, W. & Pirc, J., 2011, Cybercrime and espionage, Elsevier, Burlington.

Greenwald, G. & MacAskill, E., 2013, 'NSA Prism program taps in to user data of Apple, Google and others', The Guardian, 7 June, viewed 09 June 2013, from http://www.guardian.co.uk/world/2013/jun/06/us-tech-giants-nsa-data

Hahn, R., 2010, 'Physics of the cyber-EMS problem: Why we have the language wrong', Journal of Electronic Defence 33(11), 44–46.

Hatamoto, M., 2013, 'U.S. Army developing cyber, electronic war arsenal', Daily Tech, 31 October, viewed 13 November 2012, from http://www.dailytech.com/US+Army+Developing+Cyber+Electronic+War+Arsenal/article33660.htm

Higgins, K.J., 2013, '"Red October" attacks: The new face of cyberespionage', Dark Reading, viewed 17 January 2013, from http://www.darkreading.com/attacks-breaches/red-october-attacks-the-new-face-of-cybe/240146237

Information Warfare Monitor, 2009, 'Tracking GhostNet: Investigating a Cyber Espionage Network', viewed 01 September 2009, from http://128.100.171.10/modules.php?op=modload&name=News&file=article&sid=2386

Joint Chiefs of Staff, 1998, Joint publication 3–13: Information operations, 09 October, US Department of Defence, Washington, D.C.

Kamzi, A., 2011, 'How anonymous emerged to occupy Wall Street', The Guardian, 27 September, viewed 06 October 2013, from http://www.guardian.co.uk/commentisfree/cifamerica/2011/sep/27/occupy-wall-street-anonymous

Keller, J., 2013, 'Industry: Get ready for spectrum warfare program to cover EW, optics, GPS, and cyber operations', Military and Aerospace Electronics, viewed 18 July 2013, from http://www.militaryaerospace.com/articles/2013/07/usaf-answer-presolicitation.html

Knowles, J., 2013, 'Why two domains are better than one', Journal of Electronic Defence 36(5), 48–50.

Leyden, J., 2013, 'A post-Snowden US had better not squeal about Chinese cyber-spying', The Register, viewed 02 November 2013, from http://www.theregister.co.uk/2013/11/01/snowden_effect_us_china_cyberespionage/

Liff, A.P., 2012, 'Cyberwar: A new "absolute weapon"?: The proliferation of cyberwarfare capabilities and interstate war', Journal of Strategic Studies 35(3), 401–428. http://dx.doi.org/10.1080/01402390.2012.663252

Maasdorp, F. & Du Plessis, W., 2012, 'Using a layered model to place EW in context within the informationsphere', Proceedings of the 4th Workshop on ICT Uses in Warfare and the Safeguarding of Peace 2012 (IWSP 2012), 16 August 2012, Sandton, pp. 29–33.

Madrigal, A., 2011, 'The inside story of how Facebook responded to Tunisian hacks', The Atlantic, viewed 06 October 2013, from http://www.theatlantic.com/technology/archive/2011/01/the-inside-story-of-how-facebook-responded-to-tunisian-hacks/70044/#

Porche, I.R., Paul, C., York, M., Serena, C.C., Sollinger, J.M., Axelband, E. et al. 2013, Redefining information warfare boundaries for an army in a wireless world, RAND Institute, Santa Monica.

Prince, B., 2012, 'Project aims to detect cyber attacks using radio frequency', Security Week, viewed 21 November 2012, from http://www.securityweek.com/project-aims-detect-cyber-attacks-using-radio-frequency

Rouse, A. & Dick, M., 1994, 'The use of NUDIST, a computerized analytical tool, to support qualitative information systems research', Information Technology & People 7(3), 50–62.

Smith, R. & Knight, S., 2005, 'Applying electronic warfare solutions to network security', Canadian Military Journal 6(3), 49–58.

StrategyPage.com., 2009, 'Gaza cell phones targeted', 02 January, viewed 27 July 2009, from http://www.strategypage.com/htmw/htiw/articles/20090102.aspx

Tubbs, B., 2013, 'SAPS hack spells negligence', viewed 22 May, from http://www.itweb.co.za/index.php?option=com_content&view=article&id=64268:SAPS-hack-spells-negligence&catid=265

Van Niekerk, B., 2011, 'Vulnerability analysis of modern ICT infrastructure from an information warfare perspective', PhD thesis, University of KwaZulu-Natal.

Van Niekerk, B., 2012, 'Tools for conducting operations on social media', South African National Defence Force Psychological Operations Expertise Register Workshop, 12 October, Pretoria.

Van Niekerk, B. & Maharaj, M.S., 2009, 'The future roles of electronic warfare in the information warfare spectrum', Journal of Information Warfare 8(3), 1–13.

Van Niekerk, B. & Maharaj, M.S., 2011, 'The information warfare life cycle model', South African Journal of Information Management 13(1), 1–9. http://dx.doi.org/10.4102/sajim.v13i1.476

Van Niekerk, B. & Maharaj, M.S., 2012, 'Mobile devices and the military: Useful tool or significant threat?', Journal of Information Warfare 11(2), 1–11.

Vijayan, J., 2013, 'Is French outrage against U.S. spying misplaced?', Computer World, viewed 25 October 2013, from http://www.computerworld.com/s/article/9243414/Is_French_outrage_against_U.S._spying_misplaced

23

Health information systems to improve health care: A telemedicine case study

Authors:
Liezel Cilliers[1]
Stephen V. Flowerday[1]

Affiliations:
[1]Department of Information Systems, University of Fort Hare, South Africa

Correspondence to:
Liezel Cilliers

Email:
lcilliers@ufh.ac.za

Postal address:
50 Church Street, East London 5201, South Africa

Background: E-health has been identified as an integral part of the future of South African public healthcare. Telemedicine was first introduced in South Africa in 1997 and since then the cost of running the Telemedicine projects has increased substantially. Despite these efforts to introduce the system, only 34% of the Telemedicine sites in South Africa are functional at present.

Objectives: Literature has suggested that one of the barriers to the successful implementation of health information systems is the user acceptance by health care workers of systems such as Telemedicine. This study investigated the user acceptance of Telemedicine in the public health care system in the Eastern Cape Province, making use of the Unified Theory of the Use and Acceptance of Technology.

Method: The study employed a quantitative survey approach. A questionnaire was developed making use of existing literature and was distributed to various clinics around the province where Telemedicine has been implemented. Statistics were produced making use of Statistical Package for the Social Sciences (SPSS).

Results: In general, the health care workers did understand the value and benefit of health information systems to improve the effectiveness and efficiency of the health care system. The barriers to the effective implementation of a health information system include the lack of knowledge and the lack of awareness regarding the Telemedicine system. This in turn means that the user is apprehensive when making use of the system thus contributing to less frequent usage.

Conclusion: Health care workers do acknowledge that information systems can help to increase the effectiveness of the health care system. In general, the acceptance of Telemedicine in the Eastern Cape Department of Health is positive, but in order to integrate it into standard work practices, more must be done with regards to the promotion and education of telemedicine.

Introduction

Background

Quality healthcare is considered a fundamental human right for all citizens in South Africa. The challenge remains in providing quality health care to all, especially to people living in rural areas (Colvin *et al*. 2011). The average doctor to patient ratio in South Africa is calculated at 1:1 300 with some rural areas recording a 1:100 000 ratio (IRIN 2008; Jacobs 2007).

Health information systems have been identified as a possible solution that can be used to alleviate the disparity between rural and urban health care services (Fichman, Kohli & Krishnan 2011; Kolodner, Cohn & Friedman 2008). Information systems can provide the tools to capture, store, processes and communicate information to the relevant decision makers to coordinate health care at the individual and population levels. This improves the quality of care and reduces health care costs (Fichman *et al*. 2011). An example of such a Health Information system, which makes use of both electronic communication and information technology to provide services to the health care sector, is e-health (WHO 2013). The technology is used to expand, assist and enhance health care activities and is not a substitute for health care workers (Oh *et al*. 2005). There are several key application areas within e-health as illustrated in Figure 1. These include health informatics, Telehealth and Telemedicine (WHO 2013).

Telemedicine, meaning medicine at a distance, provides very distinct advantages for health care workers making use of the system (WHO 2013). There are two primary delivery methods that can be used: namely real-time, and a store and forward approach. The most popular method due to connectivity problems is the second approach where a message is sent to the specialist to review later or at their convenience. For this approach, all that is needed is a basic computer with Internet connectivity and camera (Singh 2006). The goal of Telemedicine is to increase the accessibility of specialised health care in rural areas. Patients in rural areas do not have to travel long distances to urban hospitals in order to access specialist care, whilst waiting times and transportation costs are reduced. Health care workers also benefit from the system as urban colleagues are able to support and teach those in rural areas making use of the system (WHO 2013; Wootton *et al.* 2009).

E-health trends in South Africa

Focus of the study

Telemedicine has become an integral part of the Department of Health's E-health plan in South Africa, with more than R15 million being invested in various Telemedicine projects in recent years (Motsoaledi 2010). Despite these investments, it has been reported that the uptake of the technology has been limited with only 34% of Telemedicine sites operational (Van Dyk, Fortuin & Schutte 2012; Motsoaledi 2010; Jack & Mars 2008). The poor uptake of Telemedicine is not unique to South Africa with many authors reporting similar results in other developing countries (Mars 2012; Ovretveit *et al.* 2007; Medecins Sans Frontiers 2007). Previous literature reported that the technology was not reliable due to frequent interruptions of electricity supply, poor connectivity and low bandwidth (Mars 2012; Fortuin & Molefi 2007; Jack & Mars 2008). Whilst these problems have been addressed since the inception of Telemedicine, the usage of the technology has remained low (Jack & Mars 2008). This has necessitated a new research focus area with particular emphasis on the human and organisational factors involved (Mars 2012; Van Gemert-Pijnen *et al.* 2012). One of the factors that has been identified as a possible obstacle for the successful implementation of Telemedicine is user acceptance (Nwabueze *et al.* 2009; Pagliari *et al.* 2005).

Telemedicine has been introduced at six district hospitals and 25 clinic sites around the Eastern Cape in the past five years. These pilot sites have not produced the desired results, and it was found that the technology was underutilised or not used at all. Therefore, an investigation is needed before any financial investment is made in further sites (Telemedicine Operation Plan E-health 2009). The objective of this article is then to investigate if user acceptance is a factor for the poor uptake of Telemedicine in the Eastern Cape Department of Health whilst making use of the Unified Theory of Acceptance and Use of Technology (UTAUT) to prove or disprove this concept.

Contribution to the field

The Unified Theory of Acceptance and Use of Technology (UTAUT) was used as a theoretical framework for this study. The UTAUT was developed by Venkatesh in order to explain behavioural intention to use a technology. The model consists of four key constructs: performance expectancy, effort expectancy, social influence, and facilitating conditions (Venkatesh, Thong & Xu *et al.* 2012). The theory was found to explain 70% of the variance in behavioural intention to use a technology and about 50% of the variance in technology use (Venkatesh *et al.* 2012). Since the inception of UTAUT, it has become a baseline model in this area of technology adoption and has been tested in a variety of settings including health information systems (Chang 2007). Additionally, it has been applied to a variety of technologies in both organisational and non-organisational settings contributing to its generalisability (Neufeld *et al.* 2007).

Research design

This research made use of a positivistic, quantitative research methodology. A questionnaire was developed and piloted. From the pilot study, it was established that the questionnaire is user friendly. The study population of this research project was defined as any health care worker for the multidisciplinary team employed at any of the Eastern Cape Department of Health telemedicine sites within the province. Statistical Package for the Social Sciences (SPSS) was used to perform the statistical analysis. Validation of the final results was conducted by four experts in Telemedicine and technology acceptance in general (Cilliers & Flowerday 2011). Feedback from these experts was then incorporated into the final recommendations and conclusions of the study. Exclusion criteria for this study included Telemedicine in the private sector, technology issues directly associated with telemedicine, as well as budgetary and other financial constraints faced by the implementers of the technology (Cilliers & Flowerday 2011).

Ethical consideration

Ethical approval was obtained from both the University of Fort Hare Ethics Committee and Department of Health Ethics Committee before the study was conducted. Study participants also received a covering letter explaining the purpose of the study and informing them that participation in the study was voluntary.

Study population

Seventy-five questionnaires were distributed to health care workers at 31 Telemedicine sites in the Eastern Cape Health Department. Health care workers from the multidisciplinary team including nurses, doctors, dentists and radiologists,

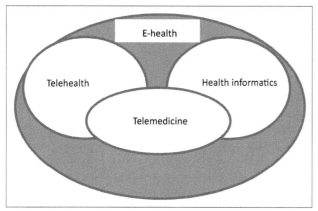

FIGURE 1: Various services as part of the E-health system.

were randomly selected to participate. The return rate for the questionnaire was 76%. The majority of the study population (86%) consisted of women. More than a third of the participants were younger than 30 years of age (36.8%), whilst 45.6% were between the ages of 31–49 years of age. The health care workers older than 50 years of age represented 17.6% of the study population. The study participants indicated that 43% worked in an urban setting and 56% in a rural area. This is consistent with the reported statistics for the larger population in the Eastern Cape. The educational level of the participants included 62% who obtained a formal qualification, 22% completed Grade 12 and 14% who completed Grade 10. The study population consisted of a multi-disciplinary team including medical doctors, dentists, pharmacists and allied health professionals including radiographers. The majority of the study population consisted of nurses (30%) and student nurses (22.8%). The following section provides insight into the four major constructs of the UTAUT model.

Results and discussion

Performance expectancy

The main objective of a health information system, such as telemedicine, is to improve health care services whilst reducing costs (Keeton 2012). Performance expectancy represents the degree to which an individual believes that using the system will assist them in attaining their goals in job performance (Venkatesh *et al.* 2003).

For the question, 'I find Telemedicine useful in my job', a significant statistical difference was found when measured against educational level as well as where the facility was located. From the health care workers with a degree qualification, 72% indicated that telemedicine would be useful in their job, whilst 100% of the health care workers with a Grade 12 or diploma qualification answered positively ($\alpha = 19.647; p < 0.05$).

Health care workers working in rural areas (clinics, community health centres and district hospitals) found Telemedicine to be more useful than those working in the secondary hospitals in urban areas ($\alpha = 29.629; p < 0.05$). Figure 2 illustrates how useful the health care workers in various settings found telemedicine. The reason for the higher percentages for the rural areas is that these areas stand the most to benefit from telemedicine.

Effort expectancy

Effort expectancy is defined as the degree of ease associated with the use of the system (Venkatesh *et al.* 2003). The majority of health care workers found the system to be user-friendly. This is illustrated by the results of the questions, 'I find the telemedicine system easy to use' and 'I found it easy to learn how to use the system'. Accordingly, 71% of the respondents found the system easy to use and 69% agreed that it was easy to learn how to use the system.

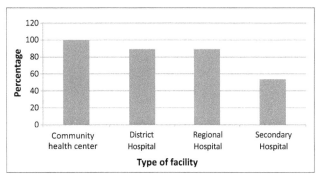

FIGURE 2: Perception of the usefulness of Telemedicine according to place of work of health care workers.

Effort expectancy was found to be statistically significant for the area in which the facility is located, as well as the general knowledge of telemedicine of the health care workers.

More health care workers in the rural areas (81.4%) agreed that the Telemedicine unit was easy to use, followed by the health care workers in urban areas (69.7%). Health care workers in both the urban (72%) and rural (81.5%) areas indicated that they felt it was easy for them to learn how to make use of the Telemedicine system ($\alpha = 21.279; p < 0.05$). This can be attributed to the increased effort that was made by the Department of Health to educate health care workers in the rural areas to not only use Telemedicine, but also the increased effort to ensure that the health care workers become computer literate. This is supported by Lungo (2008) who proposes that when education is provided to familiarise the user with a specific computer programme, it will be influenced by the computer literacy level of the user.

The majority of the participants (85.85%) who considered themselves knowledgeable regarding Telemedicine indicated that they could use the technology whilst those who did not consider themselves knowledgeable regarding the technology (52.7%) predictably felt that their interactions with the Telemedicine system were not clear and understandable. Participants who indicated they were not knowledgeable regarding telemedicine agreed that it was easy for them to learn how to make use of telemedicine (52.7%), as did those who perceived themselves knowledgeable regarding the technology (87.85%).

Social influence

Venkatesh *et al.* (2003) defined social influence as the extent to which an individual allows the opinions of others to influence their decision to use the system. In this category, a positive correlation was found for the perceived knowledge of Telemedicine. Health care workers who considered themselves knowledgeable about Telemedicine agreed with the statement that other people would influence their behaviour to use the technology (79.15%), whilst only 50% of those who did not consider themselves knowledgeable agreed with the statement ($\alpha = 19.047; p < 0.05$).

Facilitating conditions

Holden and Karsh (2010) stated that facilitating conditions when dealing with technology acceptance in health care is

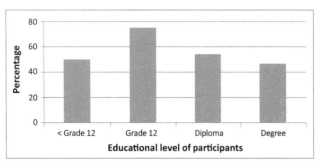

FIGURE 3: Perception of resources necessary to use telemedicine according to qualifications of health care workers.

a very important factor. Facilitating conditions include resource availability such as technical assistance, knowledge of the system and compatibility with other systems already in use (Venkatesh *et al.* 2003).

Half of the participants (54.4%) indicated that they thought they did have the resources necessary to make use of Telemedicine. Two thirds (64.9%) indicated that they did have access to technical assistance if necessary, whilst 40.3% indicated that the technology is not compatible with the systems already in use at their health care facility.

The resources necessary to make use of telemedicine tested statistically significant for qualification and knowledge of telemedicine. Qualification provided the following positive correlation with the statement: 'I have the resources, such as technical assistance, necessary to use telemedicine' ($\alpha = 18.107$; $p < 0.05$). The following graph (Figure 3) illustrates the result in percentage for this question.

Interestingly, the health care workers who considered themselves knowledgeable regarding the technology were far less confident about technical assistance (57%) than the group that perceived themselves as not knowledgeable (81.6%) ($\alpha = 19.566$; $p < 0.05$).

In general, the majority of health care workers in this study believed that Telemedicine would improve their productivity in the workplace (67%) or, at the very least, be useful during their daily activities (80%). The advantage of Telemedicine cited by health care workers in urban areas included less time being spent on outreach activities and fewer patients being referred incorrectly to urban centres. For rural based health care workers, the advantages of incorporating telemedicine in their daily activities included shorter waiting times for diagnoses and treatment as well as support from colleagues in urban centres.

Conclusion

The health care workers in the Eastern Cape Department of Health found Telemedicine to increase their productivity, quality and efficiency of work. The behavioural intent of the health care workers was also found to be favourable for the future use of the system. Most of the health care workers found the system easy to use but interestingly, those in the urban areas reported more difficulty with this aspect. As the awareness regarding Telemedicine decreased, so did the ease of use and frequency with which the system was used. Apprehension and fearfulness also increased as the knowledge of Telemedicine decreased. Social influence and facilitating conditions were also found to influence the acceptance of health care workers of telemedicine.

Awareness regarding the benefits of telemedicine must be improved in order to facilitate the acceptance of the technology. Aligned with this, is the education of health care workers regarding telemedicine in order to increase knowledge which will decrease apprehension and fearfulness, whilst at the same time increase ease of use.

Acknowledgements

Competing interest

The authors declare that they have no financial or personal relationship(s) that may have inappropriately influenced them in writing this paper.

Authors' contributions

L.C. (University of Fort Hare) completed the dissertation in fulfillment of the requirements for the degree Masters of Commerce in Information Systems in the Faculty of Management and Commerce of the University of Fort Hare. S.V.F. (University of Fort Hare) was the supervisor to this student.

References

Chang, I.C., Hwang, H.G., Hung, W.F. & Li, Y.C., 2007, 'Physicians' acceptance of pharmacokinetics-based clinical decision support systems', *Expert Systems with Applications* 33(2), 296–303. http://dx.doi.org/10.1016/j.eswa.2006.05.001

Cilliers, L. & Flowrday, S.V., 2011, 'Will computer literacy affect telemedicine acceptance among health care workers', viewed 5 January 2013, from http://www.resnes.co.za/colloquium/2011-proceedings/papers/resnes2011_p11.pdf

Colvin, R., Mia Shim, M., Brock, D. & Todd, G., 2011, 'Dermatological diagnostic acumen improves with use of a simple telemedicine system for underserved areas of South Africa', *Telemedicine and e-Health* 17(5), 363–367.

Fichman, G., Kohli, R. & Krishnan, R., 2011, 'The role of information systems in healthcare: Current research and future trends', *Information Systems Research* 22, 419–327. http://dx.doi.org/10.1287/isre.1110.0382

Fortuin, J. & Molefi, M., 2007, 'Implementing Telemedicine in South Africa - A South African Experience', International Hospital Federation Reference Book 2006/2007, Dubai.

Holden, R.J. & Karsh, B.T., 2010, 'The Technology Acceptance Model: Its past and its future in health care', *Journal of Biomed Informatics* 43(1) 159–172. http://dx.doi.org/10.1016/j.jbi.2009.07.002

IRIN, 2008, 'South Africa wanted - 4,000 doctors', viewed 5 January 2013, from http://www.plusnews.org/Report/79241/SOUTH-AFRICA-WANTED-4-000-doctors

Jack, C. & Mars, M., 2008, 'Telemedicine a need for ethical and legal guidelines in South Africa', *South African Family Practice* 50, 60–61.

Jacobs, F., 2007, '185 - The Patients per Doctor map of the world', viewed 5 January 2013, from http://bigthink.com/strange-maps/185-the-patients-per-doctor-map-of-the-world

Keeton, C., 2012, 'Measuring the impact of e-health', *Bull World Health Organisation* 90, 326–327. http://dx.doi.org/10.2471/BLT.12.020512

Kolodner, R.M., Cohn, S.P. & Friedman, P., 2008, 'Health information technology: Strategic initiatives, real progress', *Health Affairs* 27, 391–395. http://dx.doi.org/10.1377/hlthaff.27.5.w391

Lungo, J.H., 2008, 'The reliability and usability of district health information software: Case studies from Tanzania', *Tanzania Journal of Health Research* 10, 139. http://dx.doi.org/10.4314/thrb.v10i1.14340

Mars, M., 2012, 'Telepsychiatry in Africa – A way forward?', *African Journal of Psychiatry* 15, 215–217.

Medecins Sans Frontiers, 2007, 'Help wanted: Confronting the health care crises to expand HIV/AIDS treatment', viewed 6 January 2013, from http://www.doctorswithoutborders.org/publications/article.cfm?id=2881

Motsoaledi, M., 2010, 'Speaking notes for Dr. A.P Motsoaledi for the 1st Southern African Telemedicine Conference', viewed 22 February 2013, from http://www.doh.gov.za/show.php?id=2104

Neufeld, J., Dong, L. & Higgins, C., 2007, 'Charismatic leadership and user acceptance of information technology', *European Journal of Information Systems* 16, 494–510. http://dx.doi.org/10.1057/palgrave.ejis.3000682

Nwabueze, S.N., Meso, N.P., Kifle, M., Okoli, C. & Chustz, M., 2009, 'The effects of culture of adoption of Telemedicine in medically underserved communities', Proceedings of the 42nd Hawaii International Conference on System Sciences, Hawaii, United States of America, 2009, pp. 1–10.

Oh, H., Rizo, C., Enkin, M., Jadad, A., 2005, 'What is eHealth: A systematic review of published definitions', *Journal of Medical Internet Research* 24, 7.

Ovretveit, J., Scott, T., Rundall, T.G., Shortell, S.M. & Brommels, M., 2007, 'Improving quality through effective implementation of information technology in healthcare', *International Journal for Quality in Health Care* 19(5), 259–266. http://dx.doi. org/10.1093/intqhc/mzm031

Pagliari, C., Sloan, D., Gregor, P., Sullivan, F., Detmer, D., Kahan, P. *et al.*, 2005, 'What is eHealth: A scoping exercise to map the field', *Journal of Medical Internet Research* 7(1), 201–210. http://dx.doi.org/10.2196/jmir.7.1.e9 PMid:15829481

Singh, V., 2006, 'Telemedicine and Mobile Telemedicine Systems', viewed 8 January 2013, from http://works.bepress.com/vikas_singh

Telemedicine Operational Plan E-health, 2009, 'Operational Plan for Eastern Cape', viewed 7 February 2013, from http://www.ecdoh.gov.za/uploads/files/260308124225.pdf

Van Dyk, L., Fortuin, J. & Schutte, C., 2012, 'A Maturity model for Telemedicine Implementation', eTELEMED 2012: The Fourth International Conference on eHealth, Telemedicine, and Social Medicine, Cape Town, South Africa, pp. 69–71.

Van Gemert-Pijnen, J.E.W.C., Wynchank, S., Covvey, H.D. & Ossebaard, H.C., 2012, 'Improving the credibility of electronic health technologies', *Bull World Health Organ* 90, 323–323A. http://dx.doi.org/10.2471/BLT.11.099804

Venkatesh, V., Morris, M.G., Davis, G.B. & Davis, F.D., 2003, 'User acceptance of information technology: Toward a unified view', *MIS Quarterly* 27, 425–478.

Venkatesh, V., Thong, J.Y.L. & Xu, X., 2012, 'Consumer acceptance and use of information technology: Extending the unified theory of acceptance and use of technology', *MIS Quarterly* 36(1), 157–178.

WHO, 2013, 'E-Health', viewed on 6 January 2013, from http://www.who.int/trade/glossary/story021/en/index.html

Wootton, R., Patil, E., Scott, R.E. & Ho, K., 2009, '*Telemedicine in the Developing World*', Royal Society of Medicine Press, London.

24

A cost-benefit analysis of document management strategies used at a financial institution in Zimbabwe

Authors:
Rodreck David[1]
Patrick Ngulube[2]
Adock Dube[1]

Affiliations:
[1]Department of Records and Archives Management, National University of Science and Technology, Zimbabwe

[2]Department of Interdisciplinary Research and Postgraduate Studies, University of South Africa, South Africa

Correspondence to:
Patrick Ngulube

Email:
ngulup@unisa.ac.za

Postal address:
PO Box 392, Pretoria 0003, South Africa

Background: Choosing a cost-effective document management approach has become a priority to many organisations, especially in view of the rapidly changing technological environment in which information is being created and managed. A literature survey indicated that document management strategies have the potential to provide some substantial cost-saving benefits if they are used judiciously.

Objectives: This study investigated a commercial bank's document management approaches in a bid to ascertain the costs and benefits of each strategy and related issues.

Method: A quantitative research approach was employed through a case study which was used to gather data from a sampled population in the bank.

Results: The document management approaches used were not coordinated to improve operational efficiency. There were regulations governing documents management. The skills and competences of staff on both document management and cost analysis are limited. That is partly due to limited training opportunities availed to them. That means that economies are not achieved in the management of records. That has a negative impact on the overall efficiency, effectiveness and legal compliance of the banking institution.

Conclusion: The financial institutions should create regulations enabling periodical cost-benefit analysis of document management regimes used by the bank at least at quarterly intervals as recommended by the National Archives of Australia. A hybrid approach in managing records is recommended for adoption by the financial institution. There should be on-the-job staff training complimented by attendance at relevant workshops and seminars to improve the staff's understanding of both the cost-benefit analysis concept and document management.

Background to the study

Information created and used by a business is managed in documents, usually captured as records stored, maintained, distributed or communicated in some format. Broadly, electronic, paper and micrographic document management strategies are used by many organisations in managing their information (Ngulube 2011:1; Svärd 2011). Choosing a cost-effective document management approach has become a priority to most organisations, especially in view of the rapidly changing technological environment in which information is being created and managed (Wang *et al.* 2003; International Records Management Trust 2006; Ngulube 2011). Business managers have seen the importance of choosing suitable document management plans that fit with their technological environment and anticipated growth. Ngulube (2011:1) notes that 'document management strategies have the potential to provide some substantial cost-saving benefits if they are used judiciously'.

Document management challenges affect all types of business, including commercial banks. Financial institutions exist to enhance the financial welfare of citizens and to generate profit. Profit is partly used to measure the success of such business institutions. They have stakeholders such as owners, citizens, government and external funders who provide them with the resources. The effective management of documented information attracts the interest of all the stakeholders of the financial institutions. Public assurance of privacy, confidentiality and security of information; government requirements for retention and disposal; and the financial institution owners' interests on efficiency and effectiveness warrant some degree of professionalism and analysis of business processes in document management to ensure cost effective and beneficial document management.

Cost-benefit analysis (CBA) has been used to determine the most cost-effective and beneficial strategy for document management (Megill & Schantz 2000:109; National Archives of Australia 2003). The cost-benefit analysis guidelines given by the International Records Management Trust

(2006:4) define a cost-benefit analysis as 'a systematic approach to estimating the strengths and weaknesses of technology alternatives that satisfy agency business requirements'. Cost-benefit analysis is a technique that is used to determine options that provide the best approach for the adoption and practice in terms of benefits in labour, time and cost savings (Ngulube 2011; Báeza & Herrerob 2012). This article seeks to investigate a cost benefit analysis of document management strategies at a selected financial institution in Zimbabwe.

Contextual setting

The financial institution under study is one of the long-established financial institutions in Zimbabwe. It has a substantial amount of documents managed using various document management strategies and it affects a relatively large number of citizens. A quantitative case study design was employed to determine the document management strategies employed by the financial institution. Specifically, the research investigated the financial institution's two departments: namely the information technology (IT) and Software Library Department (SLD); and the Securities, Safe Custody and Archives Department (SSCAD) as these two departments were involved in the management of both electronic and paper records and documents. Their records included customer applications, records from report generating programmes, client transactional receipts and ledger registers.

The financial institutions also used computer-based databases to store and retrieve accounts payable and accounts receivable records. These databases are stripped from the information technology department which runs the database management system (DMS) for the bank. Safe Custody and Archives Department also stores these stripped-off databases on designated computers for both back-up and retention purposes. These databases mainly contain both accounts statements and general ledger statements which could be requested by the creating departments for reference. The use of information technology generates a lot of documented information that inevitably requires a documentation strategy that is both effective and efficient. The departments therefore provided a good case that would enable the researchers to answer the research questions.

Apart from handling a substantially large amount of documents that inevitably need a viable document management strategy, the two departments were chosen because their activities are regulated by law. The financial institution cannot re-engineer these departments' business processes in document management in any way it desires because the law stipulates crucial regulations regarding the retention and disposal as well as the format of the documented records that would be admissible as evidence in the case of litigation. *Statutory Instrument 23* called the *Serious Offences (Retention of Documents) Regulations of 1995 [Act 20/90] section 3(b)* prescribes that every commercial bank in Zimbabwe should retain physical documents for not less than six years (Government of Zimbabwe 1995). Furthermore, the *Banks*

Act 5/1999 of Zimbabwe requires financial institutions including banks to maintain the information they generate in a manner that will promote transparency, accountability and accessibility (Government of Zimbabwe 2004).

The proliferation of compound documents, unstructured information on local area networks (LANs), and virtual private networks (VPNs) commonly used by banking institutions; as well as mail servers, hard-drive storage solutions, and office documents (Svärd 2011:5), is posing challenges regarding the best possible document management strategy that a banking institution should take in order to realise the benefits of efficiency, effectiveness and usability of documented information. A survey on African banks by the World Bank (2009:12) reflects that documented information in banks is continuously being used, distributed, controlled, maintained and stored by electronic means.

With the increased tendency of creating too much information enabled by too many technological devices in the banking sector (Ambira & Kemoni 2011), especially from clients undertaking transactions, (Megill & Schantz 2000:109) it becomes even more difficult to efficiently and effectively select and utilise documents management methods, which impact negatively on the overall efficiency of the banking industry. Here, the choice of the strategy is even more critical. Many organisations in a East and Southern Africa Regional Branch of the International Council on Archives (ESARBICA) operate through a parallel document management plan involving electronic and paper-based systems (Ngulube & Tafor 2006; Ambira & Kemoni 2011). Whilst surrogates can be helpful as back-up, this approach often causes duplication of efforts and resources (Roper & Millar 2009). As such, strategies for identifying, adopting, implementing and maintaining cost-effective systems have become important.

Our preliminary investigation revealed that the document-creating departments were experiencing an unprecedented accumulation of paper-based and electronic records, forms and files. More so, SSCAD which acted as the intermediate storage facility for both semi-current and non-current records - mainly those records that were retained as required by law- was becoming over-capacitated by large volumes of files, withdrawal slips and other computer print-out records. There was also a high likelihood that essential records and vital records deposited with SSCAD for secure storage may possibly get mixed up with non-current records pending disposal, and this poses difficulties when it comes to the retrieval of the required information. Creating departments, the police and legal departments which often consult these departments to retrieve records when they need information for various reasons such as operational use, fraud investigation and lawsuit may find themselves failing to access the records.

This state of affairs inevitably prompted the researchers to investigate the possibility of coming up with a workable solution to champion a more standardised, coherent, cost-effective and beneficial document management strategy for enterprise-wide adoption at the institution.

Justification of the study

Cost-benefit analysis is pertinent to this study because it may provide organisations with valuable information about the status of its documents regimes and available alternatives by identifying, analysing and presenting results about the costs and benefits of documents management approaches it uses. The aim was to recommend on the more cost-effective options so as to stimulate the institution to operate effectively. The results from this study may also be used as a basis for doing research in other financial institutions about cost-benefit analyses of document management systems. It is also expected to sensitise records managers and business managers about analysing, monitoring and evaluating the costs and advantages of using different document management strategies.

Ngulube (2011:2) argues that cost-benefit analysis of document management solutions does not seem to be a major concern to many records managers, especially in sub-Saharan Africa (SSA) and worse still, in banking institutions. Furthermore, the extensive studies on document formats by ALOS Micrographics Corporation (2009:7), Alaska State Archives (2009) and Missouri State Archives (2011) further indicated that on average 34% of many corporate organisations' documents are not managed in the right format resulting in the organisation suffering increased operational overhead costs. All these studies accentuate the need for investigation into the most effective strategies of managing records in a cost effective way.

Therefore, as a narrowly researched area, this study also added to research literature on the topic. The significance of the study is mainly centred on stirring the financial institutions in Zimbabwe and SSA to realise the best available document management practice strategies, and to use cost-benefit analysis in adopting the most appropriate strategy.

Statement of the problem

Cost-benefit analysis is fundamental in choosing and utilising economic, effective and efficient document management schemes because it provides the possibility of identifying cost-effective and beneficial document management strategies for different types of information. Little research has been done in the banking and finance industry about the use of the cost-benefit analysis in document management. Arguably, cost-benefit analysis of document management approaches does not seem to be a major concern to many records managers (Ngulube 2011; Svärd 2011). Not surprisingly, many scholars have expressed concern over the deteriorating state of records management in SSA reflecting the need for such an analysis (Akotia 2003; Akussah 2002; Mnjama 2003; Ngulube & Tafor 2006; Wamukoya 2000). As stated by Ngulube (2011:14) further research is required to demonstrate both the need for the cost analysis and the efficacy of each document management approach.

Objective of the study

The main objective of the study was to investigate the costs and benefits of different document management approaches used by a selected financial institution with a view of making recommendations that may inform document management practice.

The study was guided by the following objectives:

1. Establishing the staff's understanding of document management and cost benefit analysis at the selected financial institution.
2. Identifying the document management strategies used by the selected financial institution and ascertaining their cost and benefits.
3. Determining the skills and competences of the records management staff at the financial institution about cost-benefit analysis of document management systems.

Scope of the study

The study was limited to the institution's two departments, the Software Library Department (SLD) and the Securities, Safe Custody and Archives Department (SSCAD) as these departments shepherd the management of records at many financial institutions in Zimbabwe (Commercial Bank of Zimbabwe 2011). All the staff in the two departments formed the target population of the study. The document management strategies covered by the study were paper, microforms and electronic formats. The study was not wide enough to cover related document management concepts and practices such as enterprise content management and document imaging systems. These were considered to be advanced stages of document management frameworks which are predicated on the fundamentals of electronic documents management. No organisation may embrace these without first embracing the electronic document management as a strategy.

Review of scholarship

Literature on the cost-benefit analysis of document management has been limited in Africa. An informative study by Ngulube (2011) has been the most influential in an African context. This is complemented by studies carried out on records management and risk management in banks in Kenya by Ambira and Kemoni (2011) and on the effectiveness of records management by Akotia (2003) and Mnjama (2003).

However, in the international arena great strides towards more comprehensive literature on the cost benefit analysis of documents and records management has been made. This is characterised by the manual on records keeping and cost-benefit analysis created by the National Archives of Australia (2003) and the records management project management guideline on cost-benefit analysis by the International Records Management Trust (2006). These resources were written in a consortium amalgamating several researches. There are also influential independent case studies published on document formats (Alaska State Archives, 2009; ALOS Micrographics Corporation 2009; Missouri State Archives 2011; Western Micrographics Imaging Systems 2008), on document management cost-effectiveness in the medical field (Wang *et al.* 2003), in relation to technology (Megill & Schantz 2000), and on the benefits of enterprise content management (Svärd 2011).

The cost-benefit analysis concept: A cost-benefit analysis provides an economic framework to evaluate the viability of a proposed or operating project (International Records Management Trust 2006:67). It can be defined as the systematic gathering of technical and financial data about a given business situation or function (Ngulube 2011:7). Information gathered and analysed through this method assists decision-making about resource allocation and making the right choice in selecting the appropriate alternative. A cost-benefit analysis specifies the return on investment (ROI), that is, financial inputs and expected returns from a given project. It compares the 'with' and 'without' situations (International Records Management Trust 2006). The results of this analysis can be used to evaluate alternative options. It can strongly support a bid for management endorsement and resource allocation. To undertake a cost-benefit analysis the scope, purpose and objectives of the proposed project must be explicit.

The cost-benefit principles are mostly explained in the context of undertaking design and implementation of records keeping systems (DIRKS) projects (National Archives of Australia 2003:56). This type of analysis enables records and information management staff to assess the likely impacts, advantages and disadvantages of implementing DIRKS. The same principles used are applicable to the cost-benefit analysis of documents management strategies. For instance, the need to conduct a needs assessment is equally important in conducting a cost-benefit analysis as it enables the identification of the specific needs of the institution and thereby the rationale or justification for the project.

Objectives of the cost-benefit analysis: It is important to understand the purpose and business objectives and benefits that a cost-benefit analysis project is expected to realise. The study by Ngulube (2011) identifies such justification by articulating expected benefits. He explains that the significance of any document management scheme in an organisation is primarily evident in the exploitation of available technology to reduce costs in maintenance, retrieval and storage of documented information whilst promoting the usability of the documented information, ensuring legal safeguards and thereby transparency, accountability, economy, efficiency and effectiveness of business operations.

Ngulube (2011:3) lists the expected benefits of adopting a documents management strategy as follows:

1. reduction of enterprise wide operating costs
2. high level of support on decision making
3. protection of the rights of stakeholders
4. compliance with legislation and regulations (for instance tax, company, safety, promotion of access to information)
5. provision of evidence of transparency and accountability
6. contribution to organisational efficiency and good governance
7. increase in productivity and individual accountability
8. high level of information related risk management
9. the preservation of corporate memory.

Factors to be considered in undertaking a cost-benefit analysis: The two major factors that should be considered are cost and benefits. The *DIRKS Manual – Appendix 10* attempts to provide a dollar figure for each cost incurred in purchasing and using any object in documents management (National Archives of Australia 2003). Costs to be considered include the acquisition and maintenance of equipment; the upgrade, redesign or enhancement of current networks; acquisition, testing and maintenance of software; the development and delivery of training for support staff and users; the conversion of records from the current system; and the system administration.

Costs associated with intangibles, although not easy to quantify, need to be recognised as they can impact on the overall costs of a document management approach in place or under consideration. The cost-benefit analysis should acknowledge non-quantifiable costs, even if they may not be factored into the calculations in the analysis. Depending on the document management regime in question, some intangible costs to consider may include: the impact of non-compliance with legislation; impaired document management (exacerbated by decentralised operations); diminished corporate memory (compounded by administrative change and high staff turnover); the impact of not achieving best practice standards, such as complying with the International Standards Organisation Records Management Standard (ISO 15489-1) (2001); potential litigation costs due to inadequate records management and information management; reduced accountability in decision-making and actions; and reduced organisational productivity.

On the other hand, benefits are the returns expected from a project. Most benefits are articulated in terms of improvements or cost savings. Like costs, benefits can be quantifiable (tangible) and non-quantifiable (intangible). To be precise, and for determining achievement, it is important to attempt to provide a dollar figure for each benefit. The cost-benefit analysis guideline from the National Archives of Australia (2003) stipulates that one should seek advice from financial staff and that it is important to bear in mind that secondary benefits may also be derived from a project; that is benefits that will be achieved because other benefits were delivered. They must be practical and realistic. The best way to achieve this is to investigate benefits over a reasonable time frame (National Archives of Australia 2003:34).

Benefits that may accrue to the organisation include: compliance with the International Standards Organisation Records Management Standard (ISO 15489-1) (2001) compliance with legislative requirements; compliance with government-wide policy initiatives; universal access to records; delivery of services in a consistent, coherent and equitable manner; enabling of order and in business; reduced risk of loss of vital records; meeting the requirements to create and keep records; keeping track of the documentation of all business transactions; support and maintenance of corporate memory; and cost savings generated from better recordkeeping and records management practices.

Document management: The activities involving the capture or receipt of documents, version and format control, their storage, maintenance, retrieval and disposal entail document management. The complexity of documents management is that they come in various formats and this prompts the need for critical thinking in selecting the most appropriate approach which saves resources whilst meeting documentation needs (Alaska State Archives 2009). For instance, the invoice that comes as a paper record could be quite possibly obvious however, if it comes as part of the whole relational database of an accounting system, hyperlinked to a remote server and other subsidiary databases could have different management needs than its paper counterpart (Alaska State Archives 2009:8).

The mostly discussed document management approaches in the literature (Ngulube 2011:5; Tough & Moss 2006; Williams 2006) are paper, micrographics, electronic formats and hybrid regimes. Following Ngulube (2011), document imaging which encompass software based computer systems is beyond the scope of this study because document imaging is a documents management tool that integrates various document management systems. As noted by Ngulube (2011):

> document imaging may be part and parcel of a suite of tools that may be used to capture, manage, store, preserve and deliver content and support business processes, what is often termed enterprise content management. An analysis of literature on several proprietary and open-source software systems reflects that they are much bent towards enterprise content management. Therefore, the discussion of document management systems such as Documentum®, eFileCabinet®, ImagePlus®, Hummingbird®, SharePoint®, TRIM Context®, Universal Content Management® which are proprietary systems and Open-Source Systems such as Alfresco®, Archivista®, Knowledge Tree® and OpenKM® are equally beyond the scope of this study. (pp. 5–6)

Ngulube's (2011) study reflects that document management strategies that aim to improve the effectiveness, efficiency, consistency and coherence in the management of records in a continuum, through the specific stages of the life cycle of records, require different management regimes without necessarily delving into an enterprise wide content management system.

This article focuses on three major document management strategies: paper, micrographics and electronic formats. Even though most organisations and business enterprises accept and have confidence in paper formats for document management, it has disadvantages that should not be overlooked. Dexter's (2011:34–36) study on paper documents in public sector agencies of the state of Iowa, United States of America showed that most delays in government, poor clientele service provision and even the loss of revenue, good will and competitiveness could be attributed to the paper-based records management systems widespread in the agencies. Indeed, 'changing the format of paper documents to microfilm or digital can help an organisation to maximise storage space and make records easier to access by multiple users' (Ngulube 2011:7). As a more cost-effective format than paper, micrographics can provide many advantages and

benefits. However, Ngulube (2011:8) warned that 'vendor portrayals of micrographics and its possibilities have at times been overly simplistic and misleading'. For instance, case studies by Western Micrographics Imaging Systems (2008), Missouri State Archives (2011), and by Dexter (2011) have shown that the cost of microform-based document management systems is more expensive than optical disk and the retrieval is time consuming where the film is sequential, requiring sequential retrieval.

The application of information technology to document management has been identified in literature as one of the best ways to improve records management, enabling a continuum of care of records. Electronic documents generation is growing at an increasingly alarming proportion in the banking sector (World Bank 2009). The advantages of electronic formats are well documented in the literature (ALOS Micrographics Corporation 2009; Ngulube 2011). However, the literature also identifies some drawbacks in electronic document formats if used as a strategy for managing organisational information. The Alaska State Archives (2009), Missouri State Archives (2011), Dexter (2011) and Ngulube (2011) indicated that electronic records have a serious security concern and the digital media are pricked by obsolescence.

The advantages and disadvantages of the various formats have led to the rise of hybrid systems or mixed media approach. A hybrid system is a combination of two or more approaches to document management. Saffady (2003:7) and Ngulube (2011:9) point out that because each document management strategy has different costs and benefits, the strength of one approach complements the limitations of the other. Ngulube (2011) argues that a hybrid system can be the most viable approach to managing a continuum of records through their life cycle by allocating appropriate document management regimes at different stages and being flexible enough to change to different formats and media especially in dynamic and technology-based enterprise systems. Thus, 'a hybrid approach that relies heavily on tapping into the advantages of paper, microfilming and electronic formats may offer the best records management solution in a cost-effective manner' (Ngulube 2011:9).

The theoretical framework that underpins the study

The theoretical framework is the standard or benchmark by which a researcher measures variables in a study. Unlike qualitative research which often builds up theories, quantitative research is informed by theories to investigate phenomena (Ngulube 2009). It helps the researcher see clearly the variables of the study; provides a general framework for data analysis and determines whether a topic or area of study is researchable or not (Khan 2011:5).

The researchers identified the records continuum theory as a suitable concept to use as a theoretical framework for understanding issues regarding effective document management regimes. This is because as noted by Svärd (2011:14), the model promotes a pro-active approach that emphasises the effective management of the entire records continuum. The records continuum theory promotes the effective creation, capture, dissemination, repurposing, use and preservation of documented information, for organisational businesses (An 2003).

Furthermore, the model provides a framework for understanding the continuum of records management responsibilities (McKemmish 2001; An 2003). Unlike the traditional life-cycle theory which recognises that records are created, used, maintained then disposed of, either by destruction as obsolete or by preservation as archives for their ongoing value; the continuum concept suggests that four actions continue or recur throughout the life of a record: identification of records; intellectual control of them; provision of access to them; and physical control of them (Roper & Millar 2009). It challenges the traditional view that separates records keeping phases and supports a more holistic approach that offers conituity and consistence. It may be defined as:

> a consistent and coherent regime of management processes from the time of creation of records (and before creation, in the design of record-keeping systems), through to the preservation and use of records as archives. (Chachage & Ngulube 2006:5)

According to the records continuum model records management is a continous process that focuses on activities that create records. Svärd (2011:16), supporting McKemmish (2001), also purpots that the model promotes record-keeping that connects the whole organisational functioning, and is stable enough to deal with a dynamic and changing context that can be influenced by legal, political, administrative, social, commercial, technological, cultural, and historical variables across time and space.

The records continuum model is characterised by progressive principles that can well be applied to document management in an endeavour to make choices on the best possible approach to manage documents in an effective and cost-efficient way. Therefore, the mechanisms of the best practice behind the records continuum model were observed as ideal for use as a theoretical framework for identifying effectiveness and efficiency in document management, because they focus on consistency, continuity, integration, coherence, efficiency, effectiveness, interdisciplinarism, accountability, authenticity, and appreciate the dynamism of and continous need for interface with technologies (National Archives of Australia 2003; Roper & Millar 2009; Svard 2011).

Research methodology

The quantitative research methodology was used in the study. It has a range of research approaches that include descriptive or observational studies, and experimental studies. The descriptive case study design which focuses on the grounded interpretation and understanding of research subjects by collecting data using techniques such as observation, questionnaires, interviews and documents analysis was chosen (Chimbari et al. 2011; Richards 2011; Rubin & Rubin 2005).

This study specifically used the questionnaire and interviews as research instruments for data collection. Data was collected from all the 15 employees working in the two departments working with records as outlined above (also see Table 1a and Table 1b). Of this number, four were ICTs technicians, five were records clerks two were records supervisors, one was an archivist and three were from top management comprising a Managing Director and two General Managers. All the respondents were employees of the commercial bank who had over two years' experience in handling documents and records in the institution. This was the basis of choosing these respondents for data collection.

The analysis of data entailed establishing the frequency of ideas, attitudes or concepts within the whole body of collected data and using several presentation methods to make these ideas visible. This involved the following steps: data examination, data tabling, and data charting. Examining the data involved grouping the responses under major categories according to the research question being answered. This was tabled into text, frequency, cumulative or scatter-gram tables depending on the type of data in question. From these tables, several graphs were drawn to enhance visual display of the results yielded by the study. Microsoft Access® and Microsoft Excel® application programmes were used in the data analysis and presentation processes.

Results and discussion

The aim of this section is to provide meaningful summaries through a range of presentation techniques from the collected raw data and as a quantitative study, tables, graphs, matrices and charts were basically the main presentation tools used (Chimbari et al. 2011). In analysing the data from the semi-structured interviews and questionnaires, the researcher decided to group the findings together since the interview guide was adapted from the questionnaire and created to complement data from the questionnaire. The arithmetic

TABLE 1a: Document format benefits and constraints matrix as reflected by respondents.

Format	Benefits	Constraints (Costs)
Paper	Preservation standards are known	Requires large storage space
	Legally admissible as evidence	Cumbersome nature affects retrieval
	Easy to determine authenticity	Bulky nature affects security
	Adheres to document retention regulations and legislature	Expensive to deliver were remote, multiple and simultaneous access are necessary
	Not technology dependent	Slow down business processes

TABLE 1b: Document format benefits and constraints matrix as reflected by respondents.

Format	Benefits	Constraints (Costs)
Electronic	Timely availability of information	Not legally admissible as evidence
	Promotes remote, multiple and simultaneous access	Preservation standards are unclear
	Overcomes the space problem	Difficult to determine authenticity
	Speed up business processes	Unstable or volatile storage media
		Manipulability compromises security
		Technical skill for support is expensive to employ, contract or hire
		Technology dependence triggers obsolescence

calculations and percentages were rounded off to the nearest whole number to simplify the analysis.

The population of the study comprised of 15 staff members: five from the IT and SLD and seven from the SSCAD and three from the top management. It included the managing Director, general managers, supervisors, IT staff and other clerical staff.

Questionnaire response rate was 100% from the two departments since all the respondents returned the completed questionnaires. Interviews were successfully conducted with the managing director, one general manager, two supervisors, two IT staff and two clerical staff. Though this was a purposive sample, the aim was to ensure that informants were recruited from both the two departments included in the study. There was an excellent response rate because the respondents were interested in the outcome of the study.

Staff understanding of documents management and cost-benefit analysis

Data collected showed that the top management had a higher understanding of both document management and the cost-benefit analysis concept. Using a rating scale of 1–30, the top management had a higher score of 25; followed by 13 from general managers; eight from supervisory staff and five from both technical and clerical staff as shown on the comparative scatter graph in Figure 1. However, it is evident that since technical and clerical staff was more involved in document management in their daily activities, they understood it better than their immediate supervisors who said that they need training courses to improve their appreciation of both document management and CBA.

Document management strategies used by the selected financial institution and their costs and benefits

This analysis presents the participant's responses to the question regarding the costs and benefits of document management approaches used by the institution. The document management strategies of choice were paper and electronic formats (see Figure 2).

The responses are summarised in the cost-benefit matrix shown in Table 1a and Table 1b. The responses reflect that the bank was comfortable with the paper as a records storage medium over the electronic format mainly because of its trusted security, legal acceptance and technology independence. As further shown in Figure 2, the electronic format was mostly preferred for a creation and immediate use purposes. Whilst there was mention of the computer output microfilm (COM) its wide acceptance and use in the bank had not yet been fully experimented with as a preferable document management format as evidenced by its limited utilisation in the archival stage of the records.

The following figures which were obtained from a single response by archivist regarding the rate of paper documents accumulation in the storage area are instructive:

1. 42m³ per quarter in 2009
2. 34m³ per quarter in 2010
3. 44m³ per quarter in 2011

An average for the last three years given was calculated using the mean as follows:

Mean ($\bar{x}$) = Sum of Responses OR $\sum(x)$ (Where x is the response and n is Number of Responses n the number of responses)

$$\sum(x) = 42m^3 + 34m^3 + 44m^3 \qquad \text{[Eqn 1]}$$

Therefore (x) = 120, and the Sum of the Number of Responses = 3. Therefore, Mean = 120 / 3 = 40m³. Using results from the calculation above; on average, the rate of paper accumulation at the bank is 40m³ per year. Over a year this means that a storage area of averagely 120m³ (a standard classroom) may be filled up by paper files or archival boxes. Considering that the archival repository was in an expensive city centre environment and the space was bound to be filled up in less than five years at the rate given above; the cost of the paper as a document storage medium is higher surpassing the benefits put forward for it.

Data about the name, range and types of electronic document management software used by the bank, initial installation costs, support and updates costs as well as corresponding

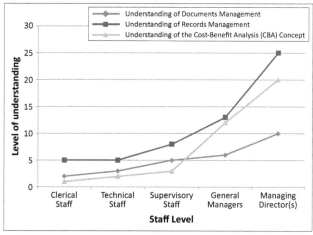

FIGURE 1: Level of staff understanding of document management, records management and the cost-benefit analysis concepts.

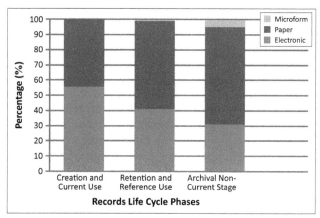

FIGURE 2: Document media ranges as the records moved in the continuum of records care through the records life cycle at the Commercial Bank of Zimbabwe.

maintenance costs was not provided on the grounds of being classified information according to the bank's Information Policy.

However, the information regarding tangible costs, which is valuable information about the bank was only one aspect of 'costs' needed to establish findings for questions guiding this study. The actual costs, or tangible costs was only a single aspect of the 'costs' of document management regimes to be measured so the other aspect, that is, intangible costs was dwelt with as illustrated in Table 1a and Table 1b. Options for electronic records storage at the financial institution are illustrated in Figure 3.

According to the respondents, electronic document formats were not fully utilised as result of costs related to acquisition and maintenance of equipment; upgrade, redesign or enhancement of networks; acquisition, testing and maintenance of software; training for support staff and users; document conversion; and system administration.

Skills and competencies of the records management staff at financial institution regarding the cost-benefit analysis of document management

Information about staff skills and competencies was categorised based on interview responses captured from different staff at different levels. Their responses regarding choosing the appropriate document format were measured against a standard drawn using the records continuum model. On the other hand, their responses regarding carrying out the cost-benefit analysis were measured against the methods of best practice set out by the cost or benefit analysis guideline set by National Archives of Australia (2003) and the International Records Management Trust (2006). The results are summarised in Table 2.

The following clustered column graph (Figure 4) shows the respondents' perceptions about each document management strategy's costs and benefits on a rating scale of 1–5. From the results it appears that the staff was unsure about the use of microforms as a document management strategy which is similar to Svärd's study results of 2011. Whilst the paper based system is portrayed as more beneficial compared to its costs; and the electronic system is considered to have both high costs and high benefits, microforms are not clearly appreciated as a storage or retention medium for bank records. Considering that many scholars have actually advocated for microforms (Western Micrographics Imaging Systems 2008; ALOS Micrographics Corporation, 2009; Ngulube 2011) because of their space efficiency, stable storage media and relatively easy retrievability, this calls for further probe.

Conclusions and recommendations

The findings may not be generalised because the case study design was used, even though these may have some significant input into the cost benefit analysis and its influence on document management strategies. As noted by

Rowley (2002), the most limiting aspect of the application of a case study research:

> is to lift the investigation from a descriptive account of 'what happens' to a piece of research that can lay claim to being a worthwhile, if modest addition to knowledge. (p. 16)

Case studies as a research method or strategy have traditionally been viewed as lacking rigour and objectivity when compared with other social research methods (Rowley 2002:16). Verification and validation of results from case study researches has often been done by comparing with other similar case studies (Rowley 2002). The study is also limited by the fact of it being a relatively new area in the

TABLE 2: Staff competencies regarding the cost-benefit analysis of document management.

Staff Level	Knowledge about the available range of alternative document formats	Choosing the appropriate document format	Carrying out the cost-benefit analysis
Clerical Staff	Paper and electronic	Low competence	Not appreciated
Technical Staff	Paper, electronic and microforms	Low competence	Not appreciated
Supervisory Staff	Paper and electronic	Low competence	Not appreciated
General Manager(s)	Paper and electronic	Low competence	Mildly appreciated
Managing Director(s)	Paper and electronic	Low competence	Appreciated

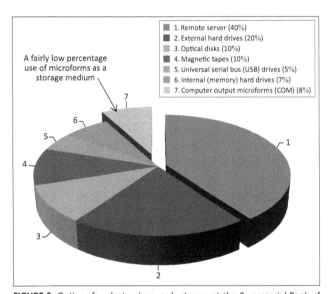

FIGURE 3: Options for electronic records storage at the Commercial Bank of Zimbabwe.

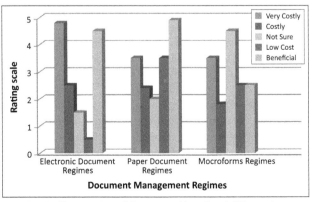

FIGURE 4: Staff perceptions of the costs and benefits of different document management regimes.

banking and finance industry in Zimbabwe and thereby restricting any potential comparisons with other similar studies in the Zimbabwean environment to verify results. We therefore, recommend that more case studies on the subject be conducted in general, and in Zimbabwe in particular in order to marshal evidence from a number of case studies in order to build theory as suggested by Rowley (2002).

A précis of the research findings from the preceding section inevitably calls for multiple conclusions. Each document management approach suited a different part of the records' life cycle and the trend at this particular financial institution was that electronic document systems were mainly employed for creation and current use whilst paper was mainly used as a retention and storage medium. Microforms were not yet considered by the bank as a major document management solution to counter the inadequacies of both electronic and paper approaches. In a nutshell:

- The financial institution is not using periodical cost-benefit analysis to determine document management approaches chosen. The document management approaches used are therefore not coordinated to improve operational efficiency.
- The skills and competences of staff on both document management and cost analysis are limited which has a negative impact on their appreciation of the need for more effective and efficient document management.
- Considering the rate of paper accumulation in the Securities, Safe Custody and Archives Department at the institution, if a document management strategy that enables miniaturisation of document is not adopted, more expensive office space will have to be acquired to store paper-based documents.
- The financial institution should create institutional regulations enabling periodical cost-benefit analysis of document management regimes used by the institution at least at quarterly intervals per year following *Appendix 10 – Recordkeeping cost-benefit analysis set out by the National Archives of Australia* (2011). The analysis should involve the finance department, archives department and relevant legal authorities. This is expected to enable more effective alternatives to be chosen since results of the cost-benefit analysis will weigh both costs and benefits of each and every strategy.
- A hybrid approach that maximises the use of electronic documents for current records management needs, paper based systems for intermediate reference and short term legal requirements and finally microforms for archival preservation is recommended for adoption by the bank.
- Electronic records may be best used for documenting current, active transactions in banks, such as recording customer transactions, filling up and updating ledger profiles capturing applications to open accounts and any other forms of current transactional billings. Paper could then be used for semi-current reference needs, especially for those records under legal obligation for retention by the *Statutory Instrument 23 of 1995, The Serious Offences (Retention of Documents) Regulations of 1995 [Act 20/90] section 3(b)* (Government of Zimbabwe 1995) which prescribes that every financial institution including banks should retain documents for not less than six years. For long term preservation however, micrographics could then be applied considering that microforms would solve the space problem whilst guaranteeing security, retrievability and legal compliance and countering the cumbersome nature and inefficiencies associated with paper based systems.
- To improve staff competencies and understanding of documents management needs, there is a need to employ a qualified records manager to interface with technicians and clerical staff on one hand and the top management on the other. Secondly, there should be on-the-job staff training complimented by attendance at relevant workshops and seminars to improve staff's understanding of both the cost-benefit analysis concept and document management and their operationalisation.

Acknowledgement

The authors would like to acknowledge the University of South Africa (South Africa) for the funding and support without which this research would not have been possible.

Competing interest

The authors declare that they have no financial or personal relationship(s) which may have inappropriately influenced them in writing this article.

Authors' contributions

R.D. (National University of Science and Technology) did the literature review, designed data collection instruments and collected and analysed the data. P.N. (University of South Africa) was the project leader, conceptualised the research and dealt with the reviewers' suggestions. A.D. (National University of Science and Technology) assisted in data analysis and the write-up of the article.

References

Akotia, P., 2003, 'Public sector records systems in Ghana: Some lessons in development management', *African Journal of Library, Archives and Information Science* 13(2), 107–117.

Akussah, H., 2002, 'Records management and preservation in government ministries and departments in Ghana,' *African Journal of Library, Archives and Information Science* 12(2), 155–165.

Alaska State Archives., 2009, 'Micrographics Lab', viewed 23 January 2011, from http://www.archives.state.ak.us/micrographics.html

ALOS Micrographics Corporation., 2009, 'Why electronic records management?', viewed 23 January 2011, from http://www.alosusa.com.why-electronic-document-management

Ambira, C. & Kemoni, H., 2011, 'Records management and risk management at Kenya Commercial Bank Limited, Nairobi', *South African Journal of Information Management* 13(1), 1–11, viewed 12 December 2011, from http://www.sajim.co.za

An, X., 2003, 'An integrated approach to records management', *Information Management Journal*, July/August, 24–30, viewed 22 December 2011, from www.interpares.org/

Báeza, A. & Herrerob, L.C., 2012, 'Using contingent valuation and cost-benefit analysis to design a policy for restoring cultural heritage', *Journal of Cultural Heritage* 13(3), 235–245. http://dx.doi.org/10.1016/j.culher.2010.12.005

Chachage, B. & Ngulube, P., 2006, 'Management of business records in Tanzania: An exploratory case study of selected companies', *South African Journal of Information Management* 8(3), 45–56, viewed 14 February 2012, from http://www.sajim.co.za

Chimbari, M.J., Mukaratirwa, S., Osman, T. & Naik, Y.S. (eds.), 2011, *Research methodology training course module for multi-disciplinary teams*, University of Botswana and Okavango Research Institute, Gaborone.

Commercial Bank of Zimbabwe, 2011, 'Company profile', viewed 14 February 2012, from http://www.cbz.co.zw/

Dexter, B., 2011, *Managing the reprographic process*, McGraw-Hill, London.

Government of Zimbabwe, 1995, *Serious Offenses (Retention of Documents) Regulations Act No. 20/90,* Government Gazette of the Republic of Zimbabwe, Government Printers, Harare.

Government of Zimbabwe, 2004, '*Banking Act Chapter 24:20*', viewed 19 May 2012, from http://www.rbz.co.zw/pdfs/BLSS/Legislation/Banking%20Act.pdf

International Records Management Trust (IRMT), 2006, *Project management guideline: Appendix D – A cost/benefit analysis guideline,* IRMT, London.

International Organization for Standardization (ISO 15489-1), 2001, 'Information and documentation – records management – Part 1: General', viewed 19 May 2012, from http://www.iso.org/

Khan, R.E., 2011, 'Developing the theoretical and conceptual framework', viewed 10 January 2012, from http://journclasses.pbworks.com/f/theoretical+framework.ppt

McKemmish, S., 2001, 'Teaching recordkeeping and archiving continuum style', *Archival Science* 6(2), 219–230.

Megill, K.A. & Schantz, H.F., 2000, 'Document management: new technologies for the information services manager', *Library Management* 21(2), 109–115.

Missouri State Archives., 2011, 'Guidelines for preservation microfilming', viewed 26 February 2012, from http://www.sos.mo.gov/records/recmgnt

Mnjama, N., 2003, 'Archives and records management in Kenya: problems and prospects', *Records Management Journal* 13(2), 91–101. http://dx.doi.org/10.1108/09565690310485315

National Archives of Australia, 2003, 'Appendix 10-record-keeping cost-benefit analysis', viewed 12 December 2011, from http://www.naa.gov.au/

National Archives of Australia, 2011, 'Appendix 10-record-keeping cost-benefit analysis', 3rd edn., viewed 12 December 2011, from http://www.naa.gov.au/

Ngulube, P., 2009, *Preservation and access to public records and archives in South Africa,* Lambert Academic Publishing Saarbrücken.

Ngulube, P., 2011, 'Cost analysis and the effective management of records throughout their life cycle', *South Africa Archives Journal* 44, 1–21.

Ngulube, P. & Tafor, V.F., 2006, 'An overview of the management of public records and archives in the member countries of the East and Southern Africa Regional Branch of the International Council on Archives (ESARBICA)', *Journal of the Society of Archivists* 27, 69–86.

Richards, T., 2011, 'Research methods in information sciences', *Academy of Management Review* 17(4), 530–539.

Roper, M. & Millar, L. (eds.), 2009, *Managing the creation, use and disposal of records: training in electronic records management,* IRMT London.

Rowley, J., 2002, 'Using case studies in research', *Management Research News* 25(1), 16–27. http://dx.doi.org/10.1108/01409170210782990

Rubin, H.J. & Rubin, I., 2005, *Case study research: Qualitative and quantitative interviewing,* Sage Publications, London.

Saffady, W., 2003, *Digital document management,* ARMA International, Prairie Village, Kan.

Svärd, P., 2011, 'The interface between enterprise content management and records management in changing organisations', Thesis for the degree of Licentiate, Härnösand, Sweden: Mid Sweden University, Dept. of Information Technology and Media.

Tough, A. & Moss, M., 2006, *Records keeping in a hybrid environment: managing the creation, use, preservation and disposal of unpublished information objects and context,* Chandos Publishing Oxford.

Wamukoya, J., 2000, 'Records and archives as a basis for good government: implications and challenges for records managers and archivists in Africa', *Records Management Journal* 10(1), 23–33. http://dx.doi.org/10.1108/EUM0000000007254

Wang, S.J., Middleton, B., Prosser, L.A., Bardon, C.G. & Spurr, C.D., 2003, 'A cost-benefit analysis of electronic medical records in primary care', *The American Journal of Medicine* 114, 397–403. http://dx.doi.org/10.1016/S0002-9343(03)00057-3

Western Micrographics Imaging Systems., 2008, 'Microfilm: the economical choice', viewed 12 February 2012, from http://www.westernmicrographic.com/html

Williams, C., 2006, *Managing archives: Foundations and practice.* Chandos Publishing, Oxford. http://dx.doi.org/10.1533/9781780630892

World Bank, 2009, 'Annual report: year in review', viewed 12 May 2012, from http://siteresources.worldbank.org

25

Information and communications technology adoption amongst township micro and small business: The case of Soweto

Author:
Carl Marnewick[1]

Affiliation:
[1]Department of Applied Information Systems, University of Johannesburg, South Africa

Correspondence to:
Carl Marnewick

Email:
cmarnewick@uj.ac.za

Postal address:
PO Box 254, Auckland Park 2004, South Africa

Background: No empirical evidence is available on whether or not information and communications technology (ICT) is adopted by South African township micro and small businesses (MSBs) in order to grow the business. ICT, as an enabler, can grow the business. It is evident from literature that ICT enables MSBs to be more productive and efficient.

Objectives: This research determines to what extent ICT is adopted by MSBs in Soweto, and whether or not a positive correlation exists between the adoption rate of ICT and the financial and growth performance of the MSB itself.

Method: A structured questionnaire was completed by 978 respondents to determine the extent of ICT adoption and for what ICT is used. This exploratory research provides new knowledge about the acceptance of ICT within township MSBs.

Results: The results indicate that ICT is not used to the fullest by MSBs. Rather, it is used as a basic tool for doing business but it does not form an integral part of the business. This research provides insight into the usage and adoption of ICT and it opens the door for further cross-analysis research.

Conclusion: Education and training are needed to ensure that MSBs use ICT to the fullest. MSBs embracing ICT can evolve from a survivalist SME to a more sustainable micro and small MSB.

Introduction

Small and medium enterprises (SMEs) are the heartbeat of any country's economy. This is even more so in developing countries where SMEs are responsible for employment and the growth of the economy (Beck, Demirguc-Kunt & Levine 2005; Cravo, Gourlay & Becker 2012). One aspect that can assist SMEs in growing the business is information and communication technology (ICT). Management literature highlights the value of ICT and information in the organisational context (Hu & Plant 2001). ICT can enable SMEs to achieve these goals, of employment and growth, if it is adopted and incorporated into the day-to-day management of the SME.

There is currently no empirical evidence of whether or not micro and small businesses (MSBs), as a special type of SME, in townships adopt any type of ICT to grow the business. The term township originated in the apartheid era and began when non-white people (black people, people of mixed-race and Indians) were limited to living near or working in white-only communities. Township MSBs play a major role in the creation of wealth and employment within the realm of townships, as there are no other forms of employment in those areas (Mbonyane 2006). According to SBP (2013):

> The contribution that small business makes in generating employment is near universally recognised. So is the corollary acknowledgement, that a healthy and much expanded small business community could be a keystone of a new economic deal for South Africa. (n.p.)

The argument is that ICT, as a business enabler, should be capable of assisting MSBs if it is adopted by the MSBs. ICT provides an opportunity for MSBs to improve their efficiency and effectiveness, and even to gain competitive advantage (Arendt 2008; Thong & Yap 1995). Research carried out, on rural SMEs in the United States of America (USA) in the late 1990s, concluded that SMEs will only adopt ICT if there is a perception that ICT will assist in overcoming a business problem or opportunity (Premkumar & Roberts 1999:470). Some of the benefits mentioned by the SMEs that had adopted ICT were reduced turnaround time, increased transaction speed, access to current information and reduction in data entry errors (Premkumar & Roberts 1999:482). There are, however, SMEs that deliberately did not adopt any ICT. One of the reasons was that the SMEs did not find any need for these technologies in their businesses.

This research is innovative as it highlights that township MSBs do not adopt ICT and that interventions are needed to cross the digital divide in townships. The results provide statistical information on the 'raw' rates of ICT adoption for a sample of MSBs in the township of Soweto. This research also provides a baseline for future research. Future research can include comparative analysis of various MSBs as well as SMEs in various townships, and analysis of developed and developing countries.

Studies within the discipline of ICT adoption have not focused on SMEs or, for that matter, MSBs within townships. Instead, research has been focused on traditional companies and SMEs and how ICT enabled those organisations to perform financially (Lucchetti & Sterlacchini 2004; Premkumar & Roberts 1999; Thong & Yap 1995).

This research addresses the lack of empirical knowledge with regard to ICT adoption and usage within township MSBs. An understanding of the problem provides various possibilities for South Africa. Firstly, the adoption of ICT will increase the revenue of the individual MSBs and ultimately the growth of the economy at large. Secondly, it also provides focus areas where ICT and the type of ICT can and should be deployed to assist MSBs.

A structured questionnaire was circulated amongst MSB owners within Soweto. This was circulated through a survey consultancy company that interviewed the population. This company deployed resources, the personnel of which interviewed the various SMB owners. The interviewers were briefed on the purpose of the research, and additionally about how each question related to the overall research hypotheses. The data were then captured and analysed using SPSS.

The article is divided into four sections. The first section focuses on the literature of MSBs, as well as the technology adoption model (TAM), and how it can and should assist MSBs in the growth of the economy. The second section focuses on the research methodology and how the results were collected from the various respondents. The third section is an analysis of the results of the 978 respondents, and focuses on the type of ICT that the MSBs used as well as the business reasons that the ICT was used. The fourth and last section specifies the impact of ICT adoption and the consequences of adopting or not adopting ICT within the realm of township MSBs.

Literature review

The value of the small business sector is recognised in economies worldwide which is irrespective of whether it is a developed or a developing economy (Thurik & Wennekers 2004; Hotho & Champion 2011). According to Mahembe (2011:13): 'the contribution towards growth, job creation and social progress is valued highly and small businesses are regarded as an essential element in a successful formula for achieving economic growth'. The contribution of SMEs in

South Africa to the economy is summarised as per Table 1. The World Bank (2006), however, estimated that SMEs would contribute 39% to the generation of employment whereas China's SME sector contributed 78% to its total employment. This is an area of concern given the high unemployment rate in South Africa. SMEs can bridge this gap.

According to Mandisa Mpahlwa, the former South African Minister of Trade and Industry, the small business sector in 2006 comprised 2 million small businesses which present almost 98% of the total number of South African companies (Njiro, Mazwai & Urban 2010). Collectively SMEs employed 55% of the country's labour force. However, 87% of these small businesses are surviving on a day-to-day basis and they are owned by black people. Women owned 41% of these. Trends such as these are very significant, as they illustrate both the potential and the challenges for small business growth (Njiro et al. 2010).

SMEs are normally defined by three components i.e. by revenue, assets (excluding fixed property) or the number of employees. Each country has varying cut-off points and these may even vary by industry. South Africa's National *Small Business Act* (Act No. 102 of 1996) defines SMEs as a 'separate and distinct business entity', and this includes cooperatives and non-governmental organisations (Kennedy, Bounds & Goldman 2011).

This *Act* uses the number of employees, the size as well as the annual turnover as measurement criteria. SMEs can be classified as follows:

- Survivalist enterprise: The income that is generated is less than the minimum income standard. Survivalist enterprises include hawkers, vendors and subsistence farmers. Survivalist enterprises are often categorised as part of the micro enterprise sector.
- Micro enterprise: The turnover is less than the stipulated South African value-added tax (VAT) registration limit. These enterprises do not formally register the enterprise and include, for example, *spaza* shops, minibus taxis and household industries. Micro enterprises employ no more than five people. The word '*spaza*' means 'camouflaged' or 'hidden' in township slang and, therefore, '*spaza* shop' refers to a camouflaged or hidden shop in a township (Terblanche 1991:37).

TABLE 1: Contribution of South Africa's small and medium enterprises to the economy.

Enterprises	Number of firms (%)	Employment (%)	GDP (%)
Survivalist	19.6	2.2	
Micro (0)	31.3	3.5	5.8
Micro (1–4)	19.8	6.5	
Very small	20.5	13	
Small enterprises	6.8	15.7	13.9
Medium enterprises	1.3	13	15
Large	0.7	46.1	65.2

Source: Falkena, H., n.d., 'SMES' access to finance in South Africa – A supply-side regulatory review', in H. Falkena, (ed.), *Financial Services and Regulation*, South Africa.
GDP, gross domestic product.

- Very small enterprise: They employ fewer than 10 employees, except for the mining, electricity, manufacturing and construction sectors, in which they employ fewer than 20 employees. These enterprises operate in the formal market and have access to ICT.
- Small enterprise: They employ up to 50 employees. Small enterprises exhibit more complex business practices.
- Medium enterprise: They employee a maximum number of 100 employees, or up to 200 employees for the mining, electricity, manufacturing and construction sectors. These enterprises might have additional management layers (Abor & Quartey 2010:221).

Another way to classify SMEs is based on the classification methods of the Bolton Committee, which classifies and describes SMEs on the basis of sectors (Abor & Quartey 2010). In the manufacturing, mining and construction sectors, it includes all companies that have 200 or fewer employees. In the road transport industry, companies are considered to be small when the number of vehicles is five or fewer. Companies operating in retail, wholesale or services are measured on the basis of their annual turnover.

The South African classification of SMEs is substantially different from that of the European definition. SMEs, as per the European definition, imply companies with less than 250 employees (Silvius 2004). The factors that mainly determine if a company is an SME are displayed in Table 2 (European Commission 2012).

An SME in South Africa's SME sector is required to fulfil the following:

> [They are] expected to fulfil a number of roles, ranging from poverty alleviation and employment creation to international competitiveness. Not only are these very divergent policy objectives, but the policy instruments introduced to meet these objectives can be equally different, ranging from literacy training to technological advice. (Blueprint Strategy & Policy (Pty) Ltd 2005:9)

It is now widely accepted that small businesses are the chief contributor to job creation worldwide and this trend is also true of South Africa, as per Table 1.

In South Africa, SMEs contribution is 56% to the employment in the private sector and 36% to the gross domestic product (Olawale & Garwe 2010:729). They also state that small businesses are one of the best ways to address unemployment through the potential of the small business itself to create employment and to promote the development of small businesses.

SMEs also play an important role within townships to uplift the local community and to create jobs. Townships are a

particularly South African phenomena and a deliberate manipulation of former urban planning that designed cities in terms of race. The creation of Soweto, which is a conglomeration of townships, was founded to house mainly black labourers who worked in mines and other industries in the city of Johannesburg. An increasing number of black people were relocated from inner city 'black spots' to Soweto, as the centre of Johannesburg was reserved for white people (Njiro et al. 2010:6). In 1963, after a public four-year competition, the name Soweto was adopted for the South Western Townships (Njiro et al. 2010:6). Apartheid planning did not provide any infrastructure to these settlements and all manner of shelters, including shacks, flourished. Residents had limited access to capital, education and basic social and economic rights. They were also prohibited from owning and running businesses.

According to Njiro et al. (2010):

> Of the 200 000 Soweto businesses, about 83% have turnovers of less than R10 000 a month. The objective is to grow these small businesses into entities with turnovers exceeding R1 million. (p.8)

To achieve this goal of growing MSBs from survivalist and micro enterprises into very small and small enterprises, ICT can be used. ICT is seen as an enabler for business (Mitra 2005). The usage of ICT can reduce the cost of operations and increase profits. This is applicable to any enterprise, irrespective of size. ICT can help MSBs to cut costs through the improvement of internal business processes, improved communication with customers as well as suppliers and an improved supply chain online (Kannabiran & Dharmalingam 2012:192). ICT can also help MSBs to manage, source, produce, plan and ultimately support decisions in their daily operations.

This is not always the case, however. ICT deployment in many Chinese MSBs resulted in negative performance which is not in parallel with the economic growth that was experienced during the same period. The critical challenges were not caused by the failure of ICT technologies. Rather, inadequate support and business processes were common obstacles in the deployment of ICT (Sidney, Tina & Choy 2010). Another case in point is Indonesia, where MSBs are one of the economic backbones. In their daily operation some of the MSBs conduct their business using ICT. However, the majority do not use ICT in an optimum way and daily operations are still performed manually (Santosa & Kusumawardani 2010).

MSBs adopt ICT to achieve efficiency and in response to a variety of environmental and internal pressures (Khalifa & Davison 2006:275). Moreover, the MSBs most likely to use ICT are very likely to be technically competent already. MSBs do not adopt ICT uniquely as a response to coercive and normative pressures from external and internal sources. They are also strongly motivated by the perceived desirability and feasibility of ICT under consideration.

The literature review indicates that there is a case to be made for the adoption and use of ICT within the day-to-day

TABLE 2: Factors determining small and medium enterprises status.

Company category	Employees	Turnover
Medium-sized	< 250	≤ € 50 million
Small	< 50	≤ € 10 million
Micro	< 10	≤ € 2 million

running of an SME. The second part of the literature review focuses on the current models which explain when and why MSBs would adopt and use ICT.

Davis (1989) emphasises that the (1) perceived usefulness and the (2) perceived ease of use determines whether someone will adopt technology or not. This thinking realised the benefits of the technology acceptance model (TAM). This model was further refined by Davis, Bagozzi and Warshaw (1989), who included (1) the attitude towards using and (2) the behavioural intention to use additional aspects of TAM. Figure 1 illustrates TAM.

Various other models have emerged since then, but all of them basically incorporate the original components of TAM (Venkatesh, Morris, Davis & Davis 2003). To relate this back to MSBs in Soweto, MSBs will only adopt ICT if there is a perception that ICT will assist in the growth and sustainability of the MSB itself and if the perception exists that it is easy to use a specified technology.

Lucchetti and Sterlacchini (2004) classify the adoption of ICT in SMEs into three categories:

1. General-use information and communication technologies (ICTs) include collaboration tools where the rate of adoption is high and do not depend on size (i.e. number of employees) and industry.
2. Production-integrating ICTs include local area network (LAN), electronic data interchange (EDI) and intranet. This type of ICTs is linked to intra and inter-firm production processes; they are more expensive than general-use ICTs and are dependent on relevant technological skills.
3. Market-oriented ICTs are jointly identified by the presence and the content of a firm's web site and are used to improve visibility and provide detailed information of products, with a view to attract potential customers (p. 152).

This is all well and good in the context of a developed nation, but access to ICT in Soweto is not a given. The results from the South African 2012 census highlight the digital divide. The 'proportion of households owning cellphones increased from 31.9% in 2001 to 88.9% in 2011' (Statistics South Africa 2012). The proportion of households with computers increased from 8.5% to 21.1% between 2001 and 2011, respectively (Statistics South Africa 2012). Figure 2 shows the percentage of South African households that have access to the Internet. A relatively high proportion of these households, 64.8%, have no access to the Internet.

The highest percentage of households reported that cellphones are used to access the Internet (Statistics South Africa 2012). A report on the status of ICT in Africa highlighted the challenges that MSBs face. The main challenges are infrastructure and a growing ICT skills gap (Yonazi et al. 2012).

The review of the literature highlighted two important aspects: (1) MSBs as well as SMEs are important for any country's economy and (2) the adoption of ICT itself can improve the profitability of an MSB.

This leads to the research problem at hand: is ICT, per se, adopted by township MSBs in order to improve the profitability and sustainability of the MSB?

The research is of an exploratory nature and, therefore, the focus is on the actual use of ICT and not necessarily on the causes of technology acceptance. Given the model in Figure 1, the focus is not on the factors that influence the use of ICT but on the actual adoption of ICT itself. The reason for this is that one first needs to understand a concept before it can be explained.

Given this rationale, the following research questions are posed:

1. What type of ICT is adopted by MSBs in Soweto?
2. Is the adoption of ICT dictated by the type of MSB?
3. Is there a correlation between the type of ICT adopted and the profitability of the MSB?
4. Is ICT applied differently based on the type of MSB?

The following section contains a discussion of the research methodology that was followed to gather the responses.

Research methodology

Research designs focus on validating the research question through a testing project and can be either quantitative research designs or qualitative research designs (Feilzer 2010; Huizingh 2007). Quantitative research focuses on answering the research question through the collection of numerical data and the statistical analysis of this data (Balnaves & Caputi 2001; Blaikie 2003).

A structured questionnaire was developed focusing on two aspects: (1) biographical information such as income and type of SME and (2) the type of ICT used, for instance cellphones, as well as the frequency of usage. The types

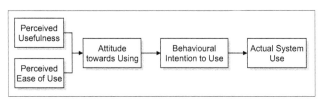

Source: Davis, F.D., Bagozzi, R.P. & Warshaw, P.R., 1989, 'User acceptance of computer technology: A comparison of two theoretical models', *Management Science* 35(8), 982–1003.
FIGURE 1: Technology acceptance model.

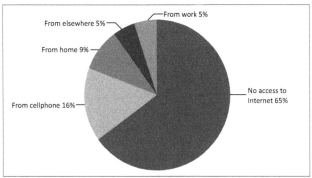

Source: Statistics South Africa, 2012, Census 2011 *Statistical Release*, Statistics South Africa, Pretoria.
FIGURE 2: Internet access.

of ICT selected are founded on research, indicating that mobile technology is a main enabling technology (Ngassam, Ntawanga & Eloff 2013). Building on mobile technology, the next levels of technology are personal computers (PCs), laptops and tablets.

Structured questionnaires make use of closed questions where the results can be analysed quantitatively for patterns and trends. The researcher opted for a structured questionnaire because it ensures that each respondent is presented with exactly the same questions in the same order. This ensures integrity in longitudinal studies as well as comparisons between various subgroups.

TAM, which informs this research, uses 28 questions to measure the perceived usefulness (14 questions) and perceived ease of use (14 questions). The intention is to adopt the TAM questions in a specific environment and for a specific application (Polun *et al.* 2004). The results can then be used to measure and correlate the perceived usefulness and ease of use. The problem that was faced in Soweto is that there are no data available on the acceptance of ICT and, therefore, the ease of use and usefulness of a specific technology is of no relevance at this point in time. It is important to understand, within the context of Soweto and its ICT adversity, what technologies are currently used as well as the purposes for which they are used. The 28 questions of TAM could, therefore, not be used as they are normally worded, and a shortened structure questionnaire, derived from TAM, was designed. The questions were grouped into two major sections focusing, firstly, on the purpose of the respective technologies and, secondly, on how frequent these technologies are used. The rationale is that the results will then be used to develop in-depth TAM questionnaires for each of the technologies, once there is an understanding of what technologies are used and how frequently.

The questionnaires were administered via a private consulting firm that was familiar with Soweto and the MSBs within the different suburbs. The consulting firm made use of runners to interview the SME owners. The runners were used as a pilot to test the questionnaire to identify potential problems and to make improvements. Using the runners as a pilot scheme, also made them aware of the type of responses that they could expect.

A briefing session was held to explain the questions to the runners, and the types of answers that should be provided by the SME owners. Soweto was divided into its suburbs (33 in total) and 30 SME owners were picked randomly to complete the questionnaire. The owners were chosen on an availability basis as the runners surveyed the suburb. The language of choice used was either English or the native language of the SME owner which consisted, in most cases, of Zulu. The contact details of the SME were also added for follow-up questionnaires and future comparative analysis. A total of 978 completed questionnaires were received. The quality of the responses was of such a nature that all the questionnaires could be used.

The data gathered in this survey were processed and analysed using SPSS, a statistical analysis software package (Argyrous 2011; Huizingh 2007). SPSS is able to perform enhanced data management and has extended reporting capabilities.

Reliability is concerned with how well the survey data can be reproduced, and validity is a measure of how well the survey measures what it is supposed to measure (Kirk & Miller 1986; Kitchenham & Pfleeger 2002; Litwin 1995). Some available reliability checks that can be done in a survey are presented by Litwin (1995):

- Test-retest is relevant when a survey is sampled at different points in time (Kitchenham & Pfleeger 2002). In this research the survey was sampled for the first time; therefore, a test-retest is only possible in future.
- As scales were used in the questionnaire, it was very important to check internal consistency. Internal consistency is a measure when assessing scales are used in the survey (Litwin 1995). Cronbach's alpha is an internal consistency measure and is used to determine whether the scale is reliable or not (Kitchenham & Pfleeger 2002; Litwin 1995). The Cronbach's alpha coefficient is a reflection of how well the different items complement one another in measuring the same variable (Cronbach 1951; Litwin 1995). The Cronbach's alpha coefficient was calculated for each of the technologies that were used and is presented in Table 3. Internal consistency levels of 0.7 or more are generally accepted as representing good reliability.

The results indicate that there is internal validity apart from the cellphone grouping of questions. The results of this grouping must be interpreted carefully and a retest might highlight some additional inconsistencies.

The purpose of any questionnaire is that it measures what it intended to measure (Cameron & Price 2009). If a questionnaire does not measure what it is supposed to measure, then the conclusions and statistical analysis might also be invalid. Validity checks are available to verify that the questionnaire is suitable (Kitchenham & Pfleeger 2002). The types of validity that can be used to assess the survey questionnaire are face, content, criterion and construct validity (Litwin 1995).

The researcher opted for face and content validity. Face validity refers to the 'obviousness' of a test that is the degree to which the purpose of the test is apparent to those taking it.

TABLE 3: Cronbach's alpha reliability tests.

ICT adoption	Cronbach's alpha	Cronbach's alpha based on standardised items	N of items
Cellphone	.570	.585	6
Smartphone	.881	.876	7
PC	.796	.837	6
Laptop	.792	.845	6
Internet	.820	.836	4

PC, personal computer.

The purpose of this research, as well as the questions, was clear to the respondents and, thus, it can be derived that there is high face validity. Content validity on the other hand focuses on extent to which the items are fairly representative of the entire domain the test seeks to measure. The questionnaire was evaluated by subject matter experts for content validity. The subject matter experts evaluated the questionnaire to ensure that (1) all the relevant technologies are listed, (2) all the relevant applications of the technology are listed and (3) the layout is logical and all relevant questions, required to collect data to answer the research questions, were included. The subject matter experts were information system experts, SME experts in Soweto itself as well as a questionnaire development expert.

Internal validity is the extent to which the questionnaire allows the researchers to draw conclusions about the relationship between variables. Internal validity was tested through various correlations and cross-tabulations. External validity, on the other hand, is the extent to which the sample genuinely represents the population from which it was drawn. In this research the sample was representative as the respondents were all SME owners within Soweto.

The results from this survey can be used with confidence as the reliability and validity of the questionnaire were proven through the reliability and validity tests.

Results and analysis

The first section of the results focuses on the biographical information of the respondents. It provides an overview of the respondents with regard to their income and type of small business that they own and manage.

The results from Figure 3 indicate that the majority (79.2%) of the SME owners earned less than R5000 a month.

What is even more astounding is that 43.3% of the respondents earned less than R2000 a month through their business. These results indicate then that close to 80% of the MSBs in this survey can be classified as micro enterprises which include survivalist MSBs.

Only 4.4% of the respondents earned more than R15 000 per month.

The next question on the questionnaire focused on the type of business that the respondents owned. These results are displayed in Figure 4.

Most of the respondents were either *spaza* shop owners (24.8%) or street vendors (23.3%). A *spaza* shop normally has a very limited floor area and is operated from a garage, shed or even a bedroom in a township.

Some 30% of the respondents owned either a tavern or *shebeen* (places that sell alcohol). Only 3.1% of the respondents owned a formal franchise. The 'Other' category made up 18.3% of the remainder of the businesses. MSBs in this grouping include

barber shops, hairdressers, daycare, shoe repair and public phone rentals.

Table 4 presents a cross-analysis of the income versus the type of business. It is evident from Table 4 that the more formal the type of MSB or SME, the more income is generated.

Street vendors and *spaza* shops accounted for 29% of the income, which was less than R2000 per month.

The results from the biographical data highlight that most of the MSBs can be classified as micro enterprises, where the income was less than R150 000 per year. Only 13.1% can be classified as small MSBs.

The second part of the analysis focuses on the type of ICT used by the owners of the MSBs, the frequency of the usage as well as the reasons for using the specific technology.

Figure 5 displays the type of ICT used and the frequency of usage. It must be noted that the respondents could select one or more of the listed technologies. The idea was to determine how many technologies were used as well as their frequency of usage.

The results indicate that the 'traditional' technologies were still used most of the time. Normal basic cellphones, without any features, as well as pen and paper were the technologies that were used the most. They were also used on a constant, daily basis. The technology that also featured fairly often (82.6% daily usage) was calculators.

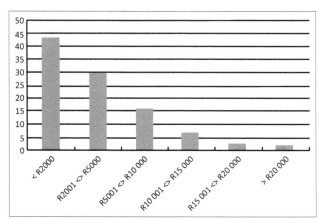

FIGURE 3: Monthly income.

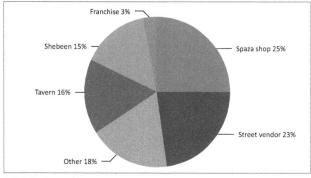

FIGURE 4: Type of business.

Although statistics indicate that smartphones are infiltrating the cellular market, only 55.3% of the respondents used them. It is quite peculiar that both cellphones and smartphones were used by the respondents, highlighting the fact that some South Africans have more than one mobile device per person.

On the other side of the scale are the technologies that were not used. These include tablet devices (98.1% never used), laptops (68.4% never used) and fax machines (65% never used). Although these technologies were mostly not used, it must be noted that where they were indeed used, fax machines (19.6%) and laptops (18%) were actually used on a daily basis.

The following section provides an analysis of the technologies to determine the purpose for which the specific technology was used.

Type of ICT and usage

The results indicate that cellphones were used for what they were intended. The respondents used them for normal day-to-day phone calls (83.2%) as well as to send SMSs (61.6%). The results are depicted in Figure 6.

It is of interest that only a small portion of the respondents used cellphones for business purposes, such as cellphone banking (8%), email (7.5%) and Internet banking (2.4%).

Although the respondents did not use smartphones as much as cellphones, it seems that those who did use them did so more for business-related activities. This indicates a paradigm shift as depicted in Figure 7.

The results must be viewed in relation to the fact that only 55% of the respondents used a smartphone on a daily basis. The implication is that those respondents who had two phones

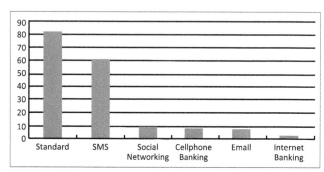

FIGURE 6: Cellphone usage.

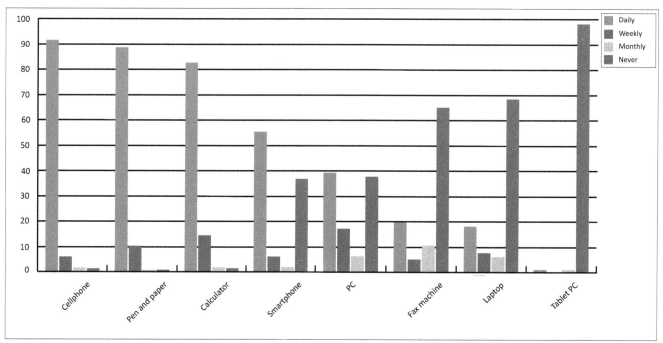

FIGURE 5: Frequency and usage of information and communications technology.

TABLE 4: Cross-analysis of income and type of business.

Type of business	< R2000 (%)	R2001 <> R5000 (%)	R5001 <> R10 000 (%)	R10 001 <> R15 000 (%)	R15 001 <> R20 000 (%)	> R20 000 (%)
Street vendor	19.0	4.0	0.3	-	0.1	-
Spaza shop	10.0	8.0	5.0	1.0	0.1	0.2
Franchise	1.0	0.4	0.2	1.0	1.0	0.3
Shebeen	4.0	7.0	3.0	1.0	0.3	0.1
Tavern	1.0	6.0	4.0	3.0	1.0	1.0
Other	8.0	5.0	3.0	1.0	1.0	1.0
TOTAL (%)	**43.00**	**30.40**	**15.50**	**7.00**	**3.50**	**2.60**

(a cellphone and smartphone) used the cellphone for normal usage and the smartphone for business-related activities.

When the usage of PCs and laptops are compared, no significant difference in the adoption and usage of the technology can be seen. A chi-squared test was done to test for independence between the usage of PCs and laptops and the results indicated that there is no dependency between the two variables. The 100% stacked bar in Figure 8 highlights these results.

The results indicate that those respondents who used a PC on a daily basis (39.2%) did not necessarily use it for business-related activities. The usage of laptops paints a similar picture and it is evident that laptops were not significantly used by the respondents. One might speculate that the high crime rate in this area could play a role in this statistic, as it is easy to steal a laptop.

The results, as depicted in Figure 6, clearly indicate that there is no difference between the usage of PCs and laptops. Each of the applications is, per ratio, the same with each technology. Figure 9 also paints an interesting picture. The Internet itself, when it was available, was used for normal browsing (47%) and social networking (19%). It was seldom used for Internet banking (10%) and email (24%).

This might result from limited Internet access in South Africa, as shown in Figure 2.

The next section investigates the correlations to determine whether or not more formal MSBs are adopting ICT and the purposes of its use.

The technique of multiple responses was used to undertake further analysis. This technique allows the analysis of a number of separate variables at the same time. According to Argyrous (2011:512): 'this is used in situations where the responses of separate variables that have a similar coding scheme all point to the same underlying variable'. In this case, the underlying variables were the four major types of technologies: cellphone, smartphone, PC and laptop. Frequencies and cross-tabulations can be performed with multiple responses.

Figure 10 shows the correlation between the type of ICT usage and the type of SME. The purpose of this correlation was to determine whether or not the more formal MSBs used more high-end technology, such as PCs and laptops.

The results in Figure 10 indicate that the more formal MSBs used more high-end technology than the informal MSBs. Cellphones were used by 47% of street vendors and *spaza* shop owners. This is in contrast with MSBs such as taverns (15.1%), which used cellphones in their day-to-day business operations.

PCs and laptops were, on the other hand, used by more formal MSBs (60.6% and 59.5%, respectively). Street

vendors and *spaza* shops used PCs (22.2%) and laptops (27.7%) for business.

Further analysis of the results indicates that the MSBs, which were categorised within the 'Other' group, adopted the usage of PCs and laptops more than the other types of business. It is important to note at this point that 44.1% of the 'Other' consists of four types of MSBs: hair salons (21.8%), fast food outlets (10.1%), barbershops (6.1%) and Internet cafés (6.1%). Figure 11 highlights that the other types of MSBs used PCs more for business-related activities than the rest of the MSBs. This might be related to the type of business, for example, fast food outlets might need a PC to transact daily sales.

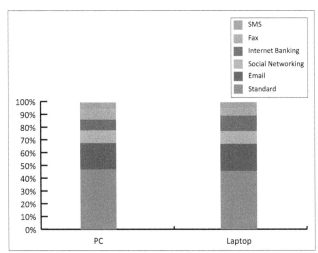

FIGURE 7: Smartphone usage.

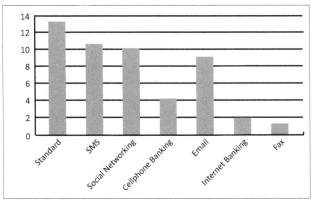

FIGURE 8: Personal computer and laptop usage.

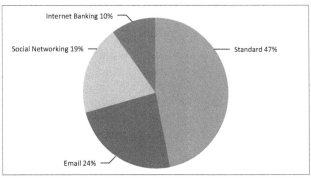

FIGURE 9: Proportional Internet usage.

Figure 12 tells the same story as with PC usage, where the other types of MSBs used laptops more frequently for business than, for instance, franchises. Table 5 is a comparison between the adoption of cellphones versus smartphones. The comparison is done per type of business.

The results as per Table 5 highlight the two major differences:

1. Cellphones were the preferred technology when the MSB used them for normal usage, such as phoning and sending SMSs. Smartphones, on the other hand, were used when the focus was on business-related transactions, such as Internet banking and emails.
2. The more formal MSBs used smartphones instead of cellphones. Street vendors and *spaza* shops were more inclined to use cellphones.

The second correlation focuses on the income and the adoption of ICT. As per the literature, the assumption is that the adoption of high-end technology will increase the profits and turnover of the SME. Figure 13 shows the correlation between the monthly income and the type of technology used.

The results clearly highlight this positive correlation between the monthly income and the type of technology adopted by the SME. The monthly income was higher where PCs and laptops were used in the day-to-day running of the SME. This raises an interesting conundrum: must MSBs invest in high-end technology hoping that it will generate money, or is it an evolving concept?

An in-depth analysis of the results indicates that a positive correlation exists between the usage of ICT and the income of the business. ICT is an enabler even in township MSBs.

Discussion

MSBs play an important role within any economy and even more so within developing economies such as South Africa. The aim of this research was to provide statistical information on the 'raw' rates of ICT adoption amongst MSBs in Soweto. Four research questions were posed and are discussed individually.

The first question focused on the type of ICT adopted by the various MSBs. The results indicate firstly that traditional pen and paper as well as cellphones are the technologies that are mostly used. A calculator is also a technology that is used on a daily basis. The interesting fact is that only a small portion of the MSBs surveyed used PCs and laptops for the daily management and running of their business. Tablet devices were not used at all even when these devices were given to the businesses for free, with the renewal of cellphone contracts. The assumption can be made that the functionality and benefits of tablet devices are not known and realised by the SME owners. This might result from a lack of education. Tablets are also not very useful without a network connection. Tablets with SIM slots are quite expensive and the cheaper versions, with Wi-Fi only, are not useful as there is no Wi-

Fi network available in Soweto. If free Wi-Fi is funded by government, private industry or both, there would be an increase in the adoption of these cheaper tablets. The Internet is an essential part in the process of technology adoption.

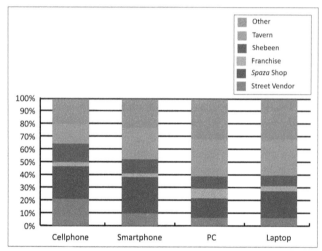

FIGURE 10: Correlation between information and communications technology usage and type of business.

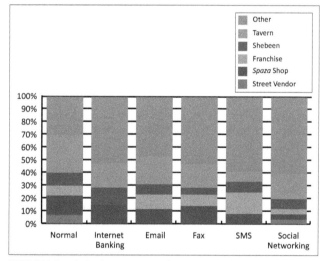

FIGURE 11: Correlation between personal computer usage and type of business.

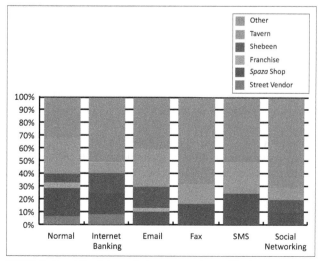

FIGURE 12: Correlation between laptop usage and type of business.

TABLE 5: Cellphone versus smartphone usage.

Type of business	Normal (%)		Internet banking (%)		Cellphone banking (%)		Email (%)		Fax (%)	SMS (%)		Social networking (%)	
	Smartphone	Cellphone	Smartphone	Cellphone	Smartphone	Cellphone	Smartphone	Cellphone	Smartphone	Smartphone	Cellphone	Smartphone	Cellphone
Street vendor	10	21.9	5	4.3	7.1	11.5	4.4	11	7.1	8.6	20.8	9	20.9
Spaza shop	26.9	25.4	20	21.7	11.9	26.9	25.6	21.9	14.3	26.7	24.1	24	17.6
Franchise	3.1	3.2	5	0	2.4	1.3	2.2	4.1	7.1	2.9	3.2	4	1.1
Shebeen	11.5	14.7	5	17.4	9.5	17.9	11.1	12.3	14.3	11.4	15.1	12	7.7
Tavern	26.5	15	30	34.8	26.2	21.8	33.3	24.7	21.4	27.6	15.1	24	15.4
Other	21.5	19.8	35	21.7	42.9	20.5	23.3	26	35.7	22.9	21.8	27	37.4

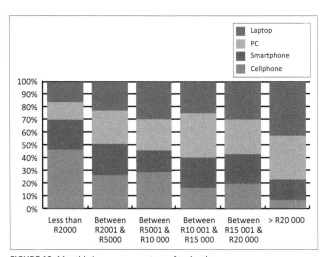

FIGURE 13: Monthly income versus type of technology.

The results of the first question highlight the fact that ICT is not that well accepted and adopted. That leads to the second question which tries to uncover whether or not the adoption of ICT is related to the type of SME that may use it. The results confirm that the usage of ICT is directly linked to the type of SME and directly to the income of the business. The more formal the type of SME and, thus, the higher the income, the more the usage of advanced ICT such as PCs and laptops. MSBs in the 'Other' type of SME grouping indicate that these MSBs use ICT to the SME's benefit. ICT is used for a wide variety of functions from social media to banking and email.

The third question focused on the correlation between the type of ICT adopted and the profitability of the SME itself. The results clearly highlight this positive correlation between the monthly income and the type of ICT adopted by the SME. The monthly income is higher where PCs and laptops are used in the day-to-day running of the SME. What is not clear from the results is whether ICT boosts the business, or whether the more formal MSBs by nature adopt and use ICT. This requires further investigation about what came first: ICT that helped the SME or the SME that used ICT and, thus, grew even further.

The fourth question interrogated the relationship between applications and ICT based on the type of SME. In other words, is the cellphone applied differently between a street vendor and a franchise? No definitive conclusion can be made. What is clear is that smartphones are the preferred technology, over cellphones, for conducting business.

It is clear that the MSBs in Soweto at best make general use of ICTs which include email and Internet access. The rates of adoption are very high and do not depend on the size of the SME. If there was a sliding scale, the MSBs would have featured fairly low on it, even as general users of ICTs. That should be a national concern about why these MSBs are not adopting ICT.

The results are quite disheartening from an ICT perspective and they also provide additional information regarding the type and size of the MSBs in Soweto. ICT is particularly easy to use these days and, thus, the adoption of ICT must rely on the perceived usefulness. This can only be overcome through training and education. Sidney *et al.* (2010) and also Santosa and Kusumawardani (2010) emphasise that there must be an effective implementation strategy that focuses on the deployment of ICT for MSBs. The strategy should serve as a guideline for MSBs to improve they utilise their ICT infrastructure.

The analysis of the results also indicates that although ICT is used by some MSBs, the usage is not necessarily linked to business. ICT is used for its intended purpose, such as word processing, but it is not used or adopted for business requirements such as marketing, Internet banking and financial analysis. It might be a matter of education or ignorance, but this should be researched further.

The results indicate that most MSBs are either survivalists or very small MSBs that barely make a living. It makes logical sense that ICT does not necessarily feature within the framework of such MSBs. However, ICT can, as an enabler, contribute to growing the business and generating more income, and, thus, move the SME to the next level.

Conclusion

The literature highlights the importance of MSBs within developing economies and their vital role in the growth of the economy. The literature also highlights the importance of ICT as an enabler for business and the argument is, thus, that ICT can or should enable MSBs to grow themselves and, thus, stimulate the economy of a country such as South Africa.

The findings indicate that the adoption and use of ICT are directly linked to the income of the respective MSBs. The more formal MSBs use more advanced technologies such as PCs and laptops, whereas the smaller MSBs revert back to pen and paper, calculators and cellphones. Another aspect that was highlighted is the fact that ICT, when it is utilised, is not fully utilised. An example is cellphones which are used mostly for normal, non-business purposes. The SME owners have not yet made the transition from traditional usage of cellphones and the intent, to applying these for business usage and growing the business. A startling aspect is that most of the MSBs are survivalist MSBs, focusing as such more on surviving and not necessarily on growing the business.

It can be concluded that work remains to be completed concerning training on and insight into the usage of ICT. The results highlight the fact that SME owners do not necessarily know what they can do with ICT and how it can grow their business. A possible solution is to liaise with the local business chambers within Soweto and provide the necessary training and awareness as a continued effort and not just a once-off scenario.

It is the first time that such research has been performed within a South African township and the results are significant for future research. The results from this research open an entirely new world of research possibilities. Various areas of research never addressed before have also been highlighted.

Future research should include a more in-depth analysis of why ICT is not used for business, and what those various barriers are to entering the world of ICT. This was not covered by this research, as the aim was to establish a common understanding of the problem at hand. The technology adoption model (TAM) is a causal model and can, thus, be used to test certain hypotheses. Future research can also be expanded to other South African townships to determine the differences between the various populations.

For township MSBs to embrace ICT and use it to the fullest, the full potential of ICT must be advocated and the benefits must be worthwhile. If this is not achieved with a concerted effort, then the digital divide will not be crossed by MSBs and they will not benefit from the potential growth and market share. ICT might help most of the MSBs to move from survivalist to micro enterprises where they can start employing other township people and, thus, reduce the unemployment statistics of South Africa.

References

Abor, J. & Quartey, P., 2010, 'Issues in SME Development in Ghana and South Africa', *International Research Journal of Finance & Economics* 39, 218–228.

Arendt, L., 2008, 'Barriers to ICT adoption in SMEs: How to bridge the digital divide?', *Journal of Systems and Information Technology* 10, 93–108. http://dx.doi.org/10.1108/13287260810897738

Argyrous, G., 2011, *Statistics for research with a guide to SPSS*, Sage Publications, London.

Balnaves, M. & Caputi, P., 2001, *Introduction to quantitative research methods – An investigative approach*, Sage Publications, London.

Beck, T., Demirguc-Kunt, A. & Levine, R., 2005, 'SMEs, growth, and poverty: Cross-country evidence', *Journal of Economic Growth* 10(3), 199–229. http://dx.doi.org/10.1007/s10887-005-3533-5

Blaikie, N., 2003, *Analyzing Quantitative Data – From Description to Explanation*, Sage Publications, London.

Blueprint Strategy & Policy (Pty) Ltd., 2005, *Promotion of small and medium enterprises in the South African chemicals sector*, Blueprint Strategy & Policy (Pty) Ltd., South Africa.

Cameron, S. & Price, D., 2009, *Business research methods – A practical approach*, Chartered Institute of Personnel and Development, London.

Cravo, T., Gourlay, A. & Becker, B., 2012, 'SMEs and regional economic growth in Brazil', *Small Business Economics* 38(2), 217–230. http://dx.doi.org/10.1007/s11187-010-9261-z

Cronbach, L., 1951, 'Coefficient alpha and the internal structure of tests', *Psychometrika* 16(3), 297–334. http://dx.doi.org/10.1007/BF02310555

Davis, F.D., 1989, 'Perceived Usefulness, Perceived Ease of Use, and User Acceptance of Information Technology', *MIS Quarterly* 13(3), 319–340. http://dx.doi.org/10.2307/249008

Davis, F.D., Bagozzi, R.P. & Warshaw, P.R., 1989, 'User acceptance of computer technology: A comparison of two theoretical models', *Management Science* 35(8), 982–1003. http://dx.doi.org/10.1287/mnsc.35.8.982

European Commission, 2012, 'Small and medium-sized enterprises (SMEs): What is an SME?', *European Commission*, viewed 04 June 2012, from http://ec.europa.eu/enterprise/policies/sme/facts-figures-analysis/sme-definition/index_en.htm

Falkena, H., n.d., 'SMES' access to finance in South Africa – A supply-side regulatory review', in H. Falkena, (ed.), *Financial Services and Regulation*, South Africa.

Feilzer, Y.M., 2010, 'Doing mixed methods research pragmatically: Implications for the rediscovery of pragmatism as a research paradigm', *Journal of Mixed Methods Research* 4(1), 6–16. http://dx.doi.org/10.1177/1558689809349691

Hotho, S. & Champion, K., 2011, 'Small businesses in the new creative industries: Innovation as a people management challenge', *Management Decision* 49(1), 29–54. http://dx.doi.org/10.1108/00251741111094428

Hu, Q. & Plant, R., 2001, 'An empirical study of the casual relationship between IT investment and firm performance', *Information Resources Management Journal* 14(3), 15–26. http://dx.doi.org/10.4018/irmj.2001070102

Huizingh, E., 2007, *Applied statistics with SPSS*, Sage Publications, London.

Kannabiran, G. & Dharmalingam, P., 2012, 'Enablers and inhibitors of advanced information technologies adoption by SMEs: An empirical study of auto ancillaries in India', *Journal of Enterprise Information Management* 25(2), 186–209. http://dx.doi.org/10.1108/17410391211204419

Kennedy, C., Bounds, M. & Goldman, G., 2011, 'Strategic planning in SMEs: conscious effort or afterthought?', in G. Goldman & G. Heyns (eds.), *The 4th International UJ Faculty of Management Conference*, 29–31 May 2012, Faculty of Management, University of Johannesburg, Amanzingwe Lodge, Broederstroom, Gauteng, South Africa.

Khalifa, M. & Davison, M., 2006, 'SME adoption of IT: the case of electronic trading systems', *IEEE Transactions on Engineering Management* 53(2), 275–284. http://dx.doi.org/10.1109/TEM.2006.872251

Kirk, J. & Miller, M.L., 1986, *Reliability and validity in qualitative research*, Sage Publications, Beverly Hills.

Kitchenham, B. & Pfleeger, S.L., 2002, 'Principles of survey research part 4: Questionnaire evaluation', *SIGSOFT Softw. Eng. Notes* 27(3), 20–23. http://dx.doi.org/10.1145/511152.511155

Litwin, M.S., 1995, *How to measure survey reliability and validity*, Sage Publications, London.

Lucchetti, R. & Sterlacchini, A., 2004, 'The adoption of ICT among SMEs: Evidence from an Italian survey', *Small Business Economics* 23(2), 151–168. http://dx.doi.org/10.1023/B:SBEJ.0000027667.55821.53

Mahembe, E., 2011, *Literature review on small and medium enterprises' access to credit and support in South Africa*, National Credit Regulator, South Africa.

Mbonyane, B.L., 2006, *An exploration of factors that lead to failure of small businesses in the Kagiso*, M.Tech Business Administration, UNISA, Pretoria.

Mitra, S., 2005, 'Information Technology as an Enabler of Growth in Firms: An Empirical Assessment', *Journal of Management Information Systems* 22(2), 279–300.

Ngassam, E.K., Ntawanga, F. & Eloff, J.H.P., 2013, 'A roadmap for rural area ICT solution deployment: A Case of Kgautswane community in South Africa,' *The African Journal of Information Systems* 5(2), 9–64.

Njiro, E., Mazwai, T. & Urban, B., 2010, 'A situational analysis of small businesses and enterprises in the townships of the Gauteng province of South Africa,' in *2010 Soweto International Conference on Entrepreneurship & Development*, Soweto, Johannesburg.

Olawale, F. & Garwe, D., 2010, 'Obstacles to the growth of new SMEs in South Africa: A principal component analysis approach', *African Journal of Business Management* 4(5), 729–738.

Polun, C., Yueh-Shuang, H., Yuann-Meei, T., Yiing-Yiing, S., Hou, I.C. & Wei-Fong, K., 2004, 'The development of intelligent, triage-based, mass-gathering emergency medical service PDA support systems', *Journal of Nursing Research (Taiwan Nurses Association)* 12(3), 227–235. http://dx.doi.org/10.1097/01.JNR.0000387506.06502.90

Premkumar, G. & Roberts, M., 1999, 'Adoption of new information technologies in rural small businesses', *Omega* 27(4), 467–484. http://dx.doi.org/10.1016/S0305-0483(98)00071-1

Santosa, P.I. & Kusumawardani, S.S., 2010, 'Improving SME ICT utilization through industrial attachment program: Indonesia case', in *Frontiers in Education Conference* (FIE), 2010 IEEE, 27–30 Oct. 2010, S1J–1–S1J–5.

SBP., 2013, *SME growth index 2012 headline report. easier/harder for small business in South Africa?* SBP, Johannesburg.

Sidney, K.T.T., Tina, A.B. & Choy, K.L., 2010, 'Efficacy of IT/IS deployment in small– and medium enterprise in China', in *2010 8th International Conference on Supply Chain Management and Information Systems (SCMIS)*, 6–9 October, 2010, Lisbon, Portugal, pp. 1–7.

Silvius, G., 2004, 'IT and small business: An unhappy marriage?', in M. Khosrow-Pour (ed.), *Innovations through information technology*, Idea Group Publishing, Hershey.

Statistics South Africa, 2012, *Census 2011 statistical release*, Statistics South Africa, Pretoria.

Terblanche, N.S., 1991, 'The spaza shop: South Africa's first own black retailing institution', *International Journal of Retail & Distribution Management* 19(5), 37–43. http://dx.doi.org/10.1108/EUM0000000002949

The World Bank, 2006, *Information and Communications for Development – Global Trends and Policies*, The World Bank, Washington D.C.

Thong, J.Y.L. & Yap, C.S., 1995, 'CEO characteristics, organizational characteristics and information technology adoption in small businesses', *Omega* 23(4), 429–442. http://dx.doi.org/10.1016/0305-0483(95)00017-I

Thurik, R. & Wennekers, S., 2004, 'Entrepreneurship, small business and economic growth', *Journal of Small Business and Enterprise Development* 11(1), 140–149. http://dx.doi.org/10.1108/14626000410519173

Venkatesh, V., Morris, M.G., Davis, G.B. & Davis, F.D., 2003, 'User acceptance of information technology: Toward a unified view', *MIS Quarterly* 27(3), 425–478.

Yonazi, E., Kelly, T., Halewood, N. & Blackman, C., 2012, *The transformational use of information and communication technologies in Africa*, eTransfrom Africa.

26

Developing a secured social networking site using information security awareness techniques

Author:
Julius O. Okesola[1]
Marthie Grobler[1]

Affiliation:
[1]School of Computing, University of South Africa, South Africa

Correspondence to:
Julius Okesola

Email:
48948535@mylife.unisa.ac.za

Postal address:
Computer Sciences Department, Tai Solarin University of Education (TASUED), Ijebu-Ode, Nigeria

Background: Ever since social network sites (SNS) became a global phenomenon in almost every industry, security has become a major concern to many SNS stakeholders. Several security techniques have been invented towards addressing SNS security, but information security awareness (ISA) remains a critical point. Whilst very few users have used social circles and applications because of a *lack of users' awareness*, the majority have found it difficult to determine the basis of categorising friends in a meaningful way for privacy and security policies settings. This has confirmed that technical control is just part of the security solutions and not necessarily a total solution. Changing human behaviour on SNSs is essential; hence the need for a privately enhanced ISA SNS.

Objective: This article presented sOcialistOnline – a newly developed SNS, duly secured and platform independent with various ISA techniques fully implemented.

Method: Following a detailed literature review of the related works, the SNS was developed on the basis of Object Oriented Programming (OOP) approach, using PhP as the coding language with the MySQL database engine at the back end.

Result: This study addressed the SNS requirements of privacy, security and services, and attributed them as the basis of architectural design for sOcialistOnline. SNS users are more aware of potential risk and the possible consequences of unsecured behaviours.

Conclusion: ISA is focussed on the users who are often the greatest security risk on SNSs, regardless of technical securities implemented. Therefore SNSs are required to incorporate effective ISA into their platform and ensure users are motivated to embrace it.

Introduction

Although Google is considered the most visited website in the world (Kyle 2011; Shamim 2011), it has been competing favourably with Facebook. For instance, as of 2010, Facebook was the second biggest website in the United States of America (USA) (HuffpostTech 2011; Kiesow 2011). Since February 2011, Facebook has become the second most visited website in the average country in the world (Shamim 2011), with statistics confirming the second place position in the USA and the United Kingdom (Kyle 2011). However, as of November 2013, Facebook has been ranked as the largest media site in the entire world (Smith 2013; Vaughan-Nichols 2013).

Despite these growing economic values, which have been traced to the opportunities social networking sites (SNSs) offer to their customers in meeting friends, and even complete strangers online, many SNSs have not been able to live up to the security and privacy issues they have created (Hopper 2010:2). Specifically, Facebook has been the centre of attention multiple times resulting from issues surrounding privacy since 2010 (HuffpostTech 2011; Kiesow 2011).

Some notable SNSs have attempted, with no success, to implement technical controls to provide for their security. Accordingly, the users were more contented with the *privacy controls* of LinkedIn, until it was hacked in 2012, than with those of Facebook (Judge 2011:15). Therefore, as technical controls have failed to secure SNS in isolation, there is a need for a new SNS to be adequately secured with effective ISA techniques.

This need for a secured SNS has become more pronounced since 2012 when cyber-attacks have remained the second greatest threat in Britain after terrorism (Smith 2012). This article designs and implements a secured SNS to address security challenges in the existing SNSs using ISA techniques. The study reveals that changing human behaviour on SNSs through ISA techniques is essential and more effective.

Securing SNSs – Technical controls

Facebook has initiated architectural features that have exposed data many times, thereby making

SNS users uncomfortable (Lucas & Borisov 2008:2). The introduction of a *news feed* is a noted example in which the activities of one's friends are amassed into one page. This then confirms that privacy breaches remain feasible whether or not the users painstakingly configure their privacy settings. It is especially the case now that privacy controls have little impact on how Facebook handles its backend data but only limits information flow within the SNS interface.

Although Giles (2007:17–24) highlights some security design patterns and measures, which can be implemented and practiced by service providers to prevent possible methods attackers may follow to attack the users' information, the risk associated with architectural features has been addressed by Lucas and Borisov (2008). They make use of encryption technology to introduce a design capable of safeguarding all data coming out of Facebook. However, their architectural design swaps security for usability in order to minimise the disturbance given to the users' workflow, and at the same time it retains universal accessibility. They have come up with a prototype Facebook application that makes use of proxy cryptography to resolve major restrictions on the Facebook platform.

In spite of all the calls and agitations by vendors necessitating the importance of security products, Stephanou and Dagada (2008:3) explain that 'many critical security activities have not and cannot be automated'. This is because, as Mataracioglu and Ozkan (2010:4) emphasise, 'only a small percentage of information security is maintained by *technical security* measures, while its greater percentage depends on the user'. Organisations have invested heavily in firewalls, antivirus systems and other technologies, yet they continue to suffer from severe IS breaches, and these problems are getting worse (Gartner 2011).

Technologies that offer security continue to require effective running by people, implying that organisations cannot achieve their security desires without *people*. However, as the individual is generally considered as the weakest link in the Information Security circle (Van Niekerk & Von Solms 2004:2), it is clearly a requirement that the users are given proper training on Information Security policies. Hence, the need for effective ISA on the SNSs is emphasised.

ISA techniques

Much research has been carried out on ISA techniques but most of these techniques are not based on a theoretical model; instead, they only guide about the right methods to use (Stephanou & Dagada 2008:6). For example, the research undertaken by Heidari (2010), Hinson (2012), and Wolf (2010) all shows detailed work on the methods used to secure SNSs.

The research of Kumaraguru *et al.* (2007) prove that security awareness materials can be effective when implemented, but online materials that create user awareness about phishing threats are more effective as users tend to recognise phishing sites more accurately. They also advocate for an improvement in the quality of awareness materials, and also improved

awareness techniques to enhance the users understanding of the same materials.

Johnson (2012:8), in his doctoral research work conducted at the University of Lagos in May 2012, argues that much is expected from the audience. This undermines the fact that security processes can only be effective when the audience has a good security support and appreciates the security requirements. On this basis and by applying background training, Jagatic *et al.* (2007:96) are able to prove that it is very easy (through SNS in particular) to capture huge amounts of data for effective phishing attacks. They also attempt, but with no success, to measure the influence of information relating to social context on phishing attacks. What makes their work different is that e-mails are spoofed to deceive users, as if they are from friends in the SNS and, in the end, the total number of victims to this phishing attack outweighed the expectation (Jagatic *et al.* 2007:97).

Research methodology used to develop sOcialistOnline

Dynamic Systems Design Methodology (DSDM) is used to develop the SNS in this research work. This is because, like Joint Application Development (JAD) methodology, DSDM has proved to be one of the best methods when handling a project that must be completed to tight deadlines. Goodwin (2011) explains DSDM thus:

> It is a set of specification and design notations for object-oriented systems, combining features from methods devised by three methodology gurus: Grady Booch, James Rumbaugh and Ivar Jakobsen. (n.p.)

The development of sOcialistOnline is handled by the development, security, and the user acceptance teams (UAT) headed by the author. As illustrated in Figure 1, it is based on an exploratory approach using an object oriented programming (OOP) methodology for application (SNS) development. To discourage security threats through exposure to third party applications, the use of such applications to secure the SNS is discouraged.

Designing the SNS

When planning to create the SNS, the development team followed the philosophy of Steve Jobs – 'Lesser artists borrow; great artists steal' (Duffy 2010) by integrating the steps developed by Timothy Duffy with the processes highlighted by Adams (2012) to develop and implement the sOcialistOnline. These integrated steps and procedures include crafting a concept, establishing a name, obtaining venture capital, and hiring the employees.

FIGURE 1: Development process for sOcialistOnline.

The Requirement

According to Aiello and Ruffo (2011:3), 'a SNS is defined, in its most general meaning, as a customisable suite of inter-operable, identity-based applications'. In this context, every user composes their own combination of applicative modules, or widgets, into a customised application suite where every widget can share data with other, possibly heterogeneous, widgets running locally or remotely.

Given this general definition, there is a set of desired network requirements as well as *password file* settings and requirements that are common to so many social widgets. Such requirements classified as privacy, service, password settings, security, and ISA are applied as the basis of architectural design of the sOcialistOnline framework.

Developmental tools

The development of sOcialistOnline is based on the Object Oriented Programming (OOP) approach, using PhP as the coding language with the MySQL database engine at the back end. The programming approach, language, and database deployed are summarised as follows:

- **Programming language:** There are several web scripting languages suitable for this research work, which include ASPX (from Microsoft Inc.), PhP (from Zend coy.), JSP (from Java), and ColdFusion (of Macromedia). However, for its additional characteristics of robustness and platform independence, as discussed in section 6.9, the development team prefers to use PhP 5.3.8, the latest version as of January 2012.
- **Database:** *MySQL* works very well with PhP because it supports MySQL natively. Using MySQL for data storage, there is no need for a third party code to connect the PhP script with the database; it has already been integrated into the PhP core. For effective security, *one-way* encryption cryptography was applied using the crypt algorithm for both the username and password. This ensures that, once encrypted, the password and username table cannot be decrypted again.
- **Programming approach:** OOP is employed as the coding style, in which all the tables have their own classes. When working with a table in the database, the class of the table provides all the functionalities needed. One notable determinant feature of OOP is inheritance. Every class inherits connect functions from the Dbconfig which connects the subclass to the database. As this is a web application that is not yet supported by PhP, polymorphism could not be applied.

Technical controls on sOcialistOnline

Fundamentally, every individual is entitled to privacy, although privacy on its own is difficult to define and formalise (Aimeur, Gambs, & Ai Ho 2010:173). Millions of internet users are accustomed to spending much time on chatting, commenting, blogging, and posting photos on SNSs, and these are the activities that eventually expose them to different privacy risks. Unfortunately, most of the current

SNSs do not value the principles of data minimisation and data sovereignty (Aimeur *et al.* 2010:173). Some of the technical controls implemented to secure sOcialistOnline are discussed below:

- **Customisation of access controls:** The access controls, as obtainable in the popular SNSs, on sOcialistOnline, are customised based on the users' groups and information type. Typically, a user has different classes of acquaintances including close friends, family members and colleagues at school or work. Unfortunately, only very few SNSs (such as Facebook, MySpace and Bebo) provide *privacy* settings that are elaborate where user profiles are broken into several small elements (Basic info, personal info, wall post, friends, etc.) (Aimeur *et al.* 2010). An experiment performed by Iyer (2009), and verified by Aimeur *et al.* (2010), confirms that the privacy settings on Facebook are erroneous and therefore not very effective, especially when a particular friend is to be restricted by his or her friend from accessing specific personal information. This ineffective access control exposes the user's privacy to security, reputation or credibility risk. sOcialistOnline is therefore designed in a way that the users can easily group their friends into user categories, making it possible to restrict the information type to the user group by means of a simple access control mechanism.
- **User-friendly way of setting privacy:** Unlike Facebook, the user's privacy settings on sOcialistOnline are flexible to customise, and are also integrated with a user-friendly interface that is easily understood by any typical SNS user.
- **Customised search:** A customised search is implemented on sOcialistOnline to further enhance the preservation of the user's privacy. It is therefore possible for a user to specify an individual who can search his or her profile, and the information types that can be searched. A screen-print of a customised search on sOcialistOnline is displayed in Figure 2.

For instance, a user may choose to ensure *unobservability* (that is, not be noticeable as a registered user on an SNS) and may want to remain totally invisible to those who are not in his or her list of friends. A user can also classify his or her personal data as 'sensitive' or 'not sensitive' relative to the search process. For example, a user may be indifferent to another user finding his or her name and sport of interest but not for

FIGURE 2: Screenshot for customised search.

sensitive information such as religion:

- **Active blocking of information related to users:** In addition to *customisation search,* which is implemented for a user to specify his or her profile information that could be searched, the sOcialistOnline offers the facility for a user to untag objects from his or her profile. Hence, an individual may consider a particular photo too sensitive and therefore choose to remove the link from his or her profile and, thus, mitigate the potential risk of the picture appearing when his or her identity is searched.

ISA techniques

Several authors such as Brodie (2009), ENISA (2007), PriceWaterHouseCoopers (2010), and Hinson (2012) have established that an SNS cannot be adequately secured without effective ISA. Hence, the author implemented the following ISA techniques into the sOcialistOnline to further enhance its security and user privacy:

- **Explicit privacy policy:** Generally, SNSs have a privacy policy but they often implement this to emphasise the significance of the users' privacy to the network and not to the users *per se.* Therefore, in most evaluations regarding the users awareness to the privacy policy, less than 10% of SNS users claim to have read and understood the policy document of their SNS (Jones & Soltren 2012:3). This is partly attributed to the fact that the document is always too long, with an average mean length of 2633 words and a median of 2.245 (Bonneau & Preibusch 2009:254). The same situations apply to the terms and conditions. sOcialistOnline addresses this situation by summarising the policy statements into three pages, and applies the *terms and conditions* as a multiple alternative option. In which case, rather than the usual *terms and conditions,* a user-friendly community guideline is published on the sOcialistOnline to educate users in *real-time.*
- **Privacy awareness and customisation:** The sOcialistOnline is flexible enough for users to express their data as a privacy policy, and makes it possible for them to automatically compare the compatibility of the privacy response of the users to that of the SNS. This is what *the terms and conditions* entail. Where there is incompatibility, a user is warned and notified instantly, although he or she may still continue with the registration. This awareness function also alerts the user of his or her unsecured privacy settings each time he or she logs on to raise his or her ISA.
- **Data minimisation:** As only the information required should be disclosed in all instances, SNS users should be able to confirm the information type that is accessible to the SNS services (providers and third party applications), and their use. SNSs should also clarify the user's personal data of interest to them, and state clearly what exactly their interest is concerned with for the data owner to decide whether or not to accept or reject the SNS services. An in-built mechanism is incorporated into the sOcialistOnline to restrict access to user information and authorised data only (Aimeur *et al.* 2010:176).

- **Privacy lens:** It is required of an SNS user to view his or her profile the exact way it will appear to others, for him or her to appreciate that his or her data are unsecured. This is exactly what the privacy lens is all about and it is targeted at raising the user's information security awareness on sOcialistOnline (Aimeur *et al.* 2010:175).
- **Password standardisation:** To guide against guessable password formulation, the sOcialistOnline incorporates Persuasive Text Password (PTP), as proposed by Forget *et al.* (2008), whereby the system auto-generates some characters and inserts them into a users' password combination. The PTP plays a middle-man role between a system generated password, which is always strong but difficult to remember, and one that is user-generated that is often weak but easily remembered. However, the sOcialistOnline makes it highly flexible and optional for SNS users to accept, reject or even request alternative characters and numbers at will.
- **Password monitoring:** In line with the user's consent, the sOcialistOnline generates and keeps personal and confidential data, including the user's passwords and photographs. This is the main input data for this research work. The development team included a *password scanner,* which scans the password, files and analyses the strength of the individual password. This solution prompts each user, at every log-on, to *inform* him or her about the strength of his or her password and advise the user to reset it accordingly, but continues to allow the user to proceed at his or her own risk. This alert pops up at the registration stage and also at every user login to eliminate the user's acclaimed ignorance of ISA, and to ensure that every individual is fully aware of the potential risk.

System testing, security and publicity

This section addresses the processes wherein the sOcialistOnline was tested, and checked to verify if it is technically secured and published for general use.

Unit and UAT testing

Available Software Development Life Cycle (SDLC) testing scripts were used to unit test the SNS. A UAT script designed by the development team was reviewed by the ICT directorate, of Tai Solarin University of Education (TASUED), Nigeria, before being presented to the testing, comprised of members of the student affairs directorate and the students' union executives. To maintain his independence, the author was not involved in the actual UAT exercise. Instead, the testing was supervised by a system analyst at the university's e-learning centre and implemented by only seven students and three non-academic staff, all of whom are knowledgeable about SNS. Informed consent forms were completed by each of the testers stating that participation was free and optional. The testers were satisfied with the sOcialistOnline, although they came up with some comments that have nothing to do with the system functionality but with the speed, stability and availability of the SNS. These problems were addressed immediately as they were problems caused by the internet service provider (ISP) who hosted the SNS server.

System security

As a result of the increasing rate at which SNSs are being attacked, Summit Technology Nig. Limited was employed to tighten up the web and application security. The focus was mostly on operating systems and the Internet Explorer platforms where the sOcialistOnline is hosted, to ensure that certain services are working correctly and securely, as they should be.

System publicity

Usually SNSs are known to experience low patronage when they are newly implemented (Khan et al. 2011). To stop or reduce this fear, the author increased user awareness amongst the university students and staff by employing the Student Affairs unit and the Staff Union government of TASUED to encourage their members to patronise the site.

Some students were invited to a presentation session on the SNSs. The author issued the invitation to some students and staff but made it clear that the participation was free, optional and anonymous. This seminar included a short question and answer session where participants were free to express their concerns about the project. The participants were also given adequate ISA guidelines towards their behaviour on SNSs in general, but with emphasis on sOcialistOnline. The seminar was organised a few days after the SNS was implemented and in the production environment, in order to promote its publicity and awareness amongst the audience and other intended users.

Results

This article discusses the development and implementation of the sOcialistOnline site. This SNS was secured by technical and ISA techniques before being migrated to the internet. Similarly, the UAT and system testing were performed but these are limited to the postulated model, and the conclusion is based on the evaluation of data obtained. Different types of technical controls, which form part of the body of a secured SNS, are evaluated with special emphasis on the incorporated ISA techniques.

Although a secured SNS is ultimately designed and implemented, the emphasis of this article is on the ISA techniques used to secure the SNS, because they are the main distinguishing factors from the existing ones.

Conclusions and recommendations

The sOcialistOnline is developed and secured by the technical and ISA techniques before being migrated to the production environment. Similarly, the UAT and system testing were performed but are limited to the postulated model and the conclusion is based on the evaluation of the data obtained. Different types of technical controls, which

form part of the body of a secured SNS, were evaluated with special emphasis on the incorporated ISA techniques. The SNS is therefore adjudged to be better secured when compared to these inadequate ISA techniques. Notwithstanding this, the *effectiveness* of these controls and techniques proposed and implemented will be subjected to absolute measurements using a non-incident statistic approach, as this is an on-going study.

It is recommended that SNSs should emulate the ISA efforts implemented in this study, and much more if possible, to raise the users' awareness maximally. Moreover, the *terms and conditions*, and the user-friendly community guidelines, should always be published on the sites to educate the users in real-time. Accessible and polite languages are also required to enhance the users' understanding and compliance with the SNS's regulations.

Acknowledgements

This scientific article is one of the final products of my research carried out during my (Julius O. Okesola) PhD study at the School of Computing, University of South Africa (UNISA). Some other final products have been published in other recognised journals.

I therefore acknowledge, with thanks, Prof. Segun Awonusi (the Vice Chancellor of TASUED) for giving me the inspiration; Abiola Okesola (my wife) for her quiet wisdom and unfailing loyalty; and, more importantly, Prof. Marthie Grobler – my project supervisor – for her foresight in identifying values, shortcomings and obstacles; her aptitude for putting an idea into context; and above everything, for being patient and understanding.

Competing interests

The authors declare that they have no financial or personal relationship(s) that may have inappropriately influenced them when they wrote this article.

Authors' contributions

J.O.O. (University of South Africa) was the lead author of this article. The contribution of M.G. (University of South Africa) was in the capacity of co-author.

References

Adams, 2012, 'Creating a social networking site like Facebook', *Advanced PHP Solution*, viewed 09 June 2013, from http://advancedphpsolutions.com/blog/social-networking/create-a-social-networking-site-like-facebook

Aiello, L.M & Ruffo, G., 2011, 'Tunable privacy for distributed online social network services', *Computer Communication*.

Aimeur, E., Gambs, S. & Ai Ho, 2010, 'Towards a privacy-enhanced social networking site', *2010 International Conference on Availability, Reliability and Security*, viewed 07 June 2011, from http://www.mendeley.com/research/towards-privacyenhanced-social-networking-site-17

Bonneau, J. & Preibusch, S., 2009, 'The privacy jungle: On the market for data protection in social networks', *The Eighth Workshop on the Economics of Information Security*, (WEIS 2009), Greece, pp. 250–261, viewed on 14 June 2014, from http://weis09.infosecon.net/files/156/index.html

Brodie, C., 2009, 'The importance of security awareness training', in *SANS Infosec Reading Room*, viewed 23 May 2011, from http://www.sans.org/reading_room/whitepapers/awareness/importance-security-awareness-training_33013

Duffy, T., 2010, Nine steps to creating a social networking site that kills Facebook, *TECHi.com*, viewed 09 February 2013, from http://www.techi.com/2010/06/9-steps-to-creating-a-social-networking-site-that-kills-facebook

ENISA, 2007, 'Information Security Awareness Initiatives: Current Practice and Measurement of Success', viewed 18 May 2011, from http://www.itu.int/osg/csd/cybersecurity/WSIS/3rd_meeting_docs/contributions/enisa_measuring_awareness_final.pdf

Forget, A., Chiasson, S., Van Oorschot, P. & Biddle, R., 2008, 'Improving text passwords through persuasion', 4th Symposium on Usable Privacy and Security (SOUPS'08), June 2008, Pittsburgh. http://dx.doi.org/10.1145/1408664.1408666

Gartner, 2011, 'User awareness in social networking', viewed 01 June 2012, from http://www.Gartner.Com/Research/Spotlight/Asset_118887_895.Jsp

Giles, H., 2007, 'Security Issues and Recommendations for Online Social Networks', in ENISA Position Paper #1, viewed 2 May 2011, from http://www.ENISA.europa.eu/act/res/ other-areas/social-networks/security-issues-and -recommendations-for-online-social-networks

Goodwin, C., 2011, Development technology in under 10 minutes, ComputerWeekly.com, viewed 12 June 2014, from http://www.computerweekly.com/feature/Development-methodology-in-under-10-minutes

Heidari, H., 2010, 'Design patterns and refactoring for security in social networking applications', in Multimedia University, Malaysia, viewed 15 December 2011, from http://www.kaspersky.com/se-asia-it-security-conference

Hinson, G., 2012, 'The true value of IS awareness', Noticebored, viewed 23 August 2011, from http://www.noticebored.com/html/why_awareness_.html

Hopper, E., 2010, 'Intelligent strategies and techniques for effective cyber security, infrastructure protection and privacy', The 5th International Conference for Internet Technology and Secured Transactions (ICITST-2010), London, UK, 8–10 November.

HuffpostTech, 2011, Facebook tops Google as most visited website of the year, viewed 23 July 2011, from http://www.huffingtonpost.com/2010/12/30/facebook-tops-google-as-m_n_802606.html

Iyer, A., 2009, 'Are Facebook's privacy settings working?', viewed 03 February 2012, from http://www.artificialignorance.net/blog/facebook/arefacebooks-privacy-settings-working

Jagatic, T.N., Johnson, M., Jakobsson, M. & Menczer, F., 2007, 'Social phishing', Communications of the ACM 50(10), 94–100. http://dx.doi.org/10.1145/1290958.1290968

Johnson, A., 2012, 'Social network settings are ineffective', Information and Communication Journal 12(3), 8.

Jones, H. & Soltren, J.H., 2012, 'Facebook: Threats to privacy', Project MAC: MIT Project on Mathematics and Computing.

Judge, P., 2011, 'Social networking security and privacy study', Barracusalabs Networks Inc., viewed 03 February 2012, from http://www.Barracudalabs.Com/Snsreport/2011socialnetworkingstudy.Pdf

Kiesow, D., 2011. Facebook, most visited website of 2010, valued at $50 billion, Poynter, viewed 23 July 2011, from http://www.poynter.org/latest-news/media-lab/social-media/112651/facebook-most-visited-website-of-2010-valued-at-50-billion/

Khan, B., Alghathbar, K.S., Nabi, S.I. & Khan, M.K., 2011, 'Effectiveness of information security awareness methods based on psychological theories', African Journal of Business Management 5(26), 10862–10868.

Kumaraguru, P., Rhee, Y., Acquisti, A., Cranor, L., Hong, J. & Nunge, E., 2007, 'Protecting people from phishing: The design and evaluation of an embedded training e-mail system', Proceedings of the SIGCHI Conference on Human Factors in Computing Systems, San Jose, California, United States of America, pp. 905–914. http://dx.doi.org/10.1145/1240624.1240760

Kyle, A.H., 2011. Top 10 most visited website of 2011, Kaleazy Creative, viewed 23 July 2011, from http://Kaleazy.com/top-10-most-visited-websites-of-2011

Lucas, M. & Borisov, N., 2008, 'Flybynight: Mitigating the privacy risks of social networking', Proceedings of the 7th ACM Workshop on Privacy in the Electronic Society, ACM New York, New York, United States of America, pp. 1–8.

Mataracioglu, T. & Ozkan, S., 2010, 'User Awareness Measurement through Social Engineering', International Journal of Managing Value and Supply Chains 1(2), 27–34.

PriceWaterHouseCoopers, 2010, 'Protecting your business – security awareness: Turning your people into your first line of defence', viewed 25 July 2011, from http://www.pwc.co.uk/eng/publications/protecting_your_business_security_awareness.html

Smith, E., 2012. 'The true cost of cyber-security – Why your company should invest in it', Enlight Research, viewed 01 August 2013, from http://www.enlightresearch.com/ideas/2012/7/9/the-true-cost-of-cyber-security-why-your-company-should-inve.html

Smith, C., 2013, 'The planet's 24 largest social media sites, and where their next wave of growth will come from', Business Insider, viewed 09 December 2013, from http://www.businessinsider.com/a-global-social-media-census-2013-10

Shamim, S., 2011, 'Top 10 most visited websites in the world', Expert Review now, viewed 25 July 2011, from http://www.expertreviewnow.com/2011/02/top-10-most-visited-websites-in-the-world/

Stephanou, A.T. & Dagada, R., 2008, 'The impact of ISA training on IS behaviour: The case for further research', Proceedings of the Information Security for South Africa - ISSA 2008: Innovative Minds, School of Tourism and hospitality, University of Johannesburg, South Africa, pp. 311–330, viewed 28 August 2012, from http://if08030.files.wordpress.com/2011/06/issa2008proceedings.pdf

Van Niekerk, J. & Von Solms, R., 2004, Organizational learning models for information security education', A Proceeding of ISSA, Johannesburg, South Africa.

Vaughan-Nichols, S.J., 2013, 'Facebook remains top social network, Google+, YouTube battle for second', in ZDNet, viewed 09 December 2013, from http://www.zdnet.com/facebook-remains-top-social-network-google-youtube-battle-for-second-7000015303/

Wolf, M.J., 2010, 'Measuring ISA programme', Master's thesis, Department of Information Systems and Quantitative Analysis, University of Nebraska, Omaha.

Permissions

All chapters in this book were first published in SAJIM, by AOSIS Publishing; hereby published with permission under the Creative Commons Attribution License or equivalent. Every chapter published in this book has been scrutinized by our experts. Their significance has been extensively debated. The topics covered herein carry significant findings which will fuel the growth of the discipline. They may even be implemented as practical applications or may be referred to as a beginning point for another development.

The contributors of this book come from diverse backgrounds, making this book a truly international effort. This book will bring forth new frontiers with its revolutionizing research information and detailed analysis of the nascent developments around the world.

We would like to thank all the contributing authors for lending their expertise to make the book truly unique. They have played a crucial role in the development of this book. Without their invaluable contributions this book wouldn't have been possible. They have made vital efforts to compile up to date information on the varied aspects of this subject to make this book a valuable addition to the collection of many professionals and students.

This book was conceptualized with the vision of imparting up-to-date information and advanced data in this field. To ensure the same, a matchless editorial board was set up. Every individual on the board went through rigorous rounds of assessment to prove their worth. After which they invested a large part of their time researching and compiling the most relevant data for our readers.

The editorial board has been involved in producing this book since its inception. They have spent rigorous hours researching and exploring the diverse topics which have resulted in the successful publishing of this book. They have passed on their knowledge of decades through this book. To expedite this challenging task, the publisher supported the team at every step. A small team of assistant editors was also appointed to further simplify the editing procedure and attain best results for the readers.

Apart from the editorial board, the designing team has also invested a significant amount of their time in understanding the subject and creating the most relevant covers. They scrutinized every image to scout for the most suitable representation of the subject and create an appropriate cover for the book.

The publishing team has been an ardent support to the editorial, designing and production team. Their endless efforts to recruit the best for this project, has resulted in the accomplishment of this book. They are a veteran in the field of academics and their pool of knowledge is as vast as their experience in printing. Their expertise and guidance has proved useful at every step. Their uncompromising quality standards have made this book an exceptional effort. Their encouragement from time to time has been an inspiration for everyone.

The publisher and the editorial board hope that this book will prove to be a valuable piece of knowledge for researchers, students, practitioners and scholars across the globe.

List of Contributors

Isaac C. Mogotsi
Department of Information Science, University of Pretoria, South Africa
Department of Accounting and Finance, University of Botswana, Botswana

J.A. (Hans) Boon
Department of Information Science, University of Pretoria, South Africa

Lizelle Fletcher
Department of Statistics, University of Pretoria, South Africa

Faeda Mohsam
Faculty of Business, Cape Peninsula University of Technology, South Africa

Pieter A. van Brakel
Faculty of Informatics and Design, Cape Peninsula University of Technology, South Africa

Wole M. Olatokun and Isioma N. Elueze
Africa Regional Centre for Information Science (ARCIS), University of Ibadan, Nigeria

Roelof Baard and George Nel
Department of Accounting, University of Stellenbosch, South Africa

Kiru Pillay and Manoj S. Maharaj
School of Management, Information Technology and Governance, University of KwaZulu-Natal, South Africa

Karin Eloff and Cornelius J. Niemand
Centre for Information and Knowledge Management, University of Johannesburg, South Africa

Mariette Visser
Human Sciences Research Council (HSRC), Pretoria, South Africa

Judy van Biljon
School of Computing, College of Science, Engineering and Technology, University of South Africa, South Africa

Marlien Herselman
Council for Scientific and Industrial Research (CSIR), Pretoria, South Africa

Joshua R. Ndiege and Stephen V. Flowerday
Department of Information Systems, University of Fort Hare, South Africa

Marlien E. Herselman
Department of Information Systems, University of Fort Hare, South Africa
Mereka Institute, CSIR, Pretoria, South Africa

Kiru Pillay and Manoj S. Maharaj
School of Management, Information Technology and Governance, University of KwaZulu-Natal, South Africa

Mpho Ngoepe
Department of Information Science, University of South Africa, South Africa

Patrick Ngulube
School of Interdisciplinary Research and Graduate Studies, University of South Africa, South Africa

Nisha Sewdass
Department of Information Science, University of Pretoria, South Africa

Zenia Barnard and Chris Rensleigh
Department of Information and Knowledge Management, University of Johannesburg, South Africa

Joel Chigada
Department of Information Science, University of South Africa, South Africa

Patrick Ngulube
School of Interdisciplinary Research and Postgraduate Studies, University of South Africa, South Africa

Phillip Nyoni
Department of Information Systems, North-West University, South Africa

Mthulisi Velempini
Department of Computer Science, University of Limpopo, South Africa

Rika Butler
School of Accountancy, Stellenbosch University, South Africa

Martin Butler
School, Stellenbosch University, South Africa

Sitali Wamundila
Department of Library and Information Science, University of Zambia, Zambia

Patrick Ngulube
School of Graduate Studies, University of South Africa, South Africa

Nonofo C. Sedimo
Department of Library and Information Studies, University of Botswana, Gaborone

Kelvin J. Bwalya
Center for Information and Knowledge Management, University of Johannesburg, South Africa

Tanya Du Plessis
Department of Information and Knowledge Management, University of Johannesburg, South Africa

Udo R. Averweg
Graduate School of Business & Leadership, College of Law and Management Studies, University of KwaZulu-Natal, South Africa
Information Services, eThekwini Municipality, Durban, South Africa

Stefan A. Sinske and Heinz E. Jacobs
Department of Civil Engineering, University of Stellenbosch, South Africa

Brett van Niekerk and Manoj S. Maharaj
School of Information Systems and Technology, University of KwaZulu-Natal, South Africa

Harsha Desai
Department of Health Informatics, School of Nursing and Public Health, University of KwaZulu-Natal, South Africa

Rubeshan Perumal
Centre for the AIDS Programme of Research in South Africa (CAPRISA), University of KwaZulu-Natal, South Africa

Rosemary Quiling
Discipline of Information Systems & Technology, School of Management, IT & Governance, College of Law & Management Studies, University of KwaZulu-Natal, Durban, South Africa

Yashik Singh
Department of Telehealth, School of Nursing and Public Health, University of KwaZulu-Natal, Durban, South Africa

Brett van Niekerk
School of Management, IT and Governance, University of KwaZulu-Natal, South Africa

Liezel Cilliers and Stephen V. Flowerday
Department of Information Systems, University of Fort Hare, South Africa

Rodreck David and Adock Dube
Department of Records and Archives Management, National University of Science and Technology, Zimbabwe

Patrick Ngulube
Department of Interdisciplinary Research and Postgraduate Studies, University of South Africa, South Africa

Carl Marnewick
Department of Applied Information Systems, University of Johannesburg, South Africa

Julius O. Okesola and Marthie Grobler
School of Computing, University of South Africa, South Africa

Index

Printed in the USA
CPSIA information can be obtained
at www.ICGtesting.com
JSHW051433221024
72173JS00006B/1454

9 781682 854105